Individuals with Disabilities Education Act (IDEA)

Special Education Law

CFR Title 34 Parts 300-399
2023 Edition

Federal Register of the
U.S. Government

The Individuals with Disabilities Education Act (IDEA) ensures children with disabilities receive a free and appropriate public education that meets their unique needs.

Comprehensive Support: IDEA provides comprehensive support for students with disabilities from birth to age 21. It mandates special education services, accommodations, and modifications for eligible students to access their education.

Access to Education: IDEA ensures that students with disabilities have access to the same educational opportunities as their peers without disabilities. It prohibits discrimination and ensures that students with disabilities are not excluded from any educational program or activity.

Parental Involvement: IDEA mandates that parents are equal partners in the educational process and must be included in all aspects of their child's education. This includes participating in Individualized Education Program (IEP) meetings, making decisions about their child's education, and being informed of their child's progress.

Individualized Education Plan: IDEA requires schools to develop an individualized education plan (IEP) for each student with a disability. The IEP outlines the student's unique needs, goals, and services necessary to meet those goals.

Funding: IDEA provides federal funding to states to support special education services. This funding is essential in ensuring that students with disabilities receive the necessary support and services to succeed in school.

Improvements: Over the years, IDEA has undergone several revisions to improve the services and support available to students with disabilities. The most recent update was in 2004, and it included changes that strengthened the law's focus on improving educational outcomes for students with disabilities.

Overall, the Individuals with Disabilities Education Act has had a significant impact on the education of students with disabilities in the United States.

CHAPTER III—OFFICE OF SPECIAL EDUCATION AND REHABILITATIVE SERVICES, DEPARTMENT OF EDUCATION

PART 300—ASSISTANCE TO STATES FOR THE EDUCATION OF CHILDREN WITH DISABILITIES

Subpart A—General

Subpart B—State Eligibility

AUTHORITY: 20 U.S.C. 1221e–3, 1406, 1411–1419, and 3474; Pub. L. 111–256, 124 Stat. 2643; unless otherwise noted.

SOURCE: 71 FR 46753, Aug. 14, 2006, unless otherwise noted.

Subpart A—General

PURPOSES AND APPLICABILITY

§ 300.1 **Purposes.**

The purposes of this part are—

(a) To ensure that all children with disabilities have available to them a free appropriate public education that emphasizes special education and related services designed to meet their unique needs and prepare them for further education, employment, and independent living;

(b) To ensure that the rights of children with disabilities and their parents are protected;

(c) To assist States, localities, educational service agencies, and Federal agencies to provide for the education of all children with disabilities; and

(d) To assess and ensure the effectiveness of efforts to educate children with disabilities.

(Authority: 20 U.S.C. 1400(d))

§ 300.2 Applicability of this part to State and local agencies.

(a) *States.* This part applies to each State that receives payments under Part B of the Act, as defined in § 300.4.

(b) *Public agencies within the State.* The provisions of this part—

(1) Apply to all political subdivisions of the State that are involved in the education of children with disabilities, including:

(i) The State educational agency (SEA).

(ii) Local educational agencies (LEAs), educational service agencies (ESAs), and public charter schools that are not otherwise included as LEAs or ESAs and are not a school of an LEA or ESA.

(iii) Other State agencies and schools (such as Departments of Mental Health and Welfare and State schools for children with deafness or children with blindness).

(iv) State and local juvenile and adult correctional facilities; and

(2) Are binding on each public agency in the State that provides special education and related services to children with disabilities, regardless of whether that agency is receiving funds under Part B of the Act.

(c) *Private schools and facilities.* Each public agency in the State is responsible for ensuring that the rights and protections under Part B of the Act are given to children with disabilities—

(1) Referred to or placed in private schools and facilities by that public agency; or

(2) Placed in private schools by their parents under the provisions of § 300.148.

(Authority: 20 U.S.C. 1412)

DEFINITIONS USED IN THIS PART

§ 300.4 Act.

Act means the Individuals with Disabilities Education Act, as amended.

(Authority: 20 U.S.C. 1400(a))

§ 300.5 Assistive technology device.

Assistive technology device means any item, piece of equipment, or product system, whether acquired commercially off the shelf, modified, or customized, that is used to increase, maintain, or improve the functional capabilities of a child with a disability. The term does not include a medical device that is surgically implanted, or the replacement of such device.

(Authority: 20 U.S.C. 1401(1))

§ 300.6 Assistive technology service.

Assistive technology service means any service that directly assists a child with a disability in the selection, acquisition, or use of an assistive technology device. The term includes—

(a) The evaluation of the needs of a child with a disability, including a functional evaluation of the child in the child's customary environment;

(b) Purchasing, leasing, or otherwise providing for the acquisition of assistive technology devices by children with disabilities;

(c) Selecting, designing, fitting, customizing, adapting, applying, maintaining, repairing, or replacing assistive technology devices;

(d) Coordinating and using other therapies, interventions, or services with assistive technology devices, such as those associated with existing education and rehabilitation plans and programs;

(e) Training or technical assistance for a child with a disability or, if appropriate, that child's family; and

(f) Training or technical assistance for professionals (including individuals providing education or rehabilitation services), employers, or other individuals who provide services to, employ, or are otherwise substantially involved in the major life functions of that child.

(Authority: 20 U.S.C. 1401(2))

§ 300.7 Charter school.

Charter school has the meaning given the term in section 4310(2) of the Elementary and Secondary Education Act of 1965, as amended, 20 U.S.C. 6301 *et seq.* (ESEA).

(Authority: 20 U.S.C. 7221i(2))

[71 FR 46753, Aug. 14, 2006, as amended at 82 FR 29759, June 30, 2017]

§ 300.8 Child with a disability.

(a) *General*—(1) *Child with a disability* means a child evaluated in accordance with §§ 300.304 through 300.311 as having an intellectual disability, a hearing impairment (including deafness), a speech or language impairment, a visual impairment (including blindness), a serious emotional disturbance (referred to in this part as "emotional disturbance"), an orthopedic impairment, autism, traumatic brain injury, an other health impairment, a specific learning disability, deaf-blindness, or multiple disabilities, and who, by reason thereof, needs special education and related services.

(2)(i) Subject to paragraph (a)(2)(ii) of this section, if it is determined, through an appropriate evaluation under §§ 300.304 through 300.311, that a child has one of the disabilities identified in paragraph (a)(1) of this section, but only needs a related service and not special education, the child is not a child with a disability under this part.

(ii) If, consistent with § 300.39(a)(2), the related service required by the child is considered special education rather than a related service under State standards, the child would be determined to be a child with a disability under paragraph (a)(1) of this section.

(b) *Children aged three through nine experiencing developmental delays.* *Child with a disability* for children aged three through nine (or any subset of that age range, including ages three through five), may, subject to the conditions described in § 300.111(b), include a child—

(1) Who is experiencing developmental delays, as defined by the State and as measured by appropriate diagnostic instruments and procedures, in one or more of the following areas: Physical development, cognitive development, communication development, social or emotional development, or adaptive development; and

(2) Who, by reason thereof, needs special education and related services.

(c) *Definitions of disability terms.* The terms used in this definition of a child with a disability are defined as follows:

(1)(i) *Autism* means a developmental disability significantly affecting verbal and nonverbal communication and social interaction, generally evident before age three, that adversely affects a child's educational performance. Other characteristics often associated with autism are engagement in repetitive activities and stereotyped movements, resistance to environmental change or change in daily routines, and unusual responses to sensory experiences.

(ii) Autism does not apply if a child's educational performance is adversely affected primarily because the child has an emotional disturbance, as defined in paragraph (c)(4) of this section.

(iii) A child who manifests the characteristics of autism after age three could be identified as having autism if the criteria in paragraph (c)(1)(i) of this section are satisfied.

(2) *Deaf-blindness* means concomitant hearing and visual impairments, the combination of which causes such severe communication and other developmental and educational needs that they cannot be accommodated in special education programs solely for children with deafness or children with blindness.

(3) *Deafness* means a hearing impairment that is so severe that the child is impaired in processing linguistic information through hearing, with or without amplification, that adversely affects a child's educational performance.

(4)(i) *Emotional disturbance* means a condition exhibiting one or more of the following characteristics over a long period of time and to a marked degree that adversely affects a child's educational performance:

(A) An inability to learn that cannot be explained by intellectual, sensory, or health factors.

(B) An inability to build or maintain satisfactory interpersonal relationships with peers and teachers.

(C) Inappropriate types of behavior or feelings under normal circumstances.

(D) A general pervasive mood of unhappiness or depression.

(E) A tendency to develop physical symptoms or fears associated with personal or school problems.

(ii) Emotional disturbance includes schizophrenia. The term does not apply to children who are socially maladjusted, unless it is determined that they have an emotional disturbance under paragraph (c)(4)(i) of this section.

(5) *Hearing impairment* means an impairment in hearing, whether permanent or fluctuating, that adversely affects a child's educational performance but that is not included under the definition of deafness in this section.

(6) *Intellectual disability* means significantly subaverage general intellectual functioning, existing concurrently with deficits in adaptive behavior and manifested during the developmental period, that adversely affects a child's educational performance. The term "intellectual disability" was formerly termed "mental retardation."

(7) *Multiple disabilities* means concomitant impairments (such as intellectual disability-blindness or intellectual disability-orthopedic impairment), the combination of which causes such severe educational needs that they cannot be accommodated in special education programs solely for one of the impairments. Multiple disabilities does not include deaf-blindness.

(8) *Orthopedic impairment* means a severe orthopedic impairment that adversely affects a child's educational performance. The term includes impairments caused by a congenital anomaly, impairments caused by disease (e.g., poliomyelitis, bone tuberculosis), and impairments from other causes (e.g., cerebral palsy, amputations, and fractures or burns that cause contractures).

(9) *Other health impairment* means having limited strength, vitality, or alertness, including a heightened alertness to environmental stimuli, that results in limited alertness with respect to the educational environment, that—

(i) Is due to chronic or acute health problems such as asthma, attention deficit disorder or attention deficit hyperactivity disorder, diabetes, epilepsy, a heart condition, hemophilia, lead poisoning, leukemia, nephritis, rheumatic fever, sickle cell anemia, and Tourette syndrome; and

(ii) Adversely affects a child's educational performance.

(10) *Specific learning disability*—(i) *General.* Specific learning disability means a disorder in one or more of the basic psychological processes involved in understanding or in using language, spoken or written, that may manifest itself in the imperfect ability to listen, think, speak, read, write, spell, or to do mathematical calculations, including conditions such as perceptual disabilities, brain injury, minimal brain dysfunction, dyslexia, and developmental aphasia.

(ii) *Disorders not included.* Specific learning disability does not include learning problems that are primarily the result of visual, hearing, or motor disabilities, of intellectual disability, of emotional disturbance, or of environmental, cultural, or economic disadvantage.

(11) *Speech or language impairment* means a communication disorder, such as stuttering, impaired articulation, a language impairment, or a voice impairment, that adversely affects a child's educational performance.

(12) *Traumatic brain injury* means an acquired injury to the brain caused by an external physical force, resulting in total or partial functional disability or psychosocial impairment, or both, that adversely affects a child's educational performance. Traumatic brain injury applies to open or closed head injuries resulting in impairments in one or more areas, such as cognition; language; memory; attention; reasoning; abstract thinking; judgment; problem-solving; sensory, perceptual, and motor abilities; psychosocial behavior; physical functions; information processing; and speech. Traumatic brain injury does not apply to brain injuries that are congenital or degenerative, or to brain injuries induced by birth trauma.

(13) *Visual impairment including blindness* means an impairment in vision that, even with correction, adversely

13

affects a child's educational performance. The term includes both partial sight and blindness.

[71 FR 46753, Aug. 14, 2006, as amended at 72 FR 61306, Oct. 30, 2007; 82 FR 31912, July 11, 2017]

§ 300.9 Consent.

Consent means that—

(a) The parent has been fully informed of all information relevant to the activity for which consent is sought, in his or her native language, or through another mode of communication;

(b) The parent understands and agrees in writing to the carrying out of the activity for which his or her consent is sought, and the consent describes that activity and lists the records (if any) that will be released and to whom; and

(c)(1) The parent understands that the granting of consent is voluntary on the part of the parent and may be revoked at any time.

(2) If a parent revokes consent, that revocation is not retroactive (i.e., it does not negate an action that has occurred after the consent was given and before the consent was revoked).

(3) If the parent revokes consent in writing for their child's receipt of special education services after the child is initially provided special education and related services, the public agency is not required to amend the child's education records to remove any references to the child's receipt of special education and related services because of the revocation of consent.

(Authority: 20 U.S.C. 1414(a)(1)(D))

[71 FR 46753, Aug. 14, 2006, as amended at 72 FR 61306, Oct. 30, 2007; 73 FR 73027, Dec. 1, 2008]

§ 300.10 [Reserved]

§ 300.11 Day; business day; school day.

(a) *Day* means calendar day unless otherwise indicated as business day or school day.

(b) *Business day* means Monday through Friday, except for Federal and State holidays (unless holidays are specifically included in the designation of business day, as in § 300.148(d)(1)(ii)).

(c)(1) *School day* means any day, including a partial day that children are in attendance at school for instructional purposes.

(2) *School day* has the same meaning for all children in school, including children with and without disabilities.

(Authority: 20 U.S.C. 1221e–3)

§ 300.12 Educational service agency.

Educational service agency means—

(a) A regional public multiservice agency—

(1) Authorized by State law to develop, manage, and provide services or programs to LEAs;

(2) Recognized as an administrative agency for purposes of the provision of special education and related services provided within public elementary schools and secondary schools of the State;

(b) Includes any other public institution or agency having administrative control and direction over a public elementary school or secondary school; and

(c) Includes entities that meet the definition of intermediate educational unit in section 602(23) of the Act as in effect prior to June 4, 1997.

(Authority: 20 U.S.C. 1401(5))

§ 300.13 Elementary school.

Elementary school means a nonprofit institutional day or residential school, including a public elementary charter school, that provides elementary education, as determined under State law.

(Authority: 20 U.S.C. 1401(6))

§ 300.14 Equipment.

Equipment means—

(a) Machinery, utilities, and built-in equipment, and any necessary enclosures or structures to house the machinery, utilities, or equipment; and

(b) All other items necessary for the functioning of a particular facility as a facility for the provision of educational services, including items such as instructional equipment and necessary furniture; printed, published and audiovisual instructional materials; telecommunications, sensory, and other technological aids and devices; and books, periodicals, documents, and other related materials.

(Authority: 20 U.S.C. 1401(7))

§ 300.15 Evaluation.

Evaluation means procedures used in accordance with §§ 300.304 through 300.311 to determine whether a child has a disability and the nature and extent of the special education and related services that the child needs.

(Authority: 20 U.S.C. 1414(a) (c))

§ 300.16 Excess costs.

Excess costs means those costs that are in excess of the average annual per-student expenditure in an LEA during the preceding school year for an elementary school or secondary school student, as may be appropriate, and that must be computed after deducting—

(a) Amounts received—

(1) Under Part B of the Act;

(2) Under Part A of title I of the ESEA; and

(3) Under Part A of title III of the ESEA and;

(b) Any State or local funds expended for programs that would qualify for assistance under any of the parts described in paragraph (a) of this section, but excluding any amounts for capital outlay or debt service. (See appendix A to part 300 for an example of how excess costs must be calculated.)

(Authority: 20 U.S.C. 1401(8))

[71 FR 46753, Aug. 14, 2006, as amended at 82 FR 29759, June 30, 2017]

§ 300.17 Free appropriate public education.

Free appropriate public education or *FAPE* means special education and related services that—

(a) Are provided at public expense, under public supervision and direction, and without charge;

(b) Meet the standards of the SEA, including the requirements of this part;

(c) Include an appropriate preschool, elementary school, or secondary school education in the State involved; and

(d) Are provided in conformity with an individualized education program (IEP) that meets the requirements of §§ 300.320 through 300.324.

(Authority: 20 U.S.C. 1401(9))

§ 300.18 [Reserved]

§ 300.19 Homeless children.

Homeless children has the meaning given the term *homeless children and youths* in section 725 (42 U.S.C. 11434a) of the McKinney-Vento Homeless Assistance Act, as amended, 42 U.S.C. 11431 *et seq.*

(Authority: 20 U.S.C. 1401(11))

§ 300.20 Include.

Include means that the items named are not all of the possible items that are covered, whether like or unlike the ones named.

(Authority: 20 U.S.C. 1221e–3)

§ 300.21 Indian and Indian tribe.

(a) *Indian* means an individual who is a member of an Indian tribe.

(b) *Indian tribe* means any Federal or State Indian tribe, band, rancheria, pueblo, colony, or community, including any Alaska Native village or regional village corporation (as defined in or established under the Alaska Native Claims Settlement Act, 43 U.S.C. 1601 *et seq.*).

(c) Nothing in this definition is intended to indicate that the Secretary of the Interior is required to provide services or funding to a State Indian tribe that is not listed in the FEDERAL REGISTER list of Indian entities recognized as eligible to receive services from the United States, published pursuant to Section 104 of the Federally Recognized Indian Tribe List Act of 1994, 25 U.S.C. 479a–1.

(Authority: 20 U.S.C. 1401(12) and (13))

§ 300.22 Individualized education program.

Individualized education program or *IEP* means a written statement for a child with a disability that is developed, reviewed, and revised in accordance with §§ 300.320 through 300.324.

(Authority: 20 U.S.C. 1401(14))

§ 300.23 Individualized education program team.

Individualized education program team or *IEP Team* means a group of individuals described in § 300.321 that is responsible for developing, reviewing, or revising an IEP for a child with a disability.

(Authority: 20 U.S.C. 1414(d)(1)(B))

§ 300.24 Individualized family service plan.

Individualized family service plan or *IFSP* has the meaning given the term in section 636 of the Act.

(Authority: 20 U.S.C. 1401(15))

§ 300.25 Infant or toddler with a disability.

Infant or toddler with a disability—

(a) Means an individual under three years of age who needs early intervention services because the individual—

(1) Is experiencing developmental delays, as measured by appropriate diagnostic instruments and procedures in one or more of the areas of cognitive development, physical development, communication development, social or emotional development, and adaptive development; or

(2) Has a diagnosed physical or mental condition that has a high probability of resulting in developmental delay; and

(b) May also include, at a State's discretion—

(1) At-risk infants and toddlers; and

(2) Children with disabilities who are eligible for services under section 619 and who previously received services under Part C of the Act until such children enter, or are eligible under State law to enter, kindergarten or elementary school, as appropriate, provided that any programs under Part C of the Act serving such children shall include—

(i) An educational component that promotes school readiness and incorporates pre-literacy, language, and numeracy skills; and

(ii) A written notification to parents of their rights and responsibilities in determining whether their child will continue to receive services under Part C of the Act or participate in preschool programs under section 619.

(Authority: 20 U.S.C. 1401(16) and 1432(5))

§ 300.26 Institution of higher education.

Institution of higher education—

(a) Has the meaning given the term in section 101 of the Higher Education Act of 1965, as amended, 20 U.S.C. 1021 *et seq.* (HEA); and

(b) Also includes any community college receiving funds from the Secretary of the Interior under the Tribally Controlled Community College or University Assistance Act of 1978, 25 U.S.C. 1801, *et seq.*

(Authority: 20 U.S.C. 1401(17))

§ 300.27 Limited English proficient.

Limited English proficient has the meaning given the term 'English learner' in section 8101 of the ESEA.

(Authority: 20 U.S.C. 1401(18))

[71 FR 46753, Aug. 14, 2006, as amended at 82 FR 29759, June 30, 2017]

§ 300.28 Local educational agency.

(a) *General. Local educational agency* or *LEA* means a public board of education or other public authority legally constituted within a State for either administrative control or direction of, or to perform a service function for, public elementary or secondary schools in a city, county, township, school district, or other political subdivision of a State, or for a combination of school districts or counties as are recognized in a State as an administrative agency for its public elementary schools or secondary schools.

(b) *Educational service agencies and other public institutions or agencies.* The term includes—

(1) An educational service agency, as defined in § 300.12; and

(2) Any other public institution or agency having administrative control and direction of a public elementary school or secondary school, including a public nonprofit charter school that is established as an LEA under State law.

(c) *BIA funded schools.* The term includes an elementary school or secondary school funded by the Bureau of Indian Affairs, and not subject to the jurisdiction of any SEA other than the Bureau of Indian Affairs, but only to the extent that the inclusion makes the school eligible for programs for which specific eligibility is not provided to the school in another provision of law and the school does not have a student population that is smaller than the student population of the LEA receiving assistance under the Act with the smallest student population.

(Authority: 20 U.S.C. 1401(19))

§300.29 Native language.

(a) *Native language*, when used with respect to an individual who is limited English proficient, means the following:

(1) The language normally used by that individual, or, in the case of a child, the language normally used by the parents of the child, except as provided in paragraph (a)(2) of this section.

(2) In all direct contact with a child (including evaluation of the child), the language normally used by the child in the home or learning environment.

(b) For an individual with deafness or blindness, or for an individual with no written language, the mode of communication is that normally used by the individual (such as sign language, Braille, or oral communication).

(Authority: 20 U.S.C. 1401(20))

§300.30 Parent.

(a) *Parent* means—

(1) A biological or adoptive parent of a child;

(2) A foster parent, unless State law, regulations, or contractual obligations with a State or local entity prohibit a foster parent from acting as a parent;

(3) A guardian generally authorized to act as the child's parent, or authorized to make educational decisions for the child (but not the State if the child is a ward of the State);

(4) An individual acting in the place of a biological or adoptive parent (including a grandparent, stepparent, or other relative) with whom the child lives, or an individual who is legally responsible for the child's welfare; or

(5) A surrogate parent who has been appointed in accordance with §300.519 or section 639(a)(5) of the Act.

(b) (1) Except as provided in paragraph (b)(2) of this section, the biological or adoptive parent, when attempting to act as the parent under this part and when more than one party is qualified under paragraph (a) of this section to act as a parent, must be presumed to

be the parent for purposes of this section unless the biological or adoptive parent does not have legal authority to make educational decisions for the child.

(2) If a judicial decree or order identifies a specific person or persons under paragraphs (a)(1) through (4) of this section to act as the "parent" of a child or to make educational decisions on behalf of a child, then such person or persons shall be determined to be the "parent" for purposes of this section.

(Authority: 20 U.S.C. 1401(23))

§300.31 Parent training and information center.

Parent training and information center means a center assisted under sections 671 or 672 of the Act.

(Authority: 20 U.S.C. 1401(25))

§300.32 Personally identifiable.

Personally identifiable means information that contains—

(a) The name of the child, the child's parent, or other family member;

(b) The address of the child;

(c) A personal identifier, such as the child's social security number or student number; or

(d) A list of personal characteristics or other information that would make it possible to identify the child with reasonable certainty.

(Authority: 20 U.S.C. 1415(a))

§300.33 Public agency.

Public agency includes the SEA, LEAs, ESAs, nonprofit public charter schools that are not otherwise included as LEAs or ESAs and are not a school of an LEA or ESA, and any other political subdivisions of the State that are responsible for providing education to children with disabilities.

(Authority: 20 U.S.C. 1412(a)(11))

§300.34 Related services.

(a) *General. Related services* means transportation and such developmental, corrective, and other supportive services as are required to assist a child with a disability to benefit from special education, and includes speech-language pathology and audiology services, interpreting services, psychological services, physical and occupational therapy, recreation, including therapeutic recreation, early identification and assessment of disabilities in children, counseling services, including rehabilitation counseling, orientation and mobility services, and medical services for diagnostic or evaluation purposes. Related services also include school health services and school nurse services, social work services in schools, and parent counseling and training.

(b) *Exception; services that apply to children with surgically implanted devices, including cochlear implants.* (1) Related services do not include a medical device that is surgically implanted, the optimization of that device's functioning (e.g., mapping), maintenance of that device, or the replacement of that device.

(2) Nothing in paragraph (b)(1) of this section—

(i) Limits the right of a child with a surgically implanted device (e.g., cochlear implant) to receive related services (as listed in paragraph (a) of this section) that are determined by the IEP Team to be necessary for the child to receive FAPE.

(ii) Limits the responsibility of a public agency to appropriately monitor and maintain medical devices that are needed to maintain the health and safety of the child, including breathing, nutrition, or operation of other bodily functions, while the child is transported to and from school or is at school; or

(iii) Prevents the routine checking of an external component of a surgically implanted device to make sure it is functioning properly, as required in § 300.113(b).

(c) *Individual related services terms defined.* The terms used in this definition are defined as follows:

(1) *Audiology* includes—

(i) Identification of children with hearing loss;

(ii) Determination of the range, nature, and degree of hearing loss, including referral for medical or other professional attention for the habilitation of hearing;

(iii) Provision of habilitative activities, such as language habilitation, auditory training, speech reading (lipreading), hearing evaluation, and speech conservation;

(iv) Creation and administration of programs for prevention of hearing loss;

(v) Counseling and guidance of children, parents, and teachers regarding hearing loss; and

(vi) Determination of children's needs for group and individual amplification, selecting and fitting an appropriate aid, and evaluating the effectiveness of amplification.

(2) *Counseling services* means services provided by qualified social workers, psychologists, guidance counselors, or other qualified personnel.

(3) *Early identification and assessment of disabilities in children* means the implementation of a formal plan for identifying a disability as early as possible in a child's life.

(4) *Interpreting services* includes—

(i) The following, when used with respect to children who are deaf or hard of hearing: Oral transliteration services, cued language transliteration services, sign language transliteration and interpreting services, and transcription services, such as communication access real-time translation (CART), C-Print, and TypeWell; and

(ii) Special interpreting services for children who are deaf-blind.

(5) *Medical services* means services provided by a licensed physician to determine a child's medically related disability that results in the child's need for special education and related services.

(6) *Occupational therapy*—

(i) Means services provided by a qualified occupational therapist; and

(ii) Includes—

(A) Improving, developing, or restoring functions impaired or lost through illness, injury, or deprivation;

(B) Improving ability to perform tasks for independent functioning if functions are impaired or lost; and

(C) Preventing, through early intervention, initial or further impairment or loss of function.

(7) *Orientation and mobility services*—

(i) Means services provided to blind or visually impaired children by qualified personnel to enable those students to attain systematic orientation to and safe movement within their environments in school, home, and community; and

(ii) Includes teaching children the following, as appropriate:

(A) Spatial and environmental concepts and use of information received by the senses (such as sound, temperature and vibrations) to establish, maintain, or regain orientation and line of travel (e.g., using sound at a traffic light to cross the street);

(B) To use the long cane or a service animal to supplement visual travel skills or as a tool for safely negotiating the environment for children with no available travel vision;

(C) To understand and use remaining vision and distance low vision aids; and

(D) Other concepts, techniques, and tools.

(8)(i) *Parent counseling and training* means assisting parents in understanding the special needs of their child;

(ii) Providing parents with information about child development; and

(iii) Helping parents to acquire the necessary skills that will allow them to support the implementation of their child's IEP or IFSP.

(9) *Physical therapy* means services provided by a qualified physical therapist.

(10) *Psychological services* includes—

(i) Administering psychological and educational tests, and other assessment procedures;

(ii) Interpreting assessment results;

(iii) Obtaining, integrating, and interpreting information about child behavior and conditions relating to learning;

(iv) Consulting with other staff members in planning school programs to meet the special educational needs of children as indicated by psychological tests, interviews, direct observation, and behavioral evaluations;

(v) Planning and managing a program of psychological services, including psychological counseling for children and parents; and

(vi) Assisting in developing positive behavioral intervention strategies.

(11) *Recreation* includes—

(i) Assessment of leisure function;

(ii) Therapeutic recreation services;

(iii) Recreation programs in schools and community agencies; and

(iv) Leisure education.

(12) *Rehabilitation counseling services* means services provided by qualified personnel in individual or group sessions that focus specifically on career development, employment preparation, achieving independence, and integration in the workplace and community of a student with a disability. The term also includes vocational rehabilitation services provided to a student with a disability by vocational rehabilitation programs funded under the Rehabilitation Act of 1973, as amended, 29 U.S.C. 701 *et seq.*

(13) *School health services and school nurse services* means health services that are designed to enable a child with a disability to receive FAPE as described in the child's IEP. School nurse services are services provided by a qualified school nurse. School health services are services that may be provided by either a qualified school nurse or other qualified person.

(14) *Social work services in schools* includes—

(i) Preparing a social or developmental history on a child with a disability;

(ii) Group and individual counseling with the child and family;

(iii) Working in partnership with parents and others on those problems in a child's living situation (home, school, and community) that affect the child's adjustment in school;

(iv) Mobilizing school and community resources to enable the child to learn as effectively as possible in his or her educational program; and

(v) Assisting in developing positive behavioral intervention strategies.

(15) *Speech-language pathology services* includes—

(i) Identification of children with speech or language impairments;

(ii) Diagnosis and appraisal of specific speech or language impairments;

(iii) Referral for medical or other professional attention necessary for the habilitation of speech or language impairments;

(iv) Provision of speech and language services for the habilitation or prevention of communicative impairments; and

(v) Counseling and guidance of parents, children, and teachers regarding speech and language impairments.

(16) *Transportation* includes—

(i) Travel to and from school and between schools;

(ii) Travel in and around school buildings; and

(iii) Specialized equipment (such as special or adapted buses, lifts, and ramps), if required to provide special transportation for a child with a disability.

(Authority: 20 U.S.C. 1401(26))

§ 300.35   [Reserved]

§ 300.36   Secondary school.

Secondary school means a nonprofit institutional day or residential school, including a public secondary charter school that provides secondary education, as determined under State law, except that it does not include any education beyond grade 12.

(Authority: 20 U.S.C. 1401(27))

§ 300.37   Services plan.

Services plan means a written statement that describes the special education and related services the LEA will provide to a parentally-placed child with a disability enrolled in a private school who has been designated to receive services, including the location of the services and any transportation necessary, consistent with § 300.132, and is developed and implemented in accordance with §§ 300.137 through 300.139.

(Authority: 20 U.S.C. 1412(a)(10)(A))

§ 300.38   Secretary.

Secretary means the Secretary of Education.

(Authority: 20 U.S.C. 1401(28))

§ 300.39   Special education.

(a) *General.* (1) *Special education* means specially designed instruction, at no cost to the parents, to meet the unique needs of a child with a disability, including—

(i) Instruction conducted in the classroom, in the home, in hospitals and institutions, and in other settings; and

(ii) Instruction in physical education.

(2) *Special education* includes each of the following, if the services otherwise meet the requirements of paragraph (a)(1) of this section—

(i) Speech-language pathology services, or any other related service, if the service is considered special education rather than a related service under State standards;

(ii) Travel training; and

(iii) Vocational education.

(b) *Individual special education terms defined.* The terms in this definition are defined as follows:

(1) *At no cost* means that all specially-designed instruction is provided without charge, but does not preclude incidental fees that are normally charged to nondisabled students or their parents as a part of the regular education program.

(2) *Physical education* means—

(i) The development of—

(A) Physical and motor fitness;

(B) Fundamental motor skills and patterns; and

(C) Skills in aquatics, dance, and individual and group games and sports (including intramural and lifetime sports); and

(ii) Includes special physical education, adapted physical education, movement education, and motor development.

(3) *Specially designed instruction* means adapting, as appropriate to the needs of an eligible child under this part, the content, methodology, or delivery of instruction—

(i) To address the unique needs of the child that result from the child's disability; and

(ii) To ensure access of the child to the general curriculum, so that the child can meet the educational standards within the jurisdiction of the public agency that apply to all children.

(4) *Travel training* means providing instruction, as appropriate, to children with significant cognitive disabilities, and any other children with disabilities who require this instruction, to enable them to—

(i) Develop an awareness of the environment in which they live; and

(ii) Learn the skills necessary to move effectively and safely from place to place within that environment (e.g., in school, in the home, at work, and in the community).

(5) *Vocational education* means organized educational programs that are directly related to the preparation of individuals for paid or unpaid employment, or for additional preparation for a career not requiring a baccalaureate or advanced degree.

(Authority: 20 U.S.C. 1401(29))

§ 300.40 State.

State means each of the 50 States, the District of Columbia, the Commonwealth of Puerto Rico, and each of the outlying areas.

(Authority: 20 U.S.C. 1401(31))

§ 300.41 State educational agency.

State educational agency or *SEA* means the State board of education or other agency or officer primarily responsible for the State supervision of public elementary schools and secondary schools, or, if there is no such officer or agency, an officer or agency designated by the Governor or by State law.

(Authority: 20 U.S.C. 1401(32))

§ 300.42 Supplementary aids and services.

Supplementary aids and services means aids, services, and other supports that are provided in regular education classes, other education-related settings, and in extracurricular and nonacademic settings, to enable children with disabilities to be educated with nondisabled children to the maximum extent appropriate in accordance with §§ 300.114 through 300.116.

(Authority: 20 U.S.C. 1401(33))

§ 300.43 Transition services.

(a) *Transition services* means a coordinated set of activities for a child with a disability that—

(1) Is designed to be within a results-oriented process, that is focused on improving the academic and functional achievement of the child with a disability to facilitate the child's movement from school to post-school activities, including postsecondary education, vocational education, integrated employment (including supported employment), continuing and adult education, adult services, independent living, or community participation;

(2) Is based on the individual child's needs, taking into account the child's strengths, preferences, and interests; and includes—

(i) Instruction;
(ii) Related services;
(iii) Community experiences;
(iv) The development of employment and other post-school adult living objectives; and
(v) If appropriate, acquisition of daily living skills and provision of a functional vocational evaluation.

(b) *Transition services* for children with disabilities may be special education, if provided as specially designed instruction, or a related service, if required to assist a child with a disability to benefit from special education.

(Authority: 20 U.S.C. 1401(34))

§ 300.44 Universal design.

Universal design has the meaning given the term in section 3 of the Assistive Technology Act of 1998, as amended, 29 U.S.C. 3002.

(Authority: 20 U.S.C. 1401(35))

§ 300.45 Ward of the State.

(a) *General.* Subject to paragraph (b) of this section, *ward of the State* means a child who, as determined by the State where the child resides, is—

(1) A foster child;
(2) A ward of the State; or
(3) In the custody of a public child welfare agency.

(b) *Exception.* Ward of the State does not include a foster child who has a foster parent who meets the definition of a *parent* in § 300.30.

(Authority: 20 U.S.C. 1401(36))

Subpart B—State Eligibility

GENERAL

§ 300.100 Eligibility for assistance.

A State is eligible for assistance under Part B of the Act for a fiscal year if the State submits a plan that provides assurances to the Secretary that the State has in effect policies and procedures to ensure that the State meets the conditions in §§ 300.101 through 300.176.

(Approved by the Office of Management and Budget under control number 1820–0030)

(Authority: 20 U.S.C. 1412(a))

FAPE REQUIREMENTS

§ 300.101   Free appropriate public education (FAPE).

(a) *General.* A free appropriate public education must be available to all children residing in the State between the ages of 3 and 21, inclusive, including children with disabilities who have been suspended or expelled from school, as provided for in § 300.530(d).

(b) *FAPE for children beginning at age 3.* (1) Each State must ensure that—

(i) The obligation to make FAPE available to each eligible child residing in the State begins no later than the child's third birthday; and

(ii) An IEP or an IFSP is in effect for the child by that date, in accordance with § 300.323(b).

(2) If a child's third birthday occurs during the summer, the child's IEP Team shall determine the date when services under the IEP or IFSP will begin.

(c) *Children advancing from grade to grade.* (1) Each State must ensure that FAPE is available to any individual child with a disability who needs special education and related services, even though the child has not failed or been retained in a course or grade, and is advancing from grade to grade.

(2) The determination that a child described in paragraph (a) of this section is eligible under this part, must be made on an individual basis by the group responsible within the child's LEA for making eligibility determinations.

(Approved by the Office of Management and Budget under control number 1820–0030)

(Authority: 20 U.S.C. 1412(a)(1)(A))

§ 300.102   Limitation—exception to FAPE for certain ages.

(a) *General.* The obligation to make FAPE available to all children with disabilities does not apply with respect to the following:

(1) Children aged 3, 4, 5, 18, 19, 20, or 21 in a State to the extent that its application to those children would be inconsistent with State law or practice, or the order of any court, respecting the provision of public education to children of those ages.

(2)(i) Children aged 18 through 21 to the extent that State law does not require that special education and related services under Part B of the Act be provided to students with disabilities who, in the last educational placement prior to their incarceration in an adult correctional facility—

(A) Were not actually identified as being a child with a disability under § 300.8; and

(B) Did not have an IEP under Part B of the Act.

(ii) The exception in paragraph (a)(2)(i) of this section does not apply to children with disabilities, aged 18 through 21, who—

(A) Had been identified as a child with a disability under § 300.8 and had received services in accordance with an IEP, but who left school prior to their incarceration; or

(B) Did not have an IEP in their last educational setting, but who had actually been identified as a child with a disability under § 300.8.

(3)(i) Children with disabilities who have graduated from high school with a regular high school diploma.

(ii) The exception in paragraph (a)(3)(i) of this section does not apply to children who have graduated from high school but have not been awarded a regular high school diploma.

(iii) Graduation from high school with a regular high school diploma constitutes a change in placement, requiring written prior notice in accordance with § 300.503.

(iv) As used in paragraphs (a)(3)(i) through (iii) of this section, the term *regular high school diploma* means the standard high school diploma awarded to the preponderance of students in the State that is fully aligned with State standards, or a higher diploma, except that a regular high school diploma shall not be aligned to the alternate academic achievement standards described in section 1111(b)(1)(E) of the

ESEA. A regular high school diploma does not include a recognized equivalent of a diploma, such as a general equivalency diploma, certificate of completion, certificate of attendance, or similar lesser credential.

(4) Children with disabilities who are eligible under subpart H of this part, but who receive early intervention services under Part C of the Act.

(b) *Documents relating to exceptions.* The State must assure that the information it has provided to the Secretary regarding the exceptions in paragraph (a) of this section, as required by § 300.700 (for purposes of making grants to States under this part), is current and accurate.

(Approved by the Office of Management and Budget under control number 1820–0030)

(Authority: 20 U.S.C. 1412(a)(1)(B)–(C) and 7801(43))

[71 FR 46753, Aug. 14, 2006, as amended at 82 FR 29759, June 30, 2017]

OTHER FAPE REQUIREMENTS

§ 300.103 FAPE—methods and payments.

(a) Each State may use whatever State, local, Federal, and private sources of support that are available in the State to meet the requirements of this part. For example, if it is necessary to place a child with a disability in a residential facility, a State could use joint agreements between the agencies involved for sharing the cost of that placement.

(b) Nothing in this part relieves an insurer or similar third party from an otherwise valid obligation to provide or to pay for services provided to a child with a disability.

(c) Consistent with § 300.323(c), the State must ensure that there is no delay in implementing a child's IEP, including any case in which the payment source for providing or paying for special education and related services to the child is being determined.

(Approved by the Office of Management and Budget under control number 1820–0030)

(Authority: 20 U.S.C. 1401(8), 1412(a)(1))

[71 FR 46753, Aug. 14, 2006, as amended at 72 FR 61306, Oct. 30, 2007]

§ 300.104 Residential placement

If placement in a public or private residential program is necessary to provide special education and related services to a child with a disability, the program, including non-medical care and room and board, must be at no cost to the parents of the child.

(Approved by the Office of Management and Budget under control number 1820–0030)

(Authority: 20 U.S.C. 1412(a)(1), 1412(a)(10)(B))

§ 300.105 Assistive technology.

(a) Each public agency must ensure that assistive technology devices or assistive technology services, or both, as those terms are defined in §§ 300.5 and 300.6, respectively, are made available to a child with a disability if required as a part of the child's—

(1) Special education under § 300.39;

(2) Related services under § 300.34; or

(3) Supplementary aids and services under §§ 300.42 and 300.114(a)(2)(ii).

(b) On a case-by-case basis, the use of school-purchased assistive technology devices in a child's home or in other settings is required if the child's IEP Team determines that the child needs access to those devices in order to receive FAPE.

(Approved by the Office of Management and Budget under control number 1820–0030)

(Authority: 20 U.S.C. 1412(a)(1), 1412(a)(12)(B)(i))

[71 FR 46753, Aug. 14, 2006, as amended at 82 FR 29759, June 30, 2017]

§ 300.106 Extended school year services.

(a) *General.* (1) Each public agency must ensure that extended school year services are available as necessary to provide FAPE, consistent with paragraph (a)(2) of this section.

(2) Extended school year services must be provided only if a child's IEP Team determines, on an individual basis, in accordance with §§ 300.320 through 300.324, that the services are necessary for the provision of FAPE to the child.

(3) In implementing the requirements of this section, a public agency may not—

(i) Limit extended school year services to particular categories of disability; or

(ii) Unilaterally limit the type, amount, or duration of those services.

(b) *Definition.* As used in this section, the term extended school year services means special education and related services that—

(1) Are provided to a child with a disability—

(i) Beyond the normal school year of the public agency;

(ii) In accordance with the child's IEP; and

(iii) At no cost to the parents of the child; and

(2) Meet the standards of the SEA.

(Approved by the Office of Management and Budget under control number 1820–0030)

(Authority: 20 U.S.C. 1412(a)(1))

§ 300.107 Nonacademic services.

The State must ensure the following:

(a) Each public agency must take steps, including the provision of supplementary aids and services determined appropriate and necessary by the child's IEP Team, to provide nonacademic and extracurricular services and activities in the manner necessary to afford children with disabilities an equal opportunity for participation in those services and activities.

(b) Nonacademic and extracurricular services and activities may include counseling services, athletics, transportation, health services, recreational activities, special interest groups or clubs sponsored by the public agency, referrals to agencies that provide assistance to individuals with disabilities, and employment of students, including both employment by the public agency and assistance in making outside employment available.

(Approved by the Office of Management and Budget under control number 1820–0030)

(Authority: 20 U.S.C. 1412(a)(1))

§ 300.108 Physical education.

The State must ensure that public agencies in the State comply with the following:

(a) *General.* Physical education services, specially designed if necessary, must be made available to every child with a disability receiving FAPE, un-less the public agency enrolls children without disabilities and does not provide physical education to children without disabilities in the same grades.

(b) *Regular physical education.* Each child with a disability must be afforded the opportunity to participate in the regular physical education program available to nondisabled children unless—

(1) The child is enrolled full time in a separate facility; or

(2) The child needs specially designed physical education, as prescribed in the child's IEP.

(c) *Special physical education.* If specially designed physical education is prescribed in a child's IEP, the public agency responsible for the education of that child must provide the services directly or make arrangements for those services to be provided through other public or private programs.

(d) *Education in separate facilities.* The public agency responsible for the education of a child with a disability who is enrolled in a separate facility must ensure that the child receives appropriate physical education services in compliance with this section.

(Approved by the Office of Management and Budget under control number 1820–0030)

(Authority: 20 U.S.C. 1412(a)(5)(A))

§ 300.109 Full educational opportunity goal (FEOG).

The State must have in effect policies and procedures to demonstrate that the State has established a goal of providing full educational opportunity to all children with disabilities, aged birth through 21, and a detailed timetable for accomplishing that goal.

(Approved by the Office of Management and Budget under control number 1820–0030)

(Authority: 20 U.S.C. 1412(a)(2))

§ 300.110 Program options.

The State must ensure that each public agency takes steps to ensure that its children with disabilities have available to them the variety of educational programs and services available to nondisabled children in the area served by the agency, including art, music, industrial arts, consumer and homemaking education, and vocational education.

(Approved by the Office of Management and Budget under control number 1820–0030)

(Authority: 20 U.S.C. 1412(a)(2), 1413(a)(1))

§ 300.111 Child find.

(a) *General.* (1) The State must have in effect policies and procedures to ensure that—

(i) All children with disabilities residing in the State, including children with disabilities who are homeless children or are wards of the State, and children with disabilities attending private schools, regardless of the severity of their disability, and who are in need of special education and related services, are identified, located, and evaluated; and

(ii) A practical method is developed and implemented to determine which children are currently receiving needed special education and related services.

(b) *Use of term developmental delay.* The following provisions apply with respect to implementing the child find requirements of this section:

(1) A State that adopts a definition of *developmental delay* under § 300.8(b) determines whether the term applies to children aged three through nine, or to a subset of that age range (*e.g.*, ages three through five).

(2) A State may not require an LEA to adopt and use the term *developmental delay* for any children within its jurisdiction.

(3) If an LEA uses the term *developmental delay* for children described in § 300.8(b), the LEA must conform to both the State's definition of that term and to the age range that has been adopted by the State.

(4) If a State does not adopt the term *developmental delay*, an LEA may not independently use that term as a basis for establishing a child's eligibility under this part.

(c) *Other children in child find.* Child find also must include—

(1) Children who are suspected of being a child with a disability under § 300.8 and in need of special education, even though they are advancing from grade to grade; and

(2) Highly mobile children, including migrant children.

(d) *Construction.* Nothing in the Act requires that children be classified by their disability so long as each child who has a disability that is listed in § 300.8 and who, by reason of that disability, needs special education and related services is regarded as a child with a disability under Part B of the Act.

(Approved by the Office of Management and Budget under control number 1820–0030)

(Authority: 20 U.S.C. 1401(3)); 1412(a)(3))

§ 300.112 Individualized education programs (IEP).

The State must ensure that an IEP, or an IFSP that meets the requirements of section 636(d) of the Act, is developed, reviewed, and revised for each child with a disability in accordance with §§ 300.320 through 300.324, except as provided in § 300.300(b)(3)(ii).

(Approved by the Office of Management and Budget under control number 1820–0030)

(Authority: 20 U.S.C. 1412(a)(4))

§ 300.113 Routine checking of hearing aids and external components of surgically implanted medical devices.

(a) *Hearing aids.* Each public agency must ensure that hearing aids worn in school by children with hearing impairments, including deafness, are functioning properly.

(b) *External components of surgically implanted medical devices.* (1) Subject to paragraph (b)(2) of this section, each public agency must ensure that the external components of surgically implanted medical devices are functioning properly.

(2) For a child with a surgically implanted medical device who is receiving special education and related services under this part, a public agency is not responsible for the post-surgical maintenance, programming, or replacement of the medical device that has been surgically implanted (or of an external component of the surgically implanted medical device).

(Approved by the Office of Management and Budget under control number 1820–0030)

(Authority: 20 U.S.C. 1401(1), 1401(26)(B))

LEAST RESTRICTIVE ENVIRONMENT
(LRE)

§ 300.114 LRE requirements.

(a) *General.* (1) Except as provided in § 300.324(d)(2) (regarding children with disabilities in adult prisons), the State must have in effect policies and procedures to ensure that public agencies in the State meet the LRE requirements of this section and §§ 300.115 through 300.120.

(2) Each public agency must ensure that—

(i) To the maximum extent appropriate, children with disabilities, including children in public or private institutions or other care facilities, are educated with children who are nondisabled; and

(ii) Special classes, separate schooling, or other removal of children with disabilities from the regular educational environment occurs only if the nature or severity of the disability is such that education in regular classes with the use of supplementary aids and services cannot be achieved satisfactorily.

(b) *Additional requirement—State funding mechanism—*(1) *General.* (i) A State funding mechanism must not result in placements that violate the requirements of paragraph (a) of this section; and

(ii) A State must not use a funding mechanism by which the State distributes funds on the basis of the type of setting in which a child is served that will result in the failure to provide a child with a disability FAPE according to the unique needs of the child, as described in the child's IEP.

(2) *Assurance.* If the State does not have policies and procedures to ensure compliance with paragraph (b)(1) of this section, the State must provide the Secretary an assurance that the State will revise the funding mechanism as soon as feasible to ensure that the mechanism does not result in placements that violate that paragraph.

(Approved by the Office of Management and Budget under control number 1820–0030)

(Authority: 20 U.S.C. 1412(a)(5))

§ 300.115 Continuum of alternative placements.

(a) Each public agency must ensure that a continuum of alternative placements is available to meet the needs of children with disabilities for special education and related services.

(b) The continuum required in paragraph (a) of this section must—

(1) Include the alternative placements listed in the definition of special education under § 300.39 (instruction in regular classes, special classes, special schools, home instruction, and instruction in hospitals and institutions); and

(2) Make provision for supplementary services (such as resource room or itinerant instruction) to be provided in conjunction with regular class placement.

(Approved by the Office of Management and Budget under control number 1820–0030)

(Authority: 20 U.S.C. 1412(a)(5))

[71 FR 46753, Aug. 14, 2006, as amended at 82 FR 29759, June 30, 2017]

§ 300.116 Placements.

In determining the educational placement of a child with a disability, including a preschool child with a disability, each public agency must ensure that—

(a) The placement decision—

(1) Is made by a group of persons, including the parents, and other persons knowledgeable about the child, the meaning of the evaluation data, and the placement options; and

(2) Is made in conformity with the LRE provisions of this subpart, including §§ 300.114 through 300.118;

(b) The child's placement—

(1) Is determined at least annually;

(2) Is based on the child's IEP; and

(3) Is as close as possible to the child's home;

(c) Unless the IEP of a child with a disability requires some other arrangement, the child is educated in the school that he or she would attend if nondisabled;

(d) In selecting the LRE, consideration is given to any potential harmful effect on the child or on the quality of services that he or she needs; and

(e) A child with a disability is not removed from education in age-appropriate regular classrooms solely because of needed modifications in the general education curriculum.

(Approved by the Office of Management and Budget under control number 1820–0030)

(Authority: 20 U.S.C. 1412(a)(5))

§ 300.117 **Nonacademic settings.**

In providing or arranging for the provision of nonacademic and extracurricular services and activities, including meals, recess periods, and the services and activities set forth in § 300.107, each public agency must ensure that each child with a disability participates with nondisabled children in the extracurricular services and activities to the maximum extent appropriate to the needs of that child. The public agency must ensure that each child with a disability has the supplementary aids and services determined by the child's IEP Team to be appropriate and necessary for the child to participate in nonacademic settings.

(Approved by the Office of Management and Budget under control number 1820–0030)

(Authority: 20 U.S.C. 1412(a)(5))

§ 300.118 **Children in public or private institutions.**

Except as provided in § 300.149(d) (regarding agency responsibility for general supervision of some individuals in adult prisons), an SEA must ensure that § 300.114 is effectively implemented, including, if necessary, making arrangements with public and private institutions (such as a memorandum of agreement or special implementation procedures).

(Approved by the Office of Management and Budget under control number 1820–0030)

(Authority: 20 U.S.C. 1412(a)(5))

[71 FR 46753, Aug. 14, 2006, as amended at 72 FR 61306, Oct. 30, 2007]

§ 300.119 **Technical assistance and training activities.**

Each SEA must carry out activities to ensure that teachers and administrators in all public agencies—

(a) Are fully informed about their responsibilities for implementing § 300.114; and

(b) Are provided with technical assistance and training necessary to assist them in this effort.

(Approved by the Office of Management and Budget under control number 1820–0030)

(Authority: 20 U.S.C. 1412(a)(5))

§ 300.120 **Monitoring activities.**

(a) The SEA must carry out activities to ensure that § 300.114 is implemented by each public agency.

(b) If there is evidence that a public agency makes placements that are inconsistent with § 300.114, the SEA must—

(1) Review the public agency's justification for its actions; and

(2) Assist in planning and implementing any necessary corrective action.

(Approved by the Office of Management and Budget under control number 1820–0030)

(Authority: 20 U.S.C. 1412(a)(5))

ADDITIONAL ELIGIBILITY REQUIREMENTS

§ 300.121 **Procedural safeguards.**

(a) *General.* The State must have procedural safeguards in effect to ensure that each public agency in the State meets the requirements of §§ 300.500 through 300.536.

(b) *Procedural safeguards identified.* Children with disabilities and their parents must be afforded the procedural safeguards identified in paragraph (a) of this section.

(Approved by the Office of Management and Budget under control number 1820–0030)

(Authority: 20 U.S.C. 1412(a)(6)(A))

§ 300.122 **Evaluation.**

Children with disabilities must be evaluated in accordance with §§ 300.300 through 300.311 of subpart D of this part.

(Approved by the Office of Management and Budget under control number 1820–0030)

(Authority: 20 U.S.C. 1412(a)(7))

§ 300.123 **Confidentiality of personally identifiable information.**

The State must have policies and procedures in effect to ensure that public agencies in the State comply with

§§ 300.610 through 300.626 related to protecting the confidentiality of any personally identifiable information collected, used, or maintained under Part B of the Act.

(Approved by the Office of Management and Budget under control number 1820–0030)

(Authority: 20 U.S.C. 1412(a)(8); 1417(c))

§ 300.124 Transition of children from the Part C program to preschool programs.

The State must have in effect policies and procedures to ensure that—

(a) Children participating in early intervention programs assisted under Part C of the Act, and who will participate in preschool programs assisted under Part B of the Act, experience a smooth and effective transition to those preschool programs in a manner consistent with section 637(a)(9) of the Act;

(b) By the third birthday of a child described in paragraph (a) of this section, an IEP or, if consistent with § 300.323(b) and section 636(d) of the Act, an IFSP, has been developed and is being implemented for the child consistent with § 300.101(b); and

(c) Each affected LEA will participate in transition planning conferences arranged by the designated lead agency under section 635(a)(10) of the Act.

(Approved by the Office of Management and Budget under control number 1820–0030)

(Authority: 20 U.S.C. 1412(a)(9))

§§ 300.125–300.128 [Reserved]

CHILDREN IN PRIVATE SCHOOLS

§ 300.129 State responsibility regarding children in private schools.

The State must have in effect policies and procedures that ensure that LEAs, and, if applicable, the SEA, meet the private school requirements in §§ 300.130 through 300.148.

(Approved by the Office of Management and Budget under control number 1820–0030)

(Authority: 20 U.S.C. 1412(a)(10))

CHILDREN WITH DISABILITIES ENROLLED BY THEIR PARENTS IN PRIVATE SCHOOLS

§ 300.130 Definition of parentally-placed private school children with disabilities.

Parentally-placed private school children with disabilities means children with disabilities enrolled by their parents in private, including religious, schools or facilities that meet the definition of elementary school in § 300.13 or secondary school in § 300.36, other than children with disabilities covered under §§ 300.145 through 300.147.

(Approved by the Office of Management and Budget under control number 1820–0030)

(Authority: 20 U.S.C. 1412(a)(10)(A))

§ 300.131 Child find for parentally-placed private school children with disabilities.

(a) *General.* Each LEA must locate, identify, and evaluate all children with disabilities who are enrolled by their parents in private, including religious, elementary schools and secondary schools located in the school district served by the LEA, in accordance with paragraphs (b) through (e) of this section, and §§ 300.111 and 300.201.

(b) *Child find design.* The child find process must be designed to ensure—

(1) The equitable participation of parentally-placed private school children; and

(2) An accurate count of those children.

(c) *Activities.* In carrying out the requirements of this section, the LEA, or, if applicable, the SEA, must undertake activities similar to the activities undertaken for the agency's public school children.

(d) *Cost.* The cost of carrying out the child find requirements in this section, including individual evaluations, may not be considered in determining if an LEA has met its obligation under § 300.133.

(e) *Completion period.* The child find process must be completed in a time period comparable to that for students attending public schools in the LEA consistent with § 300.301.

(f) *Out-of-State children.* Each LEA in which private, including religious, elementary schools and secondary schools are located must, in carrying out the child find requirements in this section, include parentally-placed private school children who reside in a State other than the State in which the private schools that they attend are located.

(Approved by the Office of Management and Budget under control number 1820–0030)

(Authority: 20 U.S.C. 1412(a)(10)(A)(ii))

§300.132 Provision of services for parentally-placed private school children with disabilities—basic requirement.

(a) *General.* To the extent consistent with the number and location of children with disabilities who are enrolled by their parents in private, including religious, elementary schools and secondary schools located in the school district served by the LEA, provision is made for the participation of those children in the program assisted or carried out under Part B of the Act by providing them with special education and related services, including direct services determined in accordance with §300.137, unless the Secretary has arranged for services to those children under the by-pass provisions in §§300.190 through 300.198.

(b) *Services plan for parentally-placed private school children with disabilities.* In accordance with paragraph (a) of this section and §§300.137 through 300.139, a services plan must be developed and implemented for each private school child with a disability who has been designated by the LEA in which the private school is located to receive special education and related services under this part.

(c) *Record keeping.* Each LEA must maintain in its records, and provide to the SEA, the following information related to parentally-placed private school children covered under §§300.130 through 300.144:

(1) The number of children evaluated;

(2) The number of children determined to be children with disabilities; and

(3) The number of children served.

(Approved by the Office of Management and Budget under control numbers 1820–0030 and 1820–0600)

(Authority: 20 U.S.C. 1412(a)(10)(A)(i))

§300.133 Expenditures.

(a) *Formula.* To meet the requirement of §300.132(a), each LEA must spend the following on providing special education and related services (including direct services) to parentally-placed private school children with disabilities:

(1) For children aged 3 through 21, an amount that is the same proportion of the LEA's total subgrant under section 611(f) of the Act as the number of private school children with disabilities aged 3 through 21 who are enrolled by their parents in private, including religious, elementary schools and secondary schools located in the school district served by the LEA, is to the total number of children with disabilities in its jurisdiction aged 3 through 21.

(2)(i) For children aged three through five, an amount that is the same proportion of the LEA's total subgrant under section 619(g) of the Act as the number of parentally-placed private school children with disabilities aged three through five who are enrolled by their parents in a private, including religious, elementary school located in the school district served by the LEA, is to the total number of children with disabilities in its jurisdiction aged three through five.

(ii) As described in paragraph (a)(2)(i) of this section, children aged three through five are considered to be parentally-placed private school children with disabilities enrolled by their parents in private, including religious, elementary schools, if they are enrolled in a private school that meets the definition of elementary school in §300.13.

(3) If an LEA has not expended for equitable services all of the funds described in paragraphs (a)(1) and (a)(2) of this section by the end of the fiscal year for which Congress appropriated the funds, the LEA must obligate the remaining funds for special education and related services (including direct services) to parentally-placed private school children with disabilities during a carry-over period of one additional year.

(b) *Calculating proportionate amount.* In calculating the proportionate amount of Federal funds to be provided for parentally-placed private school children with disabilities, the LEA, after timely and meaningful consultation with representatives of private schools under § 300.134, must conduct a thorough and complete child find process to determine the number of parentally-placed children with disabilities attending private schools located in the LEA. (See appendix B for an example of how proportionate share is calculated).

(c) *Annual count of the number of parentally-placed private school children with disabilities.* (1) Each LEA must—

(i) After timely and meaningful consultation with representatives of parentally-placed private school children with disabilities (consistent with § 300.134), determine the number of parentally-placed private school children with disabilities attending private schools located in the LEA; and

(ii) Ensure that the count is conducted on any date between October 1 and December 1, inclusive, of each year.

(2) The count must be used to determine the amount that the LEA must spend on providing special education and related services to parentally-placed private school children with disabilities in the next subsequent fiscal year.

(d) *Supplement, not supplant.* State and local funds may supplement and in no case supplant the proportionate amount of Federal funds required to be expended for parentally-placed private school children with disabilities under this part.

(Approved by the Office of Management and Budget under control number 1820–0030)

(Authority: 20 U.S.C. 1412(a)(10)(A))

§ 300.134 Consultation.

To ensure timely and meaningful consultation, an LEA, or, if appropriate, an SEA, must consult with private school representatives and representatives of parents of parentally-placed private school children with disabilities during the design and development of special education and related services for the children regarding the following:

(a) Child find. The child find process, including—

(1) How parentally-placed private school children suspected of having a disability can participate equitably; and

(2) How parents, teachers, and private school officials will be informed of the process.

(b) *Proportionate share of funds.* The determination of the proportionate share of Federal funds available to serve parentally-placed private school children with disabilities under § 300.133(b), including the determination of how the proportionate share of those funds was calculated.

(c) *Consultation process.* The consultation process among the LEA, private school officials, and representatives of parents of parentally-placed private school children with disabilities, including how the process will operate throughout the school year to ensure that parentally-placed children with disabilities identified through the child find process can meaningfully participate in special education and related services.

(d) *Provision of special education and related services.* How, where, and by whom special education and related services will be provided for parentally-placed private school children with disabilities, including a discussion of—

(1) The types of services, including direct services and alternate service delivery mechanisms; and

(2) How special education and related services will be apportioned if funds are insufficient to serve all parentally-placed private school children; and

(3) How and when those decisions will be made;

(e) *Written explanation by LEA regarding services.* How, if the LEA disagrees with the views of the private school officials on the provision of services or the types of services (whether provided directly or through a contract), the LEA will provide to the private school officials a written explanation of the reasons why the LEA chose not to provide services directly or through a contract.

(Approved by the Office of Management and Budget under control numbers 1820–0030 and 1820–0600)

(Authority: 20 U.S.C. 1412(a)(10)(A)(iii))

§300.135 Written affirmation.

(a) When timely and meaningful consultation, as required by §300.134, has occurred, the LEA must obtain a written affirmation signed by the representatives of participating private schools.

(b) If the representatives do not provide the affirmation within a reasonable period of time, the LEA must forward the documentation of the consultation process to the SEA.

(Approved by the Office of Management and Budget under control numbers 1820–0030 and 1820–0600)

(Authority: 20 U.S.C. 1412(a)(10)(A)(iv))

§300.136 Compliance.

(a) *General.* A private school official has the right to submit a complaint to the SEA that the LEA—

(1) Did not engage in consultation that was meaningful and timely; or

(2) Did not give due consideration to the views of the private school official.

(b) *Procedure.* (1) If the private school official wishes to submit a complaint, the official must provide to the SEA the basis of the noncompliance by the LEA with the applicable private school provisions in this part; and

(2) The LEA must forward the appropriate documentation to the SEA.

(3)(i) If the private school official is dissatisfied with the decision of the SEA, the official may submit a complaint to the Secretary by providing the information on noncompliance described in paragraph (b)(1) of this section; and

(ii) The SEA must forward the appropriate documentation to the Secretary.

(Approved by the Office of Management and Budget under control numbers 1820–0030 and 1820–0600)

(Authority: 20 U.S.C. 1412(a)(10)(A)(v))

§300.137 Equitable services determined.

(a) *No individual right to special education and related services.* No parentally-placed private school child with a disability has an individual right to receive some or all of the special education and related services that the child would receive if enrolled in a public school.

(b) *Decisions.* (1) Decisions about the services that will be provided to parentally-placed private school children with disabilities under §§300.130 through 300.144 must be made in accordance with paragraph (c) of this section and §300.134(d).

(2) The LEA must make the final decisions with respect to the services to be provided to eligible parentally-placed private school children with disabilities.

(c) *Services plan for each child served under §§300.130 through 300.144.* If a child with a disability is enrolled in a religious or other private school by the child's parents and will receive special education or related services from an LEA, the LEA must—

(1) Initiate and conduct meetings to develop, review, and revise a services plan for the child, in accordance with §300.138(b); and

(2) Ensure that a representative of the religious or other private school attends each meeting. If the representative cannot attend, the LEA shall use other methods to ensure participation by the religious or other private school, including individual or conference telephone calls.

(Approved by the Office of Management and Budget under control number 1820–0030)

(Authority: 20 U.S.C. 1412(a)(10)(A))

[71 FR 46753, Aug. 14, 2006, as amended at 72 FR 61306, Oct. 30, 2007]

§300.138 Equitable services provided.

(a) *General.* (1) The services provided to parentally-placed private school children with disabilities must be provided by personnel meeting the same standards as personnel providing services in the public schools, except that private elementary school and secondary school teachers who are providing equitable services to parentally-placed private school children with disabilities do not have to meet the special education teacher qualification requirements in §300.156(c).

(2) Parentally-placed private school children with disabilities may receive a different amount of services than children with disabilities in public schools.

(b) *Services provided in accordance with a services plan.* (1) Each parentally-placed private school child with a disability who has been designated to receive services under § 300.132 must have a services plan that describes the specific special education and related services that the LEA will provide to the child in light of the services that the LEA has determined, through the process described in §§ 300.134 and 300.137, it will make available to parentally-placed private school children with disabilities.

(2) The services plan must, to the extent appropriate—

(i) Meet the requirements of § 300.320, or for a child ages three through five, meet the requirements of § 300.323(b) with respect to the services provided; and

(ii) Be developed, reviewed, and revised consistent with §§ 300.321 through 300.324.

(c) *Provision of equitable services.* (1) The provision of services pursuant to this section and §§ 300.139 through 300.143 must be provided:

(i) By employees of a public agency; or

(ii) Through contract by the public agency with an individual, association, agency, organization, or other entity.

(2) Special education and related services provided to parentally-placed private school children with disabilities, including materials and equipment, must be secular, neutral, and nonideological.

(Approved by the Office of Management and Budget under control number 1820–0030)

(Authority: 20 U.S.C. 1412(a)(10)(A)(vi))

[71 FR 46753, Aug. 14, 2006, as amended at 82 FR 29759, June 30, 2017]

§ 300.139 Location of services and transportation.

(a) *Services on private school premises.* Services to parentally-placed private school children with disabilities may be provided on the premises of private, including religious, schools, to the extent consistent with law.

(b) *Transportation*—(1) *General.* (i) If necessary for the child to benefit from or participate in the services provided under this part, a parentally-placed private school child with a disability must be provided transportation—

(A) From the child's school or the child's home to a site other than the private school; and

(B) From the service site to the private school, or to the child's home, depending on the timing of the services.

(ii) LEAs are not required to provide transportation from the child's home to the private school.

(2) *Cost of transportation.* The cost of the transportation described in paragraph (b)(1)(i) of this section may be included in calculating whether the LEA has met the requirement of § 300.133.

(Approved by the Office of Management and Budget under control number 1820–0030)

(Authority: 20 U.S.C. 1412(a)(10)(A))

§ 300.140 Due process complaints and State complaints.

(a) *Due process not applicable, except for child find.* (1) Except as provided in paragraph (b) of this section, the procedures in §§ 300.504 through 300.519 do not apply to complaints that an LEA has failed to meet the requirements of §§ 300.132 through 300.139, including the provision of services indicated on the child's services plan.

(b) *Child find complaints—to be filed with the LEA in which the private school is located.* (1) The procedures in §§ 300.504 through 300.519 apply to complaints that an LEA has failed to meet the child find requirements in § 300.131, including the requirements in §§ 300.300 through 300.311.

(2) Any due process complaint regarding the child find requirements (as described in paragraph (b)(1) of this section) must be filed with the LEA in which the private school is located and a copy must be forwarded to the SEA.

(c) *State complaints.* (1) Any complaint that an SEA or LEA has failed to meet the requirements in §§ 300.132 through 300.135 and 300.137 through 300.144 must be filed in accordance with the procedures described in §§ 300.151 through 300.153.

(2) A complaint filed by a private school official under § 300.136(a) must be filed with the SEA in accordance with the procedures in § 300.136(b).

(Approved by the Office of Management and Budget under control number 1820–0030)

(Authority: 20 U.S.C. 1412(a)(10)(A))

§ 300.141 Requirement that funds not benefit a private school.

(a) An LEA may not use funds provided under section 611 or 619 of the Act to finance the existing level of instruction in a private school or to otherwise benefit the private school.

(b) The LEA must use funds provided under Part B of the Act to meet the special education and related services needs of parentally-placed private school children with disabilities, but not for meeting—

(1) The needs of a private school; or

(2) The general needs of the students enrolled in the private school.

(Approved by the Office of Management and Budget under control number 1820–0030)

(Authority: 20 U.S.C. 1412(a)(10)(A))

§ 300.142 Use of personnel.

(a) *Use of public school personnel.* An LEA may use funds available under sections 611 and 619 of the Act to make public school personnel available in other than public facilities—

(1) To the extent necessary to provide services under §§ 300.130 through 300.144 for parentally-placed private school children with disabilities; and

(2) If those services are not normally provided by the private school.

(b) *Use of private school personnel.* An LEA may use funds available under sections 611 and 619 of the Act to pay for the services of an employee of a private school to provide services under §§ 300.130 through 300.144 if—

(1) The employee performs the services outside of his or her regular hours of duty; and

(2) The employee performs the services under public supervision and control.

(Approved by the Office of Management and Budget under control number 1820–0030)

(Authority: 20 U.S.C. 1412(a)(10)(A))

§ 300.143 Separate classes prohibited.

An LEA may not use funds available under section 611 or 619 of the Act for classes that are organized separately on the basis of school enrollment or religion of the children if—'

(a) The classes are at the same site; and

(b) The classes include children enrolled in public schools and children enrolled in private schools.

(Approved by the Office of Management and Budget under control number 1820–0030)

(Authority: 20 U.S.C. 1412(a)(10)(A))

§ 300.144 Property, equipment, and supplies.

(a) A public agency must control and administer the funds used to provide special education and related services under §§ 300.137 through 300.139, and hold title to and administer materials, equipment, and property purchased with those funds for the uses and purposes provided in the Act.

(b) The public agency may place equipment and supplies in a private school for the period of time needed for the Part B program.

(c) The public agency must ensure that the equipment and supplies placed in a private school—

(1) Are used only for Part B purposes; and

(2) Can be removed from the private school without remodeling the private school facility.

(d) The public agency must remove equipment and supplies from a private school if—

(1) The equipment and supplies are no longer needed for Part B purposes; or

(2) Removal is necessary to avoid unauthorized use of the equipment and supplies for other than Part B purposes.

(e) No funds under Part B of the Act may be used for repairs, minor remodeling, or construction of private school facilities.

(Approved by the Office of Management and Budget under control number 1820–0030)

(Authority: 20 U.S.C. 1412(a)(10)(A)(vii))

CHILDREN WITH DISABILITIES IN PRIVATE SCHOOLS PLACED OR REFERRED BY PUBLIC AGENCIES

§ 300.145 Applicability of §§ 300.146 through 300.147.

Sections 300.146 through 300.147 apply only to children with disabilities who are or have been placed in or referred to a private school or facility by a public agency as a means of providing special education and related services.

(Approved by the Office of Management and Budget under control number 1820–0030)

(Authority: 20 U.S.C. 1412(a)(10)(B))

§ 300.146 Responsibility of SEA.

Each SEA must ensure that a child with a disability who is placed in or referred to a private school or facility by a public agency—

(a) Is provided special education and related services—

(1) In conformance with an IEP that meets the requirements of §§ 300.320 through 300.325; and

(2) At no cost to the parents;

(b) Is provided an education that meets the standards that apply to education provided by the SEA and LEAs including the requirements of this part, except for § 300.156(c); and

(c) Has all of the rights of a child with a disability who is served by a public agency.

(Approved by the Office of Management and Budget under control number 1820–0030)

(Authority: 20 U.S.C. 1412(a)(10)(B))

[71 FR 46753, Aug. 14, 2006, as amended at 82 FR 29759, June 30, 2017]

§ 300.147 Implementation by SEA.

In implementing § 300.146, the SEA must—

(a) Monitor compliance through procedures such as written reports, on-site visits, and parent questionnaires;

(b) Disseminate copies of applicable standards to each private school and facility to which a public agency has referred or placed a child with a disability; and

(c) Provide an opportunity for those private schools and facilities to participate in the development and revision of State standards that apply to them.

(Approved by the Office of Management and Budget under control number 1820–0030)

(Authority: 20 U.S.C. 1412(a)(10)(B))

CHILDREN WITH DISABILITIES ENROLLED BY THEIR PARENTS IN PRIVATE SCHOOLS WHEN FAPE IS AT ISSUE

§ 300.148 Placement of children by parents when FAPE is at issue.

(a) *General.* This part does not require an LEA to pay for the cost of education, including special education and related services, of a child with a disability at a private school or facility if that agency made FAPE available to the child and the parents elected to place the child in a private school or facility. However, the public agency must include that child in the population whose needs are addressed consistent with §§ 300.131 through 300.144.

(b) *Disagreements about FAPE.* Disagreements between the parents and a public agency regarding the availability of a program appropriate for the child, and the question of financial reimbursement, are subject to the due process procedures in §§ 300.504 through 300.520.

(c) *Reimbursement for private school placement.* If the parents of a child with a disability, who previously received special education and related services under the authority of a public agency, enroll the child in a private preschool, elementary school, or secondary school without the consent of or referral by the public agency, a court or a hearing officer may require the agency to reimburse the parents for the cost of that enrollment if the court or hearing officer finds that the agency had not made FAPE available to the child in a timely manner prior to that enrollment and that the private placement is appropriate. A parental placement may be found to be appropriate by a hearing officer or a court even if it does not meet the State standards that apply to education provided by the SEA and LEAs.

(d) *Limitation on reimbursement.* The cost of reimbursement described in paragraph (c) of this section may be reduced or denied—

(1) If—

(i) At the most recent IEP Team meeting that the parents attended prior to removal of the child from the public school, the parents did not inform the IEP Team that they were rejecting the placement proposed by the public agency to provide FAPE to their child, including stating their concerns and their intent to enroll their child in a private school at public expense; or

(ii) At least ten (10) business days (including any holidays that occur on a business day) prior to the removal of the child from the public school, the parents did not give written notice to the public agency of the information described in paragraph (d)(1)(i) of this section;

(2) If, prior to the parents' removal of the child from the public school, the public agency informed the parents, through the notice requirements described in § 300.503(a)(1), of its intent to evaluate the child (including a statement of the purpose of the evaluation that was appropriate and reasonable), but the parents did not make the child available for the evaluation; or

(3) Upon a judicial finding of unreasonableness with respect to actions taken by the parents.

(e) *Exception.* Notwithstanding the notice requirement in paragraph (d)(1) of this section, the cost of reimbursement—

(1) Must not be reduced or denied for failure to provide the notice if—

(i) The school prevented the parents from providing the notice;

(ii) The parents had not received notice, pursuant to § 300.504, of the notice requirement in paragraph (d)(1) of this section; or

(iii) Compliance with paragraph (d)(1) of this section would likely result in physical harm to the child; and

(2) May, in the discretion of the court or a hearing officer, not be reduced or denied for failure to provide this notice if—

(i) The parents are not literate or cannot write in English; or

(ii) Compliance with paragraph (d)(1) of this section would likely result in serious emotional harm to the child.

(Approved by the Office of Management and Budget under control number 1820–0030)

(Authority: 20 U.S.C. 1412(a)(10)(C))

SEA RESPONSIBILITY FOR GENERAL SUPERVISION AND IMPLEMENTATION OF PROCEDURAL SAFEGUARDS

§ 300.149 SEA responsibility for general supervision.

(a) The SEA is responsible for ensuring—

(1) That the requirements of this part are carried out; and

(2) That each educational program for children with disabilities administered within the State, including each program administered by any other State or local agency (but not including elementary schools and secondary schools for Indian children operated or funded by the Secretary of the Interior)—

(i) Is under the general supervision of the persons responsible for educational programs for children with disabilities in the SEA; and

(ii) Meets the educational standards of the SEA (including the requirements of this part).

(3) In carrying out this part with respect to homeless children, the requirements of subtitle B of title VII of the McKinney-Vento Homeless Assistance Act (42 U.S.C. 11431 *et seq.*) are met.

(b) The State must have in effect policies and procedures to ensure that it complies with the monitoring and enforcement requirements in §§ 300.600 through 300.602 and §§ 300.606 through 300.608.

(c) Part B of the Act does not limit the responsibility of agencies other than educational agencies for providing or paying some or all of the costs of FAPE to children with disabilities in the State.

(d) Notwithstanding paragraph (a) of this section, the Governor (or another individual pursuant to State law) may assign to any public agency in the State the responsibility of ensuring that the requirements of Part B of the Act are met with respect to students with disabilities who are convicted as adults under State law and incarcerated in adult prisons.

(Approved by the Office of Management and Budget under control number 1820–0030)

(Authority: 20 U.S.C. 1412(a)(11); 1416)

§ 300.150 SEA implementation of procedural safeguards.

The SEA (and any agency assigned responsibility pursuant to § 300.149(d)) must have in effect procedures to inform each public agency of its responsibility for ensuring effective implementation of procedural safeguards for the children with disabilities served by that public agency.

(Approved by the Office of Management and Budget under control number 1820–0030)

(Authority: 20 U.S.C. 1412(a)(11); 1415(a))

STATE COMPLAINT PROCEDURES

§ 300.151 Adoption of State complaint procedures.

(a) *General.* Each SEA must adopt written procedures for—

(1) Resolving any complaint, including a complaint filed by an organization or individual from another State, that meets the requirements of § 300.153 by—

(i) Providing for the filing of a complaint with the SEA; and

(ii) At the SEA's discretion, providing for the filing of a complaint with a public agency and the right to have the SEA review the public agency's decision on the complaint; and

(2) Widely disseminating to parents and other interested individuals, including parent training and information centers, protection and advocacy agencies, independent living centers, and other appropriate entities, the State procedures under §§ 300.151 through 300.153.

(b) *Remedies for denial of appropriate services.* In resolving a complaint in which the SEA has found a failure to provide appropriate services, an SEA, pursuant to its general supervisory authority under Part B of the Act, must address—

(1) The failure to provide appropriate services, including corrective action appropriate to address the needs of the child (such as compensatory services or monetary reimbursement); and

(2) Appropriate future provision of services for all children with disabilities.

(Approved by the Office of Management and Budget under control numbers 1820–0030 and 1820–0600)

(Authority: 20 U.S.C. 1221e–3)

§ 300.152 Minimum State complaint procedures.

(a) *Time limit; minimum procedures.* Each SEA must include in its complaint procedures a time limit of 60 days after a complaint is filed under § 300.153 to—

(1) Carry out an independent on-site investigation, if the SEA determines that an investigation is necessary;

(2) Give the complainant the opportunity to submit additional information, either orally or in writing, about the allegations in the complaint;

(3) Provide the public agency with the opportunity to respond to the complaint, including, at a minimum—

(i) At the discretion of the public agency, a proposal to resolve the complaint; and

(ii) An opportunity for a parent who has filed a complaint and the public agency to voluntarily engage in mediation consistent with § 300.506;

(4) Review all relevant information and make an independent determination as to whether the public agency is violating a requirement of Part B of the Act or of this part; and

(5) Issue a written decision to the complainant that addresses each allegation in the complaint and contains—

(i) Findings of fact and conclusions; and

(ii) The reasons for the SEA's final decision.

(b) *Time extension; final decision; implementation.* The SEA's procedures described in paragraph (a) of this section also must—

(1) Permit an extension of the time limit under paragraph (a) of this section only if—

(i) Exceptional circumstances exist with respect to a particular complaint; or

(ii) The parent (or individual or organization, if mediation or other alternative means of dispute resolution is available to the individual or organization under State procedures) and the public agency involved agree to extend the time to engage in mediation pursuant to paragraph (a)(3)(ii) of this section, or to engage in other alternative means of dispute resolution, if available in the State; and

(2) Include procedures for effective implementation of the SEA's final decision, if needed, including—

(i) Technical assistance activities;

(ii) Negotiations; and

(iii) Corrective actions to achieve compliance.

(c) *Complaints filed under this section and due process hearings under § 300.507 and §§ 300.530 through 300.532.* (1) If a written complaint is received that is also the subject of a due process hearing under § 300.507 or §§ 300.530 through 300.532, or contains multiple issues of which one or more are part of that hearing, the State must set aside any part of the complaint that is being addressed in the due process hearing until the conclusion of the hearing. However, any issue in the complaint that is not a part of the due process action must be resolved using the time limit and procedures described in paragraphs (a) and (b) of this section.

(2) If an issue raised in a complaint filed under this section has previously been decided in a due process hearing involving the same parties—

(i) The due process hearing decision is binding on that issue; and

(ii) The SEA must inform the complainant to that effect.

(3) A complaint alleging a public agency's failure to implement a due process hearing decision must be resolved by the SEA.

(Approved by the Office of Management and Budget under control numbers 1820–0030 and 1820–0600)

(Authority: 20 U.S.C. 1221e–3)

§ 300.153 Filing a complaint.

(a) An organization or individual may file a signed written complaint under the procedures described in §§ 300.151 through 300.152.

(b) The complaint must include—

(1) A statement that a public agency has violated a requirement of Part B of the Act or of this part;

(2) The facts on which the statement is based;

(3) The signature and contact information for the complainant; and

(4) If alleging violations with respect to a specific child—

(i) The name and address of the residence of the child;

(ii) The name of the school the child is attending;

(iii) In the case of a homeless child or youth (within the meaning of section 725(2) of the McKinney-Vento Homeless Assistance Act (42 U.S.C. 11434a(2)), available contact information for the child, and the name of the school the child is attending;

(iv) A description of the nature of the problem of the child, including facts relating to the problem; and

(v) A proposed resolution of the problem to the extent known and available to the party at the time the complaint is filed.

(c) The complaint must allege a violation that occurred not more than one year prior to the date that the complaint is received in accordance with § 300.151.

(d) The party filing the complaint must forward a copy of the complaint to the LEA or public agency serving the child at the same time the party files the complaint with the SEA.

(Approved by the Office of Management and Budget under control numbers 1820–0030 and 1820–0600)

(Authority: 20 U.S.C. 1221e–3)

METHODS OF ENSURING SERVICES

§ 300.154 Methods of ensuring services.

(a) *Establishing responsibility for services.* The Chief Executive Officer of a State or designee of that officer must ensure that an interagency agreement or other mechanism for interagency coordination is in effect between each noneducational public agency described in paragraph (b) of this section and the SEA, in order to ensure that all services described in paragraph (b)(1) of this section that are needed to ensure FAPE are provided, including the provision of these services during the pendency of any dispute under paragraph (a)(3) of this section. The agreement or mechanism must include the following:

(1) An identification of, or a method for defining, the financial responsibility of each agency for providing services described in paragraph (b)(1) of this section to ensure FAPE to children with disabilities. The financial responsibility of each noneducational public agency described in paragraph (b) of this section, including the State Medicaid agency and other public insurers of children with disabilities, must precede the financial responsibility of the LEA (or the State agency responsible for developing the child's IEP).

(2) The conditions, terms, and procedures under which an LEA must be reimbursed by other agencies.

(3) Procedures for resolving interagency disputes (including procedures under which LEAs may initiate proceedings) under the agreement or other mechanism to secure reimbursement from other agencies or otherwise implement the provisions of the agreement or mechanism.

(4) Policies and procedures for agencies to determine and identify the interagency coordination responsibilities of each agency to promote the coordination and timely and appropriate delivery of services described in paragraph (b)(1) of this section.

(b) *Obligation of noneducational public agencies.* (1)(i) If any public agency other than an educational agency is otherwise obligated under Federal or State law, or assigned responsibility under State policy or pursuant to paragraph (a) of this section, to provide or pay for any services that are also considered special education or related services (such as, but not limited to, services described in § 300.5 relating to assistive technology devices, § 300.6 relating to assistive technology services, § 300.34 relating to related services, § 300.42 relating to supplementary aids and services, and § 300.43 relating to transition services) that are necessary for ensuring FAPE to children with disabilities within the State, the public agency must fulfill that obligation or responsibility, either directly or through contract or other arrangement pursuant to paragraph (a) of this section or an agreement pursuant to paragraph (c) of this section.

(ii) A noneducational public agency described in paragraph (b)(1)(i) of this section may not disqualify an eligible service for Medicaid reimbursement because that service is provided in a school context.

(2) If a public agency other than an educational agency fails to provide or pay for the special education and related services described in paragraph (b)(1) of this section, the LEA (or State agency responsible for developing the child's IEP) must provide or pay for these services to the child in a timely manner. The LEA or State agency is authorized to claim reimbursement for the services from the noneducational public agency that failed to provide or pay for these services and that agency must reimburse the LEA or State agency in accordance with the terms of the interagency agreement or other mechanism described in paragraph (a) of this section.

(c) *Special rule.* The requirements of paragraph (a) of this section may be met through—

(1) State statute or regulation;

(2) Signed agreements between respective agency officials that clearly identify the responsibilities of each agency relating to the provision of services; or

(3) Other appropriate written methods as determined by the Chief Executive Officer of the State or designee of that officer and approved by the Secretary.

(d) *Children with disabilities who are covered by public benefits or insurance.* (1) A public agency may use the Medicaid or other public benefits or insurance programs in which a child participates to provide or pay for services required under this part, as permitted under the public benefits or insurance program, except as provided in paragraph (d)(2) of this section.

(2) With regard to services required to provide FAPE to an eligible child under this part, the public agency—

(i) May not require parents to sign up for or enroll in public benefits or insurance programs in order for their child to receive FAPE under Part B of the Act;

(ii) May not require parents to incur an out-of-pocket expense such as the payment of a deductible or co-pay amount incurred in filing a claim for services provided pursuant to this part, but pursuant to paragraph (g)(2) of this section, may pay the cost that the parents otherwise would be required to pay;

(iii) May not use a child's benefits under a public benefits or insurance program if that use would—

(A) Decrease available lifetime coverage or any other insured benefit;

(B) Result in the family paying for services that would otherwise be covered by the public benefits or insurance program and that are required for the child outside of the time the child is in school;

(C) Increase premiums or lead to the discontinuation of benefits or insurance; or

(D) Risk loss of eligibility for home and community-based waivers, based on aggregate health-related expenditures; and

(iv) Prior to accessing a child's or parent's public benefits or insurance for the first time, and after providing notification to the child's parents consistent with paragraph (d)(2)(v) of this section, must obtain written, parental consent that—

(A) Meets the requirements of § 99.30 of this title and § 300.622, which consent must specify the personally identifiable information that may be disclosed (e.g., records or information about the services that may be provided to a particular child), the purpose of the disclosure (e.g., billing for services under part 300), and the agency to which the disclosure may be made (e.g., the State's public benefits or insurance program (e.g., Medicaid)); and

(B) Specifies that the parent understands and agrees that the public agency may access the parent's or child's public benefits or insurance to pay for services under part 300.

(v) Prior to accessing a child's or parent's public benefits or insurance for the first time, and annually thereafter, must provide written notification, consistent with § 300.503(c), to the child's parents, that includes—

(A) A statement of the parental consent provisions in paragraphs (d)(2)(iv)(A) and (B) of this section;

(B) A statement of the "no cost" provisions in paragraphs (d)(2)(i) through (iii) of this section;

(C) A statement that the parents have the right under 34 CFR part 99 and part 300 to withdraw their consent to disclosure of their child's personally identifiable information to the agency responsible for the administration of the State's public benefits or insurance program (e.g., Medicaid) at any time; and

(D) A statement that the withdrawal of consent or refusal to provide consent under 34 CFR part 99 and part 300 to disclose personally identifiable information to the agency responsible for the administration of the State's public benefits or insurance program (e.g., Medicaid) does not relieve the public agency of its responsibility to ensure that all required services are provided at no cost to the parents.

(e) *Children with disabilities who are covered by private insurance.* (1) With regard to services required to provide FAPE to an eligible child under this part, a public agency may access the parents' private insurance proceeds only if the parents provide consent consistent with § 300.9.

(2) Each time the public agency proposes to access the parents' private insurance proceeds, the agency must—

(i) Obtain parental consent in accordance with paragraph (e)(1) of this section; and

(ii) Inform the parents that their refusal to permit the public agency to access their private insurance does not relieve the public agency of its responsibility to ensure that all required services are provided at no cost to the parents.

(f) *Use of Part B funds.* (1) If a public agency is unable to obtain parental consent to use the parents' private insurance, or public benefits or insurance when the parents would incur a cost for a specified service required under this part, to ensure FAPE the public agency may use its Part B funds to pay for the service.

(2) To avoid financial cost to parents who otherwise would consent to use private insurance, or public benefits or insurance if the parents would incur a cost, the public agency may use its Part B funds to pay the cost that the

parents otherwise would have to pay to use the parents' benefits or insurance (e.g., the deductible or co-pay amounts).

(g) *Proceeds from public benefits or insurance or private insurance.* (1) Proceeds from public benefits or insurance or private insurance will not be treated as program income for purposes of 2 CFR 200.307

(2) If a public agency spends reimbursements from Federal funds (e.g., Medicaid) for services under this part, those funds will not be considered "State or local" funds for purposes of the maintenance of effort provisions in §§ 300.163 and 300.203.

(h) *Construction.* Nothing in this part should be construed to alter the requirements imposed on a State Medicaid agency, or any other agency administering a public benefits or insurance program by Federal statute, regulations or policy under title XIX, or title XXI of the Social Security Act, 42 U.S.C. 1396 through 1396v and 42 U.S.C. 1397aa through 1397jj, or any other public benefits or insurance program.

(Approved by the Office of Management and Budget under control number 1820-0030)

(Authority: 20 U.S.C. 1412(a)(12) and (e))

[71 FR 46753, Aug. 14, 2006, as amended at 78 FR 10537, Feb. 14, 2013; 79 FR 76096, Dec. 19, 2014; 82 FR 29759, June 30, 2017]

ADDITIONAL ELIGIBILITY REQUIREMENTS

§ 300.155 Hearings relating to LEA eligibility.

The SEA must not make any final determination that an LEA is not eligible for assistance under Part B of the Act without first giving the LEA reasonable notice and an opportunity for a hearing under 34 CFR 76.401(d).

(Approved by the Office of Management and Budget under control number 1820-0030)

(Authority: 20 U.S.C. 1412(a)(13))

§ 300.156 Personnel qualifications.

(a) *General.* The SEA must establish and maintain qualifications to ensure that personnel necessary to carry out the purposes of this part are appropriately and adequately prepared and trained, including that those personnel have the content knowledge and skills to serve children with disabilities.

(b) *Related services personnel and paraprofessionals.* The qualifications under paragraph (a) of this section must include qualifications for related services personnel and paraprofessionals that—

(1) Are consistent with any State-approved or State-recognized certification, licensing, registration, or other comparable requirements that apply to the professional discipline in which those personnel are providing special education or related services; and

(2) Ensure that related services personnel who deliver services in their discipline or profession—

(i) Meet the requirements of paragraph (b)(1) of this section; and

(ii) Have not had certification or licensure requirements waived on an emergency, temporary, or provisional basis; and

(iii) Allow paraprofessionals and assistants who are appropriately trained and supervised, in accordance with State law, regulation, or written policy, in meeting the requirements of this part to be used to assist in the provision of special education and related services under this part to children with disabilities.

(c) *Qualifications for special education teachers.* (1) The qualifications described in paragraph (a) of this section must ensure that each person employed as a public school special education teacher in the State who teaches in an elementary school, middle school, or secondary school—

(i) Has obtained full State certification as a special education teacher (including certification obtained through an alternate route to certification as a special educator, if such alternate route meets minimum requirements described in 34 CFR 200.56(a)(2)(ii) as such section was in effect on November 28, 2008), or passed the State special education teacher licensing examination, and holds a license to teach in the State as a special education teacher, except that when used with respect to any teacher teaching in a public charter school, the teacher must meet the certification or licensing requirements, if any, set forth in the State's public charter school law;

(ii) Has not had special education certification or licensure requirements waived on an emergency, temporary, or provisional basis; and

(iii) Holds at least a bachelor's degree.

(2) A teacher will be considered to meet the standard in paragraph (c)(1)(i) of this section if that teacher is participating in an alternate route to special education certification program under which—

(i) The teacher—

(A) Receives high-quality professional development that is sustained, intensive, and classroom-focused in order to have a positive and lasting impact on classroom instruction, before and while teaching;

(B) Participates in a program of intensive supervision that consists of structured guidance and regular ongoing support for teachers or a teacher mentoring program;

(C) Assumes functions as a teacher only for a specified period of time not to exceed three years; and

(D) Demonstrates satisfactory progress toward full certification as prescribed by the State; and

(ii) The State ensures, through its certification and licensure process, that the provisions in paragraph (c)(2)(i) of this section are met.

(d) *Policy.* In implementing this section, a State must adopt a policy that includes a requirement that LEAs in the State take measurable steps to recruit, hire, train, and retain personnel who meet the applicable requirements described in paragraph (c) of this section to provide special education and related services under this part to children with disabilities.

(e) *Rule of construction.* Notwithstanding any other individual right of action that a parent or student may maintain under this part, nothing in this part shall be construed to create a right of action on behalf of an individual student or a class of students for the failure of a particular SEA or LEA employee to meet the applicable requirements described in paragraph (c) of this section, or to prevent a parent from filing a complaint about staff qualifications with the SEA as provided for under this part.

(Approved by the Office of Management and Budget under control number 1820–0030)

(Authority: 20 U.S.C. 1412(a)(14))

[71 FR 46753, Aug. 14, 2006, as amended at 82 FR 29759, June 30, 2017]

§ 300.157 Performance goals and indicators.

The State must—

(a) Have in effect established goals for the performance of children with disabilities in the State that—

(1) Promote the purposes of this part, as stated in § 300.1;

(2) Are the same as the State's long-term goals and measurements of interim progress for children with disabilities under section 1111(c)(4)(A)(i) of the ESEA.

(3) Address graduation rates and dropout rates, as well as such other factors as the State may determine; and

(4) Are consistent, to the extent appropriate, with any other goals and academic standards for children established by the State;

(b) Have in effect established performance indicators the State will use to assess progress toward achieving the goals described in paragraph (a) of this section, including measurements of interim progress for children with disabilities under section 1111(c)(4)(A)(i)(cc) of the ESEA, 20 U.S.C. 6311; and

(c) Annually report to the Secretary and the public on the progress of the State, and of children with disabilities in the State, toward meeting the goals established under paragraph (a) of this section, which may include elements of the reports required under section 1111(h) of the ESEA.

(Approved by the Office of Management and Budget under control number 1820–0030)

(Authority: 20 U.S.C. 1412(a)(15))

[71 FR 46753, Aug. 14, 2006, as amended at 82 FR 29760, June 30, 2017]

§§ 300.158–300.159 [Reserved]

§ 300.160 Participation in assessments.

(a) *General.* A State must ensure that all children with disabilities are included in all general State and district-wide assessment programs, including assessments described under section 1111 of the ESEA, 20 U.S.C. 6311, with appropriate accommodations and alternate assessments, if necessary, as indicated in their respective IEPs.

(b) *Accommodation guidelines.* (1) A State (or, in the case of a district-wide assessment, an LEA) must develop guidelines for the provision of appropriate accommodations.

(2) The State's (or, in the case of a district-wide assessment, the LEA's) guidelines must—

(i) Identify only those accommodations for each assessment that do not invalidate the score; and

(ii) Instruct IEP Teams to select, for each assessment, only those accommodations that do not invalidate the score.

(c) *Alternate assessments aligned with alternate academic achievement standards for students with the most significant cognitive disabilities.* (1) If a State has adopted alternate academic achievement standards for children with disabilities who are students with the most significant cognitive disabilities as permitted in section 1111(b)(1)(E) of the ESEA, the State (or, in the case of a district-wide assessment, an LEA) must develop and implement alternate assessments and guidelines for the participation in alternate assessments of those children with disabilities who cannot participate in regular assessments, even with accommodations, as indicated in their respective IEPs, as provided in paragraph (a) of this section.

(2) For assessing the academic progress of children with disabilities who are students with the most significant cognitive disabilities under title I of the ESEA, the alternate assessments and guidelines in paragraph (c)(1) of this section must—

(i) Be aligned with the challenging State academic content standards under section 1111(b)(1) of the ESEA and alternate academic achievement standards under section 1111(b)(1)(E) of the ESEA; and

(ii) Measure the achievement of children with disabilities who are students with the most significant cognitive disabilities against those standards.

(3) Consistent with section 1111(b)(1)(E)(ii) of the ESEA and 34 CFR 200.6(c)(6), a State may not adopt modified academic achievement standards or any other alternate academic achievement standards that do not meet the requirements in section 1111(b)(1)(E) of the ESEA for any children with disabilities under section 602(3) of the IDEA.

(d) *Explanation to IEP Teams.* A State (or in the case of a district-wide assessment, an LEA) must—

(1) Provide to IEP teams a clear explanation of the differences between assessments based on grade-level academic achievement standards and those based on alternate academic achievement standards, including any effects of State and local policies on a student's education resulting from taking an alternate assessment aligned with alternate academic achievement standards, such as how participation in such assessments may delay or otherwise affect the student from completing the requirements for a regular high school diploma; and

(2) Not preclude a student with the most significant cognitive disabilities who takes an alternate assessment aligned with alternate academic achievement standards from attempting to complete the requirements for a regular high school diploma.

(e) *Inform parents.* A State (or in the case of a district-wide assessment, an LEA) must ensure that parents of students selected to be assessed using an alternate assessment aligned with alternate academic achievement standards under the State's guidelines in paragraph (c)(1) of this section are informed, consistent with 34 CFR 200.2(e), that their child's achievement will be measured based on alternate academic achievement standards, and of how participation in such assessments may delay or otherwise affect the student from completing the requirements for a regular high school diploma.

(f) *Reports.* An SEA (or, in the case of a district-wide assessment, an LEA) must make available to the public, and report to the public with the same frequency and in the same detail as it reports on the assessment of nondisabled children, the following:

(1) The number of children with disabilities participating in regular assessments, and the number of those children who were provided accommodations (that did not result in an invalid score) in order to participate in those assessments.

(2) The number of children with disabilities, if any, participating in alternate assessments based on grade-level academic achievement standards in school years prior to 2017–2018.

(3) The number of children with disabilities, if any, participating in alternate assessments aligned with modified academic achievement standards in school years prior to 2016–2017.

(4) The number of children with disabilities who are students with the most significant cognitive disabilities participating in alternate assessments aligned with alternate academic achievement standards.

(5) Compared with the achievement of all children, including children with disabilities, the performance results of children with disabilities on regular assessments, alternate assessments based on grade-level academic achievement standards (prior to 2017–2018), alternate assessments based on modified academic achievement standards (prior to 2016–2017), and alternate assessments aligned with alternate academic achievement standards if—

(i) The number of children participating in those assessments is sufficient to yield statistically reliable information; and

(ii) Reporting that information will not reveal personally identifiable information about an individual student on those assessments.

(g) *Universal design.* An SEA (or, in the case of a district-wide assessment, an LEA) must, to the extent possible, use universal design principles in developing and administering any assessments under this section.

(Authority: 20 U.S.C. 1412(a)(16))

[72 FR 17781, Apr. 9, 2007, as amended at 80 FR 50785, Aug. 21, 2015; 82 FR 29760, June 30, 2017]

§ 300.161   [Reserved]

§ 300.162   Supplementation of State, local, and other Federal funds.

(a) *Expenditures.* Funds paid to a State under this part must be expended in accordance with all the provisions of this part.

(b) *Prohibition against commingling.* (1) Funds paid to a State under this part must not be commingled with State funds.

(2) The requirement in paragraph (b)(1) of this section is satisfied by the use of a separate accounting system that includes an audit trail of the expenditure of funds paid to a State under this part. Separate bank accounts are not required. (See 34 CFR 76.702 (Fiscal control and fund accounting procedures).)

(c) *State-level nonsupplanting.* (1) Except as provided in § 300.203, funds paid to a State under Part B of the Act must be used to supplement the level of Federal, State, and local funds (including funds that are not under the direct control of the SEA or LEAs) expended for special education and related services provided to children with disabilities under Part B of the Act, and in no case to supplant those Federal, State, and local funds.

(2) If the State provides clear and convincing evidence that all children with disabilities have available to them FAPE, the Secretary may waive, in whole or in part, the requirements of paragraph (c)(1) of this section if the Secretary concurs with the evidence provided by the State under § 300.164.

(Approved by the Office of Management and Budget under control number 1820–0030)

(Authority: 20 U.S.C. 1412(a)(17))

[71 FR 46753, Aug. 14, 2006, as amended at 72 FR 61306, Oct. 30, 2007]

§ 300.163   Maintenance of State financial support.

(a) *General.* A State must not reduce the amount of State financial support for special education and related services for children with disabilities, or otherwise made available because of the excess costs of educating those children, below the amount of that support for the preceding fiscal year.

(b) *Reduction of funds for failure to maintain support.* The Secretary reduces the allocation of funds under section 611 of the Act for any fiscal year following the fiscal year in which the State fails to comply with the requirement of paragraph (a) of this section by the same amount by which the State fails to meet the requirement.

(c) *Waivers for exceptional or uncontrollable circumstances.* The Secretary may waive the requirement of paragraph (a) of this section for a State, for one fiscal year at a time, if the Secretary determines that—

(1) Granting a waiver would be equitable due to exceptional or uncontrollable circumstances such as a natural disaster or a precipitous and unforeseen decline in the financial resources of the State; or

(2) The State meets the standard in § 300.164 for a waiver of the requirement to supplement, and not to supplant, funds received under Part B of the Act.

(d) *Subsequent years.* If, for any fiscal year, a State fails to meet the requirement of paragraph (a) of this section, including any year for which the State is granted a waiver under paragraph (c) of this section, the financial support required of the State in future years under paragraph (a) of this section shall be the amount that would have been required in the absence of that failure and not the reduced level of the State's support.

(Approved by the Office of Management and Budget under control number 1820–0030)

(Authority: 20 U.S.C. 1412(a)(18))

§ 300.164 Waiver of requirement regarding supplementing and not supplanting with Part B funds.

(a) Except as provided under §§ 300.202 through 300.205, funds paid to a State under Part B of the Act must be used to supplement and increase the level of Federal, State, and local funds (including funds that are not under the direct control of SEAs or LEAs) expended for special education and related services provided to children with disabilities under Part B of the Act and in no case to supplant those Federal, State, and local funds. A State may use funds it retains under § 300.704(a) and (b) without regard to the prohibition on supplanting other funds.

(b) If a State provides clear and convincing evidence that all eligible children with disabilities throughout the State have FAPE available to them, the Secretary may waive for a period of one year in whole or in part the requirement under § 300.162 (regarding State-level nonsupplanting) if the Secretary concurs with the evidence provided by the State.

(c) If a State wishes to request a waiver under this section, it must submit to the Secretary a written request that includes—

(1) An assurance that FAPE is currently available, and will remain available throughout the period that a waiver would be in effect, to all eligible children with disabilities throughout the State, regardless of the public agency that is responsible for providing FAPE to them. The assurance must be signed by an official who has the authority to provide that assurance as it applies to all eligible children with disabilities in the State;

(2) All evidence that the State wishes the Secretary to consider in determining whether all eligible children with disabilities have FAPE available to them, setting forth in detail—

(i) The basis on which the State has concluded that FAPE is available to all eligible children in the State; and

(ii) The procedures that the State will implement to ensure that FAPE remains available to all eligible children in the State, which must include—

(A) The State's procedures under § 300.111 for ensuring that all eligible children are identified, located and evaluated;

(B) The State's procedures for monitoring public agencies to ensure that they comply with all requirements of this part;

(C) The State's complaint procedures under §§ 300.151 through 300.153; and

(D) The State's hearing procedures under §§ 300.511 through 300.516 and §§ 300.530 through 300.536;

(3) A summary of all State and Federal monitoring reports, and State complaint decisions (see §§ 300.151 through 300.153) and hearing decisions (see §§ 300.511 through 300.516 and §§ 300.530 through 300.536), issued within three years prior to the date of the

State's request for a waiver under this section, that includes any finding that FAPE has not been available to one or more eligible children, and evidence that FAPE is now available to all children addressed in those reports or decisions; and

(4) Evidence that the State, in determining that FAPE is currently available to all eligible children with disabilities in the State, has consulted with the State advisory panel under § 300.167.

(d) If the Secretary determines that the request and supporting evidence submitted by the State makes a prima facie showing that FAPE is, and will remain, available to all eligible children with disabilities in the State, the Secretary, after notice to the public throughout the State, conducts a public hearing at which all interested persons and organizations may present evidence regarding the following issues:

(1) Whether FAPE is currently available to all eligible children with disabilities in the State.

(2) Whether the State will be able to ensure that FAPE remains available to all eligible children with disabilities in the State if the Secretary provides the requested waiver.

(e) Following the hearing, the Secretary, based on all submitted evidence, will provide a waiver, in whole or in part, for a period of one year if the Secretary finds that the State has provided clear and convincing evidence that FAPE is currently available to all eligible children with disabilities in the State, and the State will be able to ensure that FAPE remains available to all eligible children with disabilities in the State if the Secretary provides the requested waiver.

(f) A State may receive a waiver of the requirement of section 612(a)(18)(A) of the Act and § 300.164 if it satisfies the requirements of paragraphs (b) through (e) of this section.

(g) The Secretary may grant subsequent waivers for a period of one year each, if the Secretary determines that the State has provided clear and convincing evidence that all eligible children with disabilities throughout the State have, and will continue to have

throughout the one-year period of the waiver, FAPE available to them.

(Approved by the Office of Management and Budget under control number 1820–0030)

(Authority: 20 U.S.C. 1412(a)(17)(C), (18)(C)(ii))

§ 300.165 **Public participation.**

(a) Prior to the adoption of any policies and procedures needed to comply with Part B of the Act (including any amendments to those policies and procedures), the State must ensure that there are public hearings, adequate notice of the hearings, and an opportunity for comment available to the general public, including individuals with disabilities and parents of children with disabilities.

(b) Before submitting a State plan under this part, a State must comply with the public participation requirements in paragraph (a) of this section and those in 20 U.S.C. 1232d(b)(7).

(Approved by the Office of Management and Budget under control number 1820–0030)

(Authority: 20 U.S.C. 1412(a)(19); 20 U.S.C. 1232d(b)(7))

§ 300.166 **Rule of construction.**

In complying with §§ 300.162 and 300.163, a State may not use funds paid to it under this part to satisfy State-law mandated funding obligations to LEAs, including funding based on student attendance or enrollment, or inflation.

(Approved by the Office of Management and Budget under control number 1820–0030)

(Authority: 20 U.S.C. 1412(a)(20))

STATE ADVISORY PANEL

§ 300.167 **State advisory panel.**

The State must establish and maintain an advisory panel for the purpose of providing policy guidance with respect to special education and related services for children with disabilities in the State.

(Approved by the Office of Management and Budget under control number 1820–0030)

(Authority: 20 U.S.C. 1412(a)(21)(A))

§ 300.168 **Membership.**

(a) *General.* The advisory panel must consist of members appointed by the

Governor, or any other official authorized under State law to make such appointments, be representative of the State population and be composed of individuals involved in, or concerned with the education of children with disabilities, including—

(1) Parents of children with disabilities (ages birth through 26);

(2) Individuals with disabilities;

(3) Teachers;

(4) Representatives of institutions of higher education that prepare special education and related services personnel;

(5) State and local education officials, including officials who carry out activities under subtitle B of title VII of the McKinney-Vento Homeless Assistance Act, (42 U.S.C. 11431 *et seq.*);

(6) Administrators of programs for children with disabilities;

(7) Representatives of other State agencies involved in the financing or delivery of related services to children with disabilities;

(8) Representatives of private schools and public charter schools;

(9) Not less than one representative of a vocational, community, or business organization concerned with the provision of transition services to children with disabilities;

(10) A representative from the State child welfare agency responsible for foster care; and

(11) Representatives from the State juvenile and adult corrections agencies.

(b) *Special rule.* A majority of the members of the panel must be individuals with disabilities or parents of children with disabilities (ages birth through 26).

(Approved by the Office of Management and Budget under control number 1820–0030)

(Authority: 20 U.S.C. 1412(a)(21)(B) and (C))

§ 300.169   Duties.

The advisory panel must—

(a) Advise the SEA of unmet needs within the State in the education of children with disabilities;

(b) Comment publicly on any rules or regulations proposed by the State regarding the education of children with disabilities;

(c) Advise the SEA in developing evaluations and reporting on data to the Secretary under section 618 of the Act;

(d) Advise the SEA in developing corrective action plans to address findings identified in Federal monitoring reports under Part B of the Act; and

(e) Advise the SEA in developing and implementing policies relating to the coordination of services for children with disabilities.

(Approved by the Office of Management and Budget under control number 1820–0030)

(Authority: 20 U.S.C. 1412(a)(21)(D))

OTHER PROVISIONS REQUIRED FOR STATE ELIGIBILITY

§ 300.170   Suspension and expulsion rates.

(a) *General.* The SEA must examine data, including data disaggregated by race and ethnicity, to determine if significant discrepancies are occurring in the rate of long-term suspensions and expulsions of children with disabilities—

(1) Among LEAs in the State; or

(2) Compared to the rates for nondisabled children within those agencies.

(b) *Review and revision of policies.* If the discrepancies described in paragraph (a) of this section are occurring, the SEA must review and, if appropriate, revise (or require the affected State agency or LEA to revise) its policies, procedures, and practices relating to the development and implementation of IEPs, the use of positive behavioral interventions and supports, and procedural safeguards, to ensure that these policies, procedures, and practices comply with the Act.

(Approved by the Office of Management and Budget under control number 1820–0030)

(Authority: 20 U.S.C. 1412(a)(22))

§ 300.171   Annual description of use of Part B funds.

(a) In order to receive a grant in any fiscal year a State must annually describe—

(1) How amounts retained for State administration and State-level activities under § 300.704 will be used to meet the requirements of this part; and

(2) How those amounts will be allocated among the activities described in

§300.704 to meet State priorities based on input from LEAs.

(b) If a State's plans for use of its funds under §300.704 for the forthcoming year do not change from the prior year, the State may submit a letter to that effect to meet the requirement in paragraph (a) of this section.

(c) The provisions of this section do not apply to the Virgin Islands, Guam, American Samoa, the Commonwealth of the Northern Mariana Islands, and the freely associated States.

(Approved by the Office of Management and Budget under control number 1820–0030)

(Authority: 20 U.S.C. 1411(e)(5))

§300.172 Access to instructional materials.

(a) *General.* The State must—

(1) Adopt the National Instructional Materials Accessibility Standard (NIMAS), published as appendix C to part 300, for the purposes of providing instructional materials to blind persons or other persons with print disabilities, in a timely manner after publication of the NIMAS in the FEDERAL REGISTER on July 19, 2006 (71 FR 41084); and

(2) Establish a State definition of "timely manner" for purposes of paragraphs (b)(2) and (b)(3) of this section if the State is not coordinating with the National Instructional Materials Access Center (NIMAC) or (b)(3) and (c)(2) of this section if the State is coordinating with the NIMAC.

(b) *Rights and responsibilities of SEA.* (1) Nothing in this section shall be construed to require any SEA to coordinate with the NIMAC.

(2) If an SEA chooses not to coordinate with the NIMAC, the SEA must provide an assurance to the Secretary that it will provide instructional materials to blind persons or other persons with print disabilities in a timely manner.

(3) Nothing in this section relieves an SEA of its responsibility to ensure that children with disabilities who need instructional materials in accessible formats, but are not included under the definition of blind or other persons with print disabilities in §300.172(e)(1)(i) or who need materials that cannot be produced from NIMAS files, receive those instructional materials in a timely manner.

(4) In order to meet its responsibility under paragraphs (b)(2), (b)(3), and (c) of this section to ensure that children with disabilities who need instructional materials in accessible formats are provided those materials in a timely manner, the SEA must ensure that all public agencies take all reasonable steps to provide instructional materials in accessible formats to children with disabilities who need those instructional materials at the same time as other children receive instructional materials.

(c) *Preparation and delivery of files.* If an SEA chooses to coordinate with the NIMAC, as of December 3, 2006, the SEA must—

(1) As part of any print instructional materials adoption process, procurement contract, or other practice or instrument used for purchase of print instructional materials, enter into a written contract with the publisher of the print instructional materials to—

(i) Require the publisher to prepare and, on or before delivery of the print instructional materials, provide to NIMAC electronic files containing the contents of the print instructional materials using the NIMAS; or

(ii) Purchase instructional materials from the publisher that are produced in, or may be rendered in, specialized formats.

(2) Provide instructional materials to blind persons or other persons with print disabilities in a timely manner.

(d) *Assistive technology.* In carrying out this section, the SEA, to the maximum extent possible, must work collaboratively with the State agency responsible for assistive technology programs.

(e) *Definitions.* (1) In this section and §300.210—

(i) *Blind persons or other persons with print disabilities* means children served under this part who may qualify to receive books and other publications produced in specialized formats in accordance with the Act entitled "An Act to provide books for adult blind," approved March 3, 1931, 2 U.S.C. 135a;

(ii) *National Instructional Materials Access Center* or *NIMAC* means the center established pursuant to section 674(e) of the Act;

(iii) *National Instructional Materials Accessibility Standard* or *NIMAS* has the meaning given the term in section 674(e)(3)(B) of the Act;

(iv) *Specialized formats* has the meaning given the term in section 674(e)(3)(D) of the Act.

(2) The definitions in paragraph (e)(1) of this section apply to each State and LEA, whether or not the State or LEA chooses to coordinate with the NIMAC.

(Approved by the Office of Management and Budget under control number 1820–0030)

(Authority: 20 U.S.C. 1412(a)(23), 1474(e))

[71 FR 46753, Aug. 14, 2006, as amended at 72 FR 61306, Oct. 30, 2007]

§ 300.173 Overidentification and disproportionality.

The State must have in effect, consistent with the purposes of this part and with section 618(d) of the Act, policies and procedures designed to prevent the inappropriate overidentification or disproportionate representation by race and ethnicity of children as children with disabilities, including children with disabilities with a particular impairment described in § 300.8.

(Approved by the Office of Management and Budget under control number 1820–0030)

(Authority: 20 U.S.C. 1412(a)(24))

§ 300.174 Prohibition on mandatory medication.

(a) *General.* The SEA must prohibit State and LEA personnel from requiring parents to obtain a prescription for substances identified under schedules I, II, III, IV, or V in section 202(c) of the Controlled Substances Act (21 U.S.C. 812(c)) for a child as a condition of attending school, receiving an evaluation under §§ 300.300 through 300.311, or receiving services under this part.

(b) *Rule of construction.* Nothing in paragraph (a) of this section shall be construed to create a Federal prohibition against teachers and other school personnel consulting or sharing classroom-based observations with parents or guardians regarding a student's academic and functional performance, or behavior in the classroom or school, or

regarding the need for evaluation for special education or related services under § 300.111 (related to child find).

(Approved by the Office of Management and Budget under control number 1820–0030)

(Authority: 20 U.S.C. 1412(a)(25))

§ 300.175 SEA as provider of FAPE or direct services.

If the SEA provides FAPE to children with disabilities, or provides direct services to these children, the agency—

(a) Must comply with any additional requirements of §§ 300.201 and 300.202 and §§ 300.206 through 300.226 as if the agency were an LEA; and

(b) May use amounts that are otherwise available to the agency under Part B of the Act to serve those children without regard to § 300.202(b) (relating to excess costs).

(Approved by the Office of Management and Budget under control number 1820–0030)

(Authority: 20 U.S.C. 1412(b))

§ 300.176 Exception for prior State plans.

(a) *General.* If a State has on file with the Secretary policies and procedures approved by the Secretary that demonstrate that the State meets any requirement of § 300.100, including any policies and procedures filed under Part B of the Act as in effect before, December 3, 2004, the Secretary considers the State to have met the requirement for purposes of receiving a grant under Part B of the Act.

(b) *Modifications made by a State.* (1) Subject to paragraph (b)(2) of this section, policies and procedures submitted by a State in accordance with this subpart remain in effect until the State submits to the Secretary the modifications that the State determines necessary.

(2) The provisions of this subpart apply to a modification to an application to the same extent and in the same manner that they apply to the original plan.

(c) *Modifications required by the Secretary.* The Secretary may require a State to modify its policies and procedures, but only to the extent necessary to ensure the State's compliance with this part, if—

(1) After December 3, 2004, the provisions of the Act or the regulations in this part are amended;

(2) There is a new interpretation of this Act by a Federal court or a State's highest court; or

(3) There is an official finding of noncompliance with Federal law or regulations.

(Approved by the Office of Management and Budget under control number 1820–0030)

(Authority: 20 U.S.C. 1412(c)(2) and (3))

§ 300.177 States' sovereign immunity and positive efforts to employ and advance qualified individuals with disabilities.

(a) *States' sovereign immunity.* (1) A State that accepts funds under this part waives its immunity under the 11th amendment of the Constitution of the United States from suit in Federal court for a violation of this part.

(2) In a suit against a State for a violation of this part, remedies (including remedies both at law and in equity) are available for such a violation in the suit against any public entity other than a State.

(3) Paragraphs (a)(1) and (a)(2) of this section apply with respect to violations that occur in whole or part after the date of enactment of the Education of the Handicapped Act Amendments of 1990.

(b) *Positive efforts to employ and advance qualified individuals with disabilities.* Each recipient of assistance under Part B of the Act must make positive efforts to employ, and advance in employment, qualified individuals with disabilities in programs assisted under Part B of the Act.

(Authority: 20 U.S.C. 1403, 1405)

[73 FR 73027, Dec. 1, 2008]

DEPARTMENT PROCEDURES

§ 300.178 Determination by the Secretary that a State is eligible to receive a grant.

If the Secretary determines that a State is eligible to receive a grant under Part B of the Act, the Secretary notifies the State of that determination.

(Authority: 20 U.S.C. 1412(d)(1))

§ 300.179 Notice and hearing before determining that a State is not eligible to receive a grant.

(a) *General.* (1) The Secretary does not make a final determination that a State is not eligible to receive a grant under Part B of the Act until providing the State—

(i) With reasonable notice; and

(ii) With an opportunity for a hearing.

(2) In implementing paragraph (a)(1)(i) of this section, the Secretary sends a written notice to the SEA by certified mail with return receipt requested.

(b) *Content of notice.* In the written notice described in paragraph (a)(2) of this section, the Secretary—

(1) States the basis on which the Secretary proposes to make a final determination that the State is not eligible;

(2) May describe possible options for resolving the issues;

(3) Advises the SEA that it may request a hearing and that the request for a hearing must be made not later than 30 days after it receives the notice of the proposed final determination that the State is not eligible; and

(4) Provides the SEA with information about the hearing procedures that will be followed.

(Authority: 20 U.S.C. 1412(d)(2))

§ 300.180 Hearing official or panel.

(a) If the SEA requests a hearing, the Secretary designates one or more individuals, either from the Department or elsewhere, not responsible for or connected with the administration of this program, to conduct a hearing.

(b) If more than one individual is designated, the Secretary designates one of those individuals as the Chief Hearing Official of the Hearing Panel. If one individual is designated, that individual is the Hearing Official.

(Authority: 20 U.S.C. 1412(d)(2))

§ 300.181 Hearing procedures.

(a) As used in §§ 300.179 through 300.184 the term party or parties means the following:

(1) An SEA that requests a hearing regarding the proposed disapproval of the State's eligibility under this part.

(2) The Department official who administers the program of financial assistance under this part.

(3) A person, group or agency with an interest in and having relevant information about the case that has applied for and been granted leave to intervene by the Hearing Official or Hearing Panel.

(b) Within 15 days after receiving a request for a hearing, the Secretary designates a Hearing Official or Hearing Panel and notifies the parties.

(c) The Hearing Official or Hearing Panel may regulate the course of proceedings and the conduct of the parties during the proceedings. The Hearing Official or Hearing Panel takes all steps necessary to conduct a fair and impartial proceeding, to avoid delay, and to maintain order, including the following:

(1) The Hearing Official or Hearing Panel may hold conferences or other types of appropriate proceedings to clarify, simplify, or define the issues or to consider other matters that may aid in the disposition of the case.

(2) The Hearing Official or Hearing Panel may schedule a prehearing conference with the Hearing Official or Hearing Panel and the parties.

(3) Any party may request the Hearing Official or Hearing Panel to schedule a prehearing or other conference. The Hearing Official or Hearing Panel decides whether a conference is necessary and notifies all parties.

(4) At a prehearing or other conference, the Hearing Official or Hearing Panel and the parties may consider subjects such as—

(i) Narrowing and clarifying issues;

(ii) Assisting the parties in reaching agreements and stipulations;

(iii) Clarifying the positions of the parties;

(iv) Determining whether an evidentiary hearing or oral argument should be held; and

(v) Setting dates for—

(A) The exchange of written documents;

(B) The receipt of comments from the parties on the need for oral argument or evidentiary hearing;

(C) Further proceedings before the Hearing Official or Hearing Panel (including an evidentiary hearing or oral argument, if either is scheduled);

(D) Requesting the names of witnesses each party wishes to present at an evidentiary hearing and estimation of time for each presentation; or

(E) Completion of the review and the initial decision of the Hearing Official or Hearing Panel.

(5) A prehearing or other conference held under paragraph (c)(4) of this section may be conducted by telephone conference call.

(6) At a prehearing or other conference, the parties must be prepared to discuss the subjects listed in paragraph (b)(4) of this section.

(7) Following a prehearing or other conference the Hearing Official or Hearing Panel may issue a written statement describing the issues raised, the action taken, and the stipulations and agreements reached by the parties.

(d) The Hearing Official or Hearing Panel may require parties to state their positions and to provide all or part of the evidence in writing.

(e) The Hearing Official or Hearing Panel may require parties to present testimony through affidavits and to conduct cross-examination through interrogatories.

(f) The Hearing Official or Hearing Panel may direct the parties to exchange relevant documents or information and lists of witnesses, and to send copies to the Hearing Official or Panel.

(g) The Hearing Official or Hearing Panel may receive, rule on, exclude, or limit evidence at any stage of the proceedings.

(h) The Hearing Official or Hearing Panel may rule on motions and other issues at any stage of the proceedings.

(i) The Hearing Official or Hearing Panel may examine witnesses.

(j) The Hearing Official or Hearing Panel may set reasonable time limits for submission of written documents.

(k) The Hearing Official or Hearing Panel may refuse to consider documents or other submissions if they are not submitted in a timely manner unless good cause is shown.

(l) The Hearing Official or Hearing Panel may interpret applicable statutes and regulations but may not waive them or rule on their validity.

(m)(1) The parties must present their positions through briefs and the submission of other documents and may request an oral argument or evidentiary hearing. The Hearing Official or Hearing Panel shall determine whether an oral argument or an evidentiary hearing is needed to clarify the positions of the parties.

(2) The Hearing Official or Hearing Panel gives each party an opportunity to be represented by counsel.

(n) If the Hearing Official or Hearing Panel determines that an evidentiary hearing would materially assist the resolution of the matter, the Hearing Official or Hearing Panel gives each party, in addition to the opportunity to be represented by counsel—

(1) An opportunity to present witnesses on the party's behalf; and

(2) An opportunity to cross-examine witnesses either orally or with written questions.

(o) The Hearing Official or Hearing Panel accepts any evidence that it finds is relevant and material to the proceedings and is not unduly repetitious.

(p)(1) The Hearing Official or Hearing Panel—

(i) Arranges for the preparation of a transcript of each hearing;

(ii) Retains the original transcript as part of the record of the hearing; and

(iii) Provides one copy of the transcript to each party.

(2) Additional copies of the transcript are available on request and with payment of the reproduction fee.

(q) Each party must file with the Hearing Official or Hearing Panel all written motions, briefs, and other documents and must at the same time provide a copy to the other parties to the proceedings.

(Authority: 20 U.S.C. 1412(d)(2))

[71 FR 46753, Aug. 14, 2006, as amended at 72 FR 61306, Oct. 30, 2007]

§300.182 Initial decision; final decision.

(a) The Hearing Official or Hearing Panel prepares an initial written decision that addresses each of the points in the notice sent by the Secretary to the SEA under §300.179 including any amendments to or further clarifications of the issues, under §300.181(c)(7).

(b) The initial decision of a Hearing Panel is made by a majority of Panel members.

(c) The Hearing Official or Hearing Panel mails, by certified mail with return receipt requested, a copy of the initial decision to each party (or to the party's counsel) and to the Secretary, with a notice stating that each party has an opportunity to submit written comments regarding the decision to the Secretary.

(d) Each party may file comments and recommendations on the initial decision with the Hearing Official or Hearing Panel within 15 days of the date the party receives the Panel's decision.

(e) The Hearing Official or Hearing Panel sends a copy of a party's initial comments and recommendations to the other parties by certified mail with return receipt requested. Each party may file responsive comments and recommendations with the Hearing Official or Hearing Panel within seven days of the date the party receives the initial comments and recommendations.

(f) The Hearing Official or Hearing Panel forwards the parties' initial and responsive comments on the initial decision to the Secretary who reviews the initial decision and issues a final decision.

(g) The initial decision of the Hearing Official or Hearing Panel becomes the final decision of the Secretary unless, within 25 days after the end of the time for receipt of written comments and recommendations, the Secretary informs the Hearing Official or Hearing Panel and the parties to a hearing in writing that the decision is being further reviewed for possible modification.

(h) The Secretary rejects or modifies the initial decision of the Hearing Official or Hearing Panel if the Secretary finds that it is clearly erroneous.

(i) The Secretary conducts the review based on the initial decision, the written record, the transcript of the Hearing Official's or Hearing Panel's proceedings, and written comments.

(j) The Secretary may remand the matter to the Hearing Official or Hearing Panel for further proceedings.

(k) Unless the Secretary remands the matter as provided in paragraph (j) of this section, the Secretary issues the final decision, with any necessary modifications, within 30 days after notifying the Hearing Official or Hearing Panel that the initial decision is being further reviewed.

(Approved by the Office of Management and Budget under control number 1820-0030)

(Authority: 20 U.S.C. 1412(d)(2))

§ 300.183 Filing requirements.

(a) Any written submission by a party under §§ 300.179 through 300.184 must be filed by hand delivery, by mail, or by facsimile transmission. The Secretary discourages the use of facsimile transmission for documents longer than five pages.

(b) The filing date under paragraph (a) of this section is the date the document is—

(1) Hand-delivered;

(2) Mailed; or

(3) Sent by facsimile transmission.

(c) A party filing by facsimile transmission is responsible for confirming that a complete and legible copy of the document was received by the Department.

(d) If a document is filed by facsimile transmission, the Secretary, the Hearing Official, or the Hearing Panel, as applicable, may require the filing of a follow-up hard copy by hand delivery or by mail within a reasonable period of time.

(e) If agreed upon by the parties, service of a document may be made upon the other party by facsimile transmission.

(Authority: 20 U.S.C. 1412(d))

§ 300.184 Judicial review.

If a State is dissatisfied with the Secretary's final decision with respect to the eligibility of the State under section 612 of the Act, the State may, not later than 60 days after notice of that decision, file with the United States Court of Appeals for the circuit in which that State is located a petition for review of that decision. A copy of the petition must be transmitted by the clerk of the court to the Secretary. The Secretary then files in the court the record of the proceedings upon which the Secretary's decision was based, as provided in 28 U.S.C. 2112.

(Authority: 20 U.S.C. 1416(e)(8))

§ 300.185 [Reserved]

§ 300.186 Assistance under other Federal programs.

Part B of the Act may not be construed to permit a State to reduce medical and other assistance available, or to alter eligibility, under titles V and XIX of the Social Security Act with respect to the provision of FAPE for children with disabilities in the State.

(Authority: 20 U.S.C. 1412(e))

By-Pass for Children in Private Schools

§ 300.190 By-pass—general.

(a) If, on December 2, 1983, the date of enactment of the Education of the Handicapped Act Amendments of 1983, an SEA was prohibited by law from providing for the equitable participation in special programs of children with disabilities enrolled in private elementary schools and secondary schools as required by section 612(a)(10)(A) of the Act, or if the Secretary determines that an SEA, LEA, or other public agency has substantially failed or is unwilling to provide for such equitable participation then the Secretary shall, notwithstanding such provision of law, arrange for the provision of services to these children through arrangements which shall be subject to the requirements of section 612(a)(10)(A) of the Act.

(b) The Secretary waives the requirement of section 612(a)(10)(A) of the Act and of §§ 300.131 through 300.144 if the Secretary implements a by-pass.

(Authority: 20 U.S.C. 1412(f)(1))

§ 300.191 Provisions for services under a by-pass.

(a) Before implementing a by-pass, the Secretary consults with appropriate public and private school officials, including SEA officials, in the affected State, and as appropriate, LEA or other public agency officials to consider matters such as—

(1) Any prohibition imposed by State law that results in the need for a by-pass; and

(2) The scope and nature of the services required by private school children with disabilities in the State, and the number of children to be served under the by-pass.

(b) After determining that a by-pass is required, the Secretary arranges for the provision of services to private school children with disabilities in the State, LEA or other public agency in a manner consistent with the requirements of section 612(a)(10)(A) of the Act and §§ 300.131 through 300.144 by providing services through one or more agreements with appropriate parties.

(c) For any fiscal year that a by-pass is implemented, the Secretary determines the maximum amount to be paid to the providers of services by multiplying—

(1) A per child amount determined by dividing the total amount received by the State under Part B of the Act for the fiscal year by the number of children with disabilities served in the prior year as reported to the Secretary under section 618 of the Act; by

(2) The number of private school children with disabilities (as defined in §§ 300.8(a) and 300.130) in the State, LEA or other public agency, as determined by the Secretary on the basis of the most recent satisfactory data available, which may include an estimate of the number of those children with disabilities.

(d) The Secretary deducts from the State's allocation under Part B of the Act the amount the Secretary determines is necessary to implement a by-pass and pays that amount to the provider of services. The Secretary may withhold this amount from the State's allocation pending final resolution of any investigation or complaint that could result in a determination that a by-pass must be implemented.

(Authority: 20 U.S.C. 1412(f)(2))

§ 300.192 Notice of intent to implement a by-pass.

(a) Before taking any final action to implement a by-pass, the Secretary provides the SEA and, as appropriate, LEA or other public agency with written notice.

(b) In the written notice, the Secretary—

(1) States the reasons for the proposed by-pass in sufficient detail to allow the SEA and, as appropriate, LEA or other public agency to respond; and

(2) Advises the SEA and, as appropriate, LEA or other public agency that it has a specific period of time (at least 45 days) from receipt of the written notice to submit written objections to the proposed by-pass and that it may request in writing the opportunity for a hearing to show cause why a by-pass should not be implemented.

(c) The Secretary sends the notice to the SEA and, as appropriate, LEA or other public agency by certified mail with return receipt requested.

(Authority: 20 U.S.C. 1412(f)(3)(A))

§ 300.193 Request to show cause.

An SEA, LEA or other public agency in receipt of a notice under § 300.192 that seeks an opportunity to show cause why a by-pass should not be implemented must submit a written request for a show cause hearing to the Secretary, within the specified time period in the written notice in § 300.192(b)(2).

(Authority: 20 U.S.C. 1412(f)(3))

§ 300.194 Show cause hearing.

(a) If a show cause hearing is requested, the Secretary—

(1) Notifies the SEA and affected LEA or other public agency, and other appropriate public and private school officials of the time and place for the hearing;

(2) Designates a person to conduct the show cause hearing. The designee must not have had any responsibility for the matter brought for a hearing; and

(3) Notifies the SEA, LEA or other public agency, and representatives of private schools that they may be represented by legal counsel and submit oral or written evidence and arguments at the hearing.

(b) At the show cause hearing, the designee considers matters such as—

(1) The necessity for implementing a by-pass;

(2) Possible factual errors in the written notice of intent to implement a by-pass; and

(3) The objections raised by public and private school representatives.

(c) The designee may regulate the course of the proceedings and the conduct of parties during the pendency of the proceedings. The designee takes all steps necessary to conduct a fair and impartial proceeding, to avoid delay, and to maintain order.

(d) The designee has no authority to require or conduct discovery.

(e) The designee may interpret applicable statutes and regulations, but may not waive them or rule on their validity.

(f) The designee arranges for the preparation, retention, and, if appropriate, dissemination of the record of the hearing.

(g) Within 10 days after the hearing, the designee—

(1) Indicates that a decision will be issued on the basis of the existing record; or

(2) Requests further information from the SEA, LEA, other public agency, representatives of private schools or Department officials.

(Authority: 20 U.S.C. 1412(f)(3))

§ 300.195   Decision.

(a) The designee who conducts the show cause hearing—

(1) Within 120 days after the record of a show cause hearing is closed, issues a written decision that includes a statement of findings; and

(2) Submits a copy of the decision to the Secretary and sends a copy to each party by certified mail with return receipt requested.

(b) Each party may submit comments and recommendations on the designee's decision to the Secretary within 30 days of the date the party receives the designee's decision.

(c) The Secretary adopts, reverses, or modifies the designee's decision and notifies all parties to the show cause hearing of the Secretary's final action. That notice is sent by certified mail with return receipt requested.

(Authority: 20 U.S.C. 1412(f)(3))

§ 300.196   Filing requirements.

(a) Any written submission under § 300.194 must be filed by hand-delivery, by mail, or by facsimile transmission. The Secretary discourages the use of facsimile transmission for documents longer than five pages.

(b) The filing date under paragraph (a) of this section is the date the document is—

(1) Hand-delivered;

(2) Mailed; or

(3) Sent by facsimile transmission.

(c) A party filing by facsimile transmission is responsible for confirming that a complete and legible copy of the document was received by the Department.

(d) If a document is filed by facsimile transmission, the Secretary or the hearing officer, as applicable, may require the filing of a follow-up hard copy by hand-delivery or by mail within a reasonable period of time.

(e) If agreed upon by the parties, service of a document may be made upon the other party by facsimile transmission.

(f) A party must show a proof of mailing to establish the filing date under paragraph (b)(2) of this section as provided in 34 CFR 75.102(d).

(Authority: 20 U.S.C. 1412(f)(3))

§ 300.197   Judicial review.

If dissatisfied with the Secretary's final action, the SEA may, within 60 days after notice of that action, file a petition for review with the United States Court of Appeals for the circuit in which the State is located. The procedures for judicial review are described in section 612(f)(3) (B) through (D) of the Act.

(Authority: 20 U.S.C. 1412(f)(3)(B)–(D))

§ 300.198   Continuation of a by-pass.

The Secretary continues a by-pass until the Secretary determines that the SEA, LEA or other public agency will meet the requirements for providing services to private school children.

(Authority: 20 U.S.C. 1412(f)(2)(C))

STATE ADMINISTRATION

§300.199 State administration.

(a) *Rulemaking.* Each State that receives funds under Part B of the Act must—

(1) Ensure that any State rules, regulations, and policies relating to this part conform to the purposes of this part;

(2) Identify in writing to LEAs located in the State and the Secretary any such rule, regulation, or policy as a State-imposed requirement that is not required by Part B of the Act and Federal regulations; and

(3) Minimize the number of rules, regulations, and policies to which the LEAs and schools located in the State are subject under Part B of the Act.

(b) *Support and facilitation.* State rules, regulations, and policies under Part B of the Act must support and facilitate LEA and school-level system improvement designed to enable children with disabilities to meet the challenging State student academic achievement standards.

(Approved by the Office of Management and Budget under control number 1820–0030)

(Authority: 20 U.S.C. 1407)

Subpart C—Local Educational Agency Eligibility

§300.200 Condition of assistance.

An LEA is eligible for assistance under Part B of the Act for a fiscal year if the agency submits a plan that provides assurances to the SEA that the LEA meets each of the conditions in §§300.201 through 300.213.

(Authority: 20 U.S.C. 1413(a))

§300.201 Consistency with State policies.

The LEA, in providing for the education of children with disabilities within its jurisdiction, must have in effect policies, procedures, and programs that are consistent with the State policies and procedures established under §§300.101 through 300.163, and §§300.165 through 300.174.

(Approved by the Office of Management and Budget under control number 1820–0600)

(Authority: 20 U.S.C. 1413(a)(1))

§300.202 Use of amounts.

(a) *General.* Amounts provided to the LEA under Part B of the Act—

(1) Must be expended in accordance with the applicable provisions of this part;

(2) Must be used only to pay the excess costs of providing special education and related services to children with disabilities, consistent with paragraph (b) of this section; and

(3) Must be used to supplement State, local, and other Federal funds and not to supplant those funds.

(b) *Excess cost requirement*—(1) *General.* (i) The excess cost requirement prevents an LEA from using funds provided under Part B of the Act to pay for all of the costs directly attributable to the education of a child with a disability, subject to paragraph (b)(1)(ii) of this section.

(ii) The excess cost requirement does not prevent an LEA from using Part B funds to pay for all of the costs directly attributable to the education of a child with a disability in any of the ages 3, 4, 5, 18, 19, 20, or 21, if no local or State funds are available for nondisabled children of these ages. However, the LEA must comply with the nonsupplanting and other requirements of this part in providing the education and services for these children.

(2)(i) An LEA meets the excess cost requirement if it has spent at least a minimum average amount for the education of its children with disabilities before funds under Part B of the Act are used.

(ii) The amount described in paragraph (b)(2)(i) of this section is determined in accordance with the definition of *excess costs* in §300.16. That amount may not include capital outlay or debt service.

(3) If two or more LEAs jointly establish eligibility in accordance with §300.223, the minimum average amount is the average of the combined minimum average amounts determined in accordance with the definition of excess costs in §300.16 in those agencies for elementary or secondary school students, as the case may be.

(Approved by the Office of Management and Budget under control number 1820–0600)

(Authority: 20 U.S.C. 1413(a)(2)(A))

§ 300.203 Maintenance of effort.

(a) *Eligibility standard.* (1) For purposes of establishing the LEA's eligibility for an award for a fiscal year, the SEA must determine that the LEA budgets, for the education of children with disabilities, at least the same amount, from at least one of the following sources, as the LEA spent for that purpose from the same source for the most recent fiscal year for which information is available:

(i) Local funds only;

(ii) The combination of State and local funds;

(iii) Local funds only on a per capita basis; or

(iv) The combination of State and local funds on a per capita basis.

(2) When determining the amount of funds that the LEA must budget to meet the requirement in paragraph (a)(1) of this section, the LEA may take into consideration, to the extent the information is available, the exceptions and adjustment provided in §§ 300.204 and 300.205 that the LEA:

(i) Took in the intervening year or years between the most recent fiscal year for which information is available and the fiscal year for which the LEA is budgeting; and

(ii) Reasonably expects to take in the fiscal year for which the LEA is budgeting.

(3) Expenditures made from funds provided by the Federal government for which the SEA is required to account to the Federal government or for which the LEA is required to account to the Federal government directly or through the SEA may not be considered in determining whether an LEA meets the standard in paragraph (a)(1) of this section.

(b) *Compliance standard.* (1) Except as provided in §§ 300.204 and 300.205, funds provided to an LEA under Part B of the Act must not be used to reduce the level of expenditures for the education of children with disabilities made by the LEA from local funds below the level of those expenditures for the preceding fiscal year.

(2) An LEA meets this standard if it does not reduce the level of expenditures for the education of children with disabilities made by the LEA from at least one of the following sources below

the level of those expenditures from the same source for the preceding fiscal year, except as provided in §§ 300.204 and 300.205:

(i) Local funds only;

(ii) The combination of State and local funds;

(iii) Local funds only on a per capita basis; or

(iv) The combination of State and local funds on a per capita basis.

(3) Expenditures made from funds provided by the Federal government for which the SEA is required to account to the Federal government or for which the LEA is required to account to the Federal government directly or through the SEA may not be considered in determining whether an LEA meets the standard in paragraphs (b)(1) and (2) of this section.

(c) *Subsequent years.* (1) If, in the fiscal year beginning on July 1, 2013 or July 1, 2014, an LEA fails to meet the requirements of § 300.203 in effect at that time, the level of expenditures required of the LEA for the fiscal year subsequent to the year of the failure is the amount that would have been required in the absence of that failure, not the LEA's reduced level of expenditures.

(2) If, in any fiscal year beginning on or after July 1, 2015, an LEA fails to meet the requirement of paragraph (b)(2)(i) or (iii) of this section and the LEA is relying on local funds only, or local funds only on a per capita basis, to meet the requirements of paragraph (a) or (b) of this section, the level of expenditures required of the LEA for the fiscal year subsequent to the year of the failure is the amount that would have been required under paragraph (b)(2)(i) or (iii) in the absence of that failure, not the LEA's reduced level of expenditures.

(3) If, in any fiscal year beginning on or after July 1, 2015, an LEA fails to meet the requirement of paragraph (b)(2)(ii) or (iv) of this section and the LEA is relying on the combination of State and local funds, or the combination of State and local funds on a per capita basis, to meet the requirements of paragraph (a) or (b) of this section, the level of expenditures required of the LEA for the fiscal year subsequent to the year of the failure is the amount

that would have been required under paragraph (b)(2)(ii) or (iv) in the absence of that failure, not the LEA's reduced level of expenditures.

(d) *Consequence of failure to maintain effort.* If an LEA fails to maintain its level of expenditures for the education of children with disabilities in accordance with paragraph (b) of this section, the SEA is liable in a recovery action under section 452 of the General Education Provisions Act (20 U.S.C. 1234a) to return to the Department, using non-Federal funds, an amount equal to the amount by which the LEA failed to maintain its level of expenditures in accordance with paragraph (b) of this section in that fiscal year, or the amount of the LEA's Part B subgrant in that fiscal year, whichever is lower. (Approved by the Office of Management and Budget under control number 1820–0600)

(Authority: 20 U.S.C. 1413(a)(2)(A), Pub. L. 113–76, 128 Stat. 5, 394 (2014), Pub. L. 113–235, 128 Stat. 2130, 2499 (2014))

[80 FR 23666, Apr. 28, 2015]

§ 300.204 Exception to maintenance of effort.

Notwithstanding the restriction in § 300.203(b), an LEA may reduce the level of expenditures by the LEA under Part B of the Act below the level of those expenditures for the preceding fiscal year if the reduction is attributable to any of the following:

(a) The voluntary departure, by retirement or otherwise, or departure for just cause, of special education or related services personnel.

(b) A decrease in the enrollment of children with disabilities.

(c) The termination of the obligation of the agency, consistent with this part, to provide a program of special education to a particular child with a disability that is an exceptionally costly program, as determined by the SEA, because the child—

(1) Has left the jurisdiction of the agency;

(2) Has reached the age at which the obligation of the agency to provide FAPE to the child has terminated; or

(3) No longer needs the program of special education.

(d) The termination of costly expenditures for long-term purchases, such as the acquisition of equipment or the construction of school facilities.

(e) The assumption of cost by the high cost fund operated by the SEA under § 300.704(c).

(Approved by the Office of Management and Budget under control number 1820–0600)

(Authority: 20 U.S.C. 1413(a)(2)(B))

[71 FR 46753, Aug. 14, 2006, as amended at 80 FR 23667, Apr. 28, 2015]

§ 300.205 Adjustment to local fiscal efforts in certain fiscal years.

(a) *Amounts in excess.* Notwithstanding § 300.202(a)(2) and (b) and § 300.203(b), and except as provided in paragraph (d) of this section and § 300.230(e)(2), for any fiscal year for which the allocation received by an LEA under § 300.705 exceeds the amount the LEA received for the previous fiscal year, the LEA may reduce the level of expenditures otherwise required by § 300.203(b) by not more than 50 percent of the amount of that excess.

(b) *Use of amounts to carry out activities under ESEA.* If an LEA exercises the authority under paragraph (a) of this section, the LEA must use an amount of local funds equal to the reduction in expenditures under paragraph (a) of this section to carry out activities that could be supported with funds under the ESEA regardless of whether the LEA is using funds under the ESEA for those activities.

(c) *State prohibition.* Notwithstanding paragraph (a) of this section, if an SEA determines that an LEA is unable to establish and maintain programs of FAPE that meet the requirements of section 613(a) of the Act and this part or the SEA has taken action against the LEA under section 616 of the Act and subpart F of these regulations, the SEA must prohibit the LEA from reducing the level of expenditures under paragraph (a) of this section for that fiscal year.

(d) *Special rule.* The amount of funds expended by an LEA for early intervening services under § 300.226 shall count toward the maximum amount of expenditures that the LEA may reduce under paragraph (a) of this section.

(Approved by the Office of Management and Budget under control number 1820–0600)

(Authority: 20 U.S.C. 1413(a)(2)(C))

[71 FR 46753, Aug. 14, 2006, as amended at 80 FR 23667, Apr. 28, 2015]

§ 300.206 Schoolwide programs under title I of the ESEA.

(a) *General.* Notwithstanding the provisions of §§ 300.202 and 300.203 or any other provision of Part B of the Act, an LEA may use funds received under Part B of the Act for any fiscal year to carry out a schoolwide program under section 1114 of the ESEA, except that the amount used in any schoolwide program may not exceed—

(1)(i) The amount received by the LEA under Part B of the Act for that fiscal year; divided by

(ii) The number of children with disabilities in the jurisdiction of the LEA; and multiplied by

(2) The number of children with disabilities participating in the schoolwide program.

(b) *Funding conditions.* The funds described in paragraph (a) of this section are subject to the following conditions:

(1) The funds must be considered as Federal Part B funds for purposes of the calculations required by § 300.202(a)(2) and (a)(3).

(2) The funds may be used without regard to the requirements of § 300.202(a)(1).

(c) *Meeting other Part B requirements.* Except as provided in paragraph (b) of this section, all other requirements of Part B of the Act must be met by an LEA using Part B funds in accordance with paragraph (a) of this section, including ensuring that children with disabilities in schoolwide program schools—

(1) Receive services in accordance with a properly developed IEP; and

(2) Are afforded all of the rights and services guaranteed to children with disabilities under the Act.

(Approved by the Office of Management and Budget under control number 1820–0600)

(Authority: 20 U.S.C. 1413(a)(2)(D))

§ 300.207 Personnel development.

The LEA must ensure that all personnel necessary to carry out Part B of the Act are appropriately and adequately prepared, subject to the requirements of § 300.156 (related to personnel qualifications) and section 2102(b) of the ESEA.

(Approved by the Office of Management and Budget under control number 1820–0600)

(Authority: 20 U.S.C. 1413(a)(3))

[71 FR 46753, Aug. 14, 2006, as amended at 82 FR 29761, June 30, 2017]

§ 300.208 Permissive use of funds.

(a) *Uses.* Notwithstanding §§ 300.202, 300.203(b), and 300.162(b), funds provided to an LEA under Part B of the Act may be used for the following activities:

(1) *Services and aids that also benefit nondisabled children.* For the costs of special education and related services, and supplementary aids and services, provided in a regular class or other education-related setting to a child with a disability in accordance with the IEP of the child, even if one or more nondisabled children benefit from these services.

(2) *Early intervening services.* To develop and implement coordinated, early intervening educational services in accordance with § 300.226.

(3) *High cost special education and related services.* To establish and implement cost or risk sharing funds, consortia, or cooperatives for the LEA itself, or for LEAs working in a consortium of which the LEA is a part, to pay for high cost special education and related services.

(b) *Administrative case management.* An LEA may use funds received under Part B of the Act to purchase appropriate technology for recordkeeping, data collection, and related case management activities of teachers and related services personnel providing services described in the IEP of children with disabilities, that is needed for the implementation of those case management activities.

(Approved by the Office of Management and Budget under control number 1820–0600)

(Authority: 20 U.S.C. 1413(a)(4))

[71 FR 46753, Aug. 14, 2006, as amended at 80 FR 23667, Apr. 28, 2015]

§300.209 Treatment of charter schools and their students.

(a) *Rights of children with disabilities.* Children with disabilities who attend public charter schools and their parents retain all rights under this part.

(b) *Charter schools that are public schools of the LEA.* (1) In carrying out Part B of the Act and these regulations with respect to charter schools that are public schools of the LEA, the LEA must—

(i) Serve children with disabilities attending those charter schools in the same manner as the LEA serves children with disabilities in its other schools, including providing supplementary and related services on site at the charter school to the same extent to which the LEA has a policy or practice of providing such services on the site to its other public schools; and

(ii) Provide funds under Part B of the Act to those charter schools—

(A) On the same basis as the LEA provides funds to the LEA's other public schools, including proportional distribution based on relative enrollment of children with disabilities; and

(B) At the same time as the LEA distributes other Federal funds to the LEA's other public schools, consistent with the State's charter school law.

(2) If the public charter school is a school of an LEA that receives funding under §300.705 and includes other public schools—

(i) The LEA is responsible for ensuring that the requirements of this part are met, unless State law assigns that responsibility to some other entity; and

(ii) The LEA must meet the requirements of paragraph (b)(1) of this section.

(c) *Public charter schools that are LEAs.* If the public charter school is an LEA, consistent with §300.28, that receives funding under §300.705, that charter school is responsible for ensuring that the requirements of this part are met, unless State law assigns that responsibility to some other entity.

(d) *Public charter schools that are not an LEA or a school that is part of an LEA.* (1) If the public charter school is not an LEA receiving funding under §300.705, or a school that is part of an LEA receiving funding under §300.705, the SEA is responsible for ensuring that the requirements of this part are met.

(2) Paragraph (d)(1) of this section does not preclude a State from assigning initial responsibility for ensuring the requirements of this part are met to another entity. However, the SEA must maintain the ultimate responsibility for ensuring compliance with this part, consistent with §300.149.

(Approved by the Office of Management and Budget under control number 1820–0600)

(Authority: 20 U.S.C. 1413(a)(5))

§300.210 Purchase of instructional materials.

(a) *General.* Not later than December 3, 2006, an LEA that chooses to coordinate with the National Instructional Materials Access Center (NIMAC), when purchasing print instructional materials, must acquire those instructional materials in the same manner, and subject to the same conditions as an SEA under §300.172.

(b) *Rights of LEA.* (1) Nothing in this section shall be construed to require an LEA to coordinate with the NIMAC.

(2) If an LEA chooses not to coordinate with the NIMAC, the LEA must provide an assurance to the SEA that the LEA will provide instructional materials to blind persons or other persons with print disabilities in a timely manner.

(3) Nothing in this section relieves an LEA of its responsibility to ensure that children with disabilities who need instructional materials in accessible formats but are not included under the definition of blind or other persons with print disabilities in §300.172(e)(1)(i) or who need materials that cannot be produced from NIMAS files, receive those instructional materials in a timely manner.

(Approved by the Office of Management and Budget under control number 1820–0600)

(Authority: 20 U.S.C. 1413(a)(6))

§300.211 Information for SEA.

The LEA must provide the SEA with information necessary to enable the SEA to carry out its duties under Part B of the Act, including, with respect to §§300.157 and 300.160, information relating to the performance of children with disabilities participating in programs carried out under Part B of the Act.

(Approved by the Office of Management and Budget under control number 1820–0600)

(Authority: 20 U.S.C. 1413(a)(7))

§ 300.212 Public information.

The LEA must make available to parents of children with disabilities and to the general public all documents relating to the eligibility of the agency under Part B of the Act.

(Approved by the Office of Management and Budget under control number 1820–0600)

(Authority: 20 U.S.C. 1413(a)(8))

§ 300.213 Records regarding migratory children with disabilities.

The LEA must cooperate in the Secretary's efforts under section 1308 of the ESEA to ensure the linkage of records pertaining to migratory children with disabilities for the purpose of electronically exchanging, among the States, health and educational information regarding those children.

(Approved by the Office of Management and Budget under control number 1820–0600)

(Authority: 20 U.S.C. 1413(a)(9))

§§ 300.214–300.219 [Reserved]

§ 300.220 Exception for prior local plans.

(a) *General.* If an LEA or a State agency described in § 300.228 has on file with the SEA policies and procedures that demonstrate that the LEA or State agency meets any requirement of § 300.200, including any policies and procedures filed under Part B of the Act as in effect before December 3, 2004, the SEA must consider the LEA or State agency to have met that requirement for purposes of receiving assistance under Part B of the Act.

(b) *Modification made by an LEA or State agency.* Subject to paragraph (c) of this section, policies and procedures submitted by an LEA or a State agency in accordance with this subpart remain in effect until the LEA or State agency submits to the SEA the modifications that the LEA or State agency determines are necessary.

(c) *Modifications required by the SEA.* The SEA may require an LEA or a

State agency to modify its policies and procedures, but only to the extent necessary to ensure the LEA's or State agency's compliance with Part B of the Act or State law, if—

(1) After December 3, 2004, the effective date of the Individuals with Disabilities Education Improvement Act of 2004, the applicable provisions of the Act (or the regulations developed to carry out the Act) are amended;

(2) There is a new interpretation of an applicable provision of the Act by Federal or State courts; or

(3) There is an official finding of noncompliance with Federal or State law or regulations.

(Authority: 20 U.S.C. 1413(b))

§ 300.221 Notification of LEA or State agency in case of ineligibility.

If the SEA determines that an LEA or State agency is not eligible under Part B of the Act, then the SEA must—

(a) Notify the LEA or State agency of that determination; and

(b) Provide the LEA or State agency with reasonable notice and an opportunity for a hearing.

(Authority: 20 U.S.C. 1413(c))

§ 300.222 LEA and State agency compliance.

(a) *General.* If the SEA, after reasonable notice and an opportunity for a hearing, finds that an LEA or State agency that has been determined to be eligible under this subpart is failing to comply with any requirement described in §§ 300.201 through 300.213, the SEA must reduce or must not provide any further payments to the LEA or State agency until the SEA is satisfied that the LEA or State agency is complying with that requirement.

(b) *Notice requirement.* Any State agency or LEA in receipt of a notice described in paragraph (a) of this section must, by means of public notice, take the measures necessary to bring the pendency of an action pursuant to this section to the attention of the public within the jurisdiction of the agency.

(c) *Consideration.* In carrying out its responsibilities under this section, each SEA must consider any decision resulting from a hearing held under

§§ 300.511 through 300.533 that is adverse to the LEA or State agency involved in the decision.

(Authority: 20 U.S.C. 1413(d))

§ 300.223 Joint establishment of eligibility.

(a) *General.* An SEA may require an LEA to establish its eligibility jointly with another LEA if the SEA determines that the LEA will be ineligible under this subpart because the agency will not be able to establish and maintain programs of sufficient size and scope to effectively meet the needs of children with disabilities.

(b) *Charter school exception.* An SEA may not require a charter school that is an LEA to jointly establish its eligibility under paragraph (a) of this section unless the charter school is explicitly permitted to do so under the State's charter school statute.

(c) *Amount of payments.* If an SEA requires the joint establishment of eligibility under paragraph (a) of this section, the total amount of funds made available to the affected LEAs must be equal to the sum of the payments that each LEA would have received under § 300.705 if the agencies were eligible for those payments.

(Authority: 20 U.S.C. 1413(e)(1) and (2))

§ 300.224 Requirements for establishing eligibility.

(a) *Requirements for LEAs in general.* LEAs that establish joint eligibility under this section must—

(1) Adopt policies and procedures that are consistent with the State's policies and procedures under §§ 300.101 through 300.163, and §§ 300.165 through 300.174; and

(2) Be jointly responsible for implementing programs that receive assistance under Part B of the Act.

(b) *Requirements for educational service agencies in general.* If an educational service agency is required by State law to carry out programs under Part B of the Act, the joint responsibilities given to LEAs under Part B of the Act—

(1) Do not apply to the administration and disbursement of any payments received by that educational service agency; and

(2) Must be carried out only by that educational service agency.

(c) *Additional requirement.* Notwithstanding any other provision of §§ 300.223 through 300.224, an educational service agency must provide for the education of children with disabilities in the least restrictive environment, as required by § 300.112.

(Approved by the Office of Management and Budget under control number 1820–0600)

(Authority: 20 U.S.C. 1413(e)(3) and (4))

§ 300.225 [Reserved]

§ 300.226 Early intervening services.

(a) *General.* An LEA may not use more than 15 percent of the amount the LEA receives under Part B of the Act for any fiscal year, less any amount reduced by the LEA pursuant to § 300.205, if any, in combination with other amounts (which may include amounts other than education funds), to develop and implement coordinated, early intervening services, which may include interagency financing structures, for students in kindergarten through grade 12 (with a particular emphasis on students in kindergarten through grade three) who are not currently identified as needing special education or related services, but who need additional academic and behavioral support to succeed in a general education environment. (See appendix D for examples of how § 300.205(d), regarding local maintenance of effort, and § 300.226(a) affect one another.)

(b) *Activities.* In implementing coordinated, early intervening services under this section, an LEA may carry out activities that include—

(1) Professional development (which may be provided by entities other than LEAs) for teachers and other school staff to enable such personnel to deliver scientifically based academic and behavioral interventions, including scientifically based literacy instruction, and, where appropriate, instruction on the use of adaptive and instructional software; and

(2) Providing educational and behavioral evaluations, services, and supports, including scientifically based literacy instruction.

(c) *Construction.* Nothing in this section shall be construed to either limit or create a right to FAPE under Part B of the Act or to delay appropriate evaluation of a child suspected of having a disability.

(d) *Reporting.* Each LEA that develops and maintains coordinated, early intervening services under this section must annually report to the SEA on—

(1) The number of children served under this section who received early intervening services; and

(2) The number of children served under this section who received early intervening services and subsequently receive special education and related services under Part B of the Act during the preceding two year period.

(e) *Coordination with ESEA.* Funds made available to carry out this section may be used to carry out coordinated, early intervening services aligned with activities funded by, and carried out under the ESEA if those funds are used to supplement, and not supplant, funds made available under the ESEA for the activities and services assisted under this section.

(Approved by the Office of Management and Budget under control number 1820–0600)

(Authority: 20 U.S.C. 1413(f))

§ 300.227 Direct services by the SEA.

(a) *General.* (1) An SEA must use the payments that would otherwise have been available to an LEA or to a State agency to provide special education and related services directly to children with disabilities residing in the area served by that LEA, or for whom that State agency is responsible, if the SEA determines that the LEA or State agency—

(i) Has not provided the information needed to establish the eligibility of the LEA or State agency, or elected not to apply for its Part B allotment, under Part B of the Act;

(ii) Is unable to establish and maintain programs of FAPE that meet the requirements of this part;

(iii) Is unable or unwilling to be consolidated with one or more LEAs in order to establish and maintain the programs; or

(iv) Has one or more children with disabilities who can best be served by a regional or State program or service

delivery system designed to meet the needs of these children.

(2) *SEA administrative procedures.* (i) In meeting the requirements in paragraph (a)(1) of this section, the SEA may provide special education and related services directly, by contract, or through other arrangements.

(ii) The excess cost requirements of § 300.202(b) do not apply to the SEA.

(b) *Manner and location of education and services.* The SEA may provide special education and related services under paragraph (a) of this section in the manner and at the locations (including regional or State centers) as the SEA considers appropriate. The education and services must be provided in accordance with this part.

(Authority: 20 U.S.C. 1413(g))

§ 300.228 State agency eligibility.

Any State agency that desires to receive a subgrant for any fiscal year under § 300.705 must demonstrate to the satisfaction of the SEA that—

(a) All children with disabilities who are participating in programs and projects funded under Part B of the Act receive FAPE, and that those children and their parents are provided all the rights and procedural safeguards described in this part; and

(b) The agency meets the other conditions of this subpart that apply to LEAs.

(Authority: 20 U.S.C. 1413(h))

§ 300.229 Disciplinary information.

(a) The State may require that a public agency include in the records of a child with a disability a statement of any current or previous disciplinary action that has been taken against the child and transmit the statement to the same extent that the disciplinary information is included in, and transmitted with, the student records of nondisabled children.

(b) The statement may include a description of any behavior engaged in by the child that required disciplinary action, a description of the disciplinary action taken, and any other information that is relevant to the safety of the child and other individuals involved with the child.

(c) If the State adopts such a policy, and the child transfers from one school to another, the transmission of any of the child's records must include both the child's current IEP and any statement of current or previous disciplinary action that has been taken against the child.

(Authority: 20 U.S.C. 1413(i))

§ 300.230 SEA flexibility.

(a) *Adjustment to State fiscal effort in certain fiscal years.* For any fiscal year for which the allotment received by a State under § 300.703 exceeds the amount the State received for the previous fiscal year and if the State in school year 2003–2004 or any subsequent school year pays or reimburses all LEAs within the State from State revenue 100 percent of the non-Federal share of the costs of special education and related services, the SEA, notwithstanding §§ 300.162 through 300.163 (related to State-level nonsupplanting and maintenance of effort), and § 300.175 (related to direct services by the SEA) may reduce the level of expenditures from State sources for the education of children with disabilities by not more than 50 percent of the amount of such excess.

(b) *Prohibition.* Notwithstanding paragraph (a) of this section, if the Secretary determines that an SEA is unable to establish, maintain, or oversee programs of FAPE that meet the requirements of this part, or that the State needs assistance, intervention, or substantial intervention under § 300.603, the Secretary prohibits the SEA from exercising the authority in paragraph (a) of this section.

(c) *Education activities.* If an SEA exercises the authority under paragraph (a) of this section, the agency must use funds from State sources, in an amount equal to the amount of the reduction under paragraph (a) of this section, to support activities authorized under the ESEA, or to support need-based student or teacher higher education programs.

(d) *Report.* For each fiscal year for which an SEA exercises the authority under paragraph (a) of this section, the SEA must report to the Secretary—

(1) The amount of expenditures reduced pursuant to that paragraph; and

(2) The activities that were funded pursuant to paragraph (c) of this section.

(e) *Limitation.* (1) Notwithstanding paragraph (a) of this section, an SEA may not reduce the level of expenditures described in paragraph (a) of this section if any LEA in the State would, as a result of such reduction, receive less than 100 percent of the amount necessary to ensure that all children with disabilities served by the LEA receive FAPE from the combination of Federal funds received under Part B of the Act and State funds received from the SEA.

(2) If an SEA exercises the authority under paragraph (a) of this section, LEAs in the State may not reduce local effort under § 300.205 by more than the reduction in the State funds they receive.

(Authority: 20 U.S.C. 1413(j))

Subpart D—Evaluations, Eligibility Determinations, Individualized Education Programs, and Educational Placements

PARENTAL CONSENT

§ 300.300 Parental consent.

(a) *Parental consent for initial evaluation.* (1)(i) The public agency proposing to conduct an initial evaluation to determine if a child qualifies as a child with a disability under § 300.8 must, after providing notice consistent with §§ 300.503 and 300.504, obtain informed consent, consistent with § 300.9, from the parent of the child before conducting the evaluation.

(ii) Parental consent for initial evaluation must not be construed as consent for initial provision of special education and related services.

(iii) The public agency must make reasonable efforts to obtain the informed consent from the parent for an initial evaluation to determine whether the child is a child with a disability.

(2) For initial evaluations only, if the child is a ward of the State and is not residing with the child's parent, the public agency is not required to obtain informed consent from the parent for an initial evaluation to determine

whether the child is a child with a disability if—

(i) Despite reasonable efforts to do so, the public agency cannot discover the whereabouts of the parent of the child;

(ii) The rights of the parents of the child have been terminated in accordance with State law; or

(iii) The rights of the parent to make educational decisions have been subrogated by a judge in accordance with State law and consent for an initial evaluation has been given by an individual appointed by the judge to represent the child.

(3)(i) If the parent of a child enrolled in public school or seeking to be enrolled in public school does not provide consent for initial evaluation under paragraph (a)(1) of this section, or the parent fails to respond to a request to provide consent, the public agency may, but is not required to, pursue the initial evaluation of the child by utilizing the procedural safeguards in subpart E of this part (including the mediation procedures under § 300.506 or the due process procedures under §§ 300.507 through 300.516), if appropriate, except to the extent inconsistent with State law relating to such parental consent.

(ii) The public agency does not violate its obligation under § 300.111 and §§ 300.301 through 300.311 if it declines to pursue the evaluation.

(b) *Parental consent for services.* (1) A public agency that is responsible for making FAPE available to a child with a disability must obtain informed consent from the parent of the child before the initial provision of special education and related services to the child.

(2) The public agency must make reasonable efforts to obtain informed consent from the parent for the initial provision of special education and related services to the child.

(3) If the parent of a child fails to respond to a request for, or refuses to consent to, the initial provision of special education and related services, the public agency—

(i) May not use the procedures in subpart E of this part (including the mediation procedures under § 300.506 or the due process procedures under §§ 300.507 through 300.516) in order to obtain

agreement or a ruling that the services may be provided to the child;

(ii) Will not be considered to be in violation of the requirement to make FAPE available to the child because of the failure to provide the child with the special education and related services for which the parent refuses to or fails to provide consent; and

(iii) Is not required to convene an IEP Team meeting or develop an IEP under §§ 300.320 and 300.324 for the child.

(4) If, at any time subsequent to the initial provision of special education and related services, the parent of a child revokes consent in writing for the continued provision of special education and related services, the public agency—

(i) May not continue to provide special education and related services to the child, but must provide prior written notice in accordance with § 300.503 before ceasing the provision of special education and related services;

(ii) May not use the procedures in subpart E of this part (including the mediation procedures under § 300.506 or the due process procedures under §§ 300.507 through 300.516) in order to obtain agreement or a ruling that the services may be provided to the child;

(iii) Will not be considered to be in violation of the requirement to make FAPE available to the child because of the failure to provide the child with further special education and related services; and

(iv) Is not required to convene an IEP Team meeting or develop an IEP under §§ 300.320 and 300.324 for the child for further provision of special education and related services.

(c) *Parental consent for reevaluations.* (1) Subject to paragraph (c)(2) of this section, each public agency—

(i) Must obtain informed parental consent, in accordance with § 300.300(a)(1), prior to conducting any reevaluation of a child with a disability.

(ii) If the parent refuses to consent to the reevaluation, the public agency may, but is not required to, pursue the reevaluation by using the consent override procedures described in paragraph (a)(3) of this section.

(iii) The public agency does not violate its obligation under § 300.111 and

§§ 300.301 through 300.311 if it declines to pursue the evaluation or reevaluation.

(2) The informed parental consent described in paragraph (c)(1) of this section need not be obtained if the public agency can demonstrate that—

(i) It made reasonable efforts to obtain such consent; and

(ii) The child's parent has failed to respond.

(d) Other consent requirements.

(1) Parental consent is not required before—

(i) Reviewing existing data as part of an evaluation or a reevaluation; or

(ii) Administering a test or other evaluation that is administered to all children unless, before administration of that test or evaluation, consent is required of parents of all children.

(2) In addition to the parental consent requirements described in paragraphs (a), (b), and (c) of this section, a State may require parental consent for other services and activities under this part if it ensures that each public agency in the State establishes and implements effective procedures to ensure that a parent's refusal to consent does not result in a failure to provide the child with FAPE.

(3) A public agency may not use a parent's refusal to consent to one service or activity under paragraphs (a), (b), (c), or (d)(2) of this section to deny the parent or child any other service, benefit, or activity of the public agency, except as required by this part.

(4)(i) If a parent of a child who is home schooled or placed in a private school by the parents at their own expense does not provide consent for the initial evaluation or the reevaluation, or the parent fails to respond to a request to provide consent, the public agency may not use the consent override procedures (described in paragraphs (a)(3) and (c)(1) of this section); and

(ii) The public agency is not required to consider the child as eligible for services under §§ 300.132 through 300.144.

(5) To meet the reasonable efforts requirement in paragraphs (a)(1)(iii), (a)(2)(i), (b)(2), and (c)(2)(i) of this section, the public agency must document

its attempts to obtain parental consent using the procedures in § 300.322(d).

(Authority: 20 U.S.C. 1414(a)(1)(D) and 1414(c))

[71 FR 46753, Aug. 14, 2006, as amended at 73 FR 73027, Dec. 1, 2008]

EVALUATIONS AND REEVALUATIONS

§ 300.301 Initial evaluations.

(a) *General.* Each public agency must conduct a full and individual initial evaluation, in accordance with §§ 300.304 through 300.306, before the initial provision of special education and related services to a child with a disability under this part.

(b) *Request for initial evaluation.* Consistent with the consent requirements in § 300.300, either a parent of a child or a public agency may initiate a request for an initial evaluation to determine if the child is a child with a disability.

(c) *Procedures for initial evaluation.* The initial evaluation—

(1)(i) Must be conducted within 60 days of receiving parental consent for the evaluation; or

(ii) If the State establishes a timeframe within which the evaluation must be conducted, within that timeframe; and

(2) Must consist of procedures—

(i) To determine if the child is a child with a disability under § 300.8; and

(ii) To determine the educational needs of the child.

(d) *Exception.* The timeframe described in paragraph (c)(1) of this section does not apply to a public agency if—

(1) The parent of a child repeatedly fails or refuses to produce the child for the evaluation; or

(2) A child enrolls in a school of another public agency after the relevant timeframe in paragraph (c)(1) of this section has begun, and prior to a determination by the child's previous public agency as to whether the child is a child with a disability under § 300.8.

(e) The exception in paragraph (d)(2) of this section applies only if the subsequent public agency is making sufficient progress to ensure a prompt completion of the evaluation, and the parent and subsequent public agency agree to a specific time when the evaluation will be completed.

(Authority: 20 U.S.C. 1414(a))

[71 FR 46753, Aug. 14, 2006, as amended at 72 FR 61307, Oct. 30, 2007]

§ 300.302 Screening for instructional purposes is not evaluation.

The screening of a student by a teacher or specialist to determine appropriate instructional strategies for curriculum implementation shall not be considered to be an evaluation for eligibility for special education and related services.

(Authority: 20 U.S.C. 1414(a)(1)(E))

§ 300.303 Reevaluations.

(a) *General.* A public agency must ensure that a reevaluation of each child with a disability is conducted in accordance with §§ 300.304 through 300.311—

(1) If the public agency determines that the educational or related services needs, including improved academic achievement and functional performance, of the child warrant a reevaluation; or

(2) If the child's parent or teacher requests a reevaluation.

(b) *Limitation.* A reevaluation conducted under paragraph (a) of this section—

(1) May occur not more than once a year, unless the parent and the public agency agree otherwise; and

(2) Must occur at least once every 3 years, unless the parent and the public agency agree that a reevaluation is unnecessary.

(Authority: 20 U.S.C. 1414(a)(2))

§ 300.304 Evaluation procedures.

(a) *Notice.* The public agency must provide notice to the parents of a child with a disability, in accordance with § 300.503, that describes any evaluation procedures the agency proposes to conduct.

(b) *Conduct of evaluation.* In conducting the evaluation, the public agency must—

(1) Use a variety of assessment tools and strategies to gather relevant functional, developmental, and academic information about the child, including information provided by the parent, that may assist in determining—

(i) Whether the child is a child with a disability under § 300.8; and

(ii) The content of the child's IEP, including information related to enabling the child to be involved in and progress in the general education curriculum (or for a preschool child, to participate in appropriate activities);

(2) Not use any single measure or assessment as the sole criterion for determining whether a child is a child with a disability and for determining an appropriate educational program for the child; and

(3) Use technically sound instruments that may assess the relative contribution of cognitive and behavioral factors, in addition to physical or developmental factors.

(c) *Other evaluation procedures.* Each public agency must ensure that—

(1) Assessments and other evaluation materials used to assess a child under this part—

(i) Are selected and administered so as not to be discriminatory on a racial or cultural basis;

(ii) Are provided and administered in the child's native language or other mode of communication and in the form most likely to yield accurate information on what the child knows and can do academically, developmentally, and functionally, unless it is clearly not feasible to so provide or administer;

(iii) Are used for the purposes for which the assessments or measures are valid and reliable;

(iv) Are administered by trained and knowledgeable personnel; and

(v) Are administered in accordance with any instructions provided by the producer of the assessments.

(2) Assessments and other evaluation materials include those tailored to assess specific areas of educational need and not merely those that are designed to provide a single general intelligence quotient.

(3) Assessments are selected and administered so as best to ensure that if an assessment is administered to a child with impaired sensory, manual,

or speaking skills, the assessment results accurately reflect the child's aptitude or achievement level or whatever other factors the test purports to measure, rather than reflecting the child's impaired sensory, manual, or speaking skills (unless those skills are the factors that the test purports to measure).

(4) The child is assessed in all areas related to the suspected disability, including, if appropriate, health, vision, hearing, social and emotional status, general intelligence, academic performance, communicative status, and motor abilities;

(5) Assessments of children with disabilities who transfer from one public agency to another public agency in the same school year are coordinated with those children's prior and subsequent schools, as necessary and as expeditiously as possible, consistent with §300.301(d)(2) and (e), to ensure prompt completion of full evaluations.

(6) In evaluating each child with a disability under §§300.304 through 300.306, the evaluation is sufficiently comprehensive to identify all of the child's special education and related services needs, whether or not commonly linked to the disability category in which the child has been classified.

(7) Assessment tools and strategies that provide relevant information that directly assists persons in determining the educational needs of the child are provided.

(Authority: 20 U.S.C. 1414(b)(1)–(3), 1412(a)(6)(B))

§300.305 Additional requirements for evaluations and reevaluations.

(a) *Review of existing evaluation data.* As part of an initial evaluation (if appropriate) and as part of any reevaluation under this part, the IEP Team and other qualified professionals, as appropriate, must—

(1) Review existing evaluation data on the child, including—

(i) Evaluations and information provided by the parents of the child;

(ii) Current classroom-based, local, or State assessments, and classroom-based observations; and

(iii) Observations by teachers and related services providers; and

(2) On the basis of that review, and input from the child's parents, identify what additional data, if any, are needed to determine—

(i)(A) Whether the child is a child with a disability, as defined in §300.8, and the educational needs of the child; or

(B) In case of a reevaluation of a child, whether the child continues to have such a disability, and the educational needs of the child;

(ii) The present levels of academic achievement and related developmental needs of the child;

(iii)(A) Whether the child needs special education and related services; or

(B) In the case of a reevaluation of a child, whether the child continues to need special education and related services; and

(iv) Whether any additions or modifications to the special education and related services are needed to enable the child to meet the measurable annual goals set out in the IEP of the child and to participate, as appropriate, in the general education curriculum.

(b) *Conduct of review.* The group described in paragraph (a) of this section may conduct its review without a meeting.

(c) *Source of data.* The public agency must administer such assessments and other evaluation measures as may be needed to produce the data identified under paragraph (a) of this section.

(d) *Requirements if additional data are not needed.* (1) If the IEP Team and other qualified professionals, as appropriate, determine that no additional data are needed to determine whether the child continues to be a child with a disability, and to determine the child's educational needs, the public agency must notify the child's parents of—

(i) That determination and the reasons for the determination; and

(ii) The right of the parents to request an assessment to determine whether the child continues to be a child with a disability, and to determine the child's educational needs.

(2) The public agency is not required to conduct the assessment described in paragraph (d)(1)(ii) of this section unless requested to do so by the child's parents.

(e) *Evaluations before change in eligibility*. (1) Except as provided in paragraph (e)(2) of this section, a public agency must evaluate a child with a disability in accordance with §§ 300.304 through 300.311 before determining that the child is no longer a child with a disability.

(2) The evaluation described in paragraph (e)(1) of this section is not required before the termination of a child's eligibility under this part due to graduation from secondary school with a regular diploma, or due to exceeding the age eligibility for FAPE under State law.

(3) For a child whose eligibility terminates under circumstances described in paragraph (e)(2) of this section, a public agency must provide the child with a summary of the child's academic achievement and functional performance, which shall include recommendations on how to assist the child in meeting the child's postsecondary goals.

(Authority: 20 U.S.C. 1414(c))

[71 FR 46753, Aug. 14, 2006, as amended at 72 FR 61307, Oct. 30, 2007]

§ 300.306 Determination of eligibility.

(a) *General*. Upon completion of the administration of assessments and other evaluation measures—

(1) A group of qualified professionals and the parent of the child determines whether the child is a child with a disability, as defined in § 300.8, in accordance with paragraph (c) of this section and the educational needs of the child; and

(2) The public agency provides a copy of the evaluation report and the documentation of determination of eligibility at no cost to the parent.

(b) *Special rule for eligibility determination*. A child must not be determined to be a child with a disability under this part—

(1) If the determinant factor for that determination is—

(i) Lack of appropriate instruction in reading, including the essential components of reading instruction (as defined in section 1208(3) of the ESEA as such section was in effect on the day before the date of enactment of the Every

Student Succeeds Act (December 9, 2015));

(ii) Lack of appropriate instruction in math; or

(iii) Limited English proficiency; and

(2) If the child does not otherwise meet the eligibility criteria under § 300.8(a).

(c) *Procedures for determining eligibility and educational need*. (1) In interpreting evaluation data for the purpose of determining if a child is a child with a disability under § 300.8, and the educational needs of the child, each public agency must—

(i) Draw upon information from a variety of sources, including aptitude and achievement tests, parent input, and teacher recommendations, as well as information about the child's physical condition, social or cultural background, and adaptive behavior; and

(ii) Ensure that information obtained from all of these sources is documented and carefully considered.

(2) If a determination is made that a child has a disability and needs special education and related services, an IEP must be developed for the child in accordance with §§ 300.320 through 300.324.

(Authority: 20 U.S.C. 1414(b)(4) and (5))

[71 FR 46753, Aug. 14, 2006, as amended at 72 FR 61307, Oct. 30, 2007; 82 FR 29761, June 30, 2017]

ADDITIONAL PROCEDURES FOR IDENTIFYING CHILDREN WITH SPECIFIC LEARNING DISABILITIES

§ 300.307 Specific learning disabilities.

(a) *General*. A State must adopt, consistent with § 300.309, criteria for determining whether a child has a specific learning disability as defined in § 300.8(c)(10). In addition, the criteria adopted by the State—

(1) Must not require the use of a severe discrepancy between intellectual ability and achievement for determining whether a child has a specific learning disability, as defined in § 300.8(c)(10);

(2) Must permit the use of a process based on the child's response to scientific, research-based intervention; and

(3) May permit the use of other alternative research-based procedures for

determining whether a child has a specific learning disability, as defined in §300.8(c)(10).

(b) *Consistency with State criteria.* A public agency must use the State criteria adopted pursuant to paragraph (a) of this section in determining whether a child has a specific learning disability.

(Authority: 20 U.S.C. 1221e–3; 1401(30); 1414(b)(6))

§300.308 Additional group members.

The determination of whether a child suspected of having a specific learning disability is a child with a disability as defined in §300.8, must be made by the child's parents and a team of qualified professionals, which must include—

(a)(1) The child's regular teacher; or

(2) If the child does not have a regular teacher, a regular classroom teacher qualified to teach a child of his or her age; or

(3) For a child of less than school age, an individual qualified by the SEA to teach a child of his or her age; and

(b) At least one person qualified to conduct individual diagnostic examinations of children, such as a school psychologist, speech-language pathologist, or remedial reading teacher.

(Authority: 20 U.S.C. 1221e–3; 1401(30); 1414(b)(6))

§300.309 Determining the existence of a specific learning disability.

(a) The group described in §300.306 may determine that a child has a specific learning disability, as defined in §300.8(c)(10), if—

(1) The child does not achieve adequately for the child's age or to meet State-approved grade-level standards in one or more of the following areas, when provided with learning experiences and instruction appropriate for the child's age or State-approved grade-level standards:

(i) Oral expression.

(ii) Listening comprehension.

(iii) Written expression.

(iv) Basic reading skill.

(v) Reading fluency skills.

(vi) Reading comprehension.

(vii) Mathematics calculation.

(viii) Mathematics problem solving.

(2)(i) The child does not make sufficient progress to meet age or State-approved grade-level standards in one or more of the areas identified in paragraph (a)(1) of this section when using a process based on the child's response to scientific, research-based intervention; or

(ii) The child exhibits a pattern of strengths and weaknesses in performance, achievement, or both, relative to age, State-approved grade-level standards, or intellectual development, that is determined by the group to be relevant to the identification of a specific learning disability, using appropriate assessments, consistent with §§300.304 and 300.305; and

(3) The group determines that its findings under paragraphs (a)(1) and (2) of this section are not primarily the result of—

(i) A visual, hearing, or motor disability;

(ii) An intellectual disability;

(iii) Emotional disturbance;

(iv) Cultural factors;

(v) Environmental or economic disadvantage; or

(vi) Limited English proficiency.

(b) To ensure that underachievement in a child suspected of having a specific learning disability is not due to lack of appropriate instruction in reading or math, the group must consider, as part of the evaluation described in §§300.304 through 300.306—

(1) Data that demonstrate that prior to, or as a part of, the referral process, the child was provided appropriate instruction in regular education settings, delivered by qualified personnel; and

(2) Data-based documentation of repeated assessments of achievement at reasonable intervals, reflecting formal assessment of student progress during instruction, which was provided to the child's parents.

(c) The public agency must promptly request parental consent to evaluate the child to determine if the child needs special education and related services, and must adhere to the timeframes described in §§300.301 and 300.303, unless extended by mutual written agreement of the child's parents and a group of qualified professionals, as described in §300.306(a)(1)—

(1) If, prior to a referral, a child has not made adequate progress after an

appropriate period of time when provided instruction, as described in paragraphs (b)(1) and (b)(2) of this section; and

(2) Whenever a child is referred for an evaluation.

[71 FR 46753, Aug. 14, 2006, as amended at 82 FR 31912, July 11, 2017]

§ 300.310 Observation.

(a) The public agency must ensure that the child is observed in the child's learning environment (including the regular classroom setting) to document the child's academic performance and behavior in the areas of difficulty.

(b) The group described in § 300.306(a)(1), in determining whether a child has a specific learning disability, must decide to—

(1) Use information from an observation in routine classroom instruction and monitoring of the child's performance that was done before the child was referred for an evaluation; or

(2) Have at least one member of the group described in § 300.306(a)(1) conduct an observation of the child's academic performance in the regular classroom after the child has been referred for an evaluation and parental consent, consistent with § 300.300(a), is obtained.

(c) In the case of a child of less than school age or out of school, a group member must observe the child in an environment appropriate for a child of that age.

(Authority: 20 U.S.C. 1221e–3; 1401(30); 1414(b)(6))

§ 300.311 Specific documentation for the eligibility determination.

(a) For a child suspected of having a specific learning disability, the documentation of the determination of eligibility, as required in § 300.306(a)(2), must contain a statement of—

(1) Whether the child has a specific learning disability;

(2) The basis for making the determination, including an assurance that the determination has been made in accordance with § 300.306(c)(1);

(3) The relevant behavior, if any, noted during the observation of the child and the relationship of that behavior to the child's academic functioning;

(4) The educationally relevant medical findings, if any;

(5) Whether—

(i) The child does not achieve adequately for the child's age or to meet State-approved grade-level standards consistent with § 300.309(a)(1); and

(ii)(A) The child does not make sufficient progress to meet age or State-approved grade-level standards consistent with § 300.309(a)(2)(i); or

(B) The child exhibits a pattern of strengths and weaknesses in performance, achievement, or both, relative to age, State-approved grade level standards or intellectual development consistent with § 300.309(a)(2)(ii);

(6) The determination of the group concerning the effects of a visual, hearing, motor disability, or an intellectual disability; emotional disturbance; cultural factors; environmental or economic disadvantage; or limited English proficiency on the child's achievement level; and

(7) If the child has participated in a process that assesses the child's response to scientific, research-based intervention—

(i) The instructional strategies used and the student-centered data collected; and

(ii) The documentation that the child's parents were notified about—

(A) The State's policies regarding the amount and nature of student performance data that would be collected and the general education services that would be provided;

(B) Strategies for increasing the child's rate of learning; and

(C) The parents' right to request an evaluation.

(b) Each group member must certify in writing whether the report reflects the member's conclusion. If it does not reflect the member's conclusion, the group member must submit a separate statement presenting the member's conclusions.

[71 FR 46753, Aug. 14, 2006, as amended at 82 FR 31913, July 11, 2017]

INDIVIDUALIZED EDUCATION PROGRAMS

§ 300.320 Definition of individualized education program.

(a) *General.* As used in this part, the term individualized education program or IEP means a written statement for each child with a disability that is developed, reviewed, and revised in a meeting in accordance with §§ 300.320 through 300.324, and that must include—

(1) A statement of the child's present levels of academic achievement and functional performance, including—

(i) How the child's disability affects the child's involvement and progress in the general education curriculum (i.e., the same curriculum as for nondisabled children); or

(ii) For preschool children, as appropriate, how the disability affects the child's participation in appropriate activities;

(2)(i) A statement of measurable annual goals, including academic and functional goals designed to—

(A) Meet the child's needs that result from the child's disability to enable the child to be involved in and make progress in the general education curriculum; and

(B) Meet each of the child's other educational needs that result from the child's disability;

(ii) For children with disabilities who take alternate assessments aligned to alternate academic achievement standards, a description of benchmarks or short-term objectives;

(3) A description of—

(i) How the child's progress toward meeting the annual goals described in paragraph (2) of this section will be measured; and

(ii) When periodic reports on the progress the child is making toward meeting the annual goals (such as through the use of quarterly or other periodic reports, concurrent with the issuance of report cards) will be provided;

(4) A statement of the special education and related services and supplementary aids and services, based on peer-reviewed research to the extent practicable, to be provided to the child, or on behalf of the child, and a statement of the program modifications or supports for school personnel that will be provided to enable the child—

(i) To advance appropriately toward attaining the annual goals;

(ii) To be involved in and make progress in the general education curriculum in accordance with paragraph (a)(1) of this section, and to participate in extracurricular and other nonacademic activities; and

(iii) To be educated and participate with other children with disabilities and nondisabled children in the activities described in this section;

(5) An explanation of the extent, if any, to which the child will not participate with nondisabled children in the regular class and in the activities described in paragraph (a)(4) of this section;

(6)(i) A statement of any individual appropriate accommodations that are necessary to measure the academic achievement and functional performance of the child on State and districtwide assessments consistent with section 612(a)(16) of the Act; and

(ii) If the IEP Team determines that the child must take an alternate assessment instead of a particular regular State or districtwide assessment of student achievement, a statement of why—

(A) The child cannot participate in the regular assessment; and

(B) The particular alternate assessment selected is appropriate for the child; and

(7) The projected date for the beginning of the services and modifications described in paragraph (a)(4) of this section, and the anticipated frequency, location, and duration of those services and modifications.

(b) *Transition services.* Beginning not later than the first IEP to be in effect when the child turns 16, or younger if determined appropriate by the IEP Team, and updated annually, thereafter, the IEP must include—

(1) Appropriate measurable postsecondary goals based upon age appropriate transition assessments related to training, education, employment, and, where appropriate, independent living skills; and

(2) The transition services (including courses of study) needed to assist the child in reaching those goals.

(c) *Transfer of rights at age of majority.* Beginning not later than one year before the child reaches the age of majority under State law, the IEP must include a statement that the child has been informed of the child's rights under Part B of the Act, if any, that will transfer to the child on reaching the age of majority under § 300.520.

(d) *Construction.* Nothing in this section shall be construed to require—

(1) That additional information be included in a child's IEP beyond what is explicitly required in section 614 of the Act; or

(2) The IEP Team to include information under one component of a child's IEP that is already contained under another component of the child's IEP.

(Authority: 20 U.S.C. 1414(d)(1)(A) and (d)(6))

[71 FR 46753, Aug. 14, 2006, as amended at 72 FR 61307, Oct. 30, 2007]

§ 300.321 IEP Team.

(a) *General.* The public agency must ensure that the IEP Team for each child with a disability includes—

(1) The parents of the child;

(2) Not less than one regular education teacher of the child (if the child is, or may be, participating in the regular education environment);

(3) Not less than one special education teacher of the child, or where appropriate, not less than one special education provider of the child;

(4) A representative of the public agency who—

(i) Is qualified to provide, or supervise the provision of, specially designed instruction to meet the unique needs of children with disabilities;

(ii) Is knowledgeable about the general education curriculum; and

(iii) Is knowledgeable about the availability of resources of the public agency.

(5) An individual who can interpret the instructional implications of evaluation results, who may be a member of the team described in paragraphs (a)(2) through (a)(6) of this section;

(6) At the discretion of the parent or the agency, other individuals who have knowledge or special expertise regarding the child, including related services personnel as appropriate; and

(7) Whenever appropriate, the child with a disability.

(b) *Transition services participants.* (1) In accordance with paragraph (a)(7) of this section, the public agency must invite a child with a disability to attend the child's IEP Team meeting if a purpose of the meeting will be the consideration of the postsecondary goals for the child and the transition services needed to assist the child in reaching those goals under § 300.320(b).

(2) If the child does not attend the IEP Team meeting, the public agency must take other steps to ensure that the child's preferences and interests are considered.

(3) To the extent appropriate, with the consent of the parents or a child who has reached the age of majority, in implementing the requirements of paragraph (b)(1) of this section, the public agency must invite a representative of any participating agency that is likely to be responsible for providing or paying for transition services.

(c) *Determination of knowledge and special expertise.* The determination of the knowledge or special expertise of any individual described in paragraph (a)(6) of this section must be made by the party (parents or public agency) who invited the individual to be a member of the IEP Team.

(d) *Designating a public agency representative.* A public agency may designate a public agency member of the IEP Team to also serve as the agency representative, if the criteria in paragraph (a)(4) of this section are satisfied.

(e) *IEP Team attendance.* (1) A member of the IEP Team described in paragraphs (a)(2) through (a)(5) of this section is not required to attend an IEP Team meeting, in whole or in part, if the parent of a child with a disability and the public agency agree, in writing, that the attendance of the member is not necessary because the member's area of the curriculum or related services is not being modified or discussed in the meeting.

(2) A member of the IEP Team described in paragraph (e)(1) of this section may be excused from attending an IEP Team meeting, in whole or in part, when the meeting involves a modification to or discussion of the member's area of the curriculum or related services, if—

(i) The parent, in writing, and the public agency consent to the excusal; and

(ii) The member submits, in writing to the parent and the IEP Team, input into the development of the IEP prior to the meeting.

(f) *Initial IEP Team meeting for child under Part C.* In the case of a child who was previously served under Part C of the Act, an invitation to the initial IEP Team meeting must, at the request of the parent, be sent to the Part C service coordinator or other representatives of the Part C system to assist with the smooth transition of services.

(Authority: 20 U.S.C. 1414(d)(1)(B)–(d)(1)(D))

[71 FR 46753, Aug. 14, 2006, as amended at 72 FR 61307, Oct. 30, 2007]

§ 300.322 Parent participation.

(a) *Public agency responsibility—general.* Each public agency must take steps to ensure that one or both of the parents of a child with a disability are present at each IEP Team meeting or are afforded the opportunity to participate, including—

(1) Notifying parents of the meeting early enough to ensure that they will have an opportunity to attend; and

(2) Scheduling the meeting at a mutually agreed on time and place.

(b) *Information provided to parents.* (1) The notice required under paragraph (a)(1) of this section must—

(i) Indicate the purpose, time, and location of the meeting and who will be in attendance; and

(ii) Inform the parents of the provisions in § 300.321(a)(6) and (c) (relating to the participation of other individuals on the IEP Team who have knowledge or special expertise about the child), and § 300.321(f) (relating to the participation of the Part C service coordinator or other representatives of the Part C system at the initial IEP Team meeting for a child previously served under Part C of the Act).

(2) For a child with a disability beginning not later than the first IEP to be in effect when the child turns 16, or younger if determined appropriate by the IEP Team, the notice also must—

(i) Indicate—

(A) That a purpose of the meeting will be the consideration of the postsecondary goals and transition services for the child, in accordance with § 300.320(b); and

(B) That the agency will invite the student; and

(ii) Identify any other agency that will be invited to send a representative.

(c) *Other methods to ensure parent participation.* If neither parent can attend an IEP Team meeting, the public agency must use other methods to ensure parent participation, including individual or conference telephone calls, consistent with § 300.328 (related to alternative means of meeting participation).

(d) *Conducting an IEP Team meeting without a parent in attendance.* A meeting may be conducted without a parent in attendance if the public agency is unable to convince the parents that they should attend. In this case, the public agency must keep a record of its attempts to arrange a mutually agreed on time and place, such as—

(1) Detailed records of telephone calls made or attempted and the results of those calls;

(2) Copies of correspondence sent to the parents and any responses received; and

(3) Detailed records of visits made to the parent's home or place of employment and the results of those visits.

(e) *Use of interpreters or other action, as appropriate.* The public agency must take whatever action is necessary to ensure that the parent understands the proceedings of the IEP Team meeting, including arranging for an interpreter for parents with deafness or whose native language is other than English.

(f) *Parent copy of child's IEP.* The public agency must give the parent a copy of the child's IEP at no cost to the parent.

(Authority: 20 U.S.C. 1414(d)(1)(B)(i))

§ 300.323 When IEPs must be in effect.

(a) *General.* At the beginning of each school year, each public agency must have in effect, for each child with a disability within its jurisdiction, an IEP, as defined in § 300.320.

(b) *IEP or IFSP for children aged three through five.* (1) In the case of a child with a disability aged three through five (or, at the discretion of the SEA, a two-year-old child with a disability who will turn age three during the school year), the IEP Team must consider an IFSP that contains the IFSP content (including the natural environments statement) described in section

73

636(d) of the Act and its implementing regulations (including an educational component that promotes school readiness and incorporates pre-literacy, language, and numeracy skills for children with IFSPs under this section who are at least three years of age), and that is developed in accordance with the IEP procedures under this part. The IFSP may serve as the IEP of the child, if using the IFSP as the IEP is—

(i) Consistent with State policy; and

(ii) Agreed to by the agency and the child's parents.

(2) In implementing the requirements of paragraph (b)(1) of this section, the public agency must—

(i) Provide to the child's parents a detailed explanation of the differences between an IFSP and an IEP; and

(ii) If the parents choose an IFSP, obtain written informed consent from the parents.

(c) *Initial IEPs; provision of services.* Each public agency must ensure that—

(1) A meeting to develop an IEP for a child is conducted within 30 days of a determination that the child needs special education and related services; and

(2) As soon as possible following development of the IEP, special education and related services are made available to the child in accordance with the child's IEP.

(d) *Accessibility of child's IEP to teachers and others.* Each public agency must ensure that—

(1) The child's IEP is accessible to each regular education teacher, special education teacher, related services provider, and any other service provider who is responsible for its implementation; and

(2) Each teacher and provider described in paragraph (d)(1) of this section is informed of—

(i) His or her specific responsibilities related to implementing the child's IEP; and

(ii) The specific accommodations, modifications, and supports that must be provided for the child in accordance with the IEP.

(e) *IEPs for children who transfer public agencies in the same State.* If a child with a disability (who had an IEP that was in effect in a previous public agency in the same State) transfers to a new public agency in the same State, and enrolls in a new school within the same school year, the new public agency (in consultation with the parents) must provide FAPE to the child (including services comparable to those described in the child's IEP from the previous public agency), until the new public agency either—

(1) Adopts the child's IEP from the previous public agency; or

(2) Develops, adopts, and implements a new IEP that meets the applicable requirements in §§ 300.320 through 300.324.

(f) *IEPs for children who transfer from another State.* If a child with a disability (who had an IEP that was in effect in a previous public agency in another State) transfers to a public agency in a new State, and enrolls in a new school within the same school year, the new public agency (in consultation with the parents) must provide the child with FAPE (including services comparable to those described in the child's IEP from the previous public agency), until the new public agency—

(1) Conducts an evaluation pursuant to §§ 300.304 through 300.306 (if determined to be necessary by the new public agency); and

(2) Develops, adopts, and implements a new IEP, if appropriate, that meets the applicable requirements in §§ 300.320 through 300.324.

(g) *Transmittal of records.* To facilitate the transition for a child described in paragraphs (e) and (f) of this section—

(1) The new public agency in which the child enrolls must take reasonable steps to promptly obtain the child's records, including the IEP and supporting documents and any other records relating to the provision of special education or related services to the child, from the previous public agency in which the child was enrolled, pursuant to 34 CFR 99.31(a)(2); and

(2) The previous public agency in which the child was enrolled must take reasonable steps to promptly respond to the request from the new public agency.

(Authority: 20 U.S.C. 1414(d)(2)(A)–(C))

DEVELOPMENT OF IEP

§300.324 Development, review, and revision of IEP.

(a) *Development of IEP*—(1) *General.* In developing each child's IEP, the IEP Team must consider—

(i) The strengths of the child;

(ii) The concerns of the parents for enhancing the education of their child;

(iii) The results of the initial or most recent evaluation of the child; and

(iv) The academic, developmental, and functional needs of the child.

(2) *Consideration of special factors.* The IEP Team must—

(i) In the case of a child whose behavior impedes the child's learning or that of others, consider the use of positive behavioral interventions and supports, and other strategies, to address that behavior;

(ii) In the case of a child with limited English proficiency, consider the language needs of the child as those needs relate to the child's IEP;

(iii) In the case of a child who is blind or visually impaired, provide for instruction in Braille and the use of Braille unless the IEP Team determines, after an evaluation of the child's reading and writing skills, needs, and appropriate reading and writing media (including an evaluation of the child's future needs for instruction in Braille or the use of Braille), that instruction in Braille or the use of Braille is not appropriate for the child;

(iv) Consider the communication needs of the child, and in the case of a child who is deaf or hard of hearing, consider the child's language and communication needs, opportunities for direct communications with peers and professional personnel in the child's language and communication mode, academic level, and full range of needs, including opportunities for direct instruction in the child's language and communication mode; and

(v) Consider whether the child needs assistive technology devices and services.

(3) *Requirement with respect to regular education teacher.* A regular education teacher of a child with a disability, as a member of the IEP Team, must, to the extent appropriate, participate in the development of the IEP of the child, including the determination of—

(i) Appropriate positive behavioral interventions and supports and other strategies for the child; and

(ii) Supplementary aids and services, program modifications, and support for school personnel consistent with §300.320(a)(4).

(4) *Agreement.* (i) In making changes to a child's IEP after the annual IEP Team meeting for a school year, the parent of a child with a disability and the public agency may agree not to convene an IEP Team meeting for the purposes of making those changes, and instead may develop a written document to amend or modify the child's current IEP.

(ii) If changes are made to the child's IEP in accordance with paragraph (a)(4)(i) of this section, the public agency must ensure that the child's IEP Team is informed of those changes.

(5) *Consolidation of IEP Team meetings.* To the extent possible, the public agency must encourage the consolidation of reevaluation meetings for the child and other IEP Team meetings for the child.

(6) *Amendments.* Changes to the IEP may be made either by the entire IEP Team at an IEP Team meeting, or as provided in paragraph (a)(4) of this section, by amending the IEP rather than by redrafting the entire IEP. Upon request, a parent must be provided with a revised copy of the IEP with the amendments incorporated.

(b) *Review and revision of IEPs*—(1) *General.* Each public agency must ensure that, subject to paragraphs (b)(2) and (b)(3) of this section, the IEP Team—

(i) Reviews the child's IEP periodically, but not less than annually, to determine whether the annual goals for the child are being achieved; and

(ii) Revises the IEP, as appropriate, to address—

(A) Any lack of expected progress toward the annual goals described in §300.320(a)(2), and in the general education curriculum, if appropriate;

(B) The results of any reevaluation conducted under §300.303;

(C) Information about the child provided to, or by, the parents, as described under §300.305(a)(2);

(D) The child's anticipated needs; or

75

(E) Other matters.

(2) *Consideration of special factors.* In conducting a review of the child's IEP, the IEP Team must consider the special factors described in paragraph (a)(2) of this section.

(3) *Requirement with respect to regular education teacher.* A regular education teacher of the child, as a member of the IEP Team, must, consistent with paragraph (a)(3) of this section, participate in the review and revision of the IEP of the child.

(c) *Failure to meet transition objectives*—(1) *Participating agency failure.* If a participating agency, other than the public agency, fails to provide the transition services described in the IEP in accordance with § 300.320(b), the public agency must reconvene the IEP Team to identify alternative strategies to meet the transition objectives for the child set out in the IEP.

(2) *Construction.* Nothing in this part relieves any participating agency, including a State vocational rehabilitation agency, of the responsibility to provide or pay for any transition service that the agency would otherwise provide to children with disabilities who meet the eligibility criteria of that agency.

(d) *Children with disabilities in adult prisons*—(1) *Requirements that do not apply.* The following requirements do not apply to children with disabilities who are convicted as adults under State law and incarcerated in adult prisons:

(i) The requirements contained in section 612(a)(16) of the Act and § 300.320(a)(6) (relating to participation of children with disabilities in general assessments).

(ii) The requirements in § 300.320(b) (relating to transition planning and transition services) do not apply with respect to the children whose eligibility under Part B of the Act will end, because of their age, before they will be eligible to be released from prison based on consideration of their sentence and eligibility for early release.

(2) *Modifications of IEP or placement.* (i) Subject to paragraph (d)(2)(ii) of this section, the IEP Team of a child with a disability who is convicted as an adult under State law and incarcerated in an adult prison may modify the child's IEP or placement if the State has demonstrated a bona fide security or compelling penological interest that cannot otherwise be accommodated.

(ii) The requirements of §§ 300.320 (relating to IEPs), and 300.114 (relating to LRE), do not apply with respect to the modifications described in paragraph (d)(2)(i) of this section.

(Authority: 20 U.S.C. 1412(a)(1), 1412(a)(12)(A)(i), 1414(d)(3), (4)(B), and (7); and 1414(e))

[71 FR 46753, Aug. 14, 2006, as amended at 82 FR 29761, June 30, 2017]

§ 300.325 Private school placements by public agencies.

(a) *Developing IEPs.* (1) Before a public agency places a child with a disability in, or refers a child to, a private school or facility, the agency must initiate and conduct a meeting to develop an IEP for the child in accordance with §§ 300.320 and 300.324.

(2) The agency must ensure that a representative of the private school or facility attends the meeting. If the representative cannot attend, the agency must use other methods to ensure participation by the private school or facility, including individual or conference telephone calls.

(b) *Reviewing and revising IEPs.* (1) After a child with a disability enters a private school or facility, any meetings to review and revise the child's IEP may be initiated and conducted by the private school or facility at the discretion of the public agency.

(2) If the private school or facility initiates and conducts these meetings, the public agency must ensure that the parents and an agency representative—

(i) Are involved in any decision about the child's IEP; and

(ii) Agree to any proposed changes in the IEP before those changes are implemented.

(c) *Responsibility.* Even if a private school or facility implements a child's IEP, responsibility for compliance with this part remains with the public agency and the SEA.

(Authority: 20 U.S.C. 1412(a)(10)(B))

§300.326 [Reserved]

§300.327 Educational placements.

Consistent with §300.501(c), each public agency must ensure that the parents of each child with a disability are members of any group that makes decisions on the educational placement of their child.

(Authority: 20 U.S.C. 1414(e))

§300.328 Alternative means of meeting participation.

When conducting IEP Team meetings and placement meetings pursuant to this subpart, and subpart E of this part, and carrying out administrative matters under section 615 of the Act (such as scheduling, exchange of witness lists, and status conferences), the parent of a child with a disability and a public agency may agree to use alternative means of meeting participation, such as video conferences and conference calls.

(Authority: 20 U.S.C. 1414(f))

Subpart E—Procedural Safeguards Due Process Procedures for Parents and Children

§300.500 Responsibility of SEA and other public agencies.

Each SEA must ensure that each public agency establishes, maintains, and implements procedural safeguards that meet the requirements of §§300.500 through 300.536.

(Authority: 20 U.S.C. 1415(a))

§300.501 Opportunity to examine records; parent participation in meetings.

(a) *Opportunity to examine records.* The parents of a child with a disability must be afforded, in accordance with the procedures of §§300.613 through 300.621, an opportunity to inspect and review all education records with respect to—

(1) The identification, evaluation, and educational placement of the child; and

(2) The provision of FAPE to the child.

(b) *Parent participation in meetings.* (1) The parents of a child with a disability must be afforded an opportunity to participate in meetings with respect to—

(i) The identification, evaluation, and educational placement of the child; and

(ii) The provision of FAPE to the child.

(2) Each public agency must provide notice consistent with §300.322(a)(1) and (b)(1) to ensure that parents of children with disabilities have the opportunity to participate in meetings described in paragraph (b)(1) of this section.

(3) A meeting does not include informal or unscheduled conversations involving public agency personnel and conversations on issues such as teaching methodology, lesson plans, or coordination of service provision. A meeting also does not include preparatory activities that public agency personnel engage in to develop a proposal or response to a parent proposal that will be discussed at a later meeting.

(c) *Parent involvement in placement decisions.* (1) Each public agency must ensure that a parent of each child with a disability is a member of any group that makes decisions on the educational placement of the parent's child.

(2) In implementing the requirements of paragraph (c)(1) of this section, the public agency must use procedures consistent with the procedures described in §300.322(a) through (b)(1).

(3) If neither parent can participate in a meeting in which a decision is to be made relating to the educational placement of their child, the public agency must use other methods to ensure their participation, including individual or conference telephone calls, or video conferencing.

(4) A placement decision may be made by a group without the involvement of a parent, if the public agency is unable to obtain the parent's participation in the decision. In this case, the public agency must have a record of its attempt to ensure their involvement.

(Authority: 20 U.S.C. 1414(e), 1415(b)(1))

§ 300.502 Independent educational evaluation.

(a) *General.* (1) The parents of a child with a disability have the right under this part to obtain an independent educational evaluation of the child, subject to paragraphs (b) through (e) of this section.

(2) Each public agency must provide to parents, upon request for an independent educational evaluation, information about where an independent educational evaluation may be obtained, and the agency criteria applicable for independent educational evaluations as set forth in paragraph (e) of this section.

(3) For the purposes of this subpart—

(i) *Independent educational evaluation* means an evaluation conducted by a qualified examiner who is not employed by the public agency responsible for the education of the child in question; and

(ii) *Public expense* means that the public agency either pays for the full cost of the evaluation or ensures that the evaluation is otherwise provided at no cost to the parent, consistent with § 300.103.

(b) *Parent right to evaluation at public expense.* (1) A parent has the right to an independent educational evaluation at public expense if the parent disagrees with an evaluation obtained by the public agency, subject to the conditions in paragraphs (b)(2) through (4) of this section.

(2) If a parent requests an independent educational evaluation at public expense, the public agency must, without unnecessary delay, either—

(i) File a due process complaint to request a hearing to show that its evaluation is appropriate; or

(ii) Ensure that an independent educational evaluation is provided at public expense, unless the agency demonstrates in a hearing pursuant to §§ 300.507 through 300.513 that the evaluation obtained by the parent did not meet agency criteria.

(3) If the public agency files a due process complaint notice to request a hearing and the final decision is that the agency's evaluation is appropriate, the parent still has the right to an independent educational evaluation, but not at public expense.

(4) If a parent requests an independent educational evaluation, the public agency may ask for the parent's reason why he or she objects to the public evaluation. However, the public agency may not require the parent to provide an explanation and may not unreasonably delay either providing the independent educational evaluation at public expense or filing a due process complaint to request a due process hearing to defend the public evaluation.

(5) A parent is entitled to only one independent educational evaluation at public expense each time the public agency conducts an evaluation with which the parent disagrees.

(c) *Parent-initiated evaluations.* If the parent obtains an independent educational evaluation at public expense or shares with the public agency an evaluation obtained at private expense, the results of the evaluation—

(1) Must be considered by the public agency, if it meets agency criteria, in any decision made with respect to the provision of FAPE to the child; and

(2) May be presented by any party as evidence at a hearing on a due process complaint under subpart E of this part regarding that child.

(d) *Requests for evaluations by hearing officers.* If a hearing officer requests an independent educational evaluation as part of a hearing on a due process complaint, the cost of the evaluation must be at public expense.

(e) *Agency criteria.* (1) If an independent educational evaluation is at public expense, the criteria under which the evaluation is obtained, including the location of the evaluation and the qualifications of the examiner, must be the same as the criteria that the public agency uses when it initiates an evaluation, to the extent those criteria are consistent with the parent's right to an independent educational evaluation.

(2) Except for the criteria described in paragraph (e)(1) of this section, a public agency may not impose conditions or timelines related to obtaining an independent educational evaluation at public expense.

(Authority: 20 U.S.C. 1415(b)(1) and (d)(2)(A))

§ 300.503 Prior notice by the public agency; content of notice.

(a) *Notice.* Written notice that meets the requirements of paragraph (b) of this section must be given to the parents of a child with a disability a reasonable time before the public agency—

(1) Proposes to initiate or change the identification, evaluation, or educational placement of the child or the provision of FAPE to the child; or

(2) Refuses to initiate or change the identification, evaluation, or educational placement of the child or the provision of FAPE to the child.

(b) *Content of notice.* The notice required under paragraph (a) of this section must include—

(1) A description of the action proposed or refused by the agency;

(2) An explanation of why the agency proposes or refuses to take the action;

(3) A description of each evaluation procedure, assessment, record, or report the agency used as a basis for the proposed or refused action;

(4) A statement that the parents of a child with a disability have protection under the procedural safeguards of this part and, if this notice is not an initial referral for evaluation, the means by which a copy of a description of the procedural safeguards can be obtained;

(5) Sources for parents to contact to obtain assistance in understanding the provisions of this part;

(6) A description of other options that the IEP Team considered and the reasons why those options were rejected; and

(7) A description of other factors that are relevant to the agency's proposal or refusal.

(c) *Notice in understandable language.* (1) The notice required under paragraph (a) of this section must be—

(i) Written in language understandable to the general public; and

(ii) Provided in the native language of the parent or other mode of communication used by the parent, unless it is clearly not feasible to do so.

(2) If the native language or other mode of communication of the parent is not a written language, the public agency must take steps to ensure—

(i) That the notice is translated orally or by other means to the parent in his or her native language or other mode of communication;

(ii) That the parent understands the content of the notice; and

(iii) That there is written evidence that the requirements in paragraphs (c)(2)(i) and (ii) of this section have been met.

(Authority: 20 U.S.C. 1415(b)(3) and (4), 1415(c)(1), 1414(b)(1))

§ 300.504 Procedural safeguards notice.

(a) *General.* A copy of the procedural safeguards available to the parents of a child with a disability must be given to the parents only one time a school year, except that a copy also must be given to the parents—

(1) Upon initial referral or parent request for evaluation;

(2) Upon receipt of the first State complaint under §§ 300.151 through 300.153 and upon receipt of the first due process complaint under § 300.507 in a school year;

(3) In accordance with the discipline procedures in § 300.530(h); and

(4) Upon request by a parent.

(b) *Internet Web site.* A public agency may place a current copy of the procedural safeguards notice on its Internet Web site if a Web site exists.

(c) *Contents.* The procedural safeguards notice must include a full explanation of all of the procedural safeguards available under § 300.148, §§ 300.151 through 300.153, § 300.300, §§ 300.502 through 300.503, §§ 300.505 through 300.518, §§ 300.530 through 300.536 and §§ 300.610 through 300.625 relating to—

(1) Independent educational evaluations;

(2) Prior written notice;

(3) Parental consent;

(4) Access to education records;

(5) Opportunity to present and resolve complaints through the due process complaint and State complaint procedures, including—

(i) The time period in which to file a complaint;

(ii) The opportunity for the agency to resolve the complaint; and

(iii) The difference between the due process complaint and the State complaint procedures, including the jurisdiction of each procedure, what issues may be raised, filing and decisional timelines, and relevant procedures;

(6) The availability of mediation;

(7) The child's placement during the pendency of any due process complaint;

(8) Procedures for students who are subject to placement in an interim alternative educational setting;

(9) Requirements for unilateral placement by parents of children in private schools at public expense;

(10) Hearings on due process complaints, including requirements for disclosure of evaluation results and recommendations;

(11) State-level appeals (if applicable in the State);

(12) Civil actions, including the time period in which to file those actions; and

(13) Attorneys' fees.

(d) *Notice in understandable language.* The notice required under paragraph (a) of this section must meet the requirements of § 300.503(c).

(Approved by the Office of Management and Budget under control number 1820–0600)

(Authority: 20 U.S.C. 1415(d))

[71 FR 46753, Aug. 14, 2006, as amended at 72 FR 61307, Oct. 30, 2007]

§ 300.505 Electronic mail.

A parent of a child with a disability may elect to receive notices required by §§ 300.503, 300.504, and 300.508 by an electronic mail communication, if the public agency makes that option available.

(Authority: 20 U.S.C. 1415(n))

§ 300.506 Mediation.

(a) *General.* Each public agency must ensure that procedures are established and implemented to allow parties to disputes involving any matter under this part, including matters arising prior to the filing of a due process complaint, to resolve disputes through a mediation process.

(b) *Requirements.* The procedures must meet the following requirements:

(1) The procedures must ensure that the mediation process—

(i) Is voluntary on the part of the parties;

(ii) Is not used to deny or delay a parent's right to a hearing on the parent's due process complaint, or to deny any

other rights afforded under Part B of the Act; and

(iii) Is conducted by a qualified and impartial mediator who is trained in effective mediation techniques.

(2) A public agency may establish procedures to offer to parents and schools that choose not to use the mediation process, an opportunity to meet, at a time and location convenient to the parents, with a disinterested party—

(i) Who is under contract with an appropriate alternative dispute resolution entity, or a parent training and information center or community parent resource center in the State established under section 671 or 672 of the Act; and

(ii) Who would explain the benefits of, and encourage the use of, the mediation process to the parents.

(3)(i) The State must maintain a list of individuals who are qualified mediators and knowledgeable in laws and regulations relating to the provision of special education and related services.

(ii) The SEA must select mediators on a random, rotational, or other impartial basis.

(4) The State must bear the cost of the mediation process, including the costs of meetings described in paragraph (b)(2) of this section.

(5) Each session in the mediation process must be scheduled in a timely manner and must be held in a location that is convenient to the parties to the dispute.

(6) If the parties resolve a dispute through the mediation process, the parties must execute a legally binding agreement that sets forth that resolution and that—

(i) States that all discussions that occurred during the mediation process will remain confidential and may not be used as evidence in any subsequent due process hearing or civil proceeding; and

(ii) Is signed by both the parent and a representative of the agency who has the authority to bind such agency.

(7) A written, signed mediation agreement under this paragraph is enforceable in any State court of competent jurisdiction or in a district court of the United States.

(8) Discussions that occur during the mediation process must be confidential and may not be used as evidence in any subsequent due process hearing or civil proceeding of any Federal court or State court of a State receiving assistance under this part.

(c) *Impartiality of mediator.* (1) An individual who serves as a mediator under this part—

(i) May not be an employee of the SEA or the LEA that is involved in the education or care of the child; and

(ii) Must not have a personal or professional interest that conflicts with the person's objectivity.

(2) A person who otherwise qualifies as a mediator is not an employee of an LEA or State agency described under § 300.228 solely because he or she is paid by the agency to serve as a mediator.

(Approved by the Office of Management and Budget under control number 1820–0600)

(Authority: 20 U.S.C. 1415(e))

[71 FR 46753, Aug. 14, 2006, as amended at 72 FR 61307, Oct. 30, 2007]

§ 300.507 Filing a due process complaint.

(a) *General.* (1) A parent or a public agency may file a due process complaint on any of the matters described in § 300.503(a)(1) and (2) (relating to the identification, evaluation or educational placement of a child with a disability, or the provision of FAPE to the child).

(2) The due process complaint must allege a violation that occurred not more than two years before the date the parent or public agency knew or should have known about the alleged action that forms the basis of the due process complaint, or, if the State has an explicit time limitation for filing a due process complaint under this part, in the time allowed by that State law, except that the exceptions to the timeline described in § 300.511(f) apply to the timeline in this section.

(b) *Information for parents.* The public agency must inform the parent of any free or low-cost legal and other relevant services available in the area if—

(1) The parent requests the information; or

(2) The parent or the agency files a due process complaint under this section.

(Approved by the Office of Management and Budget under control number 1820–0600)

(Authority: 20 U.S.C. 1415(b)(6))

§ 300.508 Due process complaint.

(a) *General.* (1) The public agency must have procedures that require either party, or the attorney representing a party, to provide to the other party a due process complaint (which must remain confidential).

(2) The party filing a due process complaint must forward a copy of the due process complaint to the SEA.

(b) *Content of complaint.* The due process complaint required in paragraph (a)(1) of this section must include—

(1) The name of the child;

(2) The address of the residence of the child;

(3) The name of the school the child is attending;

(4) In the case of a homeless child or youth (within the meaning of section 725(2) of the McKinney-Vento Homeless Assistance Act (42 U.S.C. 11434a(2)), available contact information for the child, and the name of the school the child is attending;

(5) A description of the nature of the problem of the child relating to the proposed or refused initiation or change, including facts relating to the problem; and

(6) A proposed resolution of the problem to the extent known and available to the party at the time.

(c) *Notice required before a hearing on a due process complaint.* A party may not have a hearing on a due process complaint until the party, or the attorney representing the party, files a due process complaint that meets the requirements of paragraph (b) of this section.

(d) *Sufficiency of complaint.* (1) The due process complaint required by this section must be deemed sufficient unless the party receiving the due process complaint notifies the hearing officer and the other party in writing, within 15 days of receipt of the due process complaint, that the receiving party believes the due process complaint does not meet the requirements in paragraph (b) of this section.

(2) Within five days of receipt of notification under paragraph (d)(1) of this section, the hearing officer must make a determination on the face of the due process complaint of whether the due process complaint meets the requirements of paragraph (b) of this section, and must immediately notify the parties in writing of that determination.

(3) A party may amend its due process complaint only if—

(i) The other party consents in writing to the amendment and is given the opportunity to resolve the due process complaint through a meeting held pursuant to § 300.510; or

(ii) The hearing officer grants permission, except that the hearing officer may only grant permission to amend at any time not later than five days before the due process hearing begins.

(4) If a party files an amended due process complaint, the timelines for the resolution meeting in § 300.510(a) and the time period to resolve in § 300.510(b) begin again with the filing of the amended due process complaint.

(e) *LEA response to a due process complaint.* (1) If the LEA has not sent a prior written notice under § 300.503 to the parent regarding the subject matter contained in the parent's due process complaint, the LEA must, within 10 days of receiving the due process complaint, send to the parent a response that includes—

(i) An explanation of why the agency proposed or refused to take the action raised in the due process complaint;

(ii) A description of other options that the IEP Team considered and the reasons why those options were rejected;

(iii) A description of each evaluation procedure, assessment, record, or report the agency used as the basis for the proposed or refused action; and

(iv) A description of the other factors that are relevant to the agency's proposed or refused action.

(2) A response by an LEA under paragraph (e)(1) of this section shall not be construed to preclude the LEA from asserting that the parent's due process complaint was insufficient, where appropriate.

(f) *Other party response to a due process complaint.* Except as provided in paragraph (e) of this section, the party receiving a due process complaint must, within 10 days of receiving the due process complaint, send to the other party a response that specifically addresses the issues raised in the due process complaint.

(Authority: 20 U.S.C. 1415(b)(7), 1415(c)(2))

§ 300.509   Model forms.

(a) Each SEA must develop model forms to assist parents and public agencies in filing a due process complaint in accordance with §§ 300.507(a) and 300.508(a) through (c) and to assist parents and other parties in filing a State complaint under §§ 300.151 through 300.153. However, the SEA or LEA may not require the use of the model forms.

(b) Parents, public agencies, and other parties may use the appropriate model form described in paragraph (a) of this section, or another form or other document, so long as the form or document that is used meets, as appropriate, the content requirements in § 300.508(b) for filing a due process complaint, or the requirements in § 300.153(b) for filing a State complaint.

(Authority: 20 U.S.C. 1415(b)(8))

§ 300.510   Resolution process.

(a) *Resolution meeting.* (1) Within 15 days of receiving notice of the parent's due process complaint, and prior to the initiation of a due process hearing under § 300.511, the LEA must convene a meeting with the parent and the relevant member or members of the IEP Team who have specific knowledge of the facts identified in the due process complaint that—

(i) Includes a representative of the public agency who has decision-making authority on behalf of that agency; and

(ii) May not include an attorney of the LEA unless the parent is accompanied by an attorney.

(2) The purpose of the meeting is for the parent of the child to discuss the due process complaint, and the facts that form the basis of the due process complaint, so that the LEA has the opportunity to resolve the dispute that is the basis for the due process complaint.

(3) The meeting described in paragraph (a)(1) and (2) of this section need not be held if—

(i) The parent and the LEA agree in writing to waive the meeting; or

(ii) The parent and the LEA agree to use the mediation process described in § 300.506.

(4) The parent and the LEA determine the relevant members of the IEP Team to attend the meeting.

(b) *Resolution period.* (1) If the LEA has not resolved the due process complaint to the satisfaction of the parent within 30 days of the receipt of the due process complaint, the due process hearing may occur.

(2) Except as provided in paragraph (c) of this section, the timeline for issuing a final decision under § 300.515 begins at the expiration of this 30-day period.

(3) Except where the parties have jointly agreed to waive the resolution process or to use mediation, notwithstanding paragraphs (b)(1) and (2) of this section, the failure of the parent filing a due process complaint to participate in the resolution meeting will delay the timelines for the resolution process and due process hearing until the meeting is held.

(4) If the LEA is unable to obtain the participation of the parent in the resolution meeting after reasonable efforts have been made (and documented using the procedures in § 300.322(d)), the LEA may, at the conclusion of the 30-day period, request that a hearing officer dismiss the parent's due process complaint.

(5) If the LEA fails to hold the resolution meeting specified in paragraph (a) of this section within 15 days of receiving notice of a parent's due process complaint or fails to participate in the resolution meeting, the parent may seek the intervention of a hearing officer to begin the due process hearing timeline.

(c) *Adjustments to 30-day resolution period.* The 45-day timeline for the due process hearing in § 300.515(a) starts the day after one of the following events:

(1) Both parties agree in writing to waive the resolution meeting;

(2) After either the mediation or resolution meeting starts but before the end of the 30-day period, the parties agree in writing that no agreement is possible;

(3) If both parties agree in writing to continue the mediation at the end of the 30-day resolution period, but later, the parent or public agency withdraws from the mediation process.

(d) *Written settlement agreement.* If a resolution to the dispute is reached at the meeting described in paragraphs (a)(1) and (2) of this section, the parties must execute a legally binding agreement that is—

(1) Signed by both the parent and a representative of the agency who has the authority to bind the agency; and

(2) Enforceable in any State court of competent jurisdiction or in a district court of the United States, or, by the SEA, if the State has other mechanisms or procedures that permit parties to seek enforcement of resolution agreements, pursuant to § 300.537.

(e) *Agreement review period.* If the parties execute an agreement pursuant to paragraph (d) of this section, a party may void the agreement within 3 business days of the agreement's execution.

(Authority: 20 U.S.C. 1415(f)(1)(B))

[71 FR 46753, Aug. 14, 2006, as amended at 72 FR 61307, Oct. 30, 2007]

§ 300.511 Impartial due process hearing.

(a) *General.* Whenever a due process complaint is received under § 300.507 or § 300.532, the parents or the LEA involved in the dispute must have an opportunity for an impartial due process hearing, consistent with the procedures in §§ 300.507, 300.508, and 300.510.

(b) *Agency responsible for conducting the due process hearing.* The hearing described in paragraph (a) of this section must be conducted by the SEA or the public agency directly responsible for the education of the child, as determined under State statute, State regulation, or a written policy of the SEA.

(c) *Impartial hearing officer.* (1) At a minimum, a hearing officer—

(i) Must not be—

(A) An employee of the SEA or the LEA that is involved in the education or care of the child; or

(B) A person having a personal or professional interest that conflicts with the person's objectivity in the hearing;

(ii) Must possess knowledge of, and the ability to understand, the provisions of the Act, Federal and State regulations pertaining to the Act, and legal interpretations of the Act by Federal and State courts;

(iii) Must possess the knowledge and ability to conduct hearings in accordance with appropriate, standard legal practice; and

(iv) Must possess the knowledge and ability to render and write decisions in accordance with appropriate, standard legal practice.

(2) A person who otherwise qualifies to conduct a hearing under paragraph (c)(1) of this section is not an employee of the agency solely because he or she is paid by the agency to serve as a hearing officer.

(3) Each public agency must keep a list of the persons who serve as hearing officers. The list must include a statement of the qualifications of each of those persons.

(d) *Subject matter of due process hearings.* The party requesting the due process hearing may not raise issues at the due process hearing that were not raised in the due process complaint filed under § 300.508(b), unless the other party agrees otherwise.

(e) *Timeline for requesting a hearing.* A parent or agency must request an impartial hearing on their due process complaint within two years of the date the parent or agency knew or should have known about the alleged action that forms the basis of the due process complaint, or if the State has an explicit time limitation for requesting such a due process hearing under this part, in the time allowed by that State law.

(f) *Exceptions to the timeline.* The timeline described in paragraph (e) of this section does not apply to a parent if the parent was prevented from filing a due process complaint due to—

(1) Specific misrepresentations by the LEA that it had resolved the problem forming the basis of the due process complaint; or

(2) The LEA's withholding of information from the parent that was required under this part to be provided to the parent.

(Approved by the Office of Management and Budget under control number 1820–0600)

(Authority: 20 U.S.C. 1415(f)(1)(A), 1415(f)(3)(A)–(D))

§ 300.512 Hearing rights.

(a) *General.* Any party to a hearing conducted pursuant to §§ 300.507 through 300.513 or §§ 300.530 through 300.534, or an appeal conducted pursuant to § 300.514, has the right to—

(1) Be accompanied and advised by counsel and by individuals with special knowledge or training with respect to the problems of children with disabilities, except that whether parties have the right to be represented by non-attorneys at due process hearings is determined under State law;

(2) Present evidence and confront, cross-examine, and compel the attendance of witnesses;

(3) Prohibit the introduction of any evidence at the hearing that has not been disclosed to that party at least five business days before the hearing;

(4) Obtain a written, or, at the option of the parents, electronic, verbatim record of the hearing; and

(5) Obtain written, or, at the option of the parents, electronic findings of fact and decisions.

(b) *Additional disclosure of information.* (1) At least five business days prior to a hearing conducted pursuant to § 300.511(a), each party must disclose to all other parties all evaluations completed by that date and recommendations based on the offering party's evaluations that the party intends to use at the hearing.

(2) A hearing officer may bar any party that fails to comply with paragraph (b)(1) of this section from introducing the relevant evaluation or recommendation at the hearing without the consent of the other party.

(c) *Parental rights at hearings.* Parents involved in hearings must be given the right to—

(1) Have the child who is the subject of the hearing present;

(2) Open the hearing to the public; and

(3) Have the record of the hearing and the findings of fact and decisions described in paragraphs (a)(4) and (a)(5) of

this section provided at no cost to parents.

(Authority: 20 U.S.C. 1415(f)(2), 1415(h))

[71 FR 46753, Aug. 14, 2006, as amended at 73 FR 73027, Dec. 1, 2008]

§ 300.513 Hearing decisions.

(a) *Decision of hearing officer on the provision of FAPE.* (1) Subject to paragraph (a)(2) of this section, a hearing officer's determination of whether a child received FAPE must be based on substantive grounds.

(2) In matters alleging a procedural violation, a hearing officer may find that a child did not receive a FAPE only if the procedural inadequacies—

(i) Impeded the child's right to a FAPE;

(ii) Significantly impeded the parent's opportunity to participate in the decision-making process regarding the provision of a FAPE to the parent's child; or

(iii) Caused a deprivation of educational benefit.

(3) Nothing in paragraph (a) of this section shall be construed to preclude a hearing officer from ordering an LEA to comply with procedural requirements under §§ 300.500 through 300.536.

(b) *Construction clause.* Nothing in §§ 300.507 through 300.513 shall be construed to affect the right of a parent to file an appeal of the due process hearing decision with the SEA under § 300.514(b), if a State level appeal is available.

(c) *Separate request for a due process hearing.* Nothing in §§ 300.500 through 300.536 shall be construed to preclude a parent from filing a separate due process complaint on an issue separate from a due process complaint already filed.

(d) *Findings and decision to advisory panel and general public.* The public agency, after deleting any personally identifiable information, must—

(1) Transmit the findings and decisions referred to in § 300.512(a)(5) to the State advisory panel established under § 300.167; and

(2) Make those findings and decisions available to the public.

(Authority: 20 U.S.C. 1415(f)(3)(E) and (F), 1415(h)(4), 1415(o))

§ 300.514 Finality of decision; appeal; impartial review.

(a) *Finality of hearing decision.* A decision made in a hearing conducted pursuant to §§ 300.507 through 300.513 or §§ 300.530 through 300.534 is final, except that any party involved in the hearing may appeal the decision under the provisions of paragraph (b) of this section and § 300.516.

(b) *Appeal of decisions; impartial review.* (1) If the hearing required by § 300.511 is conducted by a public agency other than the SEA, any party aggrieved by the findings and decision in the hearing may appeal to the SEA.

(2) If there is an appeal, the SEA must conduct an impartial review of the findings and decision appealed. The official conducting the review must—

(i) Examine the entire hearing record;

(ii) Ensure that the procedures at the hearing were consistent with the requirements of due process;

(iii) Seek additional evidence if necessary. If a hearing is held to receive additional evidence, the rights in § 300.512 apply;

(iv) Afford the parties an opportunity for oral or written argument, or both, at the discretion of the reviewing official;

(v) Make an independent decision on completion of the review; and

(vi) Give a copy of the written, or, at the option of the parents, electronic findings of fact and decisions to the parties.

(c) *Findings and decision to advisory panel and general public.* The SEA, after deleting any personally identifiable information, must—

(1) Transmit the findings and decisions referred to in paragraph (b)(2)(vi) of this section to the State advisory panel established under § 300.167; and

(2) Make those findings and decisions available to the public.

(d) *Finality of review decision.* The decision made by the reviewing official is final unless a party brings a civil action under § 300.516.

(Authority: 20 U.S.C. 1415(g) and (h)(4), 1415(i)(1)(A), 1415(i)(2))

§ 300.515 Timelines and convenience of hearings and reviews.

(a) The public agency must ensure that not later than 45 days after the expiration of the 30 day period under § 300.510(b), or the adjusted time periods described in § 300.510(c)—

(1) A final decision is reached in the hearing; and

(2) A copy of the decision is mailed to each of the parties.

(b) The SEA must ensure that not later than 30 days after the receipt of a request for a review—

(1) A final decision is reached in the review; and

(2) A copy of the decision is mailed to each of the parties.

(c) A hearing or reviewing officer may grant specific extensions of time beyond the periods set out in paragraphs (a) and (b) of this section at the request of either party.

(d) Each hearing and each review involving oral arguments must be conducted at a time and place that is reasonably convenient to the parents and child involved.

(Authority: 20 U.S.C. 1415(f)(1)(B)(ii), 1415(g), 1415(i)(1))

§ 300.516 Civil action.

(a) *General.* Any party aggrieved by the findings and decision made under §§ 300.507 through 300.513 or §§ 300.530 through 300.534 who does not have the right to an appeal under § 300.514(b), and any party aggrieved by the findings and decision under § 300.514(b), has the right to bring a civil action with respect to the due process complaint notice requesting a due process hearing under § 300.507 or §§ 300.530 through 300.532. The action may be brought in any State court of competent jurisdiction or in a district court of the United States without regard to the amount in controversy.

(b) *Time limitation.* The party bringing the action shall have 90 days from the date of the decision of the hearing officer or, if applicable, the decision of the State review official, to file a civil action, or, if the State has an explicit time limitation for bringing civil actions under Part B of the Act, in the time allowed by that State law.

(c) *Additional requirements.* In any action brought under paragraph (a) of this section, the court—

(1) Receives the records of the administrative proceedings;

(2) Hears additional evidence at the request of a party; and

(3) Basing its decision on the preponderance of the evidence, grants the relief that the court determines to be appropriate.

(d) *Jurisdiction of district courts.* The district courts of the United States have jurisdiction of actions brought under section 615 of the Act without regard to the amount in controversy.

(e) *Rule of construction.* Nothing in this part restricts or limits the rights, procedures, and remedies available under the Constitution, the Americans with Disabilities Act of 1990, title V of the Rehabilitation Act of 1973, or other Federal laws protecting the rights of children with disabilities, except that before the filing of a civil action under these laws seeking relief that is also available under section 615 of the Act, the procedures under §§ 300.507 and 300.514 must be exhausted to the same extent as would be required had the action been brought under section 615 of the Act.

(Authority: 20 U.S.C. 1415(i)(2) and (3)(A), 1415(l))

§ 300.517 Attorneys' fees.

(a) *In general.* (1) In any action or proceeding brought under section 615 of the Act, the court, in its discretion, may award reasonable attorneys' fees as part of the costs to—

(i) The prevailing party who is the parent of a child with a disability;

(ii) To a prevailing party who is an SEA or LEA against the attorney of a parent who files a complaint or subsequent cause of action that is frivolous, unreasonable, or without foundation, or against the attorney of a parent who continued to litigate after the litigation clearly became frivolous, unreasonable, or without foundation; or

(iii) To a prevailing SEA or LEA against the attorney of a parent, or against the parent, if the parent's request for a due process hearing or subsequent cause of action was presented for any improper purpose, such as to harass, to cause unnecessary delay, or to needlessly increase the cost of litigation.

(2) Nothing in this subsection shall be construed to affect section 327 of the District of Columbia Appropriations Act, 2005.

(b) *Prohibition on use of funds.* (1) Funds under Part B of the Act may not be used to pay attorneys' fees or costs of a party related to any action or proceeding under section 615 of the Act and subpart E of this part.

(2) Paragraph (b)(1) of this section does not preclude a public agency from using funds under Part B of the Act for conducting an action or proceeding under section 615 of the Act.

(c) *Award of fees.* A court awards reasonable attorneys' fees under section 615(i)(3) of the Act consistent with the following:

(1) Fees awarded under section 615(i)(3) of the Act must be based on rates prevailing in the community in which the action or proceeding arose for the kind and quality of services furnished. No bonus or multiplier may be used in calculating the fees awarded under this paragraph.

(2)(i) Attorneys' fees may not be awarded and related costs may not be reimbursed in any action or proceeding under section 615 of the Act for services performed subsequent to the time of a written offer of settlement to a parent if—

(A) The offer is made within the time prescribed by Rule 68 of the Federal Rules of Civil Procedure or, in the case of an administrative proceeding, at any time more than 10 days before the proceeding begins;

(B) The offer is not accepted within 10 days; and

(C) The court or administrative hearing officer finds that the relief finally obtained by the parents is not more favorable to the parents than the offer of settlement.

(ii) Attorneys' fees may not be awarded relating to any meeting of the IEP Team unless the meeting is convened as a result of an administrative proceeding or judicial action, or at the discretion of the State, for a mediation described in § 300.506.

(iii) A meeting conducted pursuant to § 300.510 shall not be considered—

(A) A meeting convened as a result of an administrative hearing or judicial action; or

(B) An administrative hearing or judicial action for purposes of this section.

(3) Notwithstanding paragraph (c)(2) of this section, an award of attorneys' fees and related costs may be made to a parent who is the prevailing party and who was substantially justified in rejecting the settlement offer.

(4) Except as provided in paragraph (c)(5) of this section, the court reduces, accordingly, the amount of the attorneys' fees awarded under section 615 of the Act, if the court finds that—

(i) The parent, or the parent's attorney, during the course of the action or proceeding, unreasonably protracted the final resolution of the controversy;

(ii) The amount of the attorneys' fees otherwise authorized to be awarded unreasonably exceeds the hourly rate prevailing in the community for similar services by attorneys of reasonably comparable skill, reputation, and experience;

(iii) The time spent and legal services furnished were excessive considering the nature of the action or proceeding; or

(iv) The attorney representing the parent did not provide to the LEA the appropriate information in the due process request notice in accordance with § 300.508.

(5) The provisions of paragraph (c)(4) of this section do not apply in any action or proceeding if the court finds that the State or local agency unreasonably protracted the final resolution of the action or proceeding or there was a violation of section 615 of the Act.

(Authority: 20 U.S.C. 1415(i)(3)(B)–(G))

§ 300.518 Child's status during proceedings.

(a) Except as provided in § 300.533, during the pendency of any administrative or judicial proceeding regarding a due process complaint notice requesting a due process hearing under § 300.507, unless the State or local agency and the parents of the child agree otherwise, the child involved in the complaint must remain in his or her current educational placement.

(b) If the complaint involves an application for initial admission to public school, the child, with the consent of the parents, must be placed in the public school until the completion of all the proceedings.

(c) If the complaint involves an application for initial services under this part from a child who is transitioning from Part C of the Act to Part B and is no longer eligible for Part C services because the child has turned three, the public agency is not required to provide the Part C services that the child had been receiving. If the child is found eligible for special education and related services under Part B and the parent consents to the initial provision of special education and related services under § 300.300(b), then the public agency must provide those special education and related services that are not in dispute between the parent and the public agency.

(d) If the hearing officer in a due process hearing conducted by the SEA or a State review official in an administrative appeal agrees with the child's parents that a change of placement is appropriate, that placement must be treated as an agreement between the State and the parents for purposes of paragraph (a) of this section.

(Authority: 20 U.S.C. 1415(j))

§ 300.519 Surrogate parents.

(a) *General.* Each public agency must ensure that the rights of a child are protected when—

(1) No parent (as defined in § 300.30) can be identified;

(2) The public agency, after reasonable efforts, cannot locate a parent;

(3) The child is a ward of the State under the laws of that State; or

(4) The child is an unaccompanied homeless youth as defined in section 725(6) of the McKinney-Vento Homeless Assistance Act (42 U.S.C. 11434a(6)).

(b) *Duties of public agency.* The duties of a public agency under paragraph (a) of this section include the assignment of an individual to act as a surrogate for the parents. This must include a method—

(1) For determining whether a child needs a surrogate parent; and

(2) For assigning a surrogate parent to the child.

(c) *Wards of the State.* In the case of a child who is a ward of the State, the surrogate parent alternatively may be appointed by the judge overseeing the child's case, provided that the surrogate meets the requirements in paragraphs (d)(2)(i) and (e) of this section.

(d) *Criteria for selection of surrogate parents.* (1) The public agency may select a surrogate parent in any way permitted under State law.

(2) Public agencies must ensure that a person selected as a surrogate parent—

(i) Is not an employee of the SEA, the LEA, or any other agency that is involved in the education or care of the child;

(ii) Has no personal or professional interest that conflicts with the interest of the child the surrogate parent represents; and

(iii) Has knowledge and skills that ensure adequate representation of the child.

(e) *Non-employee requirement; compensation.* A person otherwise qualified to be a surrogate parent under paragraph (d) of this section is not an employee of the agency solely because he or she is paid by the agency to serve as a surrogate parent.

(f) *Unaccompanied homeless youth.* In the case of a child who is an unaccompanied homeless youth, appropriate staff of emergency shelters, transitional shelters, independent living programs, and street outreach programs may be appointed as temporary surrogate parents without regard to paragraph (d)(2)(i) of this section, until a surrogate parent can be appointed that meets all of the requirements of paragraph (d) of this section.

(g) *Surrogate parent responsibilities.* The surrogate parent may represent the child in all matters relating to—

(1) The identification, evaluation, and educational placement of the child; and

(2) The provision of FAPE to the child.

(h) *SEA responsibility.* The SEA must make reasonable efforts to ensure the assignment of a surrogate parent not more than 30 days after a public agency determines that the child needs a surrogate parent.

(Authority: 20 U.S.C. 1415(b)(2))

§300.520 Transfer of parental rights at age of majority.

(a) *General.* A State may provide that, when a child with a disability reaches the age of majority under State law that applies to all children (except for a child with a disability who has been determined to be incompetent under State law)—

(1)(i) The public agency must provide any notice required by this part to both the child and the parents; and

(ii) All rights accorded to parents under Part B of the Act transfer to the child;

(2) All rights accorded to parents under Part B of the Act transfer to children who are incarcerated in an adult or juvenile, State or local correctional institution; and

(3) Whenever a State provides for the transfer of rights under this part pursuant to paragraph (a)(1) or (a)(2) of this section, the agency must notify the child and the parents of the transfer of rights.

(b) *Special rule.* A State must establish procedures for appointing the parent of a child with a disability, or, if the parent is not available, another appropriate individual, to represent the educational interests of the child throughout the period of the child's eligibility under Part B of the Act if, under State law, a child who has reached the age of majority, but has not been determined to be incompetent, can be determined not to have the ability to provide informed consent with respect to the child's educational program.

(Authority: 20 U.S.C. 1415(m))

§§300.521–300.529 [Reserved]

DISCIPLINE PROCEDURES

§300.530 Authority of school personnel.

(a) *Case-by-case determination.* School personnel may consider any unique circumstances on a case-by-case basis when determining whether a change in placement, consistent with the other requirements of this section, is appropriate for a child with a disability who violates a code of student conduct.

(b) *General.* (1) School personnel under this section may remove a child with a disability who violates a code of student conduct from his or her current placement to an appropriate interim alternative educational setting, another setting, or suspension, for not more than 10 consecutive school days (to the extent those alternatives are applied to children without disabilities), and for additional removals of not more than 10 consecutive school days in that same school year for separate incidents of misconduct (as long as those removals do not constitute a change of placement under §300.536).

(2) After a child with a disability has been removed from his or her current placement for 10 school days in the same school year, during any subsequent days of removal the public agency must provide services to the extent required under paragraph (d) of this section.

(c) *Additional authority.* For disciplinary changes in placement that would exceed 10 consecutive school days, if the behavior that gave rise to the violation of the school code is determined not to be a manifestation of the child's disability pursuant to paragraph (e) of this section, school personnel may apply the relevant disciplinary procedures to children with disabilities in the same manner and for the same duration as the procedures would be applied to children without disabilities, except as provided in paragraph (d) of this section.

(d) *Services.* (1) A child with a disability who is removed from the child's current placement pursuant to paragraphs (c), or (g) of this section must—

(i) Continue to receive educational services, as provided in §300.101(a), so as to enable the child to continue to participate in the general education curriculum, although in another setting, and to progress toward meeting the goals set out in the child's IEP; and

(ii) Receive, as appropriate, a functional behavioral assessment, and behavioral intervention services and modifications, that are designed to address the behavior violation so that it does not recur.

(2) The services required by paragraph (d)(1), (d)(3), (d)(4), and (d)(5) of this section may be provided in an interim alternative educational setting.

89

(3) A public agency is only required to provide services during periods of removal to a child with a disability who has been removed from his or her current placement for 10 school days or less in that school year, if it provides services to a child without disabilities who is similarly removed.

(4) After a child with a disability has been removed from his or her current placement for 10 school days in the same school year, if the current removal is for not more than 10 consecutive school days and is not a change of placement under § 300.536, school personnel, in consultation with at least one of the child's teachers, determine the extent to which services are needed, as provided in § 300.101(a), so as to enable the child to continue to participate in the general education curriculum, although in another setting, and to progress toward meeting the goals set out in the child's IEP.

(5) If the removal is a change of placement under § 300.536, the child's IEP Team determines appropriate services under paragraph (d)(1) of this section.

(e) *Manifestation determination.* (1) Within 10 school days of any decision to change the placement of a child with a disability because of a violation of a code of student conduct, the LEA, the parent, and relevant members of the child's IEP Team (as determined by the parent and the LEA) must review all relevant information in the student's file, including the child's IEP, any teacher observations, and any relevant information provided by the parents to determine—

(i) If the conduct in question was caused by, or had a direct and substantial relationship to, the child's disability; or

(ii) If the conduct in question was the direct result of the LEA's failure to implement the IEP.

(2) The conduct must be determined to be a manifestation of the child's disability if the LEA, the parent, and relevant members of the child's IEP Team determine that a condition in either paragraph (e)(1)(i) or (1)(ii) of this section was met.

(3) If the LEA, the parent, and relevant members of the child's IEP Team determine the condition described in

paragraph (e)(1)(ii) of this section was met, the LEA must take immediate steps to remedy those deficiencies.

(f) *Determination that behavior was a manifestation.* If the LEA, the parent, and relevant members of the IEP Team make the determination that the conduct was a manifestation of the child's disability, the IEP Team must—

(1) Either—

(i) Conduct a functional behavioral assessment, unless the LEA had conducted a functional behavioral assessment before the behavior that resulted in the change of placement occurred, and implement a behavioral intervention plan for the child; or

(ii) If a behavioral intervention plan already has been developed, review the behavioral intervention plan, and modify it, as necessary, to address the behavior; and

(2) Except as provided in paragraph (g) of this section, return the child to the placement from which the child was removed, unless the parent and the LEA agree to a change of placement as part of the modification of the behavioral intervention plan.

(g) *Special circumstances.* School personnel may remove a student to an interim alternative educational setting for not more than 45 school days without regard to whether the behavior is determined to be a manifestation of the child's disability, if the child—

(1) Carries a weapon to or possesses a weapon at school, on school premises, or to or at a school function under the jurisdiction of an SEA or an LEA;

(2) Knowingly possesses or uses illegal drugs, or sells or solicits the sale of a controlled substance, while at school, on school premises, or at a school function under the jurisdiction of an SEA or an LEA; or

(3) Has inflicted serious bodily injury upon another person while at school, on school premises, or at a school function under the jurisdiction of an SEA or an LEA.

(h) *Notification.* On the date on which the decision is made to make a removal that constitutes a change of placement of a child with a disability because of a violation of a code of student conduct, the LEA must notify the parents of that decision, and provide the parents the procedural safeguards notice described in §300.504.

(i) *Definitions.* For purposes of this section, the following definitions apply:

(1) *Controlled substance* means a drug or other substance identified under schedules I, II, III, IV, or V in section 202(c) of the Controlled Substances Act (21 U.S.C. 812(c)).

(2) *Illegal drug* means a controlled substance; but does not include a controlled substance that is legally possessed or used under the supervision of a licensed health-care professional or that is legally possessed or used under any other authority under that Act or under any other provision of Federal law.

(3) *Serious bodily injury* has the meaning given the term "serious bodily injury" under paragraph (3) of subsection (h) of section 1365 of title 18, United States Code.

(4) *Weapon* has the meaning given the term "dangerous weapon" under paragraph (2) of the first subsection (g) of section 930 of title 18, United States Code.

(Authority: 20 U.S.C. 1415(k)(1) and (7))

§300.531 Determination of setting.

The child's IEP Team determines the interim alternative educational setting for services under §300.530(c), (d)(5), and (g).

(Authority: 20 U.S.C. 1415(k)(2))

§300.532 Appeal.

(a) *General.* The parent of a child with a disability who disagrees with any decision regarding placement under §§300.530 and 300.531, or the manifestation determination under §300.530(e), or an LEA that believes that maintaining the current placement of the child is substantially likely to result in injury to the child or others, may appeal the decision by requesting a hearing. The hearing is requested by filing a complaint pursuant to §§300.507 and 300.508(a) and (b).

(b) *Authority of hearing officer.* (1) A hearing officer under §300.511 hears, and makes a determination regarding an appeal under paragraph (a) of this section.

(2) In making the determination under paragraph (b)(1) of this section, the hearing officer may—

(i) Return the child with a disability to the placement from which the child was removed if the hearing officer determines that the removal was a violation of §300.530 or that the child's behavior was a manifestation of the child's disability; or

(ii) Order a change of placement of the child with a disability to an appropriate interim alternative educational setting for not more than 45 school days if the hearing officer determines that maintaining the current placement of the child is substantially likely to result in injury to the child or to others.

(3) The procedures under paragraphs (a) and (b)(1) and (2) of this section may be repeated, if the LEA believes that returning the child to the original placement is substantially likely to result in injury to the child or to others.

(c) *Expedited due process hearing.* (1) Whenever a hearing is requested under paragraph (a) of this section, the parents or the LEA involved in the dispute must have an opportunity for an impartial due process hearing consistent with the requirements of §§300.507 and 300.508(a) through (c) and §§300.510 through 300.514, except as provided in paragraph (c)(2) through (4) of this section.

(2) The SEA or LEA is responsible for arranging the expedited due process hearing, which must occur within 20 school days of the date the complaint requesting the hearing is filed. The hearing officer must make a determination within 10 school days after the hearing.

(3) Unless the parents and LEA agree in writing to waive the resolution meeting described in paragraph (c)(3)(i) of this section, or agree to use the mediation process described in §300.506—

(i) A resolution meeting must occur within seven days of receiving notice of the due process complaint; and

(ii) The due process hearing may proceed unless the matter has been resolved to the satisfaction of both parties within 15 days of the receipt of the due process complaint.

(4) A State may establish different State-imposed procedural rules for expedited due process hearings conducted under this section than it has established for other due process hearings, but, except for the timelines as modified in paragraph (c)(3) of this section, the State must ensure that the requirements in §§ 300.510 through 300.514 are met.

(5) The decisions on expedited due process hearings are appealable consistent with § 300.514.

(Authority: 20 U.S.C. 1415(k)(3) and (4)(B), 1415(f)(1)(A))

§ 300.533 Placement during appeals.

When an appeal under § 300.532 has been made by either the parent or the LEA, the child must remain in the interim alternative educational setting pending the decision of the hearing officer or until the expiration of the time period specified in § 300.530(c) or (g), whichever occurs first, unless the parent and the SEA or LEA agree otherwise.

(Authority: 20 U.S.C. 1415(k)(4)(A))

[71 FR 46753, Aug. 14, 2006, as amended at 72 FR 61307, Oct. 30, 2007]

§ 300.534 Protections for children not determined eligible for special education and related services.

(a) *General.* A child who has not been determined to be eligible for special education and related services under this part and who has engaged in behavior that violated a code of student conduct, may assert any of the protections provided for in this part if the public agency had knowledge (as determined in accordance with paragraph (b) of this section) that the child was a child with a disability before the behavior that precipitated the disciplinary action occurred.

(b) *Basis of knowledge.* A public agency must be deemed to have knowledge that a child is a child with a disability if before the behavior that precipitated the disciplinary action occurred—

(1) The parent of the child expressed concern in writing to supervisory or administrative personnel of the appropriate educational agency, or a teacher of the child, that the child is in need of special education and related services;

(2) The parent of the child requested an evaluation of the child pursuant to §§ 300.300 through 300.311; or

(3) The teacher of the child, or other personnel of the LEA, expressed specific concerns about a pattern of behavior demonstrated by the child directly to the director of special education of the agency or to other supervisory personnel of the agency.

(c) *Exception.* A public agency would not be deemed to have knowledge under paragraph (b) of this section if—

(1) The parent of the child—

(i) Has not allowed an evaluation of the child pursuant to §§ 300.300 through 300.311; or

(ii) Has refused services under this part; or

(2) The child has been evaluated in accordance with §§ 300.300 through 300.311 and determined to not be a child with a disability under this part.

(d) *Conditions that apply if no basis of knowledge.* (1) If a public agency does not have knowledge that a child is a child with a disability (in accordance with paragraphs (b) and (c) of this section) prior to taking disciplinary measures against the child, the child may be subjected to the disciplinary measures applied to children without disabilities who engage in comparable behaviors consistent with paragraph (d)(2) of this section.

(2)(i) If a request is made for an evaluation of a child during the time period in which the child is subjected to disciplinary measures under § 300.530, the evaluation must be conducted in an expedited manner.

(ii) Until the evaluation is completed, the child remains in the educational placement determined by school authorities, which can include suspension or expulsion without educational services.

(iii) If the child is determined to be a child with a disability, taking into consideration information from the evaluation conducted by the agency and information provided by the parents, the agency must provide special education and related services in accordance with this part, including the requirements of §§ 300.530 through 300.536 and section 612(a)(1)(A) of the Act.

(Authority: 20 U.S.C. 1415(k)(5))

§ 300.535 Referral to and action by law enforcement and judicial authorities.

(a) *Rule of construction.* Nothing in this part prohibits an agency from reporting a crime committed by a child with a disability to appropriate authorities or prevents State law enforcement and judicial authorities from exercising their responsibilities with regard to the application of Federal and State law to crimes committed by a child with a disability.

(b) *Transmittal of records.* (1) An agency reporting a crime committed by a child with a disability must ensure that copies of the special education and disciplinary records of the child are transmitted for consideration by the appropriate authorities to whom the agency reports the crime.

(2) An agency reporting a crime under this section may transmit copies of the child's special education and disciplinary records only to the extent that the transmission is permitted by the Family Educational Rights and Privacy Act.

(Authority: 20 U.S.C. 1415(k)(6))

§ 300.536 Change of placement because of disciplinary removals.

(a) For purposes of removals of a child with a disability from the child's current educational placement under §§ 300.530 through 300.535, a change of placement occurs if—

(1) The removal is for more than 10 consecutive school days; or

(2) The child has been subjected to a series of removals that constitute a pattern—

(i) Because the series of removals total more than 10 school days in a school year;

(ii) Because the child's behavior is substantially similar to the child's behavior in previous incidents that resulted in the series of removals; and

(iii) Because of such additional factors as the length of each removal, the total amount of time the child has been removed, and the proximity of the removals to one another.

(b)(1) The public agency determines on a case-by-case basis whether a pattern of removals constitutes a change of placement.

(2) This determination is subject to review through due process and judicial proceedings.

(Authority: 20 U.S.C. 1415(k))

§ 300.537 State enforcement mechanisms.

Notwithstanding §§ 300.506(b)(7) and 300.510(d)(2), which provide for judicial enforcement of a written agreement reached as a result of mediation or a resolution meeting, there is nothing in this part that would prevent the SEA from using other mechanisms to seek enforcement of that agreement, provided that use of those mechanisms is not mandatory and does not delay or deny a party the right to seek enforcement of the written agreement in a State court of competent jurisdiction or in a district court of the United States.

(Authority: 20 U.S.C. 1415(e)(2)(F), 1415(f)(1)(B))

§§ 300.538–300.599 [Reserved]

Subpart F—Monitoring, Enforcement, Confidentiality, and Program Information

MONITORING, TECHNICAL ASSISTANCE, AND ENFORCEMENT

§ 300.600 State monitoring and enforcement.

(a) The State must—

(1) Monitor the implementation of this part;

(2) Make determinations annually about the performance of each LEA using the categories in § 300.603(b)(1);

(3) Enforce this part, consistent with § 300.604, using appropriate enforcement mechanisms, which must include, if applicable, the enforcement mechanisms identified in § 300.604(a)(1) (technical assistance), (a)(3) (conditions on funding of an LEA), (b)(2)(i) (a corrective action plan or improvement plan), (b)(2)(v) (withholding funds, in whole or in part, by the SEA), and (c)(2) (withholding funds, in whole or in part, by the SEA); and

(4) Report annually on the performance of the State and of each LEA under this part, as provided in § 300.602(b)(1)(i)(A) and (b)(2).

(b) The primary focus of the State's monitoring activities must be on—

(1) Improving educational results and functional outcomes for all children with disabilities; and

(2) Ensuring that public agencies meet the program requirements under Part B of the Act, with a particular emphasis on those requirements that are most closely related to improving educational results for children with disabilities.

(c) As a part of its responsibilities under paragraph (a) of this section, the State must use quantifiable indicators and such qualitative indicators as are needed to adequately measure performance in the priority areas identified in paragraph (d) of this section, and the indicators established by the Secretary for the State performance plans.

(d) The State must monitor the LEAs located in the State, using quantifiable indicators in each of the following priority areas, and using such qualitative indicators as are needed to adequately measure performance in those areas:

(1) Provision of FAPE in the least restrictive environment.

(2) State exercise of general supervision, including child find, effective monitoring, the use of resolution meetings, mediation, and a system of transition services as defined in § 300.43 and in 20 U.S.C. 1437(a)(9).

(3) Disproportionate representation of racial and ethnic groups in special education and related services, to the extent the representation is the result of inappropriate identification.

(e) In exercising its monitoring responsibilities under paragraph (d) of this section, the State must ensure that when it identifies noncompliance with the requirements of this part by LEAs, the noncompliance is corrected as soon as possible, and in no case later than one year after the State's identification of the noncompliance.

(Approved by the Office of Management and Budget under control number 1820–0624)

(Authority: 20 U.S.C. 1416(a))

[71 FR 46753, Aug. 14, 2006, as amended at 73 FR 73027, Dec. 1, 2008]

§ 300.601 State performance plans and data collection.

(a) *General.* Not later than December 3, 2005, each State must have in place a performance plan that evaluates the State's efforts to implement the requirements and purposes of Part B of the Act, and describes how the State will improve such implementation.

(1) Each State must submit the State's performance plan to the Secretary for approval in accordance with the approval process described in section 616(c) of the Act.

(2) Each State must review its State performance plan at least once every six years, and submit any amendments to the Secretary.

(3) As part of the State performance plan, each State must establish measurable and rigorous targets for the indicators established by the Secretary under the priority areas described in § 300.600(d).

(b) *Data collection.* (1) Each State must collect valid and reliable information as needed to report annually to the Secretary on the indicators established by the Secretary for the State performance plans.

(2) If the Secretary permits States to collect data on specific indicators through State monitoring or sampling, and the State collects the data through State monitoring or sampling, the State must collect data on those indicators for each LEA at least once during the period of the State performance plan.

(3) Nothing in Part B of the Act shall be construed to authorize the development of a nationwide database of personally identifiable information on individuals involved in studies or other collections of data under Part B of the Act.

(Approved by the Office of Management and Budget under control number 1820–0624)

(Authority: 20 U.S.C. 1416(b))

§ 300.602 State use of targets and reporting.

(a) *General.* Each State must use the targets established in the State's performance plan under § 300.601 and the priority areas described in § 300.600(d) to analyze the performance of each LEA.

(b) *Public reporting and privacy*—(1) *Public report.*

(i) Subject to paragraph (b)(1)(ii) of this section, the State must—

(A) Report annually to the public on the performance of each LEA located in the State on the targets in the State's performance plan as soon as practicable but no later than 120 days following the State's submission of its annual performance report to the Secretary under paragraph (b)(2) of this section; and

(B) Make each of the following items available through public means: the State's performance plan, under §300.601(a); annual performance reports, under paragraph (b)(2) of this section; and the State's annual reports on the performance of each LEA located in the State, under paragraph (b)(1)(i)(A) of this section. In doing so, the State must, at a minimum, post the plan and reports on the SEA's Web site, and distribute the plan and reports to the media and through public agencies.

(ii) If the State, in meeting the requirements of paragraph (b)(1)(i) of this section, collects performance data through State monitoring or sampling, the State must include in its report under paragraph (b)(1)(i)(A) of this section the most recently available performance data on each LEA, and the date the data were obtained.

(2) *State performance report.* The State must report annually to the Secretary on the performance of the State under the State's performance plan.

(3) *Privacy.* The State must not report to the public or the Secretary any information on performance that would result in the disclosure of personally identifiable information about individual children, or where the available data are insufficient to yield statistically reliable information.

(Approved by the Office of Management and Budget under control number 1820–0624)

(Authority: 20 U.S.C. 1416(b)(2)(C))

[71 FR 46753, Aug. 14, 2006, as amended at 73 FR 73027, Dec. 1, 2008]

§ 300.603 Secretary's review and determination regarding State performance.

(a) *Review.* The Secretary annually reviews the State's performance report submitted pursuant to §300.602(b)(2).

(b) *Determination*—(1) *General.* Based on the information provided by the State in the State's annual performance report, information obtained through monitoring visits, and any other public information made available, the Secretary determines if the State—

(i) Meets the requirements and purposes of Part B of the Act;

(ii) Needs assistance in implementing the requirements of Part B of the Act;

(iii) Needs intervention in implementing the requirements of Part B of the Act; or

(iv) Needs substantial intervention in implementing the requirements of Part B of the Act.

(2) *Notice and opportunity for a hearing.* (i) For determinations made under paragraphs (b)(1)(iii) and (b)(1)(iv) of this section, the Secretary provides reasonable notice and an opportunity for a hearing on those determinations.

(ii) The hearing described in paragraph (b)(2) of this section consists of an opportunity to meet with the Assistant Secretary for Special Education and Rehabilitative Services to demonstrate why the Department should not make the determination described in paragraph (b)(1) of this section.

(Authority: 20 U.S.C. 1416(d))

§ 300.604 Enforcement.

(a) *Needs assistance.* If the Secretary determines, for two consecutive years, that a State needs assistance under §300.603(b)(1)(ii) in implementing the requirements of Part B of the Act, the Secretary takes one or more of the following actions:

(1) Advises the State of available sources of technical assistance that may help the State address the areas in which the State needs assistance, which may include assistance from the Office of Special Education Programs, other offices of the Department of Education, other Federal agencies, technical assistance providers approved by the Secretary, and other federally

funded nonprofit agencies, and requires the State to work with appropriate entities. Such technical assistance may include—

(i) The provision of advice by experts to address the areas in which the State needs assistance, including explicit plans for addressing the area for concern within a specified period of time;

(ii) Assistance in identifying and implementing professional development, instructional strategies, and methods of instruction that are based on scientifically based research;

(iii) Designating and using distinguished superintendents, principals, special education administrators, special education teachers, and other teachers to provide advice, technical assistance, and support; and

(iv) Devising additional approaches to providing technical assistance, such as collaborating with institutions of higher education, educational service agencies, national centers of technical assistance supported under Part D of the Act, and private providers of scientifically based technical assistance.

(2) Directs the use of State-level funds under section 611(e) of the Act on the area or areas in which the State needs assistance.

(3) Identifies the State as a high-risk grantee and imposes special conditions on the State's grant under Part B of the Act.

(b) *Needs intervention.* If the Secretary determines, for three or more consecutive years, that a State needs intervention under § 300.603(b)(1)(iii) in implementing the requirements of Part B of the Act, the following shall apply:

(1) The Secretary may take any of the actions described in paragraph (a) of this section.

(2) The Secretary takes one or more of the following actions:

(i) Requires the State to prepare a corrective action plan or improvement plan if the Secretary determines that the State should be able to correct the problem within one year.

(ii) Requires the State to enter into a compliance agreement under section 457 of the General Education Provisions Act, as amended, 20 U.S.C. 1221 *et seq.* (GEPA), if the Secretary has reason to believe that the State cannot correct the problem within one year.

(iii) For each year of the determination, withholds not less than 20 percent and not more than 50 percent of the State's funds under section 611(e) of the Act, until the Secretary determines the State has sufficiently addressed the areas in which the State needs intervention.

(iv) Seeks to recover funds under section 452 of GEPA.

(v) Withholds, in whole or in part, any further payments to the State under Part B of the Act.

(vi) Refers the matter for appropriate enforcement action, which may include referral to the Department of Justice.

(c) *Needs substantial intervention.* Notwithstanding paragraph (a) or (b) of this section, at any time that the Secretary determines that a State needs substantial intervention in implementing the requirements of Part B of the Act or that there is a substantial failure to comply with any condition of an SEA's or LEA's eligibility under Part B of the Act, the Secretary takes one or more of the following actions:

(1) Recovers funds under section 452 of GEPA.

(2) Withholds, in whole or in part, any further payments to the State under Part B of the Act.

(3) Refers the case to the Office of the Inspector General at the Department of Education.

(4) Refers the matter for appropriate enforcement action, which may include referral to the Department of Justice.

(d) *Report to Congress.* The Secretary reports to the Committee on Education and the Workforce of the House of Representatives and the Committee on Health, Education, Labor, and Pensions of the Senate within 30 days of taking enforcement action pursuant to paragraph (a), (b), or (c) of this section, on the specific action taken and the reasons why enforcement action was taken.

(Authority: 20 U.S.C. 1416(e)(1)–(e)(3), (e)(5))

§ 300.605 Withholding funds.

(a) *Opportunity for hearing.* Prior to withholding any funds under Part B of the Act, the Secretary provides reasonable notice and an opportunity for a hearing to the SEA involved, pursuant to the procedures in §§ 300.180 through 300.183.

(b) *Suspension.* Pending the outcome of any hearing to withhold payments under paragraph (a) of this section, the Secretary may suspend payments to a recipient, suspend the authority of the recipient to obligate funds under Part B of the Act, or both, after the recipient has been given reasonable notice and an opportunity to show cause why future payments or authority to obligate funds under Part B of the Act should not be suspended.

(c) *Nature of withholding.* (1) If the Secretary determines that it is appropriate to withhold further payments under § 300.604(b)(2) or (c)(2), the Secretary may determine—

(i) That the withholding will be limited to programs or projects, or portions of programs or projects, that affected the Secretary's determination under § 300.603(b)(1); or

(ii) That the SEA must not make further payments under Part B of the Act to specified State agencies or LEAs that caused or were involved in the Secretary's determination under § 300.603(b)(1).

(2) Until the Secretary is satisfied that the condition that caused the initial withholding has been substantially rectified—

(i) Payments to the State under Part B of the Act must be withheld in whole or in part; and

(ii) Payments by the SEA under Part B of the Act must be limited to State agencies and LEAs whose actions did not cause or were not involved in the Secretary's determination under § 300.603(b)(1), as the case may be.

(Authority: 20 U.S.C. 1416(e)(4), (e)(6))

§ 300.606 Public attention.

Whenever a State receives notice that the Secretary is proposing to take or is taking an enforcement action pursuant to § 300.604, the State must, by means of a public notice, take such actions as may be necessary to notify the public within the State of the pendency of an action pursuant to § 300.604, including, at a minimum, by posting the notice on the SEA's Web site and distributing the notice to the media and through public agencies.

(Authority: 20 U.S.C. 1416(e)(7))

[73 FR 73028, Dec. 1, 2008]

§ 300.607 Divided State agency responsibility.

For purposes of this subpart, if responsibility for ensuring that the requirements of Part B of the Act are met with respect to children with disabilities who are convicted as adults under State law and incarcerated in adult prisons is assigned to a public agency other than the SEA pursuant to § 300.149(d), and if the Secretary finds that the failure to comply substantially with the provisions of Part B of the Act are related to a failure by the public agency, the Secretary takes appropriate corrective action to ensure compliance with Part B of the Act, except that—

(a) Any reduction or withholding of payments to the State under § 300.604 must be proportionate to the total funds allotted under section 611 of the Act to the State as the number of eligible children with disabilities in adult prisons under the supervision of the other public agency is proportionate to the number of eligible individuals with disabilities in the State under the supervision of the SEA; and

(b) Any withholding of funds under § 300.604 must be limited to the specific agency responsible for the failure to comply with Part B of the Act.

(Authority: 20 U.S.C. 1416(h))

§ 300.608 State enforcement.

(a) If an SEA determines that an LEA is not meeting the requirements of Part B of the Act, including the targets in the State's performance plan, the SEA must prohibit the LEA from reducing the LEA's maintenance of effort under § 300.203 for any fiscal year.

(b) Nothing in this subpart shall be construed to restrict a State from utilizing any other authority available to it to monitor and enforce the requirements of Part B of the Act.

(Authority: 20 U.S.C. 1416(f); 20 U.S.C. 1412(a)(11))

§ 300.609 Rule of construction.

Nothing in this subpart shall be construed to restrict the Secretary from utilizing any authority under GEPA, including the provisions in 34 CFR parts 76, 77, and 81 and 2 CFR part 200 to monitor and enforce the requirements of the Act, including the imposition of special or high-risk conditions under 2 CFR 200.207 and 3474.10.

(Authority: 20 U.S.C. 1416(g))

[79 FR 76097, Dec. 19, 2014]

CONFIDENTIALITY OF INFORMATION

§ 300.610 Confidentiality.

The Secretary takes appropriate action, in accordance with section 444 of GEPA, to ensure the protection of the confidentiality of any personally identifiable data, information, and records collected or maintained by the Secretary and by SEAs and LEAs pursuant to Part B of the Act, and consistent with §§ 300.611 through 300.627.

(Authority: 20 U.S.C. 1417(c))

§ 300.611 Definitions.

As used in §§ 300.611 through 300.625—

(a) *Destruction* means physical destruction or removal of personal identifiers from information so that the information is no longer personally identifiable.

(b) *Education records* means the type of records covered under the definition of "education records" in 34 CFR part 99 (the regulations implementing the Family Educational Rights and Privacy Act of 1974, 20 U.S.C. 1232g (FERPA)).

(c) *Participating agency* means any agency or institution that collects, maintains, or uses personally identifiable information, or from which information is obtained, under Part B of the Act.

(Authority: 20 U.S.C. 1221e–3, 1412(a)(8), 1417(c))

§ 300.612 Notice to parents.

(a) The SEA must give notice that is adequate to fully inform parents about the requirements of § 300.123, including—

(1) A description of the extent that the notice is given in the native languages of the various population groups in the State;

(2) A description of the children on whom personally identifiable information is maintained, the types of information sought, the methods the State intends to use in gathering the information (including the sources from whom information is gathered), and the uses to be made of the information;

(3) A summary of the policies and procedures that participating agencies must follow regarding storage, disclosure to third parties, retention, and destruction of personally identifiable information; and

(4) A description of all of the rights of parents and children regarding this information, including the rights under FERPA and implementing regulations in 34 CFR part 99.

(b) Before any major identification, location, or evaluation activity, the notice must be published or announced in newspapers or other media, or both, with circulation adequate to notify parents throughout the State of the activity.

(Authority: 20 U.S.C. 1412(a)(8); 1417(c))

§ 300.613 Access rights.

(a) Each participating agency must permit parents to inspect and review any education records relating to their children that are collected, maintained, or used by the agency under this part. The agency must comply with a request without unnecessary delay and before any meeting regarding an IEP, or any hearing pursuant to § 300.507 or §§ 300.530 through 300.532, or resolution session pursuant to § 300.510, and in no case more than 45 days after the request has been made.

(b) The right to inspect and review education records under this section includes—

(1) The right to a response from the participating agency to reasonable requests for explanations and interpretations of the records;

(2) The right to request that the agency provide copies of the records containing the information if failure to provide those copies would effectively prevent the parent from exercising the right to inspect and review the records; and

(3) The right to have a representative of the parent inspect and review the records.

(c) An agency may presume that the parent has authority to inspect and review records relating to his or her child unless the agency has been advised that the parent does not have the authority under applicable State law governing such matters as guardianship, separation, and divorce.

(Authority: 20 U.S.C. 1412(a)(8); 1417(c))

§ 300.614 Record of access.

Each participating agency must keep a record of parties obtaining access to education records collected, maintained, or used under Part B of the Act (except access by parents and authorized employees of the participating agency), including the name of the party, the date access was given, and the purpose for which the party is authorized to use the records.

(Authority: 20 U.S.C. 1412(a)(8); 1417(c))

§ 300.615 Records on more than one child.

If any education record includes information on more than one child, the parents of those children have the right to inspect and review only the information relating to their child or to be informed of that specific information.

(Authority: 20 U.S.C. 1412(a)(8); 1417(c))

§ 300.616 List of types and locations of information.

Each participating agency must provide parents on request a list of the types and locations of education records collected, maintained, or used by the agency.

(Authority: 20 U.S.C. 1412(a)(8); 1417(c))

§ 300.617 Fees.

(a) Each participating agency may charge a fee for copies of records that are made for parents under this part if the fee does not effectively prevent the parents from exercising their right to inspect and review those records.

(b) A participating agency may not charge a fee to search for or to retrieve information under this part.

(Authority: 20 U.S.C. 1412(a)(8); 1417(c))

§ 300.618 Amendment of records at parent's request.

(a) A parent who believes that information in the education records collected, maintained, or used under this part is inaccurate or misleading or violates the privacy or other rights of the child may request the participating agency that maintains the information to amend the information.

(b) The agency must decide whether to amend the information in accordance with the request within a reasonable period of time of receipt of the request.

(c) If the agency decides to refuse to amend the information in accordance with the request, it must inform the parent of the refusal and advise the parent of the right to a hearing under § 300.619.

(Authority: 20 U.S.C. 1412(a)(8); 1417(c))

§ 300.619 Opportunity for a hearing.

The agency must, on request, provide an opportunity for a hearing to challenge information in education records to ensure that it is not inaccurate, misleading, or otherwise in violation of the privacy or other rights of the child.

(Authority: 20 U.S.C. 1412(a)(8); 1417(c))

§ 300.620 Result of hearing.

(a) If, as a result of the hearing, the agency decides that the information is inaccurate, misleading or otherwise in violation of the privacy or other rights of the child, it must amend the information accordingly and so inform the parent in writing.

(b) If, as a result of the hearing, the agency decides that the information is not inaccurate, misleading, or otherwise in violation of the privacy or other rights of the child, it must inform the parent of the parent's right to place in the records the agency maintains on the child a statement commenting on the information or setting forth any reasons for disagreeing with the decision of the agency.

(c) Any explanation placed in the records of the child under this section must—

(1) Be maintained by the agency as part of the records of the child as long as the record or contested portion is maintained by the agency; and

(2) If the records of the child or the contested portion is disclosed by the agency to any party, the explanation must also be disclosed to the party.

(Authority: 20 U.S.C. 1412(a)(8); 1417(c))

§ 300.621 Hearing procedures.

A hearing held under § 300.619 must be conducted according to the procedures in 34 CFR 99.22.

(Authority: 20 U.S.C. 1412(a)(8); 1417(c))

§ 300.622 Consent.

(a) Parental consent must be obtained before personally identifiable information is disclosed to parties, other than officials of participating agencies in accordance with paragraph (b)(1) of this section, unless the information is contained in education records, and the disclosure is authorized without parental consent under 34 CFR part 99.

(b)(1) Except as provided in paragraphs (b)(2) and (b)(3) of this section, parental consent is not required before personally identifiable information is released to officials of participating agencies for purposes of meeting a requirement of this part.

(2) Parental consent, or the consent of an eligible child who has reached the age of majority under State law, must be obtained before personally identifiable information is released to officials of participating agencies providing or paying for transition services in accordance with § 300.321(b)(3).

(3) If a child is enrolled, or is going to enroll in a private school that is not located in the LEA of the parent's residence, parental consent must be obtained before any personally identifiable information about the child is released between officials in the LEA where the private school is located and officials in the LEA of the parent's residence.

(Authority: 20 U.S.C. 1412(a)(8); 1417(c))

§ 300.623 Safeguards.

(a) Each participating agency must protect the confidentiality of personally identifiable information at collection, storage, disclosure, and destruction stages.

(b) One official at each participating agency must assume responsibility for ensuring the confidentiality of any personally identifiable information.

(c) All persons collecting or using personally identifiable information must receive training or instruction regarding the State's policies and procedures under § 300.123 and 34 CFR part 99.

(d) Each participating agency must maintain, for public inspection, a current listing of the names and positions of those employees within the agency who may have access to personally identifiable information.

(Authority: 20 U.S.C. 1412(a)(8); 1417(c))

§ 300.624 Destruction of information.

(a) The public agency must inform parents when personally identifiable information collected, maintained, or used under this part is no longer needed to provide educational services to the child.

(b) The information must be destroyed at the request of the parents. However, a permanent record of a student's name, address, and phone number, his or her grades, attendance record, classes attended, grade level completed, and year completed may be maintained without time limitation.

(Authority: 20 U.S.C. 1412(a)(8); 1417(c))

§ 300.625 Children's rights.

(a) The SEA must have in effect policies and procedures regarding the extent to which children are afforded rights of privacy similar to those afforded to parents, taking into consideration the age of the child and type or severity of disability.

(b) Under the regulations for FERPA in 34 CFR 99.5(a), the rights of parents regarding education records are transferred to the student at age 18.

(c) If the rights accorded to parents under Part B of the Act are transferred to a student who reaches the age of majority, consistent with § 300.520, the rights regarding educational records in §§ 300.613 through 300.624 must also be transferred to the student. However, the public agency must provide any notice required under section 615 of the Act to the student and the parents.

(Authority: 20 U.S.C. 1412(a)(8); 1417(c))

§ 300.626 Enforcement.

The SEA must have in effect the policies and procedures, including sanctions that the State uses, to ensure that its policies and procedures consistent with §§ 300.611 through 300.625 are followed and that the requirements of the Act and the regulations in this part are met.

(Authority: 20 U.S.C. 1412(a)(8); 1417(c))

§ 300.627 Department use of personally identifiable information.

If the Department or its authorized representatives collect any personally identifiable information regarding children with disabilities that is not subject to the Privacy Act of 1974, 5 U.S.C. 552a, the Secretary applies the requirements of 5 U.S.C. 552a(b)(1) and (b)(2), 552a(b)(4) through (b)(11); 552a(c) through 552a(e)(3)(B); 552a(e)(3)(D); 552a(e)(5) through (e)(10); 552a(h); 552a(m); and 552a(n); and the regulations implementing those provisions in 34 CFR part 5b.

(Authority: 20 U.S.C. 1412(a)(8); 1417(c))

REPORTS—PROGRAM INFORMATION

§ 300.640 Annual report of children served—report requirement.

(a) The SEA must annually report to the Secretary on the information required by section 618 of the Act at the times specified by the Secretary.

(b) The SEA must submit the report on forms provided by the Secretary.

(Approved by the Office of Management and Budget under control numbers 1820–0030, 1820–0043, 1820–0659, 1820–0621, 1820–0518, 1820–0521, 1820–0517, and 1820–0677)

(Authority: 20 U.S.C. 1418(a))

§ 300.641 Annual report of children served—information required in the report.

(a) For purposes of the annual report required by section 618 of the Act and § 300.640, the State and the Secretary of the Interior must count and report the number of children with disabilities receiving special education and related services on any date between October 1 and December 1 of each year.

(b) For the purpose of this reporting provision, a child's age is the child's actual age on the date of the child count.

(c) The SEA may not report a child under more than one disability category.

(d) If a child with a disability has more than one disability, the SEA must report that child in accordance with the following procedure:

(1) If a child has only two disabilities and those disabilities are deafness and blindness, and the child is not reported as having a developmental delay, that child must be reported under the category "deaf-blindness."

(2) A child who has more than one disability and is not reported as having deaf-blindness or as having a developmental delay must be reported under the category "multiple disabilities."

(Approved by the Office of Management and Budget under control numbers 1820–0030, 1820–0043, 1820–0621, 1820–0521, and 1820–0517)

(Authority: 20 U.S.C. 1418(a), (b))

§ 300.642 Data reporting.

(a) *Protection of personally identifiable data.* The data described in section 618(a) of the Act and in § 300.641 must be publicly reported by each State in a manner that does not result in disclosure of data identifiable to individual children.

(b) *Sampling.* The Secretary may permit States and the Secretary of the Interior to obtain data in section 618(a) of the Act through sampling.

(Approved by the Office of Management and Budget under control numbers 1820–0030, 1820–0043, 1820–0518, 1820–0521, and 1820–0517)

(Authority: 20 U.S.C. 1418(b))

§ 300.643 Annual report of children served—certification.

The SEA must include in its report a certification signed by an authorized official of the agency that the information provided under § 300.640 is an accurate and unduplicated count of children with disabilities receiving special education and related services on the dates in question.

(Approved by the Office of Management and Budget under control numbers 1820–0030 and 1820–0043)

(Authority: 20 U.S.C. 1418(a)(3))

§ 300.644 Annual report of children served—criteria for counting children.

The SEA may include in its report children with disabilities who are enrolled in a school or program that is operated or supported by a public agency, and that—

(a) Provides them with both special education and related services that meet State standards;

(b) Provides them only with special education, if a related service is not required, that meets State standards; or

(c) In the case of children with disabilities enrolled by their parents in private schools, counts those children who are eligible under the Act and receive special education or related services or both that meet State standards under §§ 300.132 through 300.144.

(Approved by the Office of Management and Budget under control numbers 1820–0030, 1820–0043, 1820–0659, 1820–0621, 1820–0521, and 1820–0517)

(Authority: 20 U.S.C. 1418(a))

§ 300.645 Annual report of children served—other responsibilities of the SEA.

In addition to meeting the other requirements of §§ 300.640 through 300.644, the SEA must—

(a) Establish procedures to be used by LEAs and other educational institutions in counting the number of children with disabilities receiving special education and related services;

(b) Set dates by which those agencies and institutions must report to the SEA to ensure that the State complies with § 300.640(a);

(c) Obtain certification from each agency and institution that an unduplicated and accurate count has been made;

(d) Aggregate the data from the count obtained from each agency and institution, and prepare the reports required under §§ 300.640 through 300.644; and

(e) Ensure that documentation is maintained that enables the State and the Secretary to audit the accuracy of the count.

(Approved by the Office of Management and Budget under control numbers 1820–0030, 1820–0043, 1820–0659, 1820–0621, 1820–0518, 1820–0521, and 1820–0517)

(Authority: 20 U.S.C. 1418(a))

§ 300.646 Disproportionality.

(a) *General.* Each State that receives assistance under Part B of the Act, and the Secretary of the Interior, must provide for the collection and examination of data to determine if significant disproportionality based on race and ethnicity is occurring in the State and the LEAs of the State with respect to—

(1) The identification of children as children with disabilities, including the identification of children as children with disabilities in accordance with a particular impairment described in section 602(3) of the Act;

(2) The placement in particular educational settings of these children; and

(3) The incidence, duration, and type of disciplinary removals from placement, including suspensions and expulsions.

(b) *Methodology.* The State must apply the methods in § 300.647 to determine if significant disproportionality based on race and ethnicity is occurring in the State and the LEAs of the State under paragraph (a) of this section.

(c) *Review and revision of policies, practices, and procedures.* In the case of a determination of significant disproportionality with respect to the identification of children as children with disabilities or the placement in particular educational settings, including disciplinary removals of such children, in accordance with paragraphs (a) and (b) of this section, the State or the Secretary of the Interior must—

(1) Provide for the annual review and, if appropriate, revision of the policies, practices, and procedures used in identification or placement in particular education settings, including disciplinary removals, to ensure that the policies, practices, and procedures comply with the requirements of the Act.

(2) Require the LEA to publicly report on the revision of policies, practices, and procedures described under paragraph (c)(1) of this section consistent with the requirements of the Family Educational Rights and Privacy Act, its implementing regulations in 34 CFR part 99, and Section 618(b)(1) of the Act.

(d) *Comprehensive coordinated early intervening services.* Except as provided in paragraph (e) of this section, the State or the Secretary of the Interior shall require any LEA identified under paragraphs (a) and (b) of this section to reserve the maximum amount of funds under section 613(f) of the Act to provide comprehensive coordinated early intervening services to address factors contributing to the significant disproportionality.

(1) In implementing comprehensive coordinated early intervening services an LEA—

(i) May carry out activities that include professional development and educational and behavioral evaluations, services, and supports.

(ii) Must identify and address the factors contributing to the significant disproportionality, which may include, among other identified factors, a lack of access to scientifically based instruction; economic, cultural, or linguistic barriers to appropriate identification or placement in particular educational settings; inappropriate use of disciplinary removals; lack of access to appropriate diagnostic screenings; differences in academic achievement levels; and policies, practices, or procedures that contribute to the significant disproportionality.

(iii) Must address a policy, practice, or procedure it identifies as contributing to the significant disproportionality, including a policy, practice or procedure that results in a failure to identify, or the inappropriate identification of, a racial or ethnic group (or groups).

(2) An LEA may use funds reserved for comprehensive coordinated early intervening services to serve children from age 3 through grade 12, particularly, but not exclusively, children in those groups that were significantly overidentified under paragraph (a) or (b) of this section, including—

(i) Children who are not currently identified as needing special education or related services but who need additional academic and behavioral support to succeed in a general education environment; and

(ii) Children with disabilities.

(3) An LEA may not limit the provision of comprehensive coordinated early intervening services under this paragraph to children with disabilities.

(e) *Exception to comprehensive coordinated early intervening services.* The State or the Secretary of the Interior shall not require any LEA that serves only children with disabilities identi-

fied under paragraphs (a) and (b) of this section to reserve funds to provide comprehensive coordinated early intervening services.

(f) *Rule of construction.* Nothing in this section authorizes a State or an LEA to develop or implement policies, practices, or procedures that result in actions that violate the requirements of this part, including requirements related to child find and ensuring that a free appropriate public education is available to all eligible children with disabilities.

(Authority: 20 U.S.C. 1413(f); 20 U.S.C. 1418(d))

[81 FR 92463, Dec. 19, 2016]

§ 300.647 Determining significant disproportionality.

(a) *Definitions.* (1) *Alternate risk ratio* is a calculation performed by dividing the risk of a particular outcome for children in one racial or ethnic group within an LEA by the risk of that outcome for children in all other racial or ethnic groups in the State.

(2) *Comparison group* consists of the children in all other racial or ethnic groups within an LEA or within the State, when reviewing a particular racial or ethnic group within an LEA for significant disproportionality.

(3) *Minimum cell size* is the minimum number of children experiencing a particular outcome, to be used as the numerator when calculating either the risk for a particular racial or ethnic group or the risk for children in all other racial or ethnic groups.

(4) *Minimum n-size* is the minimum number of children enrolled in an LEA with respect to identification, and the minimum number of children with disabilities enrolled in an LEA with respect to placement and discipline, to be used as the denominator when calculating either the risk for a particular racial or ethnic group or the risk for children in all other racial or ethnic groups.

(5) *Risk* is the likelihood of a particular outcome (identification, placement, or disciplinary removal) for a specified racial or ethnic group (or groups), calculated by dividing the

number of children from a specified racial or ethnic group (or groups) experiencing that outcome by the total number of children from that racial or ethnic group or groups enrolled in the LEA.

(6) *Risk ratio* is a calculation performed by dividing the risk of a particular outcome for children in one racial or ethnic group within an LEA by the risk for children in all other racial and ethnic groups within the LEA.

(7) *Risk ratio threshold* is a threshold, determined by the State, over which disproportionality based on race or ethnicity is significant under § 300.646(a) and (b).

(b) *Significant disproportionality determinations.* In determining whether significant disproportionality exists in a State or LEA under § 300.646(a) and (b)—

(1)(i) The State must set a:

(A) Reasonable risk ratio threshold;

(B) Reasonable minimum cell size;

(C) Reasonable minimum n-size; and

(D) Standard for measuring reasonable progress if a State uses the flexibility described in paragraph (d)(2) of this section.

(ii) The State may, but is not required to, set the standards set forth in paragraph (b)(1)(i) of this section at different levels for each of the categories described in paragraphs (b)(3) and (4) of this section.

(iii) The standards set forth in paragraph (b)(1)(i) of this section:

(A) Must be based on advice from stakeholders, including State Advisory Panels, as provided under section 612(a)(21)(D)(iii) of the Act; and

(B) Are subject to monitoring and enforcement for reasonableness by the Secretary consistent with section 616 of the Act.

(iv) When monitoring for reasonableness under paragraph (b)(1)(iii)(B) of this section, the Department finds that the following are presumptively reasonable:

(A) A minimum cell size under paragraph (b)(1)(i)(B) of this section no greater than 10; and

(B) A minimum n-size under paragraph (b)(1)(i)(C) of this section no greater than 30.

(2) The State must apply the risk ratio threshold or thresholds determined in paragraph (b)(1) of this section to risk ratios or alternate risk ratios, as appropriate, in each category described in paragraphs (b)(3) and (4) of this section and the following racial and ethnic groups:

(i) Hispanic/Latino of any race; and, for individuals who are non-Hispanic/Latino only;

(ii) American Indian or Alaska Native;

(iii) Asian;

(iv) Black or African American;

(v) Native Hawaiian or Other Pacific Islander;

(vi) White; and

(vii) Two or more races.

(3) Except as provided in paragraphs (b)(5) and (c) of this section, the State must calculate the risk ratio for each LEA, for each racial and ethnic group in paragraph (b)(2) of this section with respect to:

(i) The identification of children ages 3 through 21 as children with disabilities; and

(ii) The identification of children ages 3 through 21 as children with the following impairments:

(A) Intellectual disabilities;

(B) Specific learning disabilities;

(C) Emotional disturbance;

(D) Speech or language impairments;

(E) Other health impairments; and

(F) Autism.

(4) Except as provided in paragraphs (b)(5) and (c) of this section, the State must calculate the risk ratio for each LEA, for each racial and ethnic group in paragraph (b)(2) of this section with respect to the following placements into particular educational settings, including disciplinary removals:

(i) For children with disabilities ages 6 through 21, inside a regular class less than 40 percent of the day;

(ii) For children with disabilities ages 6 through 21, inside separate schools and residential facilities, not including homebound or hospital settings, correctional facilities, or private schools;

(iii) For children with disabilities ages 3 through 21, out-of-school suspensions and expulsions of 10 days or fewer;

(iv) For children with disabilities ages 3 through 21, out-of-school suspensions and expulsions of more than 10 days;

(v) For children with disabilities ages 3 through 21, in-school suspensions of 10 days or fewer;

(vi) For children with disabilities ages 3 through 21, in-school suspensions of more than 10 days; and

(vii) For children with disabilities ages 3 through 21, disciplinary removals in total, including in-school and out-of-school suspensions, expulsions, removals by school personnel to an interim alternative education setting, and removals by a hearing officer.

(5) The State must calculate an alternate risk ratio with respect to the categories described in paragraphs (b)(3) and (4) of this section if the comparison group in the LEA does not meet the minimum cell size or the minimum n-size.

(6) Except as provided in paragraph (d) of this section, the State must identify as having significant disproportionality based on race or ethnicity under §300.646(a) and (b) any LEA that has a risk ratio or alternate risk ratio for any racial or ethnic group in any of the categories described in paragraphs (b)(3) and (4) of this section that exceeds the risk ratio threshold set by the State for that category.

(7) The State must report all risk ratio thresholds, minimum cell sizes, minimum n-sizes, and standards for measuring reasonable progress selected under paragraphs (b)(1)(i)(A) through (D) of this section, and the rationales for each, to the Department at a time and in a manner determined by the Secretary. Rationales for minimum cell sizes and minimum n-sizes not presumptively reasonable under paragraph (b)(1)(iv) of this section must include a detailed explanation of why the numbers chosen are reasonable and how they ensure that the State is appropriately analyzing and identifying LEAs with significant disparities, based on race and ethnicity, in the identification, placement, or discipline of children with disabilities.

(c) *Exception.* A State is not required to calculate a risk ratio or alternate risk ratio, as outlined in paragraphs (b)(3), (4), and (5) of this section, to determine significant disproportionality if:

(1) The particular racial or ethnic group being analyzed does not meet the minimum cell size or minimum n-size; or

(2) In calculating the alternate risk ratio under paragraph (b)(5) of this section, the comparison group in the State does not meet the minimum cell size or minimum n-size.

(d) *Flexibility.* A State is not required to identify an LEA as having significant disproportionality based on race or ethnicity under §300.646(a) and (b) until—

(1) The LEA has exceeded a risk ratio threshold set by the State for a racial or ethnic group in a category described in paragraph (b)(3) or (4) of this section for up to three prior consecutive years preceding the identification; and

(2) The LEA has exceeded the risk ratio threshold and has failed to demonstrate reasonable progress, as determined by the State, in lowering the risk ratio or alternate risk ratio for the group and category in each of the two prior consecutive years.

(Authority: 20 U.S.C. 1418(d).)

[81 FR 92463, Dec. 19, 2016]

Subpart G—Authorization, Allotment, Use of Funds, and Authorization of Appropriations

ALLOTMENTS, GRANTS, AND USE OF FUNDS

§300.700 Grants to States.

(a) *Purpose of grants.* The Secretary makes grants to States, outlying areas, and freely associated States (as defined in §300.717), and provides funds to the Secretary of the Interior, to assist them to provide special education and related services to children with disabilities in accordance with Part B of the Act.

(b) *Maximum amount.* The maximum amount of the grant a State may receive under section 611 of the Act is—

(1) For fiscal years 2005 and 2006—

(i) The number of children with disabilities in the State who are receiving special education and related services—

(A) Aged three through five, if the State is eligible for a grant under section 619 of the Act; and

(B) Aged 6 through 21; multiplied by—

(ii) Forty (40) percent of the average per-pupil expenditure in public elementary schools and secondary schools in the United States (as defined in § 300.717); and

(2) For fiscal year 2007 and subsequent fiscal years—

(i) The number of children with disabilities in the 2004–2005 school year in the State who received special education and related services—

(A) Aged three through five if the State is eligible for a grant under section 619 of the Act; and

(B) Aged 6 through 21; multiplied by

(ii) Forty (40) percent of the average per-pupil expenditure in public elementary schools and secondary schools in the United States (as defined in § 300.717);

(iii) Adjusted by the rate of annual change in the sum of—

(A) Eighty-five (85) percent of the State's population of children aged 3 through 21 who are of the same age as children with disabilities for whom the State ensures the availability of FAPE under Part B of the Act; and

(B) Fifteen (15) percent of the State's population of children described in paragraph (b)(2)(iii)(A) of this section who are living in poverty.

(Authority: 20 U.S.C. 1411(a) and (d))

§ 300.701 Outlying areas, freely associated States, and the Secretary of the Interior.

(a) *Outlying areas and freely associated States*—(1) *Funds reserved.* From the amount appropriated for any fiscal year under section 611(i) of the Act, the Secretary reserves not more than one percent, which must be used—

(i) To provide assistance to the outlying areas in accordance with their respective populations of individuals aged 3 through 21; and

(ii) To provide each freely associated State a grant in the amount that the freely associated State received for fiscal year 2003 under Part B of the Act, but only if the freely associated State—

(A) Meets the applicable requirements of Part B of the Act that apply to States.

(B) Meets the requirements in paragraph (a)(2) of this section.

(2) *Application.* Any freely associated State that wishes to receive funds under Part B of the Act must include, in its application for assistance—

(i) Information demonstrating that it will meet all conditions that apply to States under Part B of the Act.

(ii) An assurance that, notwithstanding any other provision of Part B of the Act, it will use those funds only for the direct provision of special education and related services to children with disabilities and to enhance its capacity to make FAPE available to all children with disabilities;

(iii) The identity of the source and amount of funds, in addition to funds under Part B of the Act, that it will make available to ensure that FAPE is available to all children with disabilities within its jurisdiction; and

(iv) Such other information and assurances as the Secretary may require.

(3) *Special rule.* The provisions of Public Law 95–134, permitting the consolidation of grants by the outlying areas, do not apply to funds provided to the outlying areas or to the freely associated States under Part B of the Act.

(b) *Secretary of the Interior.* From the amount appropriated for any fiscal year under section 611(i) of the Act, the Secretary reserves 1.226 percent to provide assistance to the Secretary of the Interior in accordance with §§ 300.707 through 300.716.

(Authority: 20 U.S.C. 1411(b))

§ 300.702 Technical assistance.

(a) *In general.* The Secretary may reserve not more than one-half of one percent of the amounts appropriated under Part B of the Act for each fiscal year to support technical assistance activities authorized under section 616(i) of the Act.

(b) *Maximum amount.* The maximum amount the Secretary may reserve under paragraph (a) of this section for any fiscal year is $25,000,000, cumulatively adjusted by the rate of inflation as measured by the percentage increase, if any, from the preceding fiscal year in the Consumer Price Index For

All Urban Consumers, published by the Bureau of Labor Statistics of the Department of Labor.

(Authority: 20 U.S.C. 1411(c))

§300.703 Allocations to States.

(a) *General.* After reserving funds for technical assistance under §300.702, and for payments to the outlying areas, the freely associated States, and the Secretary of the Interior under §300.701 (a) and (b) for a fiscal year, the Secretary allocates the remaining amount among the States in accordance with paragraphs (b), (c), and (d) of this section.

(b) *Special rule for use of fiscal year 1999 amount.* If a State received any funds under section 611 of the Act for fiscal year 1999 on the basis of children aged three through five, but does not make FAPE available to all children with disabilities aged three through five in the State in any subsequent fiscal year, the Secretary computes the State's amount for fiscal year 1999, solely for the purpose of calculating the State's allocation in that subsequent year under paragraph (c) or (d) of this section, by subtracting the amount allocated to the State for fiscal year 1999 on the basis of those children.

(c) *Increase in funds.* If the amount available for allocations to States under paragraph (a) of this section for a fiscal year is equal to or greater than the amount allocated to the States under section 611 of the Act for the preceding fiscal year, those allocations are calculated as follows:

(1) *Allocation of increase*—(i) *General.* Except as provided in paragraph (c)(2) of this section, the Secretary allocates for the fiscal year—

(A) To each State the amount the State received under this section for fiscal year 1999;

(B) Eighty-five (85) percent of any remaining funds to States on the basis of the States' relative populations of children aged 3 through 21 who are of the same age as children with disabilities for whom the State ensures the availability of FAPE under Part B of the Act; and

(C) Fifteen (15) percent of those remaining funds to States on the basis of the States' relative populations of children described in paragraph (c)(1)(i)(B)

of this section who are living in poverty.

(ii) *Data.* For the purpose of making grants under this section, the Secretary uses the most recent population data, including data on children living in poverty, that are available and satisfactory to the Secretary.

(2) *Limitations.* Notwithstanding paragraph (c)(1) of this section, allocations under this section are subject to the following:

(i) *Preceding year allocation.* No State's allocation may be less than its allocation under section 611 of the Act for the preceding fiscal year.

(ii) *Minimum.* No State's allocation may be less than the greatest of—

(A) The sum of—

(*1*) The amount the State received under section 611 of the Act for fiscal year 1999; and

(*2*) One third of one percent of the amount by which the amount appropriated under section 611(i) of the Act for the fiscal year exceeds the amount appropriated for section 611 of the Act for fiscal year 1999;

(B) The sum of—

(*1*) The amount the State received under section 611 of the Act for the preceding fiscal year; and

(*2*) That amount multiplied by the percentage by which the increase in the funds appropriated for section 611 of the Act from the preceding fiscal year exceeds 1.5 percent; or

(C) The sum of—

(*1*) The amount the State received under section 611 of the Act for the preceding fiscal year; and

(*2*) That amount multiplied by 90 percent of the percentage increase in the amount appropriated for section 611 of the Act from the preceding fiscal year.

(iii) *Maximum.* Notwithstanding paragraph (c)(2)(ii) of this section, no State's allocation under paragraph (a) of this section may exceed the sum of—

(A) The amount the State received under section 611 of the Act for the preceding fiscal year; and

(B) That amount multiplied by the sum of 1.5 percent and the percentage increase in the amount appropriated under section 611 of the Act from the preceding fiscal year.

(3) *Ratable reduction.* If the amount available for allocations to States

under paragraph (c) of this section is insufficient to pay those allocations in full, those allocations are ratably reduced, subject to paragraph (c)(2)(i) of this section.

(d) *Decrease in funds.* If the amount available for allocations to States under paragraph (a) of this section for a fiscal year is less than the amount allocated to the States under section 611 of the Act for the preceding fiscal year, those allocations are calculated as follows:

(1) *Amounts greater than fiscal year 1999 allocations.* If the amount available for allocations under paragraph (a) of this section is greater than the amount allocated to the States for fiscal year 1999, each State is allocated the sum of—

(i) *1999 amount.* The amount the State received under section 611 of the Act for fiscal year 1999; and

(ii) *Remaining funds.* An amount that bears the same relation to any remaining funds as the increase the State received under section 611 of the Act for the preceding fiscal year over fiscal year 1999 bears to the total of all such increases for all States.

(2) *Amounts equal to or less than fiscal year 1999 allocations*—(i) *General.* If the amount available for allocations under paragraph (a) of this section is equal to or less than the amount allocated to the States for fiscal year 1999, each State is allocated the amount it received for fiscal year 1999.

(ii) *Ratable reduction.* If the amount available for allocations under paragraph (d) of this section is insufficient to make the allocations described in paragraph (d)(2)(i) of this section, those allocations are ratably reduced.

(Authority: 20 U.S.C. 1411(d))

§ 300.704 State-level activities.

(a) *State administration.* (1) For the purpose of administering Part B of the Act, including paragraph (c) of this section, section 619 of the Act, and the coordination of activities under Part B of the Act with, and providing technical assistance to, other programs that provide services to children with disabilities—

(i) Each State may reserve for each fiscal year not more than the maximum amount the State was eligible to

reserve for State administration under section 611 of the Act for fiscal year 2004 or $800,000 (adjusted in accordance with paragraph (a)(2) of this section), whichever is greater; and

(ii) Each outlying area may reserve for each fiscal year not more than five percent of the amount the outlying area receives under § 300.701(a) for the fiscal year or $35,000, whichever is greater.

(2) For each fiscal year, beginning with fiscal year 2005, the Secretary cumulatively adjusts—

(i) The maximum amount the State was eligible to reserve for State administration under section 611 of the Act for fiscal year 2004; and

(ii) $800,000, by the rate of inflation as measured by the percentage increase, if any, from the preceding fiscal year in the Consumer Price Index for All Urban Consumers, published by the Bureau of Labor Statistics of the Department of Labor.

(3) Prior to expenditure of funds under paragraph (a) of this section, the State must certify to the Secretary that the arrangements to establish responsibility for services pursuant to section 612(a)(12)(A) of the Act are current.

(4) Funds reserved under paragraph (a)(1) of this section may be used for the administration of Part C of the Act, if the SEA is the lead agency for the State under that Part.

(b) *Other State-level activities.* (1) States may reserve a portion of their allocations for other State-level activities. The maximum amount that a State may reserve for other State-level activities is as follows:

(i) If the amount that the State sets aside for State administration under paragraph (a) of this section is greater than $850,000 and the State opts to finance a high cost fund under paragraph (c) of this section:

(A) For fiscal years 2005 and 2006, 10 percent of the State's allocation under § 300.703.

(B) For fiscal year 2007 and subsequent fiscal years, an amount equal to 10 percent of the State's allocation for fiscal year 2006 under § 300.703 adjusted cumulatively for inflation.

(ii) If the amount that the State sets aside for State administration under paragraph (a) of this section is greater than $850,000 and the State opts not to finance a high cost fund under paragraph (c) of this section—

(A) For fiscal years 2005 and 2006, nine percent of the State's allocation under §300.703.

(B) For fiscal year 2007 and subsequent fiscal years, an amount equal to nine percent of the State's allocation for fiscal year 2006 adjusted cumulatively for inflation.

(iii) If the amount that the State sets aside for State administration under paragraph (a) of this section is less than or equal to $850,000 and the State opts to finance a high cost fund under paragraph (c) of this section:

(A) For fiscal years 2005 and 2006, 10.5 percent of the State's allocation under §300.703.

(B) For fiscal year 2007 and subsequent fiscal years, an amount equal to 10.5 percent of the State's allocation for fiscal year 2006 under §300.703 adjusted cumulatively for inflation.

(iv) If the amount that the State sets aside for State administration under paragraph (a) of this section is equal to or less than $850,000 and the State opts not to finance a high cost fund under paragraph (c) of this section:

(A) For fiscal years 2005 and 2006, nine and one-half percent of the State's allocation under §300.703.

(B) For fiscal year 2007 and subsequent fiscal years, an amount equal to nine and one-half percent of the State's allocation for fiscal year 2006 under §300.703 adjusted cumulatively for inflation.

(2) The adjustment for inflation is the rate of inflation as measured by the percentage of increase, if any, from the preceding fiscal year in the Consumer Price Index for All Urban Consumers, published by the Bureau of Labor Statistics of the Department of Labor.

(3) Some portion of the funds reserved under paragraph (b)(1) of this section must be used to carry out the following activities:

(i) For monitoring, enforcement, and complaint investigation; and

(ii) To establish and implement the mediation process required by section 615(e) of the Act, including providing for the costs of mediators and support personnel;

(4) Funds reserved under paragraph (b)(1) of this section also may be used to carry out the following activities:

(i) For support and direct services, including technical assistance, personnel preparation, and professional development and training;

(ii) To support paperwork reduction activities, including expanding the use of technology in the IEP process;

(iii) To assist LEAs in providing positive behavioral interventions and supports and mental health services for children with disabilities;

(iv) To improve the use of technology in the classroom by children with disabilities to enhance learning;

(v) To support the use of technology, including technology with universal design principles and assistive technology devices, to maximize accessibility to the general education curriculum for children with disabilities;

(vi) Development and implementation of transition programs, including coordination of services with agencies involved in supporting the transition of students with disabilities to postsecondary activities;

(vii) To assist LEAs in meeting personnel shortages;

(viii) To support capacity building activities and improve the delivery of services by LEAs to improve results for children with disabilities;

(ix) Alternative programming for children with disabilities who have been expelled from school, and services for children with disabilities in correctional facilities, children enrolled in State-operated or State-supported schools, and children with disabilities in charter schools;

(x) To support the development and provision of appropriate accommodations for children with disabilities, or the development and provision of alternate assessments that are valid and reliable for assessing the performance of children with disabilities, in accordance with sections 1111(b) and 1201 of the ESEA; and

(xi) To provide technical assistance to schools and LEAs, and direct services, including direct student services described in section 1003A(c)(3) of the ESEA, to children with disabilities, in

109

schools or LEAs implementing comprehensive support and improvement activities or targeted support and improvement activities under section 1111(d) of the ESEA on the basis of consistent underperformance of the disaggregated subgroup of children with disabilities, including providing professional development to special and regular education teachers who teach children with disabilities, based on scientifically based research to improve educational instruction, in order to improve academic achievement based on the challenging academic standards described in section 1111(b)(1) of the ESEA.

(c) *Local educational agency high cost fund.* (1) In general—

(i) For the purpose of assisting LEAs (including a charter school that is an LEA or a consortium of LEAs) in addressing the needs of high need children with disabilities, each State has the option to reserve for each fiscal year 10 percent of the amount of funds the State reserves for other State-level activities under paragraph (b)(1) of this section—

(A) To finance and make disbursements from the high cost fund to LEAs in accordance with paragraph (c) of this section during the first and succeeding fiscal years of the high cost fund; and

(B) To support innovative and effective ways of cost sharing by the State, by an LEA, or among a consortium of LEAs, as determined by the State in coordination with representatives from LEAs, subject to paragraph (c)(2)(ii) of this section.

(ii) For purposes of paragraph (c) of this section, *local educational agency* includes a charter school that is an LEA, or a consortium of LEAs.

(2)(i) A State must not use any of the funds the State reserves pursuant to paragraph (c)(1)(i) of this section, which are solely for disbursement to LEAs, for costs associated with establishing, supporting, and otherwise administering the fund. The State may use funds the State reserves under paragraph (a) of this section for those administrative costs.

(ii) A State must not use more than 5 percent of the funds the State reserves pursuant to paragraph (c)(1)(i) of

this section for each fiscal year to support innovative and effective ways of cost sharing among consortia of LEAs.

(3)(i) The SEA must develop, not later than 90 days after the State reserves funds under paragraph (c)(1)(i) of this section, annually review, and amend as necessary, a State plan for the high cost fund. Such State plan must—

(A) Establish, in consultation and coordination with representatives from LEAs, a definition of a high need child with a disability that, at a minimum—

(*1*) Addresses the financial impact a high need child with a disability has on the budget of the child's LEA; and

(*2*) Ensures that the cost of the high need child with a disability is greater than 3 times the average per pupil expenditure (as defined in section 8101 of the ESEA) in that State;

(B) Establish eligibility criteria for the participation of an LEA that, at a minimum, take into account the number and percentage of high need children with disabilities served by an LEA;

(C) Establish criteria to ensure that placements supported by the fund are consistent with the requirements of §§ 300.114 through 300.118;

(D) Develop a funding mechanism that provides distributions each fiscal year to LEAs that meet the criteria developed by the State under paragraph (c)(3)(i)(B) of this section;

(E) Establish an annual schedule by which the SEA must make its distributions from the high cost fund each fiscal year; and

(F) If the State elects to reserve funds for supporting innovative and effective ways of cost sharing under paragraph (c)(1)(i)(B) of this section, describe how these funds will be used.

(ii) The State must make its final State plan available to the public not less than 30 days before the beginning of the school year, including dissemination of such information on the State Web site.

(4)(i) Each SEA must make all annual disbursements from the high cost fund established under paragraph (c)(1)(i) of this section in accordance with the State plan published pursuant to paragraph (c)(3) of this section.

(ii) The costs associated with educating a high need child with a disability, as defined under paragraph (c)(3)(i)(A) of this section, are only those costs associated with providing direct special education and related services to the child that are identified in that child's IEP, including the cost of room and board for a residential placement determined necessary, consistent with § 300.114, to implement a child's IEP.

(iii) The funds in the high cost fund remain under the control of the State until disbursed to an LEA to support a specific child who qualifies under the State plan for the high cost funds or distributed to LEAs, consistent with paragraph (c)(9) of this section.

(5) The disbursements under paragraph (c)(4) of this section must not be used to support legal fees, court costs, or other costs associated with a cause of action brought on behalf of a child with a disability to ensure FAPE for such child.

(6) Nothing in paragraph (c) of this section—

(i) Limits or conditions the right of a child with a disability who is assisted under Part B of the Act to receive FAPE pursuant to section 612(a)(1) of the Act in the least restrictive environment pursuant to section 612(a)(5) of the Act; or

(ii) Authorizes an SEA or LEA to establish a limit on what may be spent on the education of a child with a disability.

(7) Notwithstanding the provisions of paragraphs (c)(1) through (6) of this section, a State may use funds reserved pursuant to paragraph (c)(1)(i) of this section for implementing a placement neutral cost sharing and reimbursement program of high need, low incidence, catastrophic, or extraordinary aid to LEAs that provides services to high need children based on eligibility criteria for such programs that were created not later than January 1, 2004, and are currently in operation, if such program serves children that meet the requirement of the definition of a high need child with a disability as described in paragraph (c)(3)(i)(A) of this section.

(8) Disbursements provided under paragraph (c) of this section must not

be used to pay costs that otherwise would be reimbursed as medical assistance for a child with a disability under the State Medicaid program under Title XIX of the Social Security Act.

(9) Funds reserved under paragraph (c)(1)(i) of this section from the appropriation for any fiscal year, but not expended pursuant to paragraph (c)(4) of this section before the beginning of their last year of availability for obligation, must be allocated to LEAs in the same manner as other funds from the appropriation for that fiscal year are allocated to LEAs under § 300.705 during their final year of availability.

(d) *Inapplicability of certain prohibitions.* A State may use funds the State reserves under paragraphs (a) and (b) of this section without regard to—

(1) The prohibition on commingling of funds in § 300.162(b).

(2) The prohibition on supplanting other funds in § 300.162(c).

(e) *Special rule for increasing funds.* A State may use funds the State reserves under paragraph (a)(1) of this section as a result of inflationary increases under paragraph (a)(2) of this section to carry out activities authorized under paragraph (b)(4)(i), (iii), (vii), or (viii) of this section.

(f) *Flexibility in using funds for Part C.* Any State eligible to receive a grant under section 619 of the Act may use funds made available under paragraph (a)(1) of this section, § 300.705(c), or § 300.814(e) to develop and implement a State policy jointly with the lead agency under Part C of the Act and the SEA to provide early intervention services (which must include an educational component that promotes school readiness and incorporates preliteracy, language, and numeracy skills) in accordance with Part C of the Act to children with disabilities who are eligible for services under section 619 of the Act and who previously received services under Part C of the Act until the children enter, or are eligible under State

111

law to enter, kindergarten, or elementary school as appropriate.

(Approved by the Office of Management and Budget under control number 1820–0600)

(Authority: 20 U.S.C. 1411(e))

[71 FR 46753, Aug. 14, 2006, as amended at 72 FR 61307, Oct. 30, 2007; 82 FR 29761, June 30, 2017]

§ 300.705 Subgrants to LEAs.

(a) *Subgrants required.* Each State that receives a grant under section 611 of the Act for any fiscal year must distribute any funds the State does not reserve under § 300.704 to LEAs (including public charter schools that operate as LEAs) in the State that have established their eligibility under section 613 of the Act for use in accordance with Part B of the Act. Effective with funds that become available on the July 1, 2009, each State must distribute funds to eligible LEAs, including public charter schools that operate as LEAs, even if the LEA is not serving any children with disabilities.

(b) *Allocations to LEAs.* For each fiscal year for which funds are allocated to States under § 300.703, each State shall allocate funds as follows:

(1) *Base payments.* The State first must award each LEA described in paragraph (a) of this section the amount the LEA would have received under section 611 of the Act for fiscal year 1999, if the State had distributed 75 percent of its grant for that year under section 611(d) of the Act, as that section was then in effect.

(2) *Base payment adjustments.* For any fiscal year after 1999—

(i) If a new LEA is created, the State must divide the base allocation determined under paragraph (b)(1) of this section for the LEAs that would have been responsible for serving children with disabilities now being served by the new LEA, among the new LEA and affected LEAs based on the relative numbers of children with disabilities ages 3 through 21, or ages 6 through 21 if a State has had its payment reduced under § 300.703(b), currently provided special education by each of the LEAs;

(ii) If one or more LEAs are combined into a single new LEA, the State must combine the base allocations of the merged LEAs;

(iii) If, for two or more LEAs, geographic boundaries or administrative responsibility for providing services to children with disabilities ages 3 through 21 change, the base allocations of affected LEAs must be redistributed among affected LEAs based on the relative numbers of children with disabilities ages 3 through 21, or ages 6 through 21 if a State has had its payment reduced under § 300.703(b), currently provided special education by each affected LEA; and

(iv) If an LEA received a base payment of zero in its first year of operation, the SEA must adjust the base payment for the first fiscal year after the first annual child count in which the LEA reports that it is serving any children with disabilities. The State must divide the base allocation determined under paragraph (b)(1) of this section for the LEAs that would have been responsible for serving children with disabilities now being served by the LEA, among the LEA and affected LEAs based on the relative numbers of children with disabilities ages 3 through 21, or ages 6 through 21 currently provided special education by each of the LEAs. This requirement takes effect with funds that become available on July 1, 2009.

(3) *Allocation of remaining funds.* After making allocations under paragraph (b)(1) of this section, as adjusted by paragraph (b)(2) of this section, the State must—

(i) Allocate 85 percent of any remaining funds to those LEAs on the basis of the relative numbers of children enrolled in public and private elementary schools and secondary schools within the LEA's jurisdiction; and

(ii) Allocate 15 percent of those remaining funds to those LEAs in accordance with their relative numbers of children living in poverty, as determined by the SEA.

(c) *Reallocation of LEA funds.* (1) If an SEA determines that an LEA is adequately providing FAPE to all children with disabilities residing in the area served by that agency with State and local funds, the SEA may reallocate any portion of the funds under this part that are not needed by that LEA to provide FAPE, to other LEAs in the

State that are not adequately providing special education and related services to all children with disabilities residing in the areas served by those other LEAs. The SEA may also retain those funds for use at the State level to the extent the State has not reserved the maximum amount of funds it is permitted to reserve for State-level activities pursuant to §300.704.

(2) After an SEA distributes funds under this part to an eligible LEA that is not serving any children with disabilities, as provided in paragraph (a) of this section, the SEA must determine, within a reasonable period of time prior to the end of the carryover period in 34 CFR 76.709, whether the LEA has obligated the funds. The SEA may reallocate any of those funds not obligated by the LEA to other LEAs in the State that are not adequately providing special education and related services to all children with disabilities residing in the areas served by those other LEAs. The SEA may also retain those funds for use at the State level to the extent the State has not reserved the maximum amount of funds it is permitted to reserve for State-level activities pursuant to §300.704.

(Approved by the Office of Management and Budget under control number 1820–0030)

(Authority: 20 U.S.C. 1411(f))

[71 FR 46753, Aug. 14, 2006, as amended at 73 FR 73028, Dec. 1, 2008]

§300.706 [Reserved]

SECRETARY OF THE INTERIOR

§300.707 Use of amounts by Secretary of the Interior.

(a) *Definitions.* For purposes of §§300.707 through 300.716, the following definitions apply:

(1) *Reservation* means Indian Country as defined in 18 U.S.C. 1151.

(2) *Tribal governing body* has the definition given that term in 25 U.S.C. 2021(19).

(b) *Provision of amounts for assistance.* The Secretary provides amounts to the Secretary of the Interior to meet the need for assistance for the education of children with disabilities on reservations aged 5 to 21, inclusive, enrolled in elementary schools and secondary schools for Indian children operated or funded by the Secretary of the Interior. The amount of the payment for any fiscal year is equal to 80 percent of the amount allotted under section 611(b)(2) of the Act for that fiscal year. Of the amount described in the preceding sentence, after the Secretary of the Interior reserves funds for administration under §300.710, 80 percent must be allocated to such schools by July 1 of that fiscal year and 20 percent must be allocated to such schools by September 30 of that fiscal year.

(c) *Additional requirement.* With respect to all other children aged 3 to 21, inclusive, on reservations, the SEA of the State in which the reservation is located must ensure that all of the requirements of Part B of the Act are implemented.

(Authority: 20 U.S.C. 1411(h)(1))

§300.708 Submission of information.

The Secretary may provide the Secretary of the Interior amounts under §300.707 for a fiscal year only if the Secretary of the Interior submits to the Secretary information that—

(a) Meets the requirements of section 612(a)(1), (3) through (9), (10)(B) through (C), (11) through (12), (14) through (16), (19), and (21) through (25) of the Act (including monitoring and evaluation activities);

(b) Meets the requirements of section 612(b) and (e) of the Act;

(c) Meets the requirements of section 613(a)(1), (2)(A)(i), (7) through (9) and section 613(i) of the Act (references to LEAs in these sections must be read as references to elementary schools and secondary schools for Indian children operated or funded by the Secretary of the Interior);

(d) Meets the requirements of section 616 of the Act that apply to States (references to LEAs in section 616 of the Act must be read as references to elementary schools and secondary schools for Indian children operated or funded by the Secretary of the Interior).

(e) Meets the requirements of this part that implement the sections of the Act listed in paragraphs (a) through (d) of this section;

(f) Includes a description of how the Secretary of the Interior will coordinate the provision of services under Part B of the Act with LEAs, tribes and tribal organizations, and other private and Federal service providers;

(g) Includes an assurance that there are public hearings, adequate notice of the hearings, and an opportunity for comment afforded to members of tribes, tribal governing bodies, and affected local school boards before the adoption of the policies, programs, and procedures related to the requirements described in paragraphs (a) through (d) of this section;

(h) Includes an assurance that the Secretary of the Interior provides the information that the Secretary may require to comply with section 618 of the Act;

(i)(1) Includes an assurance that the Secretary of the Interior and the Secretary of Health and Human Services have entered into a memorandum of agreement, to be provided to the Secretary, for the coordination of services, resources, and personnel between their respective Federal, State, and local offices and with the SEAs and LEAs and other entities to facilitate the provision of services to Indian children with disabilities residing on or near reservations.

(2) The agreement must provide for the apportionment of responsibilities and costs, including child find, evaluation, diagnosis, remediation or therapeutic measures, and (where appropriate) equipment and medical or personal supplies, as needed for a child with a disability to remain in a school or program; and

(j) Includes an assurance that the Department of the Interior will cooperate with the Department in its exercise of monitoring and oversight of the requirements in this section and §§ 300.709 through 300.711 and §§ 300.713 through 300.716, and any agreements entered into between the Secretary of the Interior and other entities under Part B of the Act, and will fulfill its duties under Part B of the Act. The Secretary withholds payments under § 300.707 with respect to the requirements described in this section in the same manner as the Secretary withholds payments under section 616(e)(6) of the Act.

(Authority: 20 U.S.C. 1411(h)(2) and (3))

§ 300.709 Public participation.

In fulfilling the requirements of § 300.708 the Secretary of the Interior must provide for public participation consistent with § 300.165.

(Authority: 20 U.S.C. 1411(h))

§ 300.710 Use of funds under Part B of the Act.

(a) The Secretary of the Interior may reserve five percent of its payment under § 300.707(b) in any fiscal year, or $500,000, whichever is greater, for administrative costs in carrying out the provisions of §§ 300.707 through 300.709, 300.711, and 300.713 through 300.716.

(b) Payments to the Secretary of the Interior under § 300.712 must be used in accordance with that section.

(Authority: 20 U.S.C. 1411(h)(1)(A))

§ 300.711 Early intervening services.

(a) The Secretary of the Interior may allow each elementary school and secondary school for Indian children operated or funded by the Secretary of the Interior to use not more than 15 percent of the amount the school receives under § 300.707(b) for any fiscal year, in combination with other amounts (which may include amounts other than education funds), to develop and implement coordinated, early intervening services, which may include interagency financing structures, for children in kindergarten through grade 12 (with a particular emphasis on children in kindergarten through grade three) who have not been identified as needing special education or related services but who need additional academic and behavioral support to succeed in a general education environment, in accordance with section 613(f) of the Act.

(b) Each elementary school and secondary school for Indian children operated or funded by the Secretary of the Interior that develops and maintains coordinated early intervening services in accordance with section 613(f) of the Act and § 300.226 must annually report to the Secretary of the Interior in accordance with section 613(f) of the Act.

(Authority: 20 U.S.C. 1411(h) and 1413(f))

§ 300.712 **Payments for education and services for Indian children with disabilities aged three through five.**

(a) *General.* With funds appropriated under section 611(i) of the Act, the Secretary makes payments to the Secretary of the Interior to be distributed to tribes or tribal organizations (as defined under section 4 of the Indian Self-Determination and Education Assistance Act) or consortia of tribes or tribal organizations to provide for the coordination of assistance for special education and related services for children with disabilities aged three through five on reservations served by elementary schools and secondary schools for Indian children operated or funded by the Department of the Interior. The amount of the payments under paragraph (b) of this section for any fiscal year is equal to 20 percent of the amount allotted under § 300.701(b).

(b) *Distribution of funds.* The Secretary of the Interior must distribute the total amount of the payment under paragraph (a) of this section by allocating to each tribe, tribal organization, or consortium an amount based on the number of children with disabilities aged three through five residing on reservations as reported annually, divided by the total of those children served by all tribes or tribal organizations.

(c) *Submission of information.* To receive a payment under this section, the tribe or tribal organization must submit the figures to the Secretary of the Interior as required to determine the amounts to be allocated under paragraph (b) of this section. This information must be compiled and submitted to the Secretary.

(d) *Use of funds.* (1) The funds received by a tribe or tribal organization must be used to assist in child find, screening, and other procedures for the early identification of children aged three through five, parent training, and the provision of direct services. These activities may be carried out directly or through contracts or cooperative agreements with the BIA, LEAs, and other public or private nonprofit

organizations. The tribe or tribal organization is encouraged to involve Indian parents in the development and implementation of these activities.

(2) The tribe or tribal organization, as appropriate, must make referrals to local, State, or Federal entities for the provision of services or further diagnosis.

(e) *Biennial report.* To be eligible to receive a grant pursuant to paragraph (a) of this section, the tribe or tribal organization must provide to the Secretary of the Interior a biennial report of activities undertaken under this section, including the number of contracts and cooperative agreements entered into, the number of children contacted and receiving services for each year, and the estimated number of children needing services during the two years following the year in which the report is made. The Secretary of the Interior must include a summary of this information on a biennial basis in the report to the Secretary required under section 611(h) of the Act. The Secretary may require any additional information from the Secretary of the Interior.

(f) *Prohibitions.* None of the funds allocated under this section may be used by the Secretary of the Interior for administrative purposes, including child count and the provision of technical assistance.

(Authority: 20 U.S.C. 1411(h)(4))

§ 300.713 **Plan for coordination of services.**

(a) The Secretary of the Interior must develop and implement a plan for the coordination of services for all Indian children with disabilities residing on reservations served by elementary schools and secondary schools for Indian children operated or funded by the Secretary of the Interior.

(b) The plan must provide for the coordination of services benefiting those children from whatever source, including tribes, the Indian Health Service, other BIA divisions, other Federal agencies, State educational agencies, and State, local, and tribal juvenile and adult correctional facilities.

(c) In developing the plan, the Secretary of the Interior must consult with all interested and involved parties.

115

(d) The plan must be based on the needs of the children and the system best suited for meeting those needs, and may involve the establishment of cooperative agreements between the BIA, other Federal agencies, and other entities.

(e) The plan also must be distributed upon request to States; to SEAs, LEAs, and other agencies providing services to infants, toddlers, and children with disabilities; to tribes; and to other interested parties.

(Authority: 20 U.S.C. 1411(h)(5))

§ 300.714 Establishment of advisory board.

(a) To meet the requirements of section 612(a)(21) of the Act, the Secretary of the Interior must establish, under the BIA, an advisory board composed of individuals involved in or concerned with the education and provision of services to Indian infants, toddlers, children, and youth with disabilities, including Indians with disabilities, Indian parents or guardians of such children, teachers, service providers, State and local educational officials, representatives of tribes or tribal organizations, representatives from State Interagency Coordinating Councils under section 641 of the Act in States having reservations, and other members representing the various divisions and entities of the BIA. The chairperson must be selected by the Secretary of the Interior.

(b) The advisory board must—

(1) Assist in the coordination of services within the BIA and with other local, State, and Federal agencies in the provision of education for infants, toddlers, and children with disabilities;

(2) Advise and assist the Secretary of the Interior in the performance of the Secretary of the Interior's responsibilities described in section 611(h) of the Act;

(3) Develop and recommend policies concerning effective inter- and intra-agency collaboration, including modifications to regulations, and the elimination of barriers to inter- and intra-agency programs and activities;

(4) Provide assistance and disseminate information on best practices, effective program coordination strategies, and recommendations for improved early intervention services or educational programming for Indian infants, toddlers, and children with disabilities; and

(5) Provide assistance in the preparation of information required under § 300.708(h).

(Authority: 20 U.S.C. 1411(h)(6))

§ 300.715 Annual reports.

(a) *In general.* The advisory board established under § 300.714 must prepare and submit to the Secretary of the Interior and to Congress an annual report containing a description of the activities of the advisory board for the preceding year.

(b) *Availability.* The Secretary of the Interior must make available to the Secretary the report described in paragraph (a) of this section.

(Authority: 20 U.S.C. 1411(h)(7))

§ 300.716 Applicable regulations.

The Secretary of the Interior must comply with the requirements of §§ 300.103 through 300.108, 300.110 through 300.124, 300.145 through 300.154, 300.156 through 300.160, 300.165, 300.170 through 300.186, 300.226, 300.300 through 300.606, 300.610 through 300.646, and 300.707 through 300.716.

(Authority: 20 U.S.C. 1411(h)(2)(A))

DEFINITIONS THAT APPLY TO THIS SUBPART

§ 300.717 Definitions applicable to allotments, grants, and use of funds.

As used in this subpart—

(a) *Freely associated States* means the Republic of the Marshall Islands, the Federated States of Micronesia, and the Republic of Palau;

(b) *Outlying areas* means the United States Virgin Islands, Guam, American Samoa, and the Commonwealth of the Northern Mariana Islands;

(c) *State* means each of the 50 States, the District of Columbia, and the Commonwealth of Puerto Rico; and

(d) *Average per-pupil expenditure in public elementary schools and secondary schools in the United States* means—

(1) Without regard to the source of funds—

(i) The aggregate current expenditures, during the second fiscal year preceding the fiscal year for which the determination is made (or, if satisfactory data for that year are not available, during the most recent preceding fiscal year for which satisfactory data are available) of all LEAs in the 50 States and the District of Columbia; plus

(ii) Any direct expenditures by the State for the operation of those agencies; divided by (2) The aggregate number of children in average daily attendance to whom those agencies provided free public education during that preceding year.

(Authority: 20 U.S.C. 1401(22), 1411(b)(1) (C) and (g))

ACQUISITION OF EQUIPMENT AND CONSTRUCTION OR ALTERATION OF FACILITIES

§ 300.718   Acquisition of equipment and construction or alteration of facilities.

(a) *General.* If the Secretary determines that a program authorized under Part B of the Act will be improved by permitting program funds to be used to acquire appropriate equipment, or to construct new facilities or alter existing facilities, the Secretary may allow the use of those funds for those purposes.

(b) *Compliance with certain regulations.* Any construction of new facilities or alteration of existing facilities under paragraph (a) of this section must comply with the requirements of—

(1) Appendix A of part 36 of title 28, Code of Federal Regulations (commonly known as the "Americans with Disabilities Accessibility Standards for Buildings and Facilities"); or

(2) Appendix A of subpart 101–19.6 of title 41, Code of Federal Regulations (commonly known as the "Uniform Federal Accessibility Standards").

(Authority: 20 U.S.C. 1404)

Subpart H—Preschool Grants for Children with Disabilities

§ 300.800   In general.

The Secretary provides grants under section 619 of the Act to assist States to provide special education and related services in accordance with Part B of the Act—

(a) To children with disabilities aged three through five years; and

(b) At a State's discretion, to two-year-old children with disabilities who will turn three during the school year.

(Authority: 20 U.S.C. 1419(a))

§§ 300.801–300.802   [Reserved]

§ 300.803   Definition of State.

As used in this subpart, State means each of the 50 States, the District of Columbia, and the Commonwealth of Puerto Rico.

(Authority: 20 U.S.C. 1419(i))

§ 300.804   Eligibility.

A State is eligible for a grant under section 619 of the Act if the State—

(a) Is eligible under section 612 of the Act to receive a grant under Part B of the Act; and

(b) Makes FAPE available to all children with disabilities, aged three through five, residing in the State.

(Approved by the Office of Management and Budget under control number 1820–0030)

(Authority: 20 U.S.C. 1419(b))

§ 300.805   [Reserved]

§ 300.806   Eligibility for financial assistance.

No State or LEA, or other public institution or agency, may receive a grant or enter into a contract or cooperative agreement under subpart 2 or 3 of Part D of the Act that relates exclusively to programs, projects, and activities pertaining to children aged three through five years, unless the State is eligible to receive a grant under section 619(b) of the Act.

(Authority: 20 U.S.C. 1481(e))

§ 300.807   Allocations to States.

The Secretary allocates the amount made available to carry out section 619 of the Act for a fiscal year among the States in accordance with §§ 300.808 through 300.810.

(Authority: 20 U.S.C. 1419(c)(1))

§ 300.808 Increase in funds.

If the amount available for allocation to States under § 300.807 for a fiscal year is equal to or greater than the amount allocated to the States under section 619 of the Act for the preceding fiscal year, those allocations are calculated as follows:

(a) Except as provided in § 300.809, the Secretary—

(1) Allocates to each State the amount the State received under section 619 of the Act for fiscal year 1997;

(2) Allocates 85 percent of any remaining funds to States on the basis of the States' relative populations of children aged three through five; and

(3) Allocates 15 percent of those remaining funds to States on the basis of the States' relative populations of all children aged three through five who are living in poverty.

(b) For the purpose of making grants under this section, the Secretary uses the most recent population data, including data on children living in poverty, that are available and satisfactory to the Secretary.

(Authority: 20 U.S.C. 1419(c)(2)(A))

§ 300.809 Limitations.

(a) Notwithstanding § 300.808, allocations under that section are subject to the following:

(1) No State's allocation may be less than its allocation under section 619 of the Act for the preceding fiscal year.

(2) No State's allocation may be less than the greatest of—

(i) The sum of—

(A) The amount the State received under section 619 of the Act for fiscal year 1997; and

(B) One-third of one percent of the amount by which the amount appropriated under section 619(j) of the Act for the fiscal year exceeds the amount appropriated for section 619 of the Act for fiscal year 1997;

(ii) The sum of—

(A) The amount the State received under section 619 of the Act for the preceding fiscal year; and

(B) That amount multiplied by the percentage by which the increase in the funds appropriated under section 619 of the Act from the preceding fiscal year exceeds 1.5 percent; or

(iii) The sum of—

(A) The amount the State received under section 619 of the Act for the preceding fiscal year; and

(B) That amount multiplied by 90 percent of the percentage increase in the amount appropriated under section 619 of the Act from the preceding fiscal year.

(b) Notwithstanding paragraph (a)(2) of this section, no State's allocation under § 300.808 may exceed the sum of—

(1) The amount the State received under section 619 of the Act for the preceding fiscal year; and

(2) That amount multiplied by the sum of 1.5 percent and the percentage increase in the amount appropriated under section 619 of the Act from the preceding fiscal year.

(c) If the amount available for allocation to States under § 300.808 and paragraphs (a) and (b) of this section is insufficient to pay those allocations in full, those allocations are ratably reduced, subject to paragraph (a)(1) of this section.

(Authority: 20 U.S.C. 1419(c)(2)(B) and (c)(2)(C))

§ 300.810 Decrease in funds.

If the amount available for allocations to States under § 300.807 for a fiscal year is less than the amount allocated to the States under section 619 of the Act for the preceding fiscal year, those allocations are calculated as follows:

(a) If the amount available for allocations is greater than the amount allocated to the States for fiscal year 1997, each State is allocated the sum of—

(1) The amount the State received under section 619 of the Act for fiscal year 1997; and

(2) An amount that bears the same relation to any remaining funds as the increase the State received under section 619 of the Act for the preceding fiscal year over fiscal year 1997 bears to the total of all such increases for all States.

(b) If the amount available for allocations is equal to or less than the amount allocated to the States for fiscal year 1997, each State is allocated the amount the State received for fiscal year 1997, ratably reduced, if necessary.

(Authority: 20 U.S.C. 1419(c)(3))

§ 300.811 [Reserved]

§ 300.812 Reservation for State activities.

(a) Each State may reserve not more than the amount described in paragraph (b) of this section for administration and other State-level activities in accordance with §§ 300.813 and 300.814.

(b) For each fiscal year, the Secretary determines and reports to the SEA an amount that is 25 percent of the amount the State received under section 619 of the Act for fiscal year 1997, cumulatively adjusted by the Secretary for each succeeding fiscal year by the lesser of—

(1) The percentage increase, if any, from the preceding fiscal year in the State's allocation under section 619 of the Act; or

(2) The rate of inflation, as measured by the percentage increase, if any, from the preceding fiscal year in the Consumer Price Index for All Urban Consumers, published by the Bureau of Labor Statistics of the Department of Labor.

(Authority: 20 U.S.C. 1419(d))

[71 FR 46753, Aug. 14, 2006, as amended at 72 FR 61307, Oct. 30, 2007]

§ 300.813 State administration.

(a) For the purpose of administering section 619 of the Act (including the coordination of activities under Part B of the Act with, and providing technical assistance to, other programs that provide services to children with disabilities), a State may use not more than 20 percent of the maximum amount the State may reserve under § 300.812 for any fiscal year.

(b) Funds described in paragraph (a) of this section may also be used for the administration of Part C of the Act.

(Authority: 20 U.S.C. 1419(e))

§ 300.814 Other State-level activities.

Each State must use any funds the State reserves under § 300.812 and does not use for administration under § 300.813—

(a) For support services (including establishing and implementing the mediation process required by section 615(e) of the Act), which may benefit children with disabilities younger than three or older than five as long as those services also benefit children with disabilities aged three through five;

(b) For direct services for children eligible for services under section 619 of the Act;

(c) For activities at the State and local levels to meet the performance goals established by the State under section 612(a)(15) of the Act;

(d) To supplement other funds used to develop and implement a statewide coordinated services system designed to improve results for children and families, including children with disabilities and their families, but not more than one percent of the amount received by the State under section 619 of the Act for a fiscal year;

(e) To provide early intervention services (which must include an educational component that promotes school readiness and incorporates preliteracy, language, and numeracy skills) in accordance with Part C of the Act to children with disabilities who are eligible for services under section 619 of the Act and who previously received services under Part C of the Act until such children enter, or are eligible under State law to enter, kindergarten; or

(f) At the State's discretion, to continue service coordination or case management for families who receive services under Part C of the Act, consistent with § 300.814(e).

(Authority: 20 U.S.C. 1419(f))

§ 300.815 Subgrants to LEAs.

Each State that receives a grant under section 619 of the Act for any fiscal year must distribute all of the grant funds the State does not reserve under § 300.812 to LEAs (including public charter schools that operate as LEAs) in the State that have established their eligibility under section 613 of the Act. Effective with funds that become available on July 1, 2009, each State must distribute funds to eligible LEAs that are responsible for providing education to children aged three through five years, including public charter schools that operate as LEAs, even if the LEA is not serving any preschool children with disabilities.

(Authority: 20 U.S.C. 1419(g)(1))

[73 FR 73028, Dec. 1, 2008]

§ 300.816 Allocations to LEAs.

(a) *Base payments.* The State must first award each LEA described in § 300.815 the amount that agency would have received under section 619 of the Act for fiscal year 1997 if the State had distributed 75 percent of its grant for that year under section 619(c)(3), as such section was then in effect.

(b) *Base payment adjustments.* For fiscal year 1998 and beyond—

(1) If a new LEA is created, the State must divide the base allocation determined under paragraph (a) of this section for the LEAs that would have been responsible for serving children with disabilities now being served by the new LEA, among the new LEA and affected LEAs based on the relative numbers of children with disabilities ages three through five currently provided special education by each of the LEAs;

(2) If one or more LEAs are combined into a single new LEA, the State must combine the base allocations of the merged LEAs;

(3) If for two or more LEAs, geographic boundaries or administrative responsibility for providing services to children with disabilities ages three through five changes, the base allocations of affected LEAs must be redistributed among affected LEAs based on the relative numbers of children with disabilities ages three through five currently provided special education by each affected LEA; and

(4) If an LEA received a base payment of zero in its first year of operation, the SEA must adjust the base payment for the first fiscal year after the first annual child count in which the LEA reports that it is serving any children with disabilities aged three through five years. The State must divide the base allocation determined under paragraph (a) of this section for the LEAs that would have been responsible for serving children with disabilities aged three through five years now being served by the LEA, among the LEA and affected LEAs based on the

relative numbers of children with disabilities aged three through five years currently provided special education by each of the LEAs. This requirement takes effect with funds that become available on July 1, 2009.

(c) *Allocation of remaining funds.* After making allocations under paragraph (a) of this section, the State must—

(1) Allocate 85 percent of any remaining funds to those LEAs on the basis of the relative numbers of children enrolled in public and private elementary schools and secondary schools within the LEA's jurisdiction; and

(2) Allocate 15 percent of those remaining funds to those LEAs in accordance with their relative numbers of children living in poverty, as determined by the SEA.

(d) *Use of best data.* For the purpose of making grants under this section, States must apply on a uniform basis across all LEAs the best data that are available to them on the numbers of children enrolled in public and private elementary and secondary schools and the numbers of children living in poverty.

(Authority: 20 U.S.C. 1419(g)(1))

[71 FR 46753, Aug. 14, 2006, as amended at 73 FR 73028, Dec. 1, 2008]

§ 300.817 Reallocation of LEA funds.

(a) If an SEA determines that an LEA is adequately providing FAPE to all children with disabilities aged three through five years residing in the area served by the LEA with State and local funds, the SEA may reallocate any portion of the funds under section 619 of the Act that are not needed by that LEA to provide FAPE, to other LEAs in the State that are not adequately providing special education and related services to all children with disabilities aged three through five years residing in the areas served by those other LEAs. The SEA may also retain those funds for use at the State level to the extent the State has not reserved the maximum amount of funds it is permitted to reserve for State-level activities pursuant to § 300.812.

(b) After an SEA distributes section 619 funds to an eligible LEA that is not serving any children with disabilities aged three through five years, as provided in §300.815, the SEA must determine, within a reasonable period of time prior to the end of the carryover period in 34 CFR 76.709, whether the LEA has obligated the funds. The SEA may reallocate any of those funds not obligated by the LEA to other LEAs in the State that are not adequately providing special education and related services to all children with disabilities aged three through five years residing in the areas served by those other LEAs. The SEA may also retain those funds for use at the State level to the extent the State has not reserved the maximum amount of funds it is permitted to reserve for State-level activities pursuant to §300.812.

(Authority: 20 U.S.C. 1419(g)(2))

[73 FR 73028, Dec. 1, 2008]

§300.818 Part C of the Act inapplicable.

Part C of the Act does not apply to any child with a disability receiving FAPE, in accordance with Part B of the Act, with funds received under section 619 of the Act.

(Authority: 20 U.S.C. 1419(h))

APPENDIX A TO PART 300—EXCESS COSTS
CALCULATION

Except as otherwise provided, amounts provided to an LEA under Part B of the Act may be used only to pay the excess costs of providing special education and related services to children with disabilities. Excess costs are those costs for the education of an elementary school or secondary school student with a disability that are in excess of the average annual per student expenditure in an LEA during the preceding school year for an elementary school or secondary school student, as may be appropriate. An LEA must spend at least the average annual per student expenditure on the education of an elementary school or secondary school child with a disability before funds under Part B of the Act are used to pay the excess costs of providing special education and related services.

Section 602(8) of the Act and §300.16 require the LEA to compute the minimum average amount separately for children with disabilities in its elementary schools and for children with disabilities in its secondary schools. LEAs may not compute the minimum average amount it must spend on the education of children with disabilities based on a combination of the enrollments in its elementary schools and secondary schools.

The following example shows how to compute the minimum average amount an LEA must spend for the education of each of its elementary school children with disabilities under section 602(3) of the Act before it may use funds under Part B of the Act.

a. First the LEA must determine the total amount of its expenditures for elementary school students from all sources—local, State, and Federal (including Part B)—in the preceding school year. Only capital outlay and debt services are excluded.

Example: The following is an example of a computation for children with disabilities enrolled in an LEA's elementary schools. In this example, the LEA had an average elementary school enrollment for the preceding school year of 800 (including 100 children with disabilities). The LEA spent the following amounts last year for elementary school students (including its elementary school children with disabilities):

(1)	From State and local tax funds.	$6,500,000
(2)	From Federal funds	600,000
	Total expenditures	7,100,000

Of this total, $60,000 was for capital outlay and debt service relating to the education of elementary school students. This must be subtracted from total expenditures.

(1)	Total Expenditures	$7,100,000
(2)	Less capital outlay and debt.	−60,000
	Total expenditures for elementary school students less capital outlay and debt.	$7,040,000

b. Next, the LEA must subtract from the total expenditures amounts spent for:

(1) IDEA, Part B allocation,

(2) ESEA, Title I, Part A allocation,

(3) ESEA, Title III, Parts A and B allocation,

(4) State and local funds for children with disabilities, and

(5) State or local funds for programs under ESEA, Title I, Part A, and Title III, Parts A and B.

These are funds that the LEA actually spent, not funds received last year but carried over for the current school year.

Example: The LEA spent the following amounts for elementary school students last year:

(1)	From funds under IDEA, Part B allocation.	$ 200,000
(2)	From funds under ESEA, Title I, Part A allocation.	250,000

(3)	From funds under ESEA, Title III, Parts A and B allocation.	50,000
(4)	From State funds and local funds for children with disabilities.	500,000
(5)	From State and local funds for programs under ESEA, Title I, Part A, and Title III, Parts A and B.	150,000
	Total	1,150,000
(1)	Total expenditures less capital outlay and debt.	7,040,000
(2)	Other deductions	−1,150,000
	Total	$5,890,000

c. Except as otherwise provided, the LEA next must determine the average annual per student expenditure for its elementary schools dividing the average number of students enrolled in the elementary schools of the agency during the preceding year (including its children with disabilities) into the amount computed under the above paragraph. The amount obtained through this computation is the minimum amount the LEA must spend (on the average) for the education of each of its elementary school children with disabilities. Funds under Part B of the Act may be used only for costs over and above this minimum.

(1)	Amount from Step b	$5,890,000
(2)	Average number of students enrolled.	800
(3)	$5,890,000/800 Average annual per student expenditure.	$ 7,362

d. Except as otherwise provided, to determine the total minimum amount of funds the LEA must spend for the education of its elementary school children with disabilities in the LEA (not including capital outlay and debt service), the LEA must multiply the number of elementary school children with disabilities in the LEA times the average annual per student expenditure obtained in paragraph c above. Funds under Part B of the Act can only be used for excess costs over and above this minimum.

(1)	Number of children with disabilities in the LEA's elementary schools.	100
(2)	Average annual per student expenditure.	$ 7,362
(3)	$7,362 × 100.	

| Total minimum amount of funds the LEA must spend for the education of children with disabilities enrolled in the LEA's elementary schools before using Part B funds. | $ 736,200 |

APPENDIX B TO PART 300—
PROPORTIONATE SHARE CALCULATION

Each LEA must expend, during the grant period, on the provision of special education and related services for the parentally-placed private school children with disabilities enrolled in private elementary schools and secondary schools located in the LEA an amount that is equal to—

(1) A proportionate share of the LEA's subgrant under section 611(f) of the Act for children with disabilities aged 3 through 21. This is an amount that is the same proportion of the LEA's total subgrant under section 611(f) of the Act as the number of parentally-placed private school children with disabilities aged 3 through 21 enrolled in private elementary schools and secondary schools located in the LEA is to the total number of children with disabilities enrolled in public and private elementary schools and secondary schools located in the LEA aged 3 through 21; and

(2) A proportionate share of the LEA's subgrant under section 619(g) of the Act for children with disabilities aged 3 through 5. This is an amount that is the same proportion of the LEA's total subgrant under section 619(g) of the Act as the total number of parentally-placed private school children with disabilities aged 3 through 5 enrolled in private elementary schools located in the LEA is to the total number of children with disabilities enrolled in public and private elementary schools located in the LEA aged 3 through 5.

Consistent with section 612(a)(10)(A)(i) of the Act and §300.133 of these regulations, annual expenditures for parentally-placed private school children with disabilities are calculated based on the total number of children with disabilities enrolled in public and private elementary schools and secondary schools located in the LEA eligible to receive special education and related services under Part B, as compared with the total number of eligible parentally-placed private school children with disabilities enrolled in private elementary schools located in the LEA. This ratio is used to determine the proportion of the LEA's total Part B subgrants under section 611(f) of the Act for children aged 3 through 21, and under section 619(g) of the Act for children aged 3 through 5, that is to be expended on services for parentally-placed private school children with disabilities enrolled in private elementary schools and secondary schools located in the LEA.

The following is an example of how the proportionate share is calculated:

There are 300 eligible children with disabilities enrolled in the Flintstone School District and 20 eligible parentally-placed private school children with disabilities enrolled in private elementary schools and secondary schools located in the LEA for a total of 320 eligible public and private school children with disabilities (note: proportionate share for parentally-placed private school children is based on total children eligible, not children served). The number of eligible parentally-placed private school children with disabilities (20) divided by the total number of eligible public and private school children with disabilities (320) indicates that 6.25 percent of the LEA's subgrant must be spent for the group of eligible parentally-placed children with disabilities enrolled in private elementary schools and secondary schools located in the LEA. Flintstone School District receives $152,500 in Federal flow through funds. Therefore, the LEA must spend $9,531.25 on special education or related services to the group of parentally-placed private school children with disabilities enrolled in private elementary schools and secondary schools located in the LEA. (Note: The LEA must calculate the proportionate share of IDEA funds before earmarking funds for any early intervening activities in §300.226).

The following outlines the calculations for the example of how the proportionate share is calculated.

Proportionate Share Calculation for Parentally-Placed Private School Children with Disabilities For Flintstone School District:

Number of eligible children with disabilities in public schools in the LEA	300
Number of parentally-placed eligible children with disabilities in private elementary schools and secondary schools located in the LEA	20
Total number of eligible children	320

FEDERAL FLOW-THROUGH FUNDS TO FLINTSTONE SCHOOL DISTRICT

Total allocation to Flintstone	$152,500

Calculating Proportionate Share:

Total allocation to Flinstone	152,500
Divided by total number of eligible children	320
Average allocation per eligible child	476.5625
Multiplied by the number of parentally-placed children with disabilities	20
Amount to be expended for parentally-placed children with disabilities	9,531.25

APPENDIX C TO PART 300—NATIONAL INSTRUCTIONAL MATERIALS ACCESSIBILITY STANDARD (NIMAS)

Under sections 612(a)(23)(A) and 674(e)(4) of the Individuals with Disabilities Education Act, as amended by the Individuals with Disabilities Education Improvement Act of 2004, the Secretary of Education establishes the NIMAS. Under section 674(e)(4) of the Act, the NIMAS applies to print instructional materials published after July 19, 2006. The purpose of the NIMAS is to help increase the availability and timely delivery of print instructional materials in accessible formats to blind or other persons with print disabilities in elementary and secondary schools.

TECHNICAL SPECIFICATIONS—THE BASELINE ELEMENT SET

The Baseline Element Set details the minimum requirement that must be delivered to fulfill the NIMAS. It is the responsibility of publishers to provide this NIMAS-conformant XML content file, a package file (OPF), a PDF-format copy of the title page (or whichever page(s) contain(s) ISBN and copyright information), and a full set of the content's images. All of the images included within a work must be provided in a folder and placeholders entered in the relevant XML document indicating their location (all images must be included). The preferred image type is SVG, next is either PNG or JPG format. Images should be rendered in the same size/proportion as their originals at 300 dpi. Images should be named with relative path filenames in XML files (example: img id="staricon4" src="./images/U10C02/staricon4.jpg" alt="star icon").

NIMAS-conformant content must be valid to the NIMAS 1.1 [see ANSI/NISO Z39.86 2005 or subsequent revisions]. In addition, files are required to use the tags from the Baseline Element Set when such tags are appropriate. Publishers are encouraged to augment the required Baseline Element Set with tags from the Optional Element Set (elements not included in the Standard) as applicable. For the purposes of NIMAS, appropriate usage of elements, both baseline and optional, is defined by the DAISY Structure Guidelines. Files that do not follow these guidelines in the selection and application of tags are not conformant to this Standard. Both optional elements and appropriate structure guidelines may be located within Z39.86–2002 and Z39.86–2005 available from *http://www.daisy.org/z3986/*. Use of the most current standard is recommended.

THE BASELINE ELEMENT SET

Element	Description
a. Document-level tags	
dtbook	The root element in the Digital Talking Book DTD. <dtbook>contains metadata in <head>and the contents itself in <book>.
head	Contains metainformation about the book but no actual content of the book itself, which is placed in <book>.
book	Surrounds the actual content of the document, which is divided into <frontmatter>, <bodymatter>, and <rearmatter>. <head>, which contains metadata, precedes <book>.
meta	Indicates metadata about the book. It is an empty element that may appear repeatedly only in <head>.
	For the most current usage guidelines, please refer to *http://www.daisy.org/z3986/*
b. Structure and Hierarchy	
frontmatter	Usually contains <doctitle>and <docauthor>, as well as preliminary material that is often enclosed in appropriate <level>or <level1>etc. Content may include a copyright notice, a foreword, an acknowledgements section, a table of contents, etc. <frontmatter>serves as a guide to the content and nature of a <book>.
bodymatter	Consists of the text proper of a book, as contrasted with preliminary material <frontmatter>or supplementary information in <rearmatter>.
rearmatter	Contains supplementary material such as appendices, glossaries, bibliographies, and indices. It follows the <bodymatter>of the book.
level1	The highest-level container of major divisions of a book. Used in <frontmatter>, <bodymatter>, and <rearmatter>to mark the largest divisions of the book (usually parts or chapters), inside which <level2>subdivisions (often sections) may nest. The class attribute identifies the actual name (e.g., part, chapter) of the structure it marks. Contrast with <level>.
level2	Contains subdivisions that nest within <level1>divisions. The class attribute identifies the actual name (e.g., subpart, chapter, subsection) of the structure it marks.
level3	Contains sub-subdivisions that nest within <level2>subdivisions (e.g., sub-subsections within subsections). The class attribute identifies the actual name (e.g., section, subpart, subsubsection) of the subordinate structure it marks.
level4	Contains further subdivisions that nest within <level3>subdivisions. The class attribute identifies the actual name of the subordinate structure it marks.
level5	Contains further subdivisions that nest within <level4>subdivisions. The class attribute identifies the actual name of the subordinate structure it marks.
level6	Contains further subdivisions that nest within <level5>subdivisions. The class attribute identifies the actual name of the subordinate structure it marks.
h1	Contains the text of the heading for a <level1>structure.
h2	Contains the text of the heading for a <level2>structure.
h3	Contains the text of the heading for a <level3>structure.
h4	Contains the text of the heading for a <level4>structure.
h5	Contains the text of the heading for a <level5>structure.
h6	Contains the text of the heading for a <level6>structure.
	For the most current usage guidelines, please refer to *http://www.daisy.org/z3986/*
c. Block elements	
author	Identifies the writer of a work other than this one. Contrast with <docauthor>, which identifies the author of this work. <author>typically occurs within <blockquote>and <cite>.
blockquote	Indicates a block of quoted content that is set off from the surrounding text by paragraph breaks. Compare with <q>, which marks short, inline quotations.
list	Contains some form of list, ordered or unordered. The list may have an intermixed heading <hd>(generally only one, possibly with <prodnote>), and an intermixture of list items <li>and <pagenum>. If bullets and outline enumerations are part of the print content, they are expected to prefix those list items in content, rather than be implicitly generated.
li	Marks each list item in a <list>. <li>content may be either inline or block and may include other nested lists. Alternatively it may contain a sequence of list item components, <lic>, that identify regularly occurring content, such as the heading and page number of each entry in a table of contents.
hd	Marks the text of a heading in a <list>or <sidebar>.
note	Marks a footnote, endnote, etc. Any local reference to <note id="yyy">is by <noteref idref="#yyy"">. [Attribute id]
p	Contains a paragraph, which may contain subsidiary <list>or <dl>.
sidebar	Contains information supplementary to the main text and/or narrative flow and is often boxed and printed apart from the main text block on a page. It may have a heading <hd>.
cite	Marks a reference (or citation) to another document.

THE BASELINE ELEMENT SET—Continued

Element	Description
dd	Marks a definition of the preceding term <dt>within a definition list <dl>. A definition without a preceding <dt>has no semantic interpretation, but is visually presented aligned with other <dd>.
dl	Contains a definition list, usually consisting of pairs of terms <dt>and definitions <dd>. Any definition can contain another definition list.
dt	Marks a term in a definition list <dl>for which a definition <dd>follows.
	For the most current usage guidelines, please refer to *http://www.daisy.org/z3986/*

d. Inline Elements

Element	Description
em	Indicates emphasis. Usually is rendered in italics. Compare with .
q	Contains a short, inline quotation. Compare with <blockquote>, which marks a longer quotation set off from the surrounding text.
strong	Marks stronger emphasis than . Visually is usually rendered bold.
sub	Indicates a subscript character (printed below a character's normal baseline). Can be used recursively and/or intermixed with <sup>.
sup	Marks a superscript character (printed above a character's normal baseline). Can be used recursively and/or intermixed with <sub>.
br	Marks a forced line break.
line	Marks a single logical line of text. Often used in conjunction with <linenum>in documents with numbered lines. [Use only when line breaks must be preserved to capture meaning (e.g., poems, legal texts).]
linenum	Contains a line number, for example in legal text. [Use only when <line>is used, and only for lines numbered in print book.]
pagenum	Contains one page number as it appears from the print document, usually inserted at the point within the file immediately preceding the first item of content on a new page. [NB: Only valid when it includes an id attribute].
noteref	Marks one or more characters that reference a footnote or endnote <note>. Contrast with <annoref>. <noteref>and <note>are independently skippable.
	For the most current usage guidelines, please refer to *http://www.daisy.org/z3986/*

e. Tables

Element	Description
table	Contains cells of tabular data arranged in rows and columns. A <table>may have a <caption>. It may have descriptions of the columns in <col>s or groupings of several <col>in <colgroup>. A simple <table>may be made up of just rows <tr>. A long table crossing several pages of the print book should have separate <pagenum>values for each of the pages containing that <table>indicated on the page where it starts. Note the logical order of optional <thead>, optional <tfoot>, then one or more of either <tbody>or just rows <tr>. This order accommodates simple or large, complex tables. The <thead>and <tfoot>information usually helps identify content of the <tbody>rows. For a multiple-page print <table>the <thead>and <tfoot>are repeated on each page, but not redundantly tagged.
td	Indicates a table cell containing data.
tr	Marks one row of a <table>containing <th>or <td>cells.
	For the most current usage guidelines, please refer to *http://www.daisy.org/z3986/*

f. Images

Element	Description
imggroup	Provides a container for one or more and associated <caption>(s) and <prodnote>(s). A <prodnote>may contain a description of the image. The content model allows: 1) multiple if they share a caption, with the ids of each in the <caption imgref="id1 id2 ...">, 2) multiple <caption>if several captions refer to a single where each caption has the same <caption imgref="xxx">, 3) multiple <prodnote>if different versions are needed for different media (e.g., large print, braille, or print). If several <prodnote>refer to a single , each prodnote has the same <prodnote imgref="xxx">.
img	Points to the image to be rendered. An may stand alone or be grouped using <imggroup>. Note that providing extracted images is not a requirement of the NIMAS. If they are included, it is best to refer to them using within the <imggroup>container.
caption	Describes a <table>or . If used with <table>it must follow immediately after the <table>start tag. If used with <imggroup>it is not so constrained.
	For the most current usage guidelines, please refer to *http://www.daisy.org/z3986/*

1. THE OPTIONAL ELEMENTS AND GUIDELINES FOR USE

Publishers are encouraged to apply markup beyond the baseline (required) elements. The complete DTBook Element Set reflects the tags necessary to create the six types of Digital Talking Books and Braille output.

Because of the present necessity to subdivide the creation of alternate format materials into distinct phases, the Panel determined that baseline elements would be provided by publishers, and optional elements would be added to the NIMAS-conformant files by third party conversion entities. In both circumstances the protocols for tagging digital files should conform to the most current ANSI/NISO Z39.86 specification. Content converters are directed to the most current DAISY Structure Guidelines (*http://www.daisy.org/z3986/*) for guidance on their use.

Since the publication of the original National File Format report from which the NIMAS technical specifications were derived, ANSI/NISO Z39.86–2002 was updated and is now ANSI/NISO Z39.86–2005. It may be best to avoid using the following optional elements which are no longer included in ANSI/NISO Z39.86–2005: style, notice, hr, and levelhd.

Also, the following new elements were introduced by ANSI/NISO Z39.86–2005 and should be considered optional elements for the NIMAS: bridgehead, byline, covertitle, dateline, epigraph, linegroup, and poem. Please refer to ANSI/NISO Z39.86–2005 for additional information regarding these elements. To access the ANSI/NISO Z39.86–2005 specification, go to *http://www.daisy.org/z3986/*.

2. PACKAGE FILE

A package file describes a publication. It identifies all other files in the publication and provides descriptive and access information about them. A publication must include a package file conforming to the NIMAS. The package file is based on the Open eBook Publication Structure 1.2 package file specification (For most recent detail please see *http://www.openebook.org/oebps/oebps1.2/download/oeb12-xhtml.htm#sec2*). A NIMAS package file must be an XML-valid OeB PS 1.2 package file instance and must meet the following additional standards:

The NIMAS Package File must include the following Dublin Core (dc:)metadata:

dc:Title.

dc:Creator (if applicable).

dc:Publisher.

dc:Date (Date of NIMAS-compliant file creation—yyyy-mm-dd).

dc:Format (=''NIMAS 1.0'').

dc:Identifier (a unique identifier for the NIMAS-compliant digital publication, e.g., print ISBN + ''-NIMAS''—exact format to be determined).

dc:Language (one instance, or multiple in the case of a foreign language textbook, etc.).

dc:Rights (details to be determined).

dc:Source (ISBN of print version of textbook).

And the following x-metadata items:

nimas-SourceEdition (the edition of the print textbook).

nimas-SourceDate (date of publication of the print textbook).

The following metadata were proposed also as a means of facilitating recordkeeping, storage and file retrieval:

dc:Subject (Lang Arts, Soc Studies, etc.).

nimas-grade (specific grade level of the print textbook, *e.g.*; Grade 6).

nimas gradeRange (specific grade range of the print textbook, *e.g.*; Grades 4–5).

An additional suggestion references the use of:

dc:audience:educationLevel (for the grade and gradeRange identifiers, noting that Dublin Core recommends using educationLevel with an appropriate controlled vocabulary for context, and recommends the U.S. Department of Education's Level of Education vocabulary online at *http://www.ed.gov/admin/reference/index.jsp*. Using educationLevel obviates the need for a separate field for gradeRange since dc elements can repeat more than once. A book used in more than one grade would therefore have two elements, one with value ''Grade 4'' and another with value ''Grade 5.''

A final determination as to which of these specific metadata elements to use needs to be clarified in practice. The package manifest must list all provided files (text, images, etc.).

(NOTE: For purposes of continuity and to minimize errors in transformation and processing, the NIMAS-compliant digital text should be provided as a single document.)

3. MODULAR EXTENSIONS

The most current DAISY/NISO standard, formally the *ANSI/NISO Z39.86, Specifications for the Digital Talking Book* defines a comprehensive system for creating Digital Talking Books. A part of this standard is DTBook, an XML vocabulary that provides a core set of elements needed to produce most types of books. However, DTBook is not intended to be an exhaustive vocabulary for all types of books.

Guidelines for the correct approach to extend the DAISY/NISO standard have been established. Mathematics, video support, testing, workbooks, music, dictionaries, chemistry, and searching are some of the extensions that have been discussed. Visit *http://www.daisy.org/z3986/* to learn more about modular extensions.

End

APPENDIX D TO PART 300—MAINTENANCE OF EFFORT AND EARLY INTERVENING SERVICES

LEAs that seek to reduce their local maintenance of effort in accordance with § 300.205(d) and use some of their Part B funds for early intervening services under § 300.226 must do so with caution because the local maintenance of effort reduction provision and the authority to use Part B funds for early intervening services are inter-connected. The decisions that an LEA makes about the amount of funds that it uses for one purpose affect the amount that it may use for the other. Below are examples that illustrate how §§ 300.205(d) and 300.226(a) affect one another.

Example 1: In this example, the amount that is 15 percent of the LEA's total grant (see § 300.226(a)), which is the maximum amount that the LEA may use for early intervening services (EIS), is greater than the amount that may be used for local maintenance of effort (MOE) reduction (50 percent of the increase in the LEA's grant from the prior year's grant) (see § 300.205(a)).

Prior Year's Allocation	$900,000.
Current Year's Allocation	1,000,000.
Increase	100,000.
Maximum Available for MOE Reduction	50,000.
Maximum Available for EIS	150,000.

If the LEA chooses to set aside $150,000 for EIS, it may not reduce its MOE (MOE maximum $50,000 less $150,000 for EIS means $0 can be used for MOE).

If the LEA chooses to set aside $100,000 for EIS, it may not reduce its MOE (MOE maximum $50,000 less $100,000 for EIS means $0 can be used for MOE).

If the LEA chooses to set aside $50,000 for EIS, it may not reduce its MOE (MOE maximum $50,000 less $50,000 for EIS means $0 can be used for MOE).

If the LEA chooses to set aside $30,000 for EIS, it may reduce its MOE by $20,000 (MOE maximum $50,000 less $30,000 for EIS means $20,000 can be used for MOE).

If the LEA chooses to set aside $0 for EIS, it may reduce its MOE by $50,000 (MOE maximum $50,000 less $0 for EIS means $50,000 can be used for MOE).

Example 2: In this example, the amount that is 15 percent of the LEA's total grant (see § 300.226(a)), which is the maximum amount that the LEA may use for EIS, is less than the amount that may be used for MOE reduction (50 percent of the increase in

the LEA's grant from the prior year's grant) (see § 300.205(a)).

Prior Year's Allocation	$1,000,000.
Current Year's Allocation	2,000,000.
Increase	1,000,000.
Maximum Available for MOE Reduction	500,000.
Maximum Available for EIS	300,000.

If the LEA chooses to use no funds for MOE, it may set aside $300,000 for EIS (EIS maximum $300,000 less $0 means $300,000 for EIS).

If the LEA chooses to use $100,000 for MOE, it may set aside $200,000 for EIS (EIS maximum $300,000 less $100,000 means $200,000 for EIS).

If the LEA chooses to use $150,000 for MOE, it may set aside $150,000 for EIS (EIS maximum $300,000 less $150,000 means $150,000 for EIS).

If the LEA chooses to use $300,000 for MOE, it may not set aside anything for EIS (EIS maximum $300,000 less $300,000 means $0 for EIS).

If the LEA chooses to use $500,000 for MOE, it may not set aside anything for EIS (EIS maximum $300,000 less $500,000 means $0 for EIS).

APPENDIX E TO PART 300—LOCAL EDU-CATIONAL AGENCY MAINTENANCE OF EFFORT CALCULATION EXAMPLES

The following tables provide examples of calculating LEA MOE. Figures are in $10,000s. All references to a "fiscal year" in these tables refer to the fiscal year covering that school year, unless otherwise noted.

Tables 1 through 4 provide examples of how an LEA complies with the Subsequent Years rule. In Table 1, for example, an LEA spent $1 million in Fiscal Year (FY) 2012–2013 on the education of children with disabilities. In the following year, the LEA was required to spend at least $1 million but spent only $900,000. In FY 2014–2015, therefore, the LEA was required to spend $1 million, the amount it was required to spend in FY 2013–2014, not the $900,000 it actually spent.

TABLE 1—EXAMPLE OF LEVEL OF EFFORT REQUIRED TO MEET MOE COMPLIANCE STANDARD IN YEAR FOLLOWING A YEAR IN WHICH LEA FAILED TO MEET MOE COMPLIANCE STANDARD

Fiscal year	Actual level of effort	Required level of effort	Notes
2012–2013	$100	$100	LEA met MOE.
2013–2014	90	100	LEA did not meet MOE.
2014–2015		100	Required level of effort is $100 despite LEA's failure in 2013–2014.

Table 2 shows how to calculate the required amount of effort when there are con-secutive fiscal years in which an LEA does not meet MOE.

TABLE 2—EXAMPLE OF LEVEL OF EFFORT REQUIRED TO MEET MOE COMPLIANCE STANDARD IN YEAR FOLLOWING CONSECUTIVE YEARS IN WHICH LEA FAILED TO MEET MOE COMPLIANCE STANDARD

Fiscal year	Actual level of effort	Required level of effort	Notes
2012–2013	$100	$100	LEA met MOE.
2013–2014	90	100	LEA did not meet MOE.
2014–2015	90	100	LEA did not meet MOE. Required level of effort is $100 despite LEA's failure in 2013–2014.
2015–2016		100	Required level of effort is $100 despite LEA's failure in 2013–2014 and 2014–2015.

Table 3 shows how to calculate the required level of effort in a fiscal year after the year in which an LEA spent more than the required amount on the education of children with disabilities. This LEA spent $1.1 million in FY 2015–2016 though only $1 million was required. The required level of effort in FY 2016–2017, therefore, is $1.1 million.

TABLE 3—EXAMPLE OF LEVEL OF EFFORT REQUIRED TO MEET MOE COMPLIANCE STANDARD IN YEAR FOLLOWING YEAR IN WHICH LEA MET MOE COMPLIANCE STANDARD

Fiscal year	Actual level of effort	Required level of effort	Notes
2012–2013	$100	$100	LEA met MOE.
2013–2014	90	100	LEA did not meet MOE.
2014–2015	90	100	LEA did not meet MOE. Required level of effort is $100 despite LEA's failure in 2013–2014.
2015–2016	110	100	LEA met MOE.
2016–2017		110	Required level of effort is $110 because LEA expended $110, and met MOE, in 2015–2016.

Table 4 shows the same calculation when, in an intervening fiscal year, 2016–2017, the LEA did not maintain effort.

TABLE 4—EXAMPLE OF LEVEL OF EFFORT REQUIRED TO MEET MOE COMPLIANCE STANDARD IN YEAR FOLLOWING YEAR IN WHICH LEA DID NOT MEET MOE COMPLIANCE STANDARD

Fiscal year	Actual level of effort	Required level of effort	Notes
2012–2013	$100	$100	LEA met MOE.
2013–2014	90	100	LEA did not meet MOE.
2014–2015	90	100	LEA did not meet MOE. Required level of effort is $100 despite LEA's failure in 2013–2014.
2015–2016	110	100	LEA met MOE.
2016–2017	100	110	LEA did not meet MOE. Required level of effort is $110 because LEA expended $110, and met MOE, in 2015–2016.
2017–2018		110	Required level of effort is $110, despite LEA's failure in 2016–2017.

Table 5 provides an example of how an LEA may meet the compliance standard using alternate methods from year to year without using the exceptions or adjustment in §§ 300.204 and 300.205, and provides information on the following scenario. In FY 2015–2016, the LEA meets the compliance standard using all four methods. As a result, in order to demonstrate that it met the compliance standard using any one of the four methods in FY 2016–2017, the LEA must expend at least as much as it did in FY 2015–2016 using that same method. Because the LEA spent the same amount in FY 2016–2017 as it did in FY 2015–2016, calculated using a combination of State and local funds and a combination of State and local funds on a per capita basis, the LEA met the compliance standard using both of those methods in FY 2016–2017. However, the LEA did not meet the compliance standard in FY 2016–2017 using the other two methods—local funds only or local funds only on a per capita basis—because it did not spend at least the same amount in FY 2016–

2017 as it did in FY 2015–2016 using the same methods.

TABLE 5—EXAMPLE OF HOW AN LEA MAY MEET THE COMPLIANCE STANDARD USING ALTERNATE METHODS FROM YEAR TO YEAR

Fiscal year	Local funds only	Combination of State and local funds	Local funds only on a per capita basis	Combination of State and local funds on a per capita basis	Child count
2015–2016	*$500	*$950	*$50	*$95	10
2016–2017	400	*950	40	*95	10
2017–2018	*500	900	*50	90	10

*LEA met compliance standard using this method.

Table 6 provides an example of how an LEA may meet the compliance standard using alternate methods from year to year in years in which the LEA used the exceptions or adjustment in §§ 300.204 and 300.205, including using the per capita methods.

TABLE 6—EXAMPLE OF HOW AN LEA MAY MEET THE COMPLIANCE STANDARD USING ALTERNATE METHODS FROM YEAR TO YEAR AND USING EXCEPTIONS OR ADJUSTMENT UNDER §§ 300.204 AND 300.205

Fiscal year	Local funds only	Combination of State and local funds	Local funds only on a per capita basis	Combination of State and local funds on a per capita basis	Child count
2015–2016	$500*	$950*	$50*	$95*	10
2016–2017	400	950*	40	95*	10
2017–2018	450*	1,000*	45*	100*	10
	In 2017–2018, the LEA was required to spend at least the same amount in local funds only that it spent in the preceding fiscal year, subject to the Subsequent Years rule. Therefore, prior to taking any exceptions or adjustment in §§ 300.204 and 300.205, the LEA was required to spend at least $500 in local funds only. In 2017–2018, the LEA properly reduced its expenditures, per an exception in § 300.204, by $50, and therefore, was required to spend at least $450 in local funds only ($500) from 2015–2016 per Subsequent Years rule − $50 allowable reduction per an exception under § 300.204).		In 2017–2018, the LEA was required to spend at least the same amount in local funds only on a per capita basis that it spent in the preceding fiscal year, subject to the Subsequent Years rule. Therefore, prior to taking any exceptions or adjustment in §§ 300.204 and 300.205, the LEA was required to spend at least $50 in local funds only on a per capita basis. In 2017–2018, the LEA properly reduced its aggregate expenditures, per an exception in § 300.204, by $50. $50/10 children with disabilities in the comparison year (2015–2016) = $5 per capita allowable reduction per an exception under § 300.204. $50 local funds only on a per capita basis (from 2015–2016 per Subsequent Years rule) − $5 allowable reduction per an exception under § 300.204 = $45 local funds only on a per capita basis to meet MOE.		
2018–2019	405	1,000*	45*	111.11*	9

TABLE 6—EXAMPLE OF HOW AN LEA MAY MEET THE COMPLIANCE STANDARD USING ALTERNATE METHODS FROM YEAR TO YEAR AND USING EXCEPTIONS OR ADJUSTMENT UNDER §§ 300.204 AND 300.205—Continued

Fiscal year	Local funds only	Combination of State and local funds	Local funds only on a per capita basis	Combination of State and local funds on a per capita basis	Child count
	In 2018–2019, the LEA was required to spend at least the same amount in local funds only that it spent in the preceding fiscal year, subject to the Subsequent Years rule. Therefore, prior to taking any exceptions or adjustment in §§ 300.204 and 300.205, the LEA was required to spend at least $450 in local funds only. In 2018–2019, the LEA properly reduced its expenditures, per an exception in § 300.204 by $10 and the adjustment in § 300.205 by $10. Therefore, the LEA was required to spend at least $430 in local funds only. ($450 from 2017–2018 − $20 allowable reduction per an exception and the adjustment under §§ 300.204 and 300.205).	Because the LEA did not reduce its expenditures from the comparison year (2017–2018) using a combination of State and local funds, the LEA met MOE.	In 2018–2019, the LEA was required to spend at least the same amount in local funds only on a per capita basis that it spent in the preceding fiscal year, subject to the Subsequent Years rule. Therefore, prior to taking any exceptions or adjustment in §§ 300.204 and 300.205, the LEA was required to spend at least $45 in local funds only on a per capita basis. In 2018–2019, the LEA properly reduced its aggregate expenditures, per an exception in § 300.204 by $10 and the adjustment in § 300.205 by $10. $20/10 children with disabilities in the comparison year (2017–2018) = $2 per capita allowable reduction per an exception and the adjustment under §§ 300.204 and 300.205. $45 local funds only on a per capita basis (from 2017–2018) − $2 allowable reduction per an exception and the adjustment under §§ 300.204 and 300.205 = $43 local funds only on a per capita basis required to meet MOE. Actual level of effort is $405/9 (the current year child count).	Because the LEA did not reduce its expenditures from the comparison year (2017–2018) using a combination of State and local funds on a per capita basis ($1,000/9 = $111.11 and $111.11 > $100), the LEA met MOE.	

*LEA met MOE using this method.
Note: When calculating any exception(s) and/or adjustment on a per capita basis for the purpose of determining the required level of effort, the LEA must use the child count from the comparison year, and not the child count of the year in which the LEA took the exception(s) and/or adjustment. When determining the actual level of effort on a per capita basis, the LEA must use the child count for the current year. For example, in 2018–2019, the LEA uses a child count of 9, not the child count of 10 in the comparison year, to determine the actual level of effort.

Tables 7 and 8 demonstrate how an LEA could meet the eligibility standard over a period of years using different methods from year to year. These tables assume that the LEA did not take any of the exceptions or adjustment in §§ 300.204 and 300.205. Numbers are in $10,000s budgeted and spent for the education of children with disabilities.

TABLE 7—EXAMPLE OF HOW AN LEA MAY MEET THE ELIGIBILITY STANDARD IN 2016–2017 USING DIFFERENT METHODS

Fiscal year	Local funds only	Combination of State and local funds	Local funds only on a per capita basis	Combination of State and local funds on a per capita basis	Child count	Notes
2014–2015	* $500	* $1,000	* $50	* $100	10	The LEA met the compliance standard using all 4 methods.*
2015–2016	....	....	....	....	....	Final information not available at time of budgeting for 2016–2017.
How much must the LEA budget for 2016–2017 to meet the eligibility standard in 2016–2017?	500	1,000	50	100	....	When the LEA submits a budget for 2016–2017, the most recent fiscal year for which the LEA has information is 2014–2015. It is not necessary for the LEA to consider information on expenditures for a fiscal year prior to 2014–2015 because the LEA maintained effort in 2014–2015. Therefore, the Subsequent Years rule in § 300.203(c) is not applicable.

*The LEA met the compliance standard using all 4 methods.

TABLE 8—EXAMPLE OF HOW AN LEA MAY MEET THE ELIGIBILITY STANDARD IN 2017–2018 USING DIFFERENT METHODS AND THE APPLICATION OF THE SUBSEQUENT YEARS RULE

Fiscal year	Local funds only	Combination of State and local funds	Local funds only on a per capita basis	Combination of State and local funds on a per capita basis	Child count	Notes
2014–2015	* $500	* $1,000	* $50	* $100	10	
2015–2016	450	* 1,000	45	* 100	10	
2016–2017	....	....	....	....	....	Final information not available at time of budgeting for 2017–2018.
How much must the LEA budget for 2017–2018 to meet the eligibility standard in 2017–2018?	500	1,000	50	100	....	If the LEA seeks to use a combination of State and local funds, or a combination of State and local funds on a per capita basis, to meet the eligibility standard, the LEA does not consider information on expenditures for a fiscal year prior to 2015–2016 because the LEA maintained effort in 2015–2016 using those methods. However, if the LEA seeks to use local funds only, or local funds only on a per capita basis, to meet the eligibility standard, the LEA must use information on expenditures for a fiscal year prior to 2015–2016 because the LEA did not maintain effort in 2015–2016 using either of those methods, per the Subsequent Years rule. That is, the LEA must determine what it should have spent in 2015–2016 using either of those methods, and that is the amount that the LEA must budget in 2017–2018.

*LEA met MOE using this method.

Table 9 provides an example of how an LEA may consider the exceptions and adjustment in §§ 300.204 and 300.205 when budgeting for the expenditures for the education of children with disabilities.

TABLE 9—EXAMPLE OF HOW AN LEA MAY MEET THE ELIGIBILITY STANDARD USING EXCEPTIONS AND ADJUSTMENT IN §§ 300.204 AND 300.205, 2016–2017

Fiscal year	Local funds only	Combination of State and local funds	Local funds only on a per capita basis	Combination of State and local funds on a per capita basis	Child count	Notes
Actual 2014–2015 expenditures.	*$500	*$1,000	*$50	*$100	10	The LEA met the compliance standard using all 4 methods.*
Exceptions and adjustment taken in 2015–2016.	−50	−50	−5	−5	....	LEA uses the child count number from the comparison year (2014–2015).
Exceptions and adjustment the LEA reasonably expects to take in 2016–2017.	−25	−25	−2.50	−2.50	....	LEA uses the child count number from the comparison year (2014–2015).
How much must the LEA budget to meet the eligibility standard in 2016–2017?.	425	925	42.50	92.50	....	When the LEA submits a budget for 2016–2017, the most recent fiscal year for which the LEA has information is 2014–2015. However, if the LEA has information on exceptions and adjustment taken in 2015–2016, the LEA may use that information when budgeting for 2016–2017. The LEA may also use information that it has on any exceptions and adjustment it reasonably expects to take in 2016–2017 when budgeting for that year.

Table 10 provides examples both of how to calculate the amount by which an LEA failed to maintain its level of expenditures and of the amount of non-Federal funds that an SEA must return to the Department on account of that failure.

TABLE 10—EXAMPLE OF HOW TO CALCULATE THE AMOUNT OF AN LEA'S FAILURE TO MEET THE COMPLIANCE STANDARD IN 2016–2017 AND THE AMOUNT THAT AN SEA MUST RETURN TO THE DEPARTMENT

Fiscal year	Local funds only	Combination of State and local funds	Local funds only on a per capita basis	Combination of State and local funds on a per capita basis	Child count	Amount of IDEA Part B subgrant
2015–2016	*$500	*$950	$50*	$95*	....	Not relevant.
2016–2017	400	750	40	75	10	$50
Amount by which an LEA failed to maintain its level of expenditures in 2016–2017.	100	200	100 (the amount of the failure equals the amount of the per capita shortfall ($10) times the number of children with disabilities in 2016–2017 (10)).	200 (the amount of the failure equals the amount of the per capita shortfall ($20) times the number of children with disabilities in 2016–2017 (10)).	....	

The SEA determines that the amount of the LEA's failure is $100 using the calculation method that results in the lowest amount of a failure. The SEA's liability is the lesser of the four calculated shortfalls and the amount of the LEA's Part B subgrant in the fiscal year in which the LEA failed to meet the compliance standard. In this case, the SEA must return $50 to the Department because the LEA's IDEA Part B subgrant was $50, and that is the lower amount.

*LEA met MOE using this method.

[80 FR 23667, Apr. 28, 2015]

APPENDIX F TO PART 300—INDEX FOR IDEA—PART B REGULATIONS (34 CFR PART 300)

134

- Discipline (See "Timelines—Discipline")
- School day (Definition) .... 300.11(c).
- See "Timelines".

DECREASE IN ENROLLMENT (Exception to LEA 300.204(b). maintenance of effort).

DECREASE IN FUNDS (To States) .... 300.703(d).

DEDUCTIBLE OR CO-PAY (Public benefits or insur- 300.154(d)(2)(ii). ance).

DEFINITIONS (A–D)
- Act .... 300.4.
- Assistive technology device .... 300.5.
- Assistive technology service .... 300.6.
- At no cost .... 300.39(b)(1).
- Audiology .... 300.34(c)(1).
- Autism .... 300.8(c)(1).
- Average per-pupil expenditure in public elementary 300.717(d). and secondary schools in the United States.
- Business day .... 300.11(b).
- Charter school .... 300.7.
- Child with a disability .... 300.8(a)(1).
- Consent .... 300.9.
- Controlled substance .... 300.530(i)(1).
- Core academic subjects .... 300.10.
- Counseling services .... 300.34(c)(2).
- Day; business day; school day .... 300.11.
- Deaf-blindness .... 300.8(c)(2).
- Deafness .... 300.8(c)(3).
- Destruction (Of information) .... 300.611(a).
- Developmental delays(s) .... 300.8(b).

DEFINITIONS (E–H)
- Early identification and assessment .... 300.34(c)(3).
- Education records .... 300.611(b).
- Educational service agency .... 300.12.
- Elementary school .... 300.13.
- Emotional disturbance .... 300.8(c)(4).
- Equipment .... 300.14.
- Evaluation .... 300.15.
- Excess costs .... 300.16.
- Extended school year services .... 300.106(b).
- Free appropriate public education .... 300.17.
- Freely associated States .... 300.717(a).
- Hearing impairment .... 300.8(c)(5).
- Highly qualified special education teacher .... 300.18(b).
- Homeless children .... 300.19.

DEFINITIONS (I)
- IEP Team .... 300.23.
- Illegal drug .... 300.530(i)(2).
- Include .... 300.20.
- Independent educational evaluation .... 300.502(a)(3)(i).
- Indian .... 300.21(a).
- Indian tribe .... 300.21(b).
- Individualized education program (IEP) .... 300.22.
- Individualized family service plan .... 300.24.
- Infant or toddler with a disability .... 300.25.
- Institution of higher education .... 300.26.
- Intellectual Disability .... 300.8(c)(6).
- Interpreting services .... 300.34(c)(4).

DEFINITIONS (J–O)

IEE (See "Independent educational evaluation")

IEP (A–I)
- Agency responsibilities for transition services .... 300.324(c)(1).
- Basic requirements (see §§ 300.320 through 300.324).
- Child participation when considering transition .... 300.321(b)(1).
- Consideration of special factors .... 300.324(a)(2).
- Consolidation of IEP Team meetings .... 300.324(a)(5).
- Content of IEPs .... 300.320(a).
- Definition (see §§ 300.22, 300.320).
- Development, review, and revision of .... 300.324.
- IEP or IFSP for children aged 3 through 5 .... 300.323(b).
- IEP Team .... 300.321.

IEP (J–Z)
- Modifications of IEP or placement (FAPE for children in adult prisons). 300.324(d)(2)(i).
- Modify/Amend without convening meeting (see § 300.324(a)(4), (a)(6)).
- Parent participation .... 300.322.
- Alternative means .... 300.328.
- Part C coordinator involvement .... 300.321(f).
- Private school placements by public agencies .... 300.325(a)(1).
- Regular education teacher (See "IEP Team").
- Review and revision of IEPs .... 300.324(b).
- SEA responsibility regarding private school .... 300.325(c).
- State eligibility requirement .... 300.112.
- Transition services .... 300.320(b).
- When IEPs must be in effect .... 300.323.

IEP TEAM .... 300.321.
- Alternative educational setting (Determined by) .... 300.531.
- Consideration of special factors .... 300.324(a)(2).
  - O Assistive technology .... 300.324(a)(2)(v).
  - O Behavioral interventions .... 300.324(a)(2)(i).
  - O Braille needs .... 300.324(a)(2)(iii).
  - O Communication needs (Deafness and other needs). 300.324(a)(2)(iv).
  - O Limited English proficiency .... 300.324(a)(2)(ii).
- Determination of knowledge or special expertise .... 300.321(c).
- Discipline procedures (see §§ 300.530(e), 300.531).
- Manifestation determination .... 300.530(e).
- Other individuals who have knowledge or special expertise (At parent or agency discretion). 300.321(a)(6).
- Participation by private school (public agency placement). 300.325(a).
- Regular education teacher (see §§ 300.321(a)(2), 300.324(a)(3)).

IFSP (INDIVIDUALIZED FAMILY SERVICE PLAN)
- Definition .... 300.24.
- Transition from Part C .... 300.124.
- IFSP vs. IEP .... 300.323(b).

ILLEGAL DRUG (Definition—discipline) .... 300.530(i)(2).

IMPARTIAL DUE PROCESS HEARING .... 300.511.
- See "Due process hearings and reviews".

IMPARTIAL HEARING OFFICER .... 300.511(c).

IMPARTIALITY OF MEDIATOR .... 300.506(b)(1).

INCIDENTAL BENEFITS (Permissive use of funds) .... 300.208.

INCIDENTAL FEES (In definition of "at no cost" under "Special education"). 300.39(b)(1).

150

REEVALUATION
- Frequency of occurrence .... 300.303(b).
- Parental consent required before conducting .... 300.300(c)(1).
    - O If parent fails to consent .... 300.300(c)(1)(ii).
- Parental consent not required for:
    - O Administering a test that all children take .... 300.300(d)(1)(ii).
    - O Reviewing existing data .... 300.300(d)(1)(i).
- Parent refusal to consent .... 300.300(c)(1)(ii).
- Review of existing evaluation data .... 300.305(a).
- Revision of IEP (To address reevaluation) .... 300.324(b)(1)(ii).

REFERRAL (A–M)
- Discipline:
    - O Referral to and action by law enforcement and judicial authorities.   300.535.
    - O Protections for children not determined eligible.   300.534.
- Enforcement (Referral for) .... 300.604(b)(2)(vi).
- Indian children (Referral for services or further diagnosis).   300.712(d)(2).
- Medical attention (Referral for):
    - O Audiology .... 300.34(c)(1)(ii).
    - O Speech-language pathology services .... 300.34(c)(15)(iii).

REFERRAL (N–Z)
- Nonacademic and extracurricular services (Referral to agencies regarding assistance to individuals with disabilities).   300.107(b).
- Prior notice (If not initial referral for evaluation) ...... 300.503(b)(4).
- Private school placement when FAPE is at issue (Reimbursement when no referral by public agency).   300.148(c).
- Procedural safeguards notice (Upon initial referral for evaluation).   300.504(a)(1).
- Referral to and action by law enforcement and judicial authorities.   300.535.

REGULAR EDUCATION TEACHER
- Access to IEP .... 300.323(d).
- IEP Team member .... 300.321(a)(2).
- Participate in IEP development .... 300.324(a)(3).
    - O Behavioral interventions .... 300.324(a)(3)(i).
    - O Supplementary aids and services .... 300.324(a)(3)(ii).

REGULATIONS
- Applicable regulations (Secretary of the Interior) .... 300.716.
- Applicability of this part to State, local, and private agencies.   300.2.

REHABILITATION
- Assistive technology service (see § 300.6(d), (f))
- Rehabilitation Act of 1973 (see §§ 300.34(c)(12), 300.516(e))
- Rehabilitation counseling services:
    - O Definition .... 300.34(c)(12).
    - O In vocational rehabilitation (VR) programs .... 300.34(c)(12).
- Transition services (State VR agency responsibility) .. 300.324(c)(2).

REHABILITATION COUNSELING SERVICES .... 300.34(c)(12).

REIMBURSEMENT
- Methods of ensuring services (see § 300.154(a)(3), (b)(1)(ii), (b)(2), (g)(2))
- Private school placement when FAPE is at issue:
    - O Limitation on reimbursement .... 300.148(d).
    - O Reimbursement for private school placement   300.148(c).

- Assignment of surrogate parent (Not more than 30 days).   300.519(h).
- Attorneys' fees (10 days prohibition) .... 300.517(c)(2)(i).
- Complaint procedures (State: 60 days) .... 300.152(a).
- Department hearing procedures (30 days) .... 300.179(b)(3).
      O See also §§ 300.181 through 300.184
- Due process hearings and reviews (see §§ 300.510(b)(2), 300.511(e), (f)):
      O Conducted within 20 school days; decision   300.532(c)(2).
        within 10 school days.
      O Decision within 45 days after expiration of 30   300.515(a).
        day period.
      O Disclose evaluations before hearings (5 busi-   300.512(a)(3).
        ness days).

TIMELINES (E–H)
- Hearing procedures (State eligibility: 30 days) .... 300.179(b)(3).
- Hearing rights:
      O Disclosure of evaluations (At least 5 business   300.512(b)(1).
        days before hearing).
      O Prohibit introduction of evidence not dis-   300.512(a)(3).
        closed (At least 5 business days before hearing).
      O Reviews (Decision not later than 30 days) .... 300.515(b).

TIMELINES (I–Z)
- IEP (Initial meeting: 30 days) .... 300.323(c)(1).
- Initial evaluation (60 days) .... 300.301(c)(1).
- Parent notice before private placement (At least 10   300.148(d)(2).
  business days).
- Show cause hearing .... 300.194(g).
- Decision .... 300.195(a)(1).
- State eligibility: Department hearing procedures (see §§ 300.179(b)(3), 300.181(b), 300.182(d), (e), (g), (k), 300.184)
- Timelines and convenience of hearings and reviews .... 300.515.

TIMELINES—DISCIPLINE (A–P)
- Authority of hearing officer (May order change of   300.532(b)(2)(ii).
  placement for not more than 45 school days).
- Authority of school personnel:
      O Change of placement for not more than 45   300.530(g).
        consecutive days for weapons or drugs.
      O Removal of a child for not more than 10   300.530(b).
        school days.
- Change of placement for disciplinary removals:
      O Of more than 10 consecutive school days .... 300.536(a)(1).
      O Because series of removals total more than 10   300.536(a)(2)(i).
        school days.
- Due process hearing request .... 300.507(a)(2).
- Expedited due process hearings:
      O Conducted within 20 days .... 300.532(c)(2).
      O Decision within 10 days .... 300.532(c)(3)(i).
- Hearing officer (Order change of placement for not   300.532(b)(2)(ii).
  more than 45 days).
- Manifestation determination review (Conducted in no   300.530(e).
  more than 10 school days).
- Placement during appeals (Not longer than 45 days) ... 300.532(b)(2)(ii).

TIMELINES—DISCIPLINE (Q–Z)
- Removals for not more than:
      O 10 school days (By school personnel) .... 300.530(b).
      O 45 days (To interim alternative educational   300.532(b)(2)(ii).
        setting).

[71 FR 46753, Aug. 14, 2006, as amended at 72 FR 61307, Oct. 30, 2007. Redesignated at 80 FR 23667, Apr. 28, 2015, as amended at 82 FR 31913, July 11, 2017]

PART 303—EARLY INTERVENTION PROGRAM FOR INFANTS AND TODDLERS WITH DISABILITIES

Subpart A—General

PURPOSE AND APPLICABLE REGULATIONS

Subpart B—State Eligibility for a Grant and Requirements for a Statewide System

GENERAL AUTHORITY AND ELIGIBILITY

APPENDIX A TO PART 303—INDEX FOR IDEA PART C REGULATIONS

AUTHORITY: 20 U.S.C. 1431 through 1444, unless otherwise noted.

SOURCE: 76 FR 60244, Sept. 28, 2011, unless otherwise noted.

Subpart A—General

PURPOSE AND APPLICABLE REGULATIONS

§ 303.1 Purpose of the early intervention program for infants and toddlers with disabilities.

The purpose of this part is to provide financial assistance to States to—

(a) Develop and implement a statewide, comprehensive, coordinated, multidisciplinary, interagency system that provides early intervention services for infants and toddlers with disabilities and their families;

(b) Facilitate the coordination of payment for early intervention services from Federal, State, local, and private sources (including public and private insurance coverage);

(c) Enhance State capacity to provide quality early intervention services and expand and improve existing early intervention services being provided to infants and toddlers with disabilities and their families;

(d) Enhance the capacity of State and local agencies and service providers to identify, evaluate, and meet the needs of all children, including historically underrepresented populations, particularly minority, low-income, inner-city, and rural children, and infants and toddlers in foster care; and

(e) Encourage States to expand opportunities for children under three years of age who would be at risk of having substantial developmental delay if they did not receive early intervention services.

(Authority: 20 U.S.C. 1400(d)(2), 1431(a)(5), 1431(b))

§ 303.2 Eligible recipients of an award and applicability of this part.

(a) *Eligible recipients of an award.* Eligible recipients include the 50 States, the Commonwealth of Puerto Rico, the District of Columbia, the Secretary of the Interior, and the following jurisdictions: Guam, American Samoa, the United States Virgin Islands, and the Commonwealth of the Northern Mariana Islands.

(b) *Applicability of this part.* (1) The provisions of this part apply to—

(i) The State lead agency and any EIS provider that is part of the statewide system of early intervention, regardless of whether that EIS provider receives funds under part C of the Act; and

(ii) All children referred to the part C program, including infants and toddlers with disabilities consistent with the definitions in §§ 303.6 and 303.21, and their families.

(2) The provisions of this part do not apply to any child with a disability receiving a free appropriate public education or FAPE under 34 CFR part 300.

(Authority: 20 U.S.C. 1401(31), 1434, 1435(a)(10)(A))

§ 303.3 Applicable regulations.

(a) The following regulations apply to this part:

(1) The regulations in this part 303.

(2) EDGAR, including 34 CFR parts 76 (except for § 76.103), 77, 79, 81, 82, 84, and 86.

(3) The Uniform Administrative Requirements, Cost Principles, and Audit Requirements for Federal Awards in 2 CFR part 200, as adopted in part 3474, and the OMB Guidelines to Agencies on Governmentwide Debarment and Suspension (Nonprocurement) in 2 CFR part 180, as adopted in 2 CFR part 3485.

(b) In applying the regulations cited in paragraph (a)(2) of this section, any reference to—

(1) *State educational agency* means the lead agency under this part; and

(2) *Education records* or *records* means early intervention records.

(Authority: 20 U.S.C. 1221(b), 1221e–3, 1431–1444)

[76 FR 60244, Sept. 28, 2011, as amended at 79 FR 76097, Dec. 19, 2014

DEFINITIONS USED IN THIS PART

§ 303.4 Act.

Act means the Individuals with Disabilities Education Act, as amended.

(Authority: 20 U.S.C. 1400(a))

§ 303.5 At-risk infant or toddler.

At-risk infant or toddler means an individual under three years of age who would be at risk of experiencing a substantial developmental delay if early intervention services were not provided to the individual. At the State's discretion, *at-risk infant or toddler* may include an infant or toddler who is at risk of experiencing developmental delays because of biological or environmental factors that can be identified (including low birth weight, respiratory distress as a newborn, lack of oxygen, brain hemorrhage, infection, nutritional deprivation, a history of abuse or neglect, and being directly affected by illegal substance abuse or withdrawal symptoms resulting from prenatal drug exposure).

(Authority: 20 U.S.C. 1432(1), 1432(5)(B)(i) and 1437(a)(6))

§ 303.6 Child.

Child means an individual under the age of six and may include an *infant or toddler with a disability*, as that term is defined in § 303.21.

(Authority: 20 U.S.C. 1432(5))

§ 303.7 Consent.

Consent means that—

(a) The parent has been fully informed of all information relevant to the activity for which consent is sought, in the parent's native language, as defined in § 303.25;

(b) The parent understands and agrees in writing to the carrying out of the activity for which the parent's consent is sought, and the consent form describes that activity and lists the early intervention records (if any) that will be released and to whom they will be released; and

(c)(1) The parent understands that the granting of consent is voluntary on the part of the parent and may be revoked at any time.

(2) If a parent revokes consent, that revocation is not retroactive (*i.e.*, it does not apply to an action that occurred before the consent was revoked).

(Authority: 20 U.S.C. 1439)

§ 303.8 Council.

Council means the State Interagency Coordinating Council that meets the requirements of subpart G of this part.

(Authority: 20 U.S.C. 1432(2))

§ 303.9 Day.

Day means calendar day, unless otherwise indicated.

(Authority: 20 U.S.C. 1221e–3)

§ 303.10 Developmental delay.

Developmental delay, when used with respect to a child residing in a State, has the meaning given that term by the State under § 303.111.

(Authority: 20 U.S.C. 1432(3))

§ 303.11 Early intervention service program.

Early intervention service program or *EIS program* means an entity designated by the lead agency for reporting under §§ 303.700 through 303.702.

(Authority: 20 U.S.C. 1416, 1431–1444)

§ 303.12 Early intervention service provider.

(a) *Early intervention service provider* or *EIS provider* means an entity (whether public, private, or nonprofit) or an individual that provides early intervention services under part C of the Act, whether or not the entity or individual receives Federal funds under part C of the Act, and may include, where appropriate, the lead agency and a public agency responsible for providing early intervention services to infants and toddlers with disabilities in the State under part C of the Act.

(b) An EIS provider is responsible for—

(1) Participating in the multidisciplinary individualized family service plan (IFSP) Team's ongoing assessment of an infant or toddler with a disability and a family-directed assessment of the resources, priorities, and concerns of the infant's or toddler's family, as related to the needs of the infant or toddler, in the development of integrated goals and outcomes for the IFSP;

(2) Providing early intervention services in accordance with the IFSP of the infant or toddler with a disability; and

(3) Consulting with and training parents and others regarding the provision of the early intervention services described in the IFSP of the infant or toddler with a disability.

(Authority: 20 U.S.C. 1431–1444)

§ 303.13 Early intervention services.

(a) *General. Early intervention services* means developmental services that—

(1) Are provided under public supervision;

(2) Are selected in collaboration with the parents;

(3) Are provided at no cost, except, subject to §§ 303.520 and 303.521, where Federal or State law provides for a system of payments by families, including a schedule of sliding fees;

(4) Are designed to meet the developmental needs of an infant or toddler with a disability and the needs of the family to assist appropriately in the infant's or toddler's development, as identified by the IFSP Team, in any one or more of the following areas, including—

(i) Physical development;

(ii) Cognitive development;

(iii) Communication development;

(iv) Social or emotional development; or

(v) Adaptive development;

(5) Meet the standards of the State in which the early intervention services are provided, including the requirements of part C of the Act;

(6) Include services identified under paragraph (b) of this section;

(7) Are provided by *qualified personnel* (as that term is defined in § 303.31), including the types of personnel listed in paragraph (c) of this section;

(8) To the maximum extent appropriate, are provided in natural environments, as defined in § 303.26 and consistent with §§ 303.126 and 303.344(d); and

(9) Are provided in conformity with an IFSP adopted in accordance with section 636 of the Act and § 303.20.

(b) *Types of early intervention services.* Subject to paragraph (d) of this section, early intervention services include the following services defined in this paragraph:

(1) *Assistive technology device and service* are defined as follows:

(i) *Assistive technology device* means any item, piece of equipment, or product system, whether acquired commercially off the shelf, modified, or customized, that is used to increase, maintain, or improve the functional capabilities of an infant or toddler with a disability. The term does not include a medical device that is surgically implanted, including a cochlear implant, or the optimization (*e.g.*, mapping), maintenance, or replacement of that device.

(ii) *Assistive technology service* means any service that directly assists an infant or toddler with a disability in the selection, acquisition, or use of an assistive technology device. The term includes—

(A) The evaluation of the needs of an infant or toddler with a disability, including a functional evaluation of the infant or toddler with a disability in the child's customary environment;

(B) Purchasing, leasing, or otherwise providing for the acquisition of assistive technology devices by infants or toddlers with disabilities;

(C) Selecting, designing, fitting, customizing, adapting, applying, maintaining, repairing, or replacing assistive technology devices;

(D) Coordinating and using other therapies, interventions, or services with assistive technology devices, such as those associated with existing education and rehabilitation plans and programs;

(E) Training or technical assistance for an infant or toddler with a disability or, if appropriate, that child's family; and

(F) Training or technical assistance for professionals (including individuals providing education or rehabilitation services) or other individuals who provide services to, or are otherwise substantially involved in the major life functions of, infants and toddlers with disabilities.

(2) *Audiology services* include—

(i) Identification of children with auditory impairments, using at-risk criteria and appropriate audiologic screening techniques;

(ii) Determination of the range, nature, and degree of hearing loss and communication functions, by use of audiological evaluation procedures;

(iii) Referral for medical and other services necessary for the habilitation

179

or rehabilitation of an infant or toddler with a disability who has an auditory impairment;

(iv) Provision of auditory training, aural rehabilitation, speech reading and listening devices, orientation and training, and other services;

(v) Provision of services for prevention of hearing loss; and

(vi) Determination of the child's individual amplification, including selecting, fitting, and dispensing appropriate listening and vibrotactile devices, and evaluating the effectiveness of those devices.

(3) *Family training, counseling, and home visits* means services provided, as appropriate, by social workers, psychologists, and other qualified personnel to assist the family of an infant or toddler with a disability in understanding the special needs of the child and enhancing the child's development.

(4) *Health services* has the meaning given the term in § 303.16.

(5) *Medical services* means services provided by a licensed physician for diagnostic or evaluation purposes to determine a child's developmental status and need for early intervention services.

(6) *Nursing services* include—

(i) The assessment of health status for the purpose of providing nursing care, including the identification of patterns of human response to actual or potential health problems;

(ii) The provision of nursing care to prevent health problems, restore or improve functioning, and promote optimal health and development; and

(iii) The administration of medications, treatments, and regimens prescribed by a licensed physician.

(7) *Nutrition services* include—

(i) Conducting individual assessments in—

(A) Nutritional history and dietary intake;

(B) Anthropometric, biochemical, and clinical variables;

(C) Feeding skills and feeding problems; and

(D) Food habits and food preferences;

(ii) Developing and monitoring appropriate plans to address the nutritional needs of children eligible under this part, based on the findings in paragraph (b)(7)(i) of this section; and

(iii) Making referrals to appropriate community resources to carry out nutrition goals.

(8) *Occupational therapy* includes services to address the functional needs of an infant or toddler with a disability related to adaptive development, adaptive behavior, and play, and sensory, motor, and postural development. These services are designed to improve the child's functional ability to perform tasks in home, school, and community settings, and include—

(i) Identification, assessment, and intervention;

(ii) Adaptation of the environment, and selection, design, and fabrication of assistive and orthotic devices to facilitate development and promote the acquisition of functional skills; and

(iii) Prevention or minimization of the impact of initial or future impairment, delay in development, or loss of functional ability.

(9) *Physical therapy* includes services to address the promotion of sensorimotor function through enhancement of musculoskeletal status, neurobehavioral organization, perceptual and motor development, cardiopulmonary status, and effective environmental adaptation. These services include—

(i) Screening, evaluation, and assessment of children to identify movement dysfunction;

(ii) Obtaining, interpreting, and integrating information appropriate to program planning to prevent, alleviate, or compensate for movement dysfunction and related functional problems; and

(iii) Providing individual and group services or treatment to prevent, alleviate, or compensate for, movement dysfunction and related functional problems.

(10) *Psychological services* include—

(i) Administering psychological and developmental tests and other assessment procedures;

(ii) Interpreting assessment results;

(iii) Obtaining, integrating, and interpreting information about child behavior and child and family conditions related to learning, mental health, and development; and

(iv) Planning and managing a program of psychological services, including psychological counseling for children and parents, family counseling, consultation on child development, parent training, and education programs.

(11) *Service coordination services* has the meaning given the term in §303.34.

(12) *Sign language and cued language services* include teaching sign language, cued language, and auditory/oral language, providing oral transliteration services (such as amplification), and providing sign and cued language interpretation.

(13) *Social work services* include—

(i) Making home visits to evaluate a child's living conditions and patterns of parent-child interaction;

(ii) Preparing a social or emotional developmental assessment of the infant or toddler within the family context;

(iii) Providing individual and family-group counseling with parents and other family members, and appropriate social skill-building activities with the infant or toddler and parents;

(iv) Working with those problems in the living situation (home, community, and any center where early intervention services are provided) of an infant or toddler with a disability and the family of that child that affect the child's maximum utilization of early intervention services; and

(v) Identifying, mobilizing, and coordinating community resources and services to enable the infant or toddler with a disability and the family to receive maximum benefit from early intervention services.

(14) *Special instruction* includes—

(i) The design of learning environments and activities that promote the infant's or toddler's acquisition of skills in a variety of developmental areas, including cognitive processes and social interaction;

(ii) Curriculum planning, including the planned interaction of personnel, materials, and time and space, that leads to achieving the outcomes in the IFSP for the infant or toddler with a disability;

(iii) Providing families with information, skills, and support related to enhancing the skill development of the child; and

(iv) Working with the infant or toddler with a disability to enhance the child's development.

(15) *Speech-language pathology services* include—

(i) Identification of children with communication or language disorders and delays in development of communication skills, including the diagnosis and appraisal of specific disorders and delays in those skills;

(ii) Referral for medical or other professional services necessary for the habilitation or rehabilitation of children with communication or language disorders and delays in development of communication skills; and

(iii) Provision of services for the habilitation, rehabilitation, or prevention of communication or language disorders and delays in development of communication skills.

(16) *Transportation and related costs* include the cost of travel and other costs that are necessary to enable an infant or toddler with a disability and the child's family to receive early intervention services.

(17) *Vision services* mean—

(i) Evaluation and assessment of visual functioning, including the diagnosis and appraisal of specific visual disorders, delays, and abilities that affect early childhood development;

(ii) Referral for medical or other professional services necessary for the habilitation or rehabilitation of visual functioning disorders, or both; and

(iii) Communication skills training, orientation and mobility training for all environments, visual training, and additional training necessary to activate visual motor abilities.

(c) *Qualified personnel.* The following are the types of qualified personnel who provide early intervention services under this part:

(1) Audiologists.

(2) Family therapists.

(3) Nurses.

(4) Occupational therapists.

(5) Orientation and mobility specialists.

(6) Pediatricians and other physicians for diagnostic and evaluation purposes.

(7) Physical therapists.

(8) Psychologists.

(9) Registered dieticians.

(10) Social workers.

(11) Special educators, including teachers of children with hearing impairments (including deafness) and teachers of children with visual impairments (including blindness).

(12) Speech and language pathologists.

(13) Vision specialists, including ophthalmologists and optometrists.

(d) *Other services.* The services and personnel identified and defined in paragraphs (b) and (c) of this section do not comprise exhaustive lists of the types of services that may constitute early intervention services or the types of qualified personnel that may provide early intervention services. Nothing in this section prohibits the identification in the IFSP of another type of service as an early intervention service provided that the service meets the criteria identified in paragraph (a) of this section or of another type of personnel that may provide early intervention services in accordance with this part, provided such personnel meet the requirements in § 303.31.

(Authority: 20 U.S.C. 1432(4))

§ 303.14   Elementary school.

Elementary school means a nonprofit institutional day or residential school, including a public elementary charter school, that provides elementary education, as determined under State law.

(Authority: 20 U.S.C. 1401(6))

§ 303.15   Free appropriate public education.

Free appropriate public education or *FAPE*, as used in §§ 303.211, 303.501, and 303.521, means special education and related services that—

(a) Are provided at public expense, under public supervision and direction, and without charge;

(b) Meet the standards of the State educational agency (SEA), including the requirements of part B of the Act;

(c) Include an appropriate preschool, elementary school, or secondary school education in the State involved; and

(d) Are provided in conformity with an individualized education program (IEP) that meets the requirements of 34 CFR 300.320 through 300.324.

(Authority: 20 U.S.C. 1401(9))

§ 303.16   Health services.

(a) *Health services* mean services necessary to enable an otherwise eligible child to benefit from the other early intervention services under this part during the time that the child is eligible to receive early intervention services.

(b) The term includes—

(1) Such services as clean intermittent catheterization, tracheostomy care, tube feeding, the changing of dressings or colostomy collection bags, and other health services; and

(2) Consultation by physicians with other service providers concerning the special health care needs of infants and toddlers with disabilities that will need to be addressed in the course of providing other early intervention services.

(c) The term does not include—

(1) Services that are—

(i) Surgical in nature (such as cleft palate surgery, surgery for club foot, or the shunting of hydrocephalus);

(ii) Purely medical in nature (such as hospitalization for management of congenital heart ailments, or the prescribing of medicine or drugs for any purpose); or

(iii) Related to the implementation, optimization (*e.g.*, mapping), maintenance, or replacement of a medical device that is surgically implanted, including a cochlear implant.

(A) Nothing in this part limits the right of an infant or toddler with a disability with a surgically implanted device (*e.g.*, cochlear implant) to receive the early intervention services that are identified in the child's IFSP as being needed to meet the child's developmental outcomes.

(B) Nothing in this part prevents the EIS provider from routinely checking that either the hearing aid or the external components of a surgically implanted device (*e.g.*, cochlear implant) of an infant or toddler with a disability are functioning properly;

(2) Devices (such as heart monitors, respirators and oxygen, and gastrointestinal feeding tubes and pumps) necessary to control or treat a medical condition; and

(3) Medical-health services (such as immunizations and regular "well-

baby'' care) that are routinely rec-ommended for all children.

(Authority: 20 U.S.C. 1432(4))

§ 303.17 Homeless children.

Homeless children means children who meet the definition given the term *homeless children and youths* in section 725 (42 U.S.C. 11434a) of the McKinney-Vento Homeless Assistance Act, as amended, 42 U.S.C. 11431 *et seq.*

(Authority: 20 U.S.C. 1401(11))

§ 303.18 Include; including.

Include or *including* means that the items named are not all of the possible items that are covered, whether like or unlike the ones named.

(Authority: 20 U.S.C. 1221e–3)

§ 303.19 Indian; Indian tribe.

(a) *Indian* means an individual who is a member of an Indian tribe.

(b) *Indian tribe* means any Federal or State Indian tribe, band, rancheria, pueblo, colony, or community, includ-ing any Alaska Native village or re-gional village corporation (as defined in or established under the Alaska Na-tive Claims Settlement Act, 43 U.S.C. 1601 *et seq.*).

(c) Nothing in this definition is in-tended to indicate that the Secretary of the Interior is required to provide services or funding to a State Indian Tribe that is not listed in the FEDERAL REGISTER list of Indian entities recog-nized as eligible to receive services from the United States, published pur-suant to section 104 of the Federally Recognized Indian Tribe List Act of 1994, 25 U.S.C. 479a–1.

(Authority: 20 U.S.C. 1401(12)–(13))

§ 303.20 Individualized family service plan.

Individualized family service plan or *IFSP* means a written plan for pro-viding early intervention services to an infant or toddler with a disability under this part and the infant's or tod-dler's family that—

(a) Is based on the evaluation and as-sessment described in § 303.321;

(b) Includes the content specified in § 303.344;

(c) Is implemented as soon as pos-sible once parental consent for the early intervention services in the IFSP is obtained (consistent with § 303.420); and

(d) Is developed in accordance with the IFSP procedures in §§ 303.342, 303.343, and 303.345.

(Authority: 20 U.S.C. 1401(15), 1435(a)(4), 1436)

§ 303.21 Infant or toddler with a dis-ability.

(a) *Infant or toddler with a disability* means an individual under three years of age who needs early intervention services because the individual—

(1) Is experiencing a developmental delay, as measured by appropriate di-agnostic instruments and procedures, in one or more of the following areas:

(i) Cognitive development.

(ii) Physical development, including vision and hearing.

(iii) Communication development.

(iv) Social or emotional development.

(v) Adaptive development; or

(2) Has a diagnosed physical or men-tal condition that—

(i) Has a high probability of resulting in developmental delay; and

(ii) Includes conditions such as chro-mosomal abnormalities; genetic or congenital disorders; sensory impair-ments; inborn errors of metabolism; disorders reflecting disturbance of the development of the nervous system; congenital infections; severe attach-ment disorders; and disorders sec-ondary to exposure to toxic substances, including fetal alcohol syndrome.

(b) *Infant or toddler with a disability* may include, at a State's discretion, an *at-risk infant or toddler* (as defined in § 303.5).

(c) *Infant or toddler with a disability* may include, at a State's discretion, a child with a disability who is eligible for services under section 619 of the Act and who previously received services under this part until the child enters, or is eligible under State law to enter, kindergarten or elementary school, as appropriate, provided that any pro-grams under this part must include—

(1) An educational component that promotes school readiness and incor-porates pre-literacy, language, and numeracy skills for children ages three

183

and older who receive part C services pursuant to § 303.211; and

(2) A written notification to parents of a child with a disability who is eligible for services under section 619 of the Act and who previously received services under this part of their rights and responsibilities in determining whether their child will continue to receive services under this part or participate in preschool programs under section 619 of the Act.

(Authority: 20 U.S.C. 1401(16), 1432(5))

§ 303.22 Lead agency.

Lead agency means the agency designated by the State's Governor under section 635(a)(10) of the Act and § 303.120 that receives funds under section 643 of the Act to administer the State's responsibilities under part C of the Act.

(Authority: 20 U.S.C. 1435(a)(10))

§ 303.23 Local educational agency.

(a) *General. Local educational agency* or *LEA* means a public board of education or other public authority legally constituted within a State for either administrative control or direction of, or to perform a service function for, public elementary schools or secondary schools in a city, county, township, school district, or other political subdivision of a State, or for a combination of school districts or counties as are recognized in a State as an administrative agency for its public elementary schools or secondary schools.

(b) *Educational service agencies and other public institutions or agencies.* The term includes the following:

(1) *Educational service agency,* defined as a regional public multiservice agency—

(i) Authorized by State law to develop, manage, and provide services or programs to LEAs; and

(ii) Recognized as an administrative agency for purposes of the provision of special education and related services provided within public elementary schools and secondary schools of the State.

(2) Any other public institution or agency having administrative control and direction of a public elementary school or secondary school, including a public charter school that is established as an LEA under State law.

(3) Entities that meet the definition of *intermediate educational unit* or *IEU* in section 602(23) of the Act, as in effect prior to June 4, 1997. Under that definition an *intermediate educational unit* or *IEU* means any public authority other than an LEA that—

(i) Is under the general supervision of a State educational agency;

(ii) Is established by State law for the purpose of providing FAPE on a regional basis; and

(iii) Provides special education and related services to children with disabilities within the State.

(c) *BIE-funded schools.* The term includes an elementary school or secondary school funded by the Bureau of Indian Education, and not subject to the jurisdiction of any SEA other than the Bureau of Indian Education, but only to the extent that the inclusion makes the school eligible for programs for which specific eligibility is not provided to the school in another provision of law and the school does not have a student population that is smaller than the student population of the LEA receiving assistance under the Act with the smallest student population.

(Authority: 20 U.S.C. 1401(5), 1401(19))

§ 303.24 Multidisciplinary.

Multidisciplinary means the involvement of two or more separate disciplines or professions and with respect to—

(a) Evaluation of the child in §§ 303.113 and 303.321(a)(1)(i) and assessments of the child and family in § 303.321(a)(1)(ii), may include one individual who is qualified in more than one discipline or profession; and

(b) The IFSP Team in § 303.340 must include the involvement of the parent and two or more individuals from separate disciplines or professions and one of these individuals must be the service coordinator (consistent with § 303.343(a)(1)(iv)).

(Authority: 20 U.S.C. 1221e–3, 1435(a)(3), 1436(a)(1), 1436(a)(3))

§ 303.25 Native language.

(a) *Native language*, when used with respect to an individual who is limited English proficient or LEP (as that term is defined in section 602(18) of the Act), means—

(1) The language normally used by that individual, or, in the case of a child, the language normally used by the parents of the child, except as provided in paragraph (a)(2) of this section; and

(2) For evaluations and assessments conducted pursuant to § 303.321(a)(5) and (a)(6), the language normally used by the child, if determined developmentally appropriate for the child by qualified personnel conducting the evaluation or assessment.

(b) *Native language*, when used with respect to an individual who is deaf or hard of hearing, blind or visually impaired, or for an individual with no written language, means the mode of communication that is normally used by the individual (such as sign language, braille, or oral communication).

(Authority: 20 U.S.C. 1401(20))

§ 303.26 Natural environments.

Natural environments means settings that are natural or typical for a same-aged infant or toddler without a disability, may include the home or community settings, and must be consistent with the provisions of § 303.126.

(Authority: 20 U.S.C. 1432, 1435, 1436)

§ 303.27 Parent.

(a) *Parent* means—

(1) A biological or adoptive parent of a child;

(2) A foster parent, unless State law, regulations, or contractual obligations with a State or local entity prohibit a foster parent from acting as a parent;

(3) A guardian generally authorized to act as the child's parent, or authorized to make early intervention, educational, health or developmental decisions for the child (but not the State if the child is a ward of the State);

(4) An individual acting in the place of a biological or adoptive parent (including a grandparent, stepparent, or other relative) with whom the child lives, or an individual who is legally responsible for the child's welfare; or

(5) A surrogate parent who has been appointed in accordance with § 303.422 or section 639(a)(5) of the Act.

(b)(1) Except as provided in paragraph (b)(2) of this section, the biological or adoptive parent, when attempting to act as the parent under this part and when more than one party is qualified under paragraph (a) of this section to act as a parent, must be presumed to be the parent for purposes of this section unless the biological or adoptive parent does not have legal authority to make educational or early intervention service decisions for the child.

(2) If a judicial decree or order identifies a specific person or persons under paragraphs (a)(1) through (a)(4) of this section to act as the "parent" of a child or to make educational or early intervention service decisions on behalf of a child, then the person or persons must be determined to be the "parent" for purposes of part C of the Act, except that if an EIS provider or a public agency provides any services to a child or any family member of that child, that EIS provider or public agency may not act as the parent for that child.

(Authority: 20 U.S.C. 1401(23), 1439(a)(5))

§ 303.28 Parent training and information center.

Parent training and information center means a center assisted under section 671 or 672 of the Act.

(Authority: 20 U.S.C. 1401(25))

§ 303.29 Personally identifiable information.

Personally identifiable information means personally identifiable information as defined in 34 CFR 99.3, as amended, except that the term "student" in the definition of personally identifiable information in 34 CFR 99.3 means "child" as used in this part and any reference to "school" means "EIS provider" as used in this part.

(Authority: 20 U.S.C. 1415, 1439)

§ 303.30 Public agency.

As used in this part, *public agency* means the lead agency and any other agency or political subdivision of the State.

(Authority: 20 U.S.C. 1435(a)(10))

§ 303.31 Qualified personnel.

Qualified personnel means personnel who have met State approved or recognized certification, licensing, registration, or other comparable requirements that apply to the areas in which the individuals are conducting evaluations or assessments or providing early intervention services.

(Authority: 20 U.S.C. 1432(4)(F))

§ 303.32 [Reserved]

§ 303.33 Secretary.

Secretary means the Secretary of Education.

(Authority: 20 U.S.C. 1401(28))

§ 303.34 Service coordination services (case management).

(a) *General.* (1) As used in this part, *service coordination services* mean services provided by a service coordinator to assist and enable an infant or toddler with a disability and the child's family to receive the services and rights, including procedural safeguards, required under this part.

(2) Each infant or toddler with a disability and the child's family must be provided with one service coordinator who is responsible for—

(i) Coordinating all services required under this part across agency lines; and

(ii) Serving as the single point of contact for carrying out the activities described in paragraphs (a)(3) and (b) of this section.

(3) Service coordination is an active, ongoing process that involves—

(i) Assisting parents of infants and toddlers with disabilities in gaining access to, and coordinating the provision of, the early intervention services required under this part; and

(ii) Coordinating the other services identified in the IFSP under § 303.344(e) that are needed by, or are being provided to, the infant or toddler with a disability and that child's family.

(b) *Specific service coordination services.* Service coordination services include—

(1) Assisting parents of infants and toddlers with disabilities in obtaining access to needed early intervention services and other services identified in the IFSP, including making referrals to providers for needed services and scheduling appointments for infants and toddlers with disabilities and their families;

(2) Coordinating the provision of early intervention services and other services (such as educational, social, and medical services that are not provided for diagnostic or evaluative purposes) that the child needs or is being provided;

(3) Coordinating evaluations and assessments;

(4) Facilitating and participating in the development, review, and evaluation of IFSPs;

(5) Conducting referral and other activities to assist families in identifying available EIS providers;

(6) Coordinating, facilitating, and monitoring the delivery of services required under this part to ensure that the services are provided in a timely manner;

(7) Conducting follow-up activities to determine that appropriate part C services are being provided;

(8) Informing families of their rights and procedural safeguards, as set forth in subpart E of this part and related resources;

(9) Coordinating the funding sources for services required under this part; and

(10) Facilitating the development of a transition plan to preschool, school, or, if appropriate, to other services.

(c) *Use of the term service coordination or service coordination services.* The lead agency's or an EIS provider's use of the term *service coordination* or *service coordination services* does not preclude characterization of the services as case management or any other service that is covered by another payor of last resort (including Title XIX of the Social Security Act—Medicaid), for purposes of claims in compliance with the requirements of §§ 303.501 through 303.521 (Payor of last resort provisions).

(Authority: 20 U.S.C. 1432(4), 1435(a)(4), 1436(d)(7), 1440)

§303.35 State.

Except as provided in §303.732(d)(3) (regarding State allotments under this part), *State* means each of the 50 States, the Commonwealth of Puerto Rico, the District of Columbia, and the four outlying areas and jurisdictions of Guam, American Samoa, the United States Virgin Islands, and the Commonwealth of the Northern Mariana Islands.

(Authority: 20 U.S.C. 1401(31))

§303.36 State educational agency.

(a) *State educational agency* or *SEA* means the State board of education or other agency or officer primarily responsible for the State supervision of public elementary schools and secondary schools, or, if there is no such officer or agency, an officer or agency designated by the Governor or by State law.

(b) The term includes the agency that receives funds under sections 611 and 619 of the Act to administer the State's responsibilities under part B of the Act.

(Authority: 20 U.S.C. 1401(32))

§303.37 Ward of the State.

(a) *General.* Subject to paragraph (b) of this section, *ward of the State* means a child who, as determined by the State where the child resides, is—

(1) A foster child;

(2) A ward of the State; or

(3) In the custody of a public child welfare agency.

(b) *Exception. Ward of the State* does not include a foster child who has a foster parent who meets the definition of a *parent* in §303.27.

(Authority: 20 U.S.C. 1401(36))

Subpart B—State Eligibility for a Grant and Requirements for a Statewide System

GENERAL AUTHORITY AND ELIGIBILITY

§303.100 General authority.

The Secretary, in accordance with part C of the Act, makes grants to States (from their allotments under section 643 of the Act) to assist each State to maintain and implement a statewide, comprehensive, coordinated, multidisciplinary, interagency system to provide early intervention services for infants and toddlers with disabilities and their families.

(Authority: 20 U.S.C. 1433)

§303.101 State eligibility—requirements for a grant under this part.

In order to be eligible for a grant under part C of the Act for any fiscal year, a State must meet the following conditions:

(a) *Assurances regarding early intervention services and a statewide system.* The State must provide assurances to the Secretary that—

(1) The State has adopted a policy that appropriate early intervention services, as defined in §303.13, are available to all infants and toddlers with disabilities in the State and their families, including—

(i) Indian infants and toddlers with disabilities and their families residing on a reservation geographically located in the State;

(ii) Infants and toddlers with disabilities who are homeless children and their families; and

(iii) Infants and toddlers with disabilities who are wards of the State; and

(2) The State has in effect a statewide system of early intervention services that meets the requirements of section 635 of the Act, including policies and procedures that address, at a minimum, the components required in §§303.111 through 303.126.

(b) *State application and assurances.* The State must provide information and assurances to the Secretary, in accordance with subpart C of this part, including—

(1) Information that shows that the State meets the State application requirements in §§303.200 through 303.212; and

(2) Assurances that the State also meets the requirements in §§303.221 through 303.227.

(c) *Approval before implementation.* The State must obtain approval by the Secretary before implementing any policy or procedure required to be submitted as part of the State's application in §§ 303.203, 303.204, 303.206, 303.207, 303.208, 303.209, and 303.211.

(Approved by Office of Management and Budget under control number 1820-0550)

(Authority: 20 U.S.C. 1434, 1435, 1437)

STATE CONFORMITY WITH PART C OF THE ACT AND ABROGATION OF STATE SOVEREIGN IMMUNITY

§ 303.102 State conformity with Part C of the Act.

Each State that receives funds under part C of the Act must ensure that any State rules, regulations, and policies relating to this part conform to the purposes and requirements of this part.

(Authority: 20 U.S.C. 1407(a)(1))

§ 303.103 Abrogation of State sovereign immunity.

(a) *General.* A State is not immune under the 11th amendment of the Constitution of the United States from suit in Federal court for a violation of part C of the Act.

(b) *Remedies.* In a suit against a State for a violation of part C of the Act, remedies (including remedies both at law and in equity) are available for such a violation to the same extent as those remedies are available for such a violation in a suit against any public entity other than a State.

(c) *Effective date.* Paragraphs (a) and (b) of this section apply with respect to violations that occur in whole or part after October 30, 1990, the date of enactment of the Education of the Handicapped Act Amendments of 1990.

(Authority: 20 U.S.C. 1403)

EQUIPMENT AND CONSTRUCTION

§ 303.104 Acquisition of equipment and construction or alteration of facilities.

(a) *General.* If the Secretary determines that a program authorized under part C of the Act will be improved by permitting program funds to be used to acquire appropriate equipment or to construct new facilities or alter existing facilities, the Secretary may allow the use of those funds for those purposes.

(b) *Compliance with certain regulations.* Any construction of new facilities or alteration of existing facilities under paragraph (a) of this section must comply with the requirements of—

(1) Appendix A of part 36 of title 28, Code of Federal Regulations (commonly known as the "Americans with Disabilities Act Accessibility Guidelines for Buildings and Facilities"); or

(2) Appendix A of subpart 101-19.6 of title 41, Code of Federal Regulations (commonly known as the "Uniform Federal Accessibility Standards").

(Authority: 20 U.S.C. 1404)

POSITIVE EFFORTS TO EMPLOY AND ADVANCE QUALIFIED INDIVIDUALS WITH DISABILITIES

§ 303.105 Positive efforts to employ and advance qualified individuals with disabilities.

Each recipient of assistance under part C of the Act must make positive efforts to employ and advance in employment, qualified individuals with disabilities in programs assisted under part C of the Act.

(Authority: 20 U.S.C. 1405)

MINIMUM COMPONENTS OF A STATEWIDE SYSTEM

§ 303.110 Minimum components of a statewide system.

Each statewide system (system) must include, at a minimum, the components described in §§ 303.111 through 303.126.

(Approved by Office of Management and Budget under control number 1820-0550)

(Authority: 20 U.S.C. 1435(a))

§ 303.111 State definition of developmental delay.

Each system must include the State's rigorous definition of *developmental delay*, consistent with §§ 303.10 and 303.203(c), that will be used by the State in carrying out programs under part C of the Act in order to appropriately identify infants and toddlers with disabilities who are in need of services under part C of the Act. The definition must—

(a) Describe, for each of the areas listed in § 303.21(a)(1), the evaluation and assessment procedures, consistent with §303.321, that will be used to measure a child's development; and

(b) Specify the level of developmental delay in functioning or other comparable criteria that constitute a developmental delay in one or more of the developmental areas identified in §303.21(a)(1).

(Approved by Office of Management and Budget under control number 1820–0550)

(Authority: 20 U.S.C. 1435(a)(1))

§303.112 Availability of early intervention services.

Each system must include a State policy that is in effect and that ensures that appropriate early intervention services are based on scientifically based research, to the extent practicable, and are available to all infants and toddlers with disabilities and their families, including—

(a) Indian infants and toddlers with disabilities and their families residing on a reservation geographically located in the State; and

(b) Infants and toddlers with disabilities who are homeless children and their families.

(Approved by Office of Management and Budget under control number 1820–0550)

(Authority: 20 U.S.C. 1435(a)(2))

§303.113 Evaluation, assessment, and nondiscriminatory procedures.

(a) Subject to paragraph (b) of this section, each system must ensure the performance of—

(1) A timely, comprehensive, multidisciplinary evaluation of the functioning of each infant or toddler with a disability in the State; and

(2) A family-directed identification of the needs of the family of the infant or toddler to assist appropriately in the development of the infant or toddler.

(b) The evaluation and family-directed identification required in paragraph (a) of this section must meet the requirements of §303.321.

(Approved by Office of Management and Budget under control number 1820–0550)

(Authority: 20 U.S.C. 1435(a)(3))

§303.114 Individualized family service plan (IFSP).

Each system must ensure, for each infant or toddler with a disability and his or her family in the State, that an IFSP, as defined in §303.20, is developed and implemented that meets the requirements of §§303.340 through 303.345, and that includes service coordination services, as defined in §303.34.

(Approved by Office of Management and Budget under control number 1820–0550)

(Authority: 20 U.S.C. 1435(a)(4))

§303.115 Comprehensive child find system.

Each system must include a comprehensive child find system that meets the requirements in §§303.302 and 303.303.

(Approved by Office of Management and Budget under control number 1820–0550)

(Authority: 20 U.S.C. 1435(a)(5))

§303.116 Public awareness program.

Each system must include a public awareness program that—

(a) Focuses on the early identification of infants and toddlers with disabilities; and

(b) Provides information to parents of infants and toddlers through primary referral sources in accordance with §303.301.

(Approved by Office of Management and Budget under control number 1820–0550)

(Authority: 20 U.S.C. 1435(a)(6))

§303.117 Central directory.

Each system must include a central directory that is accessible to the general public (i.e., through the lead agency's Web site and other appropriate means) and includes accurate, up-to-date information about—

(a) Public and private early intervention services, resources, and experts available in the State;

(b) Professional and other groups (including parent support, and training and information centers, such as those funded under the Act) that provide assistance to infants and toddlers with disabilities eligible under part C of the Act and their families; and

(c) Research and demonstration projects being conducted in the State relating to infants and toddlers with disabilities.

(Approved by Office of Management and Budget under control number 1820–0550)

(Authority: 20 U.S.C. 1435(a)(7))

§303.118 Comprehensive system of personnel development (CSPD).

Each system must include a comprehensive system of personnel development, including the training of paraprofessionals and the training of primary referral sources with respect to the basic components of early intervention services available in the State. A comprehensive system of personnel development—

(a) Must include—

(1) Training personnel to implement innovative strategies and activities for the recruitment and retention of EIS providers;

(2) Promoting the preparation of EIS providers who are fully and appropriately qualified to provide early intervention services under this part; and

(3) Training personnel to coordinate transition services for infants and toddlers with disabilities who are transitioning from an early intervention service program under part C of the Act to a preschool program under section 619 of the Act, Head Start, Early Head Start, an elementary school program under part B of the Act, or another appropriate program.

(b) May include—

(1) Training personnel to work in rural and inner-city areas;

(2) Training personnel in the emotional and social development of young children; and

(3) Training personnel to support families in participating fully in the development and implementation of the child's IFSP; and

(4) Training personnel who provide services under this part using standards that are consistent with early learning personnel development standards funded under the State Advisory Council on Early Childhood Education and Care established under the Head Start Act, if applicable.

(Approved by Office of Management and Budget under control number 1820–0550)

(Authority: 20 U.S.C. 1435(a)(8))

§303.119 Personnel standards.

(a) *General.* Each system must include policies and procedures relating to the establishment and maintenance of qualification standards to ensure that personnel necessary to carry out the purposes of this part are appropriately and adequately prepared and trained.

(b) *Qualification standards.* The policies and procedures required in paragraph (a) of this section must provide for the establishment and maintenance of qualification standards that are consistent with any State-approved or State-recognized certification, licensing, registration, or other comparable requirements that apply to the profession, discipline, or area in which personnel are providing early intervention services.

(c) *Use of paraprofessionals and assistants.* Nothing in part C of the Act may be construed to prohibit the use of paraprofessionals and assistants who are appropriately trained and supervised in accordance with State law, regulation, or written policy to assist in the provision of early intervention services under part C of the Act to infants and toddlers with disabilities.

(d) *Policy to address shortage of personnel.* A State may adopt a policy that includes making ongoing good-faith efforts to recruit and hire appropriately and adequately trained personnel to provide early intervention services to infants and toddlers with disabilities, including, in a geographic area of the State where there is a shortage of such personnel, the most qualified individuals available who are making satisfactory progress toward completing applicable course work necessary to meet the standards described in paragraphs (a) and (b) of this section.

(Approved by Office of Management and Budget under control number 1820–0550)

(Authority: 20 U.S.C. 1435(a)(9), 1435(b))

§303.120 Lead agency role in supervision, monitoring, funding, interagency coordination, and other responsibilities.

Each system must include a single line of responsibility in a lead agency designated or established by the Governor that is responsible for the following:

(a)(1) The general administration and supervision of programs and activities administered by agencies, institutions, organizations, and EIS providers receiving assistance under part C of the Act.

(2) The monitoring of programs and activities used by the State to carry out part C of the Act (whether or not the programs or activities are administered by agencies, institutions, organizations, and EIS providers that are receiving assistance under part C of the Act), to ensure that the State complies with part C of the Act, including—

(i) Monitoring agencies, institutions, organizations, and EIS providers used by the State to carry out part C of the Act;

(ii) Enforcing any obligations imposed on those agencies, institutions, organizations, and EIS providers under part C of the Act and these regulations;

(iii) Providing technical assistance, if necessary, to those agencies, institutions, organizations, and EIS providers;

(iv) Correcting any noncompliance identified through monitoring as soon as possible and in no case later than one year after the lead agency's identification of the noncompliance; and

(v) Conducting the activities in paragraphs (a)(2)(i) through (a)(2)(iv) of this section, consistent with §§303.700 through 303.707, and any other activities required by the State under those sections.

(b) The identification and coordination of all available resources for early intervention services within the State, including those from Federal, State, local, and private sources, consistent with subpart F of this part.

(c) The assignment of financial responsibility in accordance with subpart F of this part.

(d) The development of procedures in accordance with subpart F of this part to ensure that early intervention services are provided to infants and toddlers with disabilities and their families under part C of the Act in a timely manner, pending the resolution of any disputes among public agencies or EIS providers.

(e) The resolution of intra- and interagency disputes in accordance with subpart F of this part.

(f) The entry into formal interagency agreements or other written methods of establishing financial responsibility, consistent with §303.511, that define the financial responsibility of each agency for paying for early intervention services (consistent with State law) and procedures for resolving disputes and that include all additional components necessary to ensure meaningful cooperation and coordination as set forth in subpart F of this part.

(Approved by Office of Management and Budget under control number 1820–0550)

(Authority: 20 U.S.C. 1416, 1435(a)(10), 1442)

§303.121 Policy for contracting or otherwise arranging for services.

Each system must include a policy pertaining to the contracting or making of other arrangements with public or private individuals or agency service providers to provide early intervention services in the State, consistent with the provisions of part C of the Act, including the contents of the application, and the conditions of the contract or other arrangements. The policy must—

(a) Include a requirement that all early intervention services must meet State standards and be consistent with the provisions of this part; and

(b) Be consistent with 2 CFR part 200, as adopted at 2 CFR part 3474.

(Approved by Office of Management and Budget under control number 1820–0550)

(Authority: 20 U.S.C. 1435(a)(11))

[76 FR 60244, Sept. 28, 2011, as amended at 79 FR 76097, Dec. 19, 2014]

§303.122 Reimbursement procedures.

Each system must include procedures for securing the timely reimbursement of funds used under part C of the Act, in accordance with subpart F of this part.

(Approved by Office of Management and Budget under control number 1820–0550)

(Authority: 20 U.S.C. 1435(a)(12), 1440(a))

§ 303.123 Procedural safeguards.

Each system must include procedural safeguards that meet the requirements of subpart E of this part.

(Approved by Office of Management and Budget under control number 1820–0550)

(Authority: 20 U.S.C. 1435(a)(13), 1439)

§ 303.124 Data collection.

(a) Each statewide system must include a system for compiling and reporting timely and accurate data that meets the requirements in paragraph (b) of this section and §§ 303.700 through 303.702 and 303.720 through 303.724.

(b) The data system required in paragraph (a) of this section must include a description of the process that the State uses, or will use, to compile data on infants or toddlers with disabilities receiving early intervention services under this part, including a description of the State's sampling methods, if sampling is used, for reporting the data required by the Secretary under sections 616 and 618 of the Act and §§ 303.700 through 303.707 and 303.720 through 303.724.

(Approved by Office of Management and Budget under control number 1820–0550, 1820–0557 and 1820–0578)

(Authority: 20 U.S.C. 1416, 1418(a)-(c), 1435(a)(14), 1442)

§ 303.125 State interagency coordinating council.

Each system must include a State Interagency Coordinating Council (Council) that meets the requirements of subpart G of this part.

(Approved by Office of Management and Budget under control number 1820–0550)

(Authority: 20 U.S.C. 1435(a)(15))

§ 303.126 Early intervention services in natural environments.

Each system must include policies and procedures to ensure, consistent with §§ 303.13(a)(8) (early intervention services), 303.26 (natural environments), and 303.344(d)(1)(ii) (content of an IFSP), that early intervention services for infants and toddlers with disabilities are provided—

(a) To the maximum extent appropriate, in natural environments; and

(b) In settings other than the natural environment that are most appropriate, as determined by the parent and the IFSP Team, only when early intervention services cannot be achieved satisfactorily in a natural environment.

(Approved by Office of Management and Budget under control number 1820–0550)

(Authority: 20 U.S.C. 1435(a)(16))

Subpart C—State Application and Assurances

GENERAL

§ 303.200 State application and assurances.

Each application must contain—

(a) The specific State application requirements (including certifications, descriptions, methods, and policies and procedures) required in §§ 303.201 through 303.212; and

(b) The assurances required in §§ 303.221 through 303.227.

(Approved by Office of Management and Budget under control number 1820–0550)

(Authority: 20 U.S.C. 1437)

APPLICATION REQUIREMENTS

§ 303.201 Designation of lead agency.

Each application must include the name of the State lead agency, as designated under § 303.120, that will be responsible for the administration of funds provided under this part.

(Approved by Office of Management and Budget under control number 1820–0550)

(Authority: 20 U.S.C. 1437(a)(1))

§ 303.202 Certification regarding financial responsibility.

Each application must include a certification to the Secretary that the arrangements to establish financial responsibility for the provision of part C services among appropriate public agencies under § 303.511 and the lead agency's contracts with EIS providers regarding financial responsibility for the provision of part C services both meet the requirements in subpart F of this part (§§ 303.500 through 303.521) and are current as of the date of submission of the certification.

(Approved by Office of Management and Budget under control number 1820–0550)

(Authority: 20 U.S.C. 1437(a)(2))

§ 303.203 Statewide system and description of services.

Each application must include —

(a) A description of services to be provided under this part to infants and toddlers with disabilities and their families through the State's system;

(b) The State's policies and procedures regarding the identification and coordination of all available resources within the State from Federal, State, local, and private sources as required under subpart F of this part and including—

(1) Policies or procedures adopted by the State as its system of payments that meet the requirements in §§ 303.510, 303.520 and 303.521 (regarding the use of public insurance or benefits, private insurance, or family costs or fees); and

(2) Methods used by the State to implement the requirements in § 303.511(b)(2) and (b)(3); and

(c) The State's rigorous definition of developmental delay as required under §§ 303.10 and 303.111.

(Approved by Office of Management and Budget under control number 1820–0550)

(Authority: 20 U.S.C. 1432(3), 1432(4)(B), 1432(4)(C), 1435(a)(1), 1435(a)(10)(B), 1437(a)(3), 1440)

§ 303.204 Application's definition of at-risk infants and toddlers and description of services.

If the State provides services under this part to at-risk infants and toddlers through the statewide system, the application must include—

(a) The State's definition of at-risk infants and toddlers with disabilities who are eligible in the State for services under part C of the Act (consistent with §§ 303.5 and 303.21(b)); and

(b) A description of the early intervention services provided under this part to at-risk infants and toddlers with disabilities who meet the State's

definition described in paragraph (a) of this section.

(Approved by Office of Management and Budget under control number 1820–0550)

(Authority: 20 U.S.C. 1437(a)(4))

§ 303.205 Description of use of funds.

(a) *General.* Each State application must include a description of the uses for funds under this part for the fiscal year or years covered by the application. The description must be presented separately for the lead agency and the Council and include the information required in paragraphs (b) through (e) of this section.

(b) *State administration funds including administrative positions.* For lead agencies other than State educational agencies (SEAs), each application must include the total—

(1) Amount of funds retained by the lead agency for administration purposes, including the amount in paragraph (b)(2) of this section; and

(2) Number of full-time equivalent administrative positions to be used to implement part C of the Act, and the total amount of salaries (including benefits) for those positions.

(c) *Maintenance and implementation activities.* Each application must include a description of the nature and scope of each major activity to be carried out under this part, consistent with § 303.501, and the approximate amount of funds to be spent for each activity.

(d) *Direct services.* Each application must include a description of any direct services that the State expects to provide to infants and toddlers with disabilities and their families with funds under this part, consistent with § 303.501, and the approximate amount of funds under this part to be used for the provision of each direct service.

(e) *Activities by other public agencies.* If other public agencies are to receive funds under this part, the application must include—

(1) The name of each agency expected to receive funds;

(2) The approximate amount of funds each agency will receive; and

(3) A summary of the purposes for which the funds will be used.

(Approved by Office of Management and Budget under control number 1820–0550)

(Authority: 20 U.S.C. 1435(a)(10)(B), 1435(a)(10)(F), 1437(a)(3), 1437(a)(5))

§ 303.206 Referral policies for specific children.

Each application must include the State's policies and procedures that require the referral for early intervention services under this part of specific children under the age of three, as described in § 303.303(b).

(Approved by Office of Management and Budget under control number 1820–0550)

(Authority: 20 U.S.C. 1412(a)(3)(A), 1431, 1434(1), 1435(a)(2), 1435(a)(5), 1435(c)(2)(G), 1437(a)(6), 1437(a)(10), 1441)

§ 303.207 Availability of resources.

Each application must include a description of the procedure used by the State to ensure that resources are made available under this part for all geographic areas within the State.

(Approved by Office of Management and Budget under control number 1820–0550)

(Authority: 20 U.S.C. 1437(a)(7))

§ 303.208 Public participation policies and procedures.

(a) *Application.* At least 60 days prior to being submitted to the Department, each application for funds under this part (including any policies, procedures, descriptions, methods, certifications, assurances and other information required in the application) must be published in a manner that will ensure circulation throughout the State for at least a 60-day period, with an opportunity for public comment on the application for at least 30 days during that period.

(b) *State Policies and Procedures.* Each application must include a description of the policies and procedures used by the State to ensure that, before adopting any new policy or procedure (including any revision to an existing policy or procedure) needed to comply with part C of the Act and these regulations, the lead agency—

(1) Holds public hearings on the new policy or procedure (including any re-

vision to an existing policy or procedure);

(2) Provides notice of the hearings held in accordance with paragraph (b)(1) of this section at least 30 days before the hearings are conducted to enable public participation; and

(3) Provides an opportunity for the general public, including individuals with disabilities, parents of infants and toddlers with disabilities, EIS providers, and the members of the Council, to comment for at least 30 days on the new policy or procedure (including any revision to an existing policy or procedure) needed to comply with part C of the Act and these regulations.

(Approved by Office of Management and Budget under control number 1820–0550)

(Authority: 20 U.S.C. 1231d, 1221e–3, 1437(a)(8))

§ 303.209 Transition to preschool and other programs.

(a) *Application requirements.* Each State must include the following in its application:

(1) A description of the policies and procedures it will use to ensure a smooth transition for infants and toddlers with disabilities under the age of three and their families from receiving early intervention services under this part to—

(i) Preschool or other appropriate services (for toddlers with disabilities); or

(ii) Exiting the program for infants and toddlers with disabilities.

(2) A description of how the State will meet each of the requirements in paragraphs (b) through (f) of this section.

(3)(i)(A) If the lead agency is not the SEA, an interagency agreement between the lead agency and the SEA; or

(B) If the lead agency is the SEA, an intra-agency agreement between the program within that agency that administers part C of the Act and the program within the agency that administers section 619 of the Act.

(ii) To ensure a seamless transition between services under this part and under part B of the Act, an interagency agreement under paragraph (a)(3)(i)(A) of this section or an intra-agency agreement under paragraph (a)(3)(i)(B) of this section must address how the lead agency and the SEA will meet the requirements of paragraphs (b) through (f) of this section (including any policies adopted by the lead agency under § 303.401(d) and (e)), § 303.344(h), and 34 CFR 300.101(b), 300.124, 300.321(f), and 300.323(b).

(4) Any policy the lead agency has adopted under § 303.401(d) and (e).

(b) *Notification to the SEA and appropriate LEA.* (1) The State lead agency must ensure that—

(i) Subject to paragraph (b)(2) of this section, not fewer than 90 days before the third birthday of the toddler with a disability if that toddler may be eligible for preschool services under part B of the Act, the lead agency notifies the SEA and the LEA for the area in which the toddler resides that the toddler on his or her third birthday will reach the age of eligibility for services under part B of the Act, as determined in accordance with State law;

(ii) Subject to paragraph (b)(2) of this section, if the lead agency determines that the toddler is eligible for early intervention services under part C of the Act more than 45 but less than 90 days before that toddler's third birthday and if that toddler may be eligible for preschool services under part B of the Act, the lead agency, as soon as possible after determining the child's eligibility, notifies the SEA and the LEA for the area in which the toddler with a disability resides that the toddler on his or her third birthday will reach the age of eligibility for services under part B of the Act, as determined in accordance with State law; or

(iii) Subject to paragraph (b)(2) of this section, if a toddler is referred to the lead agency fewer than 45 days before that toddler's third birthday and that toddler may be eligible for preschool services under part B of the Act, the lead agency, with parental consent required under § 303.414, refers the toddler to the SEA and the LEA for the area in which the toddler resides; but, the lead agency is not required to conduct an evaluation, assessment, or an initial IFSP meeting under these circumstances.

(2) The State must ensure that the notification required under paragraphs (b)(1)(i) and (b)(1)(ii) of this section is consistent with any policy that the State has adopted, under § 303.401(e),

permitting a parent to object to disclosure of personally identifiable information.

(c) *Conference to discuss services.* The State lead agency must ensure that—

(1) If a toddler with a disability may be eligible for preschool services under part B of the Act, the lead agency, with the approval of the family of the toddler, convenes a conference, among the lead agency, the family, and the LEA not fewer than 90 days—and, at the discretion of all parties, not more than 9 months—before the toddler's third birthday to discuss any services the toddler may receive under part B of the Act; and.

(2) If the lead agency determines that a toddler with a disability is not potentially eligible for preschool services under part B of the Act, the lead agency, with the approval of the family of that toddler, makes reasonable efforts to convene a conference among the lead agency, the family, and providers of other appropriate services for the toddler to discuss appropriate services that the toddler may receive.

(d) *Transition plan.* The State lead agency must ensure that for all toddlers with disabilities—

(1)(i) It reviews the program options for the toddler with a disability for the period from the toddler's third birthday through the remainder of the school year; and

(ii) Each family of a toddler with a disability who is served under this part is included in the development of the transition plan required under this section and § 303.344(h);

(2) It establishes a transition plan in the IFSP not fewer than 90 days—and, at the discretion of all parties, not more than 9 months—before the toddler's third birthday; and

(3) The transition plan in the IFSP includes, consistent with § 303.344(h), as appropriate—

(i) Steps for the toddler with a disability and his or her family to exit from the part C program; and

(ii) Any transition services that the IFSP Team identifies as needed by that toddler and his or her family.

(e) *Transition conference and meeting to develop transition plan.* Any conference conducted under paragraph (c) of this section or meeting to develop the transition plan under paragraph (d) of this section (which conference and meeting may be combined into one meeting) must meet the requirements in §§ 303.342(d) and (e) and 303.343(a).

(f) *Applicability of transition requirements.* (1) The transition requirements in paragraphs (b)(1)(i) and (b)(1)(ii), (c)(1), and (d) of this section apply to all toddlers with disabilities receiving services under this part before those toddlers turn age three, including any toddler with a disability under the age of three who is served by a State that offers services under § 303.211.

(2) In a State that offers services under § 303.211, for toddlers with disabilities identified in § 303.209(b)(1)(i), the parent must be provided at the transition conference conducted under paragraph (c)(1) of this section:

(i) An explanation, consistent with § 303.211(b)(1)(ii), of the toddler's options to continue to receive early intervention services under this part or preschool services under section 619 of the Act.

(ii) The initial annual notice referenced in § 303.211(b)(1).

(3) For children with disabilities age three and older who receive services pursuant to § 303.211, the State must ensure that it satisfies the separate transition requirements in § 303.211(b)(6)(ii).

(Approved by Office of Management and Budget under control number 1820–0550)

(Authority: 20 U.S.C. 1412(a)(3) and (a)(9), 1436(a)(3), 1437(a)(9))

§ 303.210 Coordination with Head Start and Early Head Start, early education, and child care programs.

(a) Each application must contain a description of State efforts to promote collaboration among Head Start and Early Head Start programs under the Head Start Act (42 U.S.C. 9801, *et seq.,* as amended), early education and child care programs, and services under this part.

(Approved by Office of Management and Budget under control number 1820–0550)

(b) The State lead agency must participate, consistent with section 642B(b)(1)(C)(viii) of the Head Start Act, on the State Advisory Council on

Early Childhood Education and Care established under the Head Start Act.

(Authority: 20 U.S.C. 1437(a)(10))

§ 303.211 State option to make services under this part available to children ages three and older.

(a) *General.* (1) Subject to paragraphs (a)(2) and (b) of this section, a State may elect to include in its application for a grant under this part a State policy, developed and implemented jointly by the lead agency and the SEA, under which a parent of a child with a disability who is eligible for preschool services under section 619 of the Act and who previously received early intervention services under this part, may choose the continuation of early intervention services under this part for his or her child after the child turns three until the child enters, or is eligible under State law to enter, kindergarten or elementary school.

(2) A State that adopts the policy described in paragraph (a)(1) of this section may determine whether it applies to children with disabilities—

(i) From age three until the beginning of the school year following the child's third birthday;

(ii) From age three until the beginning of the school year following the child's fourth birthday; or

(iii) From age three until the beginning of the school year following the child's fifth birthday.

(3) In no case may a State provide services under this section beyond the age at which the child actually enters, or is eligible under State law to enter, kindergarten or elementary school in the State.

(b) *Requirements.* If a State's application for a grant under this part includes the State policy described in paragraph (a) of this section, the system must ensure the following:

(1) Parents of children with disabilities who are eligible for services under section 619 of the Act and who previously received early intervention services under this part will be provided an annual notice that contains—

(i) A description of the rights of the parents to elect to receive services pursuant to this section or under part B of the Act; and

(ii) An explanation of the differences between services provided pursuant to this section and services provided under part B of the Act, including—

(A) The types of services and the locations at which the services are provided;

(B) The procedural safeguards that apply; and

(C) Possible costs (including the costs or fees to be charged to families as described in §§303.520 and 303.521), if any, to parents of children eligible under this part.

(2) Consistent with §303.344(d), services provided pursuant to this section will include an educational component that promotes school readiness and incorporates preliteracy, language, and numeracy skills.

(3) The State policy ensures that any child served pursuant to this section has the right, at any time, to receive FAPE (as that term is defined at §303.15) under part B of the Act instead of early intervention services under part C of the Act.

(4) The lead agency must continue to provide all early intervention services identified in the toddler with a disability's IFSP under §303.344 (and consented to by the parent under §303.342(e)) beyond age three until that toddler's initial eligibility determination under part B of the Act is made under 34 CFR 300.306. This provision does not apply if the LEA has requested parental consent for the initial evaluation under 34 CFR 300.300(a) and the parent has not provided that consent.

(5) The lead agency must obtain informed consent from the parent of any child with a disability for the continuation of early intervention services pursuant to this section for that child. Consent must be obtained before the child reaches three years of age, where practicable.

(6)(i) For toddlers with disabilities under the age of three in a State that offers services under this section, the lead agency ensures that the transition requirements in §303.209(b)(1)(i) and (b)(1)(ii), (c)(1), and (d) are met.

(ii) For toddlers with disabilities age three and older in a State that offers services under this section, the lead agency ensures a smooth transition from services under this section to preschool, kindergarten or elementary school by—

(A) Providing the SEA and LEA where the child resides, consistent with any State policy adopted under §303.401(e), the information listed in §303.401(d)(1) not fewer than 90 days before the child will no longer be eligible under paragraph (a)(2) of this section to receive, or will no longer receive, early intervention services under this section;

(B) With the approval of the parents of the child, convening a transition conference, among the lead agency, the parents, and the LEA, not fewer than 90 days—and, at the discretion of all parties, not more than 9 months—before the child will no longer be eligible under paragraph (a)(2) of this section to receive, or no longer receives, early intervention services under this section, to discuss any services that the child may receive under part B of the Act; and

(C) Establishing a transition plan in the IFSP not fewer than 90 days—and, at the discretion of all parties, not more than 9 months—before the child will no longer be eligible under paragraph (a)(2) of this section to receive, or no longer receives, early intervention services under this section.

(7) In States that adopt the option to make services under this part available to children ages three and older pursuant to this section, there will be a referral to the part C system, dependent upon parental consent, of a child under the age of three who directly experiences a substantiated case of trauma due to exposure to family violence, as defined in section 320 of the Family Violence Prevention and Services Act, 42 U.S.C. 10401, et seq.

(c) *Reporting requirement.* If a State includes in its application a State policy described in paragraph (a) of this section, the State must submit to the Secretary, in the State's report under §303.124, the number and percentage of children with disabilities who are eligible for services under section 619 of the Act but whose parents choose for their children to continue to receive early intervention services under this part.

(d) *Available funds.* The State policy described in paragraph (a) of this section must describe the funds—including an identification as Federal, State, or local funds—that will be used to ensure that the option described in paragraph (a) of this section is available to eligible children and families who provide the consent described in paragraph (b)(5) of this section, including fees, if any, to be charged to families as described in §§ 303.520 and 303.521.

(e) *Rules of construction.* (1) If a statewide system includes a State policy described in paragraph (a) of this section, a State that provides services in accordance with this section to a child with a disability who is eligible for services under section 619 of the Act will not be required to provide the child FAPE under part B of the Act for the period of time in which the child is receiving services under this part.

(2) Nothing in this section may be construed to require a provider of services under this part to provide a child served under this part with FAPE.

(Approved by Office of Management and Budget under control number 1820–0550)

(Authority: 20 U.S.C. 1435(c), 1437(a)(11))

§ 303.212 Additional information and assurances.

Each application must contain—

(a) A description of the steps the State is taking to ensure equitable access to, and equitable participation in, the part C statewide system as required by section 427(b) of GEPA; and

(b) Other information and assurances as the Secretary may reasonably require.

(Approved by Office of Management and Budget under control number 1820–0550)

(Authority: 20 U.S.C. 1228a(b), 1437(a)(11))

ASSURANCES

§ 303.220 Assurances satisfactory to the Secretary.

Each application must contain assurances satisfactory to the Secretary that the State has met the requirements in §§ 303.221 through 303.227.

(Approved by Office of Management and Budget under control number 1820–0550)

(Authority: 20 U.S.C. 1437(b))

§ 303.221 Expenditure of funds.

The State must ensure that Federal funds made available to the State under section 643 of the Act will be expended in accordance with the provisions of this part, including §§ 303.500 and 303.501.

(Approved by Office of Management and Budget under control number 1820–0550)

(Authority: 20 U.S.C. 1437(b)(1))

§ 303.222 Payor of last resort.

The State must ensure that it will comply with the requirements in §§ 303.510 and 303.511 in subpart F of this part.

(Approved by Office of Management and Budget under control number 1820–0550)

(Authority: 20 U.S.C. 1437(b)(2))

§ 303.223 Control of funds and property.

The State must ensure that—

(a) The control of funds provided under this part, and title to property acquired with those funds, will be in a public agency for the uses and purposes provided in this part; and

(b) A public agency will administer the funds and property.

(Approved by Office of Management and Budget under control number 1820–0550)

(Authority: 20 U.S.C. 1437(b)(3))

§ 303.224 Reports and records.

The State must ensure that it will—

(a) Make reports in the form and containing the information that the Secretary may require; and

(b) Keep records and afford access to those records as the Secretary may find necessary to ensure compliance with the requirements of this part, the correctness and verification of reports, and the proper disbursement of funds provided under this part.

(Approved by Office of Management and Budget under control number 1820–0550)

(Authority: 20 U.S.C. 1437(b)(4))

§ 303.225 Prohibition against supplanting; indirect costs.

(a) Each application must provide satisfactory assurance that the Federal funds made available under section 643 of the Act to the State:

(1) Will not be commingled with State funds; and

(2) Will be used so as to supplement the level of State and local funds expended for infants and toddlers with disabilities and their families and in no case to supplant those State and local funds.

(b) To meet the requirement in paragraph (a) of this section, the total amount of State and local funds budgeted for expenditures in the current fiscal year for early intervention services for children eligible under this part and their families must be at least equal to the total amount of State and local funds actually expended for early intervention services for these children and their families in the most recent preceding fiscal year for which the information is available. Allowance may be made for—

(1) A decrease in the number of infants and toddlers who are eligible to receive early intervention services under this part; and

(2)) Unusually large amounts of funds expended for such long-term purposes as the acquisition of equipment and the construction of facilities.

(c) *Requirement regarding indirect costs.* (1) Except as provided in paragraph (c)(2) of this section, a lead agency under this part may not charge indirect costs to its part C grant.

(2) If approved by the lead agency's cognizant Federal agency or by the Secretary, the lead agency must charge indirect costs through either—

(i) A restricted indirect cost rate that meets the requirements in 34 CFR 76.560 through 76.569; or

(ii) A cost allocation plan that meets the non-supplanting requirements in paragraph (b) of this section and 34 CFR part 76 of EDGAR.

(3) In charging indirect costs under paragraph (c)(2)(i) and (c)(2)(ii) of this section, the lead agency may not charge rent, occupancy, or space maintenance costs directly to the part C grant, unless those costs are specifically approved in advance by the Secretary.

(Approved by Office of Management and Budget under control number 1820–0550)

(Authority: 20 U.S.C. 1437(b)(5))

§ 303.226 Fiscal control.

The State must ensure that fiscal control and fund accounting procedures will be adopted as necessary to ensure proper disbursement of, and accounting for, Federal funds paid under this part.

(Approved by Office of Management and Budget under control number 1820–0550)

(Authority: 20 U.S.C. 1437(b)(6))

§ 303.227 Traditionally underserved groups.

The State must ensure that policies and practices have been adopted to ensure—

(a) That traditionally underserved groups, including minority, low-income, homeless, and rural families and children with disabilities who are wards of the State, are meaningfully involved in the planning and implementation of all the requirements of this part; and

(b) That these families have access to culturally competent services within their local geographical areas.

(Approved by Office of Management and Budget under control number 1820–0550)

(Authority: 20 U.S.C. 1231d, 1437(b)(7))

SUBSEQUENT APPLICATIONS AND MODIFICATIONS, ELIGIBILITY DETERMINATIONS, AND STANDARD OF DISAPPROVAL

§ 303.228 Subsequent State application and modifications of application.

(a) *Subsequent State application.* If a State has on file with the Secretary a policy, procedure, method, or assurance that demonstrates that the State meets an application requirement in this part, including any policy, procedure, method, or assurance filed under this part (as in effect before the date of enactment of the Act, December 3, 2004), the Secretary considers the State to have met that requirement for purposes of receiving a grant under this part.

(b) *Modification of application.* An application submitted by a State that meets the requirements of this part remains in effect until the State submits to the Secretary such modifications as the State determines necessary. This section applies to a modification of an application to the same extent and in the same manner as this paragraph applies to the original application.

(c) *Modifications required by the Secretary.* The Secretary may require a State to modify its application under this part to the extent necessary to ensure the State's compliance with this part if—

(1) An amendment is made to the Act or to a Federal regulation issued under the Act;

(2) A new interpretation of the Act is made by a Federal court or the State's highest court; or

(3) An official finding of noncompliance with Federal law or regulations is made with respect to the State.

(Authority: 20 U.S.C. 1437(d)–(f))

§ 303.229 Determination by the Secretary that a State is eligible.

If the Secretary determines that a State is eligible to receive a grant under part C of the Act, the Secretary notifies the State of that determination.

(Authority: 20 U.S.C. 1437)

§ 303.230 Standard for disapproval of an application.

The Secretary does not disapprove an application under this part unless the Secretary determines, after notice and opportunity for a hearing in accordance with the procedures in §§ 303.231 through 303.236, that the application fails to comply with the requirements of this part.

(Authority: 20 U.S.C. 1437(c))

DEPARTMENT PROCEDURES

§ 303.231 Notice and hearing before determining that a State is not eligible.

(a) *General.* (1) The Secretary does not make a final determination that a State is not eligible to receive a grant under part C of the Act until providing the State—

(i) Reasonable notice; and

(ii) An opportunity for a hearing.

(2) In implementing paragraph (a)(1)(i) of this section, the Secretary sends a written notice to the lead agency by certified mail with a return receipt requested.

(b) *Content of notice.* In the written notice described in paragraph (a)(2) of this section, the Secretary—

(1) States the basis on which the Secretary proposes to make a final determination that the State is not eligible;

(2) May describe possible options for resolving the issues;

(3) Advises the lead agency that it may request a hearing and that the request for a hearing must be made not later than 30 days after it receives the notice of the proposed final determination that the State is not eligible; and

(4) Provides the lead agency with information about the hearing procedures that will be followed.

(Authority: 20 U.S.C. 1437(c))

§ 303.232 Hearing Official or Panel.

(a) If the lead agency requests a hearing, the Secretary designates one or more individuals, either from the Department or elsewhere, not responsible for or connected with the administration of this program, to conduct a hearing.

(b) If more than one individual is designated, the Secretary designates one of those individuals as the Chief Hearing Official of the Hearing Panel. If one individual is designated, that individual is the Hearing Official.

(Authority: 20 U.S.C. 1437(c))

§ 303.233 Hearing procedures.

(a) As used in §§ 303.231 through 303.235, the term *party* or *parties* means any of the following:

(1) A lead agency that requests a hearing regarding the proposed disapproval of the State's eligibility under this part.

(2) The Department official who administers the program of financial assistance under this part.

(3) A person, group, or agency with an interest in, and having relevant information about, the case that has applied for and been granted leave to intervene by the Hearing Official or Hearing Panel.

(b) Within 15 days after receiving a request for a hearing, the Secretary designates a Hearing Official or Hearing Panel and notifies the parties.

(c) The Hearing Official or Hearing Panel may regulate the course of proceedings and the conduct of the parties during the proceedings. The Hearing Official or Panel takes all steps necessary to conduct a fair and impartial proceeding, to avoid delay, and to maintain order, including the following:

(1) The Hearing Official or Hearing Panel may hold conferences or other types of appropriate proceedings to clarify, simplify, or define the issues or to consider other matters that may aid in the disposition of the case.

(2) The Hearing Official or Hearing Panel may schedule a prehearing conference with the Hearing Official or Hearing Panel and the parties.

(3) Any party may request the Hearing Official or Hearing Panel to schedule a prehearing or other conference. The Hearing Official or Hearing Panel decides whether a conference is necessary and notifies all parties.

(4) At a prehearing or other conference, the Hearing Official or Hearing Panel and the parties may consider subjects such as—

(i) Narrowing and clarifying issues;

(ii) Assisting the parties in reaching agreements and stipulations;

(iii) Clarifying the positions of the parties;

(iv) Determining whether an evidentiary hearing or oral argument should be held; and

(v) Setting dates for—

(A) The exchange of written documents;

(B) The receipt of comments from the parties on the need for oral argument or an evidentiary hearing;

(C) Further proceedings before the Hearing Official or Hearing Panel, including an evidentiary hearing or oral argument, if either is scheduled;

(D) Requesting the names of witnesses each party wishes to present at an evidentiary hearing and an estimation of time for each presentation; and

(E) Completion of the review and the initial decision of the Hearing Official or Hearing Panel.

(5) A prehearing or other conference held under paragraph (c)(4) of this section may be conducted by telephone conference call.

(6) At a prehearing or other conference, the parties must be prepared to discuss the subjects listed in paragraph (c)(4) of this section.

(7) Following a prehearing or other conference, the Hearing Official or Hearing Panel may issue a written statement describing the issues raised, the action taken, and the stipulations and agreements reached by the parties.

(d) The Hearing Official or Hearing Panel may require the parties to state their positions and to provide all or part of their evidence in writing.

(e) The Hearing Official or Hearing Panel may require the parties to present testimony through affidavits and to conduct cross-examination through interrogatories.

(f) The Hearing Official or Hearing Panel may direct the parties to exchange relevant documents, information, and lists of witnesses, and to send copies to the Hearing Official or Hearing Panel.

(g) The Hearing Official or Hearing Panel may receive, rule on, exclude, or limit evidence at any stage of the proceedings.

(h) The Hearing Official or Hearing Panel may rule on motions and other issues at any stage of the proceedings.

(i) The Hearing Official or Hearing Panel may examine witnesses.

(j) The Hearing Official or Hearing Panel may set reasonable time limits for submission of written documents.

(k) The Hearing Official or Hearing Panel may refuse to consider documents or other submissions if they are not submitted in a timely manner unless good cause is shown.

(l) The Hearing Official or Hearing Panel may interpret applicable statutes and regulations but may not waive them or rule on their validity.

(m)(1) The parties must present their positions through briefs and the submission of other documents and may request an oral argument or evidentiary hearing. The Hearing Official or Hearing Panel must determine whether an oral argument or an evidentiary hearing is needed to clarify the positions of the parties.

(2) The Hearing Official or Hearing Panel gives each party an opportunity to be represented by counsel.

(n) If the Hearing Official or Hearing Panel determines that an evidentiary hearing would materially assist the resolution of the matter, the Hearing Official or Hearing Panel gives each party, in addition to the opportunity to be represented by counsel—

(1) An opportunity to present witnesses on the party's behalf; and

(2) An opportunity to cross-examine witnesses either orally or with written questions.

(o) The Hearing Official or Hearing Panel accepts any evidence that it finds is relevant and material to the proceedings and is not unduly repetitious.

(p)(1) The Hearing Official or Hearing Panel—

(i) Arranges for the preparation of a transcript of each hearing;

(ii) Retains the original transcript as part of the record of the hearing; and

(iii) Provides one copy of the transcript to each party.

(2) Additional copies of the transcript are available on request and with payment of the reproduction fee.

(q) Each party must file with the Hearing Official or Hearing Panel all written motions, briefs, and other documents and must at the same time provide a copy to the other parties to the proceedings.

(Authority: 20 U.S.C. 1437(c))

§ 303.234   Initial decision; final decision.

(a) The Hearing Official or Hearing Panel prepares an initial written decision that addresses each of the points in the notice sent by the Secretary to the lead agency under § 303.231, including any amendments to or further clarification of the issues under § 303.233(c).

(b) The initial decision of a Hearing Panel is made by a majority of Hearing Panel members.

(c) The Hearing Official or Hearing Panel mails, by certified mail with return receipt requested, a copy of the initial decision to each party (or to the party's counsel) and to the Secretary, with a notice stating that each party has an opportunity to submit written comments regarding the decision to the Secretary.

(d) Each party may file comments and recommendations on the initial decision with the Hearing Official or Hearing Panel within 15 days of the date the party receives the Panel's decision.

(e) The Hearing Official or Hearing Panel sends a copy of a party's initial comments and recommendations to the other parties by certified mail with return receipt requested. Each party may file responsive comments and recommendations with the Hearing Official or Hearing Panel within seven days of the date the party receives the initial comments and recommendations.

(f) The Hearing Official or Hearing Panel forwards the parties' initial and responsive comments on the initial decision to the Secretary who reviews the initial decision and issues a final decision.

(g) The initial decision of the Hearing Official or Hearing Panel becomes the final decision of the Secretary unless, within 25 days after the end of the time for receipt of written comments, the Secretary informs the Hearing Official or Hearing Panel and the parties to a hearing in writing that the decision is being further reviewed for possible modification.

(h) The Secretary rejects or modifies the initial decision of the Hearing Official or Hearing Panel if the Secretary finds that it is clearly erroneous.

(i) The Secretary conducts the review based on the initial decision, the written record, the transcript of the Hearing Official's or Hearing Panel's proceedings, and written comments.

(j) The Secretary may remand the matter to the Hearing Official or Hearing Panel for further proceedings.

(k) Unless the Secretary remands the matter as provided in paragraph (j) of this section, the Secretary issues the final decision, with any necessary modifications, within 30 days after notifying the Hearing Official or Hearing Panel that the initial decision is being further reviewed.

(Authority: 20 U.S.C. 1437(c))

§ 303.235   Filing requirements.

(a) Any written submission by a party under §§ 303.230 through 303.236 must be filed with the Secretary by hand-delivery, by mail, or by facsimile transmission. The Secretary discourages the use of facsimile transmission for documents longer than five pages.

(b) The filing date under paragraph (a) of this section is the date the document is—

(1) Hand-delivered;

(2) Mailed; or

(3) Sent by facsimile transmission.

(c) A party filing by facsimile transmission is responsible for confirming that a complete and legible copy of the document was received by the Department.

(d) If a document is filed by facsimile transmission, the Secretary, the Hearing Official, or the Panel, as applicable, may require the filing of a follow-up hard copy by hand-delivery or by mail within a reasonable period of time.

(e) If agreed upon by the parties, service of a document may be made upon the other party by facsimile transmission.

(Authority: 20 U.S.C. 1437(c))

§ 303.236 Judicial review.

If a State is dissatisfied with the Secretary's final decision with respect to the eligibility of the State under part C of the Act, the State may, not later than 60 days after notice of that decision, file with the United States Court of Appeals for the circuit in which that State is located a petition for review of that decision. A copy of the petition must be transmitted by the clerk of the court to the Secretary. The Secretary then files in the court the record of the proceedings upon which the Secretary's action was based, as provided in 28 U.S.C. 2112.

(Authority: 20 U.S.C. 1437(c))

Subpart D—Child Find, Evaluations and Assessments, and Individualized Family Service Plans

§ 303.300 General.

The statewide comprehensive, coordinated, multidisciplinary interagency system to provide early intervention services for infants and toddlers with disabilities and their families referenced in § 303.100 must include the following components:

(a) Pre-referral policies and procedures that include—

(1) A public awareness program as described in § 303.301; and

(2) A comprehensive child find system as described in § 303.302.

(b) Referral policies and procedures as described in § 303.303.

(c) Post-referral policies and procedures that ensure compliance with the timeline requirements in § 303.310 and include—

(1) Screening, if applicable, as described in § 303.320;

(2) Evaluations and assessments as described in §§ 303.321 and 303.322; and

(3) Development, review, and implementation of IFSPs as described in §§ 303.340 through 303.346.

PRE-REFERRAL PROCEDURES—PUBLIC AWARENESS PROGRAM AND CHILD FIND SYSTEM

§ 303.301 Public awareness program—information for parents.

(a) *Preparation and dissemination.* In accordance with § 303.116, each system must include a public awareness program that requires the lead agency to—

(1)(i) Prepare information on the availability of early intervention services under this part, and other services, as described in paragraph (b) of this section; and

(ii) Disseminate to all primary referral sources (especially hospitals and physicians) the information to be given to parents of infants and toddlers, especially parents with premature infants or infants with other physical risk factors associated with learning or developmental complications; and

(2) Adopt procedures for assisting the primary referral sources described in § 303.303(c) in disseminating the information described in paragraph (b) of this section to parents of infants and toddlers with disabilities.

(b) *Information to be provided.* The information required to be prepared and disseminated under paragraph (a) of this section must include—

(1) A description of the availability of early intervention services under this part;

(2) A description of the child find system and how to refer a child under the

age of three for an evaluation or early intervention services; and

(3) A central directory, as described in § 303.117.

(c) *Information specific to toddlers with disabilities.* Each public awareness program also must include a requirement that the lead agency provide for informing parents of toddlers with disabilities of the availability of services under section 619 of the Act not fewer than 90 days prior to the toddler's third birthday.

(Authority: 20 U.S.C. 1435(a)(6), 1437(a)(9))

§ 303.302 Comprehensive child find system.

(a) *General.* Each system must include a comprehensive child find system that—

(1) Is consistent with part B of the Act (see 34 CFR 300.111);

(2) Includes a system for making referrals to lead agencies or EIS providers under this part that—

(i) Includes timelines; and

(ii) Provides for participation by the primary referral sources described in § 303.303(c);

(3) Ensures rigorous standards for appropriately identifying infants and toddlers with disabilities for early intervention services under this part that will reduce the need for future services; and

(4) Meets the requirements in paragraphs (b) and (c) of this section and §§ 303.303, 303.310, 303.320, and 303.321.

(b) *Scope of child find.* The lead agency, as part of the child find system, must ensure that—

(1) All infants and toddlers with disabilities in the State who are eligible for early intervention services under this part are identified, located, and evaluated, including—

(i) Indian infants and toddlers with disabilities residing on a reservation geographically located in the State (including coordination, as necessary, with tribes, tribal organizations, and consortia to identify infants and toddlers with disabilities in the State based, in part, on the information provided by them to the lead agency under § 303.731(e)(1)); and

(ii) Infants and toddlers with disabilities who are homeless, in foster care, and wards of the State; and

(iii) Infants and toddlers with disabilities that are referenced in § 303.303(b); and

(2) An effective method is developed and implemented to identify children who are in need of early intervention services.

(c) *Coordination.* (1) The lead agency, with the assistance of the Council, as defined in § 303.8, must ensure that the child find system under this part—

(i) Is coordinated with all other major efforts to locate and identify children by other State agencies responsible for administering the various education, health, and social service programs relevant to this part, including Indian tribes that receive payments under this part, and other Indian tribes, as appropriate; and

(ii) Is coordinated with the efforts of the—

(A) Program authorized under part B of the Act;

(B) Maternal and Child Health program, including the Maternal, Infant, and Early Childhood Home Visiting Program, under Title V of the Social Security Act, as amended, (MCHB or Title V) (42 U.S.C. 701(a));

(C) Early Periodic Screening, Diagnosis, and Treatment (EPSDT) under Title XIX of the Social Security Act (42 U.S.C. 1396(a)(43) and 1396(a)(4)(B));

(D) Programs under the Developmental Disabilities Assistance and Bill of Rights Act of 2000 (42 U.S.C. 15001 *et seq.*);

(E) Head Start Act (including Early Head Start programs under section 645A of the Head Start Act) (42 U.S.C. 9801 *et seq.*);

(F) Supplemental Security Income program under Title XVI of the Social Security Act (42 U.S.C. 1381);

(G) Child protection and child welfare programs, including programs administered by, and services provided through, the foster care agency and the State agency responsible for administering the Child Abuse Prevention and Treatment Act (CAPTA) (42 U.S.C. 5106(a));

(H) Child care programs in the State;

(I) The programs that provide services under the Family Violence Prevention and Services Act (42 U.S.C. 10401 *et seq.*);

(J) Early Hearing Detection and Intervention (EHDI) systems (42 U.S.C. 280g–1) administered by the Centers for Disease Control (CDC); and

(K) Children's Health Insurance Program (CHIP) authorized under Title XXI of the Social Security Act (42 U.S.C. 1397aa *et seq.*).

(2) The lead agency, with the advice and assistance of the Council, must take steps to ensure that—

(i) There will not be unnecessary duplication of effort by the programs identified in paragraph (c)(1)(ii) of this section; and

(ii) The State will make use of the resources available through each public agency and EIS provider in the State to implement the child find system in an effective manner.

(Authority: 20 U.S.C. 1412(a)(3)(A), 1431, 1434(1), 1435(a)(2), 1435(a)(5), 1435(c)(2)(G), 1437(a)(6), 1437(a)(10), 1441)

REFERRAL PROCEDURES

§ 303.303 Referral procedures.

(a) *General.* (1) The lead agency's child find system described in § 303.302 must include the State's procedures for use by primary referral sources for referring a child under the age of three to the part C program.

(2) The procedures required in paragraph (a)(1) of this section must—

(i) Provide for referring a child as soon as possible, but in no case more than seven days, after the child has been identified; and

(ii) Meet the requirements in paragraphs (b) and (c) of this section.

(b) *Referral of specific at-risk infants and toddlers.* The procedures required in paragraph (a) of this section must provide for requiring the referral of a child under the age of three who—

(1) Is the subject of a substantiated case of child abuse or neglect; or

(2) Is identified as directly affected by illegal substance abuse or withdrawal symptoms resulting from prenatal drug exposure.

(c) *Primary referral sources.* As used in this subpart, primary referral sources include—

(1) Hospitals, including prenatal and postnatal care facilities;

(2) Physicians;

(3) Parents, including parents of infants and toddlers;

(4) Child care programs and early learning programs;

(5) LEAs and schools;

(6) Public health facilities;

(7) Other public health or social service agencies;

(8) Other clinics and health care providers;

(9) Public agencies and staff in the child welfare system, including child protective service and foster care;

(10) Homeless family shelters; and

(11) Domestic violence shelters and agencies.

(Authority: 20 U.S.C. 1412(a)(3)(A), 1431, 1434(1), 1435(a)(2), 1435(a)(5), 1435(a)(6), 1435(c)(2)(G), 1437(a)(6), 1437(a)(10), 1441)

§§ 303.304–303.309 [Reserved]

POST-REFERRAL PROCEDURES— SCREENINGS, EVALUATIONS, AND ASSESSMENTS

§ 303.310 Post-referral timeline (45 days).

(a) Except as provided in paragraph (b) of this section, any screening under § 303.320 (if the State has adopted a policy and elects, and the parent consents, to conduct a screening of a child); the initial evaluation and the initial assessments of the child and family under § 303.321; and the initial IFSP meeting under § 303.342 must be completed within 45 days from the date the lead agency or EIS provider receives the referral of the child.

(b) Subject to paragraph (c) of this section, the 45-day timeline described in paragraph (a) of this section does not apply for any period when—

(1) The child or parent is unavailable to complete the screening (if applicable), the initial evaluation, the initial assessments of the child and family, or the initial IFSP meeting due to exceptional family circumstances that are documented in the child's early intervention records; or

(2) The parent has not provided consent for the screening (if applicable), the initial evaluation, or the initial assessment of the child, despite documented, repeated attempts by the lead agency or EIS provider to obtain parental consent.

(c) The lead agency must develop procedures to ensure that in the event the circumstances described in (b)(1) or (b)(2) of this section exist, the lead agency or EIS provider must—

(1) Document in the child's early intervention records the exceptional family circumstances or repeated attempts by the lead agency or EIS provider to obtain parental consent;

(2) Complete the screening (if applicable), the initial evaluation, the initial assessments (of the child and family), and the initial IFSP meeting as soon as possible after the documented exceptional family circumstances described in paragraph (b)(1) of this section no longer exist or parental consent is obtained for the screening (if applicable), the initial evaluation, and the initial assessment of the child; and

(3) Develop and implement an interim IFSP, to the extent appropriate and consistent with § 303.345.

(d) The initial family assessment must be conducted within the 45-day timeline in paragraph (a) of this section if the parent concurs and even if other family members are unavailable.

(Authority: 20 U.S.C. 1433, 1435(a), 1436(c))

§§ 303.311–303.319 [Reserved]

§ 303.320 Screening procedures (optional).

(a) *General*. (1) The lead agency may adopt procedures, consistent with the requirements of this section, to screen children under the age of three who have been referred to the part C program to determine whether they are suspected of having a disability under this part. If the lead agency or EIS provider proposes to screen a child, it must—

(i) Provide the parent notice under § 303.421 of its intent to screen the child to identify whether the child is suspected of having a disability and include in that notice a description of the parent's right to request an evaluation under § 303.321 at any time during the screening process; and

(ii) Obtain parental consent as required in § 303.420(a)(1) before conducting the screening procedures.

(2) If the parent consents to the screening and the screening or other available information indicates that the child is—

(i) Suspected of having a disability, after notice is provided under § 303.421 and once parental consent is obtained as required in § 303.420, an evaluation and assessment of the child must be conducted under § 303.321; or

(ii) Not suspected of having a disability, the lead agency or EIS provider must ensure that notice of that determination is provided to the parent under § 303.421, and that the notice describes the parent's right to request an evaluation.

(3) If the parent of the child requests and consents to an evaluation at any time during the screening process, evaluation of the child must be conducted under § 303.321, even if the lead agency or EIS provider has determined under paragraph (a)(2)(ii) of this section that the child is not suspected of having a disability.

(b) *Definition of screening procedures. Screening procedures*—

(1) Means activities under paragraphs (a)(1) and (a)(2) of this section that are carried out by, or under the supervision of, the lead agency or EIS provider to identify, at the earliest possible age, infants and toddlers suspected of having a disability and in need of early intervention services; and

(2) Includes the administration of appropriate instruments by personnel trained to administer those instruments.

(c) *Condition for evaluation or early intervention services.* For every child under the age of three who is referred to the part C program or screened in accordance with paragraph (a) of this section, the lead agency is not required to—

(1) Provide an evaluation of the child under § 303.321 unless the child is suspected of having a disability or the parent requests an evaluation under paragraph (a)(3) of this section; or

(2) Make early intervention services available under this part to the child unless a determination is made that the child meets the definition of *infant or toddler with a disability* under § 303.21.

(Authority: 20 U.S.C. 1432(4)(E)(ix), 1434(1), 1435(a)(2), 1435(a)(5) and (a)(6), 1435(c)(2)(G), 1437(a)(6), 1439(a)(6))

§303.321 Evaluation of the child and assessment of the child and family.

(a) *General.* (1) The lead agency must ensure that, subject to obtaining parental consent in accordance with §303.420(a)(2), each child under the age of three who is referred for evaluation or early intervention services under this part and suspected of having a disability, receives—

(i) A timely, comprehensive, multidisciplinary evaluation of the child in accordance with paragraph (b) of this section unless eligibility is established under paragraph (a)(3)(i) of this section; and

(ii) If the child is determined eligible as an infant or toddler with a disability as defined in §303.21—

(A) A multidisciplinary assessment of the unique strengths and needs of that infant or toddler and the identification of services appropriate to meet those needs;

(B) A family-directed assessment of the resources, priorities, and concerns of the family and the identification of the supports and services necessary to enhance the family's capacity to meet the developmental needs of that infant or toddler. The assessments of the child and family are described in paragraph (c) of this section and these assessments may occur simultaneously with the evaluation, provided that the requirements of paragraph (b) of this section are met.

(2) As used in this part—

(i) *Evaluation* means the procedures used by qualified personnel to determine a child's initial and continuing eligibility under this part, consistent with the definition of *infant or toddler with a disability* in §303.21. An *initial evaluation* refers to the child's evaluation to determine his or her initial eligibility under this part;

(ii) *Assessment* means the ongoing procedures used by qualified personnel to identify the child's unique strengths and needs and the early intervention services appropriate to meet those needs throughout the period of the child's eligibility under this part and includes the assessment of the child, consistent with paragraph (c)(1) of this section and the assessment of the child's family, consistent with paragraph (c)(2) of this section; and

(iii) *Initial assessment* refers to the assessment of the child and the family assessment conducted prior to the child's first IFSP meeting.

(3)(i) A child's medical and other records may be used to establish eligibility (without conducting an evaluation of the child) under this part if those records indicate that the child's level of functioning in one or more of the developmental areas identified in §303.21(a)(1) constitutes a developmental delay or that the child otherwise meets the criteria for an infant or toddler with a disability under §303.21. If the child's part C eligibility is established under this paragraph, the lead agency or EIS provider must conduct assessments of the child and family in accordance with paragraph (c) of this section.

(ii) Qualified personnel must use informed clinical opinion when conducting an evaluation and assessment of the child. In addition, the lead agency must ensure that informed clinical opinion may be used as an independent basis to establish a child's eligibility under this part even when other instruments do not establish eligibility; however, in no event may informed clinical opinion be used to negate the results of evaluation instruments used to establish eligibility under paragraph (b) of this section.

(4) All evaluations and assessments of the child and family must be conducted by qualified personnel, in a nondiscriminatory manner, and selected and administered so as not to be racially or culturally discriminatory.

(5) Unless clearly not feasible to do so, all evaluations and assessments of a child must be conducted in the native language of the child, in accordance with the definition of *native language* in §303.25.

(6) Unless clearly not feasible to do so, family assessments must be conducted in the native language of the family members being assessed, in accordance with the definition of *native language* in §303.25.

(b) *Procedures for evaluation of the child.* In conducting an evaluation, no single procedure may be used as the sole criterion for determining a child's eligibility under this part. Procedures must include—

(1) Administering an evaluation instrument;

(2) Taking the child's history (including interviewing the parent);

(3) Identifying the child's level of functioning in each of the developmental areas in § 303.21(a)(1);

(4) Gathering information from other sources such as family members, other care-givers, medical providers, social workers, and educators, if necessary, to understand the full scope of the child's unique strengths and needs; and

(5) Reviewing medical, educational, or other records.

(c) *Procedures for assessment of the child and family.* (1) An assessment of each infant or toddler with a disability must be conducted by qualified personnel in order to identify the child's unique strengths and needs and the early intervention services appropriate to meet those needs. The assessment of the child must include the following—

(i) A review of the results of the evaluation conducted under paragraph (b) of this section;

(ii) Personal observations of the child; and

(iii) The identification of the child's needs in each of the developmental areas in § 303.21(a)(1).

(2) A family-directed assessment must be conducted by qualified personnel in order to identify the family's resources, priorities, and concerns and the supports and services necessary to enhance the family's capacity to meet the developmental needs of the family's infant or toddler with a disability. The family-directed assessment must—

(i) Be voluntary on the part of each family member participating in the assessment;

(ii) Be based on information obtained through an assessment tool and also through an interview with those family members who elect to participate in the assessment; and

(iii) Include the family's description of its resources, priorities, and concerns related to enhancing the child's development.

(Authority: 20 U.S.C. 1435(a)(3), 1435(a)(5), 1436(a)(1)–(2))

§ 303.322 Determination that a child is not eligible.

If, based on the evaluation conducted under § 303.321, the lead agency determines that a child is not eligible under this part, the lead agency must provide the parent with prior written notice required in § 303.421, and include in the notice information about the parent's right to dispute the eligibility determination through dispute resolution mechanisms under § 303.430, such as requesting a due process hearing or mediation or filing a State complaint.

(Authority: 20 U.S.C. 1439(a)(6))

INDIVIDUALIZED FAMILY SERVICE PLAN (IFSP)

§ 303.340 Individualized family service plan—general.

For each infant or toddler with a disability, the lead agency must ensure the development, review, and implementation of an individualized family service plan or IFSP developed by a multidisciplinary team, which includes the parent, that—

(a) Is consistent with the definition of that term in § 303.20; and

(b) Meets the requirements in §§ 303.342 through 303.346 of this subpart.

(Authority: 20 U.S.C. 1435(a)(4), 1436)

§ 303.341 [Reserved]

§ 303.342 Procedures for IFSP development, review, and evaluation.

(a) *Meeting to develop initial IFSP—timelines.* For a child referred to the part C program and determined to be eligible under this part as an infant or toddler with a disability, a meeting to develop the initial IFSP must be conducted within the 45-day time period described in § 303.310.

(b) *Periodic review.* (1) A review of the IFSP for a child and the child's family must be conducted every six months, or more frequently if conditions warrant, or if the family requests such a review. The purpose of the periodic review is to determine—

(i) The degree to which progress toward achieving the results or outcomes identified in the IFSP is being made; and

(ii) Whether modification or revision of the results, outcomes, or early intervention services identified in the IFSP is necessary.

(2) The review may be carried out by a meeting or by another means that is acceptable to the parents and other participants.

(c) *Annual meeting to evaluate the IFSP.* A meeting must be conducted on at least an annual basis to evaluate and revise, as appropriate, the IFSP for a child and the child's family. The results of any current evaluations and other information available from the assessments of the child and family conducted under § 303.321 must be used in determining the early intervention services that are needed and will be provided.

(d) *Accessibility and convenience of meetings.* (1) IFSP meetings must be conducted—

(i) In settings and at times that are convenient for the family; and

(ii) In the native language of the family or other mode of communication used by the family, unless it is clearly not feasible to do so.

(2) Meeting arrangements must be made with, and written notice provided to, the family and other participants early enough before the meeting date to ensure that they will be able to attend.

(e) *Parental consent.* The contents of the IFSP must be fully explained to the parents and informed written consent, as described in § 303.7, must be obtained, as required in § 303.420(a)(3), prior to the provision of early intervention services described in the IFSP. Each early intervention service must be provided as soon as possible after the parent provides consent for that service, as required in § 303.344(f)(1).

(Authority: 20 U.S.C. 1435(a)(4), 1436)

§ 303.343 IFSP Team meeting and periodic review.

(a) *Initial and annual IFSP Team meeting.* (1) Each initial meeting and each annual IFSP Team meeting to evaluate the IFSP must include the following participants:

(i) The parent or parents of the child.

(ii) Other family members, as requested by the parent, if feasible to do so.

(iii) An advocate or person outside of the family, if the parent requests that the person participate.

(iv) The service coordinator designated by the public agency to be responsible for implementing the IFSP.

(v) A person or persons directly involved in conducting the evaluations and assessments in § 303.321.

(vi) As appropriate, persons who will be providing early intervention services under this part to the child or family.

(2) If a person listed in paragraph (a)(1)(v) of this section is unable to attend a meeting, arrangements must be made for the person's involvement through other means, including one of the following:

(i) Participating in a telephone conference call.

(ii) Having a knowledgeable authorized representative attend the meeting.

(iii) Making pertinent records available at the meeting.

(b) *Periodic review.* Each periodic review under § 303.342(b) must provide for the participation of persons in paragraphs (a)(1)(i) through (a)(1)(iv) of this section. If conditions warrant, provisions must be made for the participation of other representatives identified in paragraph (a) of this section.

(Authority: 20 U.S.C. 1435(a)(4), 1436)

§ 303.344 Content of an IFSP.

(a) *Information about the child's status.* The IFSP must include a statement of the infant or toddler with a disability's present levels of physical development (including vision, hearing, and health status), cognitive development, communication development, social or emotional development, and adaptive development based on the information from that child's evaluation and assessments conducted under § 303.321.

(b) *Family information.* With the concurrence of the family, the IFSP must include a statement of the family's resources, priorities, and concerns related to enhancing the development of the child as identified through the assessment of the family under § 303.321(c)(2).

(c) *Results or outcomes.* The IFSP must include a statement of the measurable results or measurable outcomes expected to be achieved for the child (including pre-literacy and language skills, as developmentally appropriate for the child) and family, and the criteria, procedures, and timelines used to determine—

(1) The degree to which progress toward achieving the results or outcomes identified in the IFSP is being made; and

(2) Whether modifications or revisions of the expected results or outcomes, or early intervention services identified in the IFSP are necessary.

(d) *Early intervention services.* (1) The IFSP must include a statement of the specific early intervention services, based on peer-reviewed research (to the extent practicable), that are necessary to meet the unique needs of the child and the family to achieve the results or outcomes identified in paragraph (c) of this section, including—

(i) The length, duration, frequency, intensity, and method of delivering the early intervention services;

(ii)(A) A statement that each early intervention service is provided in the natural environment for that child or service to the maximum extent appropriate, consistent with §§ 303.13(a)(8), 303.26 and 303.126, or, subject to paragraph (d)(1)(ii)(B) of this section, a justification as to why an early intervention service will not be provided in the natural environment.

(B) The determination of the appropriate setting for providing early intervention services to an infant or toddler with a disability, including any justification for not providing a particular early intervention service in the natural environment for that infant or toddler with a disability and service, must be—

(1) Made by the IFSP Team (which includes the parent and other team members);

(2) Consistent with the provisions in §§ 303.13(a)(8), 303.26, and 303.126; and

(3) Based on the child's outcomes that are identified by the IFSP Team in paragraph (c) of this section;

(iii) The location of the early intervention services; and

(iv) The payment arrangements, if any.

(2) As used in paragraph (d)(1)(i) of this section—

(i) *Frequency and intensity* mean the number of days or sessions that a service will be provided, and whether the service is provided on an individual or group basis;

(ii) *Method* means how a service is provided;

(iii) *Length* means the length of time the service is provided during each session of that service (such as an hour or other specified time period); and

(iv) *Duration* means projecting when a given service will no longer be provided (such as when the child is expected to achieve the results or outcomes in his or her IFSP).

(3) As used in paragraph (d)(1)(iii) of this section, *location* means the actual place or places where a service will be provided.

(4) For children who are at least three years of age, the IFSP must include an educational component that promotes school readiness and incorporates pre-literacy, language, and numeracy skills.

(e) *Other services.* To the extent appropriate, the IFSP also must—

(1) Identify medical and other services that the child or family needs or is receiving through other sources, but that are neither required nor funded under this part; and

(2) If those services are not currently being provided, include a description of the steps the service coordinator or family may take to assist the child and family in securing those other services.

(f) *Dates and duration of services.* The IFSP must include—

(1) The projected date for the initiation of each early intervention service in paragraph (d)(1) of this section, which date must be as soon as possible after the parent consents to the service, as required in §§ 303.342(e) and 303.420(a)(3); and

(2) The anticipated duration of each service.

(g) *Service coordinator.* (1) The IFSP must include the name of the service coordinator from the profession most relevant to the child's or family's needs (or who is otherwise qualified to carry out all applicable responsibilities under this part), who will be responsible for implementing the early intervention services identified in a child's IFSP, including transition services, and coordination with other agencies and persons.

(2) In meeting the requirements in paragraph (g)(1) of this section, the term "profession" includes "service coordination."

(h) *Transition from Part C services.* (1) The IFSP must include the steps and services to be taken to support the smooth transition of the child, in accordance with §§ 303.209 and 303.211(b)(6), from part C services to—

(i) Preschool services under part B of the Act, to the extent that those services are appropriate;

(ii) Part C services under § 303.211; or

(iii) Other appropriate services.

(2) The steps required in paragraph (h)(1) of this section must include—

(i) Discussions with, and training of, parents, as appropriate, regarding future placements and other matters related to the child's transition;

(ii) Procedures to prepare the child for changes in service delivery, including steps to help the child adjust to, and function in, a new setting;

(iii) Confirmation that child find information about the child has been transmitted to the LEA or other relevant agency, in accordance with § 303.209(b) (and any policy adopted by the State under § 303.401(e)) and, with parental consent if required under § 303.414, transmission of additional information needed by the LEA to ensure continuity of services from the part C program to the part B program, including a copy of the most recent evaluation and assessments of the child and the family and most recent IFSP developed in accordance with §§ 303.340 through 303.345; and

(iv) Identification of transition services and other activities that the IFSP Team determines are necessary to support the transition of the child.

(Authority: 20 U.S.C. 1435(a)(10)(B), 1435(a)(16), 1436(a)(3), 1436(d), 1437(a)(9)–(10), 1440)

§ 303.345 Interim IFSPs—provision of services before evaluations and assessments are completed.

Early intervention services for an eligible child and the child's family may commence before the completion of the evaluation and assessments in § 303.321, if the following conditions are met:

(a) Parental consent is obtained.

(b) An interim IFSP is developed that includes—

(1) The name of the service coordinator who will be responsible, consistent with § 303.344(g), for implementing the interim IFSP and coordinating with other agencies and persons; and

(2) The early intervention services that have been determined to be needed immediately by the child and the child's family.

(c) Evaluations and assessments are completed within the 45-day timeline in § 303.310.

(Authority: 20 U.S.C. 1436(c))

§ 303.346 Responsibility and accountability.

Each public agency or EIS provider who has a direct role in the provision of early intervention services is responsible for making a good faith effort to assist each eligible child in achieving the outcomes in the child's IFSP. However, part C of the Act does not require that any public agency or EIS provider be held accountable if an eligible child does not achieve the growth projected in the child's IFSP.

(Authority: 20 U.S.C. 1436)

Subpart E—Procedural Safeguards

GENERAL

§ 303.400 General responsibility of lead agency for procedural safeguards.

Subject to paragraph (c) of this section, each lead agency must—

(a) Establish or adopt the procedural safeguards that meet the requirements of this subpart, including the provisions on confidentiality in §§ 303.401 through 303.417, parental consent and notice in §§ 303.420 and 303.421, surrogate parents in § 303.422, and dispute resolution procedures in § 303.430;

(b) Ensure the effective implementation of the safeguards by each participating agency (including the lead agency and EIS providers) in the statewide system that is involved in the provision of early intervention services under this part; and

(c) Make available to parents an initial copy of the child's early intervention record, at no cost to the parents.

(Authority: 20 U.S.C. 1439(a))

CONFIDENTIALITY OF PERSONALLY IDENTIFIABLE INFORMATION AND EARLY INTERVENTION RECORDS

§ 303.401 Confidentiality and opportunity to examine records.

(a) *General.* Each State must ensure that the parents of a child referred under this part are afforded the right to confidentiality of personally identifiable information, including the right to written notice of, and written consent to, the exchange of that information among agencies, consistent with Federal and State laws.

(b) *Confidentiality procedures.* As required under sections 617(c) and 642 of the Act, the regulations in §§ 303.401 through 303.417 ensure the protection of the confidentiality of any personally identifiable data, information, and records collected or maintained pursuant to this part by the Secretary and by participating agencies, including the State lead agency and EIS providers, in accordance with the protections under the Family Educational Rights and Privacy Act (FERPA) in 20 U.S.C. 1232g and 34 CFR part 99. Each State must have procedures in effect to ensure that—

(1) Participating agencies (including the lead agency and EIS providers) comply with the part C confidentiality procedures in §§ 303.401 through 303.417; and

(2) The parents of infants or toddlers who are referred to, or receive services under this part, are afforded the opportunity to inspect and review all part C early intervention records about the child and the child's family that are collected, maintained, or used under this part, including records related to evaluations and assessments, screening, eligibility determinations, development and implementation of IFSPs, provision of early intervention services, individual complaints involving the child, or any part of the child's early intervention record under this part.

(c) *Applicability and timeframe of procedures.* The confidentiality procedures described in paragraph (b) of this section apply to the personally identifiable information of a child and the child's family that—

(1) Is contained in early intervention records collected, used, or maintained under this part by the lead agency or an EIS provider; and

(2) Applies from the point in time when the child is referred for early intervention services under this part until the later of when the participating agency is no longer required to maintain or no longer maintains that information under applicable Federal and State laws.

(d) *Disclosure of information.* (1) Subject to paragraph (e) of this section, the lead agency must disclose to the SEA and the LEA where the child resides, in accordance with § 303.209(b)(1)(i) and (b)(1)(ii), the following personally identifiable information under the Act:

(i) A child's name.

(ii) A child's date of birth.

(iii) Parent contact information (including parents' names, addresses, and telephone numbers).

(2) The information described in paragraph (d)(1) of this section is needed to enable the lead agency, as well as LEAs and SEAs under part B of the Act, to identify all children potentially eligible for services under § 303.211 and part B of the Act.

(e) *Option to inform a parent about intended disclosure.* (1) A lead agency, through its policies and procedures, may require EIS providers, prior to making the limited disclosure described in paragraph (d)(1) of this section, to inform parents of a toddler with a disability of the intended disclosure and allow the parents a specified time period to object to the disclosure in writing.

(2) If a parent (in a State that has adopted the policy described in paragraph (e)(1) of this section) objects during the time period provided by the State, the lead agency and EIS provider are not permitted to make such a disclosure under paragraph (d) of this section and § 303.209(b)(1)(i) and (b)(1)(ii).

(Authority: 20 U.S.C. 1412(a)(8), 1412(a)(9), 1417(c), 1435(a)(5), 1437(a)(9), 1439(a)(2), 1439(a)(4), 1439(a)(6), 1442)

§ 303.402 Confidentiality.

The Secretary takes appropriate action, in accordance with section 444 of GEPA, to ensure the protection of the confidentiality of any personally identifiable data, information, and records collected, maintained, or used by the Secretary and by lead agencies and EIS providers pursuant to part C of the Act, and consistent with §§ 303.401 through 303.417. The regulations in §§ 303.401 through 303.417 ensure the protection of the confidentiality of any personally identifiable data, information, and records collected or maintained pursuant to this part by the Secretary and by participating agencies, including the State lead agency and EIS providers, in accordance with the Family Educational Rights and Privacy Act (FERPA), 20 U.S.C. 1232g, and 34 CFR part 99.

(Authority: 20 U.S.C. 1417(c), 1435(a)(5), 1439(a)(2), 1442)

§ 303.403 Definitions.

The following definitions apply to §§ 303.402 through 303.417 in addition to the definition of personally identifiable information in § 303.29 and disclosure in 34 CFR 99.3:

(a) *Destruction* means physical destruction of the record or ensuring that personal identifiers are removed from a record so that the record is no longer personally identifiable under § 303.29.

(b) *Early intervention records* mean all records regarding a child that are required to be collected, maintained, or used under part C of the Act and the regulations in this part.

(c) *Participating agency* means any individual, agency, entity, or institution that collects, maintains, or uses personally identifiable information to implement the requirements in part C of the Act and the regulations in this part with respect to a particular child. A participating agency includes the lead agency and EIS providers and any individual or entity that provides any part C services (including service coordination, evaluations and assessments, and other part C services), but does not include primary referral sources, or public agencies (such as the State Medicaid or CHIP program) or private entities (such as private insurance companies) that act solely as funding sources for part C services.

(Authority: 20 U.S.C. 1221e-3, 1417(c), 1435(a)(5), 1439(a)(2), 1442)

§ 303.404 Notice to parents.

The lead agency must give notice when a child is referred under part C of the Act that is adequate to fully inform parents about the requirements in § 303.402, including—

(a) A description of the children on whom personally identifiable information is maintained, the types of information sought, the methods the State intends to use in gathering the information (including the sources from whom information is gathered), and the uses to be made of the information;

(b) A summary of the policies and procedures that participating agencies must follow regarding storage, disclosure to third parties, retention, and destruction of personally identifiable information;

(c) A description of all the rights of parents and children regarding this information, including their rights under the part C confidentiality provisions in §§ 303.401 through 303.417; and

(d) A description of the extent that the notice is provided in the native languages of the various population groups in the State.

(Authority: 20 U.S.C. 1417(c), 1435(a)(5), 1439(a)(2), 1442)

§ 303.405 Access rights.

(a) Each participating agency must permit parents to inspect and review any early intervention records relating to their children that are collected, maintained, or used by the agency under this part. The agency must comply with a parent's request to inspect and review records without unnecessary delay and before any meeting regarding an IFSP, or any hearing pursuant to §§ 303.430(d) and 303.435 through 303.439, and in no case more than 10 days after the request has been made.

(b) The right to inspect and review early intervention records under this section includes—

(1) The right to a response from the participating agency to reasonable requests for explanations and interpretations of the early intervention records;

(2) The right to request that the participating agency provide copies of the early intervention records containing the information if failure to provide those copies would effectively prevent the parent from exercising the right to inspect and review the records; and

(3) The right to have a representative of the parent inspect and review the early intervention records.

(c) An agency may presume that the parent has authority to inspect and review records relating to his or her child unless the agency has been provided documentation that the parent does not have the authority under applicable State laws governing such matters as custody, foster care, guardianship, separation, and divorce.

(Authority: 20 U.S.C. 1417(c), 1439(a)(2), 1439(a)(4), 1442)

§ 303.406   Record of access.

Each participating agency must keep a record of parties obtaining access to early intervention records collected, maintained, or used under part C of the Act (except access by parents and authorized representatives and employees of the participating agency), including the name of the party, the date access was given, and the purpose for which the party is authorized to use the early intervention records.

(Authority: 20 U.S.C. 1417(c), 1435(a)(5), 1439(a)(2), 1439(a)(4), 1442)

§ 303.407   Records on more than one child.

If any early intervention record includes information on more than one child, the parents of those children have the right to inspect and review only the information relating to their child or to be informed of that specific information.

(Authority: 20 U.S.C. 1417(c), 1439(a)(2), 1439(a)(4), 1442)

§ 303.408   List of types and locations of information.

Each participating agency must provide parents, on request, a list of the types and locations of early intervention records collected, maintained, or used by the agency.

(Authority: 20 U.S.C. 1417(c), 1439(a)(2), 1439(a)(4), 1442)

§ 303.409   Fees for records.

(a) Each participating agency may charge a fee for copies of records that are made for parents under this part if the fee does not effectively prevent the parents from exercising their right to inspect and review those records, except as provided in paragraph (c) of this section.

(b) A participating agency may not charge a fee to search for or to retrieve information under this part.

(c) A participating agency must provide at no cost to parents, a copy of each evaluation, assessment of the child, family assessment, and IFSP as soon as possible after each IFSP meeting.

(Authority: 20 U.S.C. 1417(c), 1432(4)(B), 1439(a)(2), 1439(a)(4), 1442)

§ 303.410   Amendment of records at a parent's request.

(a) A parent who believes that information in the early intervention records collected, maintained, or used under this part is inaccurate, misleading, or violates the privacy or other rights of the child or parent may request that the participating agency that maintains the information amend the information.

(b) The participating agency must decide whether to amend the information in accordance with the request within a reasonable period of time of receipt of the request.

(c) If the participating agency refuses to amend the information in accordance with the request, it must inform the parent of the refusal and advise the parent of the right to a hearing under § 303.411.

(Authority: 20 U.S.C. 1417(c), 1439(a)(2), 1439(a)(4), 1442)

§ 303.411   Opportunity for a hearing.

The participating agency must, on request, provide parents with the opportunity for a hearing to challenge information in their child's early intervention records to ensure that it is not inaccurate, misleading, or otherwise in violation of the privacy or other rights of the child or parents. A parent may request a due process hearing under the procedures in § 303.430(d)(1) provided that such hearing procedures meet the requirements of the hearing procedures in §303.413 or may request a hearing directly under the State's procedures in §303.413 (*i.e.*, procedures that are consistent with the FERPA hearing requirements in 34 CFR 99.22).

(Authority: 20 U.S.C. 1417(c), 1439(a)(2), 1439(a)(4), 1442)

§303.412 Result of hearing.

(a) If, as a result of the hearing, the participating agency decides that the information is inaccurate, misleading or in violation of the privacy or other rights of the child or parent, it must amend the information accordingly and so inform the parent in writing.

(b) If, as a result of the hearing, the agency decides that the information is not inaccurate, misleading, or in violation of the privacy or other rights of the child or parent, it must inform the parent of the right to place in the early intervention records it maintains on the child a statement commenting on the information or setting forth any reasons for disagreeing with the decision of the agency.

(c) Any explanation placed in the early intervention records of the child under this section must—

(1) Be maintained by the agency as part of the early intervention records of the child as long as the record or contested portion is maintained by the agency; and

(2) If the early intervention records of the child or the contested portion are disclosed by the agency to any party, the explanation must also be disclosed to the party.

(Authority: 20 U.S.C. 1417(c), 1439(a)(2), 1439(a)(4), 1442)

§303.413 Hearing procedures.

A hearing held under §303.411 must be conducted according to the procedures under 34 CFR 99.22.

(Authority: 20 U.S.C. 1417(c), 1439(a)(2), 1439(a)(4), 1442)

§303.414 Consent prior to disclosure or use.

(a) Except as provided in paragraph (b) of this section, prior parental consent must be obtained before personally identifiable information is—

(1) Disclosed to anyone other than authorized representatives, officials, or employees of participating agencies collecting, maintaining, or using the information under this part, subject to paragraph (b) of this section; or

(2) Used for any purpose other than meeting a requirement of this part.

(b) A lead agency or other participating agency may not disclose personally identifiable information, as defined in §303.29, to any party except participating agencies (including the lead agency and EIS providers) that are part of the State's part C system without parental consent unless authorized to do so under—

(1) Sections 303.401(d), 303.209(b)(1)(i) and (b)(1)(ii), and 303.211(b)(6)(ii)(A); or

(2) One of the exceptions enumerated in 34 CFR 99.31 (where applicable to part C), which are expressly adopted to apply to part C through this reference. In applying the exceptions in 34 CFR 99.31 to this part, participating agencies must also comply with the pertinent conditions in 34 CFR 99.32, 99.33, 99.34, 99.35, 99.36, 99.38, and 99.39; in applying these provisions in 34 CFR part 99 to part C, the reference to—

(i) 34 CFR 99.30 means §303.414(a);

(ii) "Education records" means early intervention records under §303.403(b);

(iii) "Educational" means early intervention under this part;

(iv) "Educational agency or institution" means the participating agency under §303.404(c);

(v) "School officials and officials of another school or school system" means qualified personnel or service coordinators under this part;

(vi) "State and local educational authorities" means the lead agency under §303.22; and

(vii) "Student" means child under this part.

(c) The lead agency must provide policies and procedures to be used when a parent refuses to provide consent under this section (such as a meeting to explain to parents how their failure to consent affects the ability of their child to receive services under this part), provided that those procedures do not override a parent's right to refuse consent under §303.420.

(Authority: 20 U.S.C. 1417(c), 1439(a)(2), 1439(a)(4), 1442)

§ 303.415 Safeguards.

(a) Each participating agency must protect the confidentiality of personally identifiable information at the collection, maintenance, use, storage, disclosure, and destruction stages.

(b) One official at each participating agency must assume responsibility for ensuring the confidentiality of any personally identifiable information.

(c) All persons collecting or using personally identifiable information must receive training or instruction regarding the State's policies and procedures under §§ 303.401 through 303.417 and 34 CFR part 99.

(d) Each participating agency must maintain, for public inspection, a current listing of the names and positions of those employees within the agency who may have access to personally identifiable information.

(Authority: 20 U.S.C. 1417(c), 1435(a)(5), 1439(a)(2), 1439(a)(4), 1442)

§ 303.416 Destruction of information.

(a) The participating agency must inform parents when personally identifiable information collected, maintained, or used under this part is no longer needed to provide services to the child under Part C of the Act, the GEPA provisions in 20 U.S.C. 1232f, EDGAR, 34 CFR part 76, and 2 CFR part 200, as adopted in 2 CFR part 3474.

(b) Subject to paragraph (a) of this section, the information must be destroyed at the request of the parents. However, a permanent record of a child's name, date of birth, parent contact information (including address and phone number), names of service coordinator(s) and EIS provider(s), and exit data (including year and age upon exit, and any programs entered into upon exiting) may be maintained without time limitation.

(Authority: 20 U.S.C. 1417(c), 1435(a)(5), 1439(a)(2), 1439(a)(4), 1442)

[76 FR 60244, Sept. 28, 2011, as amended at 79 FR 76097, Dec. 19, 2014]

§ 303.417 Enforcement.

The lead agency must have in effect the policies and procedures, including sanctions and the right to file a complaint under §§ 303.432 through 303.434, that the State uses to ensure that its policies and procedures, consistent with §§ 303.401 through 303.417, are followed and that the requirements of the Act and the regulations in this part are met.

(Authority: 20 U.S.C. 1417(c), 1435(a)(5), 1439(a)(2), 1439(a)(4), 1442)

PARENTAL CONSENT AND NOTICE

§ 303.420 Parental consent and ability to decline services.

(a) The lead agency must ensure parental consent is obtained before—

(1) Administering screening procedures under § 303.320 that are used to determine whether a child is suspected of having a disability;

(2) All evaluations and assessments of a child are conducted under § 303.321;

(3) Early intervention services are provided to the child under this part;

(4) Public benefits or insurance or private insurance is used if such consent is required under § 303.520; and

(5) Disclosure of personally identifiable information consistent with § 303.414.

(b) If a parent does not give consent under paragraph (a)(1), (a)(2), or (a)(3) of this section, the lead agency must make reasonable efforts to ensure that the parent—

(1) Is fully aware of the nature of the evaluation and assessment of the child or early intervention services that would be available; and

(2) Understands that the child will not be able to receive the evaluation, assessment, or early intervention service unless consent is given.

(c) The lead agency may not use the due process hearing procedures under this part or part B of the Act to challenge a parent's refusal to provide any consent that is required under paragraph (a) of this section.

(d) The parents of an infant or toddler with a disability—

(1) Determine whether they, their infant or toddler with a disability, or other family members will accept or decline any early intervention service under this part at any time, in accordance with State law; and

(2) May decline a service after first accepting it, without jeopardizing

other early intervention services under this part.

(Authority: 20 U.S.C. 1436(e), 1439(a)(3))

§303.421 Prior written notice and procedural safeguards notice.

(a) *General.* Prior written notice must be provided to parents a reasonable time before the lead agency or an EIS provider proposes, or refuses, to initiate or change the identification, evaluation, or placement of their infant or toddler, or the provision of early intervention services to the infant or toddler with a disability and that infant's or toddler's family.

(b) *Content of notice.* The notice must be in sufficient detail to inform parents about—

(1) The action that is being proposed or refused;

(2) The reasons for taking the action; and

(3) All procedural safeguards that are available under this subpart, including a description of mediation in §303.431, how to file a State complaint in §§303.432 through 303.434 and a due process complaint in the provisions adopted under §303.430(d), and any timelines under those procedures.

(c) *Native language.* (1) The notice must be—

(i) Written in language understandable to the general public; and

(ii) Provided in the native language, as defined in §303.25, of the parent or other mode of communication used by the parent, unless it is clearly not feasible to do so.

(2) If the native language or other mode of communication of the parent is not a written language, the public agency or designated EIS provider must take steps to ensure that—

(i) The notice is translated orally or by other means to the parent in the parent's native language or other mode of communication;

(ii) The parent understands the notice; and

(iii) There is written evidence that the requirements of this paragraph have been met.

(Authority: 20 U.S.C. 1439(a)(6)–(7))

§303.422 Surrogate parents.

(a) *General.* Each lead agency or other public agency must ensure that the rights of a child are protected when—

(1) No parent (as defined in §303.27) can be identified;

(2) The lead agency or other public agency, after reasonable efforts, cannot locate a parent; or

(3) The child is a ward of the State under the laws of that State.

(b) *Duty of lead agency and other public agencies.* (1) The duty of the lead agency, or other public agency under paragraph (a) of this section, includes the assignment of an individual to act as a surrogate for the parent. This assignment process must include a method for—

(i) Determining whether a child needs a surrogate parent; and

(ii) Assigning a surrogate parent to the child.

(2) In implementing the provisions under this section for children who are wards of the State or placed in foster care, the lead agency must consult with the public agency that has been assigned care of the child.

(c) *Wards of the State.* In the case of a child who is a ward of the State, the surrogate parent, instead of being appointed by the lead agency under paragraph (b)(1) of this section, may be appointed by the judge overseeing the infant or toddler's case provided that the surrogate parent meets the requirements in paragraphs (d)(2)(i) and (e) of this section.

(d) *Criteria for selection of surrogate parents.* (1) The lead agency or other public agency may select a surrogate parent in any way permitted under State law.

(2) Public agencies must ensure that a person selected as a surrogate parent—

(i) Is not an employee of the lead agency or any other public agency or EIS provider that provides early intervention services, education, care, or other services to the child or any family member of the child;

217

(ii) Has no personal or professional interest that conflicts with the interest of the child he or she represents; and

(iii) Has knowledge and skills that ensure adequate representation of the child.

(e) *Non-employee requirement; compensation.* A person who is otherwise qualified to be a surrogate parent under paragraph (d) of this section is not an employee of the agency solely because he or she is paid by the agency to serve as a surrogate parent.

(f) *Surrogate parent responsibilities.* The surrogate parent has the same rights as a parent for all purposes under this part.

(g) *Lead agency responsibility.* The lead agency must make reasonable efforts to ensure the assignment of a surrogate parent not more than 30 days after a public agency determines that the child needs a surrogate parent.

(Authority: 20 U.S.C. 1439(a)(5))

DISPUTE RESOLUTION OPTIONS

§ 303.430 **State dispute resolution options.**

(a) *General.* Each statewide system must include written procedures for the timely administrative resolution of complaints through mediation, State complaint procedures, and due process hearing procedures, described in paragraphs (b) through (e) of this section.

(b) *Mediation.* Each lead agency must make available to parties to disputes involving any matter under this part the opportunity for mediation that meets the requirements in § 303.431.

(c) *State complaint procedures.* Each lead agency must adopt written State complaint procedures to resolve any State complaints filed by any party regarding any violation of this part that meet the requirements in §§ 303.432 through 303.434.

(d) *Due process hearing procedures.* Each lead agency must adopt written due process hearing procedures to resolve complaints with respect to a particular child regarding any matter identified in § 303.421(a), by either adopting—

(1) The part C due process hearing procedures under section 639 of the Act that—

(i) Meet the requirements in §§ 303.435 through 303.438; and

(ii) Provide a means of filing a due process complaint regarding any matter listed in § 303.421(a); or

(2) The part B due process hearing procedures under section 615 of the Act and §§ 303.440 through 303.449 (with either a 30-day or 45-day timeline for resolving due process complaints, as provided in § 303.440(c)).

(e) *Status of a child during the pendency of a due process complaint.* (1) During the pendency of any proceeding involving a due process complaint under paragraph (d) of this section, unless the lead agency and parents of an infant or toddler with a disability otherwise agree, the child must continue to receive the appropriate early intervention services in the setting identified in the IFSP that is consented to by the parents.

(2) If the due process complaint under paragraph (d) of this section involves an application for initial services under part C of the Act, the child must receive those services that are not in dispute.

(Approved by Office of Management and Budget under control number 1820–0678 and 1820–NEW)

(Authority: 20 U.S.C. 1415(e), 1415(f)(1)(A), 1415(f)(3)(A)–(D), 1439)

MEDIATION

§ 303.431 **Mediation.**

(a) *General.* Each lead agency must ensure that procedures are established and implemented to allow parties to disputes involving any matter under this part, including matters arising prior to the filing of a due process complaint, to resolve disputes through a mediation process at any time.

(b) *Requirements.* The procedures must meet the following requirements:

(1) The procedures must ensure that the mediation process—

(i) Is voluntary on the part of the parties;

(ii) Is not used to deny or delay a parent's right to a due process hearing, or to deny any other rights afforded under part C of the Act; and

(iii) Is conducted by a qualified and impartial mediator who is trained in effective mediation techniques.

(2)(i) The State must maintain a list of individuals who are qualified mediators and knowledgeable in laws and regulations relating to the provision of early intervention services.

(ii) The lead agency must select mediators on a random, rotational, or other impartial basis.

(3) The State must bear the cost of the mediation process, including the costs of meetings described in paragraph (d) of this section.

(4) Each session in the mediation process must be scheduled in a timely manner and must be held in a location that is convenient to the parties to the dispute.

(5) If the parties resolve a dispute through the mediation process, the parties must execute a legally binding agreement that sets forth that resolution and that—

(i) States that all discussions that occurred during the mediation process will remain confidential and may not be used as evidence in any subsequent due process hearing or civil proceeding; and

(ii) Is signed by both the parent and a representative of the lead agency who has the authority to bind such agency.

(6) A written, signed mediation agreement under this paragraph is enforceable in any State court of competent jurisdiction or in a district court of the United States.

(7) Discussions that occur during the mediation process must be confidential and may not be used as evidence in any subsequent due process hearing or civil proceeding of any Federal court or State court of a State receiving assistance under this part.

(c) *Impartiality of mediator.* (1) An individual who serves as a mediator under this part—

(i) May not be an employee of the lead agency or an EIS provider that is involved in the provision of early intervention services or other services to the child; and

(ii) Must not have a personal or professional interest that conflicts with the person's objectivity.

(2) A person who otherwise qualifies as a mediator is not an employee of a lead agency or an early intervention provider solely because he or she is paid by the agency or provider to serve as a mediator.

(d) *Meeting to encourage mediation.* A lead agency may establish procedures to offer to parents and EIS providers that choose not to use the mediation process, an opportunity to meet, at a time and location convenient to the parents, with a disinterested party—

(1) Who is under contract with an appropriate alternative dispute resolution entity, or a parent training and information center or community parent resource center in the State established under section 671 or 672 of the Act; and

(2) Who would explain the benefits of, and encourage the use of, the mediation process to the parents.

(Approved by Office of Management and Budget under control number 1820–NEW)

(Authority: 20 U.S.C. 1415(e), 1439(a)(8))

STATE COMPLAINT PROCEDURES

§303.432 Adoption of State complaint procedures.

(a) *General.* Each lead agency must adopt written procedures for—

(1) Resolving any complaint, including a complaint filed by an organization or individual from another State, that meets the requirements in §303.434 by providing for the filing of a complaint with the lead agency; and

(2) Widely disseminating to parents and other interested individuals, including parent training and information centers, Protection and Advocacy (P&A) agencies, and other appropriate entities, the State procedures under §§303.432 through 303.434.

(b) *Remedies for denial of appropriate services.* In resolving a complaint in which the lead agency has found a failure to provide appropriate services, the lead agency, pursuant to its general supervisory authority under part C of the Act, must address—

(1) The failure to provide appropriate services, including corrective actions appropriate to address the needs of the infant or toddler with a disability who is the subject of the complaint and the infant's or toddler's family (such as compensatory services or monetary reimbursement); and

219

(2) Appropriate future provision of services for all infants and toddlers with disabilities and their families.

(Approved by Office of Management and Budget under control number 1820–NEW)

(Authority: 20 U.S.C. 1439(a)(1))

§ 303.433 Minimum State complaint procedures.

(a) *Time limit; minimum procedures.* Each lead agency must include in its complaint procedures a time limit of 60 days after a complaint is filed under § 303.434 to—

(1) Carry out an independent on-site investigation, if the lead agency determines that an investigation is necessary;

(2) Give the complainant the opportunity to submit additional information, either orally or in writing, about the allegations in the complaint;

(3) Provide the lead agency, public agency, or EIS provider with an opportunity to respond to the complaint, including, at a minimum—

(i) At the discretion of the lead agency, a proposal to resolve the complaint; and

(ii) An opportunity for a parent who has filed a complaint and the lead agency, public agency, or EIS provider to voluntarily engage in mediation, consistent with §§ 303.430(b) and 303.431;

(4) Review all relevant information and make an independent determination as to whether the lead agency, public agency, or EIS provider is violating a requirement of part C of the Act or of this part; and

(5) Issue a written decision to the complainant that addresses each allegation in the complaint and contains—

(i) Findings of fact and conclusions; and

(ii) The reasons for the lead agency's final decision.

(b) *Time extension; final decision; implementation.* The lead agency's procedures described in paragraph (a) of this section also must—

(1) Permit an extension of the time limit under paragraph (a) of this section only if—

(i) Exceptional circumstances exist with respect to a particular complaint; or

(ii) The parent (or individual or organization, if mediation is available to the individual or organization under State procedures) and the lead agency, public agency or EIS provider involved agree to extend the time to engage in mediation pursuant to paragraph (a)(3)(ii) of this section; and

(2) Include procedures for effective implementation of the lead agency's final decision, if needed, including—

(i) Technical assistance activities;

(ii) Negotiations; and

(iii) Corrective actions to achieve compliance.

(c) *Complaints filed under this section and due process hearings under § 303.430(d).* (1) If a written complaint is received that is also the subject of a due process hearing under § 303.430(d), or contains multiple issues of which one or more are part of that hearing, the State must set aside any part of the complaint that is being addressed in the due process hearing until the conclusion of the hearing. However, any issue in the complaint that is not a part of the due process hearing must be resolved using the time limit and procedures described in paragraphs (a) and (b) of this section.

(2) If an issue raised in a complaint filed under this section has previously been decided in a due process hearing involving the same parties—

(i) The due process hearing decision is binding on that issue; and

(ii) The lead agency must inform the complainant to that effect.

(3) A complaint alleging a lead agency, public agency, or EIS provider's failure to implement a due process hearing decision must be resolved by the lead agency.

(Approved by Office of Management and Budget under control number 1820–NEW)

(Authority: 20 U.S.C. 1439(a)(1))

§ 303.434 Filing a complaint.

(a) An organization or individual may file a signed written complaint under the procedures described in §§ 303.432 and 303.433.

(b) The complaint must include—

(1) A statement that the lead agency, public agency, or EIS provider has violated a requirement of part C of the Act;

(2) The facts on which the statement is based;

(3) The signature and contact information for the complainant; and

(4) If alleging violations with respect to a specific child—

(i) The name and address of the residence of the child;

(ii) The name of the EIS provider serving the child;

(iii) A description of the nature of the problem of the child, including facts relating to the problem; and

(iv) A proposed resolution of the problem to the extent known and available to the party at the time the complaint is filed.

(c) The complaint must allege a violation that occurred not more than one year prior to the date that the complaint is received in accordance with §303.432.

(d) The party filing the complaint must forward a copy of the complaint to the public agency or EIS provider serving the child at the same time the party files the complaint with the lead agency.

(Approved by Office of Management and Budget under control number 1820–NEW)

(Authority: 20 U.S.C. 1439(a)(1))

STATES THAT CHOOSE TO ADOPT THE PART C DUE PROCESS HEARING PROCEDURES UNDER SECTION 639 OF THE ACT

§303.435 Appointment of an impartial due process hearing officer.

(a) *Qualifications and duties.* Whenever a due process complaint is received under §303.430(d), a due process hearing officer must be appointed to implement the complaint resolution process in this subpart. The person must—

(1) Have knowledge about the provisions of this part and the needs of, and early intervention services available for, infants and toddlers with disabilities and their families; and

(2) Perform the following duties:

(i)(A) Listen to the presentation of relevant viewpoints about the due process complaint.

(B) Examine all information relevant to the issues.

(C) Seek to reach a timely resolution of the due process complaint.

(ii) Provide a record of the proceedings, including a written decision.

(b) *Definition of impartial.* (1) *Impartial* means that the due process hearing officer appointed to implement the due process hearing under this part—

(i) Is not an employee of the lead agency or an EIS provider involved in the provision of early intervention services or care of the child; and

(ii) Does not have a personal or professional interest that would conflict with his or her objectivity in implementing the process.

(2) A person who otherwise qualifies under paragraph (b)(1) of this section is not an employee of an agency solely because the person is paid by the agency to implement the due process hearing procedures or mediation procedures under this part.

(Authority: 20 U.S.C. 1439(a)(1))

§303.436 Parental rights in due process hearing proceedings.

(a) *General.* Each lead agency must ensure that the parents of a child referred to part C are afforded the rights in paragraph (b) of this section in the due process hearing carried out under §303.430(d).

(b) *Rights.* Any parent involved in a due process hearing has the right to—

(1) Be accompanied and advised by counsel and by individuals with special knowledge or training with respect to early intervention services for infants and toddlers with disabilities;

(2) Present evidence and confront, cross-examine, and compel the attendance of witnesses;

(3) Prohibit the introduction of any evidence at the hearing that has not been disclosed to the parent at least five days before the hearing;

(4) Obtain a written or electronic verbatim transcription of the hearing at no cost to the parent; and

(5) Receive a written copy of the findings of fact and decisions at no cost to the parent.

(Authority: 20 U.S.C. 1439(a))

§303.437 Convenience of hearings and timelines.

(a) Any due process hearing conducted under this subpart must be carried out at a time and place that is reasonably convenient to the parents.

(b) Each lead agency must ensure that, not later than 30 days after the receipt of a parent's due process complaint, the due process hearing required under this subpart is completed and a written decision mailed to each of the parties.

(c) A hearing officer may grant specific extensions of time beyond the period set out in paragraph (b) of this section at the request of either party.

(Authority: 20 U.S.C. 1439(a)(1))

§ 303.438 Civil action.

Any party aggrieved by the findings and decision issued pursuant to a due process complaint has the right to bring a civil action in State or Federal court under section 639(a)(1) of the Act.

(Authority: 20 U.S.C. 1439(a)(1))

STATES THAT CHOOSE TO ADOPT THE PART B DUE PROCESS HEARING PROCEDURES UNDER SECTION 615 OF THE ACT

§ 303.440 Filing a due process complaint.

(a) *General.* (1) A parent, EIS provider, or a lead agency may file a due process complaint on any of the matters described in § 303.421(a), relating to the identification, evaluation, or placement of a child, or the provision of early intervention services to the infant or toddler with a disability and his or her family under part C of the Act.

(2) The due process complaint must allege a violation that occurred not more than two years before the date the parent or EIS provider knew, or should have known, about the alleged action that forms the basis of the due process complaint, or, if the State has an explicit time limitation for filing a due process complaint under this part, in the time allowed by that State law, except that the exceptions to the timeline described in § 303.443(f) apply to the timeline in this section.

(b) *Information for parents.* The lead agency must inform the parent of any free or low-cost legal and other relevant services available in the area if—

(1) The parent requests the information; or

(2) The parent or EIS provider files a due process complaint under this section.

(c) *Timeline for Resolution.* The lead agency may adopt a 30- or 45-day timeline, subject to § 303.447(a), for the resolution of due process complaints and must specify in its written policies and procedures under § 303.123 and in its prior written notice under § 303.421, the specific timeline it has adopted.

(Approved by Office of Management and Budget under control number 1820–NEW)

(Authority: 20 U.S.C. 1415(b)(6), 1439)

§ 303.441 Due process complaint.

(a) *General.* (1) The lead agency must have procedures that require either party, or the attorney representing a party, to provide to the other party a due process complaint (which must remain confidential).

(2) The party filing a due process complaint must forward a copy of the due process complaint to the lead agency.

(b) *Content of complaint.* The due process complaint required in paragraph (a)(1) of this section must include—

(1) The name of the child;

(2) The address of the residence of the child;

(3) The name of the EIS provider serving the child;

(4) In the case of a homeless child (within the meaning of section 725(2) of the McKinney-Vento Homeless Assistance Act (42 U.S.C. 11434a(2)), available contact information for the child, and the name of the EIS provider serving the child;

(5) A description of the nature of the problem of the child relating to the proposed or refused initiation or change, including facts relating to the problem; and

(6) A proposed resolution of the problem to the extent known and available to the party at the time.

(c) *Notice required before a hearing on a due process complaint.* A party may not have a hearing on a due process complaint until the party, or the attorney representing the party, files a due process complaint that meets the requirements of paragraph (b) of this section.

(d) *Sufficiency of complaint.* (1) The due process complaint required by this section must be deemed sufficient unless the party receiving the due process complaint notifies the hearing officer and the other party in writing, within 15 days of receipt of the due process complaint, that the receiving party believes the due process complaint does not meet the requirements in paragraph (b) of this section.

(2) Within five days of receipt of notification under paragraph (d)(1) of this section, the hearing officer must make a determination on the face of the due process complaint of whether the due process complaint meets the requirements in paragraph (b) of this section, and must immediately notify the parties in writing of that determination.

(3) A party may amend its due process complaint only if—

(i) The other party consents in writing to the amendment and is given the opportunity to resolve the due process complaint through a meeting held pursuant to §303.442; or

(ii) The hearing officer grants permission, except that the hearing officer may only grant permission to amend at any time not later than five days before the due process hearing begins.

(4) If a party files an amended due process complaint, the timelines for the resolution meeting in §303.442(a) and the time period to resolve in §303.442(b) begin again with the filing of the amended due process complaint.

(e) *Lead agency response to a due process complaint.* (1) If the lead agency has not sent a prior written notice under §303.421 to the parent regarding the subject matter contained in the parent's due process complaint, the lead agency or EIS provider must, within 10 days of receiving the due process complaint, send to the parent a response that includes—

(i) An explanation of why the lead agency or EIS provider proposed or refused to take the action raised in the due process complaint;

(ii) A description of other options that the IFSP Team considered and the reasons why those options were rejected;

(iii) A description of each evaluation procedure, assessment, record, or report the lead agency or EIS provider used as the basis for the proposed or refused action; and

(iv) A description of the other factors that are relevant to the agency's or EIS provider's proposed or refused action.

(2) A response by the lead agency under paragraph (e)(1) of this section does not preclude the lead agency from asserting that the parent's due process complaint was insufficient, where appropriate.

(f) *Other party response to a due process complaint.* Except as provided in paragraph (e) of this section, the party receiving a due process complaint must, within 10 days of receiving the due process complaint, send to the other party a response that specifically addresses the issues raised in the due process complaint.

(Authority: 20 U.S.C. 1415(b)(7), 1415(c)(2), 1439)

§303.442 Resolution process.

(a) *Resolution meeting.* (1) Within 15 days of receiving notice of the parent's due process complaint, and prior to the initiation of a due process hearing under §303.443, the lead agency must convene a meeting with the parent and the relevant member or members of the IFSP Team who have specific knowledge of the facts identified in the due process complaint that—

(i) Includes a representative of the lead agency who has decision-making authority on behalf of that agency; and

(ii) May not include an attorney of the lead agency unless the parent is accompanied by an attorney.

(2) The purpose of the resolution meeting is for the parent of the child to discuss the due process complaint, and the facts that form the basis of the due process complaint, so that the lead agency has the opportunity to resolve the dispute that is the basis for the due process complaint.

(3) The meeting described in paragraphs (a)(1) and (a)(2) of this section need not be held if—

(i) The parent and lead agency agree in writing to waive the meeting; or

(ii) The parent and lead agency agree to use the mediation process described in §303.431.

(4) The parent and the lead agency must determine the relevant members of the IFSP Team to attend the meeting.

(b) *Resolution period.* (1) If the lead agency has not resolved the due process complaint to the satisfaction of the parties within 30 days of the receipt of the due process complaint, the due process hearing may occur.

(2) Except as provided in paragraph (c) of this section, the timeline for issuing a final decision under § 303.447 begins at the expiration of the 30-day period in paragraph (b)(1) of this section.

(3) Except where the parties have jointly agreed to waive the resolution process or to use mediation, notwithstanding paragraphs (b)(1) and (b)(2) of this section, the failure of the parent filing a due process complaint to participate in the resolution meeting will delay the timelines for the resolution process and due process hearing until the meeting is held.

(4) If the lead agency is unable to obtain the participation of the parent in the resolution meeting after reasonable efforts have been made, including documenting its efforts, the lead agency may, at the conclusion of the 30-day period, request that the hearing officer dismiss the parent's due process complaint.

(5) If the lead agency fails to hold the resolution meeting specified in paragraph (a) of this section within 15 days of receiving notice of a parent's due process complaint or fails to participate in the resolution meeting, the parent may seek the intervention of a hearing officer to begin the due process hearing timeline.

(c) *Adjustments to 30-day resolution period.* The 30- or 45-day timeline adopted by the lead agency under § 303.440(c) for the due process hearing described in § 303.447(a) starts the day after one of the following events:

(1) Both parties agree in writing to waive the resolution meeting.

(2) After either the mediation or resolution meeting starts but before the end of the 30-day period, the parties agree in writing that no agreement is possible.

(3) If both parties agree in writing to continue the mediation at the end of the 30-day resolution period, but later, the parent or lead agency withdraws from the mediation process.

(d) *Written settlement agreement.* If a resolution to the dispute is reached at the meeting described in paragraphs (a)(1) and (a)(2) of this section, the parties must execute a legally binding agreement that is—

(1) Signed by both the parent and a representative of the lead agency who has the authority to bind the agency; and

(2) Enforceable in any State court of competent jurisdiction or in a district court of the United States, or, by the lead agency, if the State has other mechanisms or procedures that permit parties to seek enforcement of resolution agreements pursuant to this section.

(e) *Agreement review period.* If the parties execute an agreement pursuant to paragraph (d) of this section, a party may void the agreement within three business days of the agreement's execution.

(Authority: 20 U.S.C. 1415(f)(1)(B), 1439)

§ 303.443 **Impartial due process hearing.**

(a) *General.* Whenever a due process complaint is received consistent with § 303.440, the parents or the EIS provider involved in the dispute must have an opportunity for an impartial due process hearing, consistent with the procedures in §§ 303.440 through 303.442.

(b) *Agency responsible for conducting the due process hearing.* The hearing described in paragraph (a) of this section must be conducted by the lead agency directly responsible for the early intervention services of the infant or toddler, as determined under State statute, State regulation, or a written policy of the lead agency.

(c) *Impartial hearing officer.* (1) At a minimum, a hearing officer—

(i) Must not be—

(A) An employee of the lead agency or the EIS provider that is involved in the early intervention services or care of the infant or toddler; or

(B) A person having a personal or professional interest that conflicts with the person's objectivity in the hearing;

(ii) Must possess knowledge of, and the ability to understand, the provisions of the Act, Federal and State regulations pertaining to the Act, and legal interpretations of the Act by Federal and State courts;

(iii) Must possess the knowledge and ability to conduct hearings in accordance with appropriate, standard legal practice; and

(iv) Must possess the knowledge and ability to render and write decisions in accordance with appropriate, standard legal practice.

(2) A person who otherwise qualifies to conduct a hearing under paragraph (c)(1) of this section is not an employee of the agency solely because he or she is paid by the agency to serve as a hearing officer.

(3) Each lead agency must keep a list of the persons who serve as hearing officers. The list must include a statement of the qualifications of each of those persons.

(d) *Subject matter of due process hearings.* The party requesting the due process hearing may not raise issues at the due process hearing that were not raised in the due process complaint filed under §303.441(b), unless the other party agrees otherwise.

(e) *Timeline for requesting a hearing.* A parent, lead agency, or EIS provider must request an impartial hearing on their due process complaint within two years of the date the parent, lead agency, or EIS provider knew or should have known about the alleged action that forms the basis of the due process complaint, or if the State has an explicit time limitation for requesting such a due process hearing under this part, in the time allowed by that State law.

(f) *Exceptions to the timeline.* The timeline described in paragraph (e) of this section does not apply to a parent if the parent was prevented from filing a due process complaint due to—

(1) Specific misrepresentations by the lead agency or EIS provider that it had resolved the problem forming the basis of the due process complaint; or

(2) The lead agency's or EIS provider's failure to provide the parent information that was required under this part to be provided to the parent.

(Approved by Office of Management and Budget under control number 1820–NEW)

(Authority: 20 U.S.C. 1415(f)(1)(A), 1415(f)(3)(A)–(D), 1439)

§303.444 **Hearing rights.**

(a) *General.* Any party to a hearing conducted pursuant to §§303.440 through 303.445, or an appeal conducted pursuant to §303.446, has the right to—

(1) Be accompanied and advised by counsel and by individuals with special knowledge or training with respect to the problems of infants or toddlers with disabilities;

(2) Present evidence and confront, cross-examine, and compel the attendance of witnesses;

(3) Prohibit the introduction of any evidence at the hearing that has not been disclosed to that party at least five business days before the hearing;

(4) Obtain a written or, at the option of the parents, electronic, verbatim record of the hearing; and

(5) Obtain written or, at the option of the parents, electronic findings of fact and decisions.

(b) *Additional disclosure of information.* (1) At least five business days prior to a hearing conducted pursuant to §303.443(a), each party must disclose to all other parties all evaluations completed by that date and recommendations based on the offering party's evaluations that the party intends to use at the hearing.

(2) A hearing officer may bar any party that fails to comply with paragraph (b)(1) of this section from introducing the relevant evaluation or recommendation at the hearing without the consent of the other party.

(c) *Parental rights at hearings.* Parents involved in hearings must—

(1) Be given the right to open the hearing to the public; and

(2) Receive a copy of the record of the hearing and the findings of fact and decisions described in paragraphs (a)(4) and (a)(5) of this section at no cost.

(Authority: 20 U.S.C. 1415(f)(2), 1415(h), 1439)

§303.445 **Hearing decisions.**

(a) *Decision of hearing officer.* (1) Subject to paragraph (a)(2) of this section, a hearing officer's determination of whether an infant or toddler was appropriately identified, evaluated, or placed, or whether the infant or toddler with a disability and his or her family were appropriately provided early intervention services under part C of the Act, must be based on substantive grounds.

(2) In matters alleging a procedural violation, a hearing officer may find that a child was not appropriately identified, evaluated, placed, or provided early intervention services under part C of the Act only if the procedural inadequacies—

(i) Impeded the child's right to identification, evaluation, and placement or provision of early intervention services for the child and that child's family under part C of the Act;

(ii) Significantly impeded the parent's opportunity to participate in the decision-making process regarding identification, evaluation, placement or provision of early intervention services for the child and that child's family under part C of the Act; or

(iii) Caused a deprivation of educational or developmental benefit.

(3) Nothing in paragraph (a) of this section precludes a hearing officer from ordering the lead agency or EIS provider to comply with procedural requirements under §§ 303.400 through 303.449.

(b) *Construction clause.* Nothing in §§ 303.440 through 303.445 affects the right of a parent to file an appeal of the due process hearing decision with the lead agency under § 303.446(b), if the lead agency level appeal is available.

(c) *Separate due process complaint.* Nothing in §§ 303.440 through 303.449 precludes a parent from filing a separate due process complaint on an issue separate from a due process complaint already filed.

(d) *Findings and decisions to general public.* The lead agency, after deleting any personally identifiable information, must make the findings and decisions available to the public.

(Authority: 20 U.S.C. 1415(f)(3)(E)–(F), 1415(h)(4), 1415(o), 1439)

§ 303.446   Finality of decision; appeal; impartial review.

(a) *Finality of hearing decision.* A decision made in a hearing conducted pursuant to §§ 303.440 through 303.445 is final, except that any party involved in the hearing may appeal the decision under the provisions of paragraph (b) of this section and § 303.448.

(b) *Appeal of decisions; impartial review.* (1) The lead agency may provide for procedures to allow any party aggrieved by the findings and decision in the hearing to appeal to the lead agency.

(2) If there is an appeal, the lead agency must conduct an impartial review of the findings and decision appealed. The official conducting the review must—

(i) Examine the entire hearing record;

(ii) Ensure that the procedures at the hearing were consistent with the requirements of due process;

(iii) Seek additional evidence if necessary. If a hearing is held to receive additional evidence, the rights in § 303.444 apply;

(iv) Afford the parties an opportunity for oral or written argument, or both, at the discretion of the reviewing official;

(v) Make an independent decision on completion of the review; and

(vi) Give a copy of the written or, at the option of the parents, electronic findings of fact and decisions to the parties.

(c) *Findings of fact and decision to the general public.* The lead agency, after deleting any personally identifiable information, must make the findings of fact and decisions described in paragraph (b)(2)(vi) of this section available to the general public.

(d) *Finality of review decision.* The decision made by the reviewing official is final unless a party brings a civil action under § 303.448.

(Authority: 20 U.S.C. 1415(g), 1415(h)(4), 1415(i)(1)(A), 1415(i)(2), 1439)

§ 303.447   Timelines and convenience of hearings and reviews.

(a) The lead agency must ensure that not later than either 30 days or 45 days (consistent with the lead agency's written policies and procedures adopted under § 303.440(c)) after the expiration of the 30-day period in § 303.442(b), or the adjusted 30-day time periods described in § 303.442(c))—

(1) A final decision is reached in the hearing; and

(2) A copy of the decision is mailed to each of the parties.

(b) The lead agency must ensure that not later than 30 days after the receipt of a request for a review—

(1) A final decision is reached in the review; and

(2) A copy of the decision is mailed to each of the parties.

(c) A hearing or reviewing officer may grant specific extensions of time beyond the periods set out in paragraphs (a) and (b) of this section at the request of either party.

(d) Each hearing and each review involving oral arguments must be conducted at a time and place that is reasonably convenient to the parents and child involved.

(Authority: 20 U.S.C. 1415(f)(1)(B)(ii), 1415(g), 1415(i)(1), 1439)

§303.448 Civil action.

(a) *General.* Any party aggrieved by the findings and decision made under §§303.440 through 303.445 who does not have the right to an appeal under §303.446(b), and any party aggrieved by the findings and decision under §303.446(b), has the right to bring a civil action with respect to the due process complaint under §303.440. The action may be brought in any State court of competent jurisdiction or in a district court of the United States without regard to the amount in controversy.

(b) *Time limitation.* The party bringing the action has 90 days from the date of the decision of the hearing officer or, if applicable, the decision of the State review official, to file a civil action, or, if the State has an explicit time limitation for bringing civil actions under part C of the Act, in the time allowed by that State law.

(c) *Additional requirements.* In any action brought under paragraph (a) of this section, the court—

(1) Receives the records of the administrative proceedings;

(2) Hears additional evidence at the request of a party; and

(3) Basing its decision on the preponderance of the evidence, grants the relief that the court determines to be appropriate.

(d) *Jurisdiction of district courts.* The district courts of the United States have jurisdiction of actions brought

under section 615 of the Act without regard to the amount in controversy.

(e) *Rule of construction.* Nothing in this part restricts or limits the rights, procedures, and remedies available under the Constitution, the Americans with Disabilities Act of 1990, title V of the Rehabilitation Act of 1973, or other Federal laws protecting the rights of children with disabilities, except that before the filing of a civil action under these laws seeking relief that is also available under section 615 of the Act, the procedures under §§303.440 and 303.446 must be exhausted to the same extent as would be required had the action been brought under section 615 of the Act.

(Authority: 20 U.S.C. 1415(i)(2), 1415(i)(3)(A), 1415(l), 1439)

§303.449 State enforcement mechanisms.

Notwithstanding §§303.431(b)(6) and 303.442(d)(2), which provide for judicial enforcement of a written agreement reached as a result of a mediation or a resolution meeting, there is nothing in this part that would prevent the State from using other mechanisms to seek enforcement of that agreement, provided that use of those mechanisms is not mandatory and does not delay or deny a party the right to seek enforcement of the written agreement in a State court or competent jurisdiction or in a district court of the United States.

(Authority: 20 U.S.C. 1415(e)(2)(F), 1415(f)(1)(B), 1439)

Subpart F—Use of Funds and Payor of Last Resort

GENERAL

§303.500 Use of funds, payor of last resort, and system of payments.

(a) *Statewide system.* Each statewide system must include written policies and procedures that meet the requirements of the—

(1) Use of funds provisions in §303.501; and

(2) Payor of last resort provisions in §§303.510 through 303.521 (regarding the identification and coordination of

funding resources for, and the provision of, early intervention services under part C of the Act within the State).

(b) *System of Payments.* A State may establish, consistent with §§ 303.13(a)(3) and 303.203(b), a system of payments for early intervention services under part C of the Act, including a schedule of sliding fees or cost participation fees (such as co-payments, premiums, or deductibles) required to be paid under Federal, State, local, or private programs of insurance or benefits for which the infant or toddler with a disability or the child's family is enrolled, that meets the requirements of §§ 303.520 and 303.521.

(Authority: 20 U.S.C. 1432(4)(B), 1435(a)(10)–(12), 1437(b), 1438, 1439(a), 1440)

USE OF FUNDS

§ 303.501 Permissive use of funds by the lead agency.

Consistent with §§ 303.120 through 303.122 and §§ 303.220 through 303.226, a lead agency may use funds under this part for activities or expenses that are reasonable and necessary for implementing the State's early intervention program for infants and toddlers with disabilities including funds—

(a) For direct early intervention services for infants and toddlers with disabilities and their families under this part that are not otherwise funded through other public or private sources (subject to §§ 303.510 through 303.521);

(b) To expand and improve services for infants and toddlers with disabilities and their families under this part that are otherwise available;

(c)(1) To provide FAPE as that term is defined in § 303.15, in accordance with part B of the Act, to children with disabilities from their third birthday to the beginning of the following school year;

(2) The provision of FAPE under paragraph (c)(1) of this section does not apply to children who continue to receive early intervention services under this part in accordance with paragraph (d) of this section and § 303.211;

(d) With the written consent of the parents, to continue to provide early intervention services under this part, in lieu of FAPE provided in accordance

with part B of the Act, to children with disabilities from their third birthday (pursuant to § 303.211) until those children enter, or are eligible under State law to enter, kindergarten; and

(e) In any State that does not provide services under § 303.204 for at-risk infants and toddlers, as defined in § 303.5, to strengthen the statewide system by initiating, expanding, or improving collaborative efforts related to at-risk infants and toddlers, including establishing linkages with appropriate public and private community-based organizations, services, and personnel for the purposes of—

(1) Identifying and evaluating at-risk infants and toddlers;

(2) Making referrals for the infants and toddlers identified and evaluated under paragraph (e)(1) of this section; and

(3) Conducting periodic follow-up on each referral, to determine if the status of the infant or toddler involved has changed with respect to the eligibility of the infant or toddler for services under this part.

(Authority: 20 U.S.C. 1435(a)(10)–(12), 1437(b), 1438)

PAYOR OF LAST RESORT—GENERAL PROVISIONS

§ 303.510 Payor of last resort.

(a) *Nonsubstitution of funds.* Except as provided in paragraph (b) of this section, funds under this part may not be used to satisfy a financial commitment for services that would otherwise have been paid for from another public or private source, including any medical program administered by the Department of Defense, but for the enactment of part C of the Act. Therefore, funds under this part may be used only for early intervention services that an infant or toddler with a disability needs but is not currently entitled to receive or have payment made from any other Federal, State, local, or private source (subject to §§ 303.520 and 303.521).

(b) *Interim payments—reimbursement.* If necessary to prevent a delay in the timely provision of appropriate early intervention services to a child or the child's family, funds under this part may be used to pay the provider of services (for services and functions authorized under this part, including health services, as defined in §303.16 (but not medical services), functions of the child find system described in §§303.115 through 303.117 and §§303.301 through 303.320, and evaluations and assessments in §303.321), pending reimbursement from the agency or entity that has ultimate responsibility for the payment.

(c) *Non-reduction of benefits.* Nothing in this part may be construed to permit a State to reduce medical or other assistance available in the State or to alter eligibility under Title V of the Social Security Act, 42 U.S.C. 701, *et seq.* (SSA) (relating to maternal and child health) or Title XIX of the SSA, 42 U.S.C. 1396 (relating to Medicaid), including section 1903(a) of the SSA regarding medical assistance for services furnished to an infant or toddler with a disability when those services are included in the child's IFSP adopted pursuant to part C of the Act.

(Authority: 20 U.S.C. 1435(a)(10)(B), 1437(a)(2), 1440(a), 1440(c))

§303.511 Methods to ensure the provision of, and financial responsibility for, Part C services.

(a) *General.* Each State must ensure that it has in place methods for State interagency coordination. Under these methods, the Chief Executive Officer of a State or designee of the Officer must ensure that the interagency agreement or other method for interagency coordination is in effect between each State public agency and the designated lead agency in order to ensure—

(1) The provision of, and establishing financial responsibility for, early intervention services provided under this part; and

(2) Such services are consistent with the requirement in section 635 of the Act and the State's application under section 637 of the Act, including the provision of such services during the pendency of any dispute between State agencies.

(b) The methods in paragraph (a) of this section must meet all requirements in this section and be set forth in one of the following:

(1) State law or regulation;

(2) Signed interagency and intraagency agreements between respective agency officials that clearly identify the financial and service provision responsibilities of each agency (or entity within the agency); or

(3) Other appropriate written methods determined by the Governor of the State, or the Governor's designee, and approved by the Secretary through the review and approval of the State's application.

(c) *Procedures for resolving disputes.* (1) Each method must include procedures for achieving a timely resolution of intra-agency and interagency disputes about payments for a given service, or disputes about other matters related to the State's early intervention service program. Those procedures must include a mechanism for resolution of disputes within agencies and for the Governor, Governor's designee, or the lead agency to make a final determination for interagency disputes, which determination must be binding upon the agencies involved.

(2) The method must—

(i) Permit the agency to resolve its own internal disputes (based on the agency's procedures that are included in the agreement), so long as the agency acts in a timely manner; and

(ii) Include the process that the lead agency will follow in achieving resolution of intra-agency disputes, if a given agency is unable to resolve its own internal disputes in a timely manner.

(3) If, during the lead agency's resolution of the dispute, the Governor, Governor's designee, or lead agency determines that the assignment of financial responsibility under this section was inappropriately made—

(i) The Governor, Governor's designee, or lead agency must reassign the financial responsibility to the appropriate agency; and

(ii) The lead agency must make arrangements for reimbursement of any expenditures incurred by the agency originally assigned financial responsibility.

(d) *Delivery of services in a timely manner.* The methods adopted by the State under this section must—

(1) Include a mechanism to ensure that no services that a child is entitled to receive under this part are delayed

or denied because of disputes between agencies regarding financial or other responsibilities; and

(2) Be consistent with the written funding policies adopted by the State under this subpart and include any provisions the State has adopted under § 303.520 regarding the use of insurance to pay for part C services.

(e) *Additional components.* Each method must include any additional components necessary to ensure effective cooperation and coordination among, and the lead agency's general supervision (including monitoring) of, EIS providers (including all public agencies) involved in the State's early intervention service programs.

(Authority: 20 U.S.C. 1435(a)(10), 1437(a)(2), 1440(b))

PAYOR OF LAST RESORT & SYSTEM OF PAYMENTS PROVISIONS—USE OF INSURANCE, BENEFITS, SYSTEMS OF PAYMENTS, AND FEES

§ 303.520 Policies related to use of public benefits or insurance or private insurance to pay for Part C services.

(a) *Use of public benefits or public insurance to pay for part C services.* (1) A State may not use the public benefits or insurance of a child or parent to pay for part C services unless the State provides written notification, consistent with § 303.520(a)(3), to the child's parents, and the State meets the no-cost protections identified in paragraph (a)(2) of this section.

(2) With regard to using the public benefits or insurance of a child or parent to pay for part C services, the State—

(i) May not require a parent to sign up for or enroll in public benefits or insurance programs as a condition of receiving part C services and must obtain consent prior to using the public benefits or insurance of a child or parent if that child or parent is not already enrolled in such a program;

(ii) Must obtain consent, consistent with §§ 303.7 and 303.420(a)(4), to use a child's or parent's public benefits or insurance to pay for part C services if that use would—

(A) Decrease available lifetime coverage or any other insured benefit for

that child or parent under that program;

(B) Result in the child's parents paying for services that would otherwise be covered by the public benefits or insurance program;

(C) Result in any increase in premiums or discontinuation of public benefits or insurance for that child or that child's parents; or

(D) Risk loss of eligibility for the child or that child's parents for home and community-based waivers based on aggregate health-related expenditures.

(iii) If the parent does not provide consent under paragraphs (a)(2)(i) or (a)(2)(ii) of this section, the State must still make available those part C services on the IFSP to which the parent has provided consent.

(3) Prior to using a child's or parent's public benefits or insurance to pay for part C services, the State must provide written notification to the child's parents. The notification must include—

(i) A statement that parental consent must be obtained under § 303.414, if that provision applies, before the State lead agency or EIS provider discloses, for billing purposes, a child's personally identifiable information to the State public agency responsible for the administration of the State's public benefits or insurance program (*e.g.,* Medicaid);

(ii) A statement of the no-cost protection provisions in § 303.520(a)(2) and that if the parent does not provide the consent under § 303.520(a)(2), the State lead agency must still make available those part C services on the IFSP for which the parent has provided consent;

(iii) A statement that the parents have the right under § 303.414, if that provision applies, to withdraw their consent to disclosure of personally identifiable information to the State public agency responsible for the administration of the State's public benefits or insurance program (*e.g.,* Medicaid) at any time; and

(iv) A statement of the general categories of costs that the parent would incur as a result of participating in a public benefits or insurance program (such as co-payments or deductibles, or the required use of private insurance as the primary insurance).

(4) If a State requires a parent to pay any costs that the parent would incur as a result of the State's using a child's or parent's public benefits or insurance to pay for part C services (such as co-payments or deductibles, or the required use of private insurance as the primary insurance), those costs must be identified in the State's system of payments policies under § 303.521 and included in the notification provided to the parent under paragraph (a)(3) of this section; otherwise, the State cannot charge those costs to the parent.

(b) *Use of private insurance to pay for Part C services.* (1)(i) The State may not use the private insurance of a parent of an infant or toddler with a disability to pay for part C services unless the parent provides parental consent, consistent with §§ 303.7 and 303.420(a)(4), to use private insurance to pay for part C services for his or her child or the State meets one of the exceptions in paragraph (b)(2) of this section. This includes the use of private insurance when such use is a prerequisite for the use of public benefits or insurance. Parental consent must be obtained—

(A) When the lead agency or EIS provider seeks to use the parent's private insurance or benefits to pay for the initial provision of an early intervention service in the IFSP; and

(B) Each time consent for services is required under § 303.420(a)(3) due to an increase (in frequency, length, duration, or intensity) in the provision of services in the child's IFSP.

(ii) If a State requires a parent to pay any costs that the parent would incur as a result of the State's use of private insurance to pay for early intervention services (such as co-payments, premiums, or deductibles), those costs must be identified in the State's system of payments policies under § 303.521; otherwise, the State may not charge those costs to the parent.

(iii) When obtaining parental consent required under paragraph (b)(1)(i) of this section or initially using benefits under a child or parent's private insurance policy to pay for an early intervention service under paragraph (b)(2) of this section, the State must provide to the parent a copy of the State's system of payments policies that identifies the potential costs that the parent

may incur when their private insurance is used to pay for early intervention services under this part (such as co-payments, premiums, or deductibles or other long-term costs such as the loss of benefits because of annual or lifetime health insurance coverage caps under the insurance policy).

(2) The parental consent requirements in paragraph (b)(1) of this section do not apply if the State has enacted a State statute regarding private health insurance coverage for early intervention services under part C of the Act, that expressly provides that—

(i) The use of private health insurance to pay for part C services cannot count towards or result in a loss of benefits due to the annual or lifetime health insurance coverage caps for the infant or toddler with a disability, the parent, or the child's family members who are covered under that health insurance policy;

(ii) The use of private health insurance to pay for part C services cannot negatively affect the availability of health insurance to the infant or toddler with a disability, the parent, or the child's family members who are covered under that health insurance policy, and health insurance coverage may not be discontinued for these individuals due to the use of the health insurance to pay for services under part C of the Act; and

(iii) The use of private health insurance to pay for part C services cannot be the basis for increasing the health insurance premiums of the infant or toddler with a disability, the parent, or the child's family members covered under that health insurance policy.

(3) If a State has enacted a State statute that meets the requirements in paragraph (b)(2) of this section, regarding the use of private health insurance coverage to pay for early intervention services under part C of the Act, the State may reestablish a new baseline of State and local expenditures under § 303.225(b) in the next Federal fiscal year following the effective date of the statute.

(c) *Inability to pay.* If a parent or family of an infant or toddler with a disability is determined unable to pay under the State's definition of inability to pay under § 303.521(a)(3) and does not provide consent under paragraph (b)(1), the lack of consent may not be used to delay or deny any services under this part to that child or family.

(d) *Proceeds or funds from public insurance or benefits or from private insurance.* (1) Proceeds or funds from public insurance or benefits or from private insurance are not treated as program income for purposes of 2 CFR 200.307.

(2) If the State receives reimbursements from Federal funds (*e.g.,* Medicaid reimbursements attributable directly to Federal funds) for services under part C of the Act, those funds are considered neither State nor local funds under § 303.225(b).

(3) If the State spends funds from private insurance for services under this part, those funds are considered neither State nor local funds under § 303.225.

(e) *Funds received from a parent or family member under a State's system of payments.* Funds received by the State from a parent or family member under the State's system of payments established under § 303.521 are considered program income under 2 CFR 200.307. These funds—

(1) Are not deducted from the total allowable costs charged under part C of the Act (as set forth in 2 CFR 200.307(e)(1));

(2) Must be used for the State's part C early intervention services program, consistent with 2 CFR 200.307(e)(2); and

(3) Are considered neither State nor local funds under § 303.225(b).

(Authority: 20 U.S.C. 1432(4)(B), 1435(a)(10), 1439(a))

[76 FR 60244, Sept. 28, 2011, as amended at 79 FR 76097, Dec. 19, 2014]

§ 303.521 System of payments and fees.

(a) *General.* If a State elects to adopt a system of payments in § 303.500(b), the State's system of payments policies must be in writing and specify which functions or services, if any, are subject to the system of payments (including any fees charged to the family as a result of using one or more of the family's public insurance or benefits or private insurance), and include—

(1) The payment system and schedule of sliding or cost participation fees that may be charged to the parent for early intervention services under this part;

(2) The basis and amount of payments or fees;

(3) The State's definition of ability to pay (including its definition of income and family expenses, such as extraordinary medical expenses), its definition of inability to pay, and when and how the State makes its determination of the ability or inability to pay;

(4) An assurance that—

(i) Fees will not be charged to parents for the services that a child is otherwise entitled to receive at no cost (including those services identified under paragraphs (a)(4)(ii), (b), and (c) of this section);

(ii) The inability of the parents of an infant or toddler with a disability to pay for services will not result in a delay or denial of services under this part to the child or the child's family such that, if the parent or family meets the State's definition of inability to pay, the infant or toddler with a disability must be provided all part C services at no cost.

(iii) Families will not be charged any more than the actual cost of the part C service (factoring in any amount received from other sources for payment for that service); and

(iv) Families with public insurance or benefits or private insurance will not be charged disproportionately more than families who do not have public insurance or benefits or private insurance;

(5) Provisions stating that the failure to provide the requisite income information and documentation may result in a charge of a fee on the fee schedule and specify the fee to be charged; and

(6) Provisions that permit, but do not require, the lead agency to use part C or other funds to pay for costs such as the premiums, deductibles, or co-payments.

(b) *Functions not subject to fees.* The following are required functions that must be carried out at public expense, and for which no fees may be charged to parents:

(1) Implementing the child find requirements in §§ 303.301 through 303.303.

(2) Evaluation and assessment, in accordance with §303.320, and the functions related to evaluation and assessment in §303.13(b).

(3) Service coordination services, as defined in §§303.13(b)(11) and 303.33.

(4) Administrative and coordinative activities related to—

(i) The development, review, and evaluation of IFSPs and interim IFSPs in accordance with §§303.342 through 303.345; and

(ii) Implementation of the procedural safeguards in subpart E of this part and the other components of the statewide system of early intervention services in subpart D of this part and this subpart.

(c) *States with FAPE mandates, or that use funds under Part B of the Act to serve children under age three.* If a State has in effect a State law requiring the provision of FAPE for, or uses part B funds to serve, an infant or toddler with a disability under the age of three (or any subset of infants and toddlers with disabilities under the age of three), the State may not charge the parents of the infant or toddler with a disability for any services (*e.g.*, physical or occupational therapy) under this part that are part of FAPE for that infant or toddler and the child's family, and those FAPE services must meet the requirements of both parts B and C of the Act.

(d) *Family fees.* (1) Fees or costs collected from a parent or the child's family to pay for early intervention services under a State's system of payments are program income under 2 CFR 200.307. A State may add this program income to its part C grant funds, rather than deducting the program income from the amount of the State's part C grant. Any fees collected must be used for the purposes of the grant under part C of the Act.

(2) Fees collected under a system of payments are considered neither State nor local funds under §303.225(b).

(e) *Procedural Safeguards.* (1) Each State system of payments must include written policies to inform parents that a parent who wishes to contest the imposition of a fee, or the State's determination of the parent's ability to pay, may do one of the following:

(i) Participate in mediation in accordance with §303.431.

(ii) Request a due process hearing under §303.436 or 303.441, whichever is applicable.

(iii) File a State complaint under §303.434.

(iv) Use any other procedure established by the State for speedy resolution of financial claims, provided that such use does not delay or deny the parent's procedural rights under this part, including the right to pursue, in a timely manner, the redress options described in paragraphs (e)(2)(i) through (e)(2)(iii) of this section.

(2) A State must inform parents of these procedural safeguard options by either—

(i) Providing parents with a copy of the State's system of payments policies when obtaining consent for provision of early intervention services under §303.420(a)(3); or

(ii) Including this information with the notice provided to parents under §303.421.

(Authority: 20 U.S.C. 1432(4)(B), 1439(a), 1440)

[76 FR 60244, Sept. 28, 2011, as amended at 79 FR 76097, Dec. 19, 2014]

Subpart G—State Interagency Coordinating Council

§303.600 Establishment of Council.

(a) A State that desires to receive financial assistance under part C of the Act must establish a State Interagency Coordinating Council (Council) as defined in §303.8.

(b) The Council must be appointed by the Governor. The Governor must ensure that the membership of the Council reasonably represents the population of the State.

(c) The Governor must designate a member of the Council to serve as the chairperson of the Council or require the Council to do so. Any member of the Council who is a representative of the lead agency designated under §303.201 may not serve as the chairperson of the Council.

(Authority: 20 U.S.C. 1441(a))

§303.601 Composition.

(a) The Council must be composed as follows:

(1)(i) At least 20 percent of the members must be parents, including minority parents, of infants or toddlers with disabilities or children with disabilities aged 12 years or younger, with knowledge of, or experience with, programs for infants and toddlers with disabilities.

(ii) At least one parent member must be a parent of an infant or toddler with a disability or a child with a disability aged six years or younger.

(2) At least 20 percent of the members must be public or private providers of early intervention services.

(3) At least one member must be from the State legislature.

(4) At least one member must be involved in personnel preparation.

(5) At least one member must—

(i) Be from each of the State agencies involved in the provision of, or payment for, early intervention services to infants and toddlers with disabilities and their families; and

(ii) Have sufficient authority to engage in policy planning and implementation on behalf of these agencies.

(6) At least one member must—

(i) Be from the SEA responsible for preschool services to children with disabilities; and

(ii) Have sufficient authority to engage in policy planning and implementation on behalf of the SEA.

(7) At least one member must be from the agency responsible for the State Medicaid and CHIP program.

(8) At least one member must be from a Head Start or Early Head Start agency or program in the State.

(9) At least one member must be from a State agency responsible for child care.

(10) At least one member must be from the agency responsible for the State regulation of private health insurance.

(11) At least one member must be a representative designated by the Office of the Coordination of Education of Homeless Children and Youth.

(12) At least one member must be a representative from the State child welfare agency responsible for foster care.

(13) At least one member must be from the State agency responsible for children's mental health.

(b) The Governor may appoint one member to represent more than one program or agency listed in paragraphs (a)(7) through (a)(13) of this section.

(c) The Council may include other members selected by the Governor, including a representative from the Bureau of Indian Education (BIE) or, where there is no school operated or funded by the BIE in the State, from the Indian Health Service or the tribe or tribal council.

(d) No member of the Council may cast a vote on any matter that would provide direct financial benefit to that member or otherwise give the appearance of a conflict of interest under State law.

(Authority: 20 U.S.C. 1231d, 1441(b), 1441(f))

§ 303.602 Meetings.

(a) The Council must meet, at a minimum, on a quarterly basis, and in such places as it determines necessary.

(b) The meetings must—

(1) Be publicly announced sufficiently in advance of the dates they are to be held to ensure that all interested parties have an opportunity to attend;

(2) To the extent appropriate, be open and accessible to the general public; and

(3) As needed, provide for interpreters for persons who are deaf and other necessary services for Council members and participants. The Council may use funds under this part to pay for those services.

(Authority: 20 U.S.C. 1441(c))

§ 303.603 Use of funds by the Council.

(a) Subject to the approval by the Governor, the Council may use funds under this part to—

(1) Conduct hearings and forums;

(2) Reimburse members of the Council for reasonable and necessary expenses for attending Council meetings and performing Council duties (including child care for parent representatives);

(3) Pay compensation to a member of the Council if the member is not employed or must forfeit wages from other employment when performing official Council business;

(4) Hire staff; and

(5) Obtain the services of professional, technical, and clerical personnel as may be necessary to carry out the performance of its functions under part C of the Act.

(b) Except as provided in paragraph (a) of this section, Council members must serve without compensation from funds available under part C of the Act.

(Authority: 20 U.S.C. 1441(d))

§ 303.604 Functions of the Council—required duties.

(a) *Advising and assisting the lead agency.* The Council must advise and assist the lead agency in the performance of its responsibilities in section 635(a)(10) of the Act, including—

(1) Identification of sources of fiscal and other support for services for early intervention service programs under part C of the Act;

(2) Assignment of financial responsibility to the appropriate agency;

(3) Promotion of methods (including use of intra-agency and interagency agreements) for intra-agency and inter-agency collaboration regarding child find under §§ 303.115 and 303.302, monitoring under § 303.120 and §§ 303.700 through 303.708, financial responsibility and provision of early intervention services under §§ 303.202 and 303.511, and transition under § 303.209; and

(4) Preparation of applications under this part and amendments to those applications.

(b) *Advising and assisting on transition.* The Council must advise and assist the SEA and the lead agency regarding the transition of toddlers with disabilities to preschool and other appropriate services.

(c) *Annual report to the Governor and to the Secretary.* (1) The Council must—

(i) Prepare and submit an annual report to the Governor and to the Secretary on the status of early intervention service programs for infants and toddlers with disabilities and their families under part C of the Act operated within the State; and

(ii) Submit the report to the Secretary by a date that the Secretary establishes.

(2) Each annual report must contain the information required by the Sec-

retary for the year for which the report is made.

(Authority: 20 U.S.C. 1441(e)(1))

§ 303.605 Authorized activities by the Council.

The Council may carry out the following activities:

(a) Advise and assist the lead agency and the SEA regarding the provision of appropriate services for children with disabilities from birth through age five.

(b) Advise appropriate agencies in the State with respect to the integration of services for infants and toddlers with disabilities and at-risk infants and toddlers and their families, regardless of whether at-risk infants and toddlers are eligible for early intervention services in the State.

(c) Coordinate and collaborate with the State Advisory Council on Early Childhood Education and Care for children, as described in section 642B(b)(1)(A)(i) of the Head Start Act, 42 U.S.C. 9837b(b)(1)(A)(i), if applicable, and other State interagency early learning initiatives, as appropriate.

(Authority: 20 U.S.C. 1435(a)(10), 1441(e)(2))

Subpart H—State Monitoring and Enforcement; Federal Monitoring and Enforcement; Reporting; and Allocation of Funds

FEDERAL AND STATE MONITORING AND ENFORCEMENT

§ 303.700 State monitoring and enforcement.

(a) The lead agency must—

(1) Monitor the implementation of this part;

(2) Make determinations annually about the performance of each EIS program using the categories identified in § 303.703(b);

(3) Enforce this part consistent with § 303.704, using appropriate enforcement mechanisms, which must include, if applicable, the enforcement mechanisms identified in § 303.704(a)(1) (technical assistance) and § 303.704(a)(2) (imposing conditions on the lead agency's funding of an EIS program or, if the lead agency does not provide part C funds to the

EIS program, an EIS provider), § 303.704(b)(2)(i) (corrective action or improvement plan) and § 303.704(b)(2)(iv) (withholding of funds, in whole or in part by the lead agency), and § 303.704(c)(2) (withholding of funds, in whole or in part by the lead agency); and

(4) Report annually on the performance of the State and of each EIS program under this part as provided in § 303.702.

(b) The primary focus of the State's monitoring activities must be on—

(1) Improving early intervention results and functional outcomes for all infants and toddlers with disabilities; and

(2) Ensuring that EIS programs meet the program requirements under part C of the Act, with a particular emphasis on those requirements that are most closely related to improving early intervention results for infants and toddlers with disabilities.

(c) As a part of its responsibilities under paragraph (a) of this section, the State must use quantifiable indicators and such qualitative indicators as are needed to adequately measure performance in the priority areas identified in paragraph (d) of this section, and the indicators established by the Secretary for the State performance plans.

(d) The lead agency must monitor each EIS program located in the State, using quantifiable indicators in each of the following priority areas, and using such qualitative indicators as are needed to adequately measure performance in those areas:

(1) Early intervention services in natural environments.

(2) State exercise of general supervision, including child find, effective monitoring, the use of resolution sessions (if the State adopts part B due process hearing procedures under § 303.430(d)(2)), mediation, and a system of transition services as defined in section 637(a)(9) of the Act.

(e) In exercising its monitoring responsibilities under paragraph (d) of this section, the State must ensure that when it identifies noncompliance with the requirements of this part by EIS programs and providers, the noncompliance is corrected as soon as possible and in no case later than one year after the State's identification of the noncompliance.

(Approved by Office of Management and Budget under control number 1820–0578)

(Authority: 20 U.S.C. 1416(a), 1442)

§ 303.701 State performance plans and data collection.

(a) *General.* Each State must have in place a performance plan that meets the requirements described in section 616 of the Act; is approved by the Secretary; and includes an evaluation of the State's efforts to implement the requirements and purposes of part C of the Act, a description of how the State will improve implementation, and measurable and rigorous targets for the indicators established by the Secretary under the priority areas described in § 303.700(d).

(b) *Review of State performance plan.* Each State must review its State performance plan at least once every six years and submit any amendments to the Secretary.

(c) *Data collection.* (1) Each State must collect valid and reliable information as needed to report annually to the Secretary under § 303.702(b)(2) on the indicators established by the Secretary for the State performance plans.

(2) If the Secretary permits States to collect data on specific indicators through State monitoring or sampling, and the State collects data for a particular indicator through State monitoring or sampling, the State must collect and report data on those indicators for each EIS program at least once during the six-year period of a State performance plan.

(3) Nothing in part C of the Act or these regulations may be construed to authorize the development of a nationwide database of personally identifiable information on individuals involved in studies or other collections of data under part C of the Act.

(Approved by Office of Management and Budget under control number 1820–0578)

(Authority: 20 U.S.C. 1416(b), 1442)

§ 303.702 State use of targets and reporting.

(a) *General.* Each State must use the targets established in the State's performance plan under § 303.701 and the priority areas described in §303.700(d) to analyze the performance of each EIS program in implementing part C of the Act.

(b) *Public reporting and privacy.* (1) *Public report.* (i) Subject to paragraph (b)(1)(ii) of this section, the State must—

(A) Report annually to the public on the performance of each EIS program located in the State on the targets in the State's performance plan as soon as practicable but no later than 120 days following the State's submission of its annual performance report to the Secretary under paragraph (b)(2) of this section; and

(B) Make the State's performance plan under §303.701(a), annual performance reports under paragraph (b)(2) of this section, and the State's annual reports on the performance of each EIS program under paragraph (b)(1)(i)(A) of this section available through public means, including by posting on the Web site of the lead agency, distribution to the media, and distribution to EIS programs.

(ii) If the State, in meeting the requirements of paragraph (b)(1)(i)(A) of this section, collects data through State monitoring or sampling, the State must include in its public report on EIS programs under paragraph (b)(1)(i)(A) of this section the most recently available performance data on each EIS program and the date the data were collected.

(2) *State performance report.* The State must report annually to the Secretary on the performance of the State under the State's performance plan.

(3) *Privacy.* The State must not report to the public or the Secretary any information on performance that would result in the disclosure of personally identifiable information about individual children, or where the available data are insufficient to yield statistically reliable information.

(Approved by Office of Management and Budget under control number 1820–0578)

(Authority: 20 U.S.C. 1416(b)(2)(B)–(C), 1442)

§303.703 Secretary's review and determination regarding State performance.

(a) *Review.* The Secretary annually reviews the State's performance report submitted pursuant to §303.702(b)(2).

(b) *Determination.* (1) *General.* Based on the information provided by the State in the State's annual performance report, information obtained through monitoring visits, and any other public information made available, the Secretary determines if the State—

(i) Meets the requirements and purposes of part C of the Act;

(ii) Needs assistance in implementing the requirements of part C of the Act;

(iii) Needs intervention in implementing the requirements of part C of the Act; or

(iv) Needs substantial intervention in implementing the requirements of part C of the Act.

(2) *Notice and opportunity for a hearing.* (i) For determinations made under paragraphs (b)(1)(iii) and (b)(1)(iv) of this section, the Secretary provides reasonable notice and an opportunity for a hearing on those determinations.

(ii) The hearing described in paragraph (b)(2)(i) of this section consists of an opportunity to meet with the Assistant Secretary for Special Education and Rehabilitative Services to demonstrate why the Secretary should not make the determination described in paragraph (b)(1)(iii) or (b)(1)(iv) of this section.

(Authority: 20 U.S.C. 1416(d), 1442)

§303.704 Enforcement.

(a) *Needs assistance.* If the Secretary determines, for two consecutive years, that a State needs assistance under §303.703(b)(1)(ii) in implementing the requirements of part C of the Act, the Secretary takes one or more of the following actions:

(1) Advises the State of available sources of technical assistance that may help the State address the areas in which the State needs assistance, which may include assistance from the Office of Special Education Programs, other offices of the Department of Education, other Federal agencies, technical assistance providers approved by

the Secretary, and other federally funded nonprofit agencies, and requires the State to work with appropriate entities. This technical assistance may include—

(i) The provision of advice by experts to address the areas in which the State needs assistance, including explicit plans for addressing the areas of concern within a specified period of time;

(ii) Assistance in identifying and implementing professional development, early intervention service provision strategies, and methods of early intervention service provision that are based on scientifically based research;

(iii) Designating and using administrators, service coordinators, service providers, and other personnel from the EIS program to provide advice, technical assistance, and support; and

(iv) Devising additional approaches to providing technical assistance, such as collaborating with institutions of higher education, educational service agencies, national centers of technical assistance supported under part D of the Act, and private providers of scientifically based technical assistance.

(2) Identifies the State as a high-risk grantee and imposes special conditions on the State's grant under part C of the Act.

(b) *Needs intervention.* If the Secretary determines, for three or more consecutive years, that a State needs intervention under § 303.703(b)(1)(iii) in implementing the requirements of part C of the Act, the following apply:

(1) The Secretary may take any of the actions described in paragraph (a) of this section.

(2) The Secretary takes one or more of the following actions:

(i) Requires the State to prepare a corrective action plan or improvement plan if the Secretary determines that the State should be able to correct the problem within one year.

(ii) Requires the State to enter into a compliance agreement under section 457 of the General Education Provisions Act, as amended (GEPA), 20 U.S.C. 1234f, if the Secretary has reason to believe that the State cannot correct the problem within one year.

(iii) Seeks to recover funds under section 452 of GEPA, 20 U.S.C. 1234a.

(iv) Withholds, in whole or in part, any further payments to the State under part C of the Act.

(v) Refers the matter for appropriate enforcement action, which may include referral to the Department of Justice.

(c) *Needs substantial intervention.* Notwithstanding paragraph (a) or (b) of this section, at any time that the Secretary determines that a State needs substantial intervention in implementing the requirements of part C of the Act or that there is a substantial failure to comply with any requirement under part C of the Act by the lead agency or an EIS program in the State, the Secretary takes one or more of the following actions:

(1) Recovers funds under section 452 of GEPA, 20 U.S.C. 1234a.

(2) Withholds, in whole or in part, any further payments to the State under part C of the Act.

(3) Refers the case to the Office of Inspector General of the Department of Education.

(4) Refers the matter for appropriate enforcement action, which may include referral to the Department of Justice.

(d) *Report to Congress.* The Secretary reports to the Committee on Education and Labor of the House of Representatives and the Committee on Health, Education, Labor, and Pensions of the Senate within 30 days of taking enforcement action pursuant to paragraph (a), (b), or (c) of this section, on the specific action taken and the reasons why enforcement action was taken.

(Authority: 20 U.S.C. 1416(e)(1)–(3), 1416(e)(5), 1442)

§ 303.705 Withholding funds.

(a) *Opportunity for hearing.* Prior to withholding any funds under part C of the Act, the Secretary provides reasonable notice and an opportunity for a hearing to the lead agency involved, pursuant to the procedures in §§ 303.231 through 303.236.

(b) *Suspension.* Pending the outcome of any hearing to withhold payments under paragraph (a) of this section, the Secretary may suspend payments to a recipient, suspend the authority of the recipient to obligate funds under part C of the Act, or both, after the recipient has been given reasonable notice and an opportunity to show cause why future payments or authority to obligate funds under part C of the Act should not be suspended.

(c) *Nature of withholding.* (1) *Limitation.* If the Secretary determines that it is appropriate to withhold further payments under section 616(e)(2) or (e)(3) of the Act, the Secretary may determine—

(i) That such withholding will be limited to programs or projects, or portions of programs or projects, that affected the Secretary's determination under § 303.703(b)(1); or

(ii) That the lead agency must not make further payments of funds under part C of the Act to specified State agencies, EIS programs or, if the lead agency does not provide part C funds to the EIS program, EIS providers that caused or were involved in the Secretary's determination under § 303.703(b)(1).

(2) *Withholding until rectified.* Until the Secretary is satisfied that the condition that caused the initial withholding has been substantially rectified—

(i) Payments to the State under part C of the Act must be withheld in whole or in part; and

(ii) Payments by the lead agency under part C of the Act must be limited to State agencies and EIS providers whose actions did not cause or were not involved in the Secretary's determination under § 303.703(b)(1).

(Authority: 20 U.S.C. 1416(e)(4), 1416(e)(6), 1442)

§ 303.706 Public attention.

Whenever a State receives notice that the Secretary is proposing to take or is taking an enforcement action pursuant to § 303.704, the State must, by means of a public notice, take such measures as may be necessary to bring the pendency of an action pursuant to section 616(e) of the Act and § 303.704 of the regulations to the attention of the public within the State, including by posting the notice on the Web site of the lead agency and distributing the notice to the media and to EIS programs.

(Authority: 20 U.S.C. 1416(e)(7), 1442)

§ 303.707 Rule of construction.

Nothing in this subpart may be construed to restrict the Secretary from utilizing any authority under GEPA, 20 U.S.C. 1221 *et seq.*, the regulations in 34 CFR parts 76, 77, and 81, and 2 CFR part 200, to monitor and enforce the requirements of the Act, including the imposition of special or high-risk conditions under 2 CFR 200.207 and 3474.5(e).

(Authority: 20 U.S.C. 1416(g), 1442)

[79 FR 76097, Dec. 19, 2014]

§ 303.708 State enforcement.

Nothing in this subpart may be construed to restrict a State from utilizing any other authority available to it to monitor and enforce the requirements of the Act.

(Authority: 20 U.S.C. 1416(a)(1)(C), 1442)

REPORTS—PROGRAM INFORMATION

§ 303.720 Data requirements—general.

(a) The lead agency must annually report to the Secretary and to the public on the information required by section 618 of the Act at the times specified by the Secretary.

(b) The lead agency must submit the report to the Secretary in the manner prescribed by the Secretary.

(Approved by Office of Management and Budget under control number 1820–0557)

(Authority: 20 U.S.C. 1418, 1435(a)(14), 1442)

§ 303.721 Annual report of children served—report requirement.

(a) For the purposes of the annual report required by section 618 of the Act and § 303.720, the lead agency must count and report the number of infants and toddlers receiving early intervention services on any date between October 1 and December 1 of each year. The report must include—

(1) The number and percentage of infants and toddlers with disabilities in the State, by race, gender, and ethnicity, who are receiving early intervention services (and include in this number any children reported to it by tribes, tribal organizations, and consortia under § 303.731(e)(1));

(2) The number and percentage of infants and toddlers with disabilities, by race, gender, and ethnicity, who, from

birth through age two, stopped receiving early intervention services because of program completion or for other reasons; and

(3) The number and percentage of at-risk infants and toddlers (as defined in section 632(1) of the Act), by race and ethnicity, who are receiving early intervention services under part C of the Act.

(b) If a State adopts the option under section 635(c) of the Act and § 303.211 to make services under this part available to children ages three and older, the State must submit to the Secretary a report on the number and percentage of children with disabilities who are eligible for services under section 619 of the Act but whose parents choose for those children to continue to receive early intervention services.

(c) The number of due process complaints filed under section 615 of the Act, the number of hearings conducted and the number of mediations held, and the number of settlement agreements reached through such mediations.

(Approved by Office of Management and Budget under control number 1820–0557)

(Authority: 20 U.S.C. 1418(a)(1)(B), (C), (F), (G), and (H), 1435(a)(14), 1435(c)(3), 1442)

§ 303.722 Data reporting.

(a) *Protection of identifiable data.* The data described in section 618(a) of the Act and in § 303.721 must be publicly reported by each State in a manner that does not result in disclosure of data identifiable to individual children.

(b) *Sampling.* The Secretary may permit States and outlying areas to obtain data in section 618(a) of the Act through sampling.

(Approved by Office of Management and Budget under control number 1820–0557)

(Authority: 20 U.S.C. 1418(b), 1435(a)(14), 1442)

§ 303.723 Annual report of children served—certification.

The lead agency must include in its report a certification signed by an authorized official of the agency that the information provided under § 303.721 is an accurate and unduplicated count of

infants and toddlers with disabilities receiving early intervention services.

(Approved by Office of Management and Budget under control number 1820–0557)

(Authority: 20 U.S.C. 1418(a)(3), 1435(a)(14), 1442)

§ 303.724 Annual report of children served—other responsibilities of the lead agency.

In addition to meeting the requirements of §§ 303.721 through 303.723, the lead agency must conduct its own child count or use EIS providers to complete its child count. If the lead agency uses EIS providers to complete its child count, then the lead agency must—

(a) Establish procedures to be used by EIS providers in counting the number of children with disabilities receiving early intervention services;

(b) Establish dates by which those EIS providers must report to the lead agency to ensure that the State complies with § 303.721(a);

(c) Obtain certification from each EIS provider that an unduplicated and accurate count has been made;

(d) Aggregate the data from the count obtained from each EIS provider and prepare the report required under §§ 303.721 through 303.723; and

(e) Ensure that documentation is maintained to enable the State and the Secretary to audit the accuracy of the count.

(Approved by Office of Management and Budget under control number 1820–0557)

(Authority: 20 U.S.C. 1418(a), 1435(a)(14), 1442)

ALLOCATION OF FUNDS

§ 303.730 Formula for State allocations.

(a) *Reservation of funds for outlying areas.* From the sums appropriated to carry out part C of the Act for any fiscal year, the Secretary may reserve not more than one percent for payments to American Samoa, the Commonwealth of the Northern Mariana Islands, Guam, and the United States Virgin Islands in accordance with their respective needs for assistance under part C of the Act.

(b) *Consolidation of funds.* The provisions of the Omnibus Territories Act of

Off. of Spec. Educ. and Rehab. Services, Education

§ 303.731

1977, Pub. L. 95–134, permitting the consolidation of grants to the outlying areas, do not apply to the funds provided under part C of the Act.

(Authority: 20 U.S.C. 1443(a))

§ 303.731 Payments to Indians.

(a) *General.* (1) The Secretary makes payments to the Secretary of the Interior under part C of the Act, which the Secretary of the Interior must distribute to tribes or tribal organizations (as defined under section 4 of the Indian Self-Determination and Education Assistance Act, as amended, 25 U.S.C. 450b), or consortia of those entities, for the coordination of assistance in the provision of early intervention services by States to infants and toddlers with disabilities and their families on reservations served by elementary and secondary schools for Indian children operated or funded by the Secretary of the Interior.

(2) A tribe, tribal organization, or consortium of those entities is eligible to receive a payment under this section if the tribe, tribal organization, or consortium of those entities is on a reservation that is served by an elementary or secondary school operated or funded by the Secretary of the Interior.

(3) The amount of the payment to the Secretary of the Interior under this section for any fiscal year is 1.25 percent of the aggregate amount available to all States under part C of the Act.

(b) *Allocation.* For each fiscal year, the Secretary of the Interior must distribute the entire payment received under paragraph (a)(1) of this section by providing to each tribe, tribal organization, or consortium an amount based on the number of infants and toddlers residing on the reservation, as determined annually, divided by the total number of those children served by all tribes, tribal organizations, or consortia.

(c) *Information.* To receive a payment under this section, the tribe, tribal organization, or consortium must submit the appropriate information to the Secretary of the Interior to determine the amounts to be distributed under paragraph (b) of this section.

(d) *Use of funds.* (1) The funds received by a tribe, tribal organization, or consortium must be used to assist States in child find, screening, and other procedures for the early identification of Indian children under three years of age and for parent training. The funds also may be used to provide early intervention services in accordance with part C of the Act. These activities may be carried out directly or through contracts or cooperative agreements with the Bureau of Indian Education, local educational agencies, and other public or private nonprofit organizations. The tribe, tribal organization, or consortium is encouraged to involve Indian parents in the development and implementation of these activities.

(2) The tribe, tribal organization, or consortium must, as appropriate, make referrals to local, State, or Federal entities for the provision of services or further diagnosis.

(e) *Reports.* (1) To be eligible to receive a payment under paragraph (b) of this section, a tribe, tribal organization, or consortium must make a biennial report to the Secretary of the Interior of activities undertaken under this section, including the number of contracts and cooperative agreements entered into, the number of infants and toddlers contacted and receiving services for each year, and the estimated number of infants and toddlers needing services during the two years following the year in which the report is made. This report must include an assurance that the tribe, tribal organization, or consortium has provided the lead agency in the State child find information (including the names and dates of birth and parent contact information) for infants or toddlers with disabilities who are included in the report in order to meet the child find coordination and child count requirements in sections 618 and 643 of the Act.

(2) The Secretary of the Interior must provide a summary of this information (including confirmation that each tribe, tribal organization, or consortium has provided to the Secretary of the Interior the assurance required under paragraph (e)(1) of this section) on a biennial basis to the Secretary along with such other information as

required of the Secretary of the Interior under part C of the Act. The Secretary may require additional information from the Secretary of the Interior.

(3) Within 90 days after the end of each fiscal year the Secretary of the Interior must provide the Secretary with a report on the payments distributed under this section. The report must include—

(i) The name of each tribe, tribal organization, or combination of those entities that received a payment for the fiscal year;

(ii) The amount of each payment; and

(iii) The date of each payment.

(f) *Prohibited uses of funds.* None of the funds under this section may be used by the Secretary of the Interior for administrative purposes, including child count and the provision of technical assistance.

(Authority: 20 U.S.C. 1443(b))

§ 303.732   State allotments.

(a) *General.* Except as provided in paragraphs (b) and (c) of this section, for each fiscal year, from the aggregate amount of funds available under part C of the Act for distribution to the States, the Secretary allots to each State an amount that bears the same ratio to the aggregate amount as the number of infants and toddlers in the State bears to the number of infants and toddlers in all States.

(b) *Minimum allocations.* Except as provided in paragraph (c) of this section, no State may receive less than 0.5 percent of the aggregate amount available under this section or $500,000, whichever is greater.

(c) *Ratable reduction.* (1) If the sums made available under part C of the Act for any fiscal year are insufficient to pay the full amount that all States are eligible to receive under this section for that year, the Secretary ratably reduces the allotments to those States for such year.

(2) If additional funds become available for making payments under this section, allotments that were reduced under paragraph (c)(1) of this section will be increased on the same basis the allotments were reduced.

(d) *Definitions.* For the purpose of allotting funds to the States under this section—

(1) *Aggregate amount* means the amount available for distribution to the States after the Secretary determines the amount of payments to be made to the Secretary of the Interior under § 303.731, to the outlying areas under § 303.730, and any amount to be reserved for State incentive grants under § 303.734;

(2) *Infants and toddlers* means children from birth through age two in the general population, based on the most recent satisfactory data as determined by the Secretary; and

(3) *State* means each of the 50 States, the District of Columbia, and the Commonwealth of Puerto Rico.

(Authority: 20 U.S.C. 1443(c))

§ 303.733   Reallotment of funds.

If a State (as defined in § 303.35) elects not to receive its allotment, the Secretary reallots those funds among the remaining States (as defined in § 303.732(d)(3)), in accordance with § 303.732(c)(2).

(Authority: 20 U.S.C. 1443(d))

§ 303.734   Reservation for State incentive grants.

(a) *General.* For any fiscal year for which the amount appropriated pursuant to the authorization of appropriations under section 644 of the Act exceeds $460,000,000, the Secretary reserves 15 percent of the appropriated amount exceeding $460,000,000 to provide grants to States that are carrying out the policy described in section 635(c) of the Act and in § 303.211 (including a State that makes part C services available under § 303.211(a)(2)), in order to facilitate the implementation of that policy.

(b) *Amount of grant.* (1) *General.* Notwithstanding section 643(c)(2) and (c)(3) of the Act, the Secretary provides a grant to each State under this section in an amount that bears the same ratio to the amount reserved under paragraph (a) of this section as the number of infants and toddlers in the State bears to the number of infants and toddlers in all States receiving grants under paragraph (a) of this section.

(2) *Maximum amount.* No State may receive a grant under paragraph (a) of this section for any fiscal year in an amount that is

greater than 20 percent of the amount reserved under that paragraph for the fiscal year.

(c) *Carryover of amounts pursuant to section 643(e)(3) of the Act.* (1) *First succeeding fiscal year.* Pursuant to section 421(b) of GEPA, 20 U.S.C. 1221 *et seq.,* amounts under a grant provided under paragraph (a) of this section that are not obligated and expended prior to the beginning of the first fiscal year succeeding the fiscal year for which those amounts were appropriated must remain available for obligation and expenditure during the first succeeding fiscal year.

(2) *Second succeeding fiscal year.* Amounts under a grant provided under paragraph (a) of this section that are not obligated and expended prior to the beginning of the second fiscal year succeeding the fiscal year for which those amounts were appropriated must be returned to the Secretary and used to make grants to States under section 633 of the Act (from their allotments identified in §§ 303.731 through 303.733) during the second succeeding fiscal year.

(Authority: 20 U.S.C. 1443)

249

253

SOCIAL SECURITY ACT:
- Title V—Maternal and Child Health .... 303.302(c)(1)(ii)(B).
- Title XVI:
    - Supplemental Security Income (SSI) .... 303.302(c)(1)(ii)(F).
- Title XIX:
    - EPSDT (Early Periodic Screening, Diagnosis, 303.302(c)(1)(ii)(C).
      and Treatment).
    - Medicaid .... 303.510, 303.520.

SOCIAL WORK SERVICES (Definition) .... 303.13(b)(13).
- Social workers .... 303.13(c)(10).

SPECIAL INSTRUCTION (Definition) .... 303.13(b)(14).
- Special educators .... 303.13(c)(11).

SPEECH–LANGUAGE PATHOLOGY:
- Definition .... 303.13(b)(15).
- Speech and language pathologists .... 303.13(c)(12).

SSI (Supplemental Security Income):
- Child find (Coordination) .... 303.302(c)(1)(ii)(F).
- See "Social Security Act".

STATE (Definition) .... 303.35.
- Special definition -State allocations .... 303.732(d)(3).

STATE ADVISORY COUNCIL ON EARLY EDUCATION AND CARE.
- Comprehensive system of personnel development 303.118(b)(4).
  (CSPD) (Coordination).
- Participation of State lead agency .... 303.210(b).

STATE AGENCIES:
- Child find (Coordination) .... 303.302(c)(1)(i).
- ICC (Composition of Council) .... 303.601(a)(5)(i).
- Interagency agreements .... 303.511(b)(2).

STATE APPLICATION:
- Amendments to (public participation) .... 303.208(a).
- Conditions of assistance .... 303.200.
- Components of a statewide system .... 303.110–303.126.
- Council function (Advise-assist lead agency with) .... 303.604(a)(4).
- General requirements .... 303.201–303.212.
- Public participation .... 303.208.
    - Reviewing public comments received .... 303.208(a).

STATE APPROVED OR RECOGNIZED CERTIFICATION (Quali- 303.31.
fied Personnel).

STATE COMPLAINT PROCEDURES:
- Adoption of .... 303.432.
    - (See also §§ 303.432–303.434)
- Filing a complaint .... 303.434.
- Lead agency must adopt .... 303.430(c).
- Minimum State complaint procedures .... 303.433.
    - Time extension; final decision; implementation 303.433(b).
    - Time limit (60 days) .... 303.433(a).
- Remedies for denial of appropriate services .... 303.432(b).
- State dispute resolution options .... 303.430(a), (c).
- State complaints & due process hearing procedures ..... 303.433(c).

STATE DEFINITION OF "INABILITY TO PAY":
- Private insurance .... 303.520(c).
- System of payments .... 303.521(a)(3), (4)(ii).

STATE EDUCATIONAL AGENCY (SEA):
- Applicable regulations (SEA means the lead agency) ... 303.3(b)(1).
- Confidentiality procedures—Disclosure of information 303.401(d).
- Council—Composition .... 303.601(a)(6)(i).
- Council—Functions .... 303.604(b), 303.605(a).
- Definition .... 303.36.
- Free Appropriate Public Education (FAPE) (Defini- 303.15(b).
  tion)—Standards of the SEA.
- State option—Services for children 3 and older .... 303.211(a)(1).
- Transition to preschool .... 303.209(a)(3)(i)(A)–
  (a)(3)(i)(B), (a)(3)(ii),
  (b)(2)(i)–(b)(2)(ii).

STATE ELIGIBILITY:
- Conditions of assistance .... 303.101.

- Confidentiality—Access rights .... 303.405(a).
- Department hearing procedures on State eligibility ..... 303.231(b)(3), 303.233(b), 303.234(d), (e), (g), (k), 303.236.
  - Due process procedures—Part B (see "Timelines—Due Process (Part B)")
- Enforcement—Secretary report to Congress w/in 30 days of taking enforcement action. 303.704(d).
- Evaluation and Assessment & initial Individualized Family Service Plan (IFSP) meeting. 303.310.
  - Exceptional circumstances .... 303.310(b)(1).

TIMELINES (PA–PU):
- Part C due process hearings; parental rights:
  - Decision not later than 30 days after receipt of complaint. 303.437(b).
  - Prohibit information not disclosed (at least five days before hearing). 303.436(b)(3).
- Payments to Indians—reports .... 303.731(e)(1)(3).
- Primary referral sources .... 303.303(a)(2)(i).
- Public reporting and privacy (State performance reports on targets). 303.702(b)(1)(i)(A).
- Public participation (Application, *etc.*) .... 303.208.
  - See also "Public Participation".

TIMELINES (R–Z):
- Report to Secretary on State performance .... 303.702(b)(2).
- State complaint procedures (Time limit of 60 days) ...... 303.433(a).
- Transition—Conference to discuss services .... 303.209(c).
- Transition—LEA notification .... 303.209(b).
- Transition plan .... 303.209(d).
  - Transition timelines for child receiving services under section 303.211. 303.211(b)(6).

TIMELINES–DUE PROCESS (PART B) (A–Q):
- Adjustments to 30-day resolution period .... 303.442(c).
- Agreement review period (w/in three business days of executing a settlement agreement). 303.442(e).
- Civil action (90 days from date of decision) .... 303.448(b).
- Hearing decision (30 or 45 days after expiration of 30-day period or adjustments to that period in § 303.442(b) or (c)). 303.447(a).
- Hearing rights:
  - Additional disclosure (At least five business days before hearing). 303.444(b).
  - Prohibit new evidence (Not disclosed at least five business days before hearing). 303.444(a)(3).
- Lead agency response to complaint (within ten days of receiving complaint). 303.441(e).
- Other party response (within ten days of receiving complaint). 303.441(f).

TIMELINES–DUE PROCESS (PART B) (RE):
- Resolution meeting (w/in 15 days) .... 303.442(a).
  - If no meeting in 15 days, parent may seek intervention—hearing officer. 303.442(b)(5).
- Resolution period:
  - If lead agency not resolved complaint w/in 30 days, hearing may occur. 303.442(b)(1).
  - If no parent participation in 30 days, complaint may be dismissed. 303.442(b)(4).
- Review decision (30 days after request for review) .... 303.447(b).

TIMELINES—DUE PROCESS (PART B) (S–Z):
- Sufficiency of complaint:
  - Amended complaint (Hearing officer permits— Not later than five days before hearing). 303.441(d)(3)(ii).
  - Complaint sufficient—unless party notifies hearing officer w/in 15 days. 303.441(d)(1).
  - Hearing officer determination (within five days of notice). 303.441(d)(2).

PART 304—SERVICE OBLIGATIONS UNDER SPECIAL EDUCATION—PERSONNEL DEVELOPMENT TO IMPROVE SERVICES AND RESULTS FOR CHILDREN WITH DISABILITIES

Subpart A—General

Sec.
304.1 Purpose.
304.3 Definitions.

Subpart B—Conditions That Must Be Met by Grantee

304.21 Allowable costs.
304.22 Requirements for grantees in disbursing scholarships.
304.23 Assurances that must be provided by grantee.

Subpart C—Conditions That Must Be Met by Scholar

304.30 Requirements for scholar.
304.31 Requirements for obtaining an exception or deferral to performance or repayment under an agreement.

AUTHORITY: 20 U.S.C. 1462(h), unless otherwise noted.

SOURCE: 71 FR 32398, June 5, 2006, unless otherwise noted.

Subpart A—General

§ 304.1 Purpose.

Individuals who receive scholarship assistance from projects funded under the Special Education—Personnel Development to Improve Services and Results for Children with Disabilities program are required to complete a service obligation, or repay all or part of the costs of such assistance, in accordance with section 662(h) of the Act and the regulations of this part.

(Authority: 20 U.S.C. 1462(h))

§ 304.3 Definitions.

The following definitions apply to this program:

(a) *Academic year* means—

(1) A full-time course of study—

(i) Taken for a period totaling at least nine months; or

(ii) Taken for the equivalent of at least two semesters, two trimesters, or three quarters; or

(2) For a part-time scholar, the accumulation of periods of part-time courses of study that is equivalent to an "academic year" under paragraph (a)(1) of this definition.

(b) *Act* means the Individuals with Disabilities Education Act, as amended, 20 U.S.C. 1400 *et seq.*

(c) *Early intervention services* means early intervention services as defined in section 632(4) of the Act and includes early intervention services to infants and toddlers with disabilities, and as applicable, to infants and toddlers at risk for disabilities under sections 632(1) and 632(5)(b) of the Act.

(d) *Full-time*, for purposes of determining whether an individual is employed full-time in accordance with § 304.30 means a full-time position as defined by the individual's employer or by the agencies served by the individual.

(e) *Related services* means related services as defined in section 602(26) of the Act.

(f) *Repayment* means monetary reimbursement of scholarship assistance in lieu of completion of a service obligation.

(g) *Scholar* means an individual who is pursuing a degree, license, endorsement, or certification related to special education, related services, or early intervention services and who receives scholarship assistance under section 662 of the Act.

(h) *Scholarship* means financial assistance to a scholar for training under the program and includes all disbursements or credits for tuition, fees, stipends, books, and travel in conjunction with training assignments.

(i) *Service obligation* means a scholar's employment obligation, as described in section 662(h) of the Act and § 304.30.

(j) *Special education* means special education as defined in section 602(29) of the Act.

(Authority: 20 U.S.C. 1462(h))

Subpart B—Conditions That Must be Met by Grantee

§ 304.21 Allowable costs.

In addition to the allowable costs established in the Education Department General Administrative Regulations in 34 CFR 75.530 through 75.562, the following items are allowable expenditures by projects funded under the program:

(a) Cost of attendance, as defined in Title IV of the Higher Education Act of 1965, as amended, 20 U.S.C. 1087*ll* (HEA), including the following:

(1) Tuition and fees.

(2) An allowance for books, supplies, transportation, and miscellaneous personal expenses.

(3) An allowance for room and board.

(b) Stipends.

(c) Travel in conjunction with training assignments.

(Authority: 20 U.S.C. 1462(h))

§ 304.22 Requirements for grantees in disbursing scholarships.

Before disbursement of scholarship assistance to an individual, a grantee must—

(a) Ensure that the scholar—

(1) Is a citizen or national of the United States;

(2) Is a permanent resident of—

(i) Puerto Rico, the United States Virgin Islands, Guam, American Samoa, or the Commonwealth of the Northern Mariana Islands; or

(ii) The Republic of the Marshall Islands, the Federated States of Micronesia, or the Republic of Palau during the period in which these entities are eligible to receive an award under the Personnel Development to Improve Services and Results for Children with Disabilities program; or

(3) Provides evidence from the U.S. Department of Homeland Security that the individual is—

(i) A lawful permanent resident of the United States; or

(ii) In the United States for other than a temporary purpose with the intention of becoming a citizen or permanent resident;

(b) Limit the cost of attendance portion of the scholarship assistance (as discussed in § 304.21(a)) to the amount by which the individual's cost of attendance at the institution exceeds the amount of grant assistance the scholar is to receive for the same academic year under title IV of the HEA; and

(c) Obtain a Certification of Eligibility for Federal Assistance from each scholar, as prescribed in 34 CFR 75.60, 75.61, and 75.62.

(Authority: 20 U.S.C. 1462(h))

§ 304.23 Assurances that must be provided by grantee.

Before receiving an award, a grantee that intends to grant scholarships under the program must include in its application an assurance that the following requirements will be satisfied:

(a) *Requirement for agreement.* Prior to granting a scholarship, the grantee will require each scholar to enter into a written agreement in which the scholar agrees to the terms and conditions set forth in § 304.30. This agreement must explain the Secretary's authority to grant deferrals and exceptions to the service obligation pursuant to § 304.31 and include the current Department address for purposes of the scholar's compliance with § 304.30(i), or any other purpose under this part.

(b) *Standards for satisfactory progress.* The grantee must establish, notify scholars of, and apply reasonable standards for measuring whether a scholar is maintaining satisfactory progress in the scholar's course of study.

(c) *Exit certification.* (1) At the time of exit from the program, the grantee must provide the following information to the scholar:

(i) The number of years the scholar needs to work to satisfy the work requirements in § 304.30(d);

(ii) The total amount of scholarship assistance received subject to § 304.30;

(iii) The time period, consistent with § 304.30(f)(1), during which the scholar must satisfy the work requirements; and

(iv) As applicable, all other obligations of the scholar under § 304.30.

(2) Upon receipt of this information from the grantee, the scholar must provide written certification to the grantee that the information is correct.

(d) *Information.* The grantee must forward the information and written certification required in paragraph (c) of this section to the Secretary, as well as any other information that is necessary to carry out the Secretary's functions under section 662 of the Act and this part.

(e) *Notification to the Secretary.* If the grantee is aware that the scholar has chosen not to fulfill or will be unable to fulfill the obligation under § 304.30(d), the grantee must notify the Secretary when the scholar exits the program.

(Approved by the Office of Management and Budget under control number 1820–0622)

(Authority: 20 U.S.C. 1462(h))

Subpart C—Conditions That Must Be Met by Scholar

§ 304.30 Requirements for scholar.

Individuals who receive scholarship assistance from grantees funded under section 662 of the Act must—

(a) *Training.* Receive the training at the educational institution or agency designated in the scholarship;

(b) *Educational allowances.* Not accept payment of educational allowances from any other entity if that allowance conflicts with the scholar's obligation under section 662 of the Act and this part;

(c) *Satisfactory progress.* Maintain satisfactory progress toward the degree,

certificate, endorsement, or license as determined by the grantee;

(d) *Service obligation.* Upon exiting the training program under paragraph (a) of this section, subsequently maintain employment—

(1) On a full-time or full-time equivalent basis; and

(2) For a period of at least two years for every academic year for which assistance was received;

(e) *Eligible employment.* In order to meet the requirements of paragraph (d) of this section for any project funded under section 662 of the Act, be employed in a position in which—

(1) At least 51 percent of the infants, toddlers, and children to whom the individual provides services are receiving special education, related services, or early intervention services from the individual;

(2) The individual spends at least 51 percent of his or her time providing special education, related services, or early intervention services to infants, toddlers, and children with disabilities; or

(3) If the position involves supervision (including in the capacity of a principal), teaching at the postsecondary level, research, policy, technical assistance, program development, or administration, the individual spends at least 51 percent of his or her time performing work related to the training for which a scholarship was received under section 662 of the Act.

(f) *Time period.* Meet the service obligation under paragraph (d) of this section as follows:

(1) A scholar must complete the service obligation within the period ending not more than the sum of the number of years required in paragraph (d)(2) of this section, as appropriate, plus five additional years, from the date the scholar completes the training for which the scholarship assistance was awarded.

(2) A scholar may begin eligible employment subsequent to the completion of one academic year of the training for which the scholarship assistance was received that otherwise meets the requirements of paragraph (1);

(g) *Part-time scholars.* If the scholar is pursuing coursework on a part-time basis, meet the service obligation in this section based on the accumulated academic years of training for which the scholarship is received;

(h) *Information upon exit.* Provide the grantee all requested information necessary for the grantee to meet the exit certification requirements under § 304.23(c);

(i) *Information after exit.* Within 60 days after exiting the program, and as necessary thereafter for any changes, provide the Department, via U.S. mail, all information that the Secretary needs to monitor the scholar's service obligation under this section, including social security number, address, employment setting, and employment status;

(j) *Repayment.* If not fulfilling the requirements in this section, subject to the provisions in § 304.31 regarding an exception or deferral, repay any scholarship received, plus interest, in an amount proportional to the service obligation not completed as follows:

(1) The Secretary charges the scholar interest on the unpaid balance owed in accordance with the Debt Collection Act of 1982, as amended, 31 U.S.C. 3717.

(2)(i) Interest on the unpaid balance accrues from the date the scholar is determined to have entered repayment status under paragraph (4) of this section.

(ii) Any accrued interest is capitalized at the time the scholar's repayment schedule is established.

(iii) No interest is charged for the period of time during which repayment has been deferred under § 304.31.

(3) Under the authority of the Debt Collection Act of 1982, as amended, the Secretary may impose reasonable collection costs.

(4) A scholar enters repayment status on the first day of the first calendar month after the earliest of the following dates, as applicable:

(i) The date the scholar informs the grantee or the Secretary that the scholar does not plan to fulfill the service obligation under the agreement.

(ii) Any date when the scholar's failure to begin or maintain employment makes it impossible for that individual to complete the service obligation within the number of years required in § 304.30(f).

(iii) Any date on which the scholar discontinues enrollment in the course of study under § 304.30(a).

(5) The scholar must make payments to the Secretary that cover principal, interest, and collection costs according to a schedule established by the Secretary.

(6) Any amount of the scholarship that has not been repaid pursuant to paragraphs (j)(1) through (j)(5) of this section will constitute a debt owed to the United States that may be collected by the Secretary in accordance with 34 CFR part 30.

(Approved by the Office of Management and Budget under control number 1820–0622)

(Authority: 20 U.S.C. 1462(h))

§ 304.31 Requirements for obtaining an exception or deferral to performance or repayment under an agreement.

(a) Based upon sufficient evidence to substantiate the grounds, the Secretary may grant an exception to the repayment requirement in § 304.30(j), in whole or part, if the scholar—

(1) Is unable to continue the course of study in § 304.30 or perform the service obligation because of a permanent disability; or

(2) Has died.

(b) Based upon sufficient evidence to substantiate the grounds, the Secretary may grant a deferral of the repayment requirement in § 304.30(j) during the time the scholar—

(1) Is engaging in a full-time course of study at an institution of higher education;

(2) Is serving on active duty as a member of the armed services of the United States;

(3) Is serving as a volunteer under the Peace Corps Act; or

(4) Is serving as a full-time volunteer under title I of the Domestic Volunteer Service Act of 1973.

(Authority: 20 U.S.C. 1462(h))

PART 350 [RESERVED]

PART 356 [RESERVED]

PART 359 [RESERVED]

PART 361—STATE VOCATIONAL RE-HABILITATION SERVICES PRO-GRAM

Subpart A—General

Subpart B—State Plan and Other Requirements for Vocational Rehabilitation Services

ADMINISTRATION

PROVISION AND SCOPE OF SERVICES

Subpart C—Financing of State Vocational Rehabilitation Programs

Subpart D—Unified and Combined State Plans Under Title I of the Workforce Innovation and Opportunity Act

Subpart E—Performance Accountability Under Title I of the Workforce Innovation and Opportunity Act

Subpart F—Description of the One-Stop Delivery System Under Title I of the Workforce Innovation and Opportunity Act

AUTHORITY: Section 12(c) of the Rehabilitation Act of 1973, as amended; 29 U.S.C. 709(c); Pub. L. 111–256, 124 Stat. 2643; unless otherwise noted.

SOURCE: 81 FR 55741, Aug. 19, 2016, unless otherwise noted.

Subpart A—General

§ 361.1 Purpose.

Under the State Vocational Rehabilitation Services Program, the Secretary provides grants to assist States in operating statewide comprehensive, coordinated, effective, efficient, and accountable vocational rehabilitation programs, each of which is—

(a) An integral part of a statewide workforce development system; and

(b) Designed to assess, plan, develop, and provide vocational rehabilitation services for individuals with disabilities, consistent with their unique strengths, resources, priorities, concerns, abilities, capabilities, interests, and informed choice so that they may prepare for and engage in competitive integrated employment and achieve economic self-sufficiency.

(Authority: Sections 12(c) and 100(a) of the Rehabilitation Act of 1973, as amended; 29 U.S.C. 709(c) and 720(a))

§ 361.2 Eligibility for a grant.

Any State that submits to the Secretary a vocational rehabilitation services portion of the Unified or Combined State Plan that meets the requirements of section 101(a) of the Act and this part is eligible for a grant under this program.

(Authority: Section 101(a) of the Rehabilitation Act of 1973, as amended; 29 U.S.C. 721(a))

§ 361.3 Authorized activities.

The Secretary makes payments to a State to assist in—

(a) The costs of providing vocational rehabilitation services under the vocational rehabilitation services portion of the Unified or Combined State Plan; and

(b) Administrative costs under the vocational rehabilitation services portion of the Unified or Combined State Plan, including one-stop infrastructure costs.

(Authority: Sections 12(c) and 111(a)(1) of the Rehabilitation Act of 1973, as amended; 29 U.S.C. 709(c) and 731(a)(1))

§ 361.4 Applicable regulations.

The following regulations apply to this program:

(a) The Education Department General Administrative Regulations (EDGAR) as follows:

(1) 34 CFR part 76 (State-Administered Programs).

(2) 34 CFR part 77 (Definitions that Apply to Department Regulations).

(3) 34 CFR part 79 (Intergovernmental Review of Department of Education Programs and Activities).

(4) 34 CFR part 81 (General Education Provisions Act—Enforcement).

(5) 34 CFR part 82 (New Restrictions on Lobbying).

(b) The regulations in this part 361.

(c) 2 CFR part 190 (OMB Guidelines to Agencies on Governmentwide Debarment and Suspension (Nonprocurement)) as adopted in 2 CFR part 3485.

(d) 2 CFR part 200 (Uniform Administrative Requirements, Cost Principles, and Audit Requirements for Federal Awards) as adopted in 2 CFR part 3474, except the requirements to accept third-party in-kind contributions to meet cost-sharing or matching requirements, as otherwise authorized under 2 CFR 200.306(b).

(Authority: Section 12(c) of the Rehabilitation Act of 1973, as amended; 29 U.S.C. 709(c))

§ 361.5 Applicable definitions.

The following definitions apply to this part:

(a) Definitions in EDGAR 77.1.

(b) Definitions in 2 CFR part 200, subpart A.

(c) The following definitions:

(1) *Act* means the Rehabilitation Act of 1973, as amended (29 U.S.C. 701 *et seq.*).

(2) *Administrative costs under the vocational rehabilitation services portion of the Unified or Combined State Plan* means expenditures incurred in the performance of administrative functions under the vocational rehabilitation program carried out under this part, including expenses related to program planning, development, monitoring, and evaluation, including, but not limited to, expenses for—

(i) Quality assurance;

(ii) Budgeting, accounting, financial management, information systems, and related data processing;

(iii) Providing information about the program to the public;

(iv) Technical assistance and support services to other State agencies, private nonprofit organizations, and businesses and industries, except for technical assistance and support services described in § 361.49(a)(4);

(v) The State Rehabilitation Council and other advisory committees;

(vi) Professional organization membership dues for designated State unit employees;

(vii) The removal of architectural barriers in State vocational rehabilitation agency offices and State-operated rehabilitation facilities;

(viii) Operating and maintaining designated State unit facilities, equipment, and grounds, as well as the infrastructure of the one-stop system;

(ix) Supplies;

(x) Administration of the comprehensive system of personnel development described in § 361.18, including personnel administration, administration of affirmative action plans, and training and staff development;

(xi) Administrative salaries, including clerical and other support staff salaries, in support of these administrative functions;

(xii) Travel costs related to carrying out the program, other than travel costs related to the provision of services;

(xiii) Costs incurred in conducting reviews of determinations made by personnel of the designated State unit, including costs associated with mediation and impartial due process hearings under § 361.57; and

(xiv) Legal expenses required in the administration of the program.

(Authority: Sections 7(1) and 12(c) of the Rehabilitation Act of 1973, as amended; 29 U.S.C. 705(1) and 709(c))

(3) *Applicant* means an individual who submits an application for vocational rehabilitation services in accordance with § 361.41(b)(2).

(Authority: Section 12(c) of the Rehabilitation Act of 1973, as amended; 29 U.S.C. 709(c))

(4) *Appropriate modes of communication* means specialized aids and supports that enable an individual with a disability to comprehend and respond to information that is being communicated. Appropriate modes of communication include, but are not limited to, the use of interpreters, open and closed captioned videos, specialized telecommunications services and audio recordings, Brailled and large print materials, materials in electronic formats, augmentative communication devices, graphic presentations, and simple language materials.

(Authority: Section 12(c) of the Rehabilitation Act of 1973, as amended; 29 U.S.C. 709(c))

(5) *Assessment for determining eligibility and vocational rehabilitation needs* means, as appropriate in each case—

(i)(A) A review of existing data—

(1) To determine if an individual is eligible for vocational rehabilitation services; and

(2) To assign priority for an order of selection described in § 361.36 in the States that use an order of selection; and

(B) To the extent necessary, the provision of appropriate assessment activities to obtain necessary additional data to make the eligibility determination and assignment;

(ii) To the extent additional data are necessary to make a determination of the employment outcomes and the nature and scope of vocational rehabilitation services to be included in the individualized plan for employment of an eligible individual, a comprehensive assessment to determine the unique strengths, resources, priorities, concerns, abilities, capabilities, interests, and informed choice, including the need for supported employment, of the eligible individual. This comprehensive assessment—

(A) Is limited to information that is necessary to identify the rehabilitation needs of the individual and to develop the individualized plan for employment of the eligible individual;

(B) Uses as a primary source of information, to the maximum extent possible and appropriate and in accordance with confidentiality requirements—

(1) Existing information obtained for the purposes of determining the eligibility of the individual and assigning priority for an order of selection described in § 361.36 for the individual; and

(2) Information that can be provided by the individual and, if appropriate, by the family of the individual;

(C) May include, to the degree needed to make such a determination, an assessment of the personality, interests, interpersonal skills, intelligence and related functional capacities, educational achievements, work experience, vocational aptitudes, personal and social adjustments, and employment opportunities of the individual and the medical, psychiatric, psychological, and other pertinent vocational, educational, cultural, social, recreational, and environmental factors that affect the employment and rehabilitation needs of the individual;

(D) May include, to the degree needed, an appraisal of the patterns of work behavior of the individual and services needed for the individual to acquire occupational skills and to develop work attitudes, work habits, work tolerance, and social and behavior patterns necessary for successful job performance, including the use of work in real job situations to assess and develop the capacities of the individual to perform adequately in a work environment; and

(E) To the maximum extent possible, relies on information obtained from experiences in integrated employment settings in the community and in other integrated community settings;

(iii) Referral, for the provision of rehabilitation technology services to the individual, to assess and develop the capacities of the individual to perform in a work environment; and

(iv) An exploration of the individual's abilities, capabilities, and capacity to perform in work situations, which must be assessed periodically during trial work experiences, including experiences in which the individual is provided appropriate supports and training.

(Authority: Sections 7(2) and 12(c) of the Rehabilitation Act of 1973, as amended; 29 U.S.C. 705(2) and 709(c))

(6) *Assistive technology terms*—(i) *Assistive technology* has the meaning given such term in section 3 of the Assistive Technology Act of 1998 (29 U.S.C. 3002).

(ii) *Assistive technology device* has the meaning given such term in section 3 of the Assistive Technology Act of 1998, except that the reference in such section to the term *individuals with disabilities* will be deemed to mean more than one individual with a disability as defined in paragraph (20)(A) of the Act.

(iii) *Assistive technology service* has the meaning given such term in section 3 of the Assistive Technology Act of 1998, except that the reference in such section to the term—

(A) *Individual with a disability* will be deemed to mean an individual with a disability, as defined in paragraph (20)(A) of the Act; and

(B) *Individuals with disabilities* will be deemed to mean more than one such individual.

(Authority: Sections 7(3) and 12(c) of the Rehabilitation Act of 1973, as amended; 29 U.S.C. 705(3) and 709(c))

(7) *Community rehabilitation program*—(i) *Community rehabilitation program* means a program that provides directly or facilitates the provision of one or more of the following vocational rehabilitation services to individuals with disabilities to enable those individuals to maximize their opportunities for employment, including career advancement:

(A) Medical, psychiatric, psychological, social, and vocational services that are provided under one management.

(B) Testing, fitting, or training in the use of prosthetic and orthotic devices.

(C) Recreational therapy.

(D) Physical and occupational therapy.

(E) Speech, language, and hearing therapy.

(F) Psychiatric, psychological, and social services, including positive behavior management.

(G) Assessment for determining eligibility and vocational rehabilitation needs.

(H) Rehabilitation technology.

(I) Job development, placement, and retention services.

(J) Evaluation or control of specific disabilities.

(K) Orientation and mobility services for individuals who are blind.

(L) Extended employment.

(M) Psychosocial rehabilitation services.

(N) Supported employment services and extended services.

(O) Customized employment.

(P) Services to family members if necessary to enable the applicant or eligible individual to achieve an employment outcome.

(Q) Personal assistance services.

(R) Services similar to the services described in paragraphs (c)(7)(i)(A) through (Q) of this section.

(ii) For the purposes of this definition, *program* means an agency, organization, or institution, or unit of an agency, organization, or institution, that provides directly or facilitates the provision of vocational rehabilitation services as one of its major functions.

(Authority: Section 7(4) of the Rehabilitation Act of 1973, as amended; 29 U.S.C. 705(4))

(8) *Comparable services and benefits*— (i) *Comparable services and benefits* means services and benefits, including accommodations and auxiliary aids and services, that are—

(A) Provided or paid for, in whole or in part, by other Federal, State, or local public agencies, by health insurance, or by employee benefits;

(B) Available to the individual at the time needed to ensure the progress of the individual toward achieving the employment outcome in the individual's individualized plan for employment in accordance with § 361.53; and

(C) Commensurate to the services that the individual would otherwise receive from the designated State vocational rehabilitation agency.

(ii) For the purposes of this definition, comparable services and benefits do not include awards and scholarships based on merit.

(Authority: Sections 12(c) and 101(a)(8) of the Rehabilitation Act of 1973, as amended; 29 U.S.C. 709(c) and 721(a)(8))

(9) *Competitive integrated employment* means work that—

(i) Is performed on a full-time or part-time basis (including self-employment) and for which an individual is compensated at a rate that–

(A) Is not less than the higher of the rate specified in section 6(a)(1) of the Fair Labor Standards Act of 1938 (29 U.S.C. 206(a)(1)) or the rate required under the applicable State or local minimum wage law for the place of employment;

(B) Is not less than the customary rate paid by the employer for the same or similar work performed by other employees who are not individuals with disabilities and who are similarly situated in similar occupations by the same employer and who have similar training, experience, and skills; and

(C) In the case of an individual who is self-employed, yields an income that is comparable to the income received by other individuals who are not individuals with disabilities and who are self-employed in similar occupations or on

similar tasks and who have similar training, experience, and skills; and

(D) Is eligible for the level of benefits provided to other employees; and

(ii) Is at a location—

(A) Typically found in the community; and

(B) Where the employee with a disability interacts for the purpose of performing the duties of the position with other employees within the particular work unit and the entire work site, and, as appropriate to the work performed, other persons (*e.g.*, customers and vendors), who are not individuals with disabilities (not including supervisory personnel or individuals who are providing services to such employee) to the same extent that employees who are not individuals with disabilities and who are in comparable positions interact with these persons; and

(iii) Presents, as appropriate, opportunities for advancement that are similar to those for other employees who are not individuals with disabilities and who have similar positions.

(Authority: Sections 7(5) and 12(c) of the Rehabilitation Act of 1973, as amended; 29 U.S.C. 705(5) and 709(c))

(10) *Construction of a facility for a public or nonprofit community rehabilitation program* means—

(i) The acquisition of land in connection with the construction of a new building for a community rehabilitation program;

(ii) The construction of new buildings;

(iii) The acquisition of existing buildings;

(iv) The expansion, remodeling, alteration, or renovation of existing buildings;

(v) Architect's fees, site surveys, and soil investigation, if necessary, in connection with the acquisition of land or existing buildings, or the construction, expansion, remodeling, or alteration of community rehabilitation facilities;

(vi) The acquisition of initial fixed or movable equipment of any new, newly acquired, newly expanded, newly remodeled, newly altered, or newly renovated buildings that are to be used for community rehabilitation program purposes; and

(vii) Other direct expenditures appropriate to the construction project, except costs of off-site improvements.

(Authority: Sections 7(6) and 12(c) of the Rehabilitation Act of 1973, as amended; 29 U.S.C. 705(6) and 709(c))

(11) *Customized employment* means competitive integrated employment, for an individual with a significant disability, that is—

(i) Based on an individualized determination of the unique strengths, needs, and interests of the individual with a significant disability;

(ii) Designed to meet the specific abilities of the individual with a significant disability and the business needs of the employer; and

(iii) Carried out through flexible strategies, such as—

(A) Job exploration by the individual; and

(B) Working with an employer to facilitate placement, including—

(*1*) Customizing a job description based on current employer needs or on previously unidentified and unmet employer needs;

(*2*) Developing a set of job duties, a work schedule and job arrangement, and specifics of supervision (including performance evaluation and review), and determining a job location;

(*3*) Using a professional representative chosen by the individual, or if elected self-representation, to work with an employer to facilitate placement; and

(*4*) Providing services and supports at the job location.

(Authority: Section 7(7) and 12(c) of the Rehabilitation Act of 1973, as amended; 29 U.S.C. 705(7) and 709(c))

(12) *Designated State agency* or *State agency* means the sole State agency, designated, in accordance with § 361.13(a), to administer, or supervise the local administration of, the vocational rehabilitation services portion of the Unified or Combined State Plan. The term includes the State agency for individuals who are blind, if designated as the sole State agency with respect to that part of the Unified or Combined State Plan relating to the vocational rehabilitation of individuals who are blind.

(Authority: Sections 7(8)(A) and 101(a)(2)(A) of the Rehabilitation Act of 1973, as amended; 29 U.S.C. 705(8)(A) and 721(a)(2)(A))

(13) *Designated State unit* or *State unit* means either—

(i) The State vocational rehabilitation bureau, division, or other organizational unit that is primarily concerned with vocational rehabilitation or vocational and other rehabilitation of individuals with disabilities and that is responsible for the administration of the vocational rehabilitation program of the State agency, as required under § 361.13(b); or

(ii) The State agency that is primarily concerned with vocational rehabilitation or vocational and other rehabilitation of individuals with disabilities.

(Authority: Sections 7(8)(B) and 101(a)(2)(B) of the Rehabilitation Act of 1973, as amended; 29 U.S.C. 705(8)(B) and 721(a)(2)(B))

(14) *Eligible individual* means an applicant for vocational rehabilitation services who meets the eligibility requirements of § 361.42(a).

(Authority: Sections 7(20)(A) and 102(a)(1) of the Rehabilitation Act of 1973, as amended; 29 U.S.C. 705(20)(A) and 722(a)(1))

(15) *Employment outcome* means, with respect to an individual, entering, advancing in, or retaining full-time or, if appropriate, part-time competitive integrated employment, as defined in paragraph (c)(9) of this section (including customized employment, self-employment, telecommuting, or business ownership), or supported employment as defined in paragraph (c)(53) of this section, that is consistent with an individual's unique strengths, resources, priorities, concerns, abilities, capabilities, interests, and informed choice.

NOTE TO PARAGRAPH (c)(15): A designated State unit may continue services to individuals with uncompensated employment goals on their approved individualized plans for employment prior to September 19, 2016 until June 30, 2017, unless a longer period of time is required based on the needs of the individual with the disability, as documented in the individual's service record.

(Authority: Sections 7(11), 12(c), 100(a)(2), and 102(b)(4)(A) of the Rehabilitation Act of 1973, as amended; 29 U.S.C. 705(11), 709(c), 720(a)(2), and 722(b)(4)(A))

(16) *Establishment, development, or improvement of a public or nonprofit community rehabilitation program* means—

(i) The establishment of a facility for a public or nonprofit community rehabilitation program, as defined in paragraph (c)(17) of this section, to provide vocational rehabilitation services to applicants or eligible individuals;

(ii) Staffing, if necessary to establish, develop, or improve a public or nonprofit community rehabilitation program for the purpose of providing vocational rehabilitation services to applicants or eligible individuals, for a maximum period of four years, with Federal financial participation available at the applicable matching rate for the following levels of staffing costs:

(A) 100 percent of staffing costs for the first year;

(B) 75 percent of staffing costs for the second year;

(C) 60 percent of staffing costs for the third year; and

(D) 45 percent of staffing costs for the fourth year; and

(iii) Other expenditures and activities related to the establishment, development, or improvement of a public or nonprofit community rehabilitation program that are necessary to make the program functional or increase its effectiveness in providing vocational rehabilitation services to applicants or eligible individuals, but are not ongoing operating expenses of the program.

(Authority: Sections 7(12) and 12(c) of the Rehabilitation Act of 1973, as amended; 29 U.S.C. 705(12) and 709(c))

(17) *Establishment of a facility for a public or nonprofit community rehabilitation program* means—

(i) The acquisition of an existing building and, if necessary, the land in connection with the acquisition, if the building has been completed in all respects for at least one year prior to the date of acquisition and the Federal share of the cost of acquisition is not more than $300,000;

(ii) The remodeling or alteration of an existing building, provided the estimated cost of remodeling or alteration does not exceed the appraised value of the existing building;

(iii) The expansion of an existing building, provided that—

(A) The existing building is complete in all respects;

(B) The total size in square footage of the expanded building, notwithstanding the number of expansions, is not greater than twice the size of the existing building;

(C) The expansion is joined structurally to the existing building and does not constitute a separate building; and

(D) The costs of the expansion do not exceed the appraised value of the existing building;

(iv) Architect's fees, site survey, and soil investigation, if necessary in connection with the acquisition, remodeling, alteration, or expansion of an existing building; and

(v) The acquisition of fixed or movable equipment, including the costs of installation of the equipment, if necessary to establish, develop, or improve a community rehabilitation program.

(Authority: Sections 7(12) and 12(c) of the Rehabilitation Act of 1973, as amended; 29 U.S.C. 705(12) and 709(c))

(18) *Extended employment* means work in a non-integrated or sheltered setting for a public or private nonprofit agency or organization that provides compensation in accordance with the Fair Labor Standards Act.

(Authority: Section 12(c) of the Rehabilitation Act of 1973, as amended; 29 U.S.C. 709(c))

(19) *Extended services* means ongoing support services and other appropriate services that are—

(i) Needed to support and maintain an individual with a most significant disability including a youth with a most significant disability, in supported employment;

(ii) Organized or made available, singly or in combination, in such a way as to assist an eligible individual in maintaining supported employment;

(iii) Based on the needs of an eligible individual, as specified in an individualized plan for employment;

(iv) Provided by a State agency, a private nonprofit organization, employer, or any other appropriate resource, after an individual has made the transition from support from the designated State unit; and

(v) Provided to a youth with a most significant disability by the designated State unit in accordance with requirements set forth in this part and part 363 for a period not to exceed four years, or at such time that a youth reaches age 25 and no longer meets the definition of a youth with a disability under paragraph (c)(58) of this section, whichever occurs first. The designated State unit may not provide extended services to an individual with a most significant disability who is not a youth with a most significant disability.

(Authority: Sections 7(13), 12(c), and 604(b) of the Rehabilitation Act of 1973, as amended; 29 U.S.C. 705(13), 709(c), and 795i(b))

(20) *Extreme medical risk* means a probability of substantially increasing functional impairment or death if medical services, including mental health services, are not provided expeditiously.

(Authority: Sections 12(c) and 101(a)(8)(A)(i)(III) of the Rehabilitation Act of 1973, as amended; 29 U.S.C. 709(c) and 721(a)(8)(A)(i)(III))

(21) *Fair hearing board* means a committee, body, or group of persons established by a State prior to January 1, 1985, that—

(i) Is authorized under State law to review determinations made by personnel of the designated State unit that affect the provision of vocational rehabilitation services; and

(ii) Carries out the responsibilities of the impartial hearing officer in accordance with the requirements in § 361.57(j).

(Authority: Sections 12(c) and 102(c)(6) of the Rehabilitation Act of 1973, as amended; 29 U.S.C. 709(c) and 722(c)(6))

(22) *Family member*, for purposes of receiving vocational rehabilitation services in accordance with § 361.48(b)(9), means an individual—

(i) Who either—

(A) Is a relative or guardian of an applicant or eligible individual; or

(B) Lives in the same household as an applicant or eligible individual;

(ii) Who has a substantial interest in the well-being of that individual; and

(iii) Whose receipt of vocational rehabilitation services is necessary to enable the applicant or eligible individual to achieve an employment outcome.

(Authority: Sections 12(c) and 103(a)(19) of the Rehabilitation Act of 1973, as amended; 29 U.S.C. 709(c) and 723(a)(19))

(23) *Governor* means a chief executive officer of a State.

(Authority: Section 7(15) of the Rehabilitation Act of 1973, as amended; 29 U.S.C. 705(15))

(24) *Impartial hearing officer*—(i) *Impartial hearing officer* means an individual who—

(A) Is not an employee of a public agency (other than an administrative law judge, hearing examiner, or employee of an institution of higher education);

(B) Is not a member of the State Rehabilitation Council for the designated State unit;

(C) Has not been involved previously in the vocational rehabilitation of the applicant or recipient of services;

(D) Has knowledge of the delivery of vocational rehabilitation services, the vocational rehabilitation services portion of the Unified or Combined State Plan, and the Federal and State regulations governing the provision of services;

(E) Has received training with respect to the performance of official duties; and

(F) Has no personal, professional, or financial interest that could affect the objectivity of the individual.

(ii) An individual is not considered to be an employee of a public agency for the purposes of this definition solely because the individual is paid by the agency to serve as a hearing officer.

(Authority: Sections 7(16) and 12(c) of the Rehabilitation Act of 1973, as amended; 29 U.S.C. 705(16) and 709(c))

(25) *Indian; American Indian; Indian American; Indian Tribe*—(i) *In general.* The terms "Indian", "American Indian", and "Indian American" mean an individual who is a member of an Indian tribe and include a Native and a

descendant of a Native, as such terms are defined in subsections (b) and (r) of section 3 of the Alaska Native Claims Settlement Act (43 U.S.C. 1602).

(ii) *Indian tribe.* The term "Indian tribe" means any Federal or State Indian tribe, band, rancheria, pueblo, colony, or community, including any Alaska native village or regional village corporation (as defined in or established pursuant to the Alaska Native Claims Settlement Act) and a tribal organization (as defined in section 4(l) of the Indian Self-Determination and Education Assistance Act (25 U.S.C. 450(b)(1)).

(Authority: Section 7(19) of the Rehabilitation Act of 1973, as amended; 29 U.S.C. 705(19))

(26) *Individual who is blind* means a person who is blind within the meaning of applicable State law.

(Authority: Section 12(c) of the Rehabilitation Act of 1973, as amended; 29 U.S.C. 709(c))

(27) *Individual with a disability,* except as provided in paragraph (c)(28) of this section, means an individual—

(i) Who has a physical or mental impairment;

(ii) Whose impairment constitutes or results in a substantial impediment to employment; and

(iii) Who can benefit in terms of an employment outcome from the provision of vocational rehabilitation services.

(Authority: Section 7(20)(A) of the Rehabilitation Act of 1973, as amended; 29 U.S.C. 705(20)(A))

(28) *Individual with a disability,* for purposes of §§ 361.5(c)(13), 361.13(a), 361.13(b)(1), 361.17(a), (b), (c), and (j), 361.18(b), 361.19, 361.20, 361.23(b)(2), 361.29(a) and (d)(8), and 361.51(b), means an individual—

(i) Who has a physical or mental impairment that substantially limits one or more major life activities;

(ii) Who has a record of such an impairment; or

(iii) Who is regarded as having such an impairment.

(Authority: Section 7(20)(B) of the Rehabilitation Act of 1973, as amended; 29 U.S.C. 705(20)(B))

(29) *Individual with a most significant disability* means an individual with a significant disability who meets the designated State unit's criteria for an individual with a most significant disability. These criteria must be consistent with the requirements in § 361.36(d)(1) and (2).

(Authority: Sections 7(21)(E) and 101(a)(5)(C) of the Rehabilitation Act of 1973, as amended; 29 U.S.C. 705(21)(E) and 721(a)(5)(C))

(30) *Individual with a significant disability* means an individual with a disability—

(i) Who has a severe physical or mental impairment that seriously limits one or more functional capacities (such as mobility, communication, self-care, self-direction, interpersonal skills, work tolerance, or work skills) in terms of an employment outcome;

(ii) Whose vocational rehabilitation can be expected to require multiple vocational rehabilitation services over an extended period of time; and

(iii) Who has one or more physical or mental disabilities resulting from amputation, arthritis, autism, blindness, burn injury, cancer, cerebral palsy, cystic fibrosis, deafness, head injury, heart disease, hemiplegia, hemophilia, respiratory or pulmonary dysfunction, mental illness, multiple sclerosis, muscular dystrophy, musculo-skeletal disorders, neurological disorders (including stroke and epilepsy), spinal cord conditions (including paraplegia and quadriplegia), sickle cell anemia, intellectual disability, specific learning disability, end-stage renal disease, or another disability or combination of disabilities determined on the basis of an assessment for determining eligibility and vocational rehabilitation needs to cause comparable substantial functional limitation.

(31) *Individual's representative* means any representative chosen by an applicant or eligible individual, as appropriate, including a parent, guardian, other family member, or advocate, unless a representative has been appointed by a court to represent the individual, in which case the court-appointed representative is the individual's representative.

(Authority: Sections 7(22) and 12(c) of the Rehabilitation Act of 1973, as amended; 29 U.S.C. 705(22) and 709(c))

(32) *Integrated setting* means—

(i) With respect to the provision of services, a setting typically found in the community in which applicants or eligible individuals interact with non-disabled individuals other than non-disabled individuals who are providing services to those applicants or eligible individuals; and

(ii) With respect to an employment outcome, means a setting—

(A) Typically found in the community; and

(B) Where the employee with a disability interacts, for the purpose of performing the duties of the position, with other employees within the particular work unit and the entire work site, and, as appropriate to the work performed, other persons (*e.g.*, customers and vendors) who are not individuals with disabilities (not including supervisory personnel or individuals who are providing services to such employee) to the same extent that employees who are not individuals with disabilities and who are in comparable positions interact with these persons.

(Authority: Section 12(c) of the Rehabilitation Act of 1973, as amended; 29 U.S.C. 709(c))

(33) *Local workforce development board* means a local board, as defined in section 3 of the Workforce Innovation and Opportunity Act.

(Authority: Section 7(25) of the Rehabilitation Act of 1973, as amended; 29 U.S.C. 705(25))

(34) *Maintenance* means monetary support provided to an individual for expenses, such as food, shelter, and clothing, that are in excess of the normal expenses of the individual and that are necessitated by the individual's participation in an assessment for determining eligibility and vocational rehabilitation needs or the individual's receipt of vocational rehabilitation services under an individualized plan for employment.

(Authority: Sections 12(c) and 103(a)(7) of the Rehabilitation Act of 1973, as amended; 29 U.S.C. 709(c) and 723(a)(7))

(i) *Examples:* The following are examples of expenses that would meet the definition of *maintenance*. The examples are illustrative, do not address all possible circumstances, and are not intended to substitute for individual counselor judgment.

Example 1: The cost of a uniform or other suitable clothing that is required for an individual's job placement or job-seeking activities.

Example 2: The cost of short-term shelter that is required in order for an individual to participate in assessment activities or vocational training at a site that is not within commuting distance of an individual's home.

Example 3: The initial one-time costs, such as a security deposit or charges for the initiation of utilities, that are required in order for an individual to relocate for a job placement.

(ii) [Reserved]

(35) *Mediation* means the act or process of using an independent third party to act as a mediator, intermediary, or conciliator to assist persons or parties in settling differences or disputes prior to pursuing formal administrative or other legal remedies. Mediation under the program must be conducted in accordance with the requirements in §361.57(d) by a qualified and impartial mediator as defined in §361.5(c)(43).

(Authority: Sections 12(c) and 102(c)(4) of the Rehabilitation Act of 1973, as amended; 29 U.S.C. 709(c) and 722(c)(4))

(36) *Nonprofit*, with respect to a community rehabilitation program, means a community rehabilitation program carried out by a corporation or association, no part of the net earnings of which inures, or may lawfully inure, to the benefit of any private shareholder or individual and the income of which is exempt from taxation under section 501(c)(3) of the Internal Revenue Code of 1986.

(Authority: Section 7(26) of the Rehabilitation Act of 1973, as amended; 29 U.S.C. 705(26))

(37) *Ongoing support services*, as used in the definition of *supported employment*, means services that—

(i) Are needed to support and maintain an individual with a most significant disability, including a youth with a most significant disability, in supported employment;

(ii) Are identified based on a determination by the designated State unit of the individual's need as specified in an individualized plan for employment;

293

(iii) Are furnished by the designated State unit from the time of job placement until transition to extended services, unless post-employment services are provided following transition, and thereafter by one or more extended services providers throughout the individual's term of employment in a particular job placement;

(iv) Include an assessment of employment stability and provision of specific services or the coordination of services at or away from the worksite that are needed to maintain stability based on—

(A) At a minimum, twice-monthly monitoring at the worksite of each individual in supported employment; or

(B) If under specific circumstances, especially at the request of the individual, the individualized plan for employment provides for off-site monitoring, twice monthly meetings with the individual;

(v) Consist of—

(A) Any particularized assessment supplementary to the comprehensive assessment of rehabilitation needs described in paragraph (c)(5)(ii) of this section;

(B) The provision of skilled job trainers who accompany the individual for intensive job skill training at the work site;

(C) Job development and training;

(D) Social skills training;

(E) Regular observation or supervision of the individual;

(F) Follow-up services including regular contact with the employers, the individuals, the parents, family members, guardians, advocates or authorized representatives of the individuals, and other suitable professional and informed advisors, in order to reinforce and stabilize the job placement;

(G) Facilitation of natural supports at the worksite;

(H) Any other service identified in the scope of vocational rehabilitation services for individuals, described in § 361.48(b); or

(I) Any service similar to the foregoing services.

(Authority: Sections 7(27) and 12(c) of the Rehabilitation Act of 1973, as amended; 29 U.S.C. 705(27) and 709(c))

(38) *Personal assistance services* means a range of services, including, among other things, training in managing, supervising, and directing personal assistance services, provided by one or more persons, that are—

(i) Designed to assist an individual with a disability to perform daily living activities on or off the job that the individual would typically perform without assistance if the individual did not have a disability;

(ii) Designed to increase the individual's control in life and ability to perform everyday activities on or off the job;

(iii) Necessary to the achievement of an employment outcome; and

(iv) Provided only while the individual is receiving other vocational rehabilitation services. The services may include training in managing, supervising, and directing personal assistance services.

(Authority: Sections 7(28), 12(c), 102(b)(4)(B)(i)(I)(bb), and 103(a)(9) of the Rehabilitation Act of 1973, as amended; 29 U.S.C. 705(28), 709(c), 722(b)(4)(B)(i)(I)(bb), and 723(a)(9))

(39) *Physical and mental restoration services* means—

(i) Corrective surgery or therapeutic treatment that is likely, within a reasonable period of time, to correct or modify substantially a stable or slowly progressive physical or mental impairment that constitutes a substantial impediment to employment;

(ii) Diagnosis of and treatment for mental or emotional disorders by qualified personnel in accordance with State licensure laws;

(iii) Dentistry;

(iv) Nursing services;

(v) Necessary hospitalization (either inpatient or outpatient care) in connection with surgery or treatment and clinic services;

(vi) Drugs and supplies;

(vii) Prosthetic and orthotic devices;

(viii) Eyeglasses and visual services, including visual training, and the examination and services necessary for the prescription and provision of eyeglasses, contact lenses, microscopic lenses, telescopic lenses, and other special visual aids prescribed by personnel who are qualified in accordance with State licensure laws;

(ix) Podiatry;

(x) Physical therapy;

(xi) Occupational therapy;

(xii) Speech or hearing therapy;

(xiii) Mental health services;

(xiv) Treatment of either acute or chronic medical complications and emergencies that are associated with or arise out of the provision of physical and mental restoration services, or that are inherent in the condition under treatment;

(xv) Special services for the treatment of individuals with end-stage renal disease, including transplantation, dialysis, artificial kidneys, and supplies; and

(xvi) Other medical or medically related rehabilitation services.

(Authority: Sections 12(c) and 103(a)(6) of the Rehabilitation Act of 1973, as amended; 29 U.S.C. 709(c) and 723(a)(6))

(40) *Physical or mental impairment* means—

(i) Any physiological disorder or condition, cosmetic disfigurement, or anatomical loss affecting one or more of the following body systems: neurological, musculo-skeletal, special sense organs, respiratory (including speech organs), cardiovascular, reproductive, digestive, genitourinary, hemic and lymphatic, skin, and endocrine; or

(ii) Any mental or psychological disorder such as intellectual disability, organic brain syndrome, emotional or mental illness, and specific learning disabilities.

(41) *Post-employment services* means one or more of the services identified in § 361.48(b) that are provided subsequent to the achievement of an employment outcome and that are necessary for an individual to maintain, regain, or advance in employment, consistent with the individual's unique strengths, resources, priorities, concerns, abilities, capabilities, interests, and informed choice.

(Authority: Sections 12(c) and 103(a)(20) of the Rehabilitation Act of 1973, as amended; 29 U.S.C. 709(c) and 723(a)(20))

NOTE TO PARAGRAPH (c)(41): Post-employment services are intended to ensure that the employment outcome remains consistent with the individual's unique strengths, resources, priorities, concerns, abilities, capabilities, interests, and informed choice. These services are available to meet rehabilitation needs that do not require a complex and comprehensive provision of services and, thus, should be limited in scope and duration. If more comprehensive services are required, then a new rehabilitation effort should be considered. Post-employment services are to be provided under an amended individualized plan for employment; thus, a redetermination of eligibility is not required. The provision of post-employment services is subject to the same requirements in this part as the provision of any other vocational rehabilitation service. Post-employment services are available to assist an individual to maintain employment, *e.g.,* the individual's employment is jeopardized because of conflicts with supervisors or co-workers, and the individual needs mental health services and counseling to maintain the employment, or the individual requires assistive technology to maintain the employment; to regain employment, *e.g.,* the individual's job is eliminated through reorganization and new placement services are needed; and to advance in employment, *e.g.,* the employment is no longer consistent with the individual's unique strengths, resources, priorities, concerns, abilities, capabilities, interests, and informed choice.

(42) *Pre-employment transition services* means the required activities and authorized activities specified in § 361.48(a)(2) and (3).

(Authority: Sections 7(30) and 113(b) and (c) of the Rehabilitation Act of 1973, as amended; 29 U.S.C. 705(30) and 733(b) and (c))

(43) *Qualified and impartial mediator*— (i) *Qualified and impartial mediator* means an individual who—

(A) Is not an employee of a public agency (other than an administrative law judge, hearing examiner, employee of a State office of mediators, or employee of an institution of higher education);

(B) Is not a member of the State Rehabilitation Council for the designated State unit;

(C) Has not been involved previously in the vocational rehabilitation of the applicant or recipient of services;

(D) Is knowledgeable of the vocational rehabilitation program and the applicable Federal and State laws, regulations, and policies governing the provision of vocational rehabilitation services;

(E) Has been trained in effective mediation techniques consistent with any State-approved or -recognized certification, licensing, registration, or other requirements; and

(F) Has no personal, professional, or financial interest that could affect the individual's objectivity during the mediation proceedings.

(ii) An individual is not considered to be an employee of the designated State agency or designated State unit for the purposes of this definition solely because the individual is paid by the designated State agency or designated State unit to serve as a mediator.

(Authority: Sections 12(c) and 102(c)(4) of the Rehabilitation Act of 1973, as amended; 29 U.S.C. 709(c) and 722(c)(4))

(44) *Rehabilitation engineering* means the systematic application of engineering sciences to design, develop, adapt, test, evaluate, apply, and distribute technological solutions to problems confronted by individuals with disabilities in functional areas, such as mobility, communications, hearing, vision, and cognition, and in activities associated with employment, independent living, education, and integration into the community.

(Authority: Sections 7(32) and (12(c) of the Rehabilitation Act of 1973, as amended; 29 U.S.C. 705(32) and 709(c))

(45) *Rehabilitation technology* means the systematic application of technologies, engineering methodologies, or scientific principles to meet the needs of, and address the barriers confronted by, individuals with disabilities in areas that include education, rehabilitation, employment, transportation, independent living, and recreation. The term includes rehabilitation engineering, assistive technology devices, and assistive technology services.

(Authority: Section 7(32) of the Rehabilitation Act of 1973, as amended; 29 U.S.C. 705(32))

(46) *Reservation* means a Federal or State Indian reservation, a public domain Indian allotment, a former Indian reservation in Oklahoma, and land held by incorporated Native groups, regional corporations, and village corporations under the provisions of the Alaska Native Claims Settlement Act (43 U.S.C. 1601 *et seq.*); or a defined area of land recognized by a State or the Federal Government where there is a concentration of tribal members and on which the tribal government is pro-

viding structured activities and services.

(Authority: Section 121(e) of the Rehabilitation Act of 1973, as amended; 29 U.S.C. 741(e))

(47) *Sole local agency* means a unit or combination of units of general local government or one or more Indian tribes that has the sole responsibility under an agreement with, and the supervision of, the State agency to conduct a local or tribal vocational rehabilitation program, in accordance with the vocational rehabilitation services portion of the Unified or Combined State Plan.

(Authority: Section 7(24) of the Rehabilitation Act of 1973, as amended; 29 U.S.C. 705(24))

(48) *State* means any of the 50 States, the District of Columbia, the Commonwealth of Puerto Rico, the United States Virgin Islands, Guam, American Samoa, and the Commonwealth of the Northern Mariana Islands.

(Authority: Section 7(34) of the Rehabilitation Act of 1973, as amended; 29 U.S.C. 705(34))

(49) *State workforce development board* means a State workforce development board, as defined in section 3 of the Workforce Innovation and Opportunity Act (29 U.S.C. 3102).

(Authority: Section 7(35) of the Rehabilitation Act of 1973, as amended; 29 U.S.C. 705(35))

(50) *Statewide workforce development system* means a workforce development system, as defined in section 3 of the Workforce Innovation and Opportunity Act (29 U.S.C. 3102).

(Authority: Section 7(36) of the Rehabilitation Act of 1973, as amended; 29 U.S.C. 705(36))

(51) *Student with a disability*—(i) *Student with a disability* means, in general, an individual with a disability in a secondary, postsecondary, or other recognized education program who—

(A)(*1*) Is not younger than the earliest age for the provision of transition services under section 614(d)(1)(A)(i)(VIII) of the Individuals with Disabilities Education Act (20 U.S.C. 1414(d)(1)(A)(i)(VIII)); or

(*2*) If the State involved elects to use a lower minimum age for receipt of pre-employment transition services under this Act, is not younger than that minimum age; and

(B)(*1*) Is not older than 21 years of age; or

(*2*) If the State law for the State provides for a higher maximum age for receipt of services under the Individuals with Disabilities Education Act (20 U.S.C. 1400 *et seq.*), is not older than that maximum age; and

(C)(*1*) Is eligible for, and receiving, special education or related services under Part B of the Individuals with Disabilities Education Act (20 U.S.C. 1411 *et seq.*); or

(*2*) Is a student who is an individual with a disability, for purposes of section 504.

(ii) *Students with disabilities* means more than one student with a disability.

(Authority: Sections 7(37) and 12(c) of the Rehabilitation Act of 1973, as amended; 29 U.S.C. 705(37) and 709(c))

(52) *Substantial impediment to employment* means that a physical or mental impairment (in light of attendant medical, psychological, vocational, educational, communication, and other related factors) hinders an individual from preparing for, entering into, engaging in, advancing in, or retaining employment consistent with the individual's abilities and capabilities.

(Authority: Sections 7(20)(A) and 12(c) of the Rehabilitation Act of 1973, as amended; 29 U.S.C. 705(20)(A) and 709(c))

(53) *Supported employment*—(i) *Supported employment* means competitive integrated employment, including customized employment, or employment in an integrated work setting in which an individual with a most significant disability, including a youth with a most significant disability, is working on a short-term basis toward competitive integrated employment that is individualized, and customized, consistent with the unique strengths, abilities, interests, and informed choice of the individual, including with ongoing support services for individuals with the most significant disabilities—

(A) For whom competitive integrated employment has not historically occurred, or for whom competitive inte-

grated employment has been interrupted or intermittent as a result of a significant disability; and

(B) Who, because of the nature and severity of their disabilities, need intensive supported employment services and extended services after the transition from support provided by the designated State unit, in order to perform this work.

(ii) For purposes of this part, an individual with a most significant disability, whose supported employment in an integrated setting does not satisfy the criteria of competitive integrated employment, as defined in paragraph (c)(9) of this section is considered to be working on a short-term basis toward competitive integrated employment so long as the individual can reasonably anticipate achieving competitive integrated employment—

(A) Within six months of achieving a supported employment outcome; or

(B) In limited circumstances, within a period not to exceed 12 months from the achievement of the supported employment outcome, if a longer period is necessary based on the needs of the individual, and the individual has demonstrated progress toward competitive earnings based on information contained in the service record.

(Authority: Sections 7(38), 12(c), and 602 of the Rehabilitation Act of 1973, as amended; 29 U.S.C. 705(38), 709(c), and 795g)

(54) *Supported employment services* means ongoing support services, including customized employment, and other appropriate services needed to support and maintain an individual with a most significant disability, including a youth with a most significant disability, in supported employment that are—

(i) Organized and made available, singly or in combination, in such a way as to assist an eligible individual to achieve competitive integrated employment;

(ii) Based on a determination of the needs of an eligible individual, as specified in an individualized plan for employment;

(iii) Provided by the designated State unit for a period of time not to exceed 24 months, unless under special circumstances the eligible individual and the rehabilitation counselor jointly agree to extend the time to achieve the employment outcome identified in the individualized plan for employment; and

(iv) Following transition, as post-employment services that are unavailable from an extended services provider and that are necessary to maintain or regain the job placement or advance in employment.

(Authority: Sections 7(39), 12(c), and 103(a)(16) of the Rehabilitation Act of 1973, as amended; 29 U.S.C. 705(39), 709(c), and 723(a)(16))

(55) *Transition services* means a co-ordinated set of activities for a student or youth with a disability—

(i) Designed within an outcome-oriented process that promotes movement from school to post-school activities, including postsecondary education, vocational training, competitive integrated employment, supported employment, continuing and adult education, adult services, independent living, or community participation;

(ii) Based upon the individual student's or youth's needs, taking into account the student's or youth's preferences and interests;

(iii) That includes instruction, community experiences, the development of employment and other post-school adult living objectives, and, if appropriate, acquisition of daily living skills and functional vocational evaluation;

(iv) That promotes or facilitates the achievement of the employment outcome identified in the student's or youth's individualized plan for employment; and

(v) That includes outreach to and engagement of the parents, or, as appropriate, the representative of such a student or youth with a disability.

(Authority: Sections 12(c) and 103(a)(15) and (b)(7) of the Rehabilitation Act of 1973, as amended; 29 U.S.C. 709(c) and 723(a)(15) and (b)(7))

(56) *Transportation* means travel and related expenses that are necessary to enable an applicant or eligible individual to participate in a vocational rehabilitation service, including expenses for training in the use of public transportation vehicles and systems.

(Authority: Sections 12(c) and 103(a)(8) of the Rehabilitation Act of 1973, as amended; 29 U.S.C. 709(c) and 723(a)(8))

(i) *Examples.* The following are examples of expenses that would meet the definition of *transportation*. The examples are purely illustrative, do not address all possible circumstances, and are not intended as substitutes for individual counselor judgment.

Example 1: Travel and related expenses for a personal care attendant or aide if the services of that person are necessary to enable the applicant or eligible individual to travel to participate in any vocational rehabilitation service.

Example 2: The purchase and repair of vehicles, including vans, but not the modification of these vehicles, as modification would be considered a rehabilitation technology service.

Example 3: Relocation expenses incurred by an eligible individual in connection with a job placement that is a significant distance from the eligible individual's current residence.

(ii) [Reserved]

(57) *Vocational rehabilitation services*— (i) If provided to an individual, means those services listed in § 361.48; and

(ii) If provided for the benefit of groups of individuals, means those services listed in § 361.49.

(Authority: Sections 7(40) and 103 of the Rehabilitation Act of 1973, as amended; 29 U.S.C. 705(40) and 723)

(58) *Youth with a disability*—(i) *Youth with a disability* means an individual with a disability who is not—

(A) Younger than 14 years of age; and

(B) Older than 24 years of age.

(ii) *Youth with disabilities* means more than one youth with a disability.

(Authority: Section 7(42) of the Rehabilitation Act of 1973, as amended; 29 U.S.C. 705(42))

[81 FR 55741, Aug. 19, 2016, as amended at 82 FR 31913, July 11, 2017]

Subpart B—State Plan and Other Requirements for Vocational Rehabilitation Services

§ 361.10 Submission, approval, and disapproval of the State plan.

(a) *Purpose.* (1) To be eligible to receive funds under this part for a fiscal year, a State must submit, and have approved, a vocational rehabilitation services portion of a Unified or Combined State Plan in accordance with section 102 or 103 of the Workforce Innovation and Opportunity Act.

(2) The vocational rehabilitation services portion of the Unified or Combined State Plan must satisfy all requirements set forth in this part.

(b) *Separate part relating to the vocational rehabilitation of individuals who are blind.* If a separate State agency administers or supervises the administration of a separate part of the vocational rehabilitation services portion of the Unified or Combined State Plan relating to the vocational rehabilitation of individuals who are blind, that part of the vocational rehabilitation services portion of the Unified or Combined State Plan must separately conform to all applicable requirements under this part.

(c) *Public participation.* Prior to the adoption of any substantive policies or procedures specific to the provision of vocational rehabilitation services under the vocational rehabilitation services portion of the Unified or Combined State Plan, including making any substantive amendment to those policies and procedures, the designated State agency must conduct public meetings throughout the State, in accordance with the requirements of § 361.20.

(d) *Submission, approval, disapproval, and duration.* All requirements regarding the submission, approval, disapproval, and duration of the vocational rehabilitation services portion of the Unified or Combined State Plan are governed by regulations set forth in subpart D of this part.

(e) *Submission of policies and procedures.* The State is not required to submit policies, procedures, or descriptions required under this part that have been previously submitted to the Secretary and that demonstrate that the State meets the requirements of this part, including any policies, procedures, or descriptions submitted under this part that are in effect on July 22, 2014.

(f) *Due process.* If the Secretary disapproves the vocational rehabilitation services portion of the Unified or Combined State Plan, the Secretary will follow these procedures:

(1) *Informal resolution.* Prior to disapproving the vocational rehabilitation services portion of the Unified or Combined State Plan, the Secretary attempts to resolve disputes informally with State officials.

(2) *Notice.* If, after reasonable effort has been made to resolve the dispute, no resolution has been reached, the Secretary provides notice to the State agency of the intention to disapprove the vocational rehabilitation services portion of the Unified or Combined State Plan and of the opportunity for a hearing.

(3) *State plan hearing.* If the State agency requests a hearing, the Secretary designates one or more individuals, either from the Department or elsewhere, not responsible for or connected with the administration of this program, to conduct a hearing in accordance with the provisions of 34 CFR part 81, subpart A.

(4) *Initial decision.* The hearing officer issues an initial decision in accordance with 34 CFR 81.41.

(5) *Petition for review of an initial decision.* The State agency may seek the Secretary's review of the initial decision in accordance with 34 CFR part 81.

(6) *Review by the Secretary.* The Secretary reviews the initial decision in accordance with 34 CFR 81.43.

(7) *Final decision of the Department.* The final decision of the Department is made in accordance with 34 CFR 81.44.

(8) *Judicial review.* A State may appeal the Secretary's decision to disapprove the vocational rehabilitation services portion of the Unified or Combined State Plan by filing a petition for review with the United States Court of Appeals for the circuit in

which the State is located, in accordance with section 107(d) of the Act.

(Approved by the Office of Management and Budget under control number 1205–0522)

(Authority: Sections 101(a) and (b) and 107(d) of the Rehabilitation Act of 1973, as amended; 29 U.S.C. 721(a) and (b) and 727(d); and 20 U.S.C. 1231g(a))

[81 FR 55741, Aug. 19, 2016, as amended at 81 FR 55779, Aug. 19, 2016]

§ 361.11 Withholding of funds.

(a) *Basis for withholding.* The Secretary may withhold or limit payments under section 111 or 603(a) of the Act, as provided by section 107(c) of the Act, if the Secretary determines that—

(1) The vocational rehabilitation services portion of the Unified or Combined State Plan, including the supported employment supplement, has been so changed that it no longer conforms with the requirements of this part or part 363; or

(2) In the administration of the vocational rehabilitation services portion of the Unified or Combined State Plan there is a failure to comply substantially with any provision of such plan or with an evaluation standard or performance indicator established under section 106 of the Act.

(b) *Informal resolution.* Prior to withholding or limiting payments in accordance with this section, the Secretary attempts to resolve disputed issues informally with State officials.

(c) *Notice.* If, after reasonable effort has been made to resolve the dispute, no resolution has been reached, the Secretary provides notice to the State agency of the intention to withhold or limit payments and of the opportunity for a hearing.

(d) *Withholding hearing.* If the State agency requests a hearing, the Secretary designates one or more individuals, either from the Department or elsewhere, not responsible for or connected with the administration of this program, to conduct a hearing in accordance with the provisions of 34 CFR part 81, subpart A.

(e) *Initial decision.* The hearing officer issues an initial decision in accordance with 34 CFR 81.41.

(f) *Petition for review of an initial decision.* The State agency may seek the Secretary's review of the initial decision in accordance with 34 CFR 81.42.

(g) *Review by the Secretary.* The Secretary reviews the initial decision in accordance with 34 CFR 81.43.

(h) *Final decision of the Department.* The final decision of the Department is made in accordance with 34 CFR 81.44.

(i) *Judicial review.* A State may appeal the Secretary's decision to withhold or limit payments by filing a petition for review with the United States Court of Appeals for the circuit in which the State is located, in accordance with section 107(d) of the Act.

(Authority: Sections 12(c), 101(b), and 107(c) and (d) of the Rehabilitation Act of 1973, as amended; 29 U.S.C. 709(c), 721(b) and 727(c) and (d))

ADMINISTRATION

§ 361.12 Methods of administration.

The vocational rehabilitation services portion of the Unified or Combined State Plan must assure that the State agency, and the designated State unit if applicable, employs methods of administration found necessary by the Secretary for the proper and efficient administration of the plan and for carrying out all functions for which the State is responsible under the plan and this part. These methods must include procedures to ensure accurate data collection and financial accountability.

(Approved by the Office of Management and Budget under control number 1205–0522)

(Authority: Sections 12(c) and 101(a)(6) and (a)(10)(A) of the Rehabilitation Act of 1973, as amended; 29 U.S.C. 709(c) and 721(a)(6) and (a)(10)(A))

§ 361.13 State agency for administration.

(a) *Designation of State agency.* The vocational rehabilitation services portion of the Unified or Combined State Plan must designate a State agency as the sole State agency to administer the vocational rehabilitation services portion of the Unified or Combined State Plan, or to supervise its administration in a political subdivision of the State by a sole local agency, in accordance with the following requirements:

(1) *General.* Except as provided in paragraphs (a)(2) and (3) of this section, the vocational rehabilitation services

portion of the Unified or Combined State Plan must provide that the designated State agency is one of the following types of agencies:

(i) A State agency that is primarily concerned with vocational rehabilitation or vocational and other rehabilitation of individuals with disabilities; or

(ii) A State agency that includes a vocational rehabilitation unit as provided in paragraph (b) of this section.

(2) *American Samoa.* In the case of American Samoa, the vocational rehabilitation services portion of the Unified or Combined State Plan must designate the Governor.

(3) *Designated State agency for individuals who are blind.* If a State commission or other agency that provides assistance or services to individuals who are blind is authorized under State law to provide vocational rehabilitation services to individuals who are blind, and this commission or agency is primarily concerned with vocational rehabilitation or includes a vocational rehabilitation unit as provided in paragraph (b) of this section, the vocational rehabilitation services portion of the Unified or Combined State Plan may designate that agency as the sole State agency to administer the part of the plan under which vocational rehabilitation services are provided for individuals who are blind or to supervise its administration in a political subdivision of the State by a sole local agency.

(b) *Designation of State unit*—(1) *General.* If the designated State agency is not of the type specified in paragraph (a)(1)(i) of this section or if the designated State agency specified in paragraph (a)(3) of this section is not primarily concerned with vocational rehabilitation or vocational and other rehabilitation of individuals with disabilities, the vocational rehabilitation services portion of the Unified or Combined State Plan must assure that the agency (or each agency if two agencies are designated) includes a vocational rehabilitation bureau, division, or unit that—

(i) Is primarily concerned with vocational rehabilitation or vocational and other rehabilitation of individuals with disabilities and is responsible for the administration of the State agency's

vocational rehabilitation program under the vocational rehabilitation services portion of the Unified or Combined State Plan;

(ii) Has a full-time director who is responsible for the day-to-day operations of the vocational rehabilitation program;

(iii) Has a staff, at least 90 percent of whom are employed full time on the rehabilitation work of the organizational unit;

(iv) Is located at an organizational level and has an organizational status within the State agency comparable to that of other major organizational units of the agency; and

(v) Has the sole authority and responsibility described within the designated State agency in paragraph (a) of this section to expend funds made available under the Act in a manner that is consistent with the purpose of the Act.

(2) In the case of a State that has not designated a separate State agency for individuals who are blind, as provided for in paragraph (a)(3) of this section, the State may assign responsibility for the part of the vocational rehabilitation services portion of the Unified or Combined State Plan under which vocational rehabilitation services are provided to individuals who are blind to one organizational unit of the designated State agency and may assign responsibility for the rest of the plan to another organizational unit of the designated State agency, with the provisions of paragraph (b)(1) of this section applying separately to each of these units.

(c) *Responsibility for administration*—(1) *Required activities.* At a minimum, the following activities are the responsibility of the designated State unit or the sole local agency under the supervision of the State unit:

(i) All decisions affecting eligibility for vocational rehabilitation services, the nature and scope of available services, and the provision of these services.

(ii) The determination to close the record of services of an individual who has achieved an employment outcome in accordance with §361.56.

(iii) Policy formulation and implementation.

301

(iv) The allocation and expenditure of vocational rehabilitation funds.

(v) Participation as a partner in the one-stop service delivery system established under title I of the Workforce Innovation and Opportunity Act, in accordance with 20 CFR part 678.

(2) *Non-delegable responsibility.* The responsibility for the functions described in paragraph (c)(1) of this section may not be delegated to any other agency or individual.

(Approved by the Office of Management and Budget under control number 1205–0522)

(Authority: Section 101(a)(2) of the Rehabilitation Act of 1973, as amended; 29 U.S.C. 721(a)(2))

§ 361.14 Substitute State agency.

(a) *General provisions.* (1) If the Secretary has withheld all funding from a State under § 361.11, the State may designate another agency to substitute for the designated State agency in carrying out the State's program of vocational rehabilitation services.

(2) Any public or nonprofit private organization or agency within the State or any political subdivision of the State is eligible to be a substitute agency.

(3) The substitute agency must submit a vocational rehabilitation services portion of the Unified or Combined State Plan that meets the requirements of this part.

(4) The Secretary makes no grant to a substitute agency until the Secretary approves its plan.

(b) *Substitute agency matching share.* The Secretary does not make any payment to a substitute agency unless it has provided assurances that it will contribute the same matching share as the State would have been required to contribute if the State agency were carrying out the vocational rehabilitation program.

(Authority: Section 107(c)(3) of the Rehabilitation Act of 1973, as amended; 29 U.S.C. 727(c)(3))

§ 361.15 Local administration.

(a) If the vocational rehabilitation services portion of the Unified or Combined State Plan provides for the administration of the plan by a local agency, the designated State agency must—

(1) Ensure that each local agency is under the supervision of the designated State unit and is the sole local agency as defined in § 361.5(c)(47) that is responsible for the administration of the program within the political subdivision that it serves; and

(2) Develop methods that each local agency will use to administer the vocational rehabilitation program, in accordance with the vocational rehabilitation services portion of the Unified or Combined State Plan.

(b) A separate local agency serving individuals who are blind may administer that part of the plan relating to vocational rehabilitation of individuals who are blind, under the supervision of the designated State unit for individuals who are blind.

(Approved by the Office of Management and Budget under control number 1205–0522)

(Authority: Sections 7(24) and 101(a)(2)(A) of the Rehabilitation Act of 1973, as amended; 29 U.S.C. 705(24) and 721(a)(2)(A))

§ 361.16 Establishment of an independent commission or a State Rehabilitation Council.

(a) *General requirement.* Except as provided in paragraph (b) of this section, the vocational rehabilitation services portion of the Unified or Combined State Plan must contain one of the following two assurances:

(1) An assurance that the designated State agency is an independent State commission that—

(i) Is responsible under State law for operating, or overseeing the operation of, the vocational rehabilitation program in the State and is primarily concerned with vocational rehabilitation or vocational and other rehabilitation services, in accordance with § 361.13(a)(1)(i);

(ii) Is consumer-controlled by persons who—

(A) Are individuals with physical or mental impairments that substantially limit major life activities; and

(B) Represent individuals with a broad range of disabilities, unless the designated State unit under the direction of the commission is the State agency for individuals who are blind;

(iii) Includes family members, advocates, or other representatives of individuals with mental impairments; and

(iv) Conducts the functions identified in § 361.17(h)(4).

(2) An assurance that—

(i) The State has established a State Rehabilitation Council (Council) that meets the requirements of § 361.17;

(ii) The designated State unit, in accordance with § 361.29, jointly develops, agrees to, and reviews annually State goals and priorities and jointly submits to the Secretary annual reports of progress with the Council;

(iii) The designated State unit regularly consults with the Council regarding the development, implementation, and revision of State policies and procedures of general applicability pertaining to the provision of vocational rehabilitation services;

(iv) The designated State unit transmits to the Council—

(A) All plans, reports, and other information required under this part to be submitted to the Secretary;

(B) All policies and information on all practices and procedures of general applicability provided to or used by rehabilitation personnel providing vocational rehabilitation services under this part; and

(C) Copies of due process hearing decisions issued under this part and transmitted in a manner to ensure that the identity of the participants in the hearings is kept confidential; and

(v) The vocational rehabilitation services portion of the Unified or Combined State Plan, and any revision to the vocational rehabilitation services portion of the Unified or Combined State Plan, includes a summary of input provided by the Council, including recommendations from the annual report of the Council, the review and analysis of consumer satisfaction described in § 361.17(h)(4), and other reports prepared by the Council, and the designated State unit's response to the input and recommendations, including its reasons for rejecting any input or recommendation of the Council.

(b) *Exception for separate State agency for individuals who are blind.* In the case of a State that designates a separate State agency under § 361.13(a)(3) to administer the part of the vocational rehabilitation services portion of the Unified or Combined State Plan under which vocational rehabilitation services are provided to individuals who are blind, the State must either establish a separate State Rehabilitation Council for each agency that does not meet the requirements in paragraph (a)(1) of this section or establish one State Rehabilitation Council for both agencies if neither agency meets the requirements of paragraph (a)(1) of this section.

(Approved by the Office of Management and Budget under control number 1205–0522)

(Authority: Sections 101(a)(21) of the Rehabilitation Act of 1973, as amended; 29 U.S.C. 721(a)(21))

§ 361.17 Requirements for a State Rehabilitation Council.

If the State has established a Council under § 361.16(a)(2) or (b), the Council must meet the following requirements:

(a) *Appointment.* (1) The members of the Council must be appointed by the Governor or, in the case of a State that, under State law, vests authority for the administration of the activities carried out under this part in an entity other than the Governor (such as one or more houses of the State legislature or an independent board), the chief officer of that entity.

(2) The appointing authority must select members of the Council after soliciting recommendations from representatives of organizations representing a broad range of individuals with disabilities and organizations interested in individuals with disabilities. In selecting members, the appointing authority must consider, to the greatest extent practicable, the extent to which minority populations are represented on the Council.

(b) *Composition*—(1) *General.* Except as provided in paragraph (b)(3) of this section, the Council must be composed of at least 15 members, including—

(i) At least one representative of the Statewide Independent Living Council, who must be the chairperson or other designee of the Statewide Independent Living Council;

(ii) At least one representative of a parent training and information center established pursuant to section 682(a) of the Individuals with Disabilities Education Act;

(iii) At least one representative of the Client Assistance Program established under part 370 of this chapter, who must be the director of or other individual recommended by the Client Assistance Program;

(iv) At least one qualified vocational rehabilitation counselor with knowledge of and experience with vocational rehabilitation programs who serves as an ex officio, nonvoting member of the Council if employed by the designated State agency;

(v) At least one representative of community rehabilitation program service providers;

(vi) Four representatives of business, industry, and labor;

(vii) Representatives of disability groups that include a cross section of—

(A) Individuals with physical, cognitive, sensory, and mental disabilities; and

(B) Representatives of individuals with disabilities who have difficulty representing themselves or are unable due to their disabilities to represent themselves;

(viii) Current or former applicants for, or recipients of, vocational rehabilitation services;

(ix) In a State in which one or more projects are funded under section 121 of the Act (American Indian Vocational Rehabilitation Services), at least one representative of the directors of the projects in such State;

(x) At least one representative of the State educational agency responsible for the public education of students with disabilities who are eligible to receive services under this part and part B of the Individuals with Disabilities Education Act;

(xi) At least one representative of the State workforce development board; and

(xii) The director of the designated State unit as an ex officio, nonvoting member of the Council.

(2) *Employees of the designated State agency.* Employees of the designated State agency may serve only as nonvoting members of the Council. This provision does not apply to the representative appointed pursuant to paragraph (b)(1)(iii) of this section.

(3) *Composition of a separate Council for a separate State agency for individ-*

uals who are blind. Except as provided in paragraph (b)(4) of this section, if the State establishes a separate Council for a separate State agency for individuals who are blind, that Council must—

(i) Conform with all of the composition requirements for a Council under paragraph (b)(1) of this section, except the requirements in paragraph (b)(1)(vii), unless the exception in paragraph (b)(4) of this section applies; and

(ii) Include—

(A) At least one representative of a disability advocacy group representing individuals who are blind; and

(B) At least one representative of an individual who is blind, has multiple disabilities, and has difficulty representing himself or herself or is unable due to disabilities to represent himself or herself.

(4) *Exception.* If State law in effect on October 29, 1992 requires a separate Council under paragraph (b)(3) of this section to have fewer than 15 members, the separate Council is in compliance with the composition requirements in paragraphs (b)(1)(vi) and (viii) of this section if it includes at least one representative who meets the requirements for each of those paragraphs.

(c) *Majority.* (1) A majority of the Council members must be individuals with disabilities who meet the requirements of § 361.5(c)(28) and are not employed by the designated State unit.

(2) In the case of a separate Council established under § 361.16(b), a majority of the Council members must be individuals who are blind and are not employed by the designated State unit.

(d) *Chairperson.* (1) The chairperson must be selected by the members of the Council from among the voting members of the Council, subject to the veto power of the Governor; or

(2) In States in which the Governor does not have veto power pursuant to State law, the appointing authority described in paragraph (a)(1) of this section must designate a member of the Council to serve as the chairperson of the Council or must require the Council to designate a member to serve as chairperson.

(e) *Terms of appointment.* (1) Each member of the Council must be appointed for a term of no more than three years, and each member of the Council, other than a representative identified in paragraph (b)(1)(iii) or (ix) of this section, may serve for no more than two consecutive full terms.

(2) A member appointed to fill a vacancy occurring prior to the end of the term for which the predecessor was appointed must be appointed for the remainder of the predecessor's term.

(3) The terms of service of the members initially appointed must be, as specified by the appointing authority as described in paragraph (a)(1) of this section, for varied numbers of years to ensure that terms expire on a staggered basis.

(f) *Vacancies.* (1) A vacancy in the membership of the Council must be filled in the same manner as the original appointment, except the appointing authority as described in paragraph (a)(1) of this section may delegate the authority to fill that vacancy to the remaining members of the Council after making the original appointment.

(2) No vacancy affects the power of the remaining members to execute the duties of the Council.

(g) *Conflict of interest.* No member of the Council may cast a vote on any matter that would provide direct financial benefit to the member or the member's organization or otherwise give the appearance of a conflict of interest under State law.

(h) *Functions.* The Council must, after consulting with the State workforce development board—

(1) Review, analyze, and advise the designated State unit regarding the performance of the State unit's responsibilities under this part, particularly responsibilities related to—

(i) Eligibility, including order of selection;

(ii) The extent, scope, and effectiveness of services provided; and

(iii) Functions performed by State agencies that affect or potentially affect the ability of individuals with disabilities in achieving employment outcomes under this part;

(2) In partnership with the designated State unit—

(i) Develop, agree to, and review State goals and priorities in accordance with §361.29(c); and

(ii) Evaluate the effectiveness of the vocational rehabilitation program and submit reports of progress to the Secretary in accordance with §361.29(e);

(3) Advise the designated State agency and the designated State unit regarding activities carried out under this part and assist in the preparation of the vocational rehabilitation services portion of the Unified or Combined State Plan and amendments to the plan, applications, reports, needs assessments, and evaluations required by this part;

(4) To the extent feasible, conduct a review and analysis of the effectiveness of, and consumer satisfaction with—

(i) The functions performed by the designated State agency;

(ii) The vocational rehabilitation services provided by State agencies and other public and private entities responsible for providing vocational rehabilitation services to individuals with disabilities under the Act; and

(iii) The employment outcomes achieved by eligible individuals receiving services under this part, including the availability of health and other employment benefits in connection with those employment outcomes;

(5) Prepare and submit to the Governor and to the Secretary no later than 90 days after the end of the Federal fiscal year an annual report on the status of vocational rehabilitation programs operated within the State and make the report available to the public through appropriate modes of communication;

(6) To avoid duplication of efforts and enhance the number of individuals served, coordinate activities with the activities of other councils within the State, including the Statewide Independent Living Council established under chapter 1, title VII of the Act, the advisory panel established under section 612(a)(21) of the Individuals with Disabilities Education Act, the State Developmental Disabilities Planning Council described in section 124 of the Developmental Disabilities Assistance and Bill of Rights Act, the State mental health planning council established under section 1914(a) of the Public Health Service Act, and the State workforce development board, and with the activities of entities carrying out

programs under the Assistive Technology Act of 1998;

(7) Provide for coordination and the establishment of working relationships between the designated State agency and the Statewide Independent Living Council and centers for independent living within the State; and

(8) Perform other comparable functions, consistent with the purpose of this part, as the Council determines to be appropriate, that are comparable to the other functions performed by the Council.

(i) *Resources.* (1) The Council, in conjunction with the designated State unit, must prepare a plan for the provision of resources, including staff and other personnel, that may be necessary and sufficient for the Council to carry out its functions under this part.

(2) The resource plan must, to the maximum extent possible, rely on the use of resources in existence during the period of implementation of the plan.

(3) Any disagreements between the designated State unit and the Council regarding the amount of resources necessary to carry out the functions of the Council must be resolved by the Governor, consistent with paragraphs (i)(1) and (2) of this section.

(4) The Council must, consistent with State law, supervise and evaluate the staff and personnel that are necessary to carry out its functions.

(5) Those staff and personnel that are assisting the Council in carrying out its functions may not be assigned duties by the designated State unit or any other agency or office of the State that would create a conflict of interest.

(j) *Meetings.* The Council must—

(1) Convene at least four meetings a year in locations determined by the Council to be necessary to conduct Council business. The meetings must be publicly announced, open, and accessible to the general public, including individuals with disabilities, unless there is a valid reason for an executive session; and

(2) Conduct forums or hearings, as appropriate, that are publicly announced, open, and accessible to the public, including individuals with disabilities.

(k) *Compensation.* Funds appropriated under title I of the Act, except funds to

carry out sections 112 and 121 of the Act, may be used to compensate and reimburse the expenses of Council members in accordance with section 105(g) of the Act.

(Approved by the Office of Management and Budget under control number 1205–0522)

(Authority: Section 105 of the Rehabilitation Act of 1973, as amended; 29 U.S.C. 725)

§ 361.18 Comprehensive system of personnel development.

The vocational rehabilitation services portion of the Unified or Combined State Plan must describe the procedures and activities the State agency will undertake to establish and maintain a comprehensive system of personnel development designed to ensure an adequate supply of qualified rehabilitation personnel, including professionals and paraprofessionals, for the designated State unit. If the State agency has a State Rehabilitation Council, this description must, at a minimum, specify that the Council has an opportunity to review and comment on the development of plans, policies, and procedures necessary to meet the requirements of paragraphs (b) through (d) of this section. This description must also conform with the following requirements:

(a) *Personnel and personnel development data system.* The vocational rehabilitation services portion of the Unified or Combined State Plan must describe the development and maintenance of a system by the State agency for collecting and analyzing on an annual basis data on qualified personnel needs and personnel development, in accordance with the following requirements:

(1) Data on qualified personnel needs must include—

(i) The number of personnel who are employed by the State agency in the provision of vocational rehabilitation services in relation to the number of individuals served, broken down by personnel category;

(ii) The number of personnel currently needed by the State agency to provide vocational rehabilitation services, broken down by personnel category; and

(iii) Projections of the number of personnel, broken down by personnel category, who will be needed by the State agency to provide vocational rehabilitation services in the State in five years based on projections of the number of individuals to be served, including individuals with significant disabilities, the number of personnel expected to retire or leave the field, and other relevant factors.

(2) Data on personnel development must include—

(i) A list of the institutions of higher education in the State that are preparing vocational rehabilitation professionals, by type of program;

(ii) The number of students enrolled at each of those institutions, broken down by type of program; and

(iii) The number of students who graduated during the prior year from each of those institutions with certification or licensure, or with the credentials for certification or licensure, broken down by the personnel category for which they have received, or have the credentials to receive, certification or licensure.

(b) *Plan for recruitment, preparation, and retention of qualified personnel.* The vocational rehabilitation services portion of the Unified or Combined State Plan must describe the development, updating, and implementation of a plan to address the current and projected needs for personnel who are qualified in accordance with paragraph (c) of this section. The plan must identify the personnel needs based on the data collection and analysis system described in paragraph (a) of this section and must provide for the coordination and facilitation of efforts between the designated State unit and institutions of higher education and professional associations to recruit, prepare, and retain personnel who are qualified in accordance with paragraph (c) of this section, including personnel from minority backgrounds and personnel who are individuals with disabilities.

(c) *Personnel standards.* (1) The vocational rehabilitation services portion of the Unified or Combined State Plan must include the State agency's policies and describe—

(i) Standards that are consistent with any national or State-approved or recognized certification, licensing, or registration requirements, or, in the absence of these requirements, other comparable requirements (including State personnel requirements) that apply to the profession or discipline in which that category of personnel is providing vocational rehabilitation services; and

(ii) The establishment and maintenance of education and experience requirements, to ensure that the personnel have a 21st-century understanding of the evolving labor force and the needs of individuals with disabilities, including requirements for—

(A)(*1*) Attainment of a baccalaureate degree in a field of study reasonably related to vocational rehabilitation, to indicate a level of competency and skill demonstrating basic preparation in a field of study such as vocational rehabilitation counseling, social work, psychology, disability studies, business administration, human resources, special education, supported employment, customized employment, economics, or another field that reasonably prepares individuals to work with consumers and employers; and

(*2*) Demonstrated paid or unpaid experience, for not less than one year, consisting of—

(*i*) Direct work with individuals with disabilities in a setting such as an independent living center;

(*ii*) Direct service or advocacy activities that provide such individual with experience and skills in working with individuals with disabilities; or

(*iii*) Direct experience in competitive integrated employment environments as an employer, as a small business owner or operator, or in self-employment, or other experience in human resources or recruitment, or experience in supervising employees, training, or other activities; or

(B) Attainment of a master's or doctoral degree in a field of study such as vocational rehabilitation counseling, law, social work, psychology, disability studies, business administration, human resources, special education, management, public administration, or another field that reasonably provides competence in the employment sector,

307

in a disability field, or in both business-related and rehabilitation-related fields; and

(2) As used in this section—

(i) *Profession or discipline* means a specific occupational category, including any paraprofessional occupational category, that—

(A) Provides rehabilitation services to individuals with disabilities;

(B) Has been established or designated by the State unit; and

(C) Has a specified scope of responsibility.

(ii) Ensuring that personnel have a 21st-century understanding of the evolving labor force and the needs of individuals with disabilities means that personnel have specialized training and experience that enables them to work effectively with individuals with disabilities to assist them to achieve competitive integrated employment and with employers who hire such individuals. Relevant personnel skills include, but are not limited to—

(A) Understanding the functional limitations of various disabilities and the vocational implications of functional limitations on employment, especially with regard to individuals whose disabilities may require specialized services or groups of individuals with disabilities who comprise an increasing proportion of the State VR caseloads, such as individuals with traumatic brain injury, post-traumatic stress syndrome, mental illnesses, autism, blindness or deaf-blindness;

(B) Vocational assessment tools and strategies and the interpretation of vocational assessment results, including, when appropriate, situational and work-based assessments and analysis of transferrable work skills;

(C) Counseling and guidance skills, including individual and group counseling and career guidance;

(D) Effective use of practices leading to competitive integrated employment, such as supported employment, customized employment, internships, apprenticeships, paid work experiences, etc.;

(E) Case management and employment services planning, including familiarity and use of the broad range of disability, employment, and social services programs in the state and local area, such as independent living programs, Social Security work incentives, and the Social Security Administration's Ticket-to-Work program;

(F) Caseload management, including familiarity with effective caseload management practices and the use of any available automated or information technology resources;

(G) In-depth knowledge of labor market trends, occupational requirements, and other labor market information that provides information about employers, business practices, and employer personnel needs, such as data provided by the Bureau of Labor Statistics and the Department of Labor's O*NET occupational system;

(H) The use of labor market information for vocational rehabilitation counseling, vocational planning, and the provision of information to consumers for the purposes of making informed choices, business engagement and business relationships, and job development and job placement;

(I) The use of labor market information to support building and maintaining relationships with employers and to inform delivery of job development and job placement activities that respond to today's labor market;

(J) Understanding the effective utilization of rehabilitation technology and job accommodations;

(K) Training in understanding the provisions of the Americans with Disabilities Act and other employment discrimination and employment-related laws;

(L) Advocacy skills to modify attitudinal and environmental barriers to employment for individuals with disabilities, including those with the most significant disabilities;

(M) Skills to address cultural diversity among consumers, particularly affecting workplace settings, including racial and ethnic diversity and generational differences; and

(N) Understanding confidentiality and ethical standards and practices, especially related to new challenges in use of social media, new partnerships, and data sharing.

(d) *Staff development.* (1) The vocational rehabilitation services portion of the Unified or Combined State Plan must include the State agency's policies and describe the procedures and activities the State agency will undertake to ensure that all personnel employed by the State unit receive appropriate and adequate training, including a description of—

(i) A system of staff development for rehabilitation professionals and paraprofessionals within the State unit, particularly with respect to assessment, vocational counseling, job placement, and rehabilitation technology, including training implemented in coordination with entities carrying out State programs under section 4 of the Assistive Technology Act of 1998 (29 U.S.C. 3003);

(ii) Procedures for acquiring and disseminating to rehabilitation professionals and paraprofessionals within the designated State unit significant knowledge from research and other sources; and

(iii) Policies and procedures relating to the establishment and maintenance of standards to ensure that personnel, including rehabilitation professionals and paraprofessionals, needed within the designated State unit to carry out this part are appropriately and adequately prepared and trained.

(2) The specific training areas for staff development must be based on the needs of each State unit and may include, but are not limited to—

(i) Training regarding the Workforce Innovation and Opportunity Act and the amendments it made to the Rehabilitation Act of 1973;

(ii) Training with respect to the requirements of the Americans with Disabilities Act, the Individuals with Disabilities Education Act, and Social Security work incentive programs, including programs under the Ticket to Work and Work Incentives Improvement Act of 1999, training to facilitate informed choice under this program, and training to improve the provision of services to culturally diverse populations; and

(iii) Activities related to—

(A) Recruitment and retention of qualified rehabilitation personnel;

(B) Succession planning; and

(C) Leadership development and capacity building.

(e) *Personnel to address individual communication needs.* The vocational rehabilitation services portion of the Unified or Combined State Plan must describe how the designated State unit includes among its personnel, or obtains the services of—

(1) Individuals able to communicate in the native languages of applicants, recipients of services, and eligible individuals who have limited English proficiency; and

(2) Individuals able to communicate with applicants, recipients of services, and eligible individuals in appropriate modes of communication.

(f) *Coordination with personnel development under the Individuals with Disabilities Education Act.* The vocational rehabilitation services portion of the Unified or Combined State Plan must describe the procedures and activities the State agency will undertake to coordinate its comprehensive system of personnel development under the Act with personnel development under the Individuals with Disabilities Education Act.

(Approved by the Office of Management and Budget under control number 1205–0522)

(Authority: Sections 12(c) and 101(a)(7) of the Rehabilitation Act of 1973, as amended; 29 U.S.C. 709(c) and 721(a)(7))

§361.19 Affirmative action for individuals with disabilities.

The vocational rehabilitation services portion of the Unified or Combined State Plan must assure that the State agency takes affirmative action to employ and advance in employment qualified individuals with disabilities covered under and on the same terms and conditions as stated in section 503 of the Act.

(Approved by the Office of Management and Budget under control number 1205–0522)

(Authority: Section 101(a)(6)(B) of the Rehabilitation Act of 1973, as amended; 29 U.S.C. 721(a)(6)(B))

§361.20 Public participation requirements.

(a) *Conduct of public meetings.* (1) The vocational rehabilitation services portion of the Unified or Combined State Plan must assure that prior to the adoption of any substantive policies or procedures governing the provision of vocational rehabilitation services under the Unified or Combined State Plan, the designated State agency conducts public meetings throughout the State to provide the public, including individuals with disabilities, an opportunity to comment on the policies or procedures.

(2) For purposes of this section, substantive changes to the policies or procedures governing the provision of vocational rehabilitation services that would require the conduct of public meetings are those that directly impact the nature and scope of the services provided to individuals with disabilities, or the manner in which individuals interact with the designated State agency or in matters related to the delivery of vocational rehabilitation services. Examples of substantive changes include, but are not limited to—

(i) Any changes to policies or procedures that fundamentally alter the rights and responsibilities of individuals with disabilities in the vocational rehabilitation process;

(ii) Organizational changes to the designated State agency or unit that would likely affect the manner in which services are delivered;

(iii) Any changes that affect the nature and scope of vocational rehabilitation services provided by the designated State agency or unit;

(iv) Changes in formal or informal dispute procedures;

(v) The adoption or amendment of policies instituting an order of selection; and

(vi) Changes to policies and procedures regarding the financial participation of eligible individuals.

(3) Non-substantive, *e.g.*, administrative changes that would not require the need for public hearings include:

(i) Internal procedures that do not directly affect individuals receiving vocational rehabilitation services, such as payment processing or personnel procedures;

(ii) Changes to the case management system that only affect vocational rehabilitation personnel;

(iii) Changes in indirect cost allocations, internal fiscal review procedures, or routine reporting requirements;

(iv) Minor revisions to vocational rehabilitation procedures or policies to correct production errors, such as typographical and grammatical mistakes; and

(v) Changes to contract procedures that do not affect the delivery of vocational rehabilitation services.

(b) *Notice requirements.* The vocational rehabilitation services portion of the Unified or Combined State Plan must assure that the designated State agency, prior to conducting the public meetings, provides appropriate and sufficient notice throughout the State of the meetings in accordance with—

(1) State law governing public meetings; or

(2) In the absence of State law governing public meetings, procedures developed by the designated State agency in consultation with the State Rehabilitation Council.

(c) *Summary of input of the State Rehabilitation Council.* The vocational rehabilitation services portion of the Unified or Combined State Plan must provide a summary of the input of the State Rehabilitation Council, if the State agency has a Council, into the vocational rehabilitation services portion of the Unified or Combined State Plan and any amendment to that portion of the plan, in accordance with § 361.16(a)(2)(v).

(d) *Special consultation requirements.* The vocational rehabilitation services portion of the Unified or Combined State Plan must assure that the State agency actively consults with the director of the Client Assistance Program, the State Rehabilitation Council, if the State agency has a Council, and, as appropriate, Indian tribes, tribal organizations, and native Hawaiian organizations on its policies and procedures governing the provision of vocational rehabilitation services under the vocational rehabilitation services portion of the Unified or Combined State Plan.

(e) *Appropriate modes of communication.* The State unit must provide to the public, through appropriate modes of communication, notices of the public meetings, any materials furnished prior to or during the public meetings, and the policies and procedures governing the provision of vocational rehabilitation services under the vocational rehabilitation services portion of the Unified or Combined State Plan.

(Approved by the Office of Management and Budget under control number 1205–0522)

(Authority: Sections 12(c), 101(a)(16)(A), and 105(c)(3) of the Rehabilitation Act of 1973, as amended; 29 U.S.C. 709(c), 721(a)(16)(A), and 725(c)(3))

§ 361.21 Consultations regarding the administration of the vocational rehabilitation services portion of the Unified or Combined State plan.

The vocational rehabilitation services portion of the Unified or Combined State Plan must assure that, in connection with matters of general policy arising in the administration of the vocational rehabilitation services portion of the Unified or Combined State Plan, the designated State agency takes into account the views of—

(a) Individuals and groups of individuals who are recipients of vocational rehabilitation services or, as appropriate, the individuals' representatives;

(b) Personnel working in programs that provide vocational rehabilitation services to individuals with disabilities;

(c) Providers of vocational rehabilitation services to individuals with disabilities;

(d) The director of the Client Assistance Program; and

(e) The State Rehabilitation Council, if the State has a Council.

(Approved by the Office of Management and Budget under control number 1205–0522)

(Authority: Sections 101(a)(16)(B) of the Rehabilitation Act of 1973, as amended; 29 U.S.C. 721(a)(16)(B))

§ 361.22 Coordination with education officials.

(a) *Plans, policies, and procedures.* (1) The vocational rehabilitation services portion of the Unified or Combined State Plan must contain plans, policies, and procedures for coordination between the designated State agency and education officials responsible for the public education of students with disabilities that are designed to facilitate the transition of students with disabilities from the receipt of educational services, including pre-employment transition services, in school to the receipt of vocational rehabilitation services under the responsibility of the designated State agency.

(2) These plans, policies, and procedures in paragraph (a)(1) of this section must provide for the development and approval of an individualized plan for employment in accordance with § 361.45 as early as possible during the transition planning process and not later than the time a student with a disability determined to be eligible for vocational rehabilitation services leaves the school setting or, if the designated State unit is operating under an order of selection, before each eligible student with a disability able to be served under the order leaves the school setting.

(b) *Formal interagency agreement.* The vocational rehabilitation services portion of the Unified or Combined State Plan must include information on a formal interagency agreement with the State educational agency that, at a minimum, provides for—

(1) Consultation and technical assistance, which may be provided using alternative means for meeting participation (such as video conferences and conference calls), to assist educational agencies in planning for the transition of students with disabilities from school to post-school activities, including pre-employment transition services and other vocational rehabilitation services;

(2) Transition planning by personnel of the designated State agency and educational agency personnel for students with disabilities that facilitates the development and implementation of their individualized education programs (IEPs) under section 614(d) of the Individuals with Disabilities Education Act;

(3) The roles and responsibilities, including financial responsibilities, of each agency, including provisions for determining State lead agencies and qualified personnel responsible for transition services and pre-employment transition services;

(4) Procedures for outreach to and identification of students with disabilities who are in need of transition services and pre-employment transition

311

services. Outreach to these students should occur as early as possible during the transition planning process and must include, at a minimum, a description of the purpose of the vocational rehabilitation program, eligibility requirements, application procedures, and scope of services that may be provided to eligible individuals;

(5) Coordination necessary to satisfy documentation requirements set forth in 34 CFR part 397 with regard to students and youth with disabilities who are seeking subminimum wage employment; and

(6) Assurance that, in accordance with 34 CFR 397.31, neither the State educational agency nor the local educational agency will enter into a contract or other arrangement with an entity, as defined in 34 CFR 397.5(d), for the purpose of operating a program under which a youth with a disability is engaged in work compensated at a subminimum wage.

(c) *Construction.* Nothing in this part will be construed to reduce the obligation under the Individuals with Disabilities Education Act (20 U.S.C. 1400 *et seq.*) of a local educational agency or any other agency to provide or pay for any transition services that are also considered special education or related services and that are necessary for ensuring a free appropriate public education to children with disabilities within the State involved.

(Approved by the Office of Management and Budget under control number 1205–0522)

(Authority: Sections 12(c), 101(a)(11)(D), 101(c), and 511 of the Rehabilitation Act of 1973, as amended; 29 U.S.C. 709(c), 721(a)(11)(D), 721(c), and 794g)

§ 361.23 Requirements related to the statewide workforce development system.

As a required partner in the one-stop service delivery system (which is part of the statewide workforce development system under title I of the Workforce Innovation and Opportunity Act), the designated State unit must satisfy all requirements set forth in regulations in subpart F of this part.

(Approved by the Office of Management and Budget under control number 1205–0522)

(Authority: Section 101(a)(11)(A) of the Rehabilitation Act of 1973, as amended; 29 U.S.C. 721(a)(11)(A); Section 121(b)(1)(B)(iv) of the Workforce Innovation and Opportunity Act; 29 U.S.C. 3151)

[81 FR 57779, Aug. 19, 2016]

§ 361.24 Cooperation and coordination with other entities.

(a) *Interagency cooperation.* The vocational rehabilitation services portion of the Unified or Combined State Plan must describe the designated State agency's cooperation with and use of the services and facilities of Federal, State, and local agencies and programs, including the State programs carried out under section 4 of the Assistive Technology Act of 1998 (29 U.S.C. 3003), programs carried out by the Under Secretary for Rural Development of the Department of Agriculture, noneducational agencies serving out-of-school youth, and State use contracting programs, to the extent that such Federal, State, and local agencies and programs are not carrying out activities through the statewide workforce development system.

(b) *Coordination with the Statewide Independent Living Council and independent living centers.* The vocational rehabilitation services portion of the Unified or Combined State Plan must assure that the designated State unit, the Statewide Independent Living Council established under title VII, chapter 1, part B of the Act, and the independent living centers established under title VII, Chapter 1, Part C of the Act have developed working relationships and coordinate their activities.

(c) *Coordination with Employers.* The vocational rehabilitation services portion of the Unified or Combined State Plan must describe how the designated State unit will work with employers to identify competitive integrated employment opportunities and career exploration opportunities, in order to facilitate the provision of—

(1) Vocational rehabilitation services; and

(2) Transition services for youth with disabilities and students with disabilities, such as pre-employment transition services.

(d) *Cooperative agreement with recipients of grants for services to American Indians*—(1) *General.* In applicable cases, the vocational rehabilitation services portion of the Unified or Combined State Plan must assure that the designated State agency has entered into a formal cooperative agreement with each grant recipient in the State that receives funds under part C of the Act (American Indian Vocational Rehabilitation Services).

(2) *Contents of formal cooperative agreement.* The agreement required under paragraph (d)(1) of this section must describe strategies for collaboration and coordination in providing vocational rehabilitation services to American Indians who are individuals with disabilities, including—

(i) Strategies for interagency referral and information sharing that will assist in eligibility determinations and the development of individualized plans for employment;

(ii) Procedures for ensuring that American Indians who are individuals with disabilities and are living on or near a reservation or tribal service area are provided vocational rehabilitation services;

(iii) Strategies for the provision of transition planning by personnel of the designated State unit, the State educational agency, and the recipient of funds under part C of the Act, that will facilitate the development and approval of the individualized plan for employment under §361.45; and

(iv) Provisions for sharing resources in cooperative studies and assessments, joint training activities, and other collaborative activities designed to improve the provision of services to American Indians who are individuals with disabilities.

(e) *Reciprocal referral services between two designated State units in the same State.* If there is a separate designated State unit for individuals who are blind, the two designated State units must establish reciprocal referral services, use each other's services and facilities to the extent feasible, jointly plan activities to improve services in the State for individuals with multiple impairments, including visual impairments, and otherwise cooperate to provide more effective services, including, if appropriate, entering into a written cooperative agreement.

(f) *Cooperative agreement regarding individuals eligible for home and community-based waiver programs.* The vocational rehabilitation services portion of the Unified or Combined State Plan must include an assurance that the designated State unit has entered into a formal cooperative agreement with the State agency responsible for administering the State Medicaid plan under title XIX of the Social Security Act (42 U.S.C. 1396 *et seq.*) and the State agency with primary responsibility for providing services and supports for individuals with intellectual disabilities and individuals with developmental disabilities, with respect to the delivery of vocational rehabilitation services, including extended services, for individuals with the most significant disabilities who have been determined to be eligible for home and community-based services under a Medicaid waiver, Medicaid State plan amendment, or other authority related to a State Medicaid program.

(g) *Interagency cooperation.* The vocational rehabilitation services portion of the Unified or Combined State Plan shall describe how the designated State agency will collaborate with the State agency responsible for administering the State Medicaid plan under title XIX of the Social Security Act (42 U.S.C. 1396 *et seq.*), the State agency responsible for providing services for individuals with developmental disabilities, and the State agency responsible for providing mental health services, to develop opportunities for community-based employment in integrated settings, to the greatest extent practicable.

(h) *Coordination with assistive technology programs.* The vocational rehabilitation services portion of the Unified or Combined State Plan must include an assurance that the designated State unit, and the lead agency and implementing entity (if any) designated by the Governor of the State under section 4 of the Assistive Technology Act of 1998 (29 U.S.C. 3003), have developed working relationships and will enter into agreements for the coordination of their activities, including the referral of individuals with disabilities to programs and activities described in that section.

(i) *Coordination with ticket to work and self-sufficiency program.* The vocational rehabilitation services portion of the Unified or Combined State Plan must include an assurance that the designated State unit will coordinate activities with any other State agency that is functioning as an employment network under the Ticket to Work and Self-Sufficiency Program established under section 1148 of the Social Security Act (42 U.S.C. 1320b–19).

(Approved by the Office of Management and Budget under control number 1205–0522)

(Authority: Sections 12(c) and 101(a)(11) of the Rehabilitation Act of 1973, as amended; 29 U.S.C. 709(c) and 721(a)(11))

§ 361.25 Statewideness.

The vocational rehabilitation services portion of the Unified or Combined State Plan must assure that services provided under the vocational rehabilitation services portion of the Unified or Combined State Plan will be available in all political subdivisions of the State, unless a waiver of statewideness is requested and approved in accordance with § 361.26.

(Approved by the Office of Management and Budget under control number 1205–0522)

(Authority: Section 101(a)(4) of the Rehabilitation Act of 1973, as amended; 29 U.S.C. 721(a)(4))

§ 361.26 Waiver of statewideness.

(a) *Availability.* The State unit may provide services in one or more political subdivisions of the State that increase services or expand the scope of services that are available statewide under the vocational rehabilitation services portion of the Unified or Combined State Plan if—

(1) The non-Federal share of the cost of these services is met from funds provided by a local public agency, including funds contributed to a local public agency by a private agency, organization, or individual;

(2) The services are likely to promote the vocational rehabilitation of sub-stantially larger numbers of individuals with disabilities or of individuals with disabilities with particular types of impairments; and

(3) For purposes other than those specified in § 361.60(b)(3)(i) and consistent with the requirements in § 361.60(b)(3)(ii), the State includes in its vocational rehabilitation services portion of the Unified or Combined State Plan, and the Secretary approves, a waiver of the statewideness requirement, in accordance with the requirements of paragraph (b) of this section.

(b) *Request for waiver.* The request for a waiver of statewideness must—

(1) Identify the types of services to be provided;

(2) Contain a written assurance from the local public agency that it will make available to the State unit the non-Federal share of funds;

(3) Contain a written assurance that State unit approval will be obtained for each proposed service before it is put into effect; and

(4) Contain a written assurance that all other requirements of the vocational rehabilitation services portion of the Unified or Combined State Plan, including a State's order of selection requirements, will apply to all services approved under the waiver.

(Approved by the Office of Management and Budget under control number 1205–0522)

(Authority: Section 101(a)(4) of the Rehabilitation Act of 1973, as amended; 29 U.S.C. 721(a)(4))

§ 361.27 Shared funding and administration of joint programs.

(a) If the vocational rehabilitation services portion of the Unified or Combined State Plan provides for the designated State agency to share funding and administrative responsibility with another State agency or local public agency to carry out a joint program to provide services to individuals with disabilities, the State must submit to the Secretary for approval a plan that describes its shared funding and administrative arrangement.

(b) The plan under paragraph (a) of this section must include—

(1) A description of the nature and scope of the joint program;

(2) The services to be provided under the joint program;

(3) The respective roles of each participating agency in the administration and provision of services; and

(4) The share of the costs to be assumed by each agency.

(c) If a proposed joint program does not comply with the statewideness requirement in § 361.25, the State unit must obtain a waiver of statewideness, in accordance with § 361.26.

(Approved by the Office of Management and Budget under control number 1205–0522)

(Authority: Section 101(a)(2)(A) of the Rehabilitation Act of 1973, as amended; 29 U.S.C. 721(a)(2)(A))

§ 361.28 Third-party cooperative arrangements involving funds from other public agencies.

(a) The designated State unit may enter into a third-party cooperative arrangement for providing or contracting for the provision of vocational rehabilitation services with another State agency or a local public agency that is providing part or all of the non-Federal share in accordance with paragraph (c) of this section, if the designated State unit ensures that—

(1) The services provided by the cooperating agency are not the customary or typical services provided by that agency but are new services that have a vocational rehabilitation focus or existing services that have been modified, adapted, expanded, or reconfigured to have a vocational rehabilitation focus;

(2) The services provided by the cooperating agency are only available to applicants for, or recipients of, services from the designated State unit;

(3) Program expenditures and staff providing services under the cooperative arrangement are under the administrative supervision of the designated State unit; and

(4) All requirements of the vocational rehabilitation services portion of the Unified or Combined State Plan, including a State's order of selection, will apply to all services provided under the cooperative arrangement.

(b) If a third party cooperative arrangement does not comply with the statewideness requirement in § 361.25, the State unit must obtain a waiver of statewideness, in accordance with § 361.26.

(c) The cooperating agency's contribution toward the non-Federal share required under the arrangement, as set forth in paragraph (a) of this section, may be made through:

(1) Cash transfers to the designated State unit;

(2) Certified personnel expenditures for the time cooperating agency staff spent providing direct vocational rehabilitation services pursuant to a third-party cooperative arrangement that meets the requirements of this section. Certified personnel expenditures may include the allocable portion of staff salary and fringe benefits based upon the amount of time cooperating agency staff directly spent providing services under the arrangement; and

(3) other direct expenditures incurred by the cooperating agency for the sole purpose of providing services under this section pursuant to a third-party cooperative arrangement that—

(i) Meets the requirements of this section;

(ii) Are verifiable as being incurred under the third-party cooperative arrangement; and

(iii) Do not meet the definition of third-party in-kind contributions under 2 CFR 200.96.

(Authority: Section 12(c) of the Rehabilitation Act of 1973, as amended; 29 U.S.C. 709(c))

§ 361.29 Statewide assessment; annual estimates; annual State goals and priorities; strategies; and progress reports.

(a) *Comprehensive statewide assessment.* (1) The vocational rehabilitation services portion of the Unified or Combined State Plan must include—

(i) The results of a comprehensive, statewide assessment, jointly conducted by the designated State unit and the State Rehabilitation Council (if the State unit has a Council) every three years. Results of the assessment are to be included in the vocational rehabilitation portion of the Unified or Combined State Plan, submitted in accordance with the requirements of § 361.10(a) and the joint regulations of

315

this part. The comprehensive needs assessment must describe the rehabilitation needs of individuals with disabilities residing within the State, particularly the vocational rehabilitation services needs of—

(A) Individuals with the most significant disabilities, including their need for supported employment services;

(B) Individuals with disabilities who are minorities and individuals with disabilities who have been unserved or underserved by the vocational rehabilitation program carried out under this part;

(C) Individuals with disabilities served through other components of the statewide workforce development system as identified by those individuals and personnel assisting those individuals through the components of the system; and

(D) Youth with disabilities, and students with disabilities, including

(1) Their need for pre-employment transition services or other transition services; and

(2) An assessment of the needs of individuals with disabilities for transition services and pre-employment transition services, and the extent to which such services provided under this part are coordinated with transition services provided under the Individuals with Disabilities Education Act (20 U.S.C. 1400 et seq.) in order to meet the needs of individuals with disabilities.

(ii) An assessment of the need to establish, develop, or improve community rehabilitation programs within the State.

(2) The vocational rehabilitation services portion of the Unified or Combined State Plan must assure that the State will submit to the Secretary a report containing information regarding updates to the assessments under paragraph (a) of this section for any year in which the State updates the assessments at such time and in such manner as the Secretary determines appropriate.

(b) Annual estimates. The vocational rehabilitation services portion of the Unified or Combined State Plan must include, and must assure that the State will submit a report to the Secretary (at such time and in such manner determined appropriate by the Secretary) that includes, State estimates of—

(1) The number of individuals in the State who are eligible for services under this part;

(2) The number of eligible individuals who will receive services provided with funds provided under this part and under part § 363, including, if the designated State agency uses an order of selection in accordance with § 361.36, estimates of the number of individuals to be served under each priority category within the order;

(3) The number of individuals who are eligible for services under paragraph (b)(1) of this section, but are not receiving such services due to an order of selection; and

(4) The costs of the services described in paragraph (b)(2) of this section, including, if the designated State agency uses an order of selection, the service costs for each priority category within the order.

(c) Goals and priorities—(1) In general. The vocational rehabilitation services portion of the Unified or Combined State Plan must identify the goals and priorities of the State in carrying out the program.

(2) Council. The goals and priorities must be jointly developed, agreed to, reviewed annually, and, as necessary, revised by the designated State unit and the State Rehabilitation Council, if the State unit has a Council.

(3) Submission. The vocational rehabilitation services portion of the Unified or Combined State Plan must assure that the State will submit to the Secretary a report containing information regarding revisions in the goals and priorities for any year in which the State revises the goals and priorities at such time and in such manner as determined appropriate by the Secretary.

(4) Basis for goals and priorities. The State goals and priorities must be based on an analysis of—

(i) The comprehensive statewide assessment described in paragraph (a) of this section, including any updates to the assessment;

(ii) The performance of the State on the standards and indicators established under section 106 of the Act; and

(iii) Other available information on the operation and the effectiveness of the vocational rehabilitation program carried out in the State, including any reports received from the State Rehabilitation Council under § 361.17(h) and the findings and recommendations from monitoring activities conducted under section 107 of the Act.

(5) *Service and outcome goals for categories in order of selection.* If the designated State agency uses an order of selection in accordance with § 361.36, the vocational rehabilitation services portion of the Unified or Combined State Plan must identify the State's service and outcome goals and the time within which these goals may be achieved for individuals in each priority category within the order.

(d) *Strategies.* The vocational rehabilitation services portion of the Unified or Combined State Plan must describe the strategies the State will use to address the needs identified in the assessment conducted under paragraph (a) of this section and achieve the goals and priorities identified in paragraph (c) of this section, including—

(1) The methods to be used to expand and improve services to individuals with disabilities, including how a broad range of assistive technology services and assistive technology devices will be provided to those individuals at each stage of the rehabilitation process and how those services and devices will be provided to individuals with disabilities on a statewide basis;

(2) The methods to be used to improve and expand vocational rehabilitation services for students with disabilities, including the coordination of services designed to facilitate the transition of such students from the receipt of educational services in school to postsecondary life, including the receipt of vocational rehabilitation services under the Act, postsecondary education, employment, and pre-employment transition services;

(3) Strategies developed and implemented by the State to address the needs of students and youth with disabilities identified in the assessments described in paragraph (a) of this section and strategies to achieve the goals and priorities identified by the State to improve and expand vocational rehabilitation services for students and

youth with disabilities on a statewide basis;

(4) Strategies to provide pre-employment transition services;

(5) Outreach procedures to identify and serve individuals with disabilities who are minorities and individuals with disabilities who have been unserved or underserved by the vocational rehabilitation program;

(6) As applicable, the plan of the State for establishing, developing, or improving community rehabilitation programs;

(7) Strategies to improve the performance of the State with respect to the evaluation standards and performance indicators established pursuant to section 106 of the Act and section 116 of Workforce Innovation and Opportunity Act; and

(8) Strategies for assisting other components of the statewide workforce development system in assisting individuals with disabilities.

(e) *Evaluation and reports of progress.* (1) The vocational rehabilitation services portion of the Unified or Combined State Plan must include—

(i) The results of an evaluation of the effectiveness of the vocational rehabilitation program; and

(ii) A joint report by the designated State unit and the State Rehabilitation Council, if the State unit has a Council, to the Secretary on the progress made in improving the effectiveness of the program from the previous year. This evaluation and joint report must include—

(A) An evaluation of the extent to which the goals and priorities identified in paragraph (c) of this section were achieved;

(B) A description of the strategies that contributed to the achievement of the goals and priorities;

(C) To the extent to which the goals and priorities were not achieved, a description of the factors that impeded that achievement; and

(D) An assessment of the performance of the State on the standards and indicators established pursuant to section 106 of the Act.

(2) The vocational rehabilitation services portion of the Unified or Combined State Plan must assure that the designated State unit and the State

Rehabilitation Council, if the State unit has a Council, will jointly submit to the Secretary a report that contains the information described in paragraph (e)(1) of this section at such time and in such manner the Secretary determines appropriate.

(Approved by the Office of Management and Budget under control number 1205–0522)

(Authority: Section 101(a)(15) and (25) of the Rehabilitation Act of 1973, as amended; 29 U.S.C. 721(a)(15) and (25))

§ 361.30 Services to American Indians.

The vocational rehabilitation services portion of the Unified or Combined State Plan must assure that the designated State agency provides vocational rehabilitation services to American Indians who are individuals with disabilities residing in the State to the same extent as the designated State agency provides vocational rehabilitation services to other significant populations of individuals with disabilities residing in the State.

(Approved by the Office of Management and Budget under control number 1205–0522)

(Authority: Sections 101(a)(13) and 121(b)(3) of the Rehabilitation Act of 1973, as amended; 29 U.S.C. 721(a)(13) and 741(b)(3))

§ 361.31 Cooperative agreements with private nonprofit organizations.

The vocational rehabilitation services portion of the Unified or Combined State Plan must describe the manner in which cooperative agreements with private nonprofit vocational rehabilitation service providers will be established.

(Approved by the Office of Management and Budget under control number 1205–0522)

(Authority: Section 101(a)(24)(B) of the Rehabilitation Act of 1973, as amended; 29 U.S.C. 721(a)(24)(B))

§ 361.32 Provision of training and services for employers.

The designated State unit may expend payments received under this part to educate and provide services to employers who have hired or are interested in hiring individuals with disabilities under the vocational rehabilitation program, including—

(a) Providing training and technical assistance to employers regarding the employment of individuals with disabilities, including disability awareness, and the requirements of the Americans with Disabilities Act of 1990 (42 U.S.C. 12101 *et seq.*) and other employment-related laws;

(b) Working with employers to—

(1) Provide opportunities for work-based learning experiences (including internships, short-term employment, apprenticeships, and fellowships);

(2) Provide opportunities for pre-employment transition services, in accordance with the requirements under § 361.48(a);

(3) Recruit qualified applicants who are individuals with disabilities;

(4) Train employees who are individuals with disabilities; and

(5) Promote awareness of disability-related obstacles to continued employment.

(c) Providing consultation, technical assistance, and support to employers on workplace accommodations, assistive technology, and facilities and workplace access through collaboration with community partners and employers, across States and nationally, to enable the employers to recruit, job match, hire, and retain qualified individuals with disabilities who are recipients of vocational rehabilitation services under this part, or who are applicants for such services; and

(d) Assisting employers with utilizing available financial support for hiring or accommodating individuals with disabilities.

(Approved by the Office of Management and Budget under control number 1205–0522)

(Authority: Section 109 of the Rehabilitation Act of 1973, as amended; 29 U.S.C. 728A)

§ 361.33 [Reserved]

§ 361.34 Supported employment State plan supplement.

(a) The vocational rehabilitation services portion of the Unified or Combined State Plan must assure that the State has an acceptable plan under part 363 of this chapter that provides for the use of funds under that part to supplement funds under this part for the cost of services leading to supported employment.

(b) The supported employment plan, including any needed revisions, must be submitted as a supplement to the vocational rehabilitation services portion of the Unified or Combined State Plan submitted under this part.

(Approved by the Office of Management and Budget under control number 1205–0522)

(Authority: Sections 101(a)(22) and 606 of the Rehabilitation Act of 1973, as amended; 29 U.S.C. 721(a)(22) and 795k)

§361.35 Innovation and expansion activities.

(a) The vocational rehabilitation services portion of the Unified or Combined State Plan must assure that the State will reserve and use a portion of the funds allotted to the State under section 110 of the Act—

(1) For the development and implementation of innovative approaches to expand and improve the provision of vocational rehabilitation services to individuals with disabilities, particularly individuals with the most significant disabilities, including transition services for students and youth with disabilities and pre-employment transition services for students with disabilities, consistent with the findings of the comprehensive statewide assessment of the rehabilitation needs of individuals with disabilities under §361.29(a) and the State's goals and priorities under §361.29(c);

(2) To support the funding of the State Rehabilitation Council, if the State has a Council, consistent with the resource plan identified in §361.17(i); and

(3) To support the funding of the Statewide Independent Living Council, consistent with the Statewide Independent Living Council resource plan prepared under Section 705(e)(1) of the Act.

(b) The vocational rehabilitation services portion of the Unified or Combined State Plan must—

(1) Describe how the reserved funds will be used; and

(2) Include a report describing how the reserved funds were used.

(Approved by the Office of Management and Budget under control number 1205–0522)

(Authority: Sections 12(c) and 101(a)(18) of the Rehabilitation Act of 1973, as amended; 29 U.S.C. 709(c) and 721(a) (18))

§361.36 Ability to serve all eligible individuals; order of selection for services.

(a) *General provisions*—(1) The designated State unit either must be able to provide the full range of services listed in section 103(a) of the Act and §361.48, as appropriate, to all eligible individuals or, in the event that vocational rehabilitation services cannot be provided to all eligible individuals in the State who apply for the services, include in the vocational rehabilitation services portion of the Unified or Combined State Plan the order to be followed in selecting eligible individuals to be provided vocational rehabilitation services.

(2) The ability of the designated State unit to provide the full range of vocational rehabilitation services to all eligible individuals must be supported by a determination that satisfies the requirements of paragraph (b) or (c) of this section and a determination that, on the basis of the designated State unit's projected fiscal and personnel resources and its assessment of the rehabilitation needs of individuals with significant disabilities within the State, it can—

(i) Continue to provide services to all individuals currently receiving services;

(ii) Provide assessment services to all individuals expected to apply for services in the next fiscal year;

(iii) Provide services to all individuals who are expected to be determined eligible in the next fiscal year; and

(iv) Meet all program requirements.

(3) If the designated State unit is unable to provide the full range of vocational rehabilitation services to all eligible individuals in the State who apply for the services, the vocational rehabilitation services portion of the Unified or Combined State Plan must—

(i) Show the order to be followed in selecting eligible individuals to be provided vocational rehabilitation services;

(ii) Provide a justification for the order of selection;

(iii) Identify service and outcome goals and the time within which the goals may be achieved for individuals in each priority category within the order, as required under §361.29(c)(5);

(iv) Assure that—

(A) In accordance with criteria established by the State for the order of selection, individuals with the most significant disabilities will be selected first for the provision of vocational rehabilitation services; and

(B) Individuals who do not meet the order of selection criteria will have access to services provided through the information and referral system established under § 361.37; and

(v) State whether the designated State unit will elect to serve, in its discretion, eligible individuals (whether or not the individuals are receiving vocational rehabilitation services under the order of selection) who require specific services or equipment to maintain employment, notwithstanding the assurance provided pursuant to paragraph (3)(iv)(A) of this section.

(b) *Basis for assurance that services can be provided to all eligible individuals.* (1) For a designated State unit that determined, for the current fiscal year and the preceding fiscal year, that it is able to provide the full range of services, as appropriate, to all eligible individuals, the State unit, during the current fiscal and preceding fiscal year, must have in fact—

(i) Provided assessment services to all applicants and the full range of services, as appropriate, to all eligible individuals;

(ii) Made referral forms widely available throughout the State;

(iii) Conducted outreach efforts to identify and serve individuals with disabilities who have been unserved or underserved by the vocational rehabilitation system; and

(iv) Not delayed, through waiting lists or other means, determinations of eligibility, the development of individualized plans for employment for individuals determined eligible for vocational rehabilitation services, or the provision of services for eligible individuals for whom individualized plans for employment have been developed.

(2) For a designated State unit that was unable to provide the full range of services to all eligible individuals during the current or preceding fiscal year or that has not met the requirements in paragraph (b)(1) of this section, the determination that the designated

State unit is able to provide the full range of vocational rehabilitation services to all eligible individuals in the next fiscal year must be based on—

(i) A demonstration that circumstances have changed that will allow the designated State unit to meet the requirements of paragraph (a)(2) of this section in the next fiscal year, including—

(A) An estimate of the number of and projected costs of serving, in the next fiscal year, individuals with existing individualized plans for employment;

(B) The projected number of individuals with disabilities who will apply for services and will be determined eligible in the next fiscal year and the projected costs of serving those individuals;

(C) The projected costs of administering the program in the next fiscal year, including, but not limited to, costs of staff salaries and benefits, outreach activities, and required statewide studies; and

(D) The projected revenues and projected number of qualified personnel for the program in the next fiscal year.

(ii) Comparable data, as relevant, for the current or preceding fiscal year, or for both years, of the costs listed in paragraphs (b)(2)(i)(A) through (C) of this section and the resources identified in paragraph (b)(2)(i)(D) of this section and an explanation of any projected increases or decreases in these costs and resources; and

(iii) A determination that the projected revenues and the projected number of qualified personnel for the program in the next fiscal year are adequate to cover the costs identified in paragraphs (b)(2)(i)(A) through (C) of this section to ensure the provision of the full range of services, as appropriate, to all eligible individuals.

(c) *Determining need for establishing and implementing an order of selection.* (1) The designated State unit must determine, prior to the beginning of each fiscal year, whether to establish and implement an order of selection.

(2) If the designated State unit determines that it does not need to establish an order of selection, it must reevaluate this determination whenever changed circumstances during the

course of a fiscal year, such as a decrease in its fiscal or personnel resources or an increase in its program costs, indicate that it may no longer be able to provide the full range of services, as appropriate, to all eligible individuals, as described in paragraph (a)(2) of this section.

(3) If a designated State unit establishes an order of selection, but determines that it does not need to implement that order at the beginning of the fiscal year, it must continue to meet the requirements of paragraph (a)(2) of this section, or it must implement the order of selection by closing one or more priority categories.

(d) *Establishing an order of selection—* (1) *Basis for order of selection.* An order of selection must be based on a refinement of the three criteria in the definition of *individual with a significant disability* in section 7(21)(A) of the Act and §361.5(c)(30).

(2) *Factors that cannot be used in determining order of selection of eligible individuals.* An order of selection may not be based on any other factors, including—

(i) Any duration of residency requirement, provided the individual is present in the State;

(ii) Type of disability;

(iii) Age, sex, race, color, or national origin;

(iv) Source of referral;

(v) Type of expected employment outcome;

(vi) The need for specific services except those services provided in accordance with 361.36(a)(3)(v), or anticipated cost of services required by an individual; or

(vii) The income level of an individual or an individual's family.

(e) *Administrative requirements.* In administering the order of selection, the designated State unit must—

(1) Implement the order of selection on a statewide basis;

(2) Notify all eligible individuals of the priority categories in a State's order of selection, their assignment to a particular category, and their right to appeal their category assignment;

(3) Continue to provide services to any recipient who has begun to receive services irrespective of the severity of the individual's disability as follows—

(i) The designated State unit must continue to provide pre-employment transition services to students with disabilities who were receiving such services prior to being determined eligible for vocational rehabilitation services; and

(ii) The designated State unit must continue to provide to an eligible individual all needed services listed on the individualized plan for employment if the individual had begun receiving such services prior to the effective date of the State's order of selection; and

(4) Ensure that its funding arrangements for providing services under the vocational rehabilitation services portion of the Unified or Combined State Plan, including third-party arrangements and awards under the establishment authority, are consistent with the order of selection. If any funding arrangements are inconsistent with the order of selection, the designated State unit must renegotiate these funding arrangements so that they are consistent with the order of selection.

(f) *State Rehabilitation Council.* The designated State unit must consult with the State Rehabilitation Council, if the State unit has a Council, regarding the—

(1) Need to establish an order of selection, including any reevaluation of the need under paragraph (c)(2) of this section;

(2) Priority categories of the particular order of selection;

(3) Criteria for determining individuals with the most significant disabilities; and

(4) Administration of the order of selection.

(Approved by the Office of Management and Budget under control number 1205–0522)

(Authority: Sections 12(d); 101(a)(5); 101(a)(12); 101(a)(15)(A), (B) and (C); 101(a)(21)(A)(ii); and 504(a) of the Rehabilitation Act of 1973, as amended; 29 U.S.C. 709(d), 721(a)(5), 721(a)(12), 721(a)(15)(A), (B) and (C); 721(a)(21)(A)(ii), and 794(a))

§361.37 Information and referral programs.

(a) *General provisions.* The vocational rehabilitation services portion of the Unified or Combined State Plan must assure that—

(1) The designated State agency will implement an information and referral system adequate to ensure that individuals with disabilities, including eligible individuals who do not meet the agency's order of selection criteria for receiving vocational rehabilitation services if the agency is operating on an order of selection, are provided accurate vocational rehabilitation information and guidance (which may include counseling and referral for job placement) using appropriate modes of communication to assist them in preparing for, securing, retaining, advancing in, or regaining employment; and

(2) The designated State agency will refer individuals with disabilities to other appropriate Federal and State programs, including other components of the statewide workforce development system.

(b) The designated State unit must refer to appropriate programs and service providers best suited to address the specific rehabilitation, independent living and employment needs of an individual with a disability who makes an informed choice not to pursue an employment outcome under the vocational rehabilitation program, as defined in § 361.5(c)(15). Before making the referral required by this paragraph, the State unit must—

(1) Consistent with § 361.42(a)(4)(i), explain to the individual that the purpose of the vocational rehabilitation program is to assist individuals to achieve an employment outcome as defined in § 361.5(c)(15);

(2) Consistent with § 361.52, provide the individual with information concerning the availability of employment options, and of vocational rehabilitation services, to assist the individual to achieve an appropriate employment outcome;

(3) Inform the individual that services under the vocational rehabilitation program can be provided to eligible individuals in an extended employment setting if necessary for purposes of training or otherwise preparing for employment in an integrated setting;

(4) Inform the individual that, if he or she initially chooses not to pursue an employment outcome as defined in § 361.5(c)(15), he or she can seek services from the designated State unit at a later date if, at that time, he or she chooses to pursue an employment outcome; and

(5) Refer the individual, as appropriate, to the Social Security Administration in order to obtain information concerning the ability of individuals with disabilities to work while receiving benefits from the Social Security Administration.

(c) *Criteria for appropriate referrals.* In making the referrals identified in paragraph (a)(2) of this section, the designated State unit must—

(1) Refer the individual to Federal or State programs, including programs carried out by other components of the statewide workforce development system, best suited to address the specific employment needs of an individual with a disability; and

(2) Provide the individual who is being referred—

(i) A notice of the referral by the designated State agency to the agency carrying out the program;

(ii) Information identifying a specific point of contact within the agency to which the individual is being referred; and

(iii) Information and advice regarding the most suitable services to assist the individual to prepare for, secure, retain, or regain employment.

(d) *Order of selection.* In providing the information and referral services under this section to eligible individuals who are not in the priority category or categories to receive vocational rehabilitation services under the State's order of selection, the State unit must identify, as part of its reporting under section 101(a)(10) of the Act and § 361.40, the number of eligible individuals who did not meet the agency's order of selection criteria for receiving vocational rehabilitation services and did receive information and referral services under this section.

(Approved by the Office of Management and Budget under control number 1205–0522)

(Authority: Sections 7(11), 12(c), 101(a)(5)(E), 101(a)(10)(C)(ii), and 101(a)(20) of the Rehabilitation Act of 1973, as amended; 29 U.S.C. 705(11), 709(c), 721(a)(5)(E), 721(a)(10)(C)(ii), and 721(a)(20))

§361.38 Protection, use, and release of personal information.

(a) *General provisions.* (1) The State agency and the State unit must adopt and implement written policies and procedures to safeguard the confidentiality of all personal information, including photographs and lists of names. These policies and procedures must ensure that—

(i) Specific safeguards are established to protect current and stored personal information, including a requirement that data only be released when governed by a written agreement between the designated State unit and receiving entity under paragraphs (d) and (e)(1) of this section, which addresses the requirements in this section;

(ii) All applicants and recipients of services and, as appropriate, those individuals' representatives, service providers, cooperating agencies, and interested persons are informed through appropriate modes of communication of the confidentiality of personal information and the conditions for accessing and releasing this information;

(iii) All applicants and recipients of services or their representatives are informed about the State unit's need to collect personal information and the policies governing its use, including—

(A) Identification of the authority under which information is collected;

(B) Explanation of the principal purposes for which the State unit intends to use or release the information;

(C) Explanation of whether providing requested information to the State unit is mandatory or voluntary and the effects of not providing requested information;

(D) Identification of those situations in which the State unit requires or does not require informed written consent of the individual before information may be released; and

(E) Identification of other agencies to which information is routinely released;

(iv) An explanation of State policies and procedures affecting personal information will be provided to each individual in that individual's native language or through the appropriate mode of communication; and

(v) These policies and procedures provide no fewer protections for individuals than State laws and regulations.

(2) The State unit may establish reasonable fees to cover extraordinary costs of duplicating records or making extensive searches and must establish policies and procedures governing access to records.

(b) *State program use.* All personal information in the possession of the State agency or the designated State unit must be used only for the purposes directly connected with the administration of the vocational rehabilitation program. Information containing identifiable personal information may not be shared with advisory or other bodies that do not have official responsibility for administration of the program. In the administration of the program, the State unit may obtain personal information from service providers and cooperating agencies under assurances that the information may not be further divulged, except as provided under paragraphs (c), (d), and (e) of this section.

(c) *Release to applicants and recipients of services.* (1) Except as provided in paragraphs (c)(2) and (3) of this section, if requested in writing by an applicant or recipient of services, the State unit must make all requested information in that individual's record of services accessible to and must release the information to the individual or the individual's representative in a timely manner.

(2) Medical, psychological, or other information that the State unit determines may be harmful to the individual may not be released directly to the individual, but must be provided to the individual through a third party chosen by the individual, which may include, among others, an advocate, a family member, or a qualified medical or mental health professional, unless a representative has been appointed by a court to represent the individual, in which case the information must be released to the court-appointed representative.

(3) If personal information has been obtained from another agency or organization, it may be released only by, or under the conditions established by, the other agency or organization.

(4) An applicant or recipient of services who believes that information in the individual's record of services is inaccurate or misleading may request that the designated State unit amend the information. If the information is not amended, the request for an amendment must be documented in the record of services, consistent with § 361.47(a)(12).

(d) *Release for audit, evaluation, and research.* Personal information may be released to an organization, agency, or individual engaged in audit, evaluation, or research only for purposes directly connected with the administration of the vocational rehabilitation program or for purposes that would significantly improve the quality of life for applicants and recipients of services and only if, in accordance with a written agreement, the organization, agency, or individual assures that—

(1) The information will be used only for the purposes for which it is being provided;

(2) The information will be released only to persons officially connected with the audit, evaluation, or research;

(3) The information will not be released to the involved individual;

(4) The information will be managed in a manner to safeguard confidentiality; and

(5) The final product will not reveal any personal identifying information without the informed written consent of the involved individual or the individual's representative.

(e) *Release to other programs or authorities.* (1) Upon receiving the informed written consent of the individual or, if appropriate, the individual's representative, the State unit may release personal information to another agency or organization, in accordance with a written agreement, for its program purposes only to the extent that the information may be released to the involved individual or the individual's representative and only to the extent that the other agency or organization demonstrates that the information requested is necessary for its program.

(2) Medical or psychological information that the State unit determines may be harmful to the individual may be released if the other agency or organization assures the State unit that the information will be used only for the purpose for which it is being provided and will not be further released to the individual.

(3) The State unit must release personal information if required by Federal law or regulations.

(4) The State unit must release personal information in response to investigations in connection with law enforcement, fraud, or abuse, unless expressly prohibited by Federal or State laws or regulations, and in response to an order issued by a judge, magistrate, or other authorized judicial officer.

(5) The State unit also may release personal information in order to protect the individual or others if the individual poses a threat to his or her safety or to the safety of others.

(Authority: Sections 12(c) and 101(a)(6)(A) of the Rehabilitation Act of 1973, as amended; 29 U.S.C. 709(c) and 721(a)(6)(A))

§ 361.39 State-imposed requirements.

The designated State unit must, upon request, identify those regulations and policies relating to the administration or operation of its vocational rehabilitation program that are State-imposed, including any regulations or policy based on State interpretation of any Federal law, regulation, or guideline.

(Authority: Section 17 of the Rehabilitation Act of 1973, as amended; 29 U.S.C. 714)

§ 361.40 Reports; Evaluation standards and performance indicators.

(a) *Reports.* (1) The vocational rehabilitation services portion of the Unified or Combined State Plan must assure that the designated State agency will submit reports, including reports required under sections 13, 14, and 101(a)(10) of the Act—

(i) In the form and level of detail and at the time required by the Secretary regarding applicants for and eligible individuals receiving services, including students receiving pre-employment transition services in accordance with § 361.48(a); and

(ii) In a manner that provides a complete count (other than the information obtained through sampling consistent with section 101(a)(10)(E) of the

Act) of the applicants and eligible individuals to—

(A) Permit the greatest possible cross-classification of data; and

(B) Protect the confidentiality of the identity of each individual.

(2) The designated State agency must comply with any requirements necessary to ensure the accuracy and verification of those reports.

(b) *Evaluation standards and performance indicators*—(1) *Standards and indicators.* The evaluation standards and performance indicators for the vocational rehabilitation program carried out under this part are subject to the performance accountability provisions described in section 116(b) of the Workforce Innovation and Opportunity Act and implemented in regulations set forth in subpart E of this part.

(2) *Compliance.* A State's compliance with common performance measures and any necessary corrective actions will be determined in accordance with regulations set forth in subpart E of this part.

(Approved by the Office of Management and Budget under control number 1205–0522)

(Authority: Sections 12(c), 101(a)(10)(A) and (F), and 106 of the Rehabilitation Act of 1973, as amended; 29 U.S.C. 709(c),721(a)(10)(A) and (F), and 726)

[81 FR 55741, Aug. 19, 2016, as amended at 81 FR 55780, Aug. 19, 2016]

PROVISION AND SCOPE OF SERVICES

§361.41 **Processing referrals and applications.**

(a) *Referrals.* The designated State unit must establish and implement standards for the prompt and equitable handling of referrals of individuals for vocational rehabilitation services, including referrals of individuals made through the one-stop service delivery systems under section 121 of the Workforce Innovation and Opportunity Act. The standards must include timelines for making good faith efforts to inform these individuals of application requirements and to gather information necessary to initiate an assessment for determining eligibility and priority for services.

(b) *Applications.* (1) Once an individual has submitted an application for vocational rehabilitation services, in-

cluding applications made through common intake procedures in one-stop centers under section 121 of the Workforce Innovation and Opportunity Act, an eligibility determination must be made within 60 days, unless—

(i) Exceptional and unforeseen circumstances beyond the control of the designated State unit preclude making an eligibility determination within 60 days and the designated State unit and the individual agree to a specific extension of time; or

(ii) An exploration of the individual's abilities, capabilities, and capacity to perform in work situations is carried out in accordance with §361.42(e).

(2) An individual is considered to have submitted an application when the individual or the individual's representative, as appropriate—

(i)(A) Has completed and signed an agency application form;

(B) Has completed a common intake application form in a one-stop center requesting vocational rehabilitation services; or

(C) Has otherwise requested services from the designated State unit;

(ii) Has provided to the designated State unit information necessary to initiate an assessment to determine eligibility and priority for services; and

(iii) Is available to complete the assessment process.

(3) The designated State unit must ensure that its application forms are widely available throughout the State, particularly in the one-stop centers under section 121 of the Workforce Innovation and Opportunity Act.

(Authority: Sections 12(c), 101(a)(6)(A), and 102(a)(6) of the Rehabilitation Act of 1973, as amended; 29 U.S.C. 709(c), 721(a)(6)(A), and 722(a)(6))

§361.42 **Assessment for determining eligibility and priority for services.**

In order to determine whether an individual is eligible for vocational rehabilitation services and the individual's priority under an order of selection for services (if the State is operating under an order of selection), the designated State unit must conduct an assessment for determining eligibility and priority for services. The assessment must be conducted in the most integrated setting possible, consistent with the individual's needs and informed choice, and in accordance with the following provisions:

(a) *Eligibility requirements*—(1) *Basic requirements.* The designated State unit's determination of an applicant's eligibility for vocational rehabilitation services must be based only on the following requirements:

(i) A determination by qualified personnel that the applicant has a physical or mental impairment;

(ii) A determination by qualified personnel that the applicant's physical or mental impairment constitutes or results in a substantial impediment to employment for the applicant; and

(iii) A determination by a qualified vocational rehabilitation counselor employed by the designated State unit that the applicant requires vocational rehabilitation services to prepare for, secure, retain, advance in, or regain employment that is consistent with the individual's unique strengths, resources, priorities, concerns, abilities, capabilities, interest, and informed choice. For purposes of an assessment for determining eligibility and vocational rehabilitation needs under this part, an individual is presumed to have a goal of an employment outcome.

(2) *Presumption of benefit.* The designated State unit must presume that an applicant who meets the eligibility requirements in paragraphs (a)(1)(i) and (ii) of this section can benefit in terms of an employment outcome.

(3) *Presumption of eligibility for Social Security recipients and beneficiaries.* (i) Any applicant who has been determined eligible for Social Security benefits under title II or title XVI of the Social Security Act is—

(A) Presumed eligible for vocational rehabilitation services under paragraphs (a)(1) and (2) of this section; and

(B) Considered an individual with a significant disability as defined in § 361.5(c)(29).

(ii) If an applicant for vocational rehabilitation services asserts that he or she is eligible for Social Security benefits under title II or title XVI of the Social Security Act (and, therefore, is presumed eligible for vocational rehabilitation services under paragraph

(a)(3)(i)(A) of this section), but is unable to provide appropriate evidence, such as an award letter, to support that assertion, the State unit must verify the applicant's eligibility under title II or title XVI of the Social Security Act by contacting the Social Security Administration. This verification must be made within a reasonable period of time that enables the State unit to determine the applicant's eligibility for vocational rehabilitation services within 60 days of the individual submitting an application for services in accordance with § 361.41(b)(2).

(4) *Achievement of an employment outcome.* Any eligible individual, including an individual whose eligibility for vocational rehabilitation services is based on the individual being eligible for Social Security benefits under title II or title XVI of the Social Security Act, must intend to achieve an employment outcome that is consistent with the applicant's unique strengths, resources, priorities, concerns, abilities, capabilities, interests, and informed choice.

(i) The State unit is responsible for informing individuals, through its application process for vocational rehabilitation services, that individuals who receive services under the program must intend to achieve an employment outcome.

(ii) The applicant's completion of the application process for vocational rehabilitation services is sufficient evidence of the individual's intent to achieve an employment outcome, and no additional demonstration on the part of the applicant is required for purposes of satisfying paragraph (a)(4) of this section.

(5) *Interpretation.* Nothing in this section, including paragraph (a)(3)(i), is to be construed to create an entitlement to any vocational rehabilitation service.

(b) *Interim determination of eligibility.* (1) The designated State unit may initiate the provision of vocational rehabilitation services for an applicant on the basis of an interim determination of eligibility prior to the 60-day period described in § 361.41(b)(2).

(2) If a State chooses to make interim determinations of eligibility, the designated State unit must—

(i) Establish criteria and conditions for making those determinations;

(ii) Develop and implement procedures for making the determinations; and

(iii) Determine the scope of services that may be provided pending the final determination of eligibility.

(3) If a State elects to use an interim eligibility determination, the designated State unit must make a final determination of eligibility within 60 days of the individual submitting an application for services in accordance with §361.41(b)(2).

(c) *Prohibited factors.* (1) The vocational rehabilitation services portion of the Unified or Combined State Plan must assure that the State unit will not impose, as part of determining eligibility under this section, a duration of residence requirement that excludes from services any applicant who is present in the State. The designated State unit may not require the applicant to demonstrate a presence in the State through the production of any documentation that under State or local law, or practical circumstances, results in a de facto duration of residence requirement.

(2) In making a determination of eligibility under this section, the designated State unit also must ensure that—

(i) No applicant or group of applicants is excluded or found ineligible solely on the basis of the type of disability; and

(ii) The eligibility requirements are applied without regard to the—

(A) Age, sex, race, color, or national origin of the applicant;

(B) Type of expected employment outcome;

(C) Source of referral for vocational rehabilitation services;

(D) Particular service needs or anticipated cost of services required by an applicant or the income level of an applicant or applicant's family;

(E) Applicants' employment history or current employment status; and

(F) Applicants' educational status or current educational credential.

(d) *Review and assessment of data for eligibility determination.* Except as provided in paragraph (e) of this section, the designated State unit—

(1) Must base its determination of each of the basic eligibility requirements in paragraph (a) of this section on—

(i) A review and assessment of existing data, including counselor observations, education records, information provided by the individual or the individual's family, particularly information used by education officials, and determinations made by officials of other agencies; and

(ii) To the extent existing data do not describe the current functioning of the individual or are unavailable, insufficient, or inappropriate to make an eligibility determination, an assessment of additional data resulting from the provision of vocational rehabilitation services, including trial work experiences, assistive technology devices and services, personal assistance services, and any other support services that are necessary to determine whether an individual is eligible; and

(2) Must base its presumption under paragraph (a)(3)(i) of this section that an applicant who has been determined eligible for Social Security benefits under title II or title XVI of the Social Security Act satisfies each of the basic eligibility requirements in paragraph (a) of this section on determinations made by the Social Security Administration.

(e) *Trial work experiences for individuals with significant disabilities.* (1) Prior to any determination that an individual with a disability is unable to benefit from vocational rehabilitation services in terms of an employment outcome because of the severity of that individual's disability or that the individual is ineligible for vocational rehabilitation services, the designated State unit must conduct an exploration of the individual's abilities, capabilities, and capacity to perform in realistic work situations.

(2)(i) The designated State unit must develop a written plan to assess periodically the individual's abilities, capabilities, and capacity to perform in competitive integrated work situations through the use of trial work experiences, which must be provided in competitive integrated employment settings to the maximum extent possible, consistent with the informed choice and rehabilitation needs of the individual.

(ii) Trial work experiences include supported employment, on-the-job training, and other experiences using realistic integrated work settings.

(iii) Trial work experiences must be of sufficient variety and over a sufficient period of time for the designated State unit to determine that—

(A) There is sufficient evidence to conclude that the individual can benefit from the provision of vocational rehabilitation services in terms of an employment outcome; or

(B) There is clear and convincing evidence that due to the severity of the individual's disability, the individual is incapable of benefitting from the provision of vocational rehabilitation services in terms of an employment outcome; and

(iv) The designated State unit must provide appropriate supports, including, but not limited to, assistive technology devices and services and personal assistance services, to accommodate the rehabilitation needs of the individual during the trial work experiences.

(f) *Data for determination of priority for services under an order of selection.* If the designated State unit is operating under an order of selection for services, as provided in § 361.36, the State unit must base its priority assignments on—

(1) A review of the data that was developed under paragraphs (d) and (e) of this section to make the eligibility determination; and

(2) An assessment of additional data, to the extent necessary.

(Authority: Sections 7(2), 12(c), 101(a)(12), 102(a), 103(a)(1), 103(a)(9), 103(a)(10), and 103(a)(14) of the Rehabilitation Act of 1973, as amended; 29 U.S.C. 705(2), 709(c), 721(a)(12), 722(a), 723(a)(1), 723(a)(9), 723(a)(10), and 723(a)(14))

NOTE TO § 361.42: *Clear and convincing evidence* means that the designated State unit has a high degree of certainty before it can conclude that an individual is incapable of benefiting from services in terms of an employment outcome. The clear and convincing standard constitutes the highest standard used in our civil system of law and is to be individually applied on a case-by-case basis. The term *clear* means unequivocal. For example, the use of an intelligence test result

alone would not constitute clear and convincing evidence. Clear and convincing evidence might include a description of assessments, including situational assessments and supported employment assessments, from service providers who have concluded that they would be unable to meet the individual's needs due to the severity of the individual's disability. The demonstration of "clear and convincing evidence" must include, if appropriate, a functional assessment of skill development activities, with any necessary supports (including assistive technology), in real life settings. (S. Rep. No. 357, 102d Cong., 2d. Sess. 37–38 (1992))

§ 361.43 Procedures for ineligibility determination.

If the State unit determines that an applicant is ineligible for vocational rehabilitation services or determines that an individual receiving services under an individualized plan for employment is no longer eligible for services, the State unit must—

(a) Make the determination only after providing an opportunity for full consultation with the individual or, as appropriate, with the individual's representative;

(b) Inform the individual in writing, supplemented as necessary by other appropriate modes of communication consistent with the informed choice of the individual, of the ineligibility determination, including the reasons for that determination, the requirements under this section, and the means by which the individual may express and seek remedy for any dissatisfaction, including the procedures for review of State unit personnel determinations in accordance with § 361.57;

(c) Provide the individual with a description of services available from a client assistance program established under 34 CFR part 370 and information on how to contact that program;

(d) Refer the individual—

(1) To other programs that are part of the one-stop service delivery system under the Workforce Innovation and Opportunity Act that can address the individual's training or employment-related needs; or

(2) To Federal, State, or local programs or service providers, including,

as appropriate, independent living programs and extended employment providers, best suited to meet their rehabilitation needs, if the ineligibility determination is based on a finding that the individual has chosen not to pursue, or is incapable of achieving, an employment outcome as defined in §361.5(c)(15).

(e) Review within 12 months and annually thereafter if requested by the individual or, if appropriate, by the individual's representative any ineligibility determination that is based on a finding that the individual is incapable of achieving an employment outcome. This review need not be conducted in situations in which the individual has refused it, the individual is no longer present in the State, the individual's whereabouts are unknown, or the individual's medical condition is rapidly progressive or terminal.

(Authority: Sections 12(c) and 102(a)(5) and (c) of the Rehabilitation Act of 1973, as amended; 29 U.S.C. 709(c) and 722(a)(5)and (c))

§361.44 Closure without eligibility determination.

The designated State unit may not close an applicant's record of services prior to making an eligibility determination unless the applicant declines to participate in, or is unavailable to complete, an assessment for determining eligibility and priority for services, and the State unit has made a reasonable number of attempts to contact the applicant or, if appropriate, the applicant's representative to encourage the applicant's participation.

(Authority: Section 12(c) of the Rehabilitation Act of 1973, as amended; 29 U.S.C. 709(c))

§361.45 Development of the individualized plan for employment.

(a) *General requirements.* The vocational rehabilitation services portion of the Unified or Combined State Plan must assure that—

(1) An individualized plan for employment meeting the requirements of this section and §361.46 is developed and implemented in a timely manner for each individual determined to be eligible for vocational rehabilitation services or, if the designated State unit is operating under an order of selection in accordance with §361.36, for each eligible individual to whom the State unit is able to provide services; and

(2) Services will be provided in accordance with the provisions of the individualized plan for employment.

(b) *Purpose.* (1) The designated State unit must conduct an assessment for determining vocational rehabilitation needs, if appropriate, for each eligible individual or, if the State is operating under an order of selection, for each eligible individual to whom the State is able to provide services. The purpose of this assessment is to determine the employment outcome, and the nature and scope of vocational rehabilitation services to be included in the individualized plan for employment.

(2) The individualized plan for employment must be designed to achieve a specific employment outcome, as defined in §361.5(c)(15), that is selected by the individual consistent with the individual's unique strengths, resources, priorities, concerns, abilities, capabilities, interests, and informed choice.

(c) *Required information.* The State unit must provide the following information to each eligible individual or, as appropriate, the individual's representative, in writing and, if appropriate, in the native language or mode of communication of the individual or the individual's representative:

(1) *Options for developing an individualized plan for employment.* Information on the available options for developing the individualized plan for employment, including the option that an eligible individual or, as appropriate, the individual's representative may develop all or part of the individualized plan for employment—

(i) Without assistance from the State unit or other entity; or

(ii) With assistance from—

(A) A qualified vocational rehabilitation counselor employed by the State unit;

(B) A qualified vocational rehabilitation counselor who is not employed by the State unit;

(C) A disability advocacy organization; or

(D) Resources other than those in paragraph (c)(1)(ii)(A) through (C) of this section.

(2) *Additional information.* Additional information to assist the eligible individual or, as appropriate, the individual's representative in developing the individualized plan for employment, including—

(i) Information describing the full range of components that must be included in an individualized plan for employment;

(ii) As appropriate to each eligible individual—

(A) An explanation of agency guidelines and criteria for determining an eligible individual's financial commitments under an individualized plan for employment;

(B) Information on the availability of assistance in completing State unit forms required as part of the individualized plan for employment; and

(C) Additional information that the eligible individual requests or the State unit determines to be necessary to the development of the individualized plan for employment;

(iii) A description of the rights and remedies available to the individual, including, if appropriate, recourse to the processes described in § 361.57; and

(iv) A description of the availability of a client assistance program established under part 370 of this chapter and information on how to contact the client assistance program.

(3) *Individuals entitled to benefits under title II or XVI of the Social Security Act.* For individuals entitled to benefits under title II or XVI of the Social Security Act on the basis of a disability or blindness, the State unit must provide to the individual general information on additional supports and assistance for individuals with disabilities desiring to enter the workforce, including assistance with benefits planning.

(d) *Mandatory procedures.* The designated State unit must ensure that—

(1) The individualized plan for employment is a written document prepared on forms provided by the State unit;

(2) The individualized plan for employment is developed and implemented in a manner that gives eligible individuals the opportunity to exercise informed choice, consistent with § 361.52, in selecting—

(i) The employment outcome, including the employment setting;

(ii) The specific vocational rehabilitation services needed to achieve the employment outcome, including the settings in which services will be provided;

(iii) The entity or entities that will provide the vocational rehabilitation services; and

(iv) The methods available for procuring the services;

(3) The individualized plan for employment is—

(i) Agreed to and signed by the eligible individual or, as appropriate, the individual's representative; and

(ii) Approved and signed by a qualified vocational rehabilitation counselor employed by the designated State unit;

(4) A copy of the individualized plan for employment and a copy of any amendments to the individualized plan for employment are provided to the eligible individual or, as appropriate, to the individual's representative, in writing and, if appropriate, in the native language or mode of communication of the individual or, as appropriate, the individual's representative;

(5) The individualized plan for employment is reviewed at least annually by a qualified vocational rehabilitation counselor and the eligible individual or, as appropriate, the individual's representative to assess the eligible individual's progress in achieving the identified employment outcome;

(6) The individualized plan for employment is amended, as necessary, by the individual or, as appropriate, the individual's representative, in collaboration with a representative of the State unit or a qualified vocational rehabilitation counselor (to the extent determined to be appropriate by the individual), if there are substantive changes in the employment outcome, the vocational rehabilitation services to be provided, or the providers of the vocational rehabilitation services;

(7) Amendments to the individualized plan for employment do not take effect until agreed to and signed by the eligible individual or, as appropriate, the individual's representative and by a qualified vocational rehabilitation

counselor employed by the designated State unit;

(8) The individualized plan for employment is amended, as necessary, to include the postemployment services and service providers that are necessary for the individual to maintain, advance in or regain employment, consistent with the individual's unique strengths, resources, priorities, concerns, abilities, capabilities, interests, and informed choice; and

(9) An individualized plan for employment for a student with a disability is developed—

(i) In consideration of the student's individualized education program or 504 services, as applicable; and

(ii) In accordance with the plans, policies, procedures, and terms of the interagency agreement required under § 361.22.

(e) *Standards for developing the individualized plan for employment.* The individualized plan for employment must be developed as soon as possible, but not later than 90 days after the date of determination of eligibility, unless the State unit and the eligible individual agree to the extension of that deadline to a specific date by which the individualized plan for employment must be completed.

(f) *Data for preparing the individualized plan for employment.* (1) *Preparation without comprehensive assessment.* To the extent possible, the employment outcome and the nature and scope of rehabilitation services to be included in the individual's individualized plan for employment must be determined based on the data used for the assessment of eligibility and priority for services under § 361.42.

(2) *Preparation based on comprehensive assessment.*

(i) If additional data are necessary to determine the employment outcome and the nature and scope of services to be included in the individualized plan for employment of an eligible individual, the State unit must conduct a comprehensive assessment of the unique strengths, resources, priorities, concerns, abilities, capabilities, interests, and informed choice, including the need for supported employment services, of the eligible individual, in the most integrated setting possible,

consistent with the informed choice of the individual in accordance with the provisions of § 361.5(c)(5)(ii).

(ii) In preparing the comprehensive assessment, the State unit must use, to the maximum extent possible and appropriate and in accordance with confidentiality requirements, existing information that is current as of the date of the development of the individualized plan for employment, including information—

(A) Available from other programs and providers, particularly information used by education officials and the Social Security Administration;

(B) Provided by the individual and the individual's family; and

(C) Obtained under the assessment for determining the individual's eligibility and vocational rehabilitation needs.

(Authority: Sections 7(2)(B), 101(a)(9), 102(b), and 103(a)(1) of the Rehabilitation Act of 1973, as amended; 29 U.S.C. 705(2)(B), 721(a)(9), 722(b), and 723(a)(1))

§ 361.46 Content of the individualized plan for employment.

(a) *Mandatory components.* Regardless of the approach in § 361.45(c)(1) that an eligible individual selects for purposes of developing the individualized plan for employment, each individualized plan for employment must—

(1) Include a description of the specific employment outcome, as defined in § 361.5(c)(15), that is chosen by the eligible individual and is consistent with the individual's unique strengths, resources, priorities, concerns, abilities, capabilities, career interests, and informed choice consistent with the general goal of competitive integrated employment (except that in the case of an eligible individual who is a student or a youth with a disability, the description may be a description of the individual's projected post-school employment outcome);

(2) Include a description under § 361.48 of—

(i) These specific rehabilitation services needed to achieve the employment outcome, including, as appropriate, the provision of assistive technology devices, assistive technology services,

331

and personal assistance services, including training in the management of those services; and

(ii) In the case of a plan for an eligible individual that is a student or youth with a disability, the specific transition services and supports needed to achieve the individual's employment outcome or projected post-school employment outcome.

(3) Provide for services in the most integrated setting that is appropriate for the services involved and is consistent with the informed choice of the eligible individual;

(4) Include timelines for the achievement of the employment outcome and for the initiation of services;

(5) Include a description of the entity or entities chosen by the eligible individual or, as appropriate, the individual's representative that will provide the vocational rehabilitation services and the methods used to procure those services;

(6) Include a description of the criteria that will be used to evaluate progress toward achievement of the employment outcome; and

(7) Include the terms and conditions of the individualized plan for employment, including, as appropriate, information describing—

(i) The responsibilities of the designated State unit;

(ii) The responsibilities of the eligible individual, including—

(A) The responsibilities the individual will assume in relation to achieving the employment outcome;

(B) If applicable, the extent of the individual's participation in paying for the cost of services; and

(C) The responsibility of the individual with regard to applying for and securing comparable services and benefits as described in § 361.53; and

(iii) The responsibilities of other entities as the result of arrangements made pursuant to the comparable services or benefits requirements in § 361.53.

(b) *Supported employment requirements.* An individualized plan for employment for an individual with a most significant disability for whom an employment outcome in a supported employment setting has been determined to be appropriate must—

(1) Specify the supported employment services to be provided by the designated State unit;

(2) Specify the expected extended services needed, which may include natural supports;

(3) Identify the source of extended services or, to the extent that it is not possible to identify the source of extended services at the time the individualized plan for employment is developed, include a description of the basis for concluding that there is a reasonable expectation that those sources will become available;

(4) Provide for periodic monitoring to ensure that the individual is making satisfactory progress toward meeting the weekly work requirement established in the individualized plan for employment by the time of transition to extended services;

(5) Provide for the coordination of services provided under an individualized plan for employment with services provided under other individualized plans established under other Federal or State programs;

(6) To the extent that job skills training is provided, identify that the training will be provided on site; and

(7) Include placement in an integrated setting for the maximum number of hours possible based on the unique strengths, resources, priorities, concerns, abilities, capabilities, interests, and informed choice of individuals with the most significant disabilities.

(c) *Post-employment services.* The individualized plan for employment for each individual must contain, as determined to be necessary, statements concerning—

(1) The expected need for post-employment services prior to closing the record of services of an individual who has achieved an employment outcome;

(2) A description of the terms and conditions for the provision of any post-employment services; and

(3) If appropriate, a statement of how post-employment services will be provided or arranged through other entities as the result of arrangements made pursuant to the comparable services or benefits requirements in § 361.53.

(d) *Coordination of services for students with disabilities.* The individualized plan for employment for a student with a disability must be coordinated with the individualized education program or 504 services, as applicable, for that individual in terms of the goals, objectives, and services identified in the education program.

(Approved by the Office of Management and Budget under control number 1205–0522)

(Authority: Sections 101(a)(8), 101(a)(9), and 102(b)(4) of the Rehabilitation Act of 1973, as amended; 29 U.S.C. 721(a)(8), 721(a)(9), and 722(b)(4))

§361.47 Record of services.

(a) The designated State unit must maintain for each applicant and eligible individual a record of services that includes, to the extent pertinent, the following documentation:

(1) If an applicant has been determined to be an eligible individual, documentation supporting that determination in accordance with the requirements under §361.42.

(2) If an applicant or eligible individual receiving services under an individualized plan for employment has been determined to be ineligible, documentation supporting that determination in accordance with the requirements under §361.43.

(3) Documentation that describes the justification for closing an applicant's or eligible individual's record of services if that closure is based on reasons other than ineligibility, including, as appropriate, documentation indicating that the State unit has satisfied the requirements in §361.44.

(4) If an individual has been determined to be an individual with a significant disability or an individual with a most significant disability, documentation supporting that determination.

(5) If an individual with a significant disability requires an exploration of abilities, capabilities, and capacity to perform in realistic work situations through the use of trial work experiences to determine whether the individual is an eligible individual, documentation supporting the need for, and the plan relating to, that exploration and documentation regarding the periodic assessments carried out during the trial work experiences in accordance with the requirements under §361.42(e).

(6) The individualized plan for employment, and any amendments to the individualized plan for employment, consistent with the requirements under §361.46.

(7) Documentation describing the extent to which the applicant or eligible individual exercised informed choice regarding the provision of assessment services and the extent to which the eligible individual exercised informed choice in the development of the individualized plan for employment with respect to the selection of the specific employment outcome, the specific vocational rehabilitation services needed to achieve the employment outcome, the entity to provide the services, the employment setting, the settings in which the services will be provided, and the methods to procure the services.

(8) In the event that an individual's individualized plan for employment provides for vocational rehabilitation services in a non-integrated setting, a justification to support the need for the non-integrated setting.

(9) In the event that an individual obtains competitive employment, verification that the individual is compensated at or above the minimum wage and that the individual's wage and level of benefits are not less than that customarily paid by the employer for the same or similar work performed by non-disabled individuals in accordance with §361.5(c)(9)(i).

(10) In the event an individual achieves an employment outcome in which the individual is compensated in accordance with section 14(c) of the Fair Labor Standards Act or the designated State unit closes the record of services of an individual in extended employment on the basis that the individual is unable to achieve an employment outcome consistent with §361.5(c)(15) or that an eligible individual through informed choice chooses to remain in extended employment, documentation of the results of the semi-annual and annual reviews required under §361.55, of the individual's input into those reviews, and of the individual's or, if appropriate, the individual's representative's acknowledgment that those reviews were conducted.

(11) Documentation concerning any action or decision resulting from a request by an individual under § 361.57 for a review of determinations made by designated State unit personnel.

(12) In the event that an applicant or eligible individual requests under § 361.38(c)(4) that documentation in the record of services be amended and the documentation is not amended, documentation of the request.

(13) In the event an individual is referred to another program through the State unit's information and referral system under § 361.37, including other components of the statewide workforce development system, documentation on the nature and scope of services provided by the designated State unit to the individual and on the referral itself, consistent with the requirements of § 361.37.

(14) In the event an individual's record of service is closed under § 361.56, documentation that demonstrates the services provided under the individual's individualized plan for employment contributed to the achievement of the employment outcome.

(15) In the event an individual's record of service is closed under § 361.56, documentation verifying that the provisions of § 361.56 have been satisfied.

(b) The State unit, in consultation with the State Rehabilitation Council if the State has a Council, must determine the type of documentation that the State unit must maintain for each applicant and eligible individual in order to meet the requirements in paragraph (a) of this section.

(Authority: Sections 12(c), 101(a)(6), (9), (14), and (20) and 102(a), (b), and (d) of the Rehabilitation Act of 1973, as amended; 29 U.S.C. 709(c), 721(a)(6), (9), (14), and (20), and 722(a), (b), and (d))

§ 361.48 Scope of vocational rehabilitation services for individuals with disabilities.

(a) *Pre-employment transition services.* Each State must ensure that the designated State unit, in collaboration with the local educational agencies involved, provide, or arrange for the provision of, pre-employment transition services for all students with disabilities, as defined in § 361.5(c)(51), in need of such services, without regard to the type of disability, from Federal funds reserved in accordance with § 361.65, and any funds made available from State, local, or private funding sources. Funds reserved and made available may be used for the required, authorized, and pre-employment transition coordination activities under paragraphs (2), (3) and (4) of this section.

(1) *Availability of services.* Pre-employment transition services must be made available Statewide to all students with disabilities, regardless of whether the student has applied or been determined eligible for vocational rehabilitation services.

(2) *Required activities.* The designated State unit must provide the following pre-employment transition services:

(i) Job exploration counseling;

(ii) Work-based learning experiences, which may include in-school or after school opportunities, or experience outside the traditional school setting (including internships), that is provided in an integrated environment in the community to the maximum extent possible;

(iii) Counseling on opportunities for enrollment in comprehensive transition or postsecondary educational programs at institutions of higher education;

(iv) Workplace readiness training to develop social skills and independent living; and

(v) Instruction in self-advocacy (including instruction in person-centered planning), which may include peer mentoring (including peer mentoring from individuals with disabilities working in competitive integrated employment).

(3) *Authorized activities.* Funds available and remaining after the provision of the required activities described in paragraph (a)(2) of this section may be used to improve the transition of students with disabilities from school to postsecondary education or an employment outcome by—

(i) Implementing effective strategies to increase the likelihood of independent living and inclusion in communities and competitive integrated workplaces;

(ii) Developing and improving strategies for individuals with intellectual disabilities and individuals with significant disabilities to live independently; participate in postsecondary education experiences; and obtain, advance in and retain competitive integrated employment;

(iii) Providing instruction to vocational rehabilitation counselors, school transition personnel, and other persons supporting students with disabilities;

(iv) Disseminating information about innovative, effective, and efficient approaches to achieve the goals of this section;

(v) Coordinating activities with transition services provided by local educational agencies under the Individuals with Disabilities Education Act (20 U.S.C. 1400 et seq.);

(vi) Applying evidence-based findings to improve policy, procedure, practice, and the preparation of personnel, in order to better achieve the goals of this section;

(vii) Developing model transition demonstration projects;

(viii) Establishing or supporting multistate or regional partnerships involving States, local educational agencies, designated State units, developmental disability agencies, private businesses, or other participants to achieve the goals of this section; and

(ix) Disseminating information and strategies to improve the transition to postsecondary activities of individuals who are members of traditionally unserved and underserved populations.

(4) *Pre-employment transition coordination.* Each local office of a designated State unit must carry out responsibilities consisting of—

(i) Attending individualized education program meetings for students with disabilities, when invited;

(ii) Working with the local workforce development boards, one-stop centers, and employers to develop work opportunities for students with disabilities, including internships, summer employment and other employment opportunities available throughout the school year, and apprenticeships;

(iii) Working with schools, including those carrying out activities under section 614(d) of the IDEA, to coordinate and ensure the provision of pre-employment transition services under this section;

(iv) When invited, attending person-centered planning meetings for individuals receiving services under title XIX of the Social Security Act (42 U.S.C. 1396 et seq.); and

(b) *Services for individuals who have applied for or been determined eligible for vocational rehabilitation services.* As appropriate to the vocational rehabilitation needs of each individual and consistent with each individual's individualized plan for employment, the designated State unit must ensure that the following vocational rehabilitation services are available to assist the individual with a disability in preparing for, securing, retaining, advancing in or regaining an employment outcome that is consistent with the individual's unique strengths, resources, priorities, concerns, abilities, capabilities, interests, and informed choice:

(1) Assessment for determining eligibility and priority for services by qualified personnel, including, if appropriate, an assessment by personnel skilled in rehabilitation technology, in accordance with § 361.42.

(2) Assessment for determining vocational rehabilitation needs by qualified personnel, including, if appropriate, an assessment by personnel skilled in rehabilitation technology, in accordance with § 361.45.

(3) Vocational rehabilitation counseling and guidance, including information and support services to assist an individual in exercising informed choice in accordance with § 361.52.

(4) Referral and other services necessary to assist applicants and eligible individuals to secure needed services from other agencies, including other components of the statewide workforce development system, in accordance with §§ 361.23, 361.24, and 361.37, and to advise those individuals about client assistance programs established under 34 CFR part 370.

(5) In accordance with the definition in § 361.5(c)(39), physical and mental restoration services, to the extent that financial support is not readily available from a source other than the designated State unit (such as through health insurance or a comparable service or benefit as defined in § 361.5(c)(10)).

(6) Vocational and other training services, including personal and vocational adjustment training, advanced training in, but not limited to, a field of science, technology, engineering, mathematics (including computer science), medicine, law, or business); books, tools, and other training materials, except that no training or training services in an institution of higher education (universities, colleges, community or junior colleges, vocational schools, technical institutes, or hospital schools of nursing or any other postsecondary education institution) may be paid for with funds under this part unless maximum efforts have been made by the State unit and the individual to secure grant assistance in whole or in part from other sources to pay for that training.

(7) Maintenance, in accordance with the definition of that term in § 361.5(c)(34).

(8) Transportation in connection with the provision of any vocational rehabilitation service and in accordance with the definition of that term in § 361.5(c)(57).

(9) Vocational rehabilitation services to family members, as defined in § 361.5(c)(23), of an applicant or eligible individual if necessary to enable the applicant or eligible individual to achieve an employment outcome.

(10) Interpreter services, including sign language and oral interpreter services, for individuals who are deaf or hard of hearing and tactile interpreting services for individuals who are deaf-blind provided by qualified personnel.

(11) Reader services, rehabilitation teaching services, and orientation and mobility services for individuals who are blind.

(12) Job-related services, including job search and placement assistance, job retention services, follow-up services, and follow-along services.

(13) Supported employment services in accordance with the definition of that term in § 361.5(c)(54).

(14) Personal assistance services in accordance with the definition of that term in § 361.5(c)(39).

(15) Post-employment services in accordance with the definition of that term in § 361.5(c)(42).

(16) Occupational licenses, tools, equipment, initial stocks, and supplies.

(17) Rehabilitation technology in accordance with the definition of that term in § 361.5(c)(45), including vehicular modification, telecommunications, sensory, and other technological aids and devices.

(18) Transition services for students and youth with disabilities, that facilitate the transition from school to postsecondary life, such as achievement of an employment outcome in competitive integrated employment, or pre-employment transition services for students.

(19) Technical assistance and other consultation services to conduct market analyses, develop business plans, and otherwise provide resources, to the extent those resources are authorized to be provided through the statewide workforce development system, to eligible individuals who are pursuing self-employment or telecommuting or establishing a small business operation as an employment outcome.

(20) Customized employment in accordance with the definition of that term in § 361.5(c)(11).

(21) Other goods and services determined necessary for the individual with a disability to achieve an employment outcome.

(Authority: Sections 7(37), 12(c), 103(a), and 113 of the Rehabilitation Act of 1973, as amended; 29 U.S.C. 705(37), 709(c), 723(a), and 733)

§ 361.49 Scope of vocational rehabilitation services for groups of individuals with disabilities.

(a) The designated State unit may provide for the following vocational rehabilitation services for the benefit of groups of individuals with disabilities:

(1) The establishment, development, or improvement of a public or other nonprofit community rehabilitation program that is used to provide vocational rehabilitation services that promote integration into the community and prepare individuals with disabilities for competitive integrated employment, including supported employment and customized employment, and under special circumstances, the construction of a facility for a public or nonprofit community rehabilitation

program as defined in §§361.5(c)(10), 361.5(c)(16) and 361.5(c)(17). Examples of special circumstances include the destruction by natural disaster of the only available center serving an area or a State determination that construction is necessary in a rural area because no other public agencies or private nonprofit organizations are currently able to provide vocational rehabilitation services to individuals.

(2) Telecommunications systems that have the potential for substantially improving vocational rehabilitation service delivery methods and developing appropriate programming to meet the particular needs of individuals with disabilities, including telephone, television, video description services, satellite, tactile-vibratory devices, and similar systems, as appropriate.

(3) Special services to provide nonvisual access to information for individuals who are blind, including the use of telecommunications, Braille, sound recordings, or other appropriate media; captioned television, films, or video cassettes for individuals who are deaf or hard of hearing; tactile materials for individuals who are deaf-blind; and other special services that provide information through tactile, vibratory, auditory, and visual media.

(4) Technical assistance to businesses that are seeking to employ individuals with disabilities.

(5) In the case of any small business enterprise operated by individuals with significant disabilities under the supervision of the designated State unit, including enterprises established under the Randolph-Sheppard program, management services and supervision provided by the State unit along with the acquisition by the State unit of vending facilities or other equipment, initial stocks and supplies, and initial operating expenses, in accordance with the following requirements:

(i) *Management services and supervision* includes inspection, quality control, consultation, accounting, regulating, in-service training, and related services provided on a systematic basis to support and improve small business enterprises operated by individuals with significant disabilities. Management services and supervision may be

provided throughout the operation of the small business enterprise.

(ii) *Initial stocks and supplies* includes those items necessary to the establishment of a new business enterprise during the initial establishment period, which may not exceed six months.

(iii) Costs of establishing a small business enterprise may include operational costs during the initial establishment period, which may not exceed six months.

(iv) If the designated State unit provides for these services, it must ensure that only individuals with significant disabilities will be selected to participate in this supervised program.

(v) If the designated State unit provides for these services and chooses to set aside funds from the proceeds of the operation of the small business enterprises, the State unit must maintain a description of the methods used in setting aside funds and the purposes for which funds are set aside. Funds may be used only for small business enterprises purposes, and benefits that are provided to operators from set-aside funds must be provided on an equitable basis.

(6) Consultation and technical assistance services to assist State educational agencies and local educational agencies in planning for the transition of students and youth with disabilities from school to postsecondary life, including employment.

(7) Transition services to youth with disabilities and students with disabilities who may not have yet applied or been determined eligible for vocational rehabilitation services, for which a vocational rehabilitation counselor works in concert with educational agencies, providers of job training programs, providers of services under the Medicaid program under title XIX of the Social Security Act (42 U.S.C. 1396 *et seq.*), entities designated by the State to provide services for individuals with developmental disabilities, centers for independent living (as defined in section 702 of the Act), housing and transportation authorities, workforce development systems, and businesses and employers. These specific transition services are to benefit a group of students with disabilities or

youth with disabilities and are not individualized services directly related to an individualized plan for employment goal. Services may include, but are not limited to, group tours of universities and vocational training programs, employer or business site visits to learn about career opportunities, career fairs coordinated with workforce development and employers to facilitate mock interviews and resume writing, and other general services applicable to groups of students with disabilities and youth with disabilities.

(8) The establishment, development, or improvement of assistive technology demonstration, loan, reutilization, or financing programs in coordination with activities authorized under the Assistive Technology Act of 1998 (29 U.S.C. 3001 *et seq.*) to promote access to assistive technology for individuals with disabilities and employers.

(9) Support (including, as appropriate, tuition) for advanced training in a field of science, technology, engineering, or mathematics (including computer science), medicine, law, or business, provided after an individual eligible to receive services under this title demonstrates—

(i) Such eligibility;

(ii) Previous completion of a bachelor's degree program at an institution of higher education or scheduled completion of such a degree program prior to matriculating in the program for which the individual proposes to use the support; and

(iii) Acceptance by a program at an institution of higher education in the United States that confers a master's degree in a field of science, technology, engineering, or mathematics (including computer science), a juris doctor degree, a master of business administration degree, or a doctor of medicine degree, except that—

(A) No training provided at an institution of higher education may be paid for with funds under this program unless maximum efforts have been made by the designated State unit to secure grant assistance, in whole or in part, from other sources to pay for such training; and

(B) Nothing in this paragraph prevents any designated State unit from providing similar support to individuals with disabilities within the State who are eligible to receive support under this title and who are not served under this section.

(b) If the designated State unit provides for vocational rehabilitation services for groups of individuals, it must—

(1) Develop and maintain written policies covering the nature and scope of each of the vocational rehabilitation services it provides and the criteria under which each service is provided; and

(2) Maintain information to ensure the proper and efficient administration of those services in the form and detail and at the time required by the Secretary, including the types of services provided, the costs of those services, and, to the extent feasible, estimates of the numbers of individuals benefiting from those services.

(Authority: Sections 12(c), 101(a)(6)(A), and 103(b) of the Rehabilitation Act of 1973, as amended; 29 U.S.C. 709(c), 721(a)(6), and 723(b))

§ 361.50 **Written policies governing the provision of services for individuals with disabilities.**

(a) *Policies.* The State unit must develop and maintain written policies covering the nature and scope of each of the vocational rehabilitation services specified in § 361.48 and the criteria under which each service is provided. The policies must ensure that the provision of services is based on the rehabilitation needs of each individual as identified in that individual's individualized plan for employment and is consistent with the individual's informed choice. The written policies may not establish any arbitrary limits on the nature and scope of vocational rehabilitation services to be provided to the individual to achieve an employment outcome. The policies must be developed in accordance with the following provisions:

(b) *Out-of-State services.* (1) The State unit may establish a preference for in-State services, provided that the preference does not effectively deny an individual a necessary service. If the individual chooses an out-of-State service at a higher cost than an in-State service, if either service would meet the individual's rehabilitation needs, the designated State unit is not responsible for those costs in excess of the cost of the in-State service.

(2) The State unit may not establish policies that effectively prohibit the provision of out-of-State services.

(c) *Payment for services.* (1) The State unit must establish and maintain written policies to govern the rates of payment for all purchased vocational rehabilitation services.

(2) The State unit may establish a fee schedule designed to ensure a reasonable cost to the program for each service, if the schedule is—

(i) Not so low as to effectively deny an individual a necessary service; and

(ii) Not absolute and permits exceptions so that individual needs can be addressed.

(3) The State unit may not place absolute dollar limits on specific service categories or on the total services provided to an individual.

(d) *Duration of services.* (1) The State unit may establish reasonable time periods for the provision of services provided that the time periods are—

(i) Not so short as to effectively deny an individual a necessary service; and

(ii) Not absolute and permit exceptions so that individual needs can be addressed.

(2) The State unit may not establish absolute time limits on the provision of specific services or on the provision of services to an individual. The duration of each service needed by an individual must be determined on an individual basis and reflected in that individual's individualized plan for employment.

(e) *Authorization of services.* The State unit must establish policies related to the timely authorization of services, including any conditions under which verbal authorization can be given.

(Authority: Sections 12(c) and 101(a)(6) of the Rehabilitation Act of 1973, as amended and 29 U.S.C. 709(c) and 721(a)(6))

§ 361.51 Standards for facilities and providers of services.

(a) *Accessibility of facilities.* The vocational rehabilitation services portion of the Unified or Combined State Plan must assure that any facility used in connection with the delivery of voca-

tional rehabilitation services under this part meets program accessibility requirements consistent with the requirements, as applicable, of the Architectural Barriers Act of 1968, the Americans with Disabilities Act of 1990, section 504 of the Act, and the regulations implementing these laws.

(b) *Affirmative action.* The vocational rehabilitation services portion of the Unified or Combined State Plan must assure that community rehabilitation programs that receive assistance under part B of title I of the Act take affirmative action to employ and advance in employment qualified individuals with disabilities covered under and on the same terms and conditions as in section 503 of the Act.

(c) *Special communication needs personnel.* The designated State unit must ensure that providers of vocational rehabilitation services are able to communicate—

(1) In the native language of applicants and eligible individuals who have limited English proficiency; and

(2) By using appropriate modes of communication used by applicants and eligible individuals.

(Approved by the Office of Management and Budget under control number 1205–0522)

(Authority: Sections 12(c) and 101(a)(6)(B) and (C) of the Rehabilitation Act of 1973, as amended; 29 U.S.C. 709(c) and 721(a)(6)(B) and (C))

§ 361.52 Informed choice.

(a) *General provision.* The vocational rehabilitation services portion of the Unified or Combined State Plan must assure that applicants and recipients of services or, as appropriate, their representatives are provided information and support services to assist applicants and recipients of services in exercising informed choice throughout the rehabilitation process consistent with the provisions of section 102(d) of the Act and the requirements of this section.

(b) *Written policies and procedures.* The designated State unit, in consultation with its State Rehabilitation Council, if it has a Council, must develop and implement written policies and procedures that enable an applicant or recipient of services to exercise informed choice throughout the vocational rehabilitation process. These policies and procedures must provide for—

(1) Informing each applicant and recipient of services (including students with disabilities who are making the transition from programs under the responsibility of an educational agency to programs under the responsibility of the designated State unit and including youth with disabilities), through appropriate modes of communication, about the availability of and opportunities to exercise informed choice, including the availability of support services for individuals with cognitive or other disabilities who require assistance in exercising informed choice throughout the vocational rehabilitation process;

(2) Assisting applicants and recipients of services in exercising informed choice in decisions related to the provision of assessment services;

(3) Developing and implementing flexible procurement policies and methods that facilitate the provision of vocational rehabilitation services and that afford recipients of services meaningful choices among the methods used to procure vocational rehabilitation services;

(4) Assisting eligible individuals or, as appropriate, the individuals' representatives, in acquiring information that enables them to exercise informed choice in the development of their individualized plans for employment with respect to the selection of the—

(i) Employment outcome;

(ii) Specific vocational rehabilitation services needed to achieve the employment outcome;

(iii) Entity that will provide the services;

(iv) Employment setting and the settings in which the services will be provided; and

(v) Methods available for procuring the services; and

(5) Ensuring that the availability and scope of informed choice is consistent with the obligations of the designated State agency under this part.

(c) *Information and assistance in the selection of vocational rehabilitation services and service providers.* In assisting an applicant and eligible individual in exercising informed choice during the assessment for determining eligibility and vocational rehabilitation needs and during development of the individualized plan for employment, the designated State unit must provide the individual or the individual's representative, or assist the individual or the individual's representative in acquiring, information necessary to make an informed choice about the specific vocational rehabilitation services, including the providers of those services, that are needed to achieve the individual's employment outcome. This information must include, at a minimum, information relating to the—

(1) Cost, accessibility, and duration of potential services;

(2) Consumer satisfaction with those services to the extent that information relating to consumer satisfaction is available;

(3) Qualifications of potential service providers;

(4) Types of services offered by the potential providers;

(5) Degree to which services are provided in integrated settings; and

(6) Outcomes achieved by individuals working with service providers, to the extent that such information is available.

(d) *Methods or sources of information.* In providing or assisting the individual or the individual's representative in acquiring the information required under paragraph (c) of this section, the State unit may use, but is not limited to, the following methods or sources of information:

(1) Lists of services and service providers.

(2) Periodic consumer satisfaction surveys and reports.

(3) Referrals to other consumers, consumer groups, or disability advisory councils qualified to discuss the services or service providers.

(4) Relevant accreditation, certification, or other information relating to the qualifications of service providers.

(5) Opportunities for individuals to visit or experience various work and service provider settings.

(Approved by the Office of Management and Budget under control number 1205–0522)

(Authority: Sections 12(c), 101(a)(19), 102(b)(2)(B), and 102(d) of the Rehabilitation Act of 1973, as amended; 29 U.S.C. 709(c), 721(a)(19), 722(b)(2)(B), and 722(d))

§361.53 Comparable services and benefits.

(a) *Determination of availability.* The vocational rehabilitation services portion of the Unified or Combined State Plan must assure that prior to providing an accommodation or auxiliary aid or service or any vocational rehabilitation services, except those services listed in paragraph (b) of this section, to an eligible individual or to members of the individual's family, the State unit must determine whether comparable services and benefits, as defined in §361.5(c)(8), exist under any other program and whether those services and benefits are available to the individual unless such a determination would interrupt or delay—

(1) The progress of the individual toward achieving the employment outcome identified in the individualized plan for employment;

(2) An immediate job placement; or

(3) The provision of vocational rehabilitation services to any individual who is determined to be at extreme medical risk, based on medical evidence provided by an appropriate qualified medical professional.

(b) *Exempt services.* The following vocational rehabilitation services described in §361.48(b) are exempt from a determination of the availability of comparable services and benefits under paragraph (a) of this section:

(1) Assessment for determining eligibility and vocational rehabilitation needs.

(2) Counseling and guidance, including information and support services to assist an individual in exercising informed choice.

(3) Referral and other services to secure needed services from other agencies, including other components of the statewide workforce development system, if those services are not available under this part.

(4) Job-related services, including job search and placement assistance, job retention services, follow-up services, and follow-along services.

(5) Rehabilitation technology, including telecommunications, sensory, and other technological aids and devices.

(6) Post-employment services consisting of the services listed under paragraphs (b)(1) through (5) of this section.

(c) *Provision of services.* (1) If comparable services or benefits exist under any other program and are available to the individual at the time needed to ensure the progress of the individual toward achieving the employment outcome in the individual's individualized plan for employment, the designated State unit must use those comparable services or benefits to meet, in whole or part, the costs of the vocational rehabilitation services.

(2) If comparable services or benefits exist under any other program, but are not available to the individual at the time needed to ensure the progress of the individual toward achieving the employment outcome specified in the individualized plan for employment, the designated State unit must provide vocational rehabilitation services until those comparable services and benefits become available.

(d) *Interagency coordination.* (1) The vocational rehabilitation services portion of the Unified or Combined State Plan must assure that the Governor, in consultation with the entity in the State responsible for the vocational rehabilitation program and other appropriate agencies, will ensure that an interagency agreement or other mechanism for interagency coordination takes effect between the designated State vocational rehabilitation unit and any appropriate public entity, including the State entity responsible for administering the State Medicaid program, a public institution of higher education, and a component of the statewide workforce development system, to ensure the provision of vocational rehabilitation services, and, if appropriate, accommodations or auxiliary aids and services, (other than those services listed in paragraph (b) of this section) that are included in the individualized plan for employment of an eligible individual, including the provision of those vocational rehabilitation services (including, if appropriate, accommodations or auxiliary aids and services) during the pendency of any interagency dispute in accordance with the provisions of paragraph (d)(3)(iii) of this section.

(2) The Governor may meet the requirements of paragraph (d)(1) of this section through—

(i) A State statute or regulation;

(ii) A signed agreement between the respective officials of the public entities that clearly identifies the responsibilities of each public entity for the provision of the services; or

(iii) Another appropriate mechanism as determined by the designated State vocational rehabilitation unit.

(3) The interagency agreement or other mechanism for interagency coordination must include the following:

(i) *Agency financial responsibility.* An identification of, or description of a method for defining, the financial responsibility of the designated State unit and other public entities for the provision of vocational rehabilitation services, and, if appropriate, accommodations or auxiliary aids and services other than those listed in paragraph (b) of this section and a provision stating the financial responsibility of the public entity for providing those services.

(ii) *Conditions, terms, and procedures of reimbursement.* Information specifying the conditions, terms, and procedures under which the designated State unit must be reimbursed by the other public entities for providing vocational rehabilitation services, and accommodations or auxiliary aids and services based on the terms of the interagency agreement or other mechanism for interagency coordination.

(iii) *Interagency disputes.* Information specifying procedures for resolving interagency disputes under the interagency agreement or other mechanism for interagency coordination, including procedures under which the designated State unit may initiate proceedings to secure reimbursement from other public entities or otherwise implement the provisions of the agreement or mechanism.

(iv) *Procedures for coordination of services.* Information specifying policies and procedures for public entities to determine and identify interagency coordination responsibilities of each public entity to promote the coordination and timely delivery of vocational rehabilitation services, and accommodations or auxiliary aids and services, other than those listed in paragraph (b) of this section.

(e) *Responsibilities under other law.* (1) If a public entity (other than the designated State unit) is obligated under Federal law (such as the Americans with Disabilities Act, section 504 of the Act, or section 188 of the Workforce Innovation and Opportunity Act) or State law, or assigned responsibility under State policy or an interagency agreement established under this section, to provide or pay for any services considered to be vocational rehabilitation services (*e.g.,* interpreter services under § 361.48(j)), and, if appropriate, accommodations or auxiliary aids and services other than those services listed in paragraph (b) of this section, the public entity must fulfill that obligation or responsibility through—

(i) The terms of the interagency agreement or other requirements of this section;

(ii) Providing or paying for the service directly or by contract; or

(iii) Other arrangement.

(2) If a public entity other than the designated State unit fails to provide or pay for vocational rehabilitation services, and, if appropriate, accommodations or auxiliary aids and services for an eligible individual as established under this section, the designated State unit must provide or pay for those services to the individual and may claim reimbursement for the services from the public entity that failed to provide or pay for those services. The public entity must reimburse the designated State unit pursuant to the terms of the interagency agreement or other mechanism described in paragraph (d) of this section in accordance with the procedures established in the

agreement or mechanism pursuant to paragraph (d)(3)(ii) of this section.

(Approved by the Office of Management and Budget under control number 1205–0522)

(Authority: Sections 12(c) and 101(a)(8) of the Rehabilitation Act of 1973, as amended; 29 U.S.C. 709(c) and 721(a)(8))

§ 361.54 Participation of individuals in cost of services based on financial need.

(a) *No Federal requirement.* There is no Federal requirement that the financial need of individuals be considered in the provision of vocational rehabilitation services.

(b) *State unit requirements.* (1) The State unit may choose to consider the financial need of eligible individuals or individuals who are receiving services through trial work experiences under § 361.42(e) for purposes of determining the extent of their participation in the costs of vocational rehabilitation services, other than those services identified in paragraph (b)(3) of this section.

(2) If the State unit chooses to consider financial need—

(i) It must maintain written policies—

(A) Explaining the method for determining the financial need of an eligible individual; and

(B) Specifying the types of vocational rehabilitation services for which the unit has established a financial needs test;

(ii) The policies must be applied uniformly to all individuals in similar circumstances;

(iii) The policies may require different levels of need for different geographic regions in the State, but must be applied uniformly to all individuals within each geographic region; and

(iv) The policies must ensure that the level of an individual's participation in the cost of vocational rehabilitation services is—

(A) Reasonable;

(B) Based on the individual's financial need, including consideration of any disability-related expenses paid by the individual; and

(C) Not so high as to effectively deny the individual a necessary service.

(3) The designated State unit may not apply a financial needs test, or require the financial participation of the individual—

(i) As a condition for furnishing the following vocational rehabilitation services:

(A) Assessment for determining eligibility and priority for services under § 361.48(b)(1), except those non-assessment services that are provided to an individual with a significant disability during either an exploration of the individual's abilities, capabilities, and capacity to perform in work situations through the use of trial work experiences under § 361.42(e).

(B) Assessment for determining vocational rehabilitation needs under § 361.48(b)(2).

(C) Vocational rehabilitation counseling and guidance under § 361.48(b)(3).

(D) Referral and other services under § 361.48(b)(4).

(E) Job-related services under § 361.48(b)(12).

(F) Personal assistance services under § 361.48(b)(14).

(G) Any auxiliary aid or service (*e.g.*, interpreter services under § 361.48(b)(10), reader services under § 361.48(b)(11)) that an individual with a disability requires under section 504 of the Act (29 U.S.C. 794) or the Americans with Disabilities Act (42 U.S.C. 12101, *et seq.*), or regulations implementing those laws, in order for the individual to participate in the vocational rehabilitation program as authorized under this part; or

(ii) As a condition for furnishing any vocational rehabilitation service if the individual in need of the service has been determined eligible for Social Security benefits under titles II or XVI of the Social Security Act.

(Authority: Section 12(c) of the Rehabilitation Act of 1973, as amended; 29 U.S.C. 709(c))

§ 361.55 Semi-annual and annual review of individuals in extended employment and other employment under special certificate provisions of the Fair Labor Standards Act.

(a) The vocational rehabilitation services portion of the Unified or Combined State Plan must assure that the designated State unit conducts a semi-annual review and reevaluation for the first two years of such employment and annually thereafter, in accordance with the requirements in paragraph (b) of this section for an individual with a disability served under this part—

(1) Who has a record of service, as described in § 361.47, as either an applicant or eligible individual under the vocational rehabilitation program; and

(2)(i) Who has achieved employment in which the individual is compensated in accordance with section 14(c) of the Fair Labor Standards Act; or

(ii) Who is in extended employment, including those individuals whose record of service is closed while the individual is in extended employment on the basis that the individual is unable to achieve an employment outcome consistent with § 361.5(c)(15) or that the individual made an informed choice to remain in extended employment.

(b) For each individual with a disability who meets the criteria in paragraph (a) of this section, the designated State unit must—

(1) Semi-annually review and re-evaluate the status of each individual for two years after the individual's record of services is closed (and annually thereafter) to determine the interests, priorities, and needs of the individual with respect to competitive integrated employment or training for competitive integrated employment;

(2) Enable the individual or, if appropriate, the individual's representative to provide input into the review and re-evaluation and must document that input in the record of services, consistent with § 361.47(a)(10), with the individual's or, as appropriate, the individual's representative's signed acknowledgment that the review and re-evaluation have been conducted; and

(3) Make maximum efforts, including identifying and providing vocational rehabilitation services, reasonable accommodations, and other necessary support services, to assist the individual in engaging in competitive integrated employment as defined in § 361.5(c)(9).

(Approved by the Office of Management and Budget under control number 1205–0522)

(Authority: Sections 12(c) and 101(a)(14) of the Rehabilitation Act of 1973, as amended; 29 U.S.C. 709(c) and 721(a)(14))

§ 361.56 Requirements for closing the record of services of an individual who has achieved an employment outcome.

The record of services of an individual who has achieved an employment outcome may be closed only if all of the following requirements are met:

(a) *Employment outcome achieved.* The individual has achieved the employment outcome that is described in the individual's individualized plan for employment in accordance with § 361.46(a)(1) and is consistent with the individual's unique strengths, resources, priorities, concerns, abilities, capabilities, interests, and informed choice.

(b) *Employment outcome maintained.* The individual has maintained the employment outcome for an appropriate period of time, but not less than 90 days, necessary to ensure the stability of the employment outcome, and the individual no longer needs vocational rehabilitation services.

(c) *Satisfactory outcome.* At the end of the appropriate period under paragraph (b) of this section, the individual and the qualified rehabilitation counselor employed by the designated State unit consider the employment outcome to be satisfactory and agree that the individual is performing well in the employment.

(d) *Post-employment services.* The individual is informed through appropriate modes of communication of the availability of post-employment services.

(Authority: Sections 12(c), 101(a)(6), and 106(a)(2) of the Rehabilitation Act of 1973, as amended; 29 U.S.C. 709(c), 721(a)(6), and 726(a)(2))

§ 361.57 Review of determinations made by designated State unit personnel.

(a) *Procedures.* The designated State unit must develop and implement procedures to ensure that an applicant or recipient of services who is dissatisfied with any determination made by personnel of the designated State unit that affects the provision of vocational rehabilitation services may request, or, if appropriate, may request through the individual's representative, a timely review of that determination. The procedures must be in accordance with paragraphs (b) through (k) of this section:

(b) *General requirements.* (1) *Notification.* Procedures established by the State unit under this section must provide an applicant or recipient or, as appropriate, the individual's representative notice of—

(i) The right to obtain review of State unit determinations that affect the provision of vocational rehabilitation services through an impartial due process hearing under paragraph (e) of this section;

(ii) The right to pursue mediation under paragraph (d) of this section with respect to determinations made by designated State unit personnel that affect the provision of vocational rehabilitation services to an applicant or recipient;

(iii) The names and addresses of individuals with whom requests for mediation or due process hearings may be filed;

(iv) The manner in which a mediator or impartial hearing officer may be selected consistent with the requirements of paragraphs (d) and (f) of this section; and

(v) The availability of the client assistance program, established under 34 CFR part 370, to assist the applicant or recipient during mediation sessions or impartial due process hearings.

(2) *Timing.* Notice described in paragraph (b)(1) of this section must be provided in writing—

(i) At the time the individual applies for vocational rehabilitation services under this part;

(ii) At the time the individual is assigned to a category in the State's order of selection, if the State has established an order of selection under §361.36;

(iii) At the time the individualized plan for employment is developed; and

(iv) Whenever vocational rehabilitation services for an individual are reduced, suspended, or terminated.

(3) *Evidence and representation.* Procedures established under this section must—

(i) Provide an applicant or recipient or, as appropriate, the individual's representative with an opportunity to submit during mediation sessions or due process hearings evidence and other information that supports the applicant's or recipient's position; and

(ii) Allow an applicant or recipient to be represented during mediation sessions or due process hearings by counsel or other advocate selected by the applicant or recipient.

(4) *Impact on provision of services.* The State unit may not institute a suspension, reduction, or termination of vocational rehabilitation services being provided to an applicant or recipient, including evaluation and assessment services and individualized plan for employment development, pending a resolution through mediation, pending a decision by a hearing officer or reviewing official, or pending informal resolution under this section unless—

(i) The individual or, in appropriate cases, the individual's representative requests a suspension, reduction, or termination of services; or

(ii) The State agency has evidence that the services have been obtained through misrepresentation, fraud, collusion, or criminal conduct on the part of the individual or the individual's representative.

(5) *Ineligibility.* Applicants who are found ineligible for vocational rehabilitation services and previously eligible individuals who are determined to be no longer eligible for vocational rehabilitation services pursuant to §361.43 are permitted to challenge the determinations of ineligibility under the procedures described in this section.

(c) *Informal dispute resolution.* The State unit may develop an informal process for resolving a request for review without conducting mediation or a formal hearing. A State's informal process must not be used to deny the right of an applicant or recipient to a hearing under paragraph (e) of this section or any other right provided under this part, including the right to pursue mediation under paragraph (d) of this section. If informal resolution under this paragraph or mediation under paragraph (d) of this section is not successful in resolving the dispute within the time period established under paragraph (e)(1) of this section, a formal hearing must be conducted within that same time period, unless the parties agree to a specific extension of time.

(d) *Mediation.* (1) The State must establish and implement procedures, as required under paragraph (b)(1)(ii) of this section, to allow an applicant or recipient and the State unit to resolve disputes involving State unit determinations that affect the provision of vocational rehabilitation services through a mediation process that must be made available, at a minimum, whenever an applicant or recipient or, as appropriate, the individual's representative requests an impartial due process hearing under this section.

(2) Mediation procedures established by the State unit under paragraph (d) of this section must ensure that—

(i) Participation in the mediation process is voluntary on the part of the applicant or recipient, as appropriate, and on the part of the State unit;

(ii) Use of the mediation process is not used to deny or delay the applicant's or recipient's right to pursue resolution of the dispute through an impartial hearing held within the time period specified in paragraph (e)(1) of this section or any other rights provided under this part. At any point during the mediation process, either party or the mediator may elect to terminate the mediation. In the event mediation is terminated, either party may pursue resolution through an impartial hearing;

(iii) The mediation process is conducted by a qualified and impartial mediator, as defined in § 361.5(c)(43), who must be selected from a list of qualified and impartial mediators maintained by the State—

(A) On a random basis;

(B) By agreement between the director of the designated State unit and the applicant or recipient or, as appropriate, the recipient's representative; or

(C) In accordance with a procedure established in the State for assigning mediators, provided this procedure ensures the neutrality of the mediator assigned; and

(iv) Mediation sessions are scheduled and conducted in a timely manner and are held in a location and manner that is convenient to the parties to the dispute.

(3) Discussions that occur during the mediation process must be kept confidential and may not be used as evidence in any subsequent due process hearings or civil proceedings, and the parties to the mediation process may be required to sign a confidentiality pledge prior to the commencement of the process.

(4) An agreement reached by the parties to the dispute in the mediation process must be described in a written mediation agreement that is developed by the parties with the assistance of the qualified and impartial mediator and signed by both parties. Copies of the agreement must be sent to both parties.

(5) The costs of the mediation process must be paid by the State. The State is not required to pay for any costs related to the representation of an applicant or recipient authorized under paragraph (b)(3)(ii) of this section.

(e) *Impartial due process hearings.* The State unit must establish and implement formal review procedures, as required under paragraph (b)(1)(i) of this section, that provide that—

(1) Hearing conducted by an impartial hearing officer, selected in accordance with paragraph (f) of this section, must be held within 60 days of an applicant's or recipient's request for review of a determination made by personnel of the State unit that affects the provision of vocational rehabilitation services to the individual, unless informal resolution or a mediation agreement is achieved prior to the 60th day or the parties agree to a specific extension of time;

(2) In addition to the rights described in paragraph (b)(3) of this section, the applicant or recipient or, if appropriate, the individual's representative must be given the opportunity to present witnesses during the hearing and to examine all witnesses and other relevant sources of information and evidence;

(3) The impartial hearing officer must—

(i) Make a decision based on the provisions of the approved vocational rehabilitation services portion of the Unified or Combined State Plan, the Act, Federal vocational rehabilitation regulations, and State regulations and policies that are consistent with Federal requirements; and

(ii) Provide to the individual or, if appropriate, the individual's representative and to the State unit a full written report of the findings and grounds for the decision within 30 days of the completion of the hearing; and

(4) The hearing officer's decision is final, except that a party may request an impartial review under paragraph (g)(1) of this section if the State has established procedures for that review, and a party involved in a hearing may bring a civil action under paragraph (i) of this section.

(f) *Selection of impartial hearing officers.* The impartial hearing officer for a particular case must be selected—

(1) From a list of qualified impartial hearing officers maintained by the State unit. Impartial hearing officers included on the list must be—

(i) Identified by the State unit if the State unit is an independent commission; or

(ii) Jointly identified by the State unit and the State Rehabilitation Council if the State has a Council; and

(2)(i) On a random basis; or

(ii) By agreement between the director of the designated State unit and the applicant or recipient or, as appropriate, the individual's representative.

(g) *Administrative review of hearing officer's decision.* The State may establish procedures to enable a party who is dissatisfied with the decision of the impartial hearing officer to seek an impartial administrative review of the decision under paragraph (e)(3) of this section in accordance with the following requirements:

(1) A request for administrative review under paragraph (g) of this section must be made within 20 days of the mailing of the impartial hearing officer's decision.

(2) Administrative review of the hearing officer's decision must be conducted by—

(i) The chief official of the designated State agency if the State has established both a designated State agency and a designated State unit under §361.13(b); or

(ii) An official from the office of the Governor.

(3) The reviewing official described in paragraph (g)(2)(i) of this section—

(i) Provides both parties with an opportunity to submit additional evidence and information relevant to a final decision concerning the matter under review;

(ii) May not overturn or modify the hearing officer's decision, or any part of that decision, that supports the position of the applicant or recipient unless the reviewing official concludes, based on clear and convincing evidence, that the decision of the impartial hearing officer is clearly erroneous on the basis of being contrary to the approved vocational rehabilitation services portion of the Unified or Combined State Plan, the Act, Federal vocational rehabilitation regulations, or State regulations and policies that are consistent with Federal requirements;

(iii) Makes an independent, final decision following a review of the entire hearing record and provides the decision in writing, including a full report of the findings and the statutory, regulatory, or policy grounds for the decision, to the applicant or recipient or, as appropriate, the individual's representative and to the State unit within 30 days of the request for administrative review under paragraph (g)(1) of this section; and

(iv) May not delegate the responsibility for making the final decision under paragraph (g) of this section to any officer or employee of the designated State unit.

(4) The reviewing official's decision under paragraph (g) of this section is final unless either party brings a civil action under paragraph (i) of this section.

(h) *Implementation of final decisions.* If a party brings a civil action under paragraph (h) of this section to challenge the final decision of a hearing officer under paragraph (e) of this section or to challenge the final decision of a State reviewing official under paragraph (g) of this section, the final decision of the hearing officer or State reviewing official must be implemented pending review by the court.

(i) *Civil action.* (1) Any party who disagrees with the findings and decision of an impartial hearing officer under paragraph (e) of this section in a State that has not established administrative review procedures under paragraph (g)

347

of this section and any party who disagrees with the findings and decision under paragraph (g)(3)(iii) of this section have a right to bring a civil action with respect to the matter in dispute. The action may be brought in any State court of competent jurisdiction or in a district court of the United States of competent jurisdiction without regard to the amount in controversy.

(2) In any action brought under paragraph (i) of this section, the court—

(i) Receives the records related to the impartial due process hearing and the records related to the administrative review process, if applicable;

(ii) Hears additional evidence at the request of a party; and

(iii) Basing its decision on the preponderance of the evidence, grants the relief that the court determines to be appropriate.

(j) *State fair hearing board.* A fair hearing board as defined in § 361.5(c)(21) is authorized to carry out the responsibilities of the impartial hearing officer under paragraph (e) of this section in accordance with the following criteria:

(1) The fair hearing board may conduct due process hearings either collectively or by assigning responsibility for conducting the hearing to one or more members of the fair hearing board.

(2) The final decision issued by the fair hearing board following a hearing under paragraph (j)(1) of this section must be made collectively by, or by a majority vote of, the fair hearing board.

(3) The provisions of paragraphs (b)(1), (2), and (3) of this section that relate to due process hearings and of paragraphs (e), (f), (g), and (h) of this section do not apply to fair hearing boards under this paragraph (j).

(k) *Data collection.* (1) The director of the designated State unit must collect and submit, at a minimum, the following data to the Secretary for inclusion each year in the annual report to Congress under section 13 of the Act:

(i) A copy of the standards used by State reviewing officials for reviewing decisions made by impartial hearing officers under this section.

(ii) The number of mediations held, including the number of mediation agreements reached.

(iii) The number of hearings and reviews sought from impartial hearing officers and State reviewing officials, including the type of complaints and the issues involved.

(iv) The number of hearing officer decisions that were not reviewed by administrative reviewing officials.

(v) The number of hearing decisions that were reviewed by State reviewing officials and, based on these reviews, the number of hearing decisions that were—

(A) Sustained in favor of an applicant or recipient;

(B) Sustained in favor of the designated State unit;

(C) Reversed in whole or in part in favor of the applicant or recipient; and

(D) Reversed in whole or in part in favor of the State unit.

(2) The State unit director also must collect and submit to the Secretary copies of all final decisions issued by impartial hearing officers under paragraph (e) of this section and by State review officials under paragraph (g) of this section.

(3) The confidentiality of records of applicants and recipients maintained by the State unit may not preclude the access of the Secretary to those records for the purposes described in this section.

(Authority: Sections 12(c) and 102(c) of the Rehabilitation Act of 1973, as amended; 29 U.S.C. 709(c) and 722(c))

Subpart C—Financing of State Vocational Rehabilitation Programs

§ 361.60 Matching requirements.

(a) *Federal share*—(1) *General.* Except as provided in paragraph (a)(2) of this section, the Federal share for expenditures made by the State under the vocational rehabilitation services portion of the Unified or Combined State Plan, including expenditures for the provision of vocational rehabilitation services and the administration of the vocational rehabilitation services portion of the Unified or Combined State Plan, is 78.7 percent.

(2) *Construction projects.* The Federal share for expenditures made for the construction of a facility for community rehabilitation program purposes may not be more than 50 percent of the total cost of the project.

(b) *Non-Federal share—(1) General.* Except as provided in paragraph (b)(2) and (b)(3) of this section, expenditures made under the vocational rehabilitation services portion of the Unified or Combined State Plan to meet the non-Federal share under this section must be consistent with the provisions of 2 CFR 200.306(b).

(2) *Third party in-kind contributions.* Third party in-kind contributions specified in 2 CFR 200.306(b) may not be used to meet the non-Federal share under this section.

(3) *Contributions by private entities.* Expenditures made from those cash contributions provided by private organizations, agencies, or individuals and that are deposited in the State agency's account or, if applicable, sole local agency's account, in accordance with State law prior to their expenditure and that are earmarked, under a condition imposed by the contributor, may be used as part of the non-Federal share under this section if the funds are earmarked for—

(i) Meeting in whole or in part the State's share for establishing a community rehabilitation program or constructing a particular facility for community rehabilitation program purposes;

(ii) Particular geographic areas within the State for any purpose under the vocational rehabilitation services portion of the Unified or Combined State Plan, other than those described in paragraph (b)(3)(i) of this section, in accordance with the following criteria:

(A) Before funds that are earmarked for a particular geographic area may be used as part of the non-Federal share, the State must notify the Secretary that the State cannot provide the full non-Federal share without using these funds.

(B) Funds that are earmarked for a particular geographic area may be used as part of the non-Federal share without requesting a waiver of statewideness under §361.26.

(C) Except as provided in paragraph (b)(3)(i) of this section, all Federal funds must be used on a statewide basis consistent with §361.25, unless a waiver of statewideness is obtained under §361.26; and

(iii) Any other purpose under the vocational rehabilitation services portion of the Unified or Combined State Plan, provided the expenditures do not benefit in any way the donor, employee, officer, or agent, any member of his or her immediate family, his or her partner, an individual with whom the donor has a close personal relationship, or an individual, entity, or organization with whom the donor shares a financial or other interest. The Secretary does not consider a donor's receipt from the State unit of a subaward or contract with funds allotted under this part to be a benefit for the purposes of this paragraph if the subaward or contract is awarded under the State's regular competitive procedures.

(Authority: Sections 7(14), 12(c), 101(a)(3), 101(a)(4), and 104 of the Rehabilitation Act of 1973, as amended; 29 U.S.C. 705(14), 709(c), 721(a)(3), 721(a)(4), and 724))

Example for paragraph (b)(3): Contributions may be earmarked in accordance with §361.60(b)(3)(iii) for providing particular services (*e.g.,* rehabilitation technology services); serving individuals with certain types of disabilities (*e.g.,* individuals who are blind), consistent with the State's order of selection, if applicable; providing services to special groups that State or Federal law permits to be targeted for services (*e.g.,* students with disabilities who are receiving special education services), consistent with the State's order of selection, if applicable; or carrying out particular types of administrative activities permissible under State law. Contributions also may be restricted to particular geographic areas to increase services or expand the scope of services that are available statewide under the vocational rehabilitation services portion of the Unified or Combined State Plan in accordance with the requirements in §361.60(b)(3)(ii).

§361.61 Limitation on use of funds for construction expenditures.

No more than 10 percent of a State's allotment for any fiscal year under section 110 of the Act may be spent on the construction of facilities for community rehabilitation program purposes.

(Authority: Section 101(a)(17)(A) of the Rehabilitation Act of 1973, as amended; 29 U.S.C. 721(a)(17)(A))

§ 361.62 **Maintenance of effort requirements.**

(a) *General requirements.* The Secretary reduces the amount otherwise payable to a State for any fiscal year by the amount by which the total expenditures from non-Federal sources under the vocational rehabilitation services portion of the Unified or Combined State Plan for any previous fiscal year were less than the total of those expenditures for the fiscal year two years prior to that previous fiscal year.

(b) *Specific requirements for construction of facilities.* If the State provides for the construction of a facility for community rehabilitation program purposes, the amount of the State's share of expenditures for vocational rehabilitation services under the plan, other than for the construction of a facility for community rehabilitation program purposes or the establishment of a facility for community rehabilitation purposes, must be at least equal to the expenditures for those services for the second prior fiscal year.

(c) *Separate State agency for vocational rehabilitation services for individuals who are blind.* If there is a separate part of the vocational rehabilitation services portion of the Unified or Combined State Plan administered by a separate State agency to provide vocational rehabilitation services for individuals who are blind—

(1) Satisfaction of the maintenance of effort requirements under paragraphs (a) and (b) of this section is determined based on the total amount of a State's non-Federal expenditures under both parts of the vocational rehabilitation services portion of the Unified or Combined State Plan; and

(2) If a State fails to meet any maintenance of effort requirement, the Secretary reduces the amount otherwise payable to the State for a fiscal year under each part of the plan in direct proportion to the amount by which non-Federal expenditures under each part of the plan in any previous fiscal year were less than they were for that

part of the plan for the fiscal year 2 years prior to that previous fiscal year.

(d) *Waiver or modification.* (1) The Secretary may waive or modify the maintenance of effort requirement in paragraph (a) of this section if the Secretary determines that a waiver or modification is necessary to permit the State to respond to exceptional or uncontrollable circumstances, such as a major natural disaster or a serious economic downturn, that—

(i) Cause significant unanticipated expenditures or reductions in revenue that result in a general reduction of programs within the State; or

(ii) Require the State to make substantial expenditures in the vocational rehabilitation program for long-term purposes due to the one-time costs associated with the construction of a facility for community rehabilitation program purposes, the establishment of a facility for community rehabilitation program purposes, or the acquisition of equipment.

(2) The Secretary may waive or modify the maintenance of effort requirement in paragraph (b) of this section or the 10 percent allotment limitation in § 361.61 if the Secretary determines that a waiver or modification is necessary to permit the State to respond to exceptional or uncontrollable circumstances, such as a major natural disaster, that result in significant destruction of existing facilities and require the State to make substantial expenditures for the construction of a facility for community rehabilitation program purposes or the establishment of a facility for community rehabilitation program purposes in order to provide vocational rehabilitation services.

(3) A written request for waiver or modification, including supporting justification, must be submitted to the Secretary for consideration as soon as the State has determined that it has failed to satisfy its maintenance of effort requirement due to an exceptional or uncontrollable circumstance, as described in paragraphs (d)(1) and (2) of this section.

(Authority: Sections 101(a)(17) and 111(a)(2) of the Rehabilitation Act of 1973, as amended; 29 U.S.C. 721(a)(17) and 731(a)(2))

§ 361.63 Program income.

(a) *Definition.* For purposes of this section, program income means gross income received by the State that is directly generated by a supported activity under this part or earned as a result of the Federal award during the period of performance, as defined in 2 CFR 200.80.

(b) *Sources.* Sources of program income include, but are not limited to: Payments from the Social Security Administration for assisting Social Security beneficiaries and recipients to achieve employment outcomes; payments received from workers' compensation funds; payments received by the State agency from insurers, consumers, or others for services to defray part or all of the costs of services provided to particular individuals; and income generated by a State-operated community rehabilitation program for activities authorized under this part.

(c) *Use of program income.* (1) Except as provided in paragraph (c)(2) of this section, program income, whenever earned, must be used for the provision of vocational rehabilitation services and the administration of the vocational rehabilitation services portion of the Unified or Combined State Plan. Program income—

(i) Is considered earned in the fiscal year in which it is received; and

(ii) Must be disbursed during the period of performance of the award.

(2) Payments provided to a State from the Social Security Administration for assisting Social Security beneficiaries and recipients to achieve employment outcomes may also be used to carry out programs under part B of title I of the Act (client assistance), title VI of the Act (supported employment), and title VII of the Act (independent living).

(3)(i) The State must use program income to supplement Federal funds that support program activities that are subject to this part. See, for example, 2 CFR 200.307(e)(2).

(ii) Notwithstanding 2 CFR 200.305(a) and to the extent that program income funds are available, a State must disburse those funds (including repayments to a revolving fund), rebates, refunds, contract settlements, audit recoveries, and interest earned on such funds before requesting additional funds from the Department.

(4) Program income cannot be used to meet the non-Federal share requirement under § 361.60.

(Authority: Sections 12(c) and 108 of the Rehabilitation Act of 1973, as amended; 29 U.S.C. 709(c) and 728; 2 CFR part 200)

§ 361.64 Obligation of Federal funds.

(a) Except as provided in paragraph (b) of this section, any Federal award funds, including reallotted funds, that are appropriated for a fiscal year to carry out a program under this part that are not obligated by the State by the beginning of the succeeding fiscal year remain available for obligation by the State during that succeeding fiscal year.

(b) Federal funds appropriated for a fiscal year remain available for obligation in the succeeding fiscal year only to the extent that the State met the matching requirement for those Federal funds by obligating, in accordance with 34 CFR 76.707, the non-Federal share in the fiscal year for which the funds were appropriated.

(Authority: Section 19 of the Rehabilitation Act of 1973, as amended; 29 U.S.C. 716)

§ 361.65 Allotment and payment of Federal funds for vocational rehabilitation services.

(a) *Allotment.* (1) The allotment of Federal funds for vocational rehabilitation services for each State is computed in accordance with the requirements of section 110 of the Act, and payments are made to the State on a quarterly basis, unless some other period is established by the Secretary.

(2) If the vocational rehabilitation services portion of the Unified or Combined State Plan designates one State agency to administer, or supervise the administration of, the part of the plan under which vocational rehabilitation services are provided for individuals who are blind and another State agency to administer the rest of the plan, the division of the State's allotment is a matter for State determination.

(3) *Reservation for pre-employment transition services.* (i) Pursuant to section 110(d) of the Act, the State must reserve at least 15 percent of the

351

State's allotment, received in accordance with section 110(a) of the Act for the provision of pre-employment transition services, as described in § 361.48(a) of this part.

(ii) The funds reserved in accordance with paragraph (a)(3)(i) of this section—

(A) Must only be used for pre-employment transition services specified in § 361.48(a); and

(B) Must not be used to pay for administrative costs, (as defined in § 361.5(c)(2)) associated with the provision of such services or any other vocational rehabilitation services.

(b) *Reallotment.* (1) The Secretary determines not later than 45 days before the end of a fiscal year which States, if any, will not use their full allotment.

(2) As soon as possible, but not later than the end of the fiscal year, the Secretary reallots these funds to other States that can use those additional funds during the period of performance of the award, provided the State can meet the matching requirement by obligating the non-Federal share of any reallotted funds in the fiscal year for which the funds were appropriated.

(3) In the event more funds are requested by agencies than are available, the Secretary will determine the process for allocating funds available for reallotment.

(4) Funds reallotted to another State are considered to be an increase in the recipient State's allotment for the fiscal year for which the funds were appropriated.

(Authority: Sections 12(c), 110, and 111 of the Rehabilitation Act of 1973, as amended; 29 U.S.C. 709(c), 730, and 731)

Subpart D—Unified and Combined State Plans Under Title I of the Workforce Innovation and Opportunity Act

AUTHORITY: Secs. 102, 103, and 503, Pub. L. 113–128, 128 Stat. 1425 (Jul. 22, 2014).

SOURCE: 81 FR 56022, Aug. 19, 2016, unless otherwise noted.

§ 361.100   What are the purposes of the Unified and Combined State Plans?

(a) The Unified and Combined State Plans provide the framework for States to outline a strategic vision of, and goals for, how their workforce development systems will achieve the purposes of the Workforce Innovation and Opportunity Act (WIOA).

(b) The Unified and Combined State Plans serve as 4-year action plans to develop, align, and integrate the State's systems and provide a platform to achieve the State's vision and strategic and operational goals. A Unified or Combined State Plan is intended to:

(1) Align, in strategic coordination, the six core programs required in the Unified State Plan pursuant to § 361.105(b), and additional Combined State Plan partner programs that may be part of the Combined State Plan pursuant to § 361.140;

(2) Direct investments in economic, education, and workforce training programs to focus on providing relevant education and training to ensure that individuals, including youth and individuals with barriers to employment, have the skills to compete in the job market and that employers have a ready supply of skilled workers;

(3) Apply strategies for job-driven training consistently across Federal programs; and

(4) Enable economic, education, and workforce partners to build a skilled workforce through innovation in, and alignment of, employment, training, and education programs.

§ 361.105   What are the general requirements for the Unified State Plan?

(a) The Unified State Plan must be submitted in accordance with § 361.130 and WIOA sec. 102(c), as explained in joint planning guidelines issued by the Secretaries of Labor and Education.

(b) The Governor of each State must submit, at a minimum, in accordance with § 361.130, a Unified State Plan to the Secretary of Labor to be eligible to receive funding for the workforce development system's six core programs:

(1) The adult, dislocated worker, and youth programs authorized under subtitle B of title I of WIOA and administered by the U.S. Department of Labor (DOL);

(2) The Adult Education and Family Literacy Act (AEFLA) program authorized under title II of WIOA and administered by the U.S. Department of Education (ED);

(3) The Employment Service program authorized under the Wagner-Peyser Act of 1933, as amended by WIOA title III and administered by DOL; and

(4) The Vocational Rehabilitation program authorized under title I of the Rehabilitation Act of 1973, as amended by title IV of WIOA and administered by ED.

(c) The Unified State Plan must outline the State's 4-year strategy for the core programs described in paragraph (b) of this section and meet the requirements of sec. 102(b) of WIOA, as explained in the joint planning guidelines issued by the Secretaries of Labor and Education.

(d) The Unified State Plan must include strategic and operational planning elements to facilitate the development of an aligned, coordinated, and comprehensive workforce development system. The Unified State Plan must include:

(1) Strategic planning elements that describe the State's strategic vision and goals for preparing an educated and skilled workforce under sec. 102(b)(1) of WIOA. The strategic planning elements must be informed by and include an analysis of the State's economic conditions and employer and workforce needs, including education and skill needs.

(2) Strategies for aligning the core programs and Combined State Plan partner programs as described in §361.140(d), as well as other resources available to the State, to achieve the strategic vision and goals in accordance with sec. 102(b)(1)(E) of WIOA.

(3) Operational planning elements in accordance with sec. 102(b)(2) of WIOA that support the strategies for aligning the core programs and other resources available to the State to achieve the State's vision and goals and a description of how the State Workforce Development Board (WDB) will implement its functions, in accordance with sec. 101(d) of WIOA. Operational planning elements must include:

(i) A description of how the State strategy will be implemented by each core program's lead State agency;

(ii) State operating systems, including data systems, and policies that will support the implementation of the State's strategy identified in paragraph (d)(1) of this section;

(iii) Program-specific requirements for the core programs required by WIOA sec. 102(b)(2)(D);

(iv) Assurances required by sec. 102(b)(2)(E) of WIOA, including an assurance that the lead State agencies responsible for the administration of the core programs reviewed and commented on the appropriate operational planning of the Unified State Plan and approved the elements as serving the needs of the population served by such programs, and other assurances deemed necessary by the Secretaries of Labor and Education under sec. 102(b)(2)(E)(x) of WIOA;

(v) A description of joint planning and coordination across core programs, required one-stop partner programs, and other programs and activities in the Unified State Plan; and

(vi) Any additional operational planning requirements imposed by the Secretary of Labor or the Secretary of Education under sec. 102(b)(2)(C)(viii) of WIOA.

(e) All of the requirements in this subpart that apply to States also apply to outlying areas.

§361.110 What are the program-specific requirements in the Unified State Plan for the adult, dislocated worker, and youth programs authorized under Workforce Innovation and Opportunity Act title I?

The program-specific requirements for the adult, dislocated worker, and youth programs that must be included in the Unified State Plan are described in sec. 102(b)(2)(D) of WIOA. Additional planning requirements may be explained in joint planning guidelines issued by the Secretaries of Labor and Education.

§ 361.115 What are the program-specific requirements in the Unified State Plan for the Adult Education and Family Literacy Act program authorized under Workforce Innovation and Opportunity Act title II?

The program-specific requirements for the AEFLA program in title II that must be included in the Unified State Plan are described in secs. 102(b)(2)(C) and 102(b)(2)(D)(ii) of WIOA.

(a) With regard to the description required in sec. 102(b)(2)(D)(ii)(I) of WIOA pertaining to content standards, the Unified State Plan must describe how the eligible agency will, by July 1, 2016, align its content standards for adult education with State-adopted challenging academic content standards under the Elementary and Secondary Education Act of 1965, as amended.

(b) With regard to the description required in sec. 102(b)(2)(C)(iv) of WIOA pertaining to the methods and factors the State will use to distribute funds under the core programs, for title II of WIOA, the Unified State Plan must include—

(1) How the eligible agency will award multi-year grants on a competitive basis to eligible providers in the State; and

(2) How the eligible agency will provide direct and equitable access to funds using the same grant or contract announcement and application procedure.

§ 361.120 What are the program-specific requirements in the Unified State Plan for the Employment Service program authorized under the Wagner-Peyser Act, as amended by Workforce Innovation and Opportunity Act title III?

The Employment Service program authorized under the Wagner-Peyser Act of 1933, as amended by WIOA title III, is subject to requirements in sec. 102(b) of WIOA, including any additional requirements imposed by the Secretary of Labor under secs. 102(b)(2)(C)(viii) and 102(b)(2)(D)(iv) of WIOA, as explained in joint planning guidelines issued by the Secretaries of Labor and Education.

§ 361.125 What are the program-specific requirements in the Unified State Plan for the State Vocational Rehabilitation program authorized under title I of the Rehabilitation Act of 1973, as amended by Workforce Innovation and Opportunity Act title IV?

The program specific-requirements for the vocational rehabilitation services portion of the Unified or Combined State Plan are set forth in sec. 101(a) of the Rehabilitation Act of 1973, as amended. All submission requirements for the vocational rehabilitation services portion of the Unified or Combined State Plan are in addition to the jointly developed strategic and operational content requirements prescribed by sec. 102(b) of WIOA.

§ 361.130 What is the development, submission, and approval process of the Unified State Plan?

(a) The Unified State Plan described in § 361.105 must be submitted in accordance with WIOA sec. 102(c), as explained in joint planning guidelines issued jointly by the Secretaries of Labor and Education.

(b) A State must submit its Unified State Plan to the Secretary of Labor pursuant to a process identified by the Secretary.

(1) The initial Unified State Plan must be submitted no later than 120 days prior to the commencement of the second full program year of WIOA.

(2) Subsequent Unified State Plans must be submitted no later than 120 days prior to the end of the 4-year period covered by a preceding Unified State Plan.

(3) For purposes of paragraph (b) of this section, "program year" means July 1 through June 30 of any year.

(c) The Unified State Plan must be developed with the assistance of the State WDB, as required by 20 CFR 679.130(a) and WIOA sec. 101(d), and must be developed in coordination with administrators with optimum policy-making authority for the core programs and required one-stop partners.

(d) The State must provide an opportunity for public comment on and input into the development of the Unified State Plan prior to its submission.

(1) The opportunity for public comment must include an opportunity for

comment by representatives of Local WDBs and chief elected officials, businesses, representatives of labor organizations, community-based organizations, adult education providers, institutions of higher education, other stakeholders with an interest in the services provided by the six core programs, and the general public, including individuals with disabilities.

(2) Consistent with the "Sunshine Provision" of WIOA in sec. 101(g), the State WDB must make information regarding the Unified State Plan available to the public through electronic means and regularly occurring open meetings in accordance with State law. The Unified State Plan must describe the State's process and timeline for ensuring a meaningful opportunity for public comment.

(e) Upon receipt of the Unified State Plan from the State, the Secretary of Labor will ensure that the entire Unified State Plan is submitted to the Secretary of Education pursuant to a process developed by the Secretaries.

(f) The Unified State Plan is subject to the approval of both the Secretary of Labor and the Secretary of Education.

(g) Before the Secretaries of Labor and Education approve the Unified State Plan, the vocational rehabilitation services portion of the Unified State Plan described in WIOA sec. 102(b)(2)(D)(iii) must be approved by the Commissioner of the Rehabilitation Services Administration.

(h) The Secretaries of Labor and Education will review and approve the Unified State Plan within 90 days of receipt by the Secretary of Labor, unless the Secretary of Labor or the Secretary of Education determines in writing within that period that:

(1) The plan is inconsistent with a core program's requirements;

(2) The Unified State Plan is inconsistent with any requirement of sec. 102 of WIOA; or

(3) The plan is incomplete or otherwise insufficient to determine whether it is consistent with a core program's requirements or other requirements of WIOA.

(i) If neither the Secretary of Labor nor the Secretary of Education makes the written determination described in paragraph (h) of this section within 90 days of the receipt by the Secretaries, the Unified State Plan will be considered approved.

§ 361.135 What are the requirements for modification of the Unified State Plan?

(a) In addition to the required modification review set forth in paragraph (b) of this section, a Governor may submit a modification of its Unified State Plan at any time during the 4-year period of the plan.

(b) Modifications are required, at a minimum:

(1) At the end of the first 2-year period of any 4-year State Plan, wherein the State WDB must review the Unified State Plan, and the Governor must submit modifications to the plan to reflect changes in labor market and economic conditions or other factors affecting the implementation of the Unified State Plan;

(2) When changes in Federal or State law or policy substantially affect the strategies, goals, and priorities upon which the Unified State Plan is based;

(3) When there are changes in the statewide vision, strategies, policies, State negotiated levels of performance as described in §361.170(b), the methodology used to determine local allocation of funds, reorganizations that change the working relationship with system employees, changes in organizational responsibilities, changes to the membership structure of the State WDB or alternative entity, and similar substantial changes to the State's workforce development system.

(c) Modifications to the Unified State Plan are subject to the same public review and comment requirements in §361.130(d) that apply to the development of the original Unified State Plan.

(d) Unified State Plan modifications must be approved by the Secretaries of Labor and Education, based on the approval standards applicable to the original Unified State Plan under §361.130. This approval must come after the approval of the Commissioner of the Rehabilitation Services Administration for modification of any portion of the plan described in sec. 102(b)(2)(D)(iii) of WIOA.

§ 361.140 What are the general requirements for submitting a Combined State Plan?

(a) A State may choose to develop and submit a 4-year Combined State Plan in lieu of the Unified State Plan described in §§ 361.105 through 361.125.

(b) A State that submits a Combined State Plan covering an activity or program described in paragraph (d) of this section that is, in accordance with WIOA sec. 103(c), approved or deemed complete under the law relating to the program will not be required to submit any other plan or application in order to receive Federal funds to carry out the core programs or the program or activities described under paragraph (d) of this section that are covered by the Combined State Plan.

(c) If a State develops a Combined State Plan, it must be submitted in accordance with the process described in § 361.143.

(d) If a State chooses to submit a Combined State Plan, the plan must include the six core programs and one or more of the Combined State Plan partner programs and activities described in sec. 103(a)(2) of WIOA. The Combined State Plan partner programs and activities that may be included in the Combined State Plan are:

(1) Career and technical education programs authorized under the Carl D. Perkins Career and Technical Education Act of 2006 (20 U.S.C. 2301 et seq.);

(2) Temporary Assistance for Needy Families or TANF, authorized under part A of title IV of the Social Security Act (42 U.S.C. 601 et seq.);

(3) Employment and training programs authorized under sec. 6(d)(4) of the Food and Nutrition Act of 2008 (7 U.S.C. 2015(d)(4));

(4) Work programs authorized under sec. 6(o) of the Food and Nutrition Act of 2008 (7 U.S.C. 2015(o));

(5) Trade adjustment assistance activities under chapter 2 of title II of the Trade Act of 1974 (19 U.S.C. 2271 et seq.);

(6) Services for veterans authorized under chapter 41 of title 38 United States Code;

(7) Programs authorized under State unemployment compensation laws (in accordance with applicable Federal law);

(8) Senior Community Service Employment Programs under title V of the Older Americans Act of 1965 (42 U.S.C. 3056 et seq.);

(9) Employment and training activities carried out by the Department of Housing and Urban Development (HUD);

(10) Employment and training activities carried out under the Community Services Block Grant Act (42 U.S.C. 9901 et seq.); and

(11) Reintegration of offenders programs authorized under sec. 212 of the Second Chance Act of 2007 (42 U.S.C. 17532).

(e) A Combined State Plan must contain:

(1) For the core programs, the information required by sec. 102(b) of WIOA and §§ 361.105 through 361.125, as explained in the joint planning guidelines issued by the Secretaries;

(2) For the Combined State Plan partner programs and activities, except as described in paragraph (h) of this section, the information required by the law authorizing and governing that program to be submitted to the appropriate Secretary, any other applicable legal requirements, and any common planning requirements described in sec. 102(b) of WIOA, as explained in the joint planning guidelines issued by the Secretaries;

(3) A description of the methods used for joint planning and coordination among the core programs, and with the required one-stop partner programs and other programs and activities included in the State Plan; and

(4) An assurance that all of the entities responsible for planning or administering the programs described in the Combined State Plan have had a meaningful opportunity to review and comment on all portions of the plan.

(f) Each Combined State Plan partner program included in the Combined State Plan remains subject to the applicable program-specific requirements of the Federal law and regulations, and any other applicable legal or program requirements, governing the implementation and operation of that program.

(g) For purposes of §§361.140 through 361.145 the term "appropriate Secretary" means the head of the Federal agency who exercises either plan or application approval authority for the program or activity under the Federal law authorizing the program or activity or, if there are no planning or application requirements, who exercises administrative authority over the program or activity under that Federal law.

(h) States that include employment and training activities carried out under the Community Services Block Grant (CSBG) Act (42 U.S.C. 9901 *et seq.*) under a Combined State Plan would submit all other required elements of a complete CSBG State Plan directly to the Federal agency that administers the program, according to the requirements of Federal law and regulations.

(i) States that submit employment and training activities carried out by HUD under a Combined State Plan would submit any other required planning documents for HUD programs directly to HUD, according to the requirements of Federal law and regulations.

§361.143 What is the development, submission, and approval process of the Combined State Plan?

(a) For purposes of §361.140(a), if a State chooses to develop a Combined State Plan it must submit the Combined State Plan in accordance with the requirements described below and sec. 103 of WIOA, as explained in the joint planning guidelines issued by the Secretaries of Labor and Education.

(b) The Combined State Plan must be developed with the assistance of the State WDB, as required by 20 CFR 679.130(a) and WIOA sec. 101(d), and must be developed in coordination with administrators with optimum policy-making authority for the core programs and required one-stop partners.

(c) The State must provide an opportunity for public comment on and input into the development of the Combined State Plan prior to its submission.

(1) The opportunity for public comment for the portions of the Combined State Plan that cover the core programs must include an opportunity for comment by representatives of Local WDBs and chief elected officials, businesses, representatives of labor organizations, community-based organizations, adult education providers, institutions of higher education, other stakeholders with an interest in the services provided by the six core programs, and the general public, including individuals with disabilities.

(2) Consistent with the "Sunshine Provision" of WIOA in sec. 101(g), the State WDB must make information regarding the Combined State Plan available to the public through electronic means and regularly occurring open meetings in accordance with State law. The Combined State Plan must describe the State's process and timeline for ensuring a meaningful opportunity for public comment on the portions of the plan covering core programs.

(3) The portions of the plan that cover the Combined State Plan partner programs are subject to any public comment requirements applicable to those programs.

(d) The State must submit to the Secretaries of Labor and Education and to the Secretary of the agency with responsibility for approving the program's plan or deeming it complete under the law governing the program, as part of its Combined State Plan, any plan, application, form, or any other similar document that is required as a condition for the approval of Federal funding under the applicable program or activity. Such submission must occur in accordance with a process identified by the relevant Secretaries in paragraph (a) of this section.

(e) The Combined State Plan will be approved or disapproved in accordance with the requirements of sec. 103(c) of WIOA.

(1) The portion of the Combined State Plan covering programs administered by the Departments of Labor and Education must be reviewed, and approved or disapproved, by the appropriate Secretary within 90 days beginning on the day the Combined State Plan is received by the appropriate Secretary from the State, consistent

with paragraph (f) of this section. Before the Secretaries of Labor and Education approve the Combined State Plan, the vocational rehabilitation services portion of the Combined State Plan described in WIOA sec. 102(b)(2)(D)(iii) must be approved by the Commissioner of the Rehabilitation Services Administration.

(2) If an appropriate Secretary other than the Secretary of Labor or the Secretary of Education has authority to approve or deem complete a portion of the Combined State Plan for a program or activity described in § 361.140(d), that portion of the Combined State Plan must be reviewed, and approved, disapproved, or deemed complete, by the appropriate Secretary within 120 days beginning on the day the Combined State Plan is received by the appropriate Secretary from the State consistent with paragraph (f) of this section.

(f) The appropriate Secretaries will review and approve or deem complete the Combined State Plan within 90 or 120 days, as appropriate, as described in paragraph (e) of this section, unless the Secretaries of Labor and Education or appropriate Secretary have determined in writing within that period that:

(1) The Combined State Plan is inconsistent with the requirements of the six core programs or the Federal laws authorizing or applicable to the program or activity involved, including the criteria for approval of a plan or application, or deeming the plan complete, if any, under such law;

(2) The portion of the Combined State Plan describing the six core programs or the program or activity described in paragraph (a) of this section involved does not satisfy the criteria as provided in sec. 102 or 103 of WIOA, as applicable; or

(3) The Combined State Plan is incomplete, or otherwise insufficient to determine whether it is consistent with a core program's requirements, other requirements of WIOA, or the Federal laws authorizing, or applicable to, the program or activity described in § 361.140(d), including the criteria for approval of a plan or application, if any, under such law.

(g) If the Secretary of Labor, the Secretary of Education, or the appropriate Secretary does not make the written determination described in paragraph (f) of this section within the relevant period of time after submission of the Combined State Plan, that portion of the Combined State Plan over which the Secretary has jurisdiction will be considered approved.

(h) The Secretaries of Labor and Education's written determination of approval or disapproval regarding the portion of the plan for the six core programs may be separate from the written determination of approval, disapproval, or completeness of the program-specific requirements of Combined State Plan partner programs and activities described in § 361.140(d) and included in the Combined State Plan.

(i) *Special rule.* In paragraphs (f)(1) and (3) of this section, the term "criteria for approval of a plan or application," with respect to a State or a core program or a program under the Carl D. Perkins Career and Technical Education Act of 2006 (20 U.S.C. 2301 *et seq.*), includes a requirement for agreement between the State and the appropriate Secretaries regarding State performance measures or State performance accountability measures, as the case may be, including levels of performance.

§ 361.145 **What are the requirements for modifications of the Combined State Plan?**

(a) For the core program portions of the Combined State Plan, modifications are required, at a minimum:

(1) By the end of the first 2-year period of any 4-year State Plan. The State WDB must review the Combined State Plan, and the Governor must submit modifications to the Combined State Plan to reflect changes in labor market and economic conditions or other factors affecting the implementation of the Combined State Plan;

(2) When changes in Federal or State law or policy substantially affect the strategies, goals, and priorities upon which the Combined State Plan is based;

(3) When there are changes in the statewide vision, strategies, policies, State negotiated levels of performance

as described in §361.170(b), the methodology used to determine local allocation of funds, reorganizations that change the working relationship with system employees, changes in organizational responsibilities, changes to the membership structure of the State WDB or alternative entity, and similar substantial changes to the State's workforce development system.

(b) In addition to the required modification review described in paragraph (a)(1) of this section, a State may submit a modification of its Combined State Plan at any time during the 4-year period of the plan.

(c) For any Combined State Plan partner programs and activities described in §361.140(d) that are included in a State's Combined State Plan, the State—

(1) May decide if the modification requirements under WIOA sec. 102(c)(3) that apply to the core programs will apply to the Combined State Plan partner programs, as long as consistent with any other modification requirements for the programs, or may comply with the requirements applicable to only the particular program or activity; and

(2) Must submit, in accordance with the procedure described in §361.143, any modification, amendment, or revision required by the Federal law authorizing, or applicable to, the Combined State Plan partner program or activity.

(i) If the underlying programmatic requirements change (*e.g.*, the authorizing statute is reauthorized) for Federal laws authorizing such programs, a State must either modify its Combined State Plan or submit a separate plan to the appropriate Federal agency in accordance with the new Federal law authorizing the Combined State Plan partner program or activity and other legal requirements applicable to such program or activity.

(ii) If the modification, amendment, or revision affects the administration of only that particular Combined State Plan partner program and has no impact on the Combined State Plan as a whole or the integration and administration of the core and other Combined State Plan partner programs at the State level, modifications must be sub-

mitted for approval to only the appropriate Secretary, based on the approval standards applicable to the original Combined State Plan under §361.143, if the State elects, or in accordance with the procedures and requirements applicable to the particular Combined State Plan partner program.

(3) A State also may amend its Combined State Plan to add a Combined State Plan partner program or activity described in §361.140(d).

(d) Modifications of the Combined State Plan are subject to the same public review and comment requirements that apply to the development of the original Combined State Plan as described in §361.143(c) except that, if the modification, amendment, or revision affects the administration of a particular Combined State Plan partner program and has no impact on the Combined State Plan as a whole or the integration and administration of the core and other Combined State Plan partner programs at the State level, a State may comply instead with the procedures and requirements applicable to the particular Combined State Plan partner program.

(e) Modifications for the core program portions of the Combined State Plan must be approved by the Secretaries of Labor and Education, based on the approval standards applicable to the original Combined State Plan under §361.143. This approval must come after the approval of the Commissioner of the Rehabilitation Services Administration for modification of any portion of the Combined State Plan described in sec. 102(b)(2)(D)(iii) of WIOA.

Subpart E—Performance Accountability Under Title I of the Workforce Innovation and Opportunity Act

AUTHORITY: Secs. 116, 189, and 503 of Pub. L. 113–128, 128 Stat. 1425 (Jul. 22, 2014).

SOURCE: 81 FR 56026, Aug. 19, 2016, unless otherwise noted.

§ 361.150 What definitions apply to Workforce Innovation and Opportunity Act performance accountability provisions?

(a) *Participant.* A reportable individual who has received services other than the services described in paragraph (a)(3) of this section, after satisfying all applicable programmatic requirements for the provision of services, such as eligibility determination.

(1) For the Vocational Rehabilitation (VR) program, a participant is a reportable individual who has an approved and signed Individualized Plan for Employment (IPE) and has begun to receive services.

(2) For the Workforce Innovation and Opportunity Act (WIOA) title I youth program, a participant is a reportable individual who has satisfied all applicable program requirements for the provision of services, including eligibility determination, an objective assessment, and development of an individual service strategy, and received 1 of the 14 WIOA youth program elements identified in sec. 129(c)(2) of WIOA.

(3) The following individuals are not participants:

(i) Individuals in an Adult Education and Family Literacy Act (AEFLA) program who have not completed at least 12 contact hours;

(ii) Individuals who only use the self-service system.

(A) Subject to paragraph (a)(3)(ii)(B) of this section, self-service occurs when individuals independently access any workforce development system program's information and activities in either a physical location, such as a one-stop center resource room or partner agency, or remotely via the use of electronic technologies.

(B) Self-service does not uniformly apply to all virtually accessed services. For example, virtually accessed services that provide a level of support beyond independent job or information seeking on the part of an individual would not qualify as self-service.

(iii) Individuals who receive information-only services or activities, which provide readily available information that does not require an assessment by a staff member of the individual's skills, education, or career objectives.

(4) Programs must include participants in their performance calculations.

(b) *Reportable individual.* An individual who has taken action that demonstrates an intent to use program services and who meets specific reporting criteria of the program, including:

(1) Individuals who provide identifying information;

(2) Individuals who only use the self-service system; or

(3) Individuals who only receive information-only services or activities.

(c) *Exit.* As defined for the purpose of performance calculations, exit is the point after which a participant who has received services through any program meets the following criteria:

(1) For the adult, dislocated worker, and youth programs authorized under WIOA title I, the AEFLA program authorized under WIOA title II, and the Employment Service program authorized under the Wagner-Peyser Act, as amended by WIOA title III, exit date is the last date of service.

(i) The last day of service cannot be determined until at least 90 days have elapsed since the participant last received services; services do not include self-service, information-only services or activities, or follow-up services. This also requires that there are no plans to provide the participant with future services.

(ii) [Reserved].

(2)(i) For the VR program authorized under title I of the Rehabilitation Act of 1973, as amended by WIOA title IV (VR program):

(A) The participant's record of service is closed in accordance with § 361.56 because the participant has achieved an employment outcome; or

(B) The participant's service record is closed because the individual has not achieved an employment outcome or the individual has been determined ineligible after receiving services in accordance with § 361.43.

(ii) Notwithstanding any other provision of this section, a participant will not be considered as meeting the definition of exit from the VR program if the participant's service record is closed because the participant has achieved a supported employment outcome in an integrated setting but not in competitive integrated employment.

(3)(i) A State may implement a common exit policy for all or some of the core programs in WIOA title I and the Employment Service program authorized under the Wagner-Peyser Act, as amended by WIOA title III, and any additional required partner program(s) listed in sec. 121(b)(1)(B) of WIOA that is under the authority of the U.S. Department of Labor (DOL).

(ii) If a State chooses to implement a common exit policy, the policy must require that a participant is exited only when all of the criteria in paragraph (c)(1) of this section are met for the WIOA title I core programs and the Employment Service program authorized under the Wagner-Peyser Act, as amended by WIOA title III, as well as any additional required partner programs listed in sec. 121(b)(1)(B) of WIOA under the authority of DOL to which the common exit policy applies in which the participant is enrolled.

(d) *State.* For purposes of this part, other than in regard to sanctions or the statistical adjustment model, all references to "State" include the outlying areas of American Samoa, Guam, Commonwealth of the Northern Mariana Islands, the U.S. Virgin Islands, and, as applicable, the Republic of Palau.

§ 361.155 **What are the primary indicators of performance under the Workforce Innovation and Opportunity Act?**

(a) All States submitting either a Unified or Combined State Plan under §§ 361.130 and 361.143, must propose expected levels of performance for each of the primary indicators of performance for the adult, dislocated worker, and youth programs authorized under WIOA title I; the AEFLA program authorized under WIOA title II; the Employment Service program authorized under the Wagner-Peyser Act, as amended by WIOA title III; and the VR program authorized under title I of the Rehabilitation Act of 1973, as amended by WIOA title IV.

(1) *Primary indicators of performance.* The six primary indicators of performance for the adult and dislocated work-

er programs, the AEFLA program, and the VR program are:

(i) The percentage of participants who are in unsubsidized employment during the second quarter after exit from the program;

(ii) The percentage of participants who are in unsubsidized employment during the fourth quarter after exit from the program;

(iii) Median earnings of participants who are in unsubsidized employment during the second quarter after exit from the program;

(iv)(A) The percentage of those participants enrolled in an education or training program (excluding those in on-the-job training [OJT] and customized training) who attained a recognized postsecondary credential or a secondary school diploma, or its recognized equivalent, during participation in or within 1 year after exit from the program.

(B) A participant who has attained a secondary school diploma or its recognized equivalent is included in the percentage of participants who have attained a secondary school diploma or recognized equivalent only if the participant also is employed or is enrolled in an education or training program leading to a recognized postsecondary credential within 1 year after exit from the program;

(v) The percentage of participants who, during a program year, are in an education or training program that leads to a recognized postsecondary credential or employment and who are achieving measurable skill gains, defined as documented academic, technical, occupational, or other forms of progress, towards such a credential or employment. Depending upon the type of education or training program, documented progress is defined as one of the following:

(A) Documented achievement of at least one educational functioning level of a participant who is receiving instruction below the postsecondary education level;

(B) Documented attainment of a secondary school diploma or its recognized equivalent;

(C) Secondary or postsecondary transcript or report card for a sufficient number of credit hours that shows a participant is meeting the State unit's academic standards;

(D) Satisfactory or better progress report, towards established milestones, such as completion of OJT or completion of 1 year of an apprenticeship program or similar milestones, from an employer or training provider who is providing training; or

(E) Successful passage of an exam that is required for a particular occupation or progress in attaining technical or occupational skills as evidenced by trade-related benchmarks such as knowledge-based exams.

(vi) Effectiveness in serving employers.

(2) *Participants.* For purposes of the primary indicators of performance in paragraph (a)(1) of this section, "participant" will have the meaning given to it in § 361.150(a), except that—

(i) For purposes of determining program performance levels under indicators set forth in paragraphs (a)(1)(i) through (iv) and (vi) of this section, a "participant" does not include a participant who received services under sec. 225 of WIOA and exits such program while still in a correctional institution as defined in sec. 225(e)(1) of WIOA; and

(ii) The Secretaries of Labor and Education may, as needed and consistent with the Paperwork Reduction Act (PRA), make further determinations as to the participants to be included in calculating program performance levels for purposes of any of the performance indicators set forth in paragraph (a)(1) of this section.

(b) The primary indicators in paragraphs (a)(1)(i) through (iii) and (vi) of this section apply to the Employment Service program authorized under the Wagner-Peyser Act, as amended by WIOA title III.

(c) For the youth program authorized under WIOA title I, the primary indicators are:

(1) Percentage of participants who are in education or training activities, or in unsubsidized employment, during the second quarter after exit from the program;

(2) Percentage of participants in education or training activities, or in unsubsidized employment, during the

fourth quarter after exit from the program;

(3) Median earnings of participants who are in unsubsidized employment during the second quarter after exit from the program;

(4) The percentage of those participants enrolled in an education or training program (excluding those in OJT and customized training) who obtained a recognized postsecondary credential or a secondary school diploma, or its recognized equivalent, during participation in or within 1 year after exit from the program, except that a participant who has attained a secondary school diploma or its recognized equivalent is included as having attained a secondary school diploma or recognized equivalent only if the participant is also employed or is enrolled in an education or training program leading to a recognized postsecondary credential within 1 year from program exit;

(5) The percentage of participants who during a program year, are in an education or training program that leads to a recognized postsecondary credential or employment and who are achieving measurable skill gains, defined as documented academic, technical, occupational or other forms of progress towards such a credential or employment. Depending upon the type of education or training program, documented progress is defined as one of the following:

(i) Documented achievement of at least one educational functioning level of a participant who is receiving instruction below the postsecondary education level;

(ii) Documented attainment of a secondary school diploma or its recognized equivalent;

(iii) Secondary or postsecondary transcript or report card for a sufficient number of credit hours that shows a participant is achieving the State unit's academic standards;

(iv) Satisfactory or better progress report, towards established milestones, such as completion of OJT or completion of 1 year of an apprenticeship program or similar milestones, from an employer or training provider who is providing training; or

(v) Successful passage of an exam that is required for a particular occupation or progress in attaining technical or occupational skills as evidenced by trade-related benchmarks such as knowledge-based exams.

(6) Effectiveness in serving employers.

§ 361.160 What information is required for State performance reports?

(a) The State performance report required by sec. 116(d)(2) of WIOA must be submitted annually using a template the Departments of Labor and Education will disseminate, and must provide, at a minimum, information on the actual performance levels achieved consistent with § 361.175 with respect to:

(1) The total number of participants served, and the total number of participants who exited each of the core programs identified in sec. 116(b)(3)(A)(ii) of WIOA, including disaggregated counts of those who participated in and exited a core program, by:

(i) Individuals with barriers to employment as defined in WIOA sec. 3(24); and

(ii) Co-enrollment in any of the programs in WIOA sec. 116(b)(3)(A)(ii).

(2) Information on the performance levels achieved for the primary indicators of performance for all of the core programs identified in § 361.155 including disaggregated levels for:

(i) Individuals with barriers to employment as defined in WIOA sec. 3(24);

(ii) Age;

(iii) Sex; and

(iv) Race and ethnicity.

(3) The total number of participants who received career services and the total number of participants who exited from career services for the most recent program year and the 3 preceding program years, and the total number of participants who received training services and the total number of participants who exited from training services for the most recent program year and the 3 preceding program years, as applicable to the program;

(4) Information on the performance levels achieved for the primary indicators of performance consistent with § 361.155 for career services and training services for the most recent program

year and the 3 preceding program years, as applicable to the program;

(5) The percentage of participants in a program who attained unsubsidized employment related to the training received (often referred to as training-related employment) through WIOA title I, subtitle B programs;

(6) The amount of funds spent on career services and the amount of funds spent on training services for the most recent program year and the 3 preceding program years, as applicable to the program;

(7) The average cost per participant for those participants who received career services and training services, respectively, during the most recent program year and the 3 preceding program years, as applicable to the program;

(8) The percentage of a State's annual allotment under WIOA sec. 132(b) that the State spent on administrative costs; and

(9) Information that facilitates comparisons of programs with programs in other States.

(10) For WIOA title I programs, a State performance narrative, which, for States in which a local area is implementing a pay-for-performance contracting strategy, at a minimum provides:

(i) A description of pay-for-performance contract strategies being used for programs;

(ii) The performance of service providers entering into contracts for such strategies, measured against the levels of performance specified in the contracts for such strategies; and

(iii) An evaluation of the design of the programs and performance strategies and, when available, the satisfaction of employers and participants who received services under such strategies.

(b) The disaggregation of data for the State performance report must be done in compliance with WIOA sec. 116(d)(6)(C).

(c) The State performance reports must include a mechanism of electronic access to the State's local area and eligible training provider (ETP) performance reports.

(d) States must comply with these requirements from sec. 116 of WIOA as explained in joint guidance issued by the Departments of Labor and Education, which may include information on reportable individuals as determined by the Secretaries of Labor and Education.

§ 361.165 May a State establish additional indicators of performance?

States may identify additional indicators of performance for the six core programs. If a State does so, these indicators must be included in the Unified or Combined State Plan.

§ 361.170 How are State levels of performance for primary indicators established?

(a) A State must submit in the State Plan expected levels of performance on the primary indicators of performance for each core program as required by sec. 116(b)(3)(A)(iii) of WIOA as explained in joint guidance issued by the Secretaries of Labor and Education.

(1) The initial State Plan submitted under WIOA must contain expected levels of performance for the first 2 years of the State Plan.

(2) States must submit expected levels of performance for the third and fourth year of the State Plan before the third program year consistent with §§ 361.135 and 361.145.

(b) States must reach agreement on levels of performance with the Secretaries of Labor and Education for each indicator for each core program. These are the negotiated levels of performance. The negotiated levels must be based on the following factors:

(1) How the negotiated levels of performance compare with State levels of performance established for other States;

(2) The application of an objective statistical model established by the Secretaries of Labor and Education, subject to paragraph (d) of this section;

(3) How the negotiated levels promote continuous improvement in performance based on the primary indicators and ensure optimal return on investment of Federal funds; and

(4) The extent to which the negotiated levels assist the State in meeting the performance goals established by the Secretaries of Labor and Education for the core programs in accordance with the Government Perform-

ance and Results Act of 1993, as amended.

(c) An objective statistical adjustment model will be developed and disseminated by the Secretaries of Labor and Education. The model will be based on:

(1) Differences among States in actual economic conditions, including but not limited to unemployment rates and job losses or gains in particular industries; and

(2) The characteristics of participants, including but not limited to:

(i) Indicators of poor work history;

(ii) Lack of work experience;

(iii) Lack of educational or occupational skills attainment;

(iv) Dislocation from high-wage and high-benefit employment;

(v) Low levels of literacy;

(vi) Low levels of English proficiency;

(vii) Disability status;

(viii) Homelessness;

(ix) Ex-offender status; and

(x) Welfare dependency.

(d) The objective statistical adjustment model developed under paragraph (c) of this section will be:

(1) Applied to the core programs' primary indicators upon availability of data which are necessary to populate the model and apply the model to the local core programs;

(2) Subject to paragraph (d)(1) of this section, used before the beginning of a program year in order to reach agreement on State negotiated levels for the upcoming program year; and

(3) Subject to paragraph (d)(1) of this section, used to revise negotiated levels at the end of a program year based on actual economic conditions and characteristics of participants served, consistent with sec. 116(b)(3)(A)(vii) of WIOA.

(e) The negotiated levels revised at the end of the program year, based on the statistical adjustment model, are the adjusted levels of performance.

(f) States must comply with these requirements from sec. 116 of WIOA as explained in joint guidance issued by the Departments of Labor and Education.

§361.175 What responsibility do States have to use quarterly wage record information for performance accountability?

(a)(1) States must, consistent with State laws, use quarterly wage record information in measuring a State's performance on the primary indicators of performance outlined in §361.155 and a local area's performance on the primary indicators of performance identified in §361.205.

(2) The use of social security numbers from participants and such other information as is necessary to measure the progress of those participants through quarterly wage record information is authorized.

(3) To the extent that quarterly wage records are not available for a participant, States may use other information as is necessary to measure the progress of those participants through methods other than quarterly wage record information.

(b) "Quarterly wage record information" means intrastate and interstate wages paid to an individual, the social security number (or numbers, if more than one) of the individual, and the name, address, State, and the Federal employer identification number of the employer paying the wages to the individual.

(c) The Governor may designate a State agency (or appropriate State entity) to assist in carrying out the performance reporting requirements for WIOA core programs and ETPs. The Governor or such agency (or appropriate State entity) is responsible for:

(1) Facilitating data matches;

(2) Data quality reliability; and

(3) Protection against disaggregation that would violate applicable privacy standards.

§361.180 When is a State subject to a financial sanction under the Workforce Innovation and Opportunity Act?

A State will be subject to financial sanction under WIOA sec. 116(f) if it fails to:

(a) Submit the State annual performance report required under WIOA sec. 116(d)(2); or

(b) Meet adjusted levels of performance for the primary indicators of performance in accordance with sec. 116(f) of WIOA.

§361.185 When are sanctions applied for a State's failure to submit an annual performance report?

(a) Sanctions will be applied when a State fails to submit the State annual performance report required under sec. 116(d)(2) of WIOA. A State fails to report if the State either:

(1) Does not submit a State annual performance report by the date for timely submission set in performance reporting guidance; or

(2) Submits a State annual performance report by the date for timely submission, but the report is incomplete.

(b) Sanctions will not be applied if the reporting failure is due to exceptional circumstances outside of the State's control. Exceptional circumstances may include, but are not limited to:

(1) Natural disasters;

(2) Unexpected personnel transitions; and

(3) Unexpected technology related issues.

(c) In the event that a State may not be able to submit a complete and accurate performance report by the deadline for timely reporting:

(1) The State must notify the Secretary of Labor or Secretary of Education as soon as possible, but no later than 30 days prior to the established deadline for submission, of a potential impact on the State's ability to submit its State annual performance report in order to not be considered failing to report.

(2) In circumstances where unexpected events occur less than 30 days before the established deadline for submission of the State annual performance reports, the Secretaries of Labor and Education will review requests for extending the reporting deadline in accordance with the Departments of Labor and Education's procedures that will be established in guidance.

§361.190 When are sanctions applied for failure to achieve adjusted levels of performance?

(a) States' negotiated levels of performance will be adjusted through the application of the statistical adjustment model established under §361.170

to account for actual economic conditions experienced during a program year and characteristics of participants, annually at the close of each program year.

(b) Any State that fails to meet adjusted levels of performance for the primary indicators of performance outlined in § 361.155 for any year will receive technical assistance, including assistance in the development of a performance improvement plan provided by the Secretary of Labor or Secretary of Education.

(c) Whether a State has failed to meet adjusted levels of performance will be determined using the following three criteria:

(1) The overall State program score, which is expressed as the percent achieved, compares the actual results achieved by a core program on the primary indicators of performance to the adjusted levels of performance for that core program. The average of the percentages achieved of the adjusted level of performance for each of the primary indicators by a core program will constitute the overall State program score.

(2) However, until all indicators for the core program have at least 2 years of complete data, the overall State program score will be based on a comparison of the actual results achieved to the adjusted level of performance for each of the primary indicators that have at least 2 years of complete data for that program;

(3) The overall State indicator score, which is expressed as the percent achieved, compares the actual results achieved on a primary indicator of performance by all core programs in a State to the adjusted levels of performance for that primary indicator. The average of the percentages achieved of the adjusted level of performance by all of the core programs on that indicator will constitute the overall State indicator score.

(4) However, until all indicators for the State have at least 2 years of complete data, the overall State indicator score will be based on a comparison of the actual results achieved to the adjusted level of performance for each of the primary indicators that have at

least 2 years of complete data in a State.

(5) The individual indicator score, which is expressed as the percent achieved, compares the actual results achieved by each core program on each of the individual primary indicators to the adjusted levels of performance for each of the program's primary indicators of performance.

(d) A performance failure occurs when:

(1) Any overall State program score or overall State indicator score falls below 90 percent for the program year; or

(2) Any of the States' individual indicator scores fall below 50 percent for the program year.

(e) Sanctions based on performance failure will be applied to States if, for 2 consecutive years, the State fails to meet:

(1) 90 percent of the overall State program score for the same core program;

(2) 90 percent of the overall State indicator score for the same primary indicator; or

(3) 50 percent of the same indicator score for the same program.

§ 361.195 What should States expect when a sanction is applied to the Governor's Reserve Allotment?

(a) The Secretaries of Labor and Education will reduce the Governor's Reserve Allotment by five percent of the maximum available amount for the immediately succeeding program year if:

(1) The State fails to submit the State annual performance reports as required under WIOA sec. 116(d)(2), as defined in § 361.185;

(2) The State fails to meet State adjusted levels of performance for the same primary performance indicator(s) under either § 361.190(d)(1) for the second consecutive year as defined in § 361.190; or

(3) The State's score on the same indicator for the same program falls below 50 percent under § 361.190(d)(2) for the second consecutive year as defined in § 361.190.

(b) If the State fails under paragraphs (a)(1) and either (a)(2) or (3) of this section in the same program year, the Secretaries of Labor and Education will reduce the Governor's Reserve Allotment by 10 percent of the maximum available amount for the immediately succeeding program year.

(c) If a State's Governor's Reserve Allotment is reduced:

(1) The reduced amount will not be returned to the State in the event that the State later improves performance or submits its annual performance report; and

(2) The Governor's Reserve will continue to be set at the reduced level in each subsequent year until the Secretary of Labor or the Secretary of Education, depending on which program is impacted, determines that the State met the State adjusted levels of performance for the applicable primary performance indicators and has submitted all of the required performance reports.

(d) A State may request review of a sanction the Secretary of Labor imposes in accordance with the provisions of 20 CFR 683.800.

§361.200 What other administrative actions will be applied to States' performance requirements?

(a) In addition to sanctions for failure to report or failure to meet adjusted levels of performance, States will be subject to administrative actions in the case of poor performance.

(b) States' performance achievement on the individual primary indicators will be assessed in addition to the overall State program score and overall State indicator score. Based on this assessment, as clarified and explained in guidance, for performance on any individual primary indicator, the Secretary of Labor or the Secretary of Education will require the State to establish a performance risk plan to address continuous improvement on the individual primary indicator.

§361.205 What performance indicators apply to local areas and what information must be included in local area performance reports?

(a) Each local area in a State under WIOA title I is subject to the same primary indicators of performance for the core programs for WIOA title I under §361.155(a)(1) and (c) that apply to the State.

(b) In addition to the indicators described in paragraph (a) of this section, under §361.165, the Governor may apply additional indicators of performance to local areas in the State.

(c) States must annually make local area performance reports available to the public using a template that the Departments of Labor and Education will disseminate in guidance, including by electronic means. The State must provide electronic access to the public local area performance report in its annual State performance report.

(d) The local area performance report must include:

(1) The actual results achieved under §361.155 and the information required under §361.160(a);

(2) The percentage of a local area's allotment under WIOA secs. 128(b) and 133(b) that the local area spent on administrative costs; and

(3) Other information that facilitates comparisons of programs with programs in other local areas (or planning regions if the local area is part of a planning region).

(e) The disaggregation of data for the local area performance report must be done in compliance with WIOA sec. 116(d)(6)(C).

(f) States must comply with any requirements from sec. 116(d)(3) of WIOA as explained in guidance, including the use of the performance reporting template, issued by DOL.

§361.210 How are local performance levels established?

(a) The objective statistical adjustment model required under sec. 116(b)(3)(A)(viii) of WIOA and described in §361.170(c) must be:

(1) Applied to the core programs' primary indicators upon availability of data which are necessary to populate the model and apply the model to the local core programs;

(2) Used in order to reach agreement on local negotiated levels of performance for the upcoming program year; and

(3) Used to establish adjusted levels of performance at the end of a program year based on actual conditions, consistent with WIOA sec. 116(c)(3).

(b) Until all indicators for the core program in a local area have at least 2

367

years of complete data, the comparison of the actual results achieved to the adjusted levels of performance for each of the primary indicators only will be applied where there are at least 2 years of complete data for that program.

(c) The Governor, Local Workforce Development Board (WDB), and chief elected official must reach agreement on local negotiated levels of performance based on a negotiations process before the start of a program year with the use of the objective statistical model described in paragraph (a) of this section. The negotiations will include a discussion of circumstances not accounted for in the model and will take into account the extent to which the levels promote continuous improvement. The objective statistical model will be applied at the end of the program year based on actual economic conditions and characteristics of the participants served.

(d) The negotiations process described in paragraph (c) of this section must be developed by the Governor and disseminated to all Local WDBs and chief elected officials.

(e) The Local WDBs may apply performance measures to service providers that differ from the performance indicators that apply to the local area. These performance measures must be established after considering:

(1) The established local negotiated levels;

(2) The services provided by each provider; and

(3) The populations the service providers are intended to serve.

§ 361.215 Under what circumstances are local areas eligible for State Incentive Grants?

(a) The Governor is not required to award local incentive funds, but is authorized to provide incentive grants to local areas for performance on the primary indicators of performance consistent with WIOA sec. 134(a)(3)(A)(xi).

(b) The Governor may use non-Federal funds to create incentives for the Local WDBs to implement pay-for-performance contract strategies for the delivery of training services described in WIOA sec. 134(c)(3) or activities described in WIOA sec. 129(c)(2) in the local areas served by the Local WDBs.

Pay-for-performance contract strategies must be implemented in accordance with 20 CFR part 683, subpart E and § 361.160.

§ 361.220 Under what circumstances may a corrective action or sanction be applied to local areas for poor performance?

(a) If a local area fails to meet the adjusted levels of performance agreed to under § 361.210 for the primary indicators of performance in the adult, dislocated worker, and youth programs authorized under WIOA title I in any program year, technical assistance must be provided by the Governor or, upon the Governor's request, by the Secretary of Labor.

(1) A State must establish the threshold for failure to meet adjusted levels of performance for a local area before coming to agreement on the negotiated levels of performance for the local area.

(i) A State must establish the adjusted level of performance for a local area, using the statistical adjustment model described in § 361.170(c).

(ii) At least 2 years of complete data on any indicator for any local core program are required in order to establish adjusted levels of performance for a local area.

(2) The technical assistance may include:

(i) Assistance in the development of a performance improvement plan;

(ii) The development of a modified local or regional plan; or

(iii) Other actions designed to assist the local area in improving performance.

(b) If a local area fails to meet the adjusted levels of performance agreed to under § 361.210 for the same primary indicators of performance for the same core program authorized under WIOA title I for a third consecutive program year, the Governor must take corrective actions. The corrective actions must include the development of a reorganization plan under which the Governor:

(1) Requires the appointment and certification of a new Local WDB, consistent with the criteria established under 20 CFR 679.350;

(2) Prohibits the use of eligible providers and one-stop partners that have

been identified as achieving poor levels of performance; or

(3) Takes such other significant actions as the Governor determines are appropriate.

§361.225 Under what circumstances may local areas appeal a reorganization plan?

(a) The Local WDB and chief elected official for a local area that is subject to a reorganization plan under WIOA sec. 116(g)(2)(A) may appeal to the Governor to rescind or revise the reorganization plan not later than 30 days after receiving notice of the reorganization plan. The Governor must make a final decision within 30 days after receipt of the appeal.

(b) The Local WDB and chief elected official may appeal the final decision of the Governor to the Secretary of Labor not later than 30 days after receiving the decision from the Governor. Any appeal of the Governor's final decision must be:

(1) Appealed jointly by the Local WDB and chief elected official to the Secretary of Labor under 20 CFR 683.650; and

(2) Must be submitted by certified mail, return receipt requested, to the Secretary of Labor, U.S. Department of Labor, 200 Constitution Ave. NW., Washington, DC 20210, Attention: ASET. A copy of the appeal must be simultaneously provided to the Governor.

(c) Upon receipt of the joint appeal from the Local WDB and chief elected official, the Secretary of Labor must make a final decision within 30 days. In making this determination the Secretary of Labor may consider any comments submitted by the Governor in response to the appeals.

(d) The decision by the Governor on the appeal becomes effective at the time it is issued and remains effective unless the Secretary of Labor rescinds or revises the reorganization plan under WIOA sec. 116(g)(2)(C).

§361.230 What information is required for the eligible training provider performance reports?

(a) States are required to make available and publish annually using a template the Departments of Labor and Education will disseminate including through electronic means, the ETP performance reports for ETPs who provide services under sec. 122 of WIOA that are described in 20 CFR 680.400 through 680.530. These reports at a minimum must include, consistent with §361.175 and with respect to each program of study that is eligible to receive funds under WIOA:

(1) The total number of participants as defined by §361.150(a) who received training services under the adult and dislocated worker programs authorized under WIOA title I for the most recent year and the 3 preceding program years, including:

(i) The number of participants under the adult and dislocated worker programs disaggregated by barriers to employment;

(ii) The number of participants under the adult and dislocated worker programs disaggregated by race, ethnicity, sex, and age;

(iii) The number of participants under the adult and dislocated worker programs disaggregated by the type of training entity for the most recent program year and the 3 preceding program years;

(2) The total number of participants who exit a program of study or its equivalent, including disaggregate counts by the type of training entity during the most recent program year and the 3 preceding program years;

(3) The average cost-per-participant for participants who received training services for the most recent program year and the 3 preceding program years disaggregated by type of training entity;

(4) The total number of individuals exiting from the program of study (or the equivalent) with respect to all individuals engaging in the program of study (or the equivalent); and

(5) The levels of performance achieved for the primary indicators of performance identified in §361.155(a)(1)(i) through (iv) with respect to all individuals engaging in a program of study (or the equivalent).

(b) Apprenticeship programs registered under the National Apprenticeship Act are not required to submit

ETP performance information. If a registered apprenticeship program voluntarily submits performance information to a State, the State must include this information in the report.

(c) The State must provide a mechanism of electronic access to the public ETP performance report in its annual State performance report.

(d) States must comply with any requirements from sec. 116(d)(4) of WIOA as explained in guidance issued by DOL.

(e) The Governor may designate one or more State agencies such as a State Education Agency or other State Educational Authority to assist in overseeing ETP performance and facilitating the production and dissemination of ETP performance reports. These agencies may be the same agencies that are designated as responsible for administering the ETP list as provided under 20 CFR 680.500. The Governor or such agencies, or authorities, is responsible for:

(1) Facilitating data matches between ETP records and unemployment insurance (UI) wage data in order to produce the report;

(2) The creation and dissemination of the reports as described in paragraphs (a) through (d) of this section;

(3) Coordinating the dissemination of the performance reports with the ETP list and the information required to accompany the list, as provided in 20 CFR 680.500.

§ 361.235 What are the reporting requirements for individual records for core Workforce Innovation and Opportunity Act (WIOA) title I programs; the Wagner-Peyser Act Employment Service program, as amended by WIOA title III; and the Vocational Rehabilitation program authorized under title I of the Rehabilitation Act of 1973, as amended by WIOA title IV?

(a) On a quarterly basis, each State must submit to the Secretary of Labor or the Secretary of Education, as appropriate, individual records that include demographic information, information on services received, and information on resulting outcomes, as appropriate, for each reportable individual in either of the following programs administered by the Secretary

of Labor or Secretary of Education: A WIOA title I core program; the Employment Service program authorized under the Wagner-Peyser Act, as amended by WIOA title III; or the VR program authorized under title I of the Rehabilitation Act of 1973, as amended by WIOA title IV.

(b) For individual records submitted to the Secretary of Labor, those records may be required to be integrated across all programs administered by the Secretary of Labor in one single file.

(c) States must comply with the requirements of sec. 116(d)(2) of WIOA as explained in guidance issued by the Departments of Labor and Education.

§ 361.240 What are the requirements for data validation of State annual performance reports?

(a) States must establish procedures, consistent with guidelines issued by the Secretary of Labor or the Secretary of Education, to ensure that they submit complete annual performance reports that contain information that is valid and reliable, as required by WIOA sec. 116(d)(5).

(b) If a State fails to meet standards in paragraph (a) of this section as determined by the Secretary of Labor or the Secretary of Education, the appropriate Secretary will provide technical assistance and may require the State to develop and implement corrective actions, which may require the State to provide training for its subrecipients.

(c) The Secretaries of Labor and Education will provide training and technical assistance to States in order to implement this section. States must comply with the requirements of sec. 116(d)(5) of WIOA as explained in guidance.

Subpart F—Description of the One-Stop Delivery System Under Title I of the Workforce Innovation and Opportunity Act

AUTHORITY: Secs. 503, 107, 121, 134, 189, Pub. L. 113–128, 128 Stat. 1425 (Jul. 22, 2014).

SOURCE: 81 FR 56033, Aug. 19, 2016, unless otherwise noted.

§ 361.300 What is the one-stop delivery system?

(a) The one-stop delivery system brings together workforce development, educational, and other human resource services in a seamless customer-focused service delivery network that enhances access to the programs' services and improves long-term employment outcomes for individuals receiving assistance. One-stop partners administer separately funded programs as a set of integrated streamlined services to customers.

(b) Title I of the Workforce Innovation and Opportunity Act (WIOA) assigns responsibilities at the local, State, and Federal level to ensure the creation and maintenance of a one-stop delivery system that enhances the range and quality of education and workforce development services that employers and individual customers can access.

(c) The system must include at least one comprehensive physical center in each local area as described in § 361.305.

(d) The system may also have additional arrangements to supplement the comprehensive center. These arrangements include:

(1) An affiliated site or a network of affiliated sites, where one or more partners make programs, services, and activities available, as described in § 361.310;

(2) A network of eligible one-stop partners, as described in §§ 361.400 through 361.410, through which each partner provides one or more of the programs, services, and activities that are linked, physically or technologically, to an affiliated site or access point that assures customers are provided information on the availability of career services, as well as other program services and activities, regardless of where they initially enter the public workforce system in the local area; and

(3) Specialized centers that address specific needs, including those of dislocated workers, youth, or key industry sectors, or clusters.

(e) Required one-stop partner programs must provide access to programs, services, and activities through electronic means if applicable and practicable. This is in addition to providing access to services through the mandatory comprehensive physical one-stop center and any affiliated sites or specialized centers. The provision of programs and services by electronic methods such as Web sites, telephones, or other means must improve the efficiency, coordination, and quality of one-stop partner services. Electronic delivery must not replace access to such services at a comprehensive one-stop center or be a substitute to making services available at an affiliated site if the partner is participating in an affiliated site. Electronic delivery systems must be in compliance with the nondiscrimination and equal opportunity provisions of WIOA sec. 188 and its implementing regulations at 29 CFR part 38.

(f) The design of the local area's one-stop delivery system must be described in the Memorandum of Understanding (MOU) executed with the one-stop partners, described in § 361.500.

§ 361.305 What is a comprehensive one-stop center and what must be provided there?

(a) A comprehensive one-stop center is a physical location where job seeker and employer customers can access the programs, services, and activities of all required one-stop partners. A comprehensive one-stop center must have at least one title I staff person physically present.

(b) The comprehensive one-stop center must provide:

(1) Career services, described in § 361.430;

(2) Access to training services described in 20 CFR 680.200;

(3) Access to any employment and training activities carried out under sec. 134(d) of WIOA;

(4) Access to programs and activities carried out by one-stop partners listed in §§ 361.400 through 361.410, including the Employment Service program authorized under the Wagner-Peyser Act, as amended by WIOA title III (Wagner-Peyser Act Employment Service program); and

(5) Workforce and labor market information.

(c) Customers must have access to these programs, services, and activities during regular business days at a comprehensive one-stop center. The Local

Workforce Development Board (WDB) may establish other service hours at other times to accommodate the schedules of individuals who work on regular business days. The State WDB will evaluate the hours of access to service as part of the evaluation of effectiveness in the one-stop certification process described in § 361.800(b).

(d) "Access" to each partner program and its services means:

(1) Having a program staff member physically present at the one-stop center;

(2) Having a staff member from a different partner program physically present at the one-stop center appropriately trained to provide information to customers about the programs, services, and activities available through partner programs; or

(3) Making available a direct linkage through technology to program staff who can provide meaningful information or services.

(i) A "direct linkage" means providing direct connection at the one-stop center, within a reasonable time, by phone or through a real-time Web-based communication to a program staff member who can provide program information or services to the customer.

(ii) A "direct linkage" cannot exclusively be providing a phone number or computer Web site or providing information, pamphlets, or materials.

(e) All comprehensive one-stop centers must be physically and programmatically accessible to individuals with disabilities, as described in 29 CFR part 38, the implementing regulations of WIOA sec. 188.

§ 361.310 What is an affiliated site and what must be provided there?

(a) An affiliated site, or affiliate one-stop center, is a site that makes available to job seeker and employer customers one or more of the one-stop partners' programs, services, and activities. An affiliated site does not need to provide access to every required one-stop partner program. The frequency of program staff's physical presence in the affiliated site will be determined at the local level. Affiliated sites are access points in addition to the comprehensive one-stop center(s) in each local area. If used by local areas as a part of the service delivery strategy, affiliate sites must be implemented in a manner that supplements and enhances customer access to services.

(b) As described in § 361.315, Wagner-Peyser Act employment services cannot be a stand-alone affiliated site.

(c) States, in conjunction with the Local WDBs, must examine lease agreements and property holdings throughout the one-stop delivery system in order to use property in an efficient and effective way. Where necessary and appropriate, States and Local WDBs must take expeditious steps to align lease expiration dates with efforts to consolidate one-stop operations into service points where Wagner-Peyser Act employment services are colocated as soon as reasonably possible. These steps must be included in the State Plan.

(d) All affiliated sites must be physically and programmatically accessible to individuals with disabilities, as described in 29 CFR part 38, the implementing regulations of WIOA sec. 188.

§ 361.315 Can a stand-alone Wagner-Peyser Act Employment Service office be designated as an affiliated one-stop site?

(a) Separate stand-alone Wagner-Peyser Act Employment Service offices are not permitted under WIOA, as also described in 20 CFR 652.202.

(b) If Wagner-Peyser Act employment services are provided at an affiliated site, there must be at least one or more other partners in the affiliated site with a physical presence of combined staff more than 50 percent of the time the center is open. Additionally, the other partner must not be the partner administering local veterans' employment representatives, disabled veterans' outreach program specialists, or unemployment compensation programs. If Wagner-Peyser Act employment services and any of these 3 programs are provided at an affiliated site, an additional partner or partners must have a presence of combined staff in the center more than 50 percent of the time the center is open.

§ 361.320 Are there any requirements for networks of eligible one-stop partners or specialized centers?

Any network of one-stop partners or specialized centers, as described in § 361.300(d)(3), must be connected to the comprehensive one-stop center and any appropriate affiliate one-stop centers, for example, by having processes in place to make referrals to these centers and the partner programs located in them. Wagner-Peyser Act employment services cannot stand alone in a specialized center. Just as described in § 361.315 for an affiliated site, a specialized center must include other programs besides Wagner-Peyser Act employment services, local veterans' employment representatives, disabled veterans' outreach program specialists, and unemployment compensation.

§ 361.400 Who are the required one-stop partners?

(a) Section 121(b)(1)(B) of WIOA identifies the entities that are required partners in the local one-stop delivery systems.

(b) The required partners are the entities responsible for administering the following programs and activities in the local area:

(1) Programs authorized under title I of WIOA, including:

(i) Adults;

(ii) Dislocated workers;

(iii) Youth;

(iv) Job Corps;

(v) YouthBuild;

(vi) Native American programs; and

(vii) Migrant and seasonal farm-worker programs;

(2) The Wagner-Peyser Act Employment Service program authorized under the Wagner-Peyser Act (29 U.S.C. 49 et seq.), as amended by WIOA title III;

(3) The Adult Education and Family Literacy Act (AEFLA) program authorized under title II of WIOA;

(4) The Vocational Rehabilitation (VR) program authorized under title I of the Rehabilitation Act of 1973 (29 U.S.C. 720 et seq.), as amended by WIOA title IV;

(5) The Senior Community Service Employment Program authorized under title V of the Older Americans Act of 1965 (42 U.S.C. 3056 et seq.);

(6) Career and technical education programs at the postsecondary level authorized under the Carl D. Perkins Career and Technical Education Act of 2006 (20 U.S.C. 2301 et seq.);

(7) Trade Adjustment Assistance activities authorized under chapter 2 of title II of the Trade Act of 1974 (19 U.S.C. 2271 et seq.);

(8) Jobs for Veterans State Grants programs authorized under chapter 41 of title 38, U.S.C.;

(9) Employment and training activities carried out under the Community Services Block Grant (42 U.S.C. 9901 et seq.);

(10) Employment and training activities carried out by the Department of Housing and Urban Development;

(11) Programs authorized under State unemployment compensation laws (in accordance with applicable Federal law);

(12) Programs authorized under sec. 212 of the Second Chance Act of 2007 (42 U.S.C. 17532); and

(13) Temporary Assistance for Needy Families (TANF) authorized under part A of title IV of the Social Security Act (42 U.S.C. 601 et seq.), unless exempted by the Governor under § 361.405(b).

§ 361.405 Is Temporary Assistance for Needy Families a required one-stop partner?

(a) Yes, TANF, authorized under part A of title IV of the Social Security Act (42 U.S.C. 601 et seq.), is a required partner.

(b) The Governor may determine that TANF will not be a required partner in the State, or within some specific local areas in the State. In this instance, the Governor must notify the Secretaries of the U.S. Departments of Labor and Health and Human Services in writing of this determination.

(c) In States, or local areas within a State, where the Governor has determined that TANF is not required to be a partner, local TANF programs may still work in collaboration or partnership with the local one-stop centers to deliver employment and training services to the TANF population unless inconsistent with the Governor's direction.

§ 361.410 What other entities may serve as one-stop partners?

(a) Other entities that carry out a workforce development program, including Federal, State, or local programs and programs in the private sector, may serve as additional partners in the one-stop delivery system if the Local WDB and chief elected official(s) approve the entity's participation.

(b) Additional partners may include, but are not limited to:

(1) Employment and training programs administered by the Social Security Administration, including the Ticket to Work and Self-Sufficiency Program established under sec. 1148 of the Social Security Act (42 U.S.C. 1320b–19);

(2) Employment and training programs carried out by the Small Business Administration;

(3) Supplemental Nutrition Assistance Program (SNAP) employment and training programs, authorized under secs. 6(d)(4) and 6(o) of the Food and Nutrition Act of 2008 (7 U.S.C. 2015(d)(4));

(4) Client Assistance Program authorized under sec. 112 of the Rehabilitation Act of 1973 (29 U.S.C. 732);

(5) Programs authorized under the National and Community Service Act of 1990 (42 U.S.C. 12501 *et seq.*); and

(6) Other appropriate Federal, State or local programs, including, but not limited to, employment, education, and training programs provided by public libraries or in the private sector.

§ 361.415 What entity serves as the one-stop partner for a particular program in the local area?

(a) The entity that carries out the program and activities listed in § 361.400 or § 361.410, and therefore serves as the one-stop partner, is the grant recipient, administrative entity, or organization responsible for administering the funds of the specified program in the local area. The term "entity" does not include the service providers that contract with, or are subrecipients of, the local administrative entity. For programs that do not include local administrative entities, the responsible State agency must be the partner. Specific entities for particular programs are identified in paragraphs (b) through

(e) of this section. If a program or activity listed in § 361.400 is not carried out in a local area, the requirements relating to a required one-stop partner are not applicable to such program or activity in that local one-stop delivery system.

(b) For title II of WIOA, the entity or agency that carries out the program for the purposes of paragraph (a) of this section is the sole entity or agency in the State or outlying area responsible for administering or supervising policy for adult education and literacy activities in the State or outlying area. The State eligible entity or agency may delegate its responsibilities under paragraph (a) of this section to one or more eligible providers or consortium of eligible providers.

(c) For the VR program, authorized under title I of the Rehabilitation Act of 1973, as amended by WIOA title IV, the entity that carries out the program for the purposes of paragraph (a) of this section is the designated State agencies or designated State units specified under sec. 101(a)(2) of the Rehabilitation Act that is primarily concerned with vocational rehabilitation, or vocational and other rehabilitation, of individuals with disabilities.

(d) Under WIOA title I, the national programs, including Job Corps, the Native American program, YouthBuild, and Migrant and Seasonal Farmworker programs are required one-stop partners. The entity for the Native American program, YouthBuild, and Migrant and Seasonal Farmworker programs is the grantee of those respective programs. The entity for Job Corps is the Job Corps center.

(e) For the Carl D. Perkins Career and Technical Education Act of 2006, the entity that carries out the program for the purposes of paragraph (a) of this section is the eligible recipient or recipients at the postsecondary level, or a consortium of eligible recipients at the postsecondary level in the local area. The eligible recipient at the postsecondary level may also request assistance from the State eligible agency in completing its responsibilities under paragraph (a) of this section.

§ 361.420 What are the roles and responsibilities of the required one-stop partners?

Each required partner must:

(a) Provide access to its programs or activities through the one-stop delivery system, in addition to any other appropriate locations;

(b) Use a portion of funds made available to the partner's program, to the extent consistent with the Federal law authorizing the partner's program and with Federal cost principles in 2 CFR parts 200 and 3474 (requiring, among other things, that costs are allowable, reasonable, necessary, and allocable), to:

(1) Provide applicable career services; and

(2) Work collaboratively with the State and Local WDBs to establish and maintain the one-stop delivery system. This includes jointly funding the one-stop infrastructure through partner contributions that are based upon:

(i) A reasonable cost allocation methodology by which infrastructure costs are charged to each partner based on proportionate use and relative benefit received;

(ii) Federal cost principles; and

(iii) Any local administrative cost requirements in the Federal law authorizing the partner's program. (This is further described in § 361.700.)

(c) Enter into an MOU with the Local WDB relating to the operation of the one-stop delivery system that meets the requirements of § 361.500(b);

(d) Participate in the operation of the one-stop delivery system consistent with the terms of the MOU, requirements of authorizing laws, the Federal cost principles, and all other applicable legal requirements; and

(e) Provide representation on the State and Local WDBs as required and participate in Board committees as needed.

§ 361.425 What are the applicable career services that must be provided through the one-stop delivery system by required one-stop partners?

(a) The applicable career services to be delivered by required one-stop partners are those services listed in § 361.430 that are authorized to be provided under each partner's program.

(b) One-stop centers provide services to individual customers based on individual needs, including the seamless delivery of multiple services to individual customers. There is no required sequence of services.

§ 361.430 What are career services?

Career services, as identified in sec. 134(c)(2) of WIOA, consist of three types:

(a) Basic career services must be made available and, at a minimum, must include the following services, as consistent with allowable program activities and Federal cost principles:

(1) Determinations of whether the individual is eligible to receive assistance from the adult, dislocated worker, or youth programs;

(2) Outreach, intake (including worker profiling), and orientation to information and other services available through the one-stop delivery system. For the TANF program, States must provide individuals with the opportunity to initiate an application for TANF assistance and non-assistance benefits and services, which could be implemented through the provision of paper application forms or links to the application Web site;

(3) Initial assessment of skill levels including literacy, numeracy, and English language proficiency, as well as aptitudes, abilities (including skills gaps), and supportive services needs;

(4) Labor exchange services, including—

(i) Job search and placement assistance, and, when needed by an individual, career counseling, including—

(A) Provision of information on in-demand industry sectors and occupations (as defined in sec. 3(23) of WIOA); and

(B) Provision of information on nontraditional employment; and

(ii) Appropriate recruitment and other business services on behalf of employers, including information and referrals to specialized business services other than those traditionally offered through the one-stop delivery system;

(5) Provision of referrals to and coordination of activities with other programs and services, including programs and services within the one-stop delivery system and, when appropriate,

other workforce development programs;

(6) Provision of workforce and labor market employment statistics information, including the provision of accurate information relating to local, regional, and national labor market areas, including—

(i) Job vacancy listings in labor market areas;

(ii) Information on job skills necessary to obtain the vacant jobs listed; and

(iii) Information relating to local occupations in demand and the earnings, skill requirements, and opportunities for advancement for those jobs;

(7) Provision of performance information and program cost information on eligible providers of education, training, and workforce services by program and type of providers;

(8) Provision of information, in usable and understandable formats and languages, about how the local area is performing on local performance accountability measures, as well as any additional performance information relating to the area's one-stop delivery system;

(9) Provision of information, in usable and understandable formats and languages, relating to the availability of supportive services or assistance, and appropriate referrals to those services and assistance, including: Child care; child support; medical or child health assistance available through the State's Medicaid program and Children's Health Insurance Program; benefits under SNAP; assistance through the earned income tax credit; and assistance under a State program for TANF, and other supportive services and transportation provided through that program;

(10) Provision of information and meaningful assistance to individuals seeking assistance in filing a claim for unemployment compensation.

(i) "Meaningful assistance" means:

(A) Providing assistance on-site using staff who are well-trained in unemployment compensation claims filing and the rights and responsibilities of claimants; or

(B) Providing assistance by phone or via other technology, as long as the assistance is provided by trained and available staff and within a reasonable time.

(ii) The costs associated in providing this assistance may be paid for by the State's unemployment insurance program, or the WIOA adult or dislocated worker programs, or some combination thereof.

(11) Assistance in establishing eligibility for programs of financial aid assistance for training and education programs not provided under WIOA.

(b) Individualized career services must be made available if determined to be appropriate in order for an individual to obtain or retain employment. These services include the following services, as consistent with program requirements and Federal cost principles:

(1) Comprehensive and specialized assessments of the skill levels and service needs of adults and dislocated workers, which may include—

(i) Diagnostic testing and use of other assessment tools; and

(ii) In-depth interviewing and evaluation to identify employment barriers and appropriate employment goals;

(2) Development of an individual employment plan, to identify the employment goals, appropriate achievement objectives, and appropriate combination of services for the participant to achieve his or her employment goals, including the list of, and information about, the eligible training providers (as described in 20 CFR 680.180);

(3) Group counseling;

(4) Individual counseling;

(5) Career planning;

(6) Short-term pre-vocational services including development of learning skills, communication skills, interviewing skills, punctuality, personal maintenance skills, and professional conduct services to prepare individuals for unsubsidized employment or training;

(7) Internships and work experiences that are linked to careers (as described in 20 CFR 680.170);

(8) Workforce preparation activities;

(9) Financial literacy services as described in sec. 129(b)(2)(D) of WIOA and 20 CFR 681.500;

(10) Out-of-area job search assistance and relocation assistance; and

(11) English language acquisition and integrated education and training programs.

(c) Follow-up services must be provided, as appropriate, including: Counseling regarding the workplace, for participants in adult or dislocated worker workforce investment activities who are placed in unsubsidized employment, for up to 12 months after the first day of employment.

(d) In addition to the requirements in paragraph (a)(2) of this section, TANF agencies must identify employment services and related support being provided by the TANF program (within the local area) that qualify as career services and ensure access to them via the local one-stop delivery system.

§361.435 **What are the business services provided through the one-stop delivery system, and how are they provided?**

(a) Certain career services must be made available to local employers, specifically labor exchange activities and labor market information described in §361.430(a)(4)(ii) and (a)(6). Local areas must establish and develop relationships and networks with large and small employers and their intermediaries. Local areas also must develop, convene, or implement industry or sector partnerships.

(b) Customized business services may be provided to employers, employer associations, or other such organizations. These services are tailored for specific employers and may include:

(1) Customized screening and referral of qualified participants in training services to employers;

(2) Customized services to employers, employer associations, or other such organizations, on employment-related issues;

(3) Customized recruitment events and related services for employers including targeted job fairs;

(4) Human resource consultation services, including but not limited to assistance with:

(i) Writing/reviewing job descriptions and employee handbooks;

(ii) Developing performance evaluation and personnel policies;

(iii) Creating orientation sessions for new workers;

(iv) Honing job interview techniques for efficiency and compliance;

(v) Analyzing employee turnover;

(vi) Creating job accommodations and using assistive technologies; or

(vii) Explaining labor and employment laws to help employers comply with discrimination, wage/hour, and safety/health regulations;

(5) Customized labor market information for specific employers, sectors, industries or clusters; and

(6) Other similar customized services.

(c) Local areas may also provide other business services and strategies that meet the workforce investment needs of area employers, in accordance with partner programs' statutory requirements and consistent with Federal cost principles. These business services may be provided through effective business intermediaries working in conjunction with the Local WDB, or through the use of economic development, philanthropic, and other public and private resources in a manner determined appropriate by the Local WDB and in cooperation with the State. Allowable activities, consistent with each partner's authorized activities, include, but are not limited to:

(1) Developing and implementing industry sector strategies (including strategies involving industry partnerships, regional skills alliances, industry skill panels, and sectoral skills partnerships);

(2) Customized assistance or referral for assistance in the development of a registered apprenticeship program;

(3) Developing and delivering innovative workforce investment services and strategies for area employers, which may include career pathways, skills upgrading, skill standard development and certification for recognized postsecondary credential or other employer use, and other effective initiatives for meeting the workforce investment needs of area employers and workers;

(4) Assistance to area employers in managing reductions in force in coordination with rapid response activities and with strategies for the aversion of layoffs, which may include strategies such as early identification of firms at risk of layoffs, use of feasibility studies to assess the needs of and options for

at-risk firms, and the delivery of employment and training activities to address risk factors;

(5) The marketing of business services to appropriate area employers, including small and mid-sized employers; and

(6) Assisting employers with accessing local, State, and Federal tax credits.

(d) All business services and strategies must be reflected in the local plan, described in 20 CFR 679.560(b)(3).

§ 361.440 **When may a fee be charged for the business services in this subpart?**

(a) There is no requirement that a fee-for-service be charged to employers.

(b) No fee may be charged for services provided in § 361.435(a).

(c) A fee may be charged for services provided under § 361.435(b) and (c). Services provided under § 361.435(c) may be provided through effective business intermediaries working in conjunction with the Local WDB and may also be provided on a fee-for-service basis or through the leveraging of economic development, philanthropic, and other public and private resources in a manner determined appropriate by the Local WDB. The Local WDB may examine the services provided compared with the assets and resources available within the local one-stop delivery system and through its partners to determine an appropriate cost structure for services, if any.

(d) Any fees earned are recognized as program income and must be expended by the partner in accordance with the partner program's authorizing statute, implementing regulations, and Federal cost principles identified in Uniform Guidance.

§ 361.500 **What is the Memorandum of Understanding for the one-stop delivery system and what must be included in the Memorandum of Understanding?**

(a) The MOU is the product of local discussion and negotiation, and is an agreement developed and executed between the Local WDB and the one-stop partners, with the agreement of the chief elected official and the one-stop partners, relating to the operation of the one-stop delivery system in the local area. Two or more local areas in a region may develop a single joint MOU, if they are in a region that has submitted a regional plan under sec. 106 of WIOA.

(b) The MOU must include:

(1) A description of services to be provided through the one-stop delivery system, including the manner in which the services will be coordinated and delivered through the system;

(2) Agreement on funding the costs of the services and the operating costs of the system, including:

(i) Funding of infrastructure costs of one-stop centers in accordance with §§ 361.700 through 361.755; and

(ii) Funding of the shared services and operating costs of the one-stop delivery system described in § 361.760;

(3) Methods for referring individuals between the one-stop operators and partners for appropriate services and activities;

(4) Methods to ensure that the needs of workers, youth, and individuals with barriers to employment, including individuals with disabilities, are addressed in providing access to services, including access to technology and materials that are available through the one-stop delivery system;

(5) The duration of the MOU and procedures for amending it; and

(6) Assurances that each MOU will be reviewed, and if substantial changes have occurred, renewed, not less than once every 3-year period to ensure appropriate funding and delivery of services.

(c) The MOU may contain any other provisions agreed to by the parties that are consistent with WIOA title I, the authorizing statutes and regulations of one-stop partner programs, and the WIOA regulations.

(d) When fully executed, the MOU must contain the signatures of the Local WDB, one-stop partners, the chief elected official(s), and the time period in which the agreement is effective. The MOU must be updated not less than every 3 years to reflect any changes in the signatory official of the Board, one-stop partners, and chief elected officials, or one-stop infrastructure funding.

(e) If a one-stop partner appeal to the State regarding infrastructure costs, using the process described in § 361.750, results in a change to the one-stop partner's infrastructure cost contributions, the MOU must be updated to reflect the final one-stop partner infrastructure cost contributions.

§ 361.505 Is there a single Memorandum of Understanding for the local area, or must there be different Memoranda of Understanding between the Local Workforce Development Board and each partner?

(a) A single "umbrella" MOU may be developed that addresses the issues relating to the local one-stop delivery system for the Local WDB, chief elected official and all partners. Alternatively, the Local WDB (with agreement of chief elected official) may enter into separate agreements between each partner or groups of partners.

(b) Under either approach, the requirements described in § 361.500 apply. Since funds are generally appropriated annually, the Local WDB may negotiate financial agreements with each partner annually to update funding of services and operating costs of the system under the MOU.

§ 361.510 How must the Memorandum of Understanding be negotiated?

(a) WIOA emphasizes full and effective partnerships between Local WDBs, chief elected officials, and one-stop partners. Local WDBs and partners must enter into good-faith negotiations. Local WDBs, chief elected officials, and one-stop partners may also request assistance from a State agency responsible for administering the partner program, the Governor, State WDB, or other appropriate parties on other aspects of the MOU.

(b) Local WDBs and one-stop partners must establish, in the MOU, how they will fund the infrastructure costs and other shared costs of the one-stop centers. If agreement regarding infrastructure costs is not reached when other sections of the MOU are ready, an interim infrastructure funding agreement may be included instead, as described in § 361.715(c). Once agreement on infrastructure funding is reached,

the Local WDB and one-stop partners must amend the MOU to include the infrastructure funding of the one-stop centers. Infrastructure funding is described in detail in §§ 361.700 through 361.760.

(c) The Local WDB must report to the State WDB, Governor, and relevant State agency when MOU negotiations with one-stop partners have reached an impasse.

(1) The Local WDB and partners must document the negotiations and efforts that have taken place in the MOU. The State WDB, one-stop partner programs, and the Governor may consult with the appropriate Federal agencies to address impasse situations related to issues other than infrastructure funding after attempting to address the impasse. Impasses related to infrastructure cost funding must be resolved using the State infrastructure cost funding mechanism described in § 361.730.

(2) The Local WDB must report failure to execute an MOU with a required partner to the Governor, State WDB, and the State agency responsible for administering the partner's program. Additionally, if the State cannot assist the Local WDB in resolving the impasse, the Governor or the State WDB must report the failure to the Secretary of Labor and to the head of any other Federal agency with responsibility for oversight of a partner's program.

§ 361.600 Who may operate one-stop centers?

(a) One-stop operators may be a single entity (public, private, or nonprofit) or a consortium of entities. If the consortium of entities is one of one-stop partners, it must include a minimum of three of the one-stop partners described in § 361.400.

(b) The one-stop operator may operate one or more one-stop centers. There may be more than one one-stop operator in a local area.

(c) The types of entities that may be a one-stop operator include:

(1) An institution of higher education;

(2) An Employment Service State agency established under the Wagner-Peyser Act;

(3) A community-based organization, nonprofit organization, or workforce intermediary;

(4) A private for-profit entity;

(5) A government agency;

(6) A Local WDB, with the approval of the chief elected official and the Governor; or

(7) Another interested organization or entity, which is capable of carrying out the duties of the one-stop operator. Examples may include a local chamber of commerce or other business organization, or a labor organization.

(d) Elementary schools and secondary schools are not eligible as one-stop operators, except that a nontraditional public secondary school such as a night school, adult school, or an area career and technical education school may be selected.

(e) The State and Local WDBs must ensure that, in carrying out WIOA programs and activities, one-stop operators:

(1) Disclose any potential conflicts of interest arising from the relationships of the operators with particular training service providers or other service providers (further discussed in 20 CFR 679.430);

(2) Do not establish practices that create disincentives to providing services to individuals with barriers to employment who may require longer-term career and training services; and

(3) Comply with Federal regulations and procurement policies relating to the calculation and use of profits, including those at 20 CFR 683.295, the Uniform Guidance at 2 CFR part 200, and other applicable regulations and policies.

§ 361.605 How is the one-stop operator selected?

(a) Consistent with paragraphs (b) and (c) of this section, the Local WDB must select the one-stop operator through a competitive process, as required by sec. 121(d)(2)(A) of WIOA, at least once every 4 years. A State may require, or a Local WDB may choose to implement, a competitive selection process more than once every 4 years.

(b) In instances in which a State is conducting the competitive process described in paragraph (a) of this section, the State must follow the same policies and procedures it uses for procurement with non-Federal funds.

(c) All other non-Federal entities, including subrecipients of a State (such as local areas), must use a competitive process based on local procurement policies and procedures and the principles of competitive procurement in the Uniform Guidance set out at 2 CFR 200.318 through 200.326. All references to "noncompetitive proposals" in the Uniform Guidance at 2 CFR 200.320(f) will be read as "sole source procurement" for the purposes of implementing this section.

(d) Entities must prepare written documentation explaining the determination concerning the nature of the competitive process to be followed in selecting a one-stop operator.

§ 361.610 When is the sole-source selection of one-stop operators appropriate, and how is it conducted?

(a) States may select a one-stop operator through sole source selection when allowed under the same policies and procedures used for competitive procurement with non-Federal funds, while other non-Federal entities including subrecipients of a State (such as local areas) may select a one-stop operator through sole selection when consistent with local procurement policies and procedures and the Uniform Guidance set out at 2 CFR 200.320.

(b) In the event that sole source procurement is determined necessary and reasonable, in accordance with § 361.605(c), written documentation must be prepared and maintained concerning the entire process of making such a selection.

(c) Such sole source procurement must include appropriate conflict of interest policies and procedures. These policies and procedures must conform to the specifications in 20 CFR 679.430 for demonstrating internal controls and preventing conflict of interest.

(d) A Local WDB may be selected as a one-stop operator through sole source procurement only with agreement of the chief elected official in the local area and the Governor. The Local WDB must establish sufficient conflict of interest policies and procedures and these policies and procedures must be approved by the Governor.

§361.615 May an entity currently serving as one-stop operator compete to be a one-stop operator under the procurement requirements of this subpart?

(a) Local WDBs may compete for and be selected as one-stop operators, as long as appropriate firewalls and conflict of interest policies and procedures are in place. These policies and procedures must conform to the specifications in 20 CFR 679.430 for demonstrating internal controls and preventing conflict of interest.

(b) State and local agencies may compete for and be selected as one-stop operators by the Local WDB, as long as appropriate firewalls and conflict of interest policies and procedures are in place. These policies and procedures must conform to the specifications in 20 CFR 679.430 for demonstrating internal controls and preventing conflict of interest.

(c) In the case of single-area States where the State WDB serves as the Local WDB, the State agency is eligible to compete for and be selected as operator as long as appropriate firewalls and conflict of interest policies are in place and followed for the competition. These policies and procedures must conform to the specifications in 20 CFR 679.430 for demonstrating internal controls and preventing conflicts of interest.

§361.620 What is the one-stop operator's role?

(a) At a minimum, the one-stop operator must coordinate the service delivery of required one-stop partners and service providers. Local WDBs may establish additional roles of one-stop operator, including, but not limited to: Coordinating service providers across the one-stop delivery system, being the primary provider of services within the center, providing some of the services within the center, or coordinating service delivery in a multi-center area, which may include affiliated sites. The competition for a one-stop operator must clearly articulate the role of the one-stop operator.

(b)(1) Subject to paragraph (b)(2) of this section, a one-stop operator may not perform the following functions: Convene system stakeholders to assist in the development of the local plan; prepare and submit local plans (as required under sec. 107 of WIOA); be responsible for oversight of itself; manage or significantly participate in the competitive selection process for one-stop operators; select or terminate one-stop operators, career services, and youth providers; negotiate local performance accountability measures; or develop and submit budget for activities of the Local WDB in the local area.

(2) An entity serving as a one-stop operator, that also serves a different role within the one-stop delivery system, may perform some or all of these functions when it is acting in its other role, if it has established sufficient firewalls and conflict of interest policies and procedures. The policies and procedures must conform to the specifications in 20 CFR 679.430 for demonstrating internal controls and preventing conflict of interest.

§361.625 Can a one-stop operator also be a service provider?

Yes, but there must be appropriate firewalls in place in regards to the competition, and subsequent oversight, monitoring, and evaluation of performance of the service provider. The operator cannot develop, manage, or conduct the competition of a service provider in which it intends to compete. In cases where an operator is also a service provider, there must be firewalls and internal controls within the operator-service provider entity, as well as specific policies and procedures at the Local WDB level regarding oversight, monitoring, and evaluation of performance of the service provider. The firewalls must conform to the specifications in 20 CFR 679.430 for demonstrating internal controls and preventing conflicts of interest.

§361.630 Can State merit staff still work in a one-stop center where the operator is not a governmental entity?

Yes. State merit staff can continue to perform functions and activities in the one-stop center. The Local WDB and one-stop operator must establish a system for management of merit staff in accordance with State policies and procedures. Continued use of State merit staff for the provision of Wagner-Peyser Act services or services from other programs with merit staffing requirements must be included in the competition for and final contract with the one-stop operator when Wagner-Peyser Act services or services from other programs with merit staffing requirements are being provided.

§ 361.635 What is the compliance date of the provisions of this subpart?

(a) No later than July 1, 2017, one-stop operators selected under the competitive process described in this subpart must be in place and operating the one-stop center.

(b) By November 17, 2016, every Local WDB must demonstrate it is taking steps to prepare for competition of its one-stop operator. This demonstration may include, but is not limited to, market research, requests for information, and conducting a cost and price analysis.

§ 361.700 What are the one-stop infrastructure costs?

(a) Infrastructure costs of one-stop centers are nonpersonnel costs that are necessary for the general operation of the one-stop center, including:

(1) Rental of the facilities;

(2) Utilities and maintenance;

(3) Equipment (including assessment-related products and assistive technology for individuals with disabilities); and

(4) Technology to facilitate access to the one-stop center, including technology used for the center's planning and outreach activities.

(b) Local WDBs may consider common identifier costs as costs of one-stop infrastructure.

(c) Each entity that carries out a program or activities in a local one-stop center, described in §§ 361.400 through 361.410, must use a portion of the funds available for the program and activities to maintain the one-stop delivery system, including payment of the infrastructure costs of one-stop centers. These payments must be in accordance with this subpart; Federal cost principles, which require that all costs must be allowable, reasonable, necessary, and allocable to the pro-

gram; and all other applicable legal requirements.

§ 361.705 What guidance must the Governor issue regarding one-stop infrastructure funding?

(a) The Governor, after consultation with chief elected officials, the State WDB, and Local WDBs, and consistent with guidance and policies provided by the State WDB, must develop and issue guidance for use by local areas, specifically:

(1) Guidelines for State-administered one-stop partner programs for determining such programs' contributions to a one-stop delivery system, based on such programs' proportionate use of such system, and relative benefit received, consistent with Office of Management and Budget (OMB) Uniform Administrative Requirements, Cost Principles, and Audit Requirements for Federal Awards in 2 CFR part 200, including determining funding for the costs of infrastructure; and

(2) Guidance to assist Local WDBs, chief elected officials, and one-stop partners in local areas in determining equitable and stable methods of funding the costs of infrastructure at one-stop centers based on proportionate use and relative benefit received, and consistent with Federal cost principles contained in the Uniform Guidance at 2 CFR part 200.

(b) The guidance must include:

(1) The appropriate roles of the one-stop partner programs in identifying one-stop infrastructure costs;

(2) Approaches to facilitate equitable and efficient cost allocation that results in a reasonable cost allocation methodology where infrastructure costs are charged to each partner based on its proportionate use of the one-stop centers and relative benefit received, consistent with Federal cost principles at 2 CFR part 200; and

(3) The timelines regarding notification to the Governor for not reaching local agreement and triggering the State funding mechanism described in § 361.730, and timelines for a one-stop partner to submit an appeal in the State funding mechanism.

§361.710 How are infrastructure costs funded?

Infrastructure costs are funded either through the local funding mechanism described in §361.715 or through the State funding mechanism described in §361.730.

§361.715 How are one-stop infrastructure costs funded in the local funding mechanism?

(a) In the local funding mechanism, the Local WDB, chief elected officials, and one-stop partners agree to amounts and methods of calculating amounts each partner will contribute for one-stop infrastructure funding, include the infrastructure funding terms in the MOU, and sign the MOU. The local funding mechanism must meet all of the following requirements:

(1) The infrastructure costs are funded through cash and fairly evaluated non-cash and third-party in-kind partner contributions and include any funding from philanthropic organizations or other private entities, or through other alternative financing options, to provide a stable and equitable funding stream for ongoing one-stop delivery system operations;

(2) Contributions must be negotiated between one-stop partners, chief elected officials, and the Local WDB and the amount to be contributed must be included in the MOU;

(3) The one-stop partner program's proportionate share of funding must be calculated in accordance with the Uniform Administrative Requirements, Cost Principles, and Audit Requirements for Federal Awards in 2 CFR part 200 based upon a reasonable cost allocation methodology whereby infrastructure costs are charged to each partner in proportion to its use of the one-stop center, relative to benefits received. Such costs must also be allowable, reasonable, necessary, and allocable;

(4) Partner shares must be periodically reviewed and reconciled against actual costs incurred, and adjusted to ensure that actual costs charged to any one-stop partners are proportionate to the use of the one-stop center and relative to the benefit received by the one-stop partners and their respective programs or activities.

(b) In developing the section of the MOU on one-stop infrastructure funding described in §361.755, the Local WDB and chief elected officials will:

(1) Ensure that the one-stop partners adhere to the guidance identified in §361.705 on one-stop delivery system infrastructure costs.

(2) Work with one-stop partners to achieve consensus and informally mediate any possible conflicts or disagreements among one-stop partners.

(3) Provide technical assistance to new one-stop partners and local grant recipients to ensure that those entities are informed and knowledgeable of the elements contained in the MOU and the one-stop infrastructure costs arrangement.

(c) The MOU may include an interim infrastructure funding agreement, including as much detail as the Local WDB has negotiated with one-stop partners, if all other parts of the MOU have been negotiated, in order to allow the partner programs to operate in the one-stop centers. The interim infrastructure funding agreement must be finalized within 6 months of when the MOU is signed. If the interim infrastructure funding agreement is not finalized within that timeframe, the Local WDB must notify the Governor, as described in §361.725.

§361.720 What funds are used to pay for infrastructure costs in the local one-stop infrastructure funding mechanism?

(a) In the local funding mechanism, one-stop partner programs may determine what funds they will use to pay for infrastructure costs. The use of these funds must be in accordance with the requirements in this subpart, and with the relevant partner's authorizing statutes and regulations, including, for example, prohibitions against supplanting non-Federal resources, statutory limitations on administrative costs, and all other applicable legal requirements. In the case of partners administering programs authorized by title I of WIOA, these infrastructure costs may be considered program costs. In the case of partners administering adult education and literacy programs authorized by title II of WIOA, these funds must include Federal funds made available for the local administration of adult education and literacy programs authorized by title II of WIOA. These funds may also include non-Federal resources that are cash, in-kind or third-party contributions. In the case of partners administering the Carl D. Perkins Career and Technical Education Act of 2006, funds used to pay for infrastructure costs may include funds available for local administrative expenses, non-Federal resources that are cash, in-kind or third-party contributions, and may include other funds made available by the State.

(b) There are no specific caps on the amount or percent of overall funding a one-stop partner may contribute to fund infrastructure costs under the local funding mechanism, except that contributions for administrative costs may not exceed the amount available for administrative costs under the authorizing statute of the partner program. However, amounts contributed for infrastructure costs must be allowable and based on proportionate use of the one-stop centers and relative benefit received by the partner program, taking into account the total cost of the one-stop infrastructure as well as alternate financing options, and must be consistent with 2 CFR part 200, including the Federal cost principles.

(c) Cash, non-cash, and third-party in-kind contributions may be provided by one-stop partners to cover their proportionate share of infrastructure costs.

(1) Cash contributions are cash funds provided to the Local WDB or its designee by one-stop partners, either directly or by an interagency transfer.

(2) Non-cash contributions are comprised of—

(i) Expenditures incurred by one-stop partners on behalf of the one-stop center; and

(ii) Non-cash contributions or goods or services contributed by a partner program and used by the one-stop center.

(3) Non-cash contributions, especially those set forth in paragraph (c)(2)(ii) of this section, must be valued consistent with 2 CFR 200.306 to ensure they are fairly evaluated and meet the partners' proportionate share.

(4) Third-party in-kind contributions are:

(i) Contributions of space, equipment, technology, non-personnel services, or other like items to support the infrastructure costs associated with one-stop operations, by a non-one-stop partner to support the one-stop center in general, not a specific partner; or

(ii) Contributions by a non-one-stop partner of space, equipment, technology, non-personnel services, or other like items to support the infrastructure costs associated with one-stop operations, to a one-stop partner to support its proportionate share of one-stop infrastructure costs.

(iii) In-kind contributions described in paragraphs (c)(4)(i) and (ii) of this section must be valued consistent with 2 CFR 200.306 and reconciled on a regular basis to ensure they are fairly evaluated and meet the proportionate share of the partner.

(5) All partner contributions, regardless of the type, must be reconciled on a regular basis (i.e., monthly or quarterly), comparing actual expenses incurred to relative benefits received, to ensure each partner program is contributing its proportionate share in accordance with the terms of the MOU.

§ 361.725 What happens if consensus on infrastructure funding is not reached at the local level between the Local Workforce Development Board, chief elected officials, and one-stop partners?

With regard to negotiations for infrastructure funding for Program Year (PY) 2017 and for each subsequent program year thereafter, if the Local WDB, chief elected officials, and one-stop partners do not reach consensus on methods of sufficiently funding local infrastructure through the local funding mechanism in accordance with the Governor's guidance issued under § 361.705 and consistent with the regulations in §§ 361.715 and 361.720, and include that consensus agreement in the signed MOU, then the Local WDB must notify the Governor by the deadline established by the Governor under § 361.705(b)(3). Once notified, the Governor must administer funding through the State funding mechanism, as described in §§ 361.730 through 361.738, for the program year impacted by the local area's failure to reach consensus.

§ 361.730 What is the State one-stop infrastructure funding mechanism?

(a) Consistent with sec. 121(h)(1)(A)(i)(II) of WIOA, if the Local WDB, chief elected official, and one-stop partners in a local area do not reach consensus agreement on methods of sufficiently funding the costs of infrastructure of one-stop centers for a program year, the State funding mechanism is applicable to the local area for that program year.

(b) In the State funding mechanism, the Governor, subject to the limitations in paragraph (c) of this section, determines one-stop partner contributions after consultation with the chief elected officials, Local WDBs, and the State WDB. This determination involves:

(1) The application of a budget for one-stop infrastructure costs as described in § 361.735, based on either agreement reached in the local area negotiations or the State WDB formula outlined in § 361.745;

(2) The determination of each local one-stop partner program's proportionate use of the one-stop delivery system and relative benefit received, consistent with the Uniform Guidance at 2 CFR part 200, including the Federal cost principles, the partner programs' authorizing laws and regulations, and other applicable legal requirements described in § 361.736; and

(3) The calculation of required statewide program caps on contributions to infrastructure costs from one-stop partner programs in areas operating under the State funding mechanism as described in § 361.738.

(c) In certain situations, the Governor does not determine the infrastructure cost contributions for some one-stop partner programs under the State funding mechanism.

(1) The Governor will not determine the contribution amounts for infrastructure funds for Native American program grantees described in 20 CFR part 684. The appropriate portion of funds to be provided by Native American program grantees to pay for one-stop infrastructure must be determined as part of the development of the MOU described in § 361.500 and specified in that MOU.

(2) In States in which the policy-making authority is placed in an entity or official that is independent of the authority of the Governor with respect to the funds provided for adult education and literacy activities authorized under title II of WIOA, postsecondary career and technical education activities authorized under the Carl D. Perkins Career and Technical Education Act of 2006, or VR services authorized under title I of the Rehabilitation Act of 1973 (other than sec. 112 or part C), as amended by WIOA title IV, the determination of the amount each of the applicable partners must contribute to assist in paying the infrastructure costs of one-stop centers must be made by the official or chief officer of the entity with such authority, in consultation with the Governor.

(d) Any duty, ability, choice, responsibility, or other action otherwise related to the determination of infrastructure costs contributions that is assigned to the Governor in §§ 361.730 through 361.745 also applies to this decision-making process performed by the official or chief officer described in paragraph (c)(2) of this section.

§ 361.731 What are the steps to determine the amount to be paid under the State one-stop infrastructure funding mechanism?

(a) To initiate the State funding mechanism, a Local WDB that has not reached consensus on methods of sufficiently funding local infrastructure through the local funding mechanism as provided in § 361.725 must notify the Governor by the deadline established by the Governor under § 361.705(b)(3).

(b) Once a Local WDB has informed the Governor that no consensus has been reached:

(1) The Local WDB must provide the Governor with local negotiation materials in accordance with § 361.735(a).

(2) The Governor must determine the one-stop center budget by either:

(i) Accepting a budget previously agreed upon by partner programs in the local negotiations, in accordance with § 361.735(b)(1); or

(ii) Creating a budget for the one-stop center using the State WDB formula (described in § 361.745) in accordance with § 361.735(b)(3).

(3) The Governor then must establish a cost allocation methodology to determine the one-stop partner programs' proportionate shares of infrastructure costs, in accordance with § 361.736.

(4)(i) Using the methodology established under paragraph (b)(2)(ii) of this section, and taking into consideration the factors concerning individual partner programs listed in § 361.737(b)(2), the Governor must determine each partner's proportionate share of the infrastructure costs, in accordance with § 361.737(b)(1), and

(ii) In accordance with § 361.730(c), in some instances, the Governor does not determine a partner program's proportionate share of infrastructure funding costs, in which case it must be determined by the entities named in § 361.730(c)(1) and (2).

(5) The Governor must then calculate the statewide caps on the amounts that partner programs may be required to contribute toward infrastructure funding, according to the steps found at § 361.738(a)(1) through (4).

(6) The Governor must ensure that the aggregate total of the infrastructure contributions according to proportionate share required of all local partner programs in local areas under the State funding mechanism do not exceed the cap for that particular program, in accordance with § 361.738(b)(1). If the total does not exceed the cap, the Governor must direct each one-stop partner program to pay the amount determined under § 361.737(a) toward the infrastructure funding costs of the one-stop center. If the total does exceed the cap, then to determine the amount to direct each one-stop program to pay, the Governor may:

(i) Ascertain, in accordance with § 361.738(b)(2)(i), whether the local partner or partners whose proportionate shares are calculated above the individual program caps are willing to voluntarily contribute above the capped amount to equal that program's proportionate share; or

(ii) Choose from the options provided in § 361.738(b)(2)(ii), including having the local area re-enter negotiations to reassess each one-stop partner's proportionate share and make adjustments or identify alternate sources of funding to make up the difference between the capped amount and the proportionate share of infrastructure funding of the one-stop partner.

(7) If none of the solutions given in paragraphs (b)(6)(i) and (ii) of this section prove to be viable, the Governor must reassess the proportionate shares of each one-stop partner so that the aggregate amount attributable to the local partners for each program is less than that program's cap amount. Upon such reassessment, the Governor must direct each one-stop partner program to pay the reassessed amount toward the infrastructure funding costs of the one-stop center.

§ 361.735 How are infrastructure cost budgets for the one-stop centers in a local area determined in the State one-stop infrastructure funding mechanism?

(a) Local WDBs must provide to the Governor appropriate and relevant materials and documents used in the negotiations under the local funding mechanism, including but not limited to: the local WIOA plan, the cost allocation method or methods proposed by the partners to be used in determining proportionate share, the proposed amounts or budget to fund infrastructure, the amount of total partner funds included, the type of funds or non-cash contributions, proposed one-stop center budgets, and any agreed upon or proposed MOUs.

(b)(1) If a local area has reached agreement as to the infrastructure budget for the one-stop centers in the local area, it must provide this budget to the Governor as required by paragraph (a) of this section. If, as a result of the agreed upon infrastructure budget, only the individual programmatic contributions to infrastructure funding based upon proportionate use of the one-stop centers and relative benefit received are at issue, the Governor may accept the budget, from which the Governor must calculate each partner's contribution consistent with the cost allocation methodologies contained in the Uniform Guidance found in 2 CFR part 200, as described in § 361.736.

(2) The Governor may also take into consideration the extent to which the partners in the local area have agreed in determining the proportionate shares, including any agreements reached at the local level by one or more partners, as well as any other element or product of the negotiating process provided to the Governor as required by paragraph (a) of this section.

(3) If a local area has not reached agreement as to the infrastructure budget for the one-stop centers in the local area, or if the Governor determines that the agreed upon budget does not adequately meet the needs of the local area or does not reasonably work within the confines of the local area's resources in accordance with the Governor's one-stop budget guidance (which is required to be issued by WIOA sec. 121(h)(1)(B) and under § 361.705), then, in accordance with § 361.745, the Governor must use the formula developed by the State WDB based on at least the factors required under § 361.745, and any associated weights to determine the local area budget.

§ 361.736 How does the Governor establish a cost allocation methodology used to determine the one-stop partner programs' proportionate shares of infrastructure costs under the State one-stop infrastructure funding mechanism?

Once the appropriate budget is determined for a local area through either method described in § 361.735 (by acceptance of a budget agreed upon in local negotiation or by the Governor applying the formula detailed in § 361.745), the Governor must determine the appropriate cost allocation methodology to be applied to the one-stop partners in such local area, consistent with the Federal cost principles permitted under 2 CFR part 200, to fund the infrastructure budget.

§ 361.737 How are one-stop partner programs' proportionate shares of infrastructure costs determined under the State one-stop infrastructure funding mechanism?

(a) The Governor must direct the one-stop partners in each local area that have not reached agreement under the local funding mechanism to pay what the Governor determines is each partner program's proportionate share of infrastructure funds for that area, subject to the application of the caps described in § 361.738.

(b)(1) The Governor must use the cost allocation methodology—as determined under § 361.736—to determine each partner's proportionate share of the infrastructure costs under the State funding mechanism, subject to considering the factors described in paragraph (b)(2) of this section.

(2) In determining each partner program's proportionate share of infrastructure costs, the Governor must take into account the costs of administration of the one-stop delivery system for purposes not related to one-stop centers for each partner (such as costs associated with maintaining the Local WDB or information technology systems), as well as the statutory requirements for each partner program, the partner program's ability to fulfill such requirements, and all other applicable legal requirements. The Governor may also take into consideration the extent to which the partners in the local area have agreed in determining the proportionate shares, including any agreements reached at the local level by one or more partners, as well as any other materials or documents of the negotiating process, which must be provided to the Governor by the Local WDB and described in § 361.735(a).

§ 361.738 How are statewide caps on the contributions for one-stop infrastructure funding determined in the State one-stop infrastructure funding mechanism?

(a) The Governor must calculate the statewide cap on the contributions for one-stop infrastructure funding required to be provided by each one-stop partner program for those local areas that have not reached agreement. The cap is the amount determined under paragraph (a)(4) of this section, which the Governor derives by:

(1) First, determining the amount resulting from applying the percentage for the corresponding one-stop partner program provided in paragraph (d) of this section to the amount of Federal funds provided to carry out the one-stop partner program in the State for the applicable fiscal year;

(2) Second, selecting a factor (or factors) that reasonably indicates the use of one-stop centers in the State, applying such factor(s) to all local areas in the State, and determining the percentage of such factor(s) applicable to the local areas that reached agreement under the local funding mechanism in the State;

(3) Third, determining the amount resulting from applying the percentage determined in paragraph (a)(2) of this section to the amount determined under paragraph (a)(1) of this section for the one-stop partner program; and

(4) Fourth, determining the amount that results from subtracting the amount determined under paragraph (a)(3) of this section from the amount determined under paragraph (a)(1) of this section. The outcome of this final calculation results in the partner program's cap.

(b)(1) The Governor must ensure that the funds required to be contributed by each partner program in the local areas in the State under the State funding mechanism, in aggregate, do not exceed the statewide cap for each program as determined under paragraph (a) of this section.

(2) If the contributions initially determined under § 361.737 would exceed the applicable cap determined under paragraph (a) of this section, the Governor may:

(i) Ascertain if the one-stop partner whose contribution would otherwise exceed the cap determined under paragraph (a) of this section will voluntarily contribute above the capped amount, so that the total contributions equal that partner's proportionate share. The one-stop partner's contribution must still be consistent with the program's authorizing laws and regulations, the Federal cost principles in 2 CFR part 200, and other applicable legal requirements; or

(ii) Direct or allow the Local WDB, chief elected officials, and one-stop partners to: Re-enter negotiations, as necessary; reduce the infrastructure costs to reflect the amount of funds that are available for such costs without exceeding the cap levels; reassess the proportionate share of each one-stop partner; or identify alternative sources of financing for one-stop infrastructure funding, consistent with the requirement that each one-stop partner pay an amount that is consistent with the proportionate use of the one-stop center and relative benefit received by the partner, the program's authorizing laws and regulations, the Federal cost principles in 2 CFR part 200, and other applicable legal requirements.

(3) If applicable under paragraph (b)(2)(ii) of this section, the Local WDB, chief elected officials, and one-stop partners, after renegotiation, may come to agreement, sign an MOU, and proceed under the local funding mechanism. Such actions do not require the redetermination of the applicable caps under paragraph (a) of this section.

(4) If, after renegotiation, agreement among partners still cannot be reached or alternate financing cannot be identified, the Governor may adjust the specified allocation, in accordance with the amounts available and the limitations described in paragraph (d) of this section. In determining these adjustments, the Governor may take into account information relating to the renegotiation as well as the information described in § 361.735(a).

(c) *Limitations.* Subject to paragraph (a) of this section and in accordance with WIOA sec. 121(h)(2)(D), the following limitations apply to the Governor's calculations of the amount that one-stop partners in local areas that have not reached agreement under the local funding mechanism may be required under § 361.736 to contribute to one-stop infrastructure funding:

(1) *WIOA formula programs and Wagner-Peyser Act Employment Service.* The portion of funds required to be contributed under the WIOA youth, adult, or dislocated worker programs, or under the Wagner-Peyser Act (29 U.S.C. 49 *et seq.*) must not exceed three percent of the amount of the program in the State for a program year.

(2) *Other one-stop partners.* For required one-stop partners other than those specified in paragraphs (c)(1), (3), (5), and (6) of this section, the portion of funds required to be contributed must not exceed 1.5 percent of the amount of Federal funds provided to carry out that program in the State for a fiscal year. For purposes of the Carl

D. Perkins Career and Technical Education Act of 2006, the cap on contributions is determined based on the funds made available by the State for postsecondary level programs and activities under sec. 132 of the Carl D. Perkins Career and Technical Education Act and the amount of funds used by the State under sec. 112(a)(3) of the Perkins Act during the prior year to administer postsecondary level programs and activities, as applicable.

(3) *Vocational rehabilitation.* (i) Within a State, for the entity or entities administering the programs described in WIOA sec. 121(b)(1)(B)(iv) and §361.400, the allotment is based on the one State Federal fiscal year allotment, even in instances where that allotment is shared between two State agencies, and the cumulative portion of funds required to be contributed must not exceed—

(A) 0.75 percent of the amount of Federal funds provided to carry out such program in the State for Fiscal Year 2016 for purposes of applicability of the State funding mechanism for PY 2017;

(B) 1.0 percent of the amount provided to carry out such program in the State for Fiscal Year 2017 for purposes of applicability of the State funding mechanism for PY 2018;

(C) 1.25 percent of the amount provided to carry out such program in the State for Fiscal Year 2018 for purposes of applicability of the State funding mechanism for PY 2019;

(D) 1.5 percent of the amount provided to carry out such program in the State for Fiscal Year 2019 and following years for purposes of applicability of the State funding mechanism for PY 2020 and subsequent years.

(ii) The limitations set forth in paragraph (d)(3)(i) of this section for any given fiscal year must be based on the final VR allotment to the State in the applicable Federal fiscal year.

(4) *Federal direct spending programs.* For local areas that have not reached a one-stop infrastructure funding agreement by consensus, an entity administering a program funded with direct Federal spending, as defined in sec. 250(c)(8) of the Balanced Budget and Emergency Deficit Control Act of 1985, as in effect on February 15, 2014 (2 U.S.C. 900(c)(8)), must not be required to provide more for infrastructure costs than the amount that the Governor determined (as described in §361.737).

(5) *TANF programs.* For purposes of TANF, the cap on contributions is determined based on the total Federal TANF funds expended by the State for work, education, and training activities during the prior Federal fiscal year (as reported to the Department of Health and Human Services (HHS) on the quarterly TANF Financial Report form), plus any additional amount of Federal TANF funds that the State TANF agency reasonably determines was expended for administrative costs in connection with these activities but that was separately reported to HHS as an administrative cost. The State's contribution to the one-stop infrastructure must not exceed 1.5 percent of these combined expenditures.

(6) *Community Services Block Grant (CSBG) programs.* For purposes of CSBG, the cap on contributions will be based on the total amount of CSBG funds determined by the State to have been expended by local CSBG-eligible entities for the provision of employment and training activities during the prior Federal fiscal year for which information is available (as reported to HHS on the CSBG Annual Report) and any additional amount that the State CSBG agency reasonably determines was expended for administrative purposes in connection with these activities and was separately reported to HHS as an administrative cost. The State's contribution must not exceed 1.5 percent of these combined expenditures.

(d) For programs for which it is not otherwise feasible to determine the amount of Federal funding used by the program until the end of that program's operational year—because, for example, the funding available for education, employment, and training activities is included within funding for the program that may also be used for other unrelated activities—the determination of the Federal funds provided to carry out the program for a fiscal year under paragraph (a)(1) of this section may be determined by:

(1) The percentage of Federal funds available to the one-stop partner program that were used by the one-stop partner program for education, employment, and training activities in the previous fiscal year for which data are available; and

(2) Applying the percentage determined under paragraph (d)(1) of this section to the total amount of Federal funds available to the one-stop partner program for the fiscal year for which the determination under paragraph (a)(1) of this section applies.

§ 361.740 What funds are used to pay for infrastructure costs in the State one-stop infrastructure funding mechanism?

(a) In the State funding mechanism, infrastructure costs for WIOA title I programs, including Native American Programs described in 20 CFR part 684, may be paid using program funds, administrative funds, or both. Infrastructure costs for the Senior Community Service Employment Program under title V of the Older Americans Act (42 U.S.C. 3056 *et seq.*) may also be paid using program funds, administrative funds, or both.

(b) In the State funding mechanism, infrastructure costs for other required one-stop partner programs (listed in §§ 361.400 through 361.410) are limited to the program's administrative funds, as appropriate.

(c) In the State funding mechanism, infrastructure costs for the adult education program authorized by title II of WIOA must be paid from the funds that are available for local administration and may be paid from funds made available by the State or non-Federal resources that are cash, in-kind, or third-party contributions.

(d) In the State funding mechanism, infrastructure costs for the Carl D. Perkins Career and Technical Education Act of 2006 must be paid from funds available for local administration of postsecondary level programs and activities to eligible recipients or consortia of eligible recipients and may be paid from funds made available by the State or non-Federal resources that are cash, in-kind, or third-party contributions.

§ 361.745 What factors does the State Workforce Development Board use to develop the formula described in Workforce Innovation and Opportunity Act, which is used by the Governor to determine the appropriate one-stop infrastructure budget for each local area operating under the State infrastructure funding mechanism, if no reasonably implementable locally negotiated budget exists?

The State WDB must develop a formula, as described in WIOA sec. 121(h)(3)(B), to be used by the Governor under § 361.735(b)(3) in determining the appropriate budget for the infrastructure costs of one-stop centers in the local areas that do not reach agreement under the local funding mechanism and are, therefore, subject to the State funding mechanism. The formula identifies the factors and corresponding weights for each factor that the Governor must use, which must include: The number of one-stop centers in a local area; the population served by such centers; the services provided by such centers; and any factors relating to the operations of such centers in the local area that the State WDB determines are appropriate. As indicated in § 361.735(b)(1), if the local area has agreed on such a budget, the Governor may accept that budget in lieu of applying the formula factors.

§ 361.750 When and how can a one-stop partner appeal a one-stop infrastructure amount designated by the State under the State infrastructure funding mechanism?

(a) The Governor must establish a process, described under sec. 121(h)(2)(E) of WIOA, for a one-stop partner administering a program described in §§ 361.400 through 361.410 to appeal the Governor's determination regarding the one-stop partner's portion of funds to be provided for one-stop infrastructure costs. This appeal process must be described in the Unified State Plan.

(b) The appeal may be made on the ground that the Governor's determination is inconsistent with proportionate share requirements in § 361.735(a), the cost contribution limitations in § 361.735(b), the cost contribution caps in §361.738, consistent with the process described in the State Plan.

(c) The process must ensure prompt resolution of the appeal in order to ensure the funds are distributed in a timely manner, consistent with the requirements of 20 CFR 683.630.

(d) The one-stop partner must submit an appeal in accordance with State's deadlines for appeals specified in the guidance issued under §361.705(b)(3), or if the State has not set a deadline, within 21 days from the Governor's determination.

§361.755 What are the required elements regarding infrastructure funding that must be included in the one-stop Memorandum of Understanding?

The MOU, fully described in §361.500, must contain the following information whether the local areas use either the local one-stop or the State funding method:

(a) The period of time in which this infrastructure funding agreement is effective. This may be a different time period than the duration of the MOU.

(b) Identification of an infrastructure and shared services budget that will be periodically reconciled against actual costs incurred and adjusted accordingly to ensure that it reflects a cost allocation methodology that demonstrates how infrastructure costs are charged to each partner in proportion to its use of the one-stop center and relative benefit received, and that complies with 2 CFR part 200 (or any corresponding similar regulation or ruling).

(c) Identification of all one-stop partners, chief elected officials, and Local WDB participating in the infrastructure funding arrangement.

(d) Steps the Local WDB, chief elected officials, and one-stop partners used to reach consensus or an assurance that the local area followed the guidance for the State funding process.

(e) Description of the process to be used among partners to resolve issues during the MOU duration period when consensus cannot be reached.

(f) Description of the periodic modification and review process to ensure equitable benefit among one-stop partners.

§361.760 How do one-stop partners jointly fund other shared costs under the Memorandum of Understanding?

(a) In addition to jointly funding infrastructure costs, one-stop partners listed in §§361.400 through 361.410 must use a portion of funds made available under their programs' authorizing Federal law (or fairly evaluated in-kind contributions) to pay the additional costs relating to the operation of the one-stop delivery system. These other costs must include applicable career services and may include other costs, including shared services.

(b) For the purposes of paragraph (a) of this section, shared services' costs may include the costs of shared services that are authorized for and may be commonly provided through the one-stop partner programs to any individual, such as initial intake, assessment of needs, appraisal of basic skills, identification of appropriate services to meet such needs, referrals to other one-stop partners, and business services. Shared operating costs may also include shared costs of the Local WDB's functions.

(c) Contributions to the additional costs related to operation of the one-stop delivery system may be cash, non-cash, or third-party in-kind contributions, consistent with how these are described in §361.720(c).

(d) The shared costs described in paragraph (a) of this section must be allocated according to the proportion of benefit received by each of the partners, consistent with the Federal law authorizing the partner's program, and consistent with all other applicable legal requirements, including Federal cost principles in 2 CFR part 200 (or any corresponding similar regulation or ruling) requiring that costs are allowable, reasonable, necessary, and allocable.

(e) Any shared costs agreed upon by the one-stop partners must be included in the MOU.

§ 361.800 How are one-stop centers and one-stop delivery systems certified for effectiveness, physical and programmatic accessibility, and continuous improvement?

(a) The State WDB, in consultation with chief elected officials and Local WDBs, must establish objective criteria and procedures for Local WDBs to use when certifying one-stop centers.

(1) The State WDB, in consultation with chief elected officials and Local WDBs, must review and update the criteria every 2 years as part of the review and modification of State Plans pursuant to § 361.135.

(2) The criteria must be consistent with the Governor's and State WDB's guidelines, guidance, and policies on infrastructure funding decisions, described in § 361.705. The criteria must evaluate the one-stop centers and one-stop delivery system for effectiveness, including customer satisfaction, physical and programmatic accessibility, and continuous improvement.

(3) When the Local WDB is the one-stop operator as described in 20 CFR 679.410, the State WDB must certify the one-stop center.

(b) Evaluations of effectiveness must include how well the one-stop center integrates available services for participants and businesses, meets the workforce development needs of participants and the employment needs of local employers, operates in a cost-efficient manner, coordinates services among the one-stop partner programs, and provides access to partner program services to the maximum extent practicable, including providing services outside of regular business hours where there is a workforce need, as identified by the Local WDB. These evaluations must take into account feedback from one-stop customers. They must also include evaluations of how well the one-stop center ensures equal opportunity for individuals with disabilities to participate in or benefit from one-stop center services. These evaluations must include criteria evaluating how well the centers and delivery systems take actions to comply with the disability-related regulations implementing WIOA sec. 188, set forth at 29 CFR part 38. Such actions include, but are not limited to:

(1) Providing reasonable accommodations for individuals with disabilities;

(2) Making reasonable modifications to policies, practices, and procedures where necessary to avoid discrimination against persons with disabilities;

(3) Administering programs in the most integrated setting appropriate;

(4) Communicating with persons with disabilities as effectively as with others;

(5) Providing appropriate auxiliary aids and services, including assistive technology devices and services, where necessary to afford individuals with disabilities an equal opportunity to participate in, and enjoy the benefits of, the program or activity; and

(6) Providing for the physical accessibility of the one-stop center to individuals with disabilities.

(c) Evaluations of continuous improvement must include how well the one-stop center supports the achievement of the negotiated local levels of performance for the indicators of performance for the local area described in sec. 116(b)(2) of WIOA and part 361. Other continuous improvement factors may include a regular process for identifying and responding to technical assistance needs, a regular system of continuing professional staff development, and having systems in place to capture and respond to specific customer feedback.

(d) Local WDBs must assess at least once every 3 years the effectiveness, physical and programmatic accessibility, and continuous improvement of one-stop centers and the one-stop delivery systems using the criteria and procedures developed by the State WDB. The Local WDB may establish additional criteria, or set higher standards for service coordination, than those set by the State criteria. Local WDBs must review and update the criteria every 2 years as part of the Local Plan update process described in § 361.580. Local WDBs must certify one-stop centers in order to be eligible to use infrastructure funds in the State funding mechanism described in § 361.730.

(e) All one-stop centers must comply with applicable physical and programmatic accessibility requirements, as set forth in 29 CFR part 38, the implementing regulations of WIOA sec. 188.

§361.900 What is the common identifier to be used by each one-stop delivery system?

(a) The common one-stop delivery system identifier is "American Job Center."

(b) As of November 17, 2016, each one-stop delivery system must include the "American Job Center" identifier or "a proud partner of the American Job Center network" on all primary electronic resources used by the one-stop delivery system, and on any newly printed, purchased, or created materials.

(c) As of July 1, 2017, each one-stop delivery system must include the "American Job Center" identifier or "a proud partner of the American Job Center network" on all products, programs, activities, services, electronic resources, facilities, and related property and new materials used in the one-stop delivery system.

(d) One-stop partners, States, or local areas may use additional identifiers on their products, programs, activities, services, facilities, and related property and materials.

PART 363—THE STATE SUPPORTED EMPLOYMENT SERVICES PROGRAM

Subpart A—General

Subpart B—How Does a State Apply for a Grant?

Subpart C—How Are State Supported Employment Services Programs Financed?

Subparts D–E [Reserved]

Subpart F—What Post-Award Conditions Must Be Met by a State?

AUTHORITY: Sections 602–608 of the Rehabilitation Act of 1973, as amended; 29 U.S.C. 795g–795m, unless otherwise noted.

SOURCE: 81 FR 55780, Aug. 19, 2016, unless otherwise noted.

Subpart A—General

§363.1 What is the State Supported Employment Services program?

(a) Under the State supported employment services program, the Secretary provides grants to assist States in developing and implementing collaborative programs with appropriate entities to provide programs of supported employment services for individuals with the most significant disabilities, including youth with the most significant disabilities, to enable them to achieve an employment outcome of supported employment in competitive integrated employment. Grants made under the State supported employment services program supplement a State's vocational rehabilitation program grants under 34 CFR part 361.

(b) For purposes of this part and 34 CFR part 361, "supported employment" means competitive integrated employment, including customized employment, or employment in an integrated work setting in which an individual with a most significant disability, including a youth with a most significant disability, is working on a short-term basis toward competitive integrated employment, that is individualized and customized, consistent with the unique strengths, abilities, interests, and informed choice of the individual, including with ongoing support services for individuals with the most significant disabilities—

(1)(i) For whom competitive integrated employment has not historically occurred; or

(ii) For whom competitive integrated employment has been interrupted or intermittent as a result of a significant disability; and

(2) Who, because of the nature and severity of the disability, need intensive supported employment services, and extended services after the transition from support provided by the designated State unit in order to perform the work.

(c) *Short-term basis.* For purposes of this part, an individual with a most significant disability, whose supported employment in an integrated setting does not satisfy the criteria of competitive integrated employment, as defined in 34 CFR 361.5(c)(9), is considered to be working on a short-term toward competitive integrated employment so long as the individual can reasonably anticipate achieving competitive integrated employment—

(1) Within six months of achieving a supported employment outcome; or,

(2) In limited circumstances, within a period not to exceed 12 months from the achievement of the supported employment outcome, if a longer period is necessary based on the needs of the individual, and the individual has demonstrated progress toward competitive

earnings based on information contained in the service record.

(Authority: Sections 7(38), 7(39), 12(c), and 602 of the Rehabilitation Act of 1973, as amended; 29 U.S.C. 705(38) 705(39), 709(c), and 795g)

§ 363.2   Who is eligible for an award?

Any State that submits the documentation required by § 363.10, as part of the vocational rehabilitation services portion of the Unified or Combined State Plan under 34 CFR part 361, is eligible for an award under this part.

(Authority: Section 606(a) of the Rehabilitation Act of 1973, as amended; 29 U.S.C. 795k(a))

§ 363.3   Who is eligible for services?

A State may provide services under this part to any individual, including a youth with a disability, if—

(a) The individual has been determined to be—

(1) Eligible for vocational rehabilitation services in accordance with 34 CFR 361.42; and

(2) An individual with a most significant disability;

(b) For purposes of activities carried out under § 363.4(a)(2), the individual is a youth with a disability, as defined in 34 CFR 361.5(c)(59), who satisfies the requirements of this section; and

(c) Supported employment has been identified as the appropriate employment outcome for the individual on the basis of a comprehensive assessment of rehabilitation needs, as defined in 34 CFR 361.5(c)(5), including an evaluation of rehabilitation, career, and job needs.

(Authority: Section 605 of the Rehabilitation Act of 1973, as amended; 29 U.S.C. 795j)

§ 363.4   What are the authorized activities under the State Supported Employment Services program?

(a) The State may use funds allotted under this part to—

(1) Provide supported employment services, as defined in 34 CFR 361.5(c)(54);

(2) Provide extended services, as defined in 34 CFR 361.5(c)(19), to youth with the most significant disabilities, in accordance with § 363.11(f), for a period of time not to exceed four years, or until such time that a youth reaches the age of 25 and no longer meets the

definition of a youth with a disability under 34 CFR 361.5(c)(58), whichever occurs first; and

(3) With funds reserved, in accordance with §363.22 for the provision of supported employment services to youth with the most significant disabilities, leverage other public and private funds to increase resources for extended services and expand supported employment opportunities.

(b) Except as provided in paragraph (a)(2) of this section, a State may not use funds under this part to provide extended services to individuals with the most significant disabilities.

(c) Nothing in this part will be construed to prohibit a State from providing—

(1) Supported employment services in accordance with the vocational rehabilitation services portion of the Unified or Combined State Plan submitted under 34 CFR part 361 by using funds made available through a State allotment under that part.

(2) Discrete postemployment services in accordance with 34 CFR 361.48(b) by using funds made available under 34 CFR part 361 to an individual who is eligible under this part.

(d) A State must coordinate with the entities described in §363.50(a) regarding the services provided to individuals with the most significant disabilities, including youth with the most significant disabilities, under this part and under 34 CFR part 361 to ensure that the services are complementary and not duplicative.

(Authority: Sections 7(39), 12(c), 604, 606(b)(6), and 608 of the Rehabilitation Act of 1973, as amended; 29 U.S.C. 705(39), 709(c), 795i, 795k(b)(6), and 795m)

§363.5 What regulations apply?

The following regulations apply to the State supported employment services program:

(a) The Education Department General Administrative Regulations (EDGAR) as follows:

(1) 34 CFR part 76 (State-Administered Programs).

(2) 34 CFR part 77 (Definitions that Apply to Department Regulations).

(3) 34 CFR part 79 (Intergovernmental Review of Department of Education Programs and Activities).

(4) 34 CFR part 81 (General Education Provisions Act—Enforcement).

(5) 34 CFR part 82 (New Restrictions on Lobbying).

(b) The regulations in this part 363.

(c) The following regulations in 34 CFR part 361 (The State Vocational Rehabilitation Services Program): §§361.5, 361.31, 361.32, 361.34, 361.35, 361.39, 361.40, 361.41, 361.42, 361.47(a), 361.48, 361.49, and 361.53.

(d) 2 CFR part 200 (Uniform Administrative Requirements, Cost Principles, and Audit Requirements for Federal Awards), as adopted in 2 CFR part 3474.

(e) 2 CFR part 180 (OMB Guidelines to Agencies on Governmentwide Debarment and Suspension (Nonprocurement)), as adopted in 2 CFR part 3485.

(Authority: Section 12(c) of the Rehabilitation Act of 1973, as amended; 29 U.S.C. 709(c))

§363.6 What definitions apply?

The following definitions apply to this part:

(a) Definitions in 34 CFR part 361.

(b) Definitions in 34 CFR part 77.

(c) Definitions in 2 CFR part 200, subpart A.

(Authority: Sections 7 and 12(c) of the Rehabilitation Act of 1973, as amended; 29 U.S.C. 705 and 709(c))

Subpart B—How Does a State Apply for a Grant?

§363.10 What documents must a State submit to receive a grant?

(a) To be eligible to receive a grant under this part, a State must submit to the Secretary, as part of the vocational rehabilitation services portion of the Unified or Combined State Plan under 34 CFR part 361, a State plan supplement that meets the requirements of §363.11.

(b) A State must submit revisions to the vocational rehabilitation services portion of the Unified or Combined State Plan supplement submitted under this part as may be necessary.

(Approved by the Office of Management and Budget under control number 1205–0522)

(Authority: Section 606(a) of the Rehabilitation Act of 1973, as amended; 29 U.S.C. 795k(a))

§ 363.11 What are the vocational rehabilitation services portion of the Unified or Combined State Plan supplement requirements?

Each State plan supplement, submitted in accordance with § 363.10, must—

(a) Designate a designated State unit or, as applicable, units, as defined in 34 CFR 361.5(c)(13), as the State agency or agencies to administer the Supported Employment program under this part;

(b) Summarize the results of the needs assessment of individuals with most significant disabilities, including youth with the most significant disabilities, conducted under 34 CFR 361.29(a), with respect to the rehabilitation and career needs of individuals with most significant disabilities and their need for supported employment services. The results of the needs assessment must also address needs relating to coordination;

(c) Describe the quality, scope, and extent of supported employment services to be provided to eligible individuals with the most significant disabilities under this part, including youth with the most significant disabilities;

(d) Describe the State's goals and plans with respect to the distribution of funds received under § 363.20;

(e) Demonstrate evidence of the designated State unit's efforts to identify and make arrangements, including entering into cooperative agreements, with—

(1) Other State agencies and other appropriate entities to assist in the provision of supported employment services; and

(2) Other public or non-profit agencies or organizations within the State, employers, natural supports, and other entities with respect to the provision of extended services;

(f) Describe the activities to be conducted for youth with the most significant disabilities with the funds reserved in accordance with § 363.22, including—

(1) The provision of extended services to youth with the most significant disabilities for a period not to exceed four years, in accordance with § 363.4(a)(2); and

(2) How the State will use supported employment funds reserved under

§ 363.22 to leverage other public and private funds to increase resources for extended services and expand supported employment opportunities for youth with the most significant disabilities;

(g) Assure that—

(1) Funds made available under this part will only be used to provide authorized supported employment services to individuals who are eligible under this part to receive such services;

(2) The comprehensive assessments of individuals with significant disabilities, including youth with the most significant disabilities, conducted under 34 CFR part 361 will include consideration of supported employment as an appropriate employment outcome;

(3) An individualized plan for employment, as described in 34 CFR 361.45 and 361.46, will be developed and updated, using funds received under 34 CFR part 361, in order to—

(i) Specify the supported employment services to be provided, including, as appropriate, transition services and pre-employment transition services to be provided for youth with the most significant disabilities;

(ii) Specify the expected extended services needed, including the extended services that may be provided under this part to youth with the most significant disabilities in accordance with an approved individualized plan for employment for a period not to exceed four years; and

(iii) Identify, as appropriate, the source of extended services, which may include natural supports, programs, or other entities, or an indication that it is not possible to identify the source of extended services at the time the individualized plan for employment is developed;

(4) The State will use funds provided under this part only to supplement, and not supplant, the funds received under 34 CFR part 361, in providing supported employment services specified in the individualized plan for employment;

(5) Services provided under an individualized plan for employment will be coordinated with services provided under other individualized plans established under other Federal or State programs;

(6) To the extent job skills training is provided, the training will be provided onsite;

(7) Supported employment services will include placement in an integrated setting based on the unique strengths, resources, interests, concerns, abilities, and capabilities of individuals with the most significant disabilities, including youth with the most significant disabilities;

(8) The designated State agency or agencies, as described in paragraph (a) of this section, will expend no more than 2.5 percent of the State's allotment under this part for administrative costs of carrying out this program; and

(9) The designated State agency or agencies will provide, directly or indirectly through public or private entities, non-Federal contributions in an amount that is not less than 10 percent of the costs of carrying out supported employment services provided to youth with the most significant disabilities with the funds reserved for such purpose under §363.22; and

(h) Contain any other information and be submitted in the form and in accordance with the procedures that the Secretary may require.

(Approved by the Office of Management and Budget under control number 1205–0522)

(Authority: Section 606 of the Rehabilitation Act of 1973, as amended; 29 U.S.C. 795k)

Subpart C—How Are State Supported Employment Services Programs Financed?

§363.20 How does the Secretary allot funds?

(a) *States.* The Secretary will allot the sums appropriated for each fiscal year to carry out the activities of this part among the States on the basis of relative population of each State, except that—

(1) No State will receive less than $250,000, or ⅓ of 1 percent of the sums appropriated for the fiscal year for which the allotment is made, whichever amount is greater; and

(2) If the sums appropriated to carry out this part for the fiscal year exceed the sums appropriated to carry out this part (as in effect on September 30, 1992) in fiscal year 1992 by $1,000,000 or more, no State will receive less than $300,000, or ⅓ of 1 percent of the sums appropriated for the fiscal year for which the allotment is made, whichever amount is greater.

(b) *Certain Territories.* (1) For the purposes of this section, Guam, American Samoa, the United States Virgin Islands, and the Commonwealth of the Northern Mariana Islands are not considered to be States.

(2) Each jurisdiction described in paragraph (b)(1) of this section will be allotted not less than ⅛ of 1 percent of the amounts appropriated for the fiscal year for which the allotment is made.

(Authority: Section 603(a) of the Rehabilitation Act of 1973, as amended; 29 U.S.C. 795h(a))

§363.21 How does the Secretary reallot funds?

(a) Whenever the Secretary determines that any amount of an allotment to a State under §363.20 for any fiscal year will not be expended by such State for carrying out the provisions of this part, the Secretary will make such amount available for carrying out the provisions of this part to one or more of the States that the Secretary determines will be able to use additional amounts during such year for carrying out such provisions.

(b) Any amount made available to a State for any fiscal year in accordance with paragraph (a) will be regarded as an increase in the State's allotment under this part for such year.

(Authority: Section 603(b) of the Rehabilitation Act of 1973, as amended; 29 U.S.C. 795h(b))

§363.22 How are funds reserved for youth with the most significant disabilities?

A State that receives an allotment under this part must reserve and expend 50 percent of such allotment for the provision of supported employment services, including extended services, to youth with the most significant disabilities in order to assist those youth in achieving an employment outcome in supported employment.

(Authority: Sections 12(c) and 603(d) of the Rehabilitation Act of 1973, as amended; 29 U.S.C. 709(c) and 795h(d))

§ 363.23 What are the matching requirements?

(a) *Non-Federal share.* (1) For funds allotted under § 363.20 and not reserved under § 363.22 for the provision of supported employment services to youth with the most significant disabilities, there is no non-Federal share requirement.

(2)(i) For funds allotted under § 363.20 and reserved under § 363.22 for the provision of supported employment services to youth with the most significant disabilities, a designated State agency must provide non-Federal expenditures in an amount that is not less than 10 percent of the total expenditures, including the Federal reserved funds and the non-Federal share, incurred for the provision of supported employment services to youth with the most significant disabilities, including extended services.

(ii) In the event that a designated State agency uses more than 50 percent of its allotment under this part to provide supported employment services to youth with the most significant disabilities as required by § 363.22, there is no requirement that a designated State agency provide non-Federal expenditures to match the excess Federal funds spent for this purpose.

(3) Except as provided under paragraphs (b) and (c) of this section, non-Federal expenditures made under the vocational rehabilitation services portion of the Unified or Combined State Plan supplement to meet the non-Federal share requirement under this section must be consistent with the provision of 2 CFR 200.306.

(b) *Third-party in-kind contributions.* Third-party in-kind contributions, as described in 2 CFR 200.306(b), may not be used to meet the non-Federal share under this section.

(c)(1) *Contributions by private entities.* Expenditures made from contributions by private organizations, agencies, or individuals that are deposited into the sole account of the State agency, in accordance with State law may be used as part of the non-Federal share under this section, provided the expenditures under the vocational rehabilitation services portion of the Unified or Combined State Plan supplement, as described in § 363.11, do not benefit in any way the donor, an individual to whom the donor is related by blood or marriage or with whom the donor shares a financial interest.

(2) The Secretary does not consider a donor's receipt from the State unit of a contract or subaward with funds allotted under this part to be a benefit for the purpose of this paragraph if the contract or subaward is awarded under the State's regular competitive procedures.

(Authority: Sections 12(c) and 606(b)(7)(I) of the Rehabilitation Act of 1973, as amended; 29 U.S.C. 709(c) and 795k(b)(7)(I))

§ 363.24 What is program income and how may it be used?

(a) *Definition.* (1) *Program income* means gross income earned by the State that is directly generated by authorized activities supported under this part or earned as a result of the Federal award during the period of performance.

(2) Program income received through the transfer of Social Security Administration payments from the State Vocational Rehabilitation Services program, in accordance with 34 CFR 361.63(c)(2), will be treated as program income received under this part.

(b) *Use of program income.* (1) Program income must be used for the provision of services authorized under § 363.4. Program income earned or received during the fiscal year must be disbursed during the period of performance of the award, prior to requesting additional cash payments.

(2) States are authorized to treat program income as an addition to the grant funds to be used for additional allowable program expenditures, in accordance with 2 CFR 200.307(e)(2).

(3) Program income cannot be used to meet the non-Federal share requirement under § 363.23.

(Authority: Sections 12(c) and 108 of the Rehabilitation Act of 1973, as amended; 29 U.S.C. 709(c) and 728)

§ 363.25 What is the period of availability of funds?

(a) Except as provided in paragraph (b) of this section, any Federal award funds, including reallotted funds, that are appropriated for a fiscal year to carry out a program under this part that are not obligated by the State by the beginning of the succeeding fiscal year, and any program income received during a fiscal year that is not obligated or expended by the State prior to the beginning of the succeeding fiscal year in which the program income was received, remain available for obligation by the State during that succeeding fiscal year.

(b) Federal funds appropriated for a fiscal year and reserved for the provision of supported employment services to youth with the most significant disabilities, in accordance with §363.22 of this part, remain available for obligation in the succeeding fiscal year only to the extent that the State met the matching requirement, as described in §363.23, for those Federal funds by obligating, in accordance with 34 CFR 76.707, the non-Federal share in the fiscal year for which the funds were appropriated. Any reserved funds carried over may only be obligated and expended in that succeeding Federal fiscal year for the provision of supported employment services to youth with the most significant disabilities.

(Authority: Sections 12(c) and 19 of the Rehabilitation Act of 1973, as amended; 29 U.S.C. 709(c) and 716)

Subparts D–E [Reserved]

Subpart F—What Post-Award Conditions Must Be Met by a State?

§363.50 What collaborative agreements must the State develop?

(a) A designated State unit must enter into one or more written collaborative agreements, memoranda of understanding, or other appropriate mechanisms with other public agencies, private nonprofit organizations, and other available funding sources, including employers and other natural supports, as appropriate, to assist with the provision of supported employment services and extended services to individuals with the most significant disabilities in the State, including youth with the most significant disabilities, to enable them to achieve an employment outcome of supported employ-

ment in competitive integrated employment.

(b) These agreements provide the mechanism for collaboration at the State level that is necessary to ensure the smooth transition from supported employment services to extended services, the transition of which is inherent to the definition of "supported employment" in §363.1(b). The agreement may contain information regarding the—

(1) Supported employment services to be provided, for a period not to exceed 24 months, by the designated State unit with funds received under this part;

(2) Extended services to be provided to youth with the most significant disabilities, for a period not to exceed four years, by the designated State unit with the funds reserved under §363.22 of this part;

(3) Extended services to be provided by other public agencies, private non-profit organizations, or other sources, including employers and other natural supports, following the provision of authorized supported employment services, or extended services as appropriate for youth with the most significant disabilities, under this part; and

(4) Collaborative efforts that will be undertaken by all relevant entities to increase opportunities for competitive integrated employment in the State for individuals with the most significant disabilities, especially youth with the most significant disabilities.

(Authority: Sections 7(38), 7(39), 12(c), 602, and 606(b) of the Rehabilitation Act of 1973, as amended; 29 U.S.C. 705(38), 705(39), 709(c), 795g, and 795k(b))

§363.51 What are the allowable administrative costs?

(a) A State may use funds under this part to pay for expenditures incurred in the administration of activities carried out under this part, consistent with the definition of administrative costs in 34 CFR 361.5(c)(2).

(b) A designated State agency may not expend more than 2.5 percent of a State's allotment under this part for administrative costs for carrying out the State supported employment program.

(Authority: Sections 7(1), 12(c), and 603(c) of the Rehabilitation Act of 1973, as amended; 29 U.S.C. 705(1), 709(c), and 795h(c))

§ 363.52 What are the information collection and reporting requirements?

Each State agency designated in § 363.11(a) must collect and report separately the information required under 34 CFR 361.40 for—

(a) Eligible individuals receiving supported employment services under this part;

(b) Eligible individuals receiving supported employment services under 34 CFR part 361;

(c) Eligible youth receiving supported employment services and extended services under this part; and

(d) Eligible youth receiving supported employment services under 34 CFR part 361 and extended services.

(Authority: Sections 13 and 607 of the Rehabilitation Act of 1973, as amended; 29 U.S.C. 710 and 795l)

§ 363.53 What requirements must a designated State unit meet for the transition of an individual to extended services?

(a) A designated State unit must provide for the transition of an individual with a most significant disability, including a youth with a most significant disability, to extended services, as defined in 34 CFR 361.5(c)(19), no later than 24 months after the individual enters supported employment, unless a longer period is established in the individualized plan for employment.

(b) Prior to assisting the individual in transitioning from supported employment services to extended services, the designated State unit must ensure—

(1) The counselor and individual have considered extending the provision of supported employment services beyond 24 months, as appropriate, and have determined that no further supported employment services are necessary to support and maintain the individual in supported employment before the individual transitions to extended services; and

(2) The source of extended services for the individual has been identified in order to ensure there will be no interruption of services. The providers of extended services may include—

(i) A State agency, a private nonprofit organization, employer, or any other appropriate resource, after an individual has made the transition from support from the designated State unit; or,

(ii) The designated State unit, in the case of a youth with a most significant disability, in accordance with requirements set forth in 34 CFR 361.5(c)(19) and this part for a period not to exceed four years, or at such time that a youth reaches the age of 25 and no longer meets the definition of a youth with a disability under 34 CFR 361.5(c)(58), whichever occurs first. For youth who still require extended services after they can no longer receive them from the designated State unit, the designated State unit must identify another source of extended services for those youth in order to ensure there will be no interruption of services. The designated State unit may not provide extended services to individuals with the most significant disabilities who are not youth with the most significant disabilities.

(Authority: Sections 7(13), 12(c), and 604(b) of the Rehabilitation Act of 1973, as amended; 29 U.S.C. 705(13), 709(c) and 795i)

§ 363.54 When will an individual be considered to have achieved an employment outcome in supported employment?

An individual with a most significant disability, including a youth with a most significant disability, who is employed in competitive integrated employment or who is employed in an integrated setting working on a short-term basis to achieve competitive integrated employment will be considered to have achieved an employment outcome, including customized employment, in supported employment when—

(a) The individual has completed supported employment services provided under this part and 34 CFR part 361, except for any other vocational rehabilitation services listed on the individualized plan for employment provided to individuals who are working on a short-term basis toward the achievement of competitive integrated employment in supported employment. An individual has completed supported employment services when—

(1) The individual has received up to 24 months of supported employment services; or

(2) The counselor and individual have determined that an extension of time to provide supported employment services beyond 24 months is necessary to support and maintain the individual in supported employment before the individual transitions to extended services and that extension of time has concluded; and

(b) The individual has transitioned to extended services provided by either the designated State unit for youth with the most significant disabilities, or another provider, consistent with the provisions of §§363.4(a)(2) and 363.22; and

(c) The individual has maintained employment and achieved stability in the work setting for at least 90 days after transitioning to extended services; and

(d) The employment is individualized and customized consistent with the strengths, abilities, interests, and informed choice of the individual.

(Authority: Sections 7(11), 7(13), 7(38), 7(39), 7(40), 12(c), 602, and 606(b) of the Rehabilitation Act of 1973, as amended; 29 U.S.C. 705(11), 705(13), 705(38), 705(39), 705(40), 709(c), 795g, and 795k(b))

§363.55 When will the service record of an individual who has achieved an employment outcome in supported employment be closed?

(a) The service record of an individual with a most significant disability, including a youth with a most significant disability, who has achieved an employment outcome in supported employment in competitive integrated employment will be closed concurrently with the achievement of the employment outcome in supported employment when the individual—

(1) Satisfies requirements for case closure, as set forth in 34 CFR 361.56; and

(2) Is not receiving extended services or any other vocational rehabilitation service provided by the designated State unit with funds under this part or 34 CFR part 361.

(b) The service record of an individual with a most significant disability, including a youth with a most significant disability who is working toward competitive integrated employment on a short-term basis and is receiving extended services from funds other than those allotted under this part and 34 CFR part 361 will be closed when the individual—

(1) Achieves competitive integrated employment within the short-term basis period established pursuant to §363.1(c); and the individual—

(i) Satisfies requirements for case closure, as set forth in 34 CFR 361.56; and

(ii) Is no longer receiving vocational rehabilitation services provided by the designated State unit with funds under 34 CFR part 361; or

(2) Does not achieve competitive integrated employment within the short-term basis period established pursuant to §363.1(c).

(c) The service record of a youth with a most significant disability who is receiving extended services provided by the designated State unit from funds under this part or 34 CFR part 361 will be closed when—

(1) The youth with a most significant disability achieves an employment outcome in supported employment in competitive integrated employment without entering the short-term basis period; and

(i) Is no longer eligible to receive extended services provided by the designated State unit with funds allotted under this part and 34 CFR part 361 because the individual—

(A) No longer meets age requirements established in the definition of a youth with a disability pursuant to 34 CFR 361.5(c)(58); or

(B) Has received extended services for a period of four years; or

(C) Has transitioned to extended services provided with funds other than those allotted under this part or part 361 prior to meeting the age or time restrictions established under paragraphs (c)(1)(i)(A) and (B) of this section, respectively; and

(ii) Satisfies requirements for case closure, as set forth in 34 CFR 361.56; and

(iii) The individual is no longer receiving any other vocational rehabilitation service from the designated State unit provided with funds under 34 CFR part 361; or

(2) The youth with a most significant disability who is working toward competitive integrated employment on a short-term basis—

(i) Achieves competitive integrated employment within the short-term basis period established pursuant to § 363.1(c);

(ii) Is no longer eligible to receive extended services provided by the designated State unit with funds allotted under this part and 34 CFR part 361 because the individual—

(A) No longer meets age requirements established in the definition of a youth with a disability pursuant to 34 CFR 361.5(c)(58); or

(B) Has received extended services for a period of four years; or

(C) Has transitioned to extended services provided with funds other than those allotted under this part or 34 CFR part 361 prior to meeting the age or time restrictions established under paragraphs (c)(2)(ii)(A) and (B) of this section, respectively; and

(iii) Satisfies requirements for case closure, as set forth in 34 CFR 361.56; or

(3) The youth with a most significant disability working toward competitive integrated employment on a short-term basis does not achieve competitive integrated employment within the short-term basis period established pursuant to § 363.1(c).

(Authority: Sections 7(11), 7(13), 7(38), 7(39), 7(40), 7(42), 12(c), 602, and 606(b) of the Rehabilitation Act of 1973, as amended; 29 U.S.C. 705(11), 705(13), 705(38), 705(39), 705(40), 705(42), 709(c), 795g, and 795k(b))

§ 363.56 What notice requirements apply to this program?

Each grantee must advise applicants for or recipients of services under this part, or as appropriate, the parents, family members, guardians, advocates, or authorized representatives of those individuals, including youth with the most significant disabilities, of the availability and purposes of the Client Assistance Program, including information on seeking assistance from that program.

(Authority: Section 20 of the Rehabilitation Act of 1973, as amended; 29 U.S.C. 717)

PARTS 364–366 [RESERVED]

PART 367—INDEPENDENT LIVING SERVICES FOR OLDER INDIVIDUALS WHO ARE BLIND

Subpart A—General

AUTHORITY: Sections 751–753 of the Rehabilitation Act of 1973, as amended; 29 U.S.C. 796j–7961, unless otherwise noted.

SOURCE: 81 FR 55583, Aug. 19, 2016, unless otherwise noted.

Subpart A—General

§ 367.1 **What is the Independent Living Services for Older Individuals Who Are Blind program?**

This program supports projects that—

(a) Provide any of the independent living (IL) services to older individuals who are blind that are described in § 367.3(b);

(b) Conduct activities that will improve or expand services for these individuals; and

(c) Conduct activities to help improve public understanding of the challenges of these individuals.

(Authority: Section 752 of the Rehabilitation Act of 1973, as amended; 29 U.S.C. 796k(a) and (d))

§ 367.2 **Who is eligible for an award?**

Any designated State agency (DSA) is eligible for an award under this program if the DSA—

(a) Is authorized to provide rehabilitation services to individuals who are blind; and

(b) Submits to and obtains approval from the Secretary of an application that meets the requirements of section 752(h) of the Act and §§ 367.30–367.31.

(Authority: Section 752(a)(2) and 752(h) of the Rehabilitation Act of 1973, as amended; 29 U.S.C. 796k(a)(2) and (h))

§ 367.3 **What activities may the Secretary fund?**

(a) The DSA may use funds awarded under this part for the activities described in § 367.1 and paragraph (b) of this section.

(b) For purposes of § 367.1(a), IL services for older individuals who are blind include—

(1) Services to help correct blindness, such as—

(i) Outreach services;

(ii) Visual screening;

(iii) Surgical or therapeutic treatment to prevent, correct, or modify disabling eye conditions; and

(iv) Hospitalization related to these services;

(2) The provision of eyeglasses and other visual aids;

(3) The provision of services and equipment to assist an older individual who is blind to become more mobile and more self-sufficient;

(4) Mobility training, Braille instruction, and other services and equipment to help an older individual who is blind adjust to blindness;

(5) Guide services, reader services, and transportation;

(6) Any other appropriate service designed to assist an older individual who is blind in coping with daily living activities, including supportive services and rehabilitation teaching services;

(7) IL skills training, information and referral services, peer counseling, individual advocacy training, facilitating the transition from nursing homes and other institutions to home and community-based residences with the requisite supports and services, and providing assistance to older individuals who are blind who are at risk of

entering institutions so that the individuals may remain in the community; and

(8) Other IL services, as defined in § 367.5.

(Authority: Section 752(d) and (e) of the Rehabilitation Act of 1973, as amended; 29 U.S.C. 796k (d) and (e))

§ 367.4 What regulations apply?

The following regulations apply to the Independent Living Services for Older Individuals Who Are Blind program:

(a) The Education Department General Administrative Regulations (EDGAR) as follows:

(1) 34 CFR part 75 (Direct Grant Programs), with respect to grants under subpart B and D.

(2) 34 CFR part 76 (State-Administered Programs), with respect to grants under subpart E.

(3) 34 CFR part 77 (Definitions That Apply to Department Regulations).

(4) 34 CFR part 79 (Intergovernmental Review of Department of Education Programs and Activities).

(5) 34 CFR part 81 (General Education Provisions Act—Enforcement).

(6) 34 CFR part 82 (New Restrictions on Lobbying).

(7) 2 CFR part 180 (OMB Guidelines to Agencies on Debarment and Suspension (Nonprocurement)), as adopted at 2 CFR part 3485.

(8) 2 CFR part 200 (Uniform Administrative Requirements, Cost Principles, and Audit Requirements for Federal Awards), as adopted at 2 CFR part 3474.

(b) The regulations in this part 367.

(Authority: Sections 12(c) and 752 of the Rehabilitation Act of 1973, as amended; 29 U.S.C. 709(c) and 796k)

§ 367.5 What definitions apply?

(a) The definitions of terms used in this part that are included in the regulations identified in § 367.4 as applying to this program.

(b) In addition, the following definitions also apply to this part:

(1) *Act* means the Rehabilitation Act, as amended by WIOA.

(2) *Advocacy* means pleading an individual's cause or speaking or writing in support of an individual. To the extent permitted by State law or the rules of the agency before which an individual is appearing, a non-lawyer may engage in advocacy on behalf of another individual. Advocacy may—

(i) Involve representing an individual—

(A) Before private entities or organizations, government agencies (whether State, local, or Federal), or in a court of law (whether State or Federal); or

(B) In negotiations or mediation, in formal or informal administrative proceedings before government agencies (whether State, local, or Federal), or in legal proceedings in a court of law; and

(ii) Be on behalf of—

(A) A single individual, in which case it is individual advocacy;

(B) A group or class of individuals, in which case it is systems (or systemic) advocacy; or

(C) Oneself, in which case it is self advocacy.

(3) *Attendant care* means a personal assistance service provided to an individual with significant disabilities in performing a variety of tasks required to meet essential personal needs in areas such as bathing, communicating, cooking, dressing, eating, homemaking, toileting, and transportation.

(4) *Contract* means a legal instrument by which RSA in subpart B or the DSA receiving a grant under this part purchases property or services needed to carry out the program under this Part. The term as used in this part does not include a legal instrument, even if RSA or the DSA considers it a contract, when the substance of the transaction meets the definition of a Federal award or subaward.

(Authority: 20 U.S.C. 1221e–3)

(5) *Designated State Agency* means the agency described in section 101(a)(2)(A)(i) of the Rehabilitation Act as the sole State agency authorized to provide rehabilitation services to individuals who are blind and administer the OIB grant.

(6) *Independent living services for older individuals who are blind* means those services listed in § 367.3(b).

(7) *Legally authorized advocate or representative* means an individual who is authorized under State law to act or advocate on behalf of another individual. Under certain circumstances, State law permits only an attorney,

legal guardian, or individual with a power of attorney to act or advocate on behalf of another individual. In other circumstances, State law may permit other individuals to act or advocate on behalf of another individual.

(8) *Minority group* means Alaska Natives, American Indians, Asians, Blacks (African Americans), Hispanics (Latinos), Native Hawaiians, and Pacific Islanders.

(9) *Older individual who is blind* means an individual age fifty-five or older whose severe visual impairment makes competitive employment extremely difficult to obtain but for whom IL goals are feasible.

(10) *Other IL services* include:

(i) Counseling services, including psychological, psychotherapeutic, and related services;

(ii) Services related to securing housing or shelter, including services related to community group living, that are supportive of the purposes of the Act, and adaptive housing services, including appropriate accommodations to and modifications of any space used to serve, or to be occupied by, older individuals who are blind;

(iii) Rehabilitation technology;

(iv) Services and training for older individuals who are blind who also have cognitive and sensory disabilities, including life skills training and interpreter services;

(v) Personal assistance services, including attendant care and the training of personnel providing these services;

(vi) Surveys, directories, and other activities to identify appropriate housing, recreation opportunities, and accessible transportation, and other support services;

(vii) Consumer information programs on rehabilitation and IL services available under the Act, especially for minorities and other older individuals who are blind who have traditionally been unserved or underserved by programs under the Act;

(viii) Education and training necessary for living in a community and participating in community activities;

(ix) Supported living;

(x) Transportation, including referral and assistance for transportation;

(xi) Physical rehabilitation;

(xii) Therapeutic treatment;

(xiii) Provision of needed prostheses and other appliances and devices;

(xiv) Individual and group social and recreational services;

(xv) Services under other Federal, State, or local programs designed to provide resources, training, counseling, or other assistance of substantial benefit in enhancing the independence, productivity, and quality of life of older individuals who are blind;

(xvi) Appropriate preventive services to decrease the need of older individuals who are blind who are assisted under the Act for similar services in the future;

(xvii) Community awareness programs to enhance the understanding and integration into society of older individuals who are blind; and

(xviii) Any other services that may be necessary to improve the ability of an older individual who is blind to function, continue functioning, or move toward functioning independently in the family or community or to continue in employment and that are not inconsistent with any other provisions of the Act.

(11) *Peer relationships* mean relationships involving mutual support and assistance among individuals with significant disabilities who are actively pursuing IL goals.

(12) *Peer role models* means individuals with significant disabilities whose achievements can serve as a positive example for other older individuals who are blind.

(13) *Personal assistance services* means a range of IL services, provided by one or more persons, designed to assist an older individual who is blind to perform daily living activities on or off the job that the individual would typically perform if the individual was not blind. These IL services must be designed to increase the individual's control in life and ability to perform everyday activities on or off the job.

(14) *Service provider* means—

(i) The DSA that directly provides services authorized under §367.3; or

(ii) Any other entity that receives a subaward or contract from the DSA to provide services authorized under §367.3.

(15) *Significant disability* means a severe physical, mental, cognitive, or sensory impairment that substantially limits an individual's ability to function independently in the family or community or to obtain, maintain, or advance in employment.

(16) *State* means, except where otherwise specified in the Act, in addition to each of the several States of the United States, the District of Columbia, the Commonwealth of Puer5to Rico, the United States Virgin Islands, Guam, American Samoa, and the Commonwealth of the Northern Mariana Islands.

(17) *Subaward* means a grant or a cooperative agreement provided by the DSA to a subrecipient for the subrecipient to carry out part of the Federal award received by the DSA under this part. It does not include payments to a contractor or payments to an individual that is a beneficiary of a program funded under this part. A subaward may be provided through any form of legal agreement, including an agreement that the DSA considers a contract.

(Authority: 20 U.S.C. 1221e-3)

(18) *Subrecipient* means a non-Federal entity that receives a subaward from the DSA to carry out part of the program funded under this part; but does not include an individual that is a beneficiary of such program. A subrecipient may also be a recipient of other Federal awards directly from a Federal awarding agency.

(Authority: 20 U.S.C. 1221e-3)

(19) *Transportation* means travel and related expenses that are necessary to enable an older individual who is blind to benefit from another IL service and travel and related expenses for an attendant or aide if the services of that attendant or aide are necessary to enable an older individual who is blind to benefit from that IL service.

(20) *Unserved and underserved groups or populations*, with respect to groups or populations of older individuals who are blind in a State, include, but are not limited to, groups or populations of older individuals who are blind who—

(i) Have cognitive and sensory impairments;

(ii) Are members of racial and ethnic minority groups;

(iii) Live in rural areas; or

(iv) Have been identified by the DSA as unserved or underserved.

(Authority: Unless otherwise noted, Section 7 of the Rehabilitation Act of 1973, as amended; 29 U.S.C. 705)

Subpart B—Training and Technical Assistance

§ 367.20   What are the requirements for funding training and technical assistance under this chapter?

For any fiscal year, beginning with fiscal year 2015, the Secretary shall first reserve not less than 1.8 percent and not more than 2 percent of funds appropriated and made available to carry out this chapter to provide training and technical assistance to DSAs, or other providers of independent living services for older individuals who are blind, that are funded under this chapter for such fiscal year.

(Authority: Section 751A(a) of the Rehabilitation Act of 1973, as amended; 29 U.S.C. 796j-1(a))

§ 367.21   How does the Secretary use these funds to provide training and technical assistance?

(a) The Secretary uses these funds to provide training and technical assistance, either directly or through grants, contracts, or cooperative agreements with State and public or non-profit agencies and organizations and institutions of higher education that have the capacity to provide technical assistance and training in the provision of independent living services for older individuals who are blind.

(b) An entity receiving assistance in accordance with paragraph (a) of this section shall provide training and technical assistance to DSAs or other service providers to assist them in improving the operation and performance of programs and services for older individuals who are blind resulting in their enhanced independence and self-sufficiency.

(Authority: Section 751A(a) and (c) of the Rehabilitation Act of 1973, as amended; 29 U.S.C. 796j-1(a) and (c))

§367.22 How does the Secretary make an award?

(a) To be eligible to receive a grant or enter into a contract or cooperative agreement under section 751A of the Act and this subpart, an applicant shall submit an application to the Secretary containing a proposal to provide training and technical assistance to DSAs or other service providers of IL services to older individuals who are blind and any additional information at the time and in the manner that the Secretary may require.

(b) The Secretary shall provide for peer review of applications by panels that include persons who are not Federal or State government employees and who have experience in the provision of services to older individuals who are blind.

(Authority: Section 751A(a) and (c) of the Rehabilitation Act of 1973, as amended; 29 U.S.C. 796j–1(a) and (c))

§367.23 How does the Secretary determine funding priorities?

The Secretary shall conduct a survey of DSAs that receive grants under section 752 regarding training and technical assistance needs in order to inform funding priorities for such training and technical assistance.

(Authority: Section 751A(b) of the Rehabilitation Act of 1973, as amended; 29 U.S.C. 796j–1(b))

§367.24 How does the Secretary evaluate an application?

(a) The Secretary evaluates each application for a grant, cooperative agreement or contract under this subpart on the basis of the selection criteria chosen from the general selection criteria found in EDGAR regulations at 34 CFR 75.210.

(b) If using a contract to award funds under this subpart, the Secretary may conduct the application process and make the subsequent award in accordance with 34 CFR part 75.

(Authority: Section 751A of the Rehabilitation Act of 1973, as amended; 29 U.S.C. 796j–1(b), 20 U.S.C. 1221e–3, and 3474)

Subpart C—What Are the Application Requirements Under This Part?

§367.30 How does a designated State agency (DSA) apply for an award?

To receive a grant under section 752(h) or a reallotment grant under section 752(i)(4) of the Act, a DSA must submit to and obtain approval from the Secretary of an application for assistance under this program at the time, in the form and manner, and containing the agreements, assurances, and information, that the Secretary determines to be necessary to carry out this program.

(Approved by the Office of Management and Budget under control number 1820–0660)

(Authority: Sections 752 (h) and (i)(4) of the Rehabilitation Act of 1973, as amended; 29 U.S.C. 796k(h) and (i))

§367.31 What assurances must a DSA include in its application?

An application for a grant under section 752(h) or a reallotment grant under section 752(i)(4) of the Act must contain an assurance that—

(a) Grant funds will be expended only for the purposes described in §367.1;

(b) With respect to the costs of the program to be carried out by the State pursuant to this part, the State will make available, directly or through donations from public or private entities, non-Federal contributions toward these costs in an amount that is not less than $1 for each $9 of Federal funds provided in the grant;

(c) At the end of each fiscal year, the DSA will prepare and submit to the Secretary a report, with respect to each project or program the DSA operates or administers under this part, whether directly or through a grant or contract, that contains information that the Secretary determines necessary for the proper and efficient administration of this program, including—

(1) The number and demographics of older individuals who are blind, including older individuals who are blind from minority backgrounds, and are receiving services;

(2) The types of services provided and the number of older individuals who

407

are blind and are receiving each type of service;

(3) The sources and amounts of funding for the operation of each project or program;

(4) The amounts and percentages of resources committed to each type of service provided;

(5) Data on actions taken to employ, and advance in employment, qualified—

(i) Individuals with significant disabilities; and

(ii) Older individuals with significant disabilities who are blind;

(6) A comparison, if appropriate, of prior year activities with the activities of the most recent year; and

(7) Any new methods and approaches relating to IL services for older individuals who are blind that are developed by projects funded under this part;

(d) The DSA will—

(1) Provide services that contribute to the maintenance of, or the increased independence of, older individuals who are blind; and

(2) Engage in—

(i) Capacity-building activities, including collaboration with other agencies and organizations;

(ii) Activities to promote community awareness, involvement, and assistance; and

(iii) Outreach efforts; and

(e) The applicant has been designated by the State as the sole State agency authorized to provide rehabilitation services to individuals who are blind.

(Approved by the Office of Management and Budget under control numbers 1820–0660 and 1820–0608)

(Authority: Section 752(h) of the Rehabilitation Act of 1973, as amended; 29 U.S.C. 796k(h))

Subpart D—How does the Secretary award discretionary grants?

§ 367.40 Under what circumstances does the Secretary award discretionary grants to States?

(a) In the case of a fiscal year for which the amount appropriated under section 753 of the Act is less than $13,000,000, the Secretary awards discretionary grants under this part on a competitive basis to States in accordance with section 752(b) of the Act and EDGAR regulations at 34 CFR part 75 (Direct Grant Programs).

(b) The Secretary awards noncompetitive continuation grants for a multi-year project to pay for the costs of activities for which a grant was awarded under this part—as long as the grantee satisfies the applicable requirements in this part, the terms of the grant, and 34 CFR 75.250 through 75.253 (Approval of Multi-year Projects).

(c) Subparts A, C, D, and F of this part govern the award of competitive grants under this part.

(Authority: Section 752(b) of the Rehabilitation Act of 1973, as amended; 29 U.S.C. 796k(b); 20 U.S.C. 1221e–3 and 3474)

§ 367.41 How does the Secretary evaluate an application for a discretionary grant?

(a) The Secretary evaluates an application for a discretionary grant based on the selection criteria chosen from the general selection criteria found in EDGAR regulations at 34 CFR 75.210.

(b) In addition to the selection criteria, the Secretary considers the geographic distribution of projects in making an award.

(Authority: Section 752(b) of the Rehabilitation Act of 1973, as amended; 29 U.S.C. 796k(b); 20 U.S.C. 1221e–3 and 3474)

Subpart E—How Does the Secretary Award Formula Grants?

§ 367.50 Under what circumstances does the Secretary award formula grants to States?

(a) In the case of a fiscal year for which the amount appropriated under section 753 of the Act is equal to or greater than $13,000,000, grants under this part are made to States from allotments under section 752(c)(2) of the Act.

(b) Subparts A, C, E, and F of this part govern the award of formula grants under this part.

(Authority: Section 752(c) of the Rehabilitation Act of 1973, as amended; 29 U.S.C. 796k(c))

§367.51 How are allotments made?

(a) For purposes of making grants under section 752(c) of the Act and this subpart, the Secretary makes an allotment to each State in an amount determined in accordance with section 752(i) of the Act.

(b) The Secretary makes a grant to a DSA in the amount of the allotment to the State under section 752(i) of the Act if the DSA submits to and obtains approval from the Secretary of an application for assistance under this program that meets the requirements of section 752(h) of the Act and §§367.30 and 367.31.

(Approved by the Office of Management and Budget under control number 1820–0660)

(Authority: Section 752(c)(2) of the Rehabilitation Act of 1973, as amended; 29 U.S.C. 796k(c)(2))

§367.52 How does the Secretary reallot funds under this program?

(a) From the amounts specified in paragraph (b) of this section, the Secretary may make reallotment grants to States, as determined by the Secretary, whose population of older individuals who are blind has a substantial need for the services specified in section 752(d) of the Act and §367.3(b), relative to the populations in other States of older individuals who are blind.

(b) The amounts referred to in paragraph (a) of this section are any amounts that are not paid to States under section 752(c)(2) of the Act and §367.51 as a result of—

(1) The failure of a DSA to prepare, submit, and receive approval of an application under section 752(h) of the Act and in accordance with §§367.30 and 367.31; or

(2) Information received by the Secretary from the DSA that the DSA does not intend to expend the full amount of the State's allotment under section 752(c) of the Act and this subpart.

(c) A reallotment grant to a State under paragraph (a) of this section is subject to the same conditions as grants made under section 752(a) of the Act and this part.

(d) Any funds made available to a State for any fiscal year pursuant to this section are regarded as an increase in the allotment of the State under §367.51 for that fiscal year only.

(e) A State that does not intend to expend the full amount of its allotment must notify RSA at least 45 days prior to the end of the fiscal year that its grant, or a portion of it, is available for reallotment.

(Approved by the Office of Management and Budget under control number 1820–0660)

(Authority: Section 752(i)(4) of the Rehabilitation Act of 1973, as amended; 29 U.S.C. 796k(i)(4))

Subpart F—What Conditions Must Be Met After an Award?

§367.60 When may a DSA make subawards or contracts?

A DSA may operate or administer the program or projects under this part to carry out the purposes specified in §367.1, either directly or through—

(a) Subawards to public or private nonprofit agencies or organizations; or

(b) Contracts with individuals, entities, or organizations that are not public or private nonprofit agencies or organizations.

(Authority: Sections 752(g) and (h) of the Rehabilitation Act of 1973, as amended; 29 U.S.C. 796k(g) and (h)(2)(A))

§367.61 What matching requirements apply?

Non-Federal contributions required by §367.31(b) must meet the requirements in 2 CFR 200.306 (Cost sharing or matching).

(Authority: Section 752(f) of the Rehabilitation Act of 1973, as amended; 29 U.S.C. 796k(f))

§367.62 What requirements apply if the State's non-Federal share is in cash?

(a) Expenditures that meet the non-Federal share requirements of 2 CFR 200.306 may be used to meet the non-Federal share matching requirement. Expenditures used as non-Federal share must also meet the following requirements:

(1) The expenditures are made with funds made available by appropriation directly to the DSA or with funds made available by allotment or transfer from

any other unit of State or local government;

(2) The expenditures are made with cash contributions from a donor that are deposited in the account of the DSA in accordance with State law for expenditure by, and at the sole discretion of, the DSA for activities authorized by § 367.3; or

(3) The expenditures are made with cash contributions from a donor that are earmarked for meeting the State's share for activities listed in § 367.3;

(b) Cash contributions are permissible under paragraph (a)(3) of this section only if the cash contributions are not used for expenditures that benefit or will benefit in any way the donor, an individual to whom the donor is related by blood or marriage or with whom the donor has a close personal relationship, or an individual, entity, or organization with whom the donor shares a financial interest.

(c) The receipt of a subaward or contract under section 752(g) of the Act from the DSA is not considered a benefit to the donor of a cash contribution for purposes of paragraph (b) of this section if the subaward or contract was awarded under the State's regular competitive procedures. The State may not exempt the awarding of the subaward or contract from its regular competitive procedures.

(d) For purposes of this section, a donor may be a private agency, a profit-making or nonprofit organization, or an individual.

(Authority: Section 752(f) of the Rehabilitation Act of 1973, as amended; 29 U.S.C. 796k(f))

§ 367.63 What requirements apply if the State's non-Federal share is in kind?

In-kind contributions may be—

(a) Used to meet the matching requirement under section 752(f) of the Act if the in-kind contributions meet the requirements and are allowable under 2 CFR 200.306; and

(b) Made to the program or project by the State or by a third party (*i.e.*, an individual, entity, or organization, whether local, public, private, for profit, or nonprofit), including a third party that is a subrecipient or contractor that is receiving or will receive

assistance under section 752(g) of the Rehabilitation Act.

(Authority: Section 752(f) and (g) of the Rehabilitation Act of 1973, as amended; 29 U.S.C. 796k(f) and (g))

§ 367.64 What is the prohibition against a State's condition of an award of a sub-award or contract based on cash or in-kind contributions?

(a) A State may not condition the making of a subaward or contract under section 752(g) of the Act on the requirement that the applicant for the subaward or contract make a cash or in-kind contribution of any particular amount or value to the State.

(b) An individual, entity, or organization that is a subrecipient or contractor of the State, may not condition the award of a subcontract on the requirement that the applicant for the subcontract make a cash or in-kind contribution of any particular amount or value to the State or to the subrecipient or contractor of the State.

(Authority: Section 752(f) and (g) of the Rehabilitation Act of 1973, as amended; 29 U.S.C. 796k(f) and (g))

§ 367.65 What is program income and how may it be used?

(a) *Definition—Program income* means gross income earned by the grantee, subrecipient, or contractor that is directly generated by a supported activity or earned as a result of the grant, subaward, or contract.

(1) Program income received through the transfer of Social Security Administration program income from the State Vocational Rehabilitation Services program (Title I) in accordance with 34 CFR 361.63(c)(2) will be treated as program income received under this part.

(2) Payments received by the State agency, subrecipients, or contractors from insurers, consumers, or other for IL services provided under the Independent Living Services for Older Individuals Who Are Blind program to defray part or all of the costs of services provided to individual consumers will be treated as program income received under this part.

(b) *Use of program income.* (1) Program income, whenever earned, must be used for the provision of services authorized under §367.3.

(2) Program income must be added to the Federal Award in accordance with 2 CFR 200.307(e)(2).

(3) Program income may not be used to meet the non-Federal share requirement under §367.31(b).

(Authority: Section 12(c) of the Rehabilitation Act of 1973, as amended; 29 U.S.C. 709(c))

§367.66 What requirements apply to the obligation of Federal funds and program income?

(a) Except as provided in paragraph (b) of this section, any Federal funds, including reallotted funds, that are appropriated for a fiscal year to carry out a program under this part that are not obligated or expended by the DSA prior to the beginning of the succeeding fiscal year, and any program income received during a fiscal year that is not obligated or expended by the DSA prior to the beginning of the succeeding fiscal year in which the program income was received, remain available for obligation and expenditure by the DSA during that succeeding fiscal year.

(b) Federal funds appropriated for a fiscal year under this part remain available for obligation in the succeeding fiscal year only to the extent that the DSA complied with its matching requirement by obligating, in accordance with 34 CFR 76.707, the non-Federal share in the fiscal year for which the funds were appropriated.

(c) Program income is considered earned in the fiscal year in which it is received. Program income earned during the fiscal year must be disbursed during the time in which new obligations may be incurred to carry out the work authorized under the award, and prior to requesting additional cash payments.

(Authority: Section 12(c) of the Rehabilitation Act of 1973, as amended; 29 U.S.C. 709(c))

§367.67 May an individual's ability to pay be considered in determining his or her participation in the costs of OIB services?

(a) *Participation of individuals in cost of services.* (1) A State is neither required to charge nor prohibited from charging consumers for the cost of IL services provided under the Independent Living Services for Older Individuals Who Are Blind program;

(2) If a State charges consumers or allows other service providers to charge for the cost of IL services provided under the Independent Living Services for Older Individuals Who Are Blind program, a State is neither required to nor prohibited from considering the ability of individual consumers to pay for the cost of these services in determining how much a particular consumer must contribute to the costs of a particular service.

(b) *State policies on cost of services.* If a State chooses to charge or allow other service providers to charge consumers for the cost of IL services provided under the Independent Living Services for Older Individuals Who Are Blind program and if a State chooses to consider and allow other service providers to consider the ability of individual consumers to pay for the cost of IL services provided under the Independent Living Services for Older Individual Who Are Blind program, the State must maintain policies that—

(1) Specify the type of IL services for which costs may be charged and the type of IL services for which a financial need test may be applied;

(2) Explain the method for determining the amount charged for the IL services and how any financial need test will be applied;

(3) Ensure costs are charged uniformly so that all individuals are treated equally;

(4) Ensure that if costs are charged or financial need is considered, the consumer's required participation is not so high that it effectively denies the individual a necessary service;

(5) Require documentation of an individual's participation in the cost of any IL services provided, including the determination of an individual's financial need; and

(6) Provide that individuals who have been determined eligible for Social Security benefits under Titles II and XVI of the Social Security Act may not be charged any cost to receive IL services under this program.

(c) *Policies on consumer financial participation.* If a State permits other service providers to charge the costs of IL services provided under the Independent Living Services for Older Individuals Who Are Blind program, or chooses to allow other service providers to consider the ability of individual consumers to contribute to the cost of IL services provided through the Independent Living Services for Older Individuals Who Are Blind program, the State must require that such service providers comply with the State's written policies regarding consumer financial participation in the cost of IL services.

(Authority: Section 12(c) of the Rehabilitation Act of 1973, as amended; 29 U.S.C. 709(c)).

§ 367.68 What notice must be given about the Client Assistance Program (CAP)?

The DSA and all other service providers under this part shall use formats that are accessible to notify individuals seeking or receiving services under this part about—

(a) The availability of CAP authorized by section 112 of the Act;

(b) The purposes of the services provided under the CAP; and

(c) How to contact the CAP.

(Authority: Section 20 of the Rehabilitation Act of 1973, as amended; 29 U.S.C. 717)

§ 367.69 What are the special requirements pertaining to the protection, use, and release of personal information?

(a) *General provisions.* The DSA and all other service providers under this part shall adopt and implement policies and procedures to safeguard the confidentiality of all personal information, including photographs and lists of names. These policies and procedures must assure that—

(1) Specific safeguards protect current and stored personal information, including a requirement that data only be released when governed by a written agreement between the DSA and other service providers and the receiving entity under paragraphs (d) and (e)(1) of this section, which addresses the requirements in this section;

(2) All applicants for, or recipients of, services under this part and, as appropriate, those individuals' legally authorized representatives, service providers, cooperating agencies, and interested persons are informed of the confidentiality of personal information and the conditions for gaining access to and releasing this information;

(3) All applicants or their legally authorized representatives are informed about the service provider's need to collect personal information and the policies governing its use, including—

(i) Identification of the authority under which information is collected;

(ii) Explanation of the principal purposes for which the service provider intends to use or release the information;

(iii) Explanation of whether providing requested information to the service provider is mandatory or voluntary and the effects to the individual of not providing requested information;

(iv) Identification of those situations in which the service provider requires or does not require informed written consent of the individual or his or her legally authorized representative before information may be released; and

(v) Identification of other agencies to which information is routinely released;

(4) Persons who do not speak, listen, read, or write English proficiently or who rely on alternative modes of communication must be provided an explanation of service provider policies and procedures affecting personal information through methods that can be meaningfully understood by them;

(5) At least the same protections are provided to individuals served under this part as provided by State laws and regulations; and

(6) Access to records is governed by rules established by the service provider and any fees charged for copies of records are reasonable and cover only extraordinary costs of duplication or making extensive searches.

(b) *Service provider use.* All personal information in the possession of the service provider may be used only for the purposes directly connected with the provision of services under this part and the administration of the program under which services are provided under this part. Information containing identifiable personal information may not be shared with advisory or other bodies that do not have official responsibility for the provision of services under this part or the administration of the program under which services are provided under this part. In the provision of services under this part or the administration of the program under which services are provided under this part, the service provider may obtain personal information from other service providers and cooperating agencies under assurances that the information may not be further divulged, except as provided under paragraphs (c), (d), and (e) of this section.

(c) *Release to recipients of services under this part.* (1) Except as provided in paragraphs (c)(2) and (3) of this section, if requested in writing by a recipient of services under this part, the service provider shall release all information in that individual's record of services to the individual or the individual's legally authorized representative in a timely manner.

(2) Medical, psychological, or other information that the service provider determines may be harmful to the individual may not be released directly to the individual, but must be provided through a qualified medical or psychological professional or the individual's legally authorized representative.

(3) If personal information has been obtained from another agency or organization, it may be released only by, or under the conditions established by, the other agency or organization.

(d) *Release for audit, evaluation, and research.* Personal information may be released to an organization, agency, or individual engaged in audit, evaluation, or research activities only for purposes directly connected with the administration of a program under this part, or for purposes that would significantly improve the quality of life for individuals served under this part and only if, in accordance with a written agreement, the organization, agency, or individual assures that—

(1) The information will be used only for the purposes for which it is being provided;

(2) The information will be released only to persons officially connected with the audit, evaluation, or research;

(3) The information will not be released to the involved individual;

(4) The information will be managed in a manner to safeguard confidentiality; and

(5) The final product will not reveal any personally identifying information without the informed written consent of the involved individual or the individual's legally authorized representative.

(e) *Release to other programs or authorities.* (1) Upon receiving the informed written consent of the individual or, if appropriate, the individual's legally authorized representative, the service provider may release personal information to another agency or organization, in accordance with a written agreement, for the latter's program purposes only to the extent that the information may be released to the involved individual and only to the extent that the other agency or organization demonstrates that the information requested is necessary for the proper administration of its program.

(2) Medical or psychological information may be released pursuant to paragraph (e)(1) of this section if the other agency or organization assures the service provider that the information will be used only for the purpose for which it is being provided and will not be further released to the individual.

(3) The service provider shall release personal information if required by Federal laws or regulations.

(4) The service provider shall release personal information in response to investigations in connection with law enforcement, fraud, or abuse, unless expressly prohibited by Federal or State laws or regulations, and in response to judicial order.

(5) The service provider also may release personal information to protect the individual or others if the individual poses a threat to his or her safety or to the safety of others.

(Authority: Section 12(c) of the Rehabilitation Act of 1973, as amended; 29 U.S.C. 709(c))

§367.70 **What access to records must be provided?**

For the purpose of conducting audits, examinations, and compliance reviews, the DSA and all other service providers shall provide access to the Secretary and the Comptroller General, or any of their duly authorized representatives, to—

(a) The records maintained under this part;

(b) Any other books, documents, papers, and records of the recipients that are pertinent to the financial assistance received under this part; and

(c) All individual case records or files or consumer service records of individuals served under this part, including names, addresses, photographs, and records of evaluation included in those individual case records or files or consumer service records.

(Authority: Section 12(c) of the Rehabilitation Act of 1973, as amended; 29 U.S.C. 709(c))

§ 367.71 What records must be maintained?

The DSA and all other service providers shall maintain—

(a) Records that fully disclose and document—

(1) The amount and disposition by the recipient of that financial assistance;

(2) The total cost of the project or undertaking in connection with which the financial assistance is given or used;

(3) The amount of that portion of the cost of the project or undertaking supplied by other sources; and

(4) Compliance with the requirements of this part; and

(b) Other records that the Secretary determines to be appropriate to facilitate an effective audit.

(Authority: Section 12(c) of the Rehabilitation Act of 1973, as amended; 29 U.S.C. 709(c))

PART 369 [RESERVED]

PART 370—CLIENT ASSISTANCE PROGRAM

Subpart A—General

AUTHORITY: Section 112 of the Rehabilitation Act of 1973, as amended; 29 U.S.C. 732, unless otherwise noted.

SOURCE: 81 FR 55590, Aug. 19. 2016, unless otherwise noted.

Subpart A—General

§ 370.1 What is the Client Assistance Program (CAP)?

The purpose of this program is to establish and carry out CAPs that—

(a) Advise and inform clients and client-applicants of all services and benefits available to them through programs authorized under the Rehabilitation Act of 1973, as amended (Act), including activities carried out under sections 113 and 511;

(b) Assist and advocate for clients and client-applicants in their relationships with projects, programs, and community rehabilitation programs providing services under the Act; and

(c) Inform individuals with disabilities in the State, especially individuals with disabilities who have traditionally been unserved or underserved by vocational rehabilitation programs, of the services and benefits available to them under the Act and under title I of the Americans with Disabilities Act of 1990 (ADA) (42 U.S.C. 12111 *et seq.*).

(Authority: Section 112(a) of the Rehabilitation Act of 1973, as amended; 29 U.S.C. 732(a))

§ 370.2 Who is eligible for an award?

(a)(1) Any State, through its Governor, and the protection and advocacy system serving the American Indian Consortium are eligible for an award under this part if the State or eligible protection and advocacy system submits, and receives approval of, an application in accordance with § 370.20.

(2) For purposes of this part, the terms—

(i) "American Indian Consortium" has the meaning given the term in section 102 of the Developmental Disabilities Assistance and Bill of Rights Act of 2000 (DD Act) (42 U.S.C. 15002); and

(ii) "Protection and advocacy system" means a protection and advocacy system established under subtitle C of title I of the DD Act (42 U.S.C. 15041 *et seq.*).

(b) Notwithstanding the protection and advocacy system serving the American Indian Consortium, the Governor of each State shall designate a public or private agency to conduct the State's CAP under this part.

(c) Except as provided in paragraph (d) of this section, the Governor shall designate an agency that is independent of any agency that provides treatment, services, or rehabilitation to individuals under the Act.

(d) The Governor may, in the initial designation, designate an agency that provides treatment, services, or rehabilitation to individuals with disabilities under the Act if, at any time before February 22, 1984, there was an agency in the State that both—

(1) Was a grantee under section 112 of the Act by serving as a client assistance agency and directly carrying out a CAP; and

(2) Was, at the same time, a grantee under any other provision of the Act.

(e) An agency designated by the Governor of a State to conduct the State's CAP or the protection and advocacy system serving the American Indian Consortium under this part may not make a subaward to or enter into a contract with an agency that provides services under this Act either to carry out the CAP or to provide services under the CAP.

(f) A designated agency, including the protection and advocacy system serving the American Indian Consortium, that contracts to provide CAP services with another entity or individual remains responsible for—

(1) The conduct of a CAP that meets all of the requirements of this part;

(2) Ensuring that the entity or individual expends CAP funds in accordance with—

(i) The regulations in this part; and

(ii) The regulations at 2 CFR part 200 applicable to the designated agency identified in paragraph (b) or the protection and advocacy system serving the American Indian Consortium, as described in paragraph (a) of this section; and

(3) The direct day-to-day supervision of the CAP services being carried out by the contractor. This day-to-day supervision must include the direct supervision of the individuals who are

employed or used by the contractor to provide CAP services.

(Authority: Sections 12(c) and 112(a), (c)(1)(A), and (e)(1)(E) of the Rehabilitation Act of 1973, as amended; 29 U.S.C. 709(c) and 732(a), (c)(1)(A), and (e)(1)(E))

§ 370.3   Who is eligible for services and information under the CAP?

(a) Any client or client-applicant is eligible for the services described in § 370.4.

(b) Any individual with a disability is eligible to receive information on the services and benefits available to individuals with disabilities under the Act and title I of the ADA.

(Authority: Section 112(a) of the Rehabilitation Act of 1973, as amended; 29 U.S.C. 732(a))

§ 370.4   What kinds of activities may the Secretary fund?

(a) Funds made available under this part must be used for activities consistent with the purposes of this program, including—

(1) Advising and informing clients, client-applicants, and individuals with disabilities in the State, especially individuals with disabilities who have traditionally been unserved or underserved by vocational rehabilitation programs, of—

(i) All services and benefits available to them through programs authorized under the Act; and

(ii) Their rights in connection with those services and benefits;

(2) Informing individuals with disabilities in the State, especially individuals with disabilities who have traditionally been unserved or underserved by vocational rehabilitation programs, of the services and benefits available to them under title I of the ADA;

(3) Upon the request of the client or client-applicant, assisting and advocating on behalf of the client or client-applicant in his or her relationship with projects, programs, and community rehabilitation programs that provide services under the Act by engaging in individual or systemic advocacy and pursuing, or assisting and advocating on behalf of the client or client-applicant to pursue, legal, administrative, and other available remedies, if necessary—

(i) To ensure the protection of the rights of a client or client-applicant under the Act; and

(ii) To facilitate access by individuals with disabilities, including students and youth with disabilities who are making the transition from school programs, to services funded under the Act; and

(4) Providing information to the public concerning the CAP.

(b) In providing assistance and advocacy services under this part with respect to services under title I of the Act, a designated agency may provide assistance and advocacy services to a client or client-applicant to facilitate the individual's employment, including assistance and advocacy services with respect to the individual's claims under title I of the ADA, if those claims under title I of the ADA are directly related to services under title I of the Act that the individual is receiving or seeking.

(Authority: Sections 12(c) and 112(a) of the Rehabilitation Act of 1973, as amended; 29 U.S.C. 709(c) and 732(a))

§ 370.5   What regulations apply?

The following regulations apply to the expenditure of funds and the administration of the program under this part:

(a) The Education Department General Administrative Regulations (EDGAR) as follows:

(1) 34 CFR part 75 (Direct Grant Programs) for purposes of an award made under § 370.30(d)(1) when the CAP appropriation equals or exceeds $14,000,000.

(2) 34 CFR part 76 (State-Administered Programs) applies to the State and, if the designated agency is a State or local government agency, to the designated agency, except for—

(i) Section 76.103;

(ii) Sections 76.125 through 76.137;

(iii) Sections 76.300 through 76.401;

(iv) Section 76.708;

(v) Section 76.734; and

(vi) Section 76.740.

(3) 34 CFR part 77 (Definitions That Apply to Department Regulations).

(4) 34 CFR part 79 (Intergovernmental Review of Department of Education Programs and Activities).

(5) 34 CFR part 81 (General Education Provisions Act—Enforcement) applies

to both the State and the designated agency, whether or not the designated agency is the actual recipient of the CAP grant. As the entity that eventually, if not directly, receives the CAP grant funds, the designated agency is considered a recipient for purposes of Part 81.

(6) 34 CFR part 82 (New Restrictions on Lobbying).

(b) Other regulations as follows:

(1) 2 CFR part 180 (OMB Guidelines to Agencies on Debarment and Suspension (Nonprocurement)), as adopted at 2 CFR part 3485.

(2) 2 CFR part 200 (Uniform Administrative Requirements, Cost Principles, and Audit Requirements for Federal Awards), as adopted at 2 CFR part 3474.

(c) The regulations in this part 370.

NOTE TO §370.5: Any funds made available to a State under this program that are transferred by a State to a designated agency do not make a subaward as that term is defined in 2 CFR 200.330. The designated agency is not, therefore, in these circumstances a subrecipient, as that term is defined in 2 CFR 200.330.

(Authority: Sections 12(c) and 112 of the Rehabilitation Act, as amended; 29 U.S.C. 709(c) and 732)

§370.6 What definitions apply?

(a) Definitions in EDGAR at 34 CFR part 77.

(b) Definitions in 2 CFR part 200, subpart A.

(c) Other definitions. The following definitions also apply to this part:

Act means the Rehabilitation Act of 1973, as amended.

Advocacy means pleading an individual's cause or speaking or writing in support of an individual. Advocacy may be formal, as in the case of a lawyer representing an individual in a court of law or in formal administrative proceedings before government agencies (whether tribal, State, local, or Federal). Advocacy also may be informal, as in the case of a lawyer or non-lawyer representing an individual in negotiations, mediation, or informal administrative proceedings before government agencies (whether tribal, State, local, or Federal), or as in the case of a lawyer or non-lawyer representing an individual's cause before private entities or organizations, or

government agencies (whether tribal, State, local, or Federal). Advocacy may be on behalf of—

(1) A single individual, in which case it is individual advocacy;

(2) More than one individual or a group of individuals, in which case it is systems (or systemic) advocacy, but systems or systemic advocacy, for the purposes of this part, does not include class actions, or

(3) Oneself, in which case it is self advocacy.

American Indian Consortium means that entity described in §370.2(a).

Class action means a formal legal suit on behalf of a group or class of individuals filed in a Federal or State court that meets the requirements for a "class action" under Federal or State law. "Systems (or systemic) advocacy" that does not include filing a formal class action in a Federal or State court is not considered a class action for purposes of this part.

Client or client-applicant means an individual receiving or seeking services under the Act, respectively.

Designated agency means the agency designated by the Governor under §370.2 or the protection and advocacy system serving the American Indian Consortium that is conducting a CAP under this part.

Mediation means the act or process of using an independent third party to act as a mediator, intermediary, or conciliator to settle differences or disputes between persons or parties. The third party who acts as a mediator, intermediary, or conciliator may not be any entity or individual who is connected in any way with the eligible system or the agency, entity, or individual with whom the individual with a disability has a dispute. Mediation may involve the use of professional mediators or any other independent third party mutually agreed to by the parties to the dispute.

Protection and Advocacy System has the meaning set forth at §370.2(a).

Services under the Act means vocational rehabilitation, independent living, supported employment, and other similar rehabilitation services provided under the Act. For purposes of the CAP, the term "services under the Act" does not include activities carried out under the protection and advocacy program authorized by section 509 of the Act (*i.e.*, the Protection and Advocacy of Individual Rights (PAIR) program, 34 CFR part 381).

State means, in addition to each of the several States of the United States, the District of Columbia, the Commonwealth of Puerto Rico, The United States Virgin Islands, Guam, American Samoa, and the Commonwealth of the Northern Mariana Islands, except for purposes of the allotments under § 370.30, in which case "State" does not mean or include Guam, American Samoa, the United States Virgin Islands, and the Commonwealth of the Northern Mariana Islands.

(Authority: Sections 7(34), 12(c), and 112 of the Rehabilitation Act of 1973, as amended; 29 U.S.C. 705(34), 709(c), and 732)

§ 370.7 What shall the designated agency do to make its services accessible?

The designated agency shall provide, as appropriate, the CAP services described in § 370.4 in formats that are accessible to clients or client-applicants who seek or receive CAP services.

(Authority: Section 12(c) of the Rehabilitation Act of 1973, as amended; 29 U.S.C. 709(c))

Subpart B—What Requirements Apply to Redesignation?

§ 370.10 When do the requirements for redesignation apply?

(a) The Governor shall redesignate the designated agency for carrying out the CAP to an agency that is independent of any agency that provides treatment, services, or rehabilitation to individuals under the Act if, after August 7, 1998—

(1) The designated State agency undergoes any change in the organizational structure of the agency that results in one or more new State agencies or departments, or results in the merger with one or more other State agencies or departments, and

(2) The designated State agency contains an office or unit conducting the CAP.

(3) For purposes of paragraph (a) of this section, the designated State agency has the meaning given to that term

at 34 CFR 361.5(c)(12) and described at 34 CFR 361.13.

(b) The Governor may not redesignate the agency designated pursuant to section 112(c) of the Act and § 370.2(b) without good cause and without complying with the requirements of §§ 370.10 through 370.17.

(c) For purposes of §§ 370.10 through 370.17, a "redesignation of" or "to redesignate" a designated agency means any change in or transfer of the designation of an agency previously designated by the Governor to conduct the State's CAP to a new or different agency, unit, or organization, including—

(1) A decision by a designated agency to cancel its existing contract with another entity with which it has previously contracted to carry out and operate all or part of its responsibilities under the CAP (including providing advisory, assistance, or advocacy services to eligible clients and client-applicants); or

(2) A decision by a designated agency not to renew its existing contract with another entity with which it has previously contracted. Therefore, an agency that is carrying out a State's CAP under a contract with a designated agency is considered a designated agency for purposes of §§ 370.10 through 370.17.

(d) For purposes of paragraph (b) of this section, a designated agency that does not renew a contract for CAP services because it is following State procurement laws that require contracts to be awarded through a competitive bidding process is presumed to have good cause for not renewing an existing contract. However, this presumption may be rebutted.

(e) If State procurement laws require a designated agency to award a contract through a competitive bidding process, the designated agency must hold public hearings on the request for proposal before awarding the new contract.

(Authority: Sections 12(c) and 112(c)(1)(B) of the Rehabilitation Act of 1973, as amended; 29 U.S.C. 709(c) and 732(c)(1)(B))

§ 370.11 What requirements apply to a notice of proposed redesignation?

(a) Prior to any redesignation of the agency that conducts the CAP, the

Governor shall give written notice of the proposed redesignation to the designated agency, the State Rehabilitation Council (SRC), and the State Independent Living Council (SILC) and publish a public notice of the Governor's intention to redesignate. Both the notice to the designated agency, the SRC, and the SILC and the public notice must include, at a minimum, the following:

(1) The Federal requirements for the CAP (section 112 of the Act).

(2) The goals and function of the CAP.

(3) The name of the current designated agency.

(4) A description of the current CAP and how it is administered.

(5) The reason or reasons for proposing the redesignation, including why the Governor believes good cause exists for the proposed redesignation.

(6) The effective date of the proposed redesignation.

(7) The name of the agency the Governor proposes to administer the CAP.

(8) A description of the system that the redesignated (*i.e.*, new) agency would administer.

(b) The notice to the designated agency must—

(1) Be given at least 30 days in advance of the Governor's written decision to redesignate; and

(2) Advise the designated agency that it has at least 30 days from receipt of the notice of proposed redesignation to respond to the Governor and that the response must be in writing.

(c) The notice of proposed redesignation must be published in a place and manner that provides the SRC, the SILC, individuals with disabilities or their representatives, and the public with at least 30 days to submit oral or written comments to the Governor.

(d) Following public notice, public hearings concerning the proposed redesignation must be conducted in an accessible format that provides individuals with disabilities or their representatives an opportunity for comment. The Governor shall maintain a written public record of these hearings.

(e) The Governor shall fully consider any public comments before issuing a written decision to redesignate.

(Authority: Sections 12(c) and 112(c)(1)(B) of the Rehabilitation Act of 1973, as amended; 29 U.S.C. 709(c) and 732(c)(1)(B))

§370.12 How does a designated agency preserve its right to appeal a redesignation?

(a) To preserve its right to appeal a Governor's written decision to redesignate (see §370.13), a designated agency must respond in writing to the Governor within 30 days after it receives the Governor's notice of proposed redesignation.

(b) The designated agency shall send its response to the Governor by registered or certified mail, return receipt requested, or other means that provides a record that the Governor received the designated agency's response.

(Approved by the Office of Management and Budget under control number 1820–0520)

(Authority: Sections 12(c) and 112(c)(1)(B) of the Rehabilitation Act of 1973, as amended; 29 U.S.C. 709(c) and 732(c)(1)(B))

§370.13 What are the requirements for a decision to redesignate?

(a) If, after complying with the requirements of §370.11, the Governor decides to redesignate the designated agency, the Governor shall provide to the designated agency a written decision to redesignate that includes the rationale for the redesignation. The Governor shall send the written decision to redesignate to the designated agency by registered or certified mail, return receipt requested, or other means that provides a record that the designated agency received the Governor's written decision to redesignate.

(b) If the designated agency submitted to the Governor a timely response to the Governor's notice of proposed redesignation, the Governor shall inform the designated agency that it has at least 15 days from receipt of the

Governor's written decision to redesignate to file a formal written appeal with the Secretary.

(Approved by the Office of Management and Budget under control number 1820–0520)

(Authority: Sections 12(c) and 112(c)(1)(B) of the Rehabilitation Act of 1973, as amended; 29 U.S.C. 709(c) and 732(c)(1)(B))

§ 370.14 How does a designated agency appeal a written decision to redesignate?

(a) A designated agency may appeal to the Secretary a Governor's written decision to redesignate only if the designated agency submitted to the Governor a timely written response to the Governor's notice of proposed redesignation in accordance with § 370.12.

(b) To appeal to the Secretary a Governor's written decision to redesignate, a designated agency shall file a formal written appeal with the Secretary within 15 days after the designated agency's receipt of the Governor's written decision to redesignate. The date of filing of the designated agency's written appeal with the Secretary will be determined in a manner consistent with the requirements of 34 CFR 81.12.

(c) If the designated agency files a written appeal with the Secretary, the designated agency shall send a separate copy of this appeal to the Governor by registered or certified mail, return receipt requested, or other means that provides a record that the Governor received a copy of the designated agency's appeal to the Secretary.

(d) The designated agency's written appeal to the Secretary must state why the Governor has not met the burden of showing that good cause for the redesignation exists or has not met the procedural requirements under §§ 370.11 and 370.13.

(e) The designated agency's written appeal must be accompanied by the designated agency's written response to the Governor's notice of proposed redesignation and may be accompanied by any other written submissions or documentation the designated agency wishes the Secretary to consider.

(f) As part of its submissions under this section, the designated agency may request an informal meeting with the Secretary at which representatives of both parties will have an oppor-

tunity to present their views on the issues raised in the appeal.

(Approved by the Office of Management and Budget under control number 1820–0520)

(Authority: Sections 12(c) and 112(c)(1)(B) of the Rehabilitation Act of 1973, as amended; 29 U.S.C. 709(c) and 732(c)(1)(B))

§ 370.15 What must the Governor of a State do upon receipt of a copy of a designated agency's written appeal to the Secretary?

(a) If the designated agency files a formal written appeal in accordance with § 370.14, the Governor shall, within 15 days of receipt of the designated agency's appeal, submit to the Secretary copies of the following:

(1) The written notice of proposed redesignation sent to the designated agency.

(2) The public notice of proposed redesignation.

(3) Transcripts of all public hearings held on the proposed redesignation.

(4) Written comments received by the Governor in response to the public notice of proposed redesignation.

(5) The Governor's written decision to redesignate, including the rationale for the decision.

(6) Any other written documentation or submissions the Governor wishes the Secretary to consider.

(7) Any other information requested by the Secretary.

(b) As part of the submissions under this section, the Governor may request an informal meeting with the Secretary at which representatives of both parties will have an opportunity to present their views on the issues raised in the appeal.

(Approved by the Office of Management and Budget under control number 1820–0520)

(Authority: Sections 12(c) and 112(c)(1)(B) of the Rehabilitation Act of 1973, as amended; 29 U.S.C. 709(c) and 732(c)(1)(B))

§ 370.16 How does the Secretary review an appeal of a redesignation?

(a) If either party requests a meeting under § 370.14(f) or § 370.15(b), the meeting is to be held within 30 days of the submissions by the Governor under § 370.15, unless both parties agree to waive this requirement. The Secretary promptly notifies the parties of the date and place of the meeting.

(b) Within 30 days of the informal meeting permitted under paragraph (a) of this section or, if neither party has requested an informal meeting, within 60 days of the submissions required from the Governor under §370.15, the Secretary issues to the parties a final written decision on whether the redesignation was for good cause.

(c) The Secretary reviews a Governor's decision based on the record submitted under §§370.14 and 370.15 and any other relevant submissions of other interested parties. The Secretary may affirm or, if the Secretary finds that the redesignation is not for good cause, remand for further findings or reverse a Governor's redesignation.

(d) The Secretary sends copies of the decision to the parties by registered or certified mail, return receipt requested, or other means that provide a record of receipt by both parties.

(Approved by the Office of Management and Budget under control number 1820–0520)

(Authority: Sections 12(c) and 112(c)(1)(B) of the Rehabilitation Act of 1973, as amended; 29 U.S.C. 709(c) and 732(c)(1)(B))

§370.17 When does a redesignation become effective?

A redesignation does not take effect for at least 15 days following the designated agency's receipt of the Governor's written decision to redesignate or, if the designated agency appeals, for at least 5 days after the Secretary has affirmed the Governor's written decision to redesignate.

(Authority: Sections 12(c) and 112(c)(1)(B) of the Rehabilitation Act of 1973, as amended; 29 U.S.C. 709(c) and 732(c)(1)(B))

Subpart C—What are the Requirements for Requesting a Grant?

§370.20 What must be included in a request for a grant?

(a) Each State and the protection and advocacy system serving the American Indian Consortium seeking assistance under this part shall submit to the Secretary, in writing, at the time and in the manner determined by the Secretary to be appropriate, an application that includes, at a minimum—

(1) The name of the designated agency; and

(2) An assurance that the designated agency meets the independence requirement of section 112(c)(1)(A) of the Act and §370.2(c), or that the State is exempted from that requirement under section 112(c)(1)(A) of the Act and §370.2(d).

(b)(1) Each State and the protection and advocacy system serving the American Indian Consortium also shall submit to the Secretary an assurance that the designated agency has the authority to pursue legal, administrative, and other appropriate remedies to ensure the protection of the rights of clients or client-applicants within the State or American Indian Consortium.

(2) The authority to pursue remedies described in paragraph (b)(1) of this section must include the authority to pursue those remedies against the State vocational rehabilitation agency and other appropriate State agencies. The designated agency meets this requirement if it has the authority to pursue those remedies either on its own behalf or by obtaining necessary services, such as legal representation, from outside sources.

(c) Each State and the protection and advocacy system serving the American Indian Consortium also shall submit to the Secretary assurances that—

(1) All entities conducting, administering, operating, or carrying out programs within the State that provide services under the Act to individuals with disabilities in the State will advise all clients and client-applicants of the existence of the CAP, the services provided under the program, and how to contact the designated agency;

(2) The designated agency will meet each of the requirements in this part; and

(3) The designated agency will provide the Secretary with the annual report required by section 112(g)(4) of the Act and §370.44.

(d) To allow a designated agency to receive direct payment of funds under this part, a State or the protection and advocacy system serving the American Indian Consortium must provide to the Secretary, as part of its application for assistance, an assurance that direct payment to the designated agency is not prohibited by or inconsistent with State or tribal law, regulation, or policy.

(Approved by the Office of Management and Budget under control number 1820–0520)

(Authority: Sections 12(c) and 112(b) and (f) of the Rehabilitation Act of 1973, as amended; 29 U.S.C. 709(c) and 732(b) and (f))

Subpart D—How Does the Secretary Allocate and Reallocate Funds to a State?

§ 370.30 How does the Secretary allocate funds?

(a) After reserving funds required under paragraphs (c) and (d) of this section, the Secretary shall allot the remainder of the sums appropriated for each fiscal year under this section among the States on the basis of relative population of each State, except that no such entity shall receive less than $50,000.

(b) The Secretary allocates $30,000 each, unless the provisions of section 112(e)(1)(D) of the Act are applicable, to American Samoa, Guam, the Virgin Islands, and the Commonwealth of Northern Mariana Islands.

(c) The Secretary shall reserve funds, from the amount appropriated to carry out this part, to make a grant to the protection and advocacy system serving the American Indian Consortium to provide services in accordance with this part. The amount of the grant to the protection and advocacy system serving the American Indian Consortium shall be the same amount as is provided to a territory under paragraph (b) of this section.

(d)(1) For any fiscal year for which the amount appropriated equals or exceeds $14,000,000, the Secretary may reserve not less than 1.8 percent and not more than 2.2 percent of such amount to provide a grant for training and technical assistance for the programs established under this part.

(2) All training and technical assistance shall be coordinated with activities provided under 34 CFR 381.22.

(3) The Secretary shall make a grant pursuant to paragraph (d)(1) of this section to an entity that has experience in or knowledge related to the provision of services authorized under this part.

(4) An entity receiving a grant under paragraph (d)(1) of this section shall provide training and technical assistance to the designated agencies or entities carrying out the CAP to assist them in improving the provision of services authorized under this part and the administration of the program.

(e)(1) Unless prohibited or otherwise provided by State or tribal law, regulation, or policy, the Secretary pays to the designated agency, from the State allotment under paragraph (a), (b), or (c) of this section, the amount specified in the State's or the eligible protection and advocacy system's approved request. Because the designated agency, including the protection and advocacy system serving the American Indian Consortium, is the eventual, if not the direct, recipient of the CAP funds, 34 CFR part 81 and 2 CFR part 200 apply to the designated agency, whether or not the designated agency is the actual recipient of the CAP grant.

(2) Notwithstanding the grant made to the protection and advocacy system serving the American Indian Consortium under paragraph (c) of this section, the State remains the grantee for purposes of 34 CFR part 76 and 2 CFR part 200 because it is the State that submits an application for and receives the CAP grant. In addition, both the State and the designated agency are considered recipients for purposes of 34 CFR part 81.

(Authority: Sections 12(c) and 112(b) and (e) of the Rehabilitation Act of 1973, as amended; 29 U.S.C. 709(c) and 732(b) and (e))

§ 370.31 How does the Secretary reallocate funds?

(a) The Secretary reallocates funds in accordance with section 112(e)(2) of the Act.

(b) A designated agency shall inform the Secretary at least 45 days before the end of the fiscal year for which CAP funds were received whether the designated agency is making available for reallotment any of those CAP funds that it will be unable to obligate in that fiscal year or the succeeding fiscal year.

(Approved by the Office of Management and Budget under control number 1820–0520)

(Authority: Sections 12(c), 19, and 112(e)(2) of the Rehabilitation Act of 1973, as amended; 29 U.S.C. 709(c), 716, and 732(e)(2))

Subpart E—What Post-Award Conditions Must Be Met by a Designated Agency?

§370.40 What are allowable costs?

(a) The designated agency, including the eligible protection and advocacy system serving the American Indian Consortium, shall apply the regulations at 2 CFR part 200.

(b) Consistent with the program activities listed in §370.4, the cost of travel in connection with the provision to a client or client-applicant of assistance under this program is allowable, in accordance with 2 CFR part 200. The cost of travel includes the cost of travel for an attendant if the attendant must accompany the client or client-applicant.

(c)(1) The State and the designated agency are accountable, both jointly and severally, to the Secretary for the proper use of funds made available under this part. However, the Secretary may choose to recover funds under the procedures in 34 CFR part 81 from either the State or the designated agency, or both, depending on the circumstances of each case.

(2) For purposes of the grant made under this part to the protection and advocacy system serving the American Indian Consortium, such entity will be solely accountable to the Secretary for the proper use of funds made available under this part. If the Secretary determines it necessary, the Secretary may recover funds from the protection and advocacy system serving the American Indian Consortium pursuant to the procedures in 34 CFR part 81.

(Authority: Sections 12(c) and 112(c)(3) of the Rehabilitation Act of 1973, as amended; 29 U.S.C. 709(c) and 732(c)(3))

§370.41 What conflict of interest provision applies to employees of a designated agency?

(a) Except as permitted by paragraph (b) of this section, an employee of a designated agency, or of an entity or individual under contract with a designated agency, who carries out any CAP duties or responsibilities, while so employed, may not—

(1) Serve concurrently as a staff member of, consultant to, or in any other capacity within, any other rehabilitation project, program, or community rehabilitation program receiving assistance under the Act in the State; or

(2) Provide any services under the Act, other than CAP and PAIR services.

(b) An employee of a designated agency under contract with a designated agency, may—

(1) Receive a traineeship under section 302 of the Act;

(2) Provide services under the PAIR program;

(3) Represent the CAP on any board or council (such as the SRC) if CAP representation on the board or council is specifically permitted or mandated by the Act; and

(4) Consult with policymaking and administrative personnel in State and local rehabilitation programs, projects, and community rehabilitation programs, if consultation with the designated agency is specifically permitted or mandated by the Act.

(Authority: Sections 12(c) and 112(g)(1) of the Rehabilitation Act of 1973, as amended; 29 U.S.C. 709(c) and 732(g)(1))

§370.42 What access must the CAP be afforded to policymaking and administrative personnel?

The CAP must be afforded reasonable access to policymaking and administrative personnel in State and local rehabilitation programs, projects, and community rehabilitation programs. One way in which the CAP may be provided that access would be to include the director of the designated agency among the individuals to be consulted on matters of general policy development and implementation, as required by section 101(a)(16) of the Act.

(Authority: Sections 12(c), 101(a)(16), and 112(g)(2) of the Rehabilitation Act of 1973, as amended; 29 U.S.C. 709(c), 721(a)(16), and 732(g)(2))

§ 370.43 What requirement applies to the use of mediation procedures?

(a) Each designated agency shall implement procedures designed to ensure that, to the maximum extent possible, good faith negotiations and mediation procedures are used before resorting to formal administrative or legal remedies. In designing these procedures, the designated agency may take into account its level of resources.

(b) For purposes of this section, mediation may involve the use of professional mediators, other independent third parties mutually agreed to by the parties to the dispute, or an employee of the designated agency who—

(1) Is not assigned to advocate for or otherwise represent or is not involved with advocating for or otherwise representing the client or client-applicant who is a party to the mediation; and

(2) Has not previously advocated for or otherwise represented or been involved with advocating for or otherwise representing that same client or client-applicant.

(Authority: Section 112(g)(3) of the Rehabilitation Act of 1973, as amended; 29 U.S.C. 732(g)(3))

§ 370.44 What reporting requirement applies to each designated agency?

In addition to the program and fiscal reporting requirements in 34 CFR 76.720 and 2 CFR 200.327 that are applicable to this program, each designated agency shall submit to the Secretary, no later than 90 days after the end of each fiscal year, an annual report on the operation of its CAP during the previous year, including a summary of the work done and the uniform statistical tabulation of all cases handled by the program. The annual report must contain information on—

(a) The number of requests received by the designated agency for information on services and benefits under the Act and title I of the ADA;

(b) The number of referrals to other agencies made by the designated agency and the reason or reasons for those referrals;

(c) The number of requests for advocacy services received by the designated agency from clients or client-applicants;

(d) The number of requests for advocacy services from clients or client-applicants that the designated agency was unable to serve;

(e) The reasons that the designated agency was unable to serve all of the requests for advocacy services from clients or client-applicants; and

(f) Any other information that the Secretary may require.

(Approved by the Office of Management and Budget under control number 1820–0520)

(Authority: Sections 12(c) and 112(g)(4) of the Rehabilitation Act of 1973, as amended; 29 U.S.C. 709(c) and 732(g)(4))

§ 370.45 What limitation applies to the pursuit of legal remedies?

A designated agency may not bring any class action in carrying out its responsibilities under this part.

(Authority: Section 112(d) of the Rehabilitation Act of 1973, as amended; 29 U.S.C. 732(d))

§ 370.46 What consultation requirement applies to a Governor of a State?

In designating a client assistance agency under § 370.2, redesignating a client assistance agency under § 370.10, and carrying out the other provisions of this part, the Governor shall consult with the director of the State vocational rehabilitation agency (or, in States with both a general agency and an agency for the blind, the directors of both agencies), the head of the developmental disability protection and advocacy agency, and representatives of professional and consumer organizations serving individuals with disabilities in the State.

(Authority: Section 112(c)(2) of the Rehabilitation Act of 1973, as amended; 29 U.S.C. 732(c)(2))

§ 370.47 What is program income and how may it be used?

(a) *Definition.* (1) Consistent with 2 CFR 200.80 and for purposes of this part, *program income* means gross income earned by the designated agency that is directly generated by an activity supported under this part.

(2) Funds received through the transfer of Social Security Administration payments from the designated State unit, as defined in 34 CFR 361.5(c)(13), in accordance with 34 CFR 361.63(c)(2) will be treated as program income received under this part.

(b) *Use of program income.* (1) Program income, whenever earned or received, must be used for the provision of services authorized under §370.4.

(2)(i) The designated agency must use program income to supplement Federal funds that support program activities that are subject to this part. See, for example 2 CFR 200.307(e)(2).

(ii) Notwithstanding 2 CFR 200.305(a) and consistent with 2 CFR 200.305(b)(5), and to the extent that program income funds are available, a designated agency, regardless of whether it is a State agency, must disburse those funds (including repayments to a revolving fund), rebates, refunds, contract settlements, audit recoveries, and interest earned on such funds before requesting additional funds from the Department.

(Authority: Sections 12(c) and 108 of the Rehabilitation Act of 1973, as amended; 29 U.S.C. 709(c) and 728; and 20 U.S.C. 3474);

§370.48 When must grant funds and program income be obligated?

Any Federal funds, including reallotted funds, that are appropriated for a fiscal year to carry out the activities under this part that are not obligated or expended by the designated agency prior to the beginning of the succeeding fiscal year, and any program income received during a fiscal year that is not obligated or expended by the designated agency prior to the beginning of the succeeding fiscal year in which the program income was received, remain available for obligation and expenditure by the designated agency during that succeeding fiscal year in accordance with section 19 of the Act.

(Authority: Sections 12(c) and 19 of the Rehabilitation Act of 1973, as amended; 29 U.S.C. 709(c) and 716)

§370.49 What are the special requirements pertaining to the protection, use, and release of personal information?

(a) All personal information about individuals served by any designated agency under this part, including lists of names, addresses, photographs, and records of evaluation, must be held strictly confidential.

(b) The designated agency's use of information and records concerning individuals must be limited only to purposes directly connected with the CAP, including program evaluation activities. Except as provided in paragraphs (c) and (e) of this section, this information may not be disclosed, directly or indirectly, other than in the administration of the CAP, unless the consent of the individual to whom the information applies, or his or her parent, legal guardian, or other legally authorized representative or advocate (including the individual's advocate from the designated agency), has been obtained in writing. A designated agency may not produce any report, evaluation, or study that reveals any personally identifying information without the written consent of the individual or his or her representative.

(c) Except as limited in paragraphs (d) and (e) of this section, the Secretary or other Federal or State officials responsible for enforcing legal requirements are to have complete access to all—

(1) Records of the designated agency that receives funds under this program; and

(2) All individual case records of clients served under this part without the consent of the client.

(d) For purposes of conducting any periodic audit, preparing or producing any report, or conducting any evaluation of the performance of the CAP established or assisted under this part, the Secretary does not require the designated agency to disclose the identity of, or any other personally identifiable information related to, any individual requesting assistance under the CAP.

(e) Notwithstanding paragraph (d) of this section and consistent with paragraph (f) of this section, a designated agency shall disclose to the Secretary, if the Secretary so requests, the identity of, or any other personally identifiable information (*i.e.*, name, address, telephone number, social security number, or any other official code or number by which an individual may be readily identified) related to, any individual requesting assistance under the CAP if—

(1) An audit, evaluation, monitoring review, State plan assurance review, or other investigation produces reliable evidence that there is probable cause to believe that the designated agency has violated its legislative mandate or misused Federal funds; or

(2) The Secretary determines that this information may reasonably lead to further evidence that is directly related to alleged misconduct of the designated agency.

(f) In addition to the protection afforded by paragraph (d) of this section, the right of a person or designated agency not to produce documents or disclose information to the Secretary is governed by the common law of privileges, as interpreted by the courts of the United States.

(Authority: Sections 12(c) and 112(g)(4) of the Rehabilitation Act of 1973, as amended; 29 U.S.C. 709(c) and 732(g)(4))

PART 371—AMERICAN INDIAN VOCATIONAL REHABILITATION SERVICES

Subpart A—General

Sec.

AUTHORITY: Sections 12(c) and 121 of the Rehabilitation Act of 1973, as amended; 29 U.S.C. 709(c) and 741, unless otherwise noted.

SOURCE: 81 FR 55596, Aug. 19, 2016, unless otherwise noted.

Subpart A—General

§ 371.1 What is the American Indian Vocational Rehabilitation Services program?

This program is designed to provide vocational rehabilitation services, including culturally appropriate services, to American Indians with disabilities who reside on or near Federal or State reservations, consistent with such eligible individual's strengths, resources, priorities, concerns, abilities, capabilities, interests, and informed choice, so that such individual may prepare for, and engage in, high-quality employment that will increase opportunities for economic self-sufficiency.

(Authority: Section 121(a) of the Rehabilitation Act of 1973, as amended; 29 U.S.C. 741(a))

§ 371.2 Who is eligible for assistance under this program?

(a) Applications may be made only by Indian tribes and consortia of those Indian tribes located on Federal and State reservations.

(1) The applicant for the grant must be

(i) The governing body of an Indian tribe, either on behalf the Indian tribe or on behalf of a consortium of Indian tribes; or

(ii) A tribal organization that is a separate legal organization from an Indian tribe.

(2) In order to receive a grant under this section, a tribal organization that is not a governing body of an Indian tribe must:

(i) Have as one of its functions the vocational rehabilitation of American Indians with disabilities; and

(ii) Have the approval of the tribe to be served by such organization.

(3) If a grant is made to the governing body of an Indian tribe, either on its own behalf or on behalf of a consortium, or to a tribal organization to perform services benefiting more than one Indian tribe, the approval of each such Indian tribe shall be a prerequisite to the making of such a grant.

(b) Applications for awards under Subpart B may be made by State, local or tribal governments, non-profit organizations, or institutions of higher education.

(Authority: Sections 12(c) and 121(a) of the Rehabilitation Act of 1973, as amended; 29 U.S.C. 709(c) and 741(a))

§ 371.3 What types of projects are authorized under this program?

The American Indian Vocational Rehabilitation Services program provides financial assistance for the establishment and operation of tribal vocational rehabilitation services programs for American Indians with disabilities who reside on or near Federal or State reservations.

(Authority: Sections 12(c) and 121(a) of the Rehabilitation Act of 1973, as amended Act, 29 U.S.C. 709(c) and 741(a))

§ 371.4 What is the length of the project period under this program?

The Secretary approves a project period of up to sixty months.

(Authority: Sections 12(c) and 121(b)(3) of the Rehabilitation Act of 1973, as amended, 29 U.S.C. 709(c) and 121(b)(3))

§ 371.5 What regulations apply to this program?

The following regulations apply to this program—

(a) The regulations in this part 371.

(b) 2 CFR part 180 (OMB Guidelines to Agencies on Debarment and Suspension (Nonprocurement)), as adopted at 2 CFR part 3485;

(c) 2 CFR part 200 (Uniform Administrative Requirements, Cost Principles, and Audit Requirements for Federal Awards) as adopted at 2 CFR part 3474.

(d) 34 CFR part 75 Direct Grant Programs

(e) 34 CFR part 77 Definitions that Apply to Department Regulations

(f) 34 CFR part 81 General Education Provisions Act—Enforcement

(g) 34 CFR part 82 New Restrictions on Lobbying

(h) 34 CFR part 84 Governmentwide Requirements for Drug-Free Workplace

(Authority: Section 12(c) of the Rehabilitation Act of 1973, as amended; 29 U.S.C. 709(c))

§ 371.6 What definitions apply to this program?

(a) The definitions of terms included in the applicable regulations listed in § 371.5;

(b) The following definitions also apply to this program—

Act means the Rehabilitation Act of 1973, as amended.

Assessment for determining eligibility and vocational rehabilitation needs means as appropriate in each case—

(i)(A) A review of existing data—

(1) To determine if an individual is eligible for vocational rehabilitation services; and

(2) To assign priority for an order of selection described in an approved plan or the approved grant application; and

(B) To the extent necessary, the provision of appropriate assessment activities to obtain necessary additional data to make the eligibility determination and assignment;

(ii) To the extent additional data are necessary to make a determination of the employment outcomes, and the nature and scope of vocational rehabilitation services, to be included in the individualized plan for employment of an eligible individual, a comprehensive assessment to determine the unique strengths, resources, priorities, concerns, abilities, capabilities, interests, and informed choice, including the need for supported employment, of the eligible individual, this comprehensive assessment—

(A) Is limited to information that is necessary to identify the rehabilitation needs of the individual and to develop the individualized plan for employment of the eligible individual;

(B) Uses as a primary source of information, to the maximum extent possible and appropriate and in accordance with confidentiality requirements—

(1) Existing information obtained for the purposes of determining the eligibility of the individual and assigning priority for an order of selection described in an approved plan or the approved grant application for the individual; and

(2) Information that can be provided by the individual and, if appropriate, by the family of the individual;

(C) May include, to the degree needed to make such a determination, an assessment of the personality, interests, interpersonal skills, intelligence and related functional capacities, educational achievements, work experience, vocational aptitudes, personal and social adjustments, and employment opportunities of the individual, and the medical, psychiatric, psychological, and other pertinent vocational, educational, cultural, social, recreational, and environmental factors, that affect the employment and rehabilitation needs of the individual;

(D) May include, to the degree needed, an appraisal of the patterns of work behavior of the individual and services needed for the individual to acquire occupational skills, and to develop work attitudes, work habits, work tolerance,

and social and behavior patterns necessary for successful job performance, including the use of work in real job situations to assess and develop the capacities of the individual to perform adequately in a work environment; and

(E) To the maximum extent possible, relies on information obtained from experiences in integrated employment settings in the community, and other integrated community settings;

(iii) Referral, for the provision of rehabilitation technology services to the individual, to assess and develop the capacities of the individual to perform in a work environment; and

(iv) An exploration of the individual's abilities, capabilities, and capacity to perform in work situations, which must be assessed periodically during trial work experiences, including experiences in which the individual is provided appropriate supports and training.

(Authority: Sections 7(2) and 12(c) of the Rehabilitation Act of 1973, as amended, 29 U.S.C. 705(2) and 709(c))

Community rehabilitation program means a program that provides directly, or facilitates the provision of, one or more of the following vocational rehabilitation services to individuals with disabilities to enable those individuals to maximize their opportunities for employment, including career advancement—

(i) Medical, psychiatric, psychological, social, and vocational services that are provided under one management;

(ii) Testing, fitting, or training in the use of prosthetic and orthotic devices;

(iii) Recreational therapy;

(iv) Physical and occupational therapy;

(v) Speech, language, and hearing therapy;

(vi) Psychiatric, psychological, and social services, including positive behavior management;

(vii) Assessment for determining eligibility and vocational rehabilitation needs;

(viii) Rehabilitation technology;

(ix) Job development, placement, and retention services;

(x) Evaluation or control of specific disabilities;

(xi) Orientation and mobility services for individuals who are blind;

(xii) Extended employment;

(xiii) Psychosocial rehabilitation services;

(xiv) Supported employment services and extended services;

(xv) Customized employment;

(xvi) Services to family members if necessary to enable the applicant or eligible individual to achieve an employment outcome;

(xvii) Personal assistance services; or

(xviii) Services similar to the services described in paragraphs (i) through (xvii) of this definition.

(Authority: Sections 7(4) and 12(c) of the Rehabilitation Act of 1973, as amended, 29 U.S.C. 705(4) and 709(c))

Comparable services and benefits means—

(i) Services and benefits, including accommodations and auxiliary aids and services, that are—

(A) Provided or paid for, in whole or in part, by other Federal, State, or local public agencies, by health insurance, or by employee benefits;

(B) Available to the individual at the time needed to ensure the progress of the individual toward achieving the employment outcome in the individual's individualized plan for employment; and

(C) Commensurate to the services that the individual would otherwise receive from the Tribal Vocational Rehabilitation unit.

(ii) For the purposes of this definition, comparable benefits do not include awards and scholarships based on merit.

(Authority: Sections 12(c) and 101(a)(8)(A) of the Rehabilitation Act of 1973, as amended, 29 U.S.C. 709(c) and 721(a)(8)(A))

Competitive integrated employment means work that—

(i) Is performed on a full-time or part-time basis (including self-employment) and for which an individual is compensated at a rate that—

(A) Is not less than the higher of the rate specified in section 6(a)(1) of the Fair Labor Standards Act of 1938 (29 U.S.C. 206(a)(1)) or the rate required under the applicable State or local minimum wage law;

(B) Is not less than the customary rate paid by the employer for the same or similar work performed by other employees who are not individuals with disabilities and who are similarly situated in similar occupations by the same employer and who have similar training, experience, and skills; and

(C) In the case of an individual who is self-employed, yields an income that is comparable to the income received by other individuals who are not individuals with disabilities and who are self-employed in similar occupations or on similar tasks and who have similar training, experience, and skills; and

(D) Is eligible for the level of benefits provided to other employees; and

(ii) Is at a location—

(A) Typically found in the community; and

(B) Where the employee with a disability interacts for the purpose of performing the duties of the position with other employees within the particular work unit and the entire work site, and, as appropriate to the work performed, other persons (*e.g.*, customers and vendors), who are not individuals with disabilities (not including supervisory personnel or individuals who are providing services to such employee) to the same extent that employees who are not individuals with disabilities and who are in comparable positions interact with these persons; and

(C) Presents, as appropriate, opportunities for advancement that are similar to those for other employees who are not individuals with disabilities and who have similar positions.

(Authority: Sections 7(5) and 12(c) of the Rehabilitation Act of 1973, as amended; 29 U.S.C. 705(5) and 709(c))

Consortium means two or more eligible governing bodies of Indian tribes that apply for an award under this program by either:

(i) Designating one governing body to apply for the grant; or

(ii) Establishing and designating a tribal organization to apply for a grant.

(Authority: Sections 12(c) and 121 of the Rehabilitation Act of 1973, as amended; 29 U.S.C. 709(c) and 741(a))

Customized employment means competitive integrated employment, for an individual with a significant disability, that is based on an individualized determination of the unique strengths, needs, and interests of the individual with a significant disability, is designed to meet the specific abilities of the individual with a significant disability and the business needs of the employer, and is carried out through flexible strategies, such as—

(i) Job exploration by the individual;

(ii) Working with an employer to facilitate placement, including—

(A) Customizing a job description based on current employer needs or on previously unidentified and unmet employer needs; and

(B) Developing a set of job duties, a work schedule and job arrangement, and specifics of supervision (including performance evaluation and review), and determining a job location;

(iii) Using a professional representative chosen by the individual, or if elected self-representation, to work with an employer to facilitate placement; and

(iv) Providing services and supports at the job location.

(Authority: Sections 7(7) and 12(c) of the Rehabilitation Act of 1973, as amended, 29 U.S.C. 705(7) and 709(c))

Eligible individual means an applicant for vocational rehabilitation services who meets the eligibility requirements of Section 102(a)(1) of the Act.

(Authority: Sections 7(20)(A), 12(c), and 102(a)(1) of the Rehabilitation Act of 1973, as amended, 29 U.S.C. 705(20)(A), 709(c), and 722)

Employment outcome means, with respect to an individual, entering, advancing in or retaining full-time or, if appropriate, part-time competitive integrated employment (including customized employment, self-employment, telecommuting or business ownership), or supported employment, that is consistent with an individual's unique strengths, resources, priorities, concerns, abilities, capabilities, interests, and informed choice.

(Authority: Sections 7(11) and 12(c) of the Rehabilitation Act of 1973, as amended, 29 U.S.C. 705(11), and 709(c))

Family member for purposes of receiving vocational rehabilitation services means an individual—

(i) Who either—

(A) Is a relative or guardian of an applicant or eligible individual; or

(B) Lives in the same household as an applicant or eligible individual;

(ii) Who has a substantial interest in the well-being of that individual; and

(iii) Whose receipt of vocational rehabilitation services is necessary to enable the applicant or eligible individual to achieve an employment outcome.

(Authority: Sections 12(c) and 103(a)(19) of the Rehabilitation Act of 1973, as amended; 29 U.S.C. 709(c) and 723(a)(19))

Governing bodies of Indian tribes means those duly elected or appointed representatives of an Indian tribe or of an Alaskan native village. These representatives must have the authority to enter into contracts, agreements, and grants on behalf of their constituency.

(Authority: Sections 12(c) and 121(a) of the Rehabilitation Act of 1973, as amended; 29 U.S.C. 709(c) and 741(a))

Indian; American Indian; Indian American; Indian tribe means—

(i) *Indian, American Indian,* and *Indian American* mean an individual who is a member of an Indian tribe and includes a Native and a descendant of a Native, as such terms are defined in subsections (b) and (r) of section 3 of the Alaska Native Claims Settlement Act (43 U.S.C. 1602).

(ii) *Indian tribe* means any Federal or State Indian tribe, band, rancheria, pueblo, colony, or community, including any Alaskan native village or regional village corporation (as defined in or established pursuant to the Alaska Native Claims Settlement Act) and a tribal organization (as defined in section 4(l) of the Indian Self-Determination and Education Assistance Act (25 U.S.C. 450(b)(1)) and this section.

(Authority: Section 7(19) of the Rehabilitation Act of 1973, as amended, 29 U.S.C. 705(19))

Individual with a disability means—

In general any individual—

(i) Who has a physical or mental impairment;

(ii) Whose impairment constitutes or results in a substantial impediment to employment; and

(iii) Who can benefit in terms of an employment outcome from the provision of vocational rehabilitation services.

(Authority: Section 7(20)(A) of the Rehabilitation Act of 1973, as amended; 29 U.S.C. 705(20)(A))

Individual with a significant disability means—

In general an individual with a disability—

(i) Who has a severe physical or mental impairment that seriously limits one or more functional capacities (such as mobility, communication, self-care, self-direction, interpersonal skills, work tolerance, or work skills) in terms of an employment outcome;

(ii) Whose vocational rehabilitation can be expected to require multiple vocational rehabilitation services over an extended period of time; and

(iii) Who has one or more physical or mental disabilities resulting from amputation, arthritis, autism, blindness, burn injury, cancer, cerebral palsy, cystic fibrosis, deafness, head injury, heart disease, hemiplegia, hemophilia, respiratory or pulmonary dysfunction, intellectual disability, mental illness, multiple sclerosis, muscular dystrophy, musculo-skeletal disorders, neurological disorders (including stroke and epilepsy), spinal cord conditions (including paraplegia and quadriplegia), sickle cell anemia, specific learning disability, end-stage renal disease, or another disability or combination of disabilities determined on the basis of an assessment for determining eligibility and vocational rehabilitation needs to cause comparable substantial functional limitation.

(Authority: Section 7(21) of the Rehabilitation Act of 1973, as amended, 29 U.S.C. 705(21))

Maintenance means monetary support provided to an individual for expenses, such as food, shelter, and clothing, that are in excess of the normal expenses of the individual and that are necessitated by the individual's participation in an assessment for determining eligibility and vocational rehabilitation needs or the individual's receipt of vocational rehabilitation services under an individualized plan for employment.

(Authority: Sections 12(c) and 103(a)(7) of the Rehabilitation Act of 1973, as amended; 29 U.S.C. 709(c) and 723(a)(7))

Examples: The following are examples of expenses that would meet the definition of maintenance. The examples are illustrative, do not address all possible circumstances, and are not intended to substitute for individual counselor judgment.

Example 1: The cost of a uniform or other suitable clothing that is required for an individual's job placement or job-seeking activities.

Example 2: The cost of short-term shelter that is required in order for an individual to participate in assessment activities or vocational training at a site that is not within commuting distance of an individual's home.

Example 3: The initial one-time costs, such as a security deposit or charges for the initiation of utilities, that are required in order for an individual to relocate for a job placement.

Physical and mental restoration services means—

(i) Corrective surgery or therapeutic treatment that is likely, within a reasonable period of time, to correct or modify substantially a stable or slowly progressive physical or mental impairment that constitutes a substantial impediment to employment;

(ii) Diagnosis of and treatment for mental or emotional disorders by qualified personnel in accordance with State licensure laws;

(iii) Dentistry;

(iv) Nursing services;

(v) Necessary hospitalization (either inpatient or outpatient care) in connection with surgery or treatment and clinic services;

(vi) Drugs and supplies;

(vii) Prosthetic and orthotic devices;

(viii) Eyeglasses and visual services, including visual training, and the examination and services necessary for the prescription and provision of eyeglasses, contact lenses, microscopic lenses, telescopic lenses, and other special visual aids prescribed by personnel that are qualified in accordance with State licensure laws;

(ix) Podiatry;

(x) Physical therapy;

(xi) Occupational therapy;

(xii) Speech or hearing therapy;

(xiii) Mental health services;

(xiv) Treatment of either acute or chronic medical complications and emergencies that are associated with or arise out of the provision of physical and mental restoration services, or that are inherent in the condition under treatment;

(xv) Special services for the treatment of individuals with end-stage renal disease, including transplantation, dialysis, artificial kidneys, and supplies; and

(xvi) Other medical or medically related rehabilitation services.

(xvii) Services reflecting the cultural background of the American Indian being served, including treatment provided by native healing practitioners in accordance with 34 CFR 371.41(a)(2).

(Authority: Sections 12(c), 103(a)(6), and 121(b)(1)(B) of the Rehabilitation Act of 1973, as amended; 29 U.S.C. 709(c), 723(a)(6), and 741(b)(1)(B))

Physical or mental impairment means—

(i) Any physiological disorder or condition, cosmetic disfigurement, or anatomical loss affecting one or more of the following body systems: Neurological, musculo-skeletal, special sense organs, respiratory (including speech organs), cardiovascular, reproductive, digestive, genitourinary, hemic and lymphatic, skin, and endocrine; or

(ii) Any mental or psychological disorder such as intellectual or developmental disability, organic brain syndrome, emotional or mental illness, and specific learning disabilities.

(Authority: Sections 7(20)(A) and 12(c) of the Rehabilitation Act of 1973, as amended; 29 U.S.C. 705(20)(A) and 709(c))

Post-employment services means one or more of the services that are provided subsequent to the achievement of an employment outcome and that are necessary for an individual to maintain, regain, or advance in employment, consistent with the individual's unique strengths, resources, priorities, concerns, abilities, capabilities, interests, and informed choice.

(Authority: Sections 12(c) and 103(a)(18) of the Rehabilitation Act of 1973, as amended; 29 U.S.C. 709(c)) and 723(a)(18))

NOTE TO DEFINITION OF POST-EMPLOYMENT SERVICES: Post-employment services are in-

tended to ensure that the employment outcome remains consistent with the individual's unique strengths, resources, priorities, concerns, abilities, capabilities, interests, and informed choice. These services are available to meet rehabilitation needs that do not require a complex and comprehensive provision of services and, thus, should be limited in scope and duration. If more comprehensive services are required, then a new rehabilitation effort should be considered. Post-employment services are to be provided under an amended individualized plan for employment; thus, a re-determination of eligibility is not required. The provision of post-employment services is subject to the same requirements in this part as the provision of any other vocational rehabilitation service. Post-employment services are available to assist an individual to maintain employment, *e.g.,* the individual's employment is jeopardized because of conflicts with supervisors or co-workers, and the individual needs mental health services and counseling to maintain the employment; or the individual requires assistive technology to maintain the employment; to regain employment, *e.g.,* the individual's job is eliminated through reorganization and new placement services are needed; and to advance in employment, *e.g.,* the employment is no longer consistent with the individual's unique strengths, resources, priorities, concerns, abilities, capabilities, interests, and informed choice.

Representatives of the Tribal Vocational Rehabilitation program means, consistent with 34 CFR 371.21(b), those individuals specifically responsible for determining eligibility, the nature and scope of vocational rehabilitation services, and the provision of those services.

(Authority: Sections 12(c) and 121(b)(1)(D) of the Rehabilitation Act of 1973, as amended, 29 U.S.C. 709(c) and 741(b)(1)(D))

Reservation means a Federal or State Indian reservation, public domain Indian allotment, former Indian reservation in Oklahoma, land held by incorporated Native groups, regional corporations and village corporations under the provisions of the Alaska Native Claims Settlement Act; or a defined area of land recognized by a State or the Federal Government where there is a concentration of tribal members and on which the tribal government is providing structured activities and services.

(Authority: Sections 12(c) and 121(e) of the Rehabilitation Act of 1973, as amended; 29 U.S.C. 709(c) and 741(e))

Subsistence means a form of self-employment in which individuals produce, using culturally relevant and traditional methods, goods or services that are predominantly consumed by their own household or used for noncommercial customary trade or barter and that constitute an important basis for the worker's livelihood.

(Authority: Section 12(c) of the Rehabilitation Act of 1973, as amended; 29 U.S.C. 709(c))

Substantial impediment to employment means that a physical or mental impairment (in light of attendant medical, psychological, vocational, educational, communication, and other related factors) hinders an individual from preparing for, entering into, engaging in, advancing in or retaining employment consistent with the individual's abilities and capabilities.

(Authority: Sections 7(20)(A) and 12(c) of the Rehabilitation Act of 1973, as amended; 29 U.S.C. 705(20)(A) and 709(c))

Supported employment—(i) *Supported employment* means competitive integrated employment, including customized employment, or employment in an integrated work setting in which an individual with a most significant disability, including a youth with a most significant disability, is working on a short-term basis toward competitive integrated employment that is individualized, consistent with the unique strengths, abilities, interests, and informed choice of the individual, including with ongoing support services for individuals with the most significant disabilities—

(A) For whom competitive integrated employment has not historically occurred, or for whom competitive integrated employment has been interrupted or intermittent as a result of a significant disability; and

(B) Who, because of the nature and severity of their disability, need intensive supported employment services and extended services after the transition from support provided by the Trib-

al Vocational Rehabilitation Unit, in order to perform this work.

(ii) For purposes of this part, an individual with the most significant disabilities, whose supported employment in an integrated setting does not satisfy the criteria of competitive integrated employment is considered to be working on a short-term basis toward competitive integrated employment so long as the individual can reasonably anticipate achieving competitive integrated employment:

(A) Within six months of achieving a supported employment outcome; or

(B) Within a period not to exceed 12 months from the achievement of the supported employment outcome, if a longer period is necessary based on the needs of the individual, and the individual has demonstrated progress toward competitive earnings based on information contained in the service record.

(Authority: Sections 7(38) and 12(c) of the Rehabilitation Act of 1973, as amended; 29 U.S.C. 705(38) and 709(c))

Supported employment services means ongoing support services, including customized employment, and other appropriate services needed to support and maintain an individual with a most significant disability, including a youth with a most significant disability, in supported employment that are:

(i) Organized and made available, singly or in combination, in such a way as to assist an eligible individual to achieve competitive integrated employment;

(ii) Based on a determination of the needs of an eligible individual, as specified in an individualized plan for employment;

(iii) Provided by the Tribal Vocational Rehabilitation Unit for a period of time not to exceed 24 months, unless under special circumstances the eligible individual and the rehabilitation counselor or coordinator jointly agree to extend the time to achieve the employment outcome identified in the individualized plan for employment; and

(iv) Following transition, as post-employment services that are unavailable from an extended services provider and that are necessary to maintain or regain the job placement or advance in employment.

(Authority: Sections 7(39) and 12(c) of the Rehabilitation Act of 1973, as amended; 29 U.S.C. 705(39) and 709(c))

Transition services means a coordinated set of activities for a student or youth with a disability—

(i) Designed within an outcome-oriented process that promotes movement from school to post-school activities, including postsecondary education, vocational training, competitive integrated employment, supported employment, continuing and adult education, adult services, independent living, or community participation;

(ii) Based upon the individual student's or youth's needs, taking into account the student's or youth's preferences and interests;

(iii) That includes instruction, community experiences, the development of employment and other post-school adult living objectives, and, if appropriate, acquisition of daily living skills and functional vocational evaluation;

(iv) That promotes or facilitates the achievement of the employment outcome identified in the student's or youth's individualized plan for employment; and

(v) That includes outreach to and engagement of the parents, or, as appropriate, the representative of such a student or youth with a disability.

(Authority: Sections 12(c), 103(a)(15), and (b)(7) of the Rehabilitation Act of 1973, as amended; 29 U.S.C. 709(c), 723(a)(15), and (b)(7))

Transportation means travel and related expenses that are necessary to enable an applicant or eligible individual to participate in a vocational rehabilitation service, including expenses for training in the use of public transportation vehicles and systems.

(Authority: Sections 12(c) and 103(a)(8) of the Rehabilitation Act of 1973, as amended, 29 U.S.C. 709(c) and 723(a)(8))

Tribal organization means the recognized governing body of any Indian tribe or any legally established organization of Indians which is controlled, sanctioned, or chartered by such governing body or which is democratically elected by the adult members of the Indian community to be served by such organization and which includes the maximum participation of Indians in all phases of its activities.

(Authority: Sections 7(19) and 12(c) of the Rehabilitation Act of 1973, as amended; 29 U.S.C. 705(19) and 709(c); Section 4 of the Indian Self-Determination and Education Assistance Act, 25 U.S.C. 450(b))

Tribal Vocational Rehabilitation program means the unit designated by the governing bodies of an Indian Tribe, or consortia of governing bodies, to implement and administer the grant under this program in accordance with the purpose of the grant and all applicable programmatic and fiscal requirements.

(Authority: Sections 12(c) and 121(b)(1) of the Rehabilitation Act of 1973, as amended, 29 U.S.C. 709(c) and 741(b)(1))

Vocational Rehabilitation Services for Individuals means any services described in an individualized plan for employment necessary to assist an individual with a disability in preparing for, securing, retaining, advancing in or regaining an employment outcome that is consistent with the unique strengths, resources, priorities, concerns, abilities, capabilities, interests, and informed choice of the individual, including, but not limited to—

(i) An assessment for determining eligibility, priority for services, and vocational rehabilitation needs by qualified personnel, including, if appropriate, an assessment by personnel skilled in rehabilitation technology.

(ii) Vocational rehabilitation counseling and guidance, including information and support services to assist an individual in exercising informed choice.

(iii) Referral and other services necessary to assist applicants and eligible individuals to secure needed services from other agencies and to advise those individuals about client assistance programs established under 34 CFR part 370.

(iv) Physical and mental restoration services, to the extent that financial support is not readily available from a source other than the Tribal Vocational Rehabilitation unit (such as through health insurance or a comparable service or benefit).

(v) Vocational and other training services, including personal and vocational adjustment training, advanced training (particularly advanced training in a field of science, technology, engineering, or mathematics (including computer science), medicine, law or business); books, tools, and other training materials, except that no training or training services in an institution of higher education (universities, colleges, community or junior colleges, vocational schools, technical institutes, or hospital schools of nursing or any other postsecondary education institution) may be paid for with funds under this part unless maximum efforts have been made by the Tribal Vocational Rehabilitation unit and the individual to secure grant assistance in whole or in part from other sources to pay for that training.

(vi) Maintenance.

(vii) Transportation in connection with the provision of any vocational rehabilitation service.

(viii) Vocational rehabilitation services to family members of an applicant or eligible individual if necessary to enable the applicant or eligible individual to achieve an employment outcome.

(ix) Interpreter services, including sign language and oral interpreter services, for individuals who are deaf or hard of hearing and tactile interpreting services for individuals who are deaf-blind provided by qualified personnel.

(x) Reader services, rehabilitation teaching services, and orientation and mobility services for individuals who are blind.

(xi) Job-related services, including job search and placement assistance, job retention services, follow-up services, and follow-along services.

(xii) Supported employment services.

(xiii) Personal assistance services.

(xiv) Post-employment services.

(xv) Occupational licenses, tools, equipment, initial stocks, and supplies.

(xvi) Rehabilitation technology, including vehicular modification, telecommunications, sensory, and other technological aids and devices.

(xvii) Transition services for students and youth with disabilities that facilitate the transition from school to post-secondary life, such as achievement of an employment outcome in competitive integrated employment.

(xviii) Technical assistance and other consultation services to conduct market analyses, develop business plans, and otherwise provide resources to eligible individuals who are pursuing self-employment or telecommuting or establishing a small business operation as an employment outcome.

(xix) Customized employment.

(x) Other goods and services determined necessary for the individual with a disability to achieve an employment outcome.

Vocational Rehabilitation Services for Groups of Individuals provided for the benefit of groups of individuals with disabilities—

(i) May be provided by the Tribal Vocational Rehabilitation Unit and may include the following:

(A) In the case of any small business enterprise operated by individuals with significant disabilities under the supervision of the Tribal Vocational Rehabilitation unit, management services and supervision provided by the Tribal Vocational Rehabilitation unit, along with the acquisition by the Tribal Vocational Rehabilitation unit of vending facilities or other equipment and initial stocks and supplies in accordance with the following requirements:

(1) Management services and supervision includes inspection, quality control, consultation, accounting, regulating, in-service training, and related services provided on a systematic basis to support and improve small business enterprises operated by individuals with significant disabilities. Management services and supervision may be provided throughout the operation of the small business enterprise.

(2) Initial stocks and supplies include those items necessary to the establishment of a new business enterprise during the initial establishment period, which may not exceed 6 months.

(3) Costs of establishing a small business enterprise may include operational costs during the initial establishment period, which may not exceed six months.

(4) If the Tribal Vocational Rehabilitation unit provides for these services,

it must ensure that only individuals with significant disabilities will be selected to participate in this supervised program.

(5) If the Tribal Vocational Rehabilitation unit provides for these services and chooses to set aside funds from the proceeds of the operation of the small business enterprises, the Tribal Vocational Rehabilitation unit must maintain a description of the methods used in setting aside funds and the purposes for which funds are set aside. Funds may be used only for small business enterprises purposes, and benefits that are provided to operators from set-aside funds must be provided on an equitable basis.

(B) The establishment, development, or improvement of a community rehabilitation program that is used to provide vocational rehabilitation services that promote integration into the community and prepare individuals with disabilities for competitive integrated employment, including supported employment and customized employment, and under special circumstances, the construction of a community rehabilitation facility. Examples of "special circumstances" include the destruction by natural disaster of the only available center serving an area or a Tribal Vocational Rehabilitation unit determination that construction is necessary in a rural area because no other public agencies or private nonprofit organizations are currently able to provide vocational rehabilitation services to individuals.

(C) Telecommunications systems (that have the potential for substantially improving vocational rehabilitation service delivery methods and developing appropriate programming to meet the particular needs of individuals with disabilities including telephone, television, video description services, satellite, tactile-vibratory devices, and similar systems, as appropriate.

(D) Special services to provide nonvisual access to information for individuals who are blind, including the use of telecommunications, Braille, sound recordings, or other appropriate media; captioned television, films, or video cassettes for individuals who are deaf or hard of hearing; tactile mate-

rials for individuals who are deaf-blind; and other special services that provide information through tactile, vibratory, auditory, and visual media.

(E) Technical assistance to businesses that are seeking to employ individuals with disabilities.

(F) Consultation and technical assistance services to assist State educational agencies and local educational agencies, and, where appropriate, Tribal Educational agencies, in planning for the transition of students with disabilities from school to postsecondary life, including employment.

(G) Transition services to youth with disabilities and students with disabilities, for which a vocational rehabilitation counselor works in concert with educational agencies, providers of job training programs, providers of services under the Medicaid program under title XIX of the Social Security Act (42 U.S.C. 1396 et seq.), entities designated by the Tribal Vocational Rehabilitation unit to provide services for individuals with developmental disabilities, centers for independent living (as defined in section 702 of the Act), housing and transportation authorities, workforce development systems, and businesses and employers. These specific transition services are to benefit a group of students with disabilities or youth with disabilities and are not individualized services directly related to a goal in an individualized plan for employment (IPE). Services may include, but are not limited to group tours of universities and vocational training programs, employer or business site visits to learn about career opportunities, career fairs coordinated with workforce development and employers to facilitate mock interviews and resume writing, and other general services applicable to groups of students with disabilities and youth with disabilities.

(H) The establishment, development, or improvement of assistive technology demonstration, loan, reutilization, or financing programs in coordination with activities authorized under the Assistive Technology Act of 1998 (29 U.S.C. 3001 et seq.) to promote access to assistive technology for individuals with disabilities and employers.

(I) Support (including, as appropriate, tuition) for advanced training in a field of science, technology, engineering, or mathematics (including computer science), medicine, law, or business, provided after an individual eligible to receive services under this title, demonstrates:

(*1*) Such eligibility;

(*2*) Previous completion of a bachelor's degree program at an institution of higher education or scheduled completion of such degree program prior to matriculating in the program for which the individual proposes to use the support; and

(*3*) Acceptance by a program at an institution of higher education in the United States that confers a master's degree in a field of science, technology, engineering, or mathematics (including computer science), a juris doctor degree, a master of business administration degree, or a doctor of medicine degree, except that—

(*i*) No training provided at an institution of higher education shall be paid for with funds under this program unless maximum efforts have been made by the Tribal Vocational Rehabilitation unit and the individual to secure grant assistance, in whole or in part, from other sources to pay for such training; and

(*ii*) Nothing in this paragraph prevents any Tribal Vocational Rehabilitation unit from providing similar support to individuals with disabilities pursuant to their approved IPEs who are eligible to receive support under this program and who are not served under this paragraph.

(ii) If the Tribal Vocational Rehabilitation Unit provides for vocational rehabilitation services for groups of individuals it must —

(A) Develop and maintain written policies covering the nature and scope of each of the vocational rehabilitation services it provides and the criteria under which each service is provided; and

(B) Maintain information to ensure the proper and efficient administration of those services in the form and detail and at the time required by the Secretary, including the types of services provided, the costs of those services, and to the extent feasible, estimates of the numbers of individuals benefiting from those services.

(Authority: Sections 12(c) and 103(a) and (b) of the Rehabilitation Act of 1973, as amended, 29 U.S.C. 709(c) and 723(a) and (b))

Subpart B—Training and Technical Assistance

§371.10 What are the requirements for funding training and technical assistance under this subpart?

The Secretary shall first reserve not less than 1.8 percent and not more than 2 percent of funds appropriated and made available to carry out this program to provide training and technical assistance to the governing bodies of Indian tribes and consortia of those governing bodies awarded a grant under this program.

(Authority: Sections 12(c) and Section 121(c) of the Rehabilitation Act of 1973, as amended; 29 U.S.C. 709(c) and 741(c))

§371.11 How does the Secretary use these funds to provide training and technical assistance?

(a) The Secretary uses these funds to make grants to, or enter into contracts or other cooperative agreements with, entities that have staff with experience in the operation of vocational rehabilitation services programs under this part.

(b) An entity receiving assistance in accordance with paragraph (a) of this section shall provide training and technical assistance with respect to developing, conducting, administering, and evaluating tribal vocational rehabilitation programs funded under this part.

(Authority: Sections 12(c) and Section 121(c) of the Rehabilitation Act of 1973, as amended; 29 U.S.C. 709(c) and 741(c))

§371.12 How does the Secretary make an award?

(a) To be eligible to receive a grant or enter into a contract or cooperative agreement under section 121(c) of the Act and this subpart, an applicant shall submit an application to the Secretary at such time, in such manner, and containing a proposal to provide such training and technical assistance, and any additional information as the Secretary may require.

437

(b) The Secretary shall provide for peer review of applications by panels that include persons who are not Federal or State government employees and who have experience in the operation of vocational rehabilitation services programs under this part.

(Authority: Sections 12(c) and Section 121(c) of the Rehabilitation Act of 1973, as amended; 29 U.S.C. 709(c) and 741(c))

§ 371.13   How does the Secretary determine funding priorities?

The Secretary shall conduct a survey of the governing bodies of Indian tribes funded under this part regarding training and technical assistance needs in order to determine funding priorities for such training and technical assistance.

(Authority: Sections 12(c) and Section 121(c) of the Rehabilitation Act of 1973, as amended; 29 U.S.C. 709(c) and 741(c))

§ 371.14   How does the Secretary evaluate an application?

(a) The Secretary evaluates each application for a grant, cooperative agreement or contract under this subpart on the basis of the selection criteria chosen from the general selection criteria found in EDGAR regulations at 34 CFR 75.210.

(b) The Secretary may award a competitive preference consistent with 34 CFR 75.102(c)(2) to applications that include as project personnel in a substantive role, individuals that have been employed as a project director or VR counselor by a Tribal Vocational Rehabilitation unit funded under this part.

(c) If using a contract to award funds under this subpart, the Secretary may conduct the application process and make the subsequent award in accordance with 34 CFR part 75.

(Authority: Sections 12(c) and Section 121(c) of the Rehabilitation Act of 1973, as amended; 29 U.S.C. 709(c) and 741(c))

Subpart C—How Does One Apply for a Grant?

§ 371.20   What are the application procedures for this program?

(a) In the development of an application, the applicant is required to con-

sult with the designated State unit (DSU) for the state vocational rehabilitation program in the State or States in which vocational rehabilitation services are to be provided.

(b) The procedures for the review and comment by the DSU or the DSUs of the State or States in which vocational rehabilitation services are to be provided on applications submitted from within the State that the DSU or DSUs serve are in 34 CFR 75.155–75.159.

(Authority: Sections 12(c) and 121(b)(1)(C) of the Rehabilitation Act of 1973, as amended; 29 U.S.C. 709(c) and 741(b)(1)(C))

§ 371.21   What are the special application requirements related to the projects funded under this part?

Each applicant under this program must provide evidence that—

(a) Effort will be made to provide a broad scope of vocational rehabilitation services in a manner and at a level of quality at least comparable to those services provided by the designated State unit.

(Authority: Sections 12(c) and 121(b)(1)(B) of the Rehabilitation Act of 1973, as amended; 29 U.S.C. 709(c) and 741(b)(1)(B))

(b) All decisions affecting eligibility for vocational rehabilitation services, the nature and scope of available vocational rehabilitation services and the provision of such services will be made by a representative of the tribal vocational rehabilitation program funded through this grant and such decisions will not be delegated to another agency or individual.

(Authority: Sections 12(c) and 121(b)(1)(D) of the Rehabilitation Act of 1973, as amended; 29 U.S.C. 709(c) and 741(b)(1)(D))

(c) Priority in the delivery of vocational rehabilitation services will be given to those American Indians with disabilities who are the most significantly disabled.

(Authority: Sections 12(c) and 101(a)(5) of the Rehabilitation Act of 1973, as amended; 29 U.S.C. 709(c) and 721(a)(5))

(d) An order of selection of individuals with disabilities to be served under the program will be specified if services cannot be provided to all eligible American Indians with disabilities who apply.

(Authority: Sections 12(c) and 101(a)(5) of the Rehabilitation Act of 1973, as amended; 29 U.S.C. 709 (c) and 721(a)(5))

(e) All vocational rehabilitation services will be provided according to an individualized plan for employment which has been developed jointly by the representative of the tribal vocational rehabilitation program and each American Indian with disabilities being served.

(Authority: Sections 12(c) and 101(a)(9) of the Rehabilitation Act of 1973, as amended; 29 U.S.C. 709(c) and 721 (a)(9))

(f) American Indians with disabilities living on or near Federal or State reservations where tribal vocational rehabilitation service programs are being carried out under this part will have an opportunity to participate in matters of general policy development and implementation affecting vocational rehabilitation service delivery by the tribal vocational rehabilitation program.

(Authority: Sections 12(c) and 101(a)(16) of the Rehabilitation Act of 1973, as amended; 29 U.S.C. 709(c) and 721(a)(16))

(g) Cooperative working arrangements will be developed with the DSU, or DSUs, as appropriate, which are providing vocational rehabilitation services to other individuals with disabilities who reside in the State or States being served.

(Authority: Sections 12(c) and 101(a)(11)(F) of the Rehabilitation Act of 1973, as amended; 29 U.S.C. 709(c) and 721(a)(11)(F))

(h) Any comparable services and benefits available to American Indians with disabilities under any other program, which might meet in whole or in part the cost of any vocational rehabilitation service, will be fully considered in the provision of vocational rehabilitation services.

(Authority: Sections 12(c) and 101(a)(8) of the Rehabilitation Act of 1973, as amended; 29 U.S.C. 709(c) and 721(a)(8))

(i) Any American Indian with disabilities who is an applicant or recipient of services, and who is dissatisfied with a determination made by a representa-

tive of the tribal vocational rehabilitation program and files a request for a review, will be afforded a review under procedures developed by the grantee comparable to those under the provisions of section 102(c)(1)–(5) and (7) of the Act.

(Authority: Sections 12(c) and 102(c) of the Rehabilitation Act of 1973, as amended; 29 U.S.C. 709(c) and 722(c)(1)–(5) and (7))

(j) The tribal vocational rehabilitation program funded under this part must assure that any facility used in connection with the delivery of vocational rehabilitation services meets facility and program accessibility requirements consistent with the requirements, as applicable, of the Architectural Barriers Act of 1968, the Americans with Disabilities Act of 1990, section 504 of the Act, and the regulations implementing these laws.

(Authority: Sections 12(c) and 101(a)(6)(C) of the Rehabilitation Act of 1973, as amended; 29 U.S.C. 709(c) and 721(a)(6)(C))

(k) The tribal vocational rehabilitation program funded under this part must ensure that providers of vocational rehabilitation services are able to communicate in the native language of, or by using an appropriate mode of communication with, applicants and eligible individuals who have limited English proficiency, unless it is clearly not feasible to do so.

(Authority: Sections 12(c) and 101(a)(6)(A) of the Rehabilitation Act of 1973, as amended; 29 U.S.C. 709(c) and 721(a)(6)(A))

Subpart D—How Does the Secretary Make a Grant?

§371.31 How are grants awarded?

To the extent that funds have been appropriated under this program, the Secretary approves all applications which meet acceptable standards of program quality. If any application is not approved because of deficiencies in proposed program standards, the Secretary provides technical assistance to the applicant Indian tribe with respect to any areas of the proposal which were judged to be deficient.

(Authority: Sections 12(c) and 121(b)(1)(A) of the Rehabilitation Act of 1973, as amended; 29 U.S.C. 709(c) and 741(b)(1)(A))

§ 371.32 What other factors does the Secretary consider in reviewing an application?

(a) In addition to the selection criteria used in accordance with the procedures in 34 CFR part 75, the Secretary, in making an award under this program, considers the past performance of the applicant in carrying out similar activities under previously awarded grants, as indicated by such factors as compliance with grant conditions, soundness of programmatic and financial management practices and attainment of established project objectives.

(b) The Secretary may award a competitive preference consistent with 34 CFR 75.102(c)(2) to applications for the continuation of programs which have been funded under this program.

(Authority: Sections 12(c), 121(b)(1)(A), and 121(b)(4) of the Rehabilitation Act of 1973, as amended; 29 U.S.C. 709(c), 741(b)(1)(A)), and 741(b)(4).

Subpart E—What Conditions Apply to a Grantee Under this Program?

§ 371.40 What are the matching requirements?

(a) *Federal share* Except as provided in paragraph (c) of this section, the Federal share may not be more than 90 percent of the total cost of the project.

(b) *Non-Federal share* The non-Federal share of the cost of the project may be in cash or in kind, fairly valued pursuant to match requirements in 2 CFR 200.306.

(c) *Waiver of non-Federal share* In order to carry out the purposes of the program, the Secretary may waive the non-Federal share requirement, in part or in whole, only if the applicant demonstrates that it does not have sufficient resources to contribute the non-Federal share of the cost of the project.

(Authority: Sections 12(c) and 121(a) of the Rehabilitation Act of 1973, as amended; 29 U.S.C. 709(c) and 741(a))

§ 371.41 What are allowable costs?

(a) In addition to those allowable cost established in 2 CFR 200.400–200.475, the following items are allowable costs under this program—

(1) Expenditures for the provision of vocational rehabilitation services and for the administration, including staff development, of a program of vocational rehabilitation services.

(2) Expenditures for services reflecting the cultural background of the American Indians being served, including treatment provided by native healing practitioners who are recognized as such by the tribal vocational rehabilitation program when the services are necessary to assist an individual with disabilities to achieve his or her vocational rehabilitation objective.

(b) Expenditures may not be made under this program to cover the costs of providing vocational rehabilitation services to individuals with disabilities not residing on or near Federal or State reservations.

(Authority: Sections 12(c) and 121(a) and (b)(1) of the Rehabilitation Act of 1973, as amended; 29 U.S.C. 709(c) and 741(a) and (b)(1))

§ 371.42 How are services to be administered under this program?

(a) *Directly or by contract.* A grantee under this part may provide the vocational rehabilitation services directly or it may contract or otherwise enter into an agreement with a DSU, a community rehabilitation program, or another agency to assist in the implementation of the tribal vocational rehabilitation program.

(b) *Inter-tribal agreement.* A grantee under this part may enter into an inter-tribal arrangement with governing bodies of other Indian tribes for carrying out a project that serves more than one Indian tribe.

(c) *Comparable services.* To the maximum extent feasible, services provided by a grantee under this part must be comparable to vocational rehabilitation services provided under the State vocational rehabilitation program to other individuals with disabilities residing in the State.

(Authority: Sections 12(c) and 121(b)(1)(B) of the Rehabilitation Act of 1973, as amended; 29 U.S.C. 709(c) and 741(b)(1)(B))

§ 371.43 What other special conditions apply to this program?

(a) Any American Indian with disabilities who is eligible for services under this program but who wishes to be provided services by the DSU must be referred to the DSU for such services.

(Authority: Sec. 12(c) and 121(b)(3) of the Rehabilitation Act of 1973, as amended; 29 U.S.C. 709(c) and 741(b)(3))

(b) Preference in employment in connection with the provision of vocational rehabilitation services under this section must be given to American Indians, with a special priority being given to American Indians with disabilities.

(Authority: Sections 12(c) and 121(b)(2) of the Rehabilitation Act of 1973, as amended; 29 U.S.C. 709(c) and 741(b)(2))

(c) The provisions of sections 5, 6, 7, and 102(a) of the Indian Self-Determination and Education Assistance Act also apply under this program (25 U.S.C. 450c, 450d, 450e, and 450f(a)). These provisions relate to grant reporting and audit requirements, maintenance of records, access to records, availability of required reports and information to Indian people served or represented, repayment of unexpended Federal funds, criminal activities involving grants, penalties, wage and labor standards, preference requirements for American Indians in the conduct and administration of the grant, and requirements affecting requests of tribal organizations to enter into contracts. For purposes of applying these requirements to this program, the Secretary carries out those responsibilities assigned to the Secretary of Interior.

(Authority: Sec. 12(c) and 121(b)(2) of the Rehabilitation Act of 1973, as amended; 29 U.S.C 709(c) and 741(b)(2))

(d) The Tribal Vocational Rehabilitation unit must develop and maintain written policies regarding the provision of vocational rehabilitation services that ensure that the provision of services is based on the vocational rehabilitation needs of each individual as identified in that individual's IPE and is consistent with the individual's informed choice. The written policies may not establish any arbitrary limits on the nature and scope of vocational rehabilitation services to be provided to the individual to achieve an employment outcome. The policies must be developed in accordance with the following provisions:

(1) *Off-reservation services.* (i) The Tribal Vocational Rehabilitation unit may establish a preference for on- or near-reservation services, provided that the preference does not effectively deny an individual a necessary service. If the individual chooses an equivalent off-reservation service at a higher cost than an available on- or near-reservation service, the Tribal Vocational Rehabilitation unit is not responsible for those costs in excess of the cost of the on- or near-reservation service, if either service would meet the individual's rehabilitation needs.

(ii) The Tribal Vocational Rehabilitation unit may not establish policies that effectively prohibit the provision of off-reservation services.

(2) *Payment for services* (i) The Tribal Vocational Rehabilitation unit must establish and maintain written policies to govern the rates of payment for all purchased vocational rehabilitation services.

(ii) The Tribal Vocational Rehabilitation unit may establish a fee schedule designed to ensure the program pays a reasonable cost for each service, as long as the fee schedule—

(A) Is not so low as effectively to deny an individual a necessary service; and

(B) permits exceptions so that individual needs can be addressed.

(C) The Tribal Vocational Rehabilitation unit may not place absolute dollar limits on the amount it will pay for specific service categories or on the total services provided to an individual.

(3) *Duration of services* (i) The Tribal Vocational Rehabilitation unit may establish reasonable time periods for the provision of services provided that the time periods—

(A) Are not so short as effectively to deny an individual a necessary service; and

(B) Permit exceptions so that individual needs can be addressed.

(ii) The Tribal Vocational Rehabilitation unit may not place time limits on the provision of specific services or on the provision of services to an individual. The duration of each service

441

needed by an individual must be determined on the basis of that individual's needs and reflected in that individual's individualized plan for employment.

(4) *Authorization of services.* The Tribal Vocational Rehabilitation unit must establish policies related to the timely authorization of services.

(Authority: Sections 12(c) and 121(b) of the Rehabilitation Act of 1973, as amended, 29 U.S.C. 709(c) and 741(b))

(e) *Informed choice.* Each individual who is an applicant for or eligible to receive vocational rehabilitation services must be afforded the opportunity to exercise informed choice throughout the vocational rehabilitation process carried out under programs funded under this part. The Tribal Vocational Rehabilitation unit must develop and maintain written policies and procedures that require it—

(1) To inform each applicant and eligible individual, through appropriate modes of communication, about the availability of, and opportunities to exercise, informed choice, including the availability of support services for individuals with cognitive or other disabilities who require assistance in exercising informed choice, throughout the vocational rehabilitation process;

(2) To assist applicants and eligible individuals in exercising informed choice in decisions related to the provision of assessment services;

(3) To develop and implement flexible procurement policies and methods that facilitate the provision of vocational rehabilitation services, and that afford eligible individuals meaningful choices among the methods used to procure vocational rehabilitation services;

(4) To provide or assist eligible individuals in acquiring information that enables them to exercise informed choice in the development of their IPEs and selection of—

(i) The employment outcome;

(ii) The specific vocational rehabilitation services needed to achieve the employment outcome;

(iii) The entity that will provide the services;

(iv) The employment setting and the settings in which the services will be provided; and

(v) The methods available for procuring the services; and

(5) To ensure that the availability and scope of informed choice is consistent with the obligations of the Tribal Vocational Rehabilitation unit.

(6) Information and assistance in the selection of vocational rehabilitation services and service providers: In assisting an applicant and eligible individual in exercising informed choice during the assessment for determining eligibility and vocational rehabilitation needs and during development of the IPE, the Tribal Vocational Rehabilitation unit must provide the individual or the individual's representative, or assist the individual or the individual's representative in acquiring, information necessary to make an informed choice about the specific vocational rehabilitation services, including the providers of those services, that are needed to achieve the individual's employment outcome. This information must include, at a minimum, information relating to the—

(i) Cost, accessibility, and duration of potential services;

(ii) Consumer satisfaction with those services to the extent that information relating to consumer satisfaction is available;

(iii) Qualifications of potential service providers;

(iv) Types of services offered by the potential providers;

(v) Degree to which services are provided in integrated settings; and

(vi) Outcomes achieved by individuals working with service providers, to the extent that such information is available.

(7) Methods or sources of information: In providing or assisting the individual or the individual's representative in acquiring the information required under paragraph (c) of this section, the Tribal Vocational Rehabilitation unit may use, but is not limited to, the following methods or sources of information:

(i) Lists of services and service providers.

(ii) Periodic consumer satisfaction surveys and reports.

(iii) Referrals to other consumers, consumer groups, or disability advisory councils qualified to discuss the services or service providers.

(iv) Relevant accreditation, certification, or other information relating to the qualifications of service providers.

(v) Opportunities for individuals to visit or experience various work and service provider settings.

(Approved by the Office of Management and Budget under control number 1820–0500)

(Authority: Sections 12(c), 102(b)(2)(B), and 102(d) of the Rehabilitation Act of 1973, as amended; 29 U.S.C. 709(c), 722(b)(2)(B), and 722(d))

§371.44 What are the special requirements pertaining to the protection, use, and release of personal information?

(a) *General provisions.* (1) The Tribal Vocational Rehabilitation unit must adopt and implement written policies and procedures to safeguard the confidentiality of all personal information, including photographs and lists of names. These policies and procedures must ensure that—

(i) Specific safeguards are established to protect current and stored personal information, including a requirement that data only be released when governed by a written agreement between the Tribal Vocational Rehabilitation unit and receiving entity under paragraphs (d) and (e)(1) of this section, which addresses the requirements in this section;

(ii) All applicants and eligible individuals and, as appropriate, those individuals' representatives, service providers, cooperating agencies, and interested persons are informed through appropriate modes of communication of the confidentiality of personal information and the conditions for accessing and releasing this information;

(iii) All applicants or their representatives are informed about the Tribal Vocational Rehabilitation unit's need to collect personal information and the policies governing its use, including—

(A) Identification of the authority under which information is collected;

(B) Explanation of the principal purposes for which the Tribal Vocational Rehabilitation unit intends to use or release the information;

(C) Explanation of whether providing requested information to the Tribal Vocational Rehabilitation unit is man-datory or voluntary and the effects of not providing requested information;

(D) Identification of those situations in which the Tribal Vocational Rehabilitation unit requires or does not require informed written consent of the individual before information may be released; and

(E) Identification of other agencies to which information is routinely released;

(iv) An explanation of the Tribal Vocational Rehabilitation unit's policies and procedures affecting personal information will be provided to each individual in that individual's native language or through the appropriate mode of communication; and

(v) These policies and procedures provide no fewer protections for individuals than State laws and regulations.

(2) The Tribal Vocational Rehabilitation unit may establish reasonable fees to cover extraordinary costs of duplicating records or making extensive searches and must establish policies and procedures governing access to records.

(b) *Tribal Vocational Rehabilitation Program Use.* All personal information in the possession of the Tribal Vocational Rehabilitation unit must be used only for the purposes directly connected with the administration of the Tribal Vocational Rehabilitation program. Information containing identifiable personal information may not be shared with advisory or other bodies or other tribal agencies that do not have official responsibility for administration of the program. In the administration of the program, the Tribal Vocational Rehabilitation unit may obtain personal information from service providers and cooperating agencies under assurances that the information may not be further divulged, except as provided under paragraphs (c), (d), and (e) of this section.

(c) *Release to applicants and eligible individuals.* (1) Except as provided in paragraphs (c)(2) and (3) of this section, if requested in writing by an applicant or eligible individual, the Tribal Vocational Rehabilitation unit must make all requested information in that individual's record of services accessible to and must release the information to

443

the individual or the individual's representative in a timely manner.

(2) Medical, psychological, or other information that the Tribal Vocational Rehabilitation unit determines may be harmful to the individual may not be released directly to the individual, but must be provided to the individual through a third party chosen by the individual, which may include, among others, an advocate, a family member, or a qualified medical or mental health professional, unless a representative has been appointed by a court to represent the individual, in which case the information must be released to the court-appointed representative.

(3) If personal information has been obtained from another agency or organization, it may be released only by, or under the conditions established by, the other agency or organization.

(4) An applicant or eligible individual who believes that information in the individual's record of services is inaccurate or misleading may request that the Tribal Vocational Rehabilitation unit amend the information. If the information is not amended, the request for an amendment must be documented in the record of services.

(d) *Release for audit, evaluation, and research.* Personal information may be released to an organization, agency, or individual engaged in audit, evaluation, or research only for purposes directly connected with the administration of the tribal vocational rehabilitation program or for purposes that would significantly improve the quality of life for applicants and eligible individuals and only if, in accordance with a written agreement, the organization, agency, or individual assures that—

(1) The information will be used only for the purposes for which it is being provided;

(2) The information will be released only to persons officially connected with the audit, evaluation, or research;

(3) The information will not be released to the involved individual;

(4) The information will be managed in a manner to safeguard confidentiality; and

(5) The final product will not reveal any personal identifying information without the informed written consent of the involved individual or the individual's representative.

(e) *Release to other programs or authorities.* (1) Upon receiving the informed written consent of the individual or, if appropriate, the individual's representative, the Tribal Vocational Rehabilitation unit may release personal information to another agency or organization, in accordance with a written agreement, for its program purposes only to the extent that the information may be released to the involved individual or the individual's representative and only to the extent that the other agency or organization demonstrates that the information requested is necessary for its program.

(2) Medical or psychological information that the Tribal Vocational Rehabilitation unit determines may be harmful to the individual may be released if the other agency or organization assures the Tribal Vocational Rehabilitation unit that the information will be used only for the purpose for which it is being provided and will not be further released to the individual.

(3) The Tribal Vocational Rehabilitation unit must release personal information if required by Federal law or regulations.

(4) The Tribal Vocational Rehabilitation unit must release personal information in response to investigations in connection with law enforcement, fraud, or abuse, unless expressly prohibited by Federal or State laws or regulations, and in response to an order issued by a judge, magistrate, or other authorized judicial officer.

(5) The Tribal Vocational Rehabilitation unit also may release personal information in order to protect the individual or others if the individual poses a threat to his or her safety or to the safety of others.

(Authority: Sections 12(c) and 121(b)(1) of the Rehabilitation Act of 1973, as amended; 29 U.S.C. 709(c) and 741(b)(1))

§ 371.45 What notice must be given about the Client Assistance Program (CAP)?

The Tribal Vocational Rehabilitation unit shall use formats that are accessible to notify individuals seeking or receiving services under this part, or as appropriate, the parents, family members, guardians, advocates, or authorized representatives of those individuals, about—

(a) The availability of CAP authorized by section 112 of the Act;

(b) The purposes of the services provided under the CAP; and

(c) How to contact the CAP.

(Authority: Section 20 of the Rehabilitation Act of 1973, as amended; 29 U.S.C. 717)

PART 373—REHABILITATION NATIONAL ACTIVITIES PROGRAM

Subpart A—General

Subpart B—How Does the Secretary Make a Grant?

Subpart C—What Conditions Must Be Met By a Grantee?

AUTHORITY: Section 303(b) of the Rehabilitation Act of 1973, as amended; 29 U.S.C. 773(b); Pub. L. 111–256, 124 Stat. 2643; unless otherwise noted.

SOURCE: 81 FR 55607, Aug. 19, 2016, unless otherwise noted.

Subpart A—General

§373.1 What is the purpose of the Rehabilitation National Activities program?

The purpose of this program is to provide competitive grants, including cooperative agreements, to, or enter into contracts with, eligible entities to expand and improve the provision of vocational rehabilitation and other services authorized under the Rehabilitation Act of 1973, as amended (Act), or to further the purposes and policies in sections 2(b) and (c) of the Act by supporting activities that increase the provision, extent, availability, scope, and quality of rehabilitation services under the Act, including related research and evaluation activities.

(Authority: Sections 2(b) and (c), 7(40), 12(c), and 303(b) of the Rehabilitation Act of 1973, as amended; 29 U.S.C. 701(b) and (c), 705(40), 709(c), and 773(b))

§373.2 Who is eligible for assistance?

(a) The following types of organizations are eligible for assistance under this program:

(1) State vocational rehabilitation agencies.

(2) Community rehabilitation programs.

(3) Indian tribes or tribal organizations.

(4) Other public or nonprofit agencies or organizations, including institutions of higher education.

(5) For-profit organizations, if the Secretary considers them to be appropriate.

(6) Consortia that meet the requirements of 34 CFR 75.128 and 75.129.

(7) Other organizations identified by the Secretary and published in the FEDERAL REGISTER.

(b) In competitions held under this program, the Secretary may limit competitions to one or more types of these organizations.

(Authority: Sections 12(c) and 303(b)(2) of the Rehabilitation Act of 1973, as amended; 29 U.S.C. 709(c) and 773(b)(2))

§373.3 What regulations apply?

The following regulations apply to this program:

(a) The Education Department General Administrative Regulations (EDGAR) as follows:

(1) 34 CFR part 75 (Direct Grant Programs).

(2) 34 CFR part 77 (Definitions that Apply to Department Regulations).

(3) 34 CFR part 79 (Intergovernmental Review of Department of Education Programs and Activities).

(4) 34 CFR part 81 (General Education Provisions Act—Enforcement).

(5) 35 CFR part 82 (New Restrictions on Lobbying).

(6) 34 CFR part 84 (Governmentwide Requirements for Drug-Free Workplace (Financial Assistance).

(7) 34 CFR part 86 (Drug and Alcohol Abuse Prevention).

(8) 34 CFR part 97 (Protection of Human Subjects).

(9) 34 CFR part 98 (Student Rights in Research, Experimental Programs, and Testing.

(10) 34 CFR part 99 (Family Educational Rights and Privacy).

(b) The regulations in this part 373.

(c) The regulations in 48 CFR part 31 (Contracts Cost Principles and Procedures).

(d)(1) 2 CFR part 180 (Nonprocurement Debarment and Suspension), as adopted at 2 CFR part 3485; and

(2) 2 CFR part 200 (Uniform Administrative Requirements, Cost Principles, and Audit Requirements for Federal Awards) as adopted at 2 CFR part 3474.

(Authority: Sections 12(c) and 303(b) of the Rehabilitation Act of 1973, as amended; 29 U.S.C. 709(c) and 773(b))

§ 373.4 What definitions apply?

The following definitions apply to this part:

Act means the Rehabilitation Act of 1973, as amended.

(Authority: 29 U.S.C. 701 *et seq.*)

Competitive integrated employment is defined in 34 CFR 361.5(c)(9).

(Authority: Section 7(5) of the Rehabilitation Act of 1973, as amended; 29 U.S.C. 705(5))

Early intervention means a service delivery or model demonstration program for adults with disabilities designed to begin the rehabilitation services as soon as possible after the onset or identification of actually or potentially disabling conditions. The populations served may include, but are not limited to, the following:

(1) Individuals with chronic and progressive diseases that may become more disabling, such as multiple sclerosis, progressive visual disabilities, or HIV.

(2) Individuals in the acute stages of injury or illness, including, but not limited to, diabetes, traumatic brain injury, stroke, burns, or amputation.

(3) Individuals receiving an employer's short-term or long-term disability insurance benefits.

(Authority: Sections 12(c) and 303(b) of the Rehabilitation Act of 1973, as amended; 29 U.S.C. 709(c) and 773(b))

Employment outcome is defined in 34 CFR 361.5.

(Authority: Section 7(11) of the Rehabilitation Act of 1973, as amended; 29 U.S.C. 705(11))

Individual with a disability is defined as follows:

(1) For an individual who will receive rehabilitation services under this part, an individual with a disability means an individual—

(i) Who has a physical or mental impairment which, for that individual, constitutes or results in a substantial impediment to employment; and

(ii) Who can benefit in terms of an employment outcome from vocational rehabilitation services.

(2) For all other purposes of this part, an individual with a disability means an individual—

(i) Who has a physical or mental impairment that substantially limits one or more major life activities;

(ii) Who has a record of such an impairment; or

(iii) Who is regarded as having such an impairment.

(3) For purposes of paragraph (2) of this definition, projects that carry out services or activities pertaining to Title V of the Act must also meet the requirements for "an individual with a disability" in section 7(20)(c) through (e) of the Act, as applicable.

(Authority: Section 7(20) of the Rehabilitation Act of 1973, as amended; 29 U.S.C. 705(20))

Individual with a significant disability means an individual—

(1) Who has a severe physical or mental impairment that seriously limits one or more functional capacities (such as mobility, communication, self-care, self-direction, interpersonal skills, work tolerance, or work skills) in terms of an employment outcome;

(2) Whose vocational rehabilitation can be expected to require multiple vocational rehabilitation services over an extended period of time; and

(3) Who has one or more physical or mental disabilities resulting from amputation, arthritis, autism, blindness, burn injury, cancer, cerebral palsy, cystic fibrosis, deafness, head injury, heart disease, hemiplegia, hemophilia, intellectual disability, respiratory or pulmonary dysfunction, mental illness, multiple sclerosis, muscular dystrophy, musculo-skeletal disorders, neurological disorders (including stroke and epilepsy), paraplegia, quadriplegia and other spinal cord conditions, sickle-cell anemia, specific learning disabilities, end-stage renal disease, or another disability or combination of disabilities determined on the basis of an assessment for determining eligibility and vocational rehabilitation needs to cause comparable substantial functional limitation.

Informed choice means the provision of activities whereby individuals with disabilities served by projects under this part have the opportunity to be active, full partners in the rehabilitation process, making meaningful and informed choices as follows:

(1) During assessments of eligibility and vocational rehabilitation needs.

(2) In the selection of employment outcomes, services needed to achieve the outcomes, entities providing these services, and the methods used to secure these services.

(Authority: Sections 2(c) and 12(c) of the Act 29 U.S.C. 701(c) and 709(c))

Rehabilitation services means services, including vocational, medical, social, and psychological rehabilitation services and other services under the Rehabilitation Act, provided to individuals with disabilities in performing functions necessary in preparing for, secur-ing, retaining, or regaining an employment or independent living outcome.

(Authority: Section 12(c) of the Rehabilitation Act of 1973, as amended; 29 U.S.C. 709(c))

Substantial impediment to employment means that a physical or mental impairment (in light of attendant medical, psychological, vocational, educational, and other related factors) hinders an individual from preparing for, entering into, engaging in, or retaining employment consistent with the individual's abilities and capabilities.

(Authority: Section 7(20)(A) and 12(c) of the Act 29; U.S.C. 705(20)(A) and 709(c))

Supported employment is defined in 34 CFR 361.5(c)(53).

(Authority: Section 7(38) of the Rehabilitation Act of 1973, as amended; 29 U.S.C. 705(38))

Vocational Rehabilitation Services means services provided to an individual with a disability in preparing for, securing, retaining, or regaining an employment outcome that is consistent with the strengths, resources, priorities, concerns, abilities, capabilities, interests, and informed choice of the individual. Vocational Rehabilitation Services for an individual with a disability may include—

(1) An assessment for determining eligibility and vocational rehabilitation needs by qualified personnel, including, if appropriate, an assessment by personnel skilled in rehabilitation technology;

(2) Counseling and guidance, including information and support services to assist an individual in exercising informed choice;

(3) Referral and other services to secure needed services from other agencies;

(4) Job-related services, including job search and placement assistance, job retention services, follow-up services, and follow-along services;

(5) Vocational and other training services, including the provision of personal and vocational adjustment services, books, tools, and other training materials;

(6) Diagnosis and treatment of physical and mental impairments;

447

(7) Maintenance for additional costs incurred while the individual is receiving services;

(8) Transportation;

(9) On-the-job or other related personal assistance services;

(10) Interpreter and reader services;

(11) Rehabilitation teaching services, and orientation and mobility services;

(12) Occupational licenses, tools, equipment, and initial stocks and supplies;

(13) Technical assistance and other consultation services to conduct market analysis, develop business plans, and otherwise provide resources to eligible individuals who are pursuing self-employment or telecommuting or establishing a small business operation as an employment outcome;

(14) Rehabilitation technology, including telecommunications, sensory, and other technological aids and devices;

(15) Transition services for individuals with disabilities that facilitate the achievement of employment outcomes;

(16) Supported employment services;

(17) Services to the family of an individual with a disability necessary to assist the individual to achieve an employment outcome;

(18) Post-employment services necessary to assist an individual with a disability to retain, regain, or advance in employment; and

(19) Expansion of employment opportunities for individuals with disabilities, which includes, but is not limited to—

(i) Self-employment, business ownership, and entreprenuership;

(ii) Non-traditional jobs, professional employment, and work settings;

(iii) Collaborating with employers, Economic Development Councils, and others in creating new jobs and career advancement options in local job markets through the use of job restructuring and other methods; and

(iv) Other services as identified by the Secretary and published in the FEDERAL REGISTER.

(Authority: Section 7(40) of the Rehabilitation Act of 1973, as amended; 29 U.S.C. 705(40))

Youth or Young adults with disabilities means individuals with disabilities who are between the ages of 14 and 24 inclusive when entering the program.

(Authority: Section 7(42) of the Rehabilitation Act of 1973, as amended; 29 U.S.C. 705(42)

(Authority: Sections 7(40), 12(c), and 103(a) of the Rehabilitation Act of 1973, as amended; 29 U.S.C. 705(40), 709(c) and 723(a))

[81 FR 55607, Aug. 19, 2016, as amended at 82 FR 31913, July 11, 2017]

§ 373.5 Who is eligible to receive services and to benefit from activities conducted by eligible entities?

(a)(1) For projects that provide rehabilitation services or activities to expand and improve the provision of rehabilitation services and other services authorized under Titles I, III, and VI of the Act, individuals are eligible who meet the definition in paragraph (a) of an "individual with a disability" as stated in § 373.4.

(2) For projects that provide independent living services or activities, individuals are eligible who meet the definition in paragraph (b) of an "individual with a disability" as stated in § 373.4.

(3) For projects that provide other services or activities that further the purposes of the Act, individuals are eligible who meet the definition in paragraph (b) of an "individual with a disability" as stated in § 373.4.

(b) By publishing a notice in the FEDERAL REGISTER, the Secretary may identify individuals determined to be eligible under one or more of the provisions in paragraph (a) of this section.

(Authority: Sections 12(c), 103(a), and 303(b) of the Rehabilitation Act of 1973, as amended; 29 U.S.C. 709(c), 723(a), and 773(b))

§ 373.6 What types of projects may be funded?

The Secretary may fund the following types of projects under this program:

(a) Special projects of service delivery.

(b) Model demonstration.

(c) Technical assistance.

(d) Systems change.

(e) Special studies, research, or evaluations.

(f) Dissemination and utilization.

(Authority: Sections 12(c) and 303(b)(4) of the Rehabilitation Act of 1973, as amended; 29 U.S.C. 709(c) and 773(b)(4))

§373.7 What are the priorities and other factors and requirements for competitions?

(a) In announcing competitions for grants and contracts, the Secretary gives priority consideration to—

(1) Initiatives focused on improving transition from education, including postsecondary education, to employment, particularly in competitive integrated employment, for youth who are individuals with significant disabilities.

(2) Supported employment, including community-based supported employment programs to meet the needs of individuals with the most significant disabilities or to provide technical assistance to States and community organizations to improve and expand the provision of supported employment services.

(3) Increasing competitive integrated employment for individuals with significant disabilities.

(b) In announcing competitions for grants and contracts, the Secretary may also identify one or more of the following as priorities—

(1) Expansion of employment opportunities for individuals with disabilities, as authorized in paragraph(s) of the definition of "vocational rehabilitation services" as stated in §373.4.

(2) System change projects to promote meaningful access of individuals with disabilities to employment-related services under subtitle B of title I of the Workforce Innovation and Opportunity Act and under other Federal laws.

(3) Innovative methods of promoting achievement of high-quality employment outcomes.

(4) The demonstration of the effectiveness of early intervention activities in improving employment outcomes.

(5) Projects to find alternative methods of providing affordable transportation services to individuals with disabilities.

(6) Technical assistance to designated State units and their personnel in working with employers to identify competitive integrated employment opportunities and career exploration opportunities in order to facilitate the provision of vocational rehabilitation services and transition services for youth with disabilities and students with disabilities.

(7) Consultation, training and technical assistance to businesses that have hired or are interested in hiring individuals with disabilities.

(8) Technical assistance and training to designated State units and their personnel on establishment and maintenance of education and experience requirements, to ensure that the personnel have a 21st century understanding of the evolving labor force and the needs of individuals with disabilities.

(9) Technical assistance to State vocational rehabilitation agencies or State vocational rehabilitation units to improve management practices that will improve the provision of vocational rehabilitation services and increase competitive employment outcomes for individuals with disabilities.

(10) Other projects that will expand and improve the provision, extent, availability, scope, and quality of rehabilitation and other services under the Act or that further the purpose and policy of the Act as stated in sections 2(b) and (c) of the Act.

(c) In announcing competitions of grants and contract the Secretary may limit the priorities listed in paragraphs (a) and (b) of this section to address one or more of the following factors:

(1) Age ranges.

(2) Types of disabilities.

(3) Types of services.

(4) Models of service delivery.

(5) Stages of the vocational rehabilitation process;

(6) Unserved and underserved populations.

(7) Unserved and underserved geographical areas.

(8) Individuals with significant disabilities.

(9) Low-incidence disability populations.

(10) Individuals residing in federally designated Empowerment Zones and Enterprise Communities.

(d) The Secretary may require that an applicant certify that the project does not include building upon or expanding activities that have previously been conducted or funded, for that applicant or in that service area.

(e) The Secretary may require that the project widely disseminate the methods of vocational rehabilitation service delivery or model proven to be effective, so that they may be adapted, replicated, or purchased under fee-for-service arrangements by State vocational rehabilitation agencies and other disability organizations in the project's targeted service area or other locations.

(Authority: Sections 12(c), 101(a)(7)(B)(ii) and (11)(E), 103(b)(5), 108a, and 303(b)(5) of the Rehabilitation Act of 1973, as amended; 29 U.S.C. 709(c), 721(a)(7)(B)(ii) and (11)(E), 723(b)(5), 728a, and 773(b)(5))

Subpart B—How Does the Secretary Make a Grant?

§ 373.10   What selection criteria does the Secretary use?

The Secretary publishes in the FEDERAL REGISTER or includes in the application package the selection criteria for each competition under this program. To evaluate the applications for new grants under this program, the Secretary may use the following:

(a) Selection criteria established under 34 CFR 75.209.

(b) Selection criteria in 34 CFR 75.210.

(c) Any combination of selection criteria from paragraphs (a) and (b) of this section.

(Authority: Sections 12(c) and 103(a) of the Rehabilitation Act of 1973, as amended; 29 U.S.C. 709(c) and 723(a))

§ 373.11   What other factors does the Secretary consider when making a grant?

(a) The Secretary funds only those applications submitted in response to competitions announced in the FEDERAL REGISTER.

(b) The Secretary may consider the past performance of the applicant in carrying out activities under previously awarded grants.

(c) The Secretary awards bonus points if identified and published in the

FEDERAL REGISTER for specific competitions.

(Authority: Sections 12(c) and 103(a) of the Rehabilitation Act of 1973, as amended; 29 U.S.C. 709(c) and 723(a))

Subpart C—What Conditions Must Be Met By a Grantee?

§ 373.20   What are the matching requirements?

The Secretary may make grants to pay all or part of the cost of activities covered under this program. If the Secretary determines that the grantee is required to pay part of the costs, the amount of grantee participation is specified in the application notice, and the Secretary will not require grantee participation to be more than 10 percent of the total cost of the project.

(Authority: Sections 12(c) and 303(b)(1) of the Rehabilitation Act of 1973, as amended; 29 U.S.C. 709(c) and 773(b)(1))

§ 373.21   What are the reporting requirements under this part?

(a) In addition to the program and fiscal reporting requirements in 34 CFR 75.720 and 2 CFR 200.327 that are applicable to projects funded under this program, the Secretary may require that recipients of grants under this part submit information determined by the Secretary to be necessary to measure project outcomes and performance, including any data needed to comply with the Government Performance and Results Act.

(b) Specific reporting requirements for competitions will be identified by the Secretary and published in the FEDERAL REGISTER.

(Authority: Sections 12(c), 303(b)(2)(B), and 306 of the Rehabilitation Act of 1973, as amended; 29 U.S.C. 709(c), 773(b)(2)(B), and 776)

§ 373.22   What are the limitations on indirect costs?

(a) Indirect cost reimbursement for grants under this program is limited to the recipient's actual indirect costs, as determined by its negotiated indirect cost rate agreement, or 10 percent of the total direct cost base, whichever amount is less.

(b) Indirect costs in excess of the 10 percent limit may be used to satisfy matching or cost-sharing requirements.

(c) The 10 percent limit does not apply to federally recognized Indian tribal governments and their tribal representatives.

(Authority: Section 12(c) of the Rehabilitation Act of 1973, as amended; 29 U.S.C. 709(c))

§ 373.23 What additional requirements must be met?

(a) Each grantee must do the following:

(1) Ensure equal access and treatment for eligible project participants who are members of groups that have traditionally been underrepresented based on race, color, national origin, gender, age, or disabilities.

(2) Encourage applications for employment from persons who are members of groups that have traditionally been underrepresented based on race, color, national origin, gender, age, or disabilities.

(3) Advise individuals with disabilities who are applicants for or recipients of the services, or the applicants' representatives or the individuals' representatives, of the availability and purposes of the Client Assistance Program, including information on means of seeking assistance under that program.

(4) Provide, through a careful appraisal and study, an assessment and evaluation of the project that indicates the significance or worth of processes, methodologies, and practices implemented by the project.

(b) A grantee may not make a subgrant under this part. However, a grantee may contract for supplies, equipment, and other services, in accordance with 2 CFR part 200 (Uniform Administrative Requirements, Cost Principles, and Audit Requirements for Federal Awards) as adopted at 2 CFR part 3474.

(Authority: Sections 12(c) and 303(b)(2)(B) of the Rehabilitation Act of 1973, as amended; 29 U.S.C. 709(c) and 773(b)(2)(B))

§ 373.24 What are the special requirements pertaining to the protection, use, and release of personal information?

(a) All personal information about individuals served by any project under this part, including lists of names, addresses, photographs, and records of evaluation, must be confidential.

(b) The use of information and records concerning individuals must be limited only to purposes directly connected with the project, including project reporting and evaluation activities. This information may not be disclosed, directly or indirectly, other than in the administration of the project unless the consent of the agency providing the information and the individual to whom the information applies, or his or her representative, has been obtained in writing. The Secretary or other Federal officials responsible for enforcing legal requirements have access to this information without written consent being obtained. The final products of the project may not reveal any personal identifying information without written consent of the individual or his or her representative.

(Authority: Sections 12(c) and 303(b)(2)(B) of the Rehabilitation Act of 1973, as amended; 29 U.S.C. 709(c), and 773(b)(2)(B))

PARTS 376–377 [RESERVED]

PARTS 379–380 [RESERVED]

PART 381—PROTECTION AND ADVOCACY OF INDIVIDUAL RIGHTS

Subpart A—General

Subpart C—How Does the Secretary Make an Award?

Subpart D—What Conditions Must Be Met After an Award?

AUTHORITY: Section 509 of the Rehabilitation Act of 1973, as amended; 29 U.S.C. 794e, unless otherwise noted.

SOURCE: 81 FR 55611, Aug. 19, 2016, unless otherwise noted.

Subpart A—General

§ 381.1 What is the Protection and Advocacy of Individual Rights program?

This program is designed to support a system in each State to protect the legal and human rights of eligible individuals with disabilities.

(Authority: Section 509(a) of the Rehabilitation Act of 1973, as amended; 29 U.S.C. 794e(a))

§ 381.2 Who is eligible for an award?

(a)(1) A protection and advocacy system that is established under part C of title I of the Developmental Disabilities Assistance and Bill of Rights Act of 2000 (DD Act), 42 U.S.C. 15041 *et seq.*, and that meets the requirements of § 381.10 is eligible to apply for a grant award under this part.

(2)(i) For any fiscal year in which the appropriation to carry out the activities of this part equals or exceeds $10,500,000, the eligible system serving the American Indian Consortium is eligible to apply for a grant award under this part.

(ii) For purposes of this part, an eligible system is defined at § 381.5(c).

(iii) For purposes of this part, the American Indian Consortium means a consortium established as described in section 102 of the DD Act (42 U.S.C. 15002).

(b) In any fiscal year in which the amount appropriated to carry out this part is less than $5,500,000, a protection and advocacy system from any State or from Guam, American Samoa, the United States Virgin Islands, or the Commonwealth of the Northern Mariana Islands, may apply for a grant under the Protection and Advocacy of Individual Rights (PAIR) program to plan for, develop outreach strategies for, and carry out a protection and advocacy program authorized under this part.

(c) In any fiscal year in which the amount appropriated to carry out this part is equal to or greater than $5,500,000, an eligible system from any State and from any of the jurisdictions named in paragraph (b) of this section may apply to receive the amount allotted pursuant to section 509(c)-(e) of the Act.

(Authority: Section 509(b), (c), and (m) of the Rehabilitation Act of 1973, as amended; 29 U.S.C. 794e(b), (c), and (m))

§ 381.3 What activities may the Secretary fund?

(a) Funds made available under this part must be used for the following activities:

(1) Establishing a system to protect, and advocate for, the rights of individuals with disabilities.

(2) Pursuing legal, administrative, and other appropriate remedies or approaches to ensure the protection of, and advocacy for, the rights of eligible individuals with disabilities within the State or the American Indian Consortium.

(3) Providing information on and making referrals to programs and services addressing the needs of individuals with disabilities in the State or American Indian Consortium, including individuals with disabilities who are exiting from school programs.

(4) Coordinating the protection and advocacy program provided through an eligible system with the advocacy programs under—

(i) Section 112 of the Act (the Client Assistance Program (CAP));

(ii) The Older Americans Act of 1965 (the State long-term care ombudsman program) (42 U.S.C. 3001 *et seq.*);

(iii) Part C of the DD Act; and

(iv) The Protection and Advocacy for Individuals with Mental Illness Act of 2000 (PAIMI) (42 U.S.C. 10801–10807).

(5) Developing a statement of objectives and priorities on an annual basis and a plan for achieving these objectives and priorities.

(6) Providing to the public, including individuals with disabilities and, as appropriate, their representatives, an opportunity to comment on the objectives and priorities described in §381.10(a)(6).

(7) Establishing a grievance procedure for clients or prospective clients of the eligible system to ensure that individuals with disabilities are afforded equal access to the services of the eligible system.

(b) Funds made available under this part also may be used to carry out any other activities consistent with the purpose of this part and the activities listed in paragraph (a) of this section.

(Authority: Sections 12(c) and 509(f) of the Rehabilitation Act of 1973, as amended; 29 U.S.C. 709(c) and 794e(f)).

§381.4 What regulations apply?

The following regulations apply to the PAIR program:

(a) The Education Department General Administrative Regulations (EDGAR) as follows:

(1) 34 CFR part 75 (Direct Grant Programs) for purposes of an award made under §§381.20 or 381.22(a)(1).

(2) 34 CFR part 76 (State-Administered Programs), if the appropriation for the PAIR program is equal to or greater than $5,500,000 and the eligible system is a State or local government agency, except for—

(i) Section 76.103;
(ii) Sections 76.125 through 76.137;
(iii) Sections 76.300 through 76.401;
(iv) Section 76.704;
(v) Section 76.734; and
(vi) Section 76.740.

(3) 34 CFR part 77 (Definitions that Apply to Department Regulations).

(4) 34 CFR part 79 (Intergovernmental Review of Department of Education Programs and Activities).

(5) 34 CFR part 81 (General Education Provisions Act—Enforcement).

(6) 34 CFR part 82 (New Restrictions on Lobbying).

(b) 2 CFR part 180 (OMB Guidelines to Agencies on Debarment and Suspension (Nonprocurement)), as adopted at 2 CFR part 3485.

(c) 2 CFR part 200 (Uniform Administrative Requirements, Cost Principles, and Audit Requirements for Federal Awards), as adopted at 2 CFR part 3474.

(d) The regulations in this part 381.

(Authority: Sections 12(c) and 509 of the Rehabilitation Act of 1973, as amended; 29 U.S.C. 709(c) and 794e)

§381.5 What definitions apply?

(a) Definitions in EDGAR at 34 CFR part 77.

(b) Definitions in 2 CFR part 200 subpart A.

(c) *Other definitions.* The following definitions also apply to this part:

Act means the Rehabilitation Act of 1973, as amended.

Advocacy means pleading an individual's cause or speaking or writing in support of an individual. Advocacy may be formal, as in the case of a lawyer representing an individual in a court of law or in formal administrative proceedings before government agencies (whether tribal, State, local, or Federal). Advocacy also may be informal, as in the case of a lawyer or non-lawyer representing an individual in negotiations, mediation, or informal administrative proceedings before government agencies (whether tribal, State, local, or Federal), or as in the case of a lawyer or non-lawyer representing an individual's cause before private entities or organizations, or government agencies (whether tribal, State, local, or Federal). Advocacy may be on behalf of—

(i) A single individual, in which case it is individual advocacy;

(ii) More than one individual or a group or class of individuals, in which case it is systems (or systemic) advocacy; or

(iii) Oneself, in which case it is self advocacy.

Eligible individual with a disability means an individual who—

(i) Needs protection and advocacy services that are beyond the scope of services authorized to be provided by the CAP under section 112 of the Act; and

(ii) Is ineligible for—

453

(A) Protection and advocacy programs under part C of the DD Act; and

(B) Protection and advocacy programs under the PAIMI.

Eligible system means a protection and advocacy system that is established under part C of the DD Act and that meets the requirements of § 381.10.

Mediation means the act or process of using an independent third party to act as a mediator, intermediary, or conciliator to settle differences or disputes between persons or parties. The third party who acts as a mediator, intermediary, or conciliator must not be any entity or individual who is connected in any way with the eligible system or the agency, entity, or individual with whom the individual with a disability has a dispute. Mediation may involve the use of professional mediators or any other independent third party mutually agreed to by the parties to the dispute.

State means, in addition to each of the several States of the United States, the District of Columbia, the Commonwealth of Puerto Rico, the United States Virgin Islands, Guam, American Samoa, and the Commonwealth of the Northern Mariana Islands, except for purposes of sections 509(c)(3)(B) and (c)(4) of the Act, in which case State does not mean or include Guam, American Samoa, the United States Virgin Islands, and the Commonwealth of the Northern Mariana Islands.

(Authority: Sections 7(34), 12(c), and 509 of the Rehabilitation Act of 1973, as amended; 29 U.S.C. 705(34), 709(c) and 794e)

Subpart B—How Does One Apply for an Award?

§ 381.10 What are the application requirements?

(a) Regardless of the amount of funds appropriated for the PAIR program in a fiscal year, an eligible system shall submit to the Secretary an application for assistance under this part at the time and in the form and manner determined by the Secretary that contains all information that the Secretary determines necessary, including assurances that the eligible system will—

(1) Have in effect a system to protect, and advocate for, the rights of eligible individuals with disabilities;

(2) Have the same general authorities, including the authority to access records and program income, as in part C of title I of the DD Act;

(3) Have the authority to pursue legal, administrative, and other appropriate remedies or approaches to ensure the protection of, and advocacy for, the rights of eligible individuals with disabilities within the State and the American Indian Consortium;

(4) Provide information on and make referrals to programs and services addressing the needs of individuals with disabilities in the State and the American Indian Consortium, including individuals with disabilities who are exiting from school programs;

(5) Develop a statement of objectives and priorities on an annual basis and a plan for achieving these objectives and priorities;

(6) Provide to the public, including individuals with disabilities and, as appropriate, their representatives, an opportunity to comment on the objectives and priorities established by, and activities of, the eligible system including—

(i) The objectives and priorities for the activities of the eligible system for each year and the rationale for the establishment of those objectives and priorities; and

(ii) The coordination of the PAIR program provided through eligible systems with the advocacy programs under—

(A) Section 112 of the Act (CAP);

(B) The Older Americans Act of 1965 (the State long-term care ombudsman program);

(C) Part C of the DD Act; and

(D) The PAIMI;

(7) Establish a grievance procedure for clients or prospective clients of the eligible system to ensure that individuals with disabilities are afforded equal access to the services of the eligible system;

(8) Use funds made available under this part to supplement and not supplant the non-Federal funds that would otherwise be made available for the purpose for which Federal funds are provided; and

(9) Implement procedures designed to ensure that, to the maximum extent possible, mediation (and other alternative dispute resolution) procedures, which include good faith negotiation, are used before resorting to formal administrative or legal remedies.

(b) To receive direct payment of funds under this part, an eligible system must provide to the Secretary, as part of its application for assistance, an assurance that direct payment is not prohibited by or inconsistent with tribal or State law, regulation, or policy.

(Approved by the Office of Management and Budget under control number 1820–0018)

(Authority: Sections 12(c) and 509(f) and (g)(1) of the Rehabilitation Act of 1973, as amended; 29 U.S.C. 709(c) and 794e(f) and (g)(1))

Subpart C—How Does the Secretary Make an Award?

§381.20 How does the Secretary evaluate an application?

In any fiscal year in which the amount appropriated for the PAIR program is less than $5,500,000, the Secretary evaluates applications under the procedures in 34 CFR part 75.

(Authority: Sections 12(c) and 509(b) and (f) of the Rehabilitation Act of 1973, as amended; 29 U.S.C. 709(c) and 794e(b) and (f))

§381.22 How does the Secretary allocate funds under this program?

(a) In any fiscal year in which the amount appropriated for this program is equal to or greater than $5,500,000—

(1) The Secretary sets aside not less than 1.8 percent but not more than 2.2 percent of the amount appropriated to provide a grant, contract, or cooperative agreement for training and technical assistance to eligible systems carrying out activities under this part.

(2) After the reservation required by paragraph (a)(1) of this section, the Secretary makes allotments from the remainder of the amount appropriated in accordance with section 509(c)(2)–(d) of the Act.

(b) Notwithstanding any other provision of law, in any fiscal year in which the amount appropriated for this program is equal to or greater than

$5,500,000, the Secretary pays directly to an eligible system that submits an application that meets the requirements of §381.10 the amount of the allotment to the State pursuant to section 509 of the Act, unless the State provides otherwise.

(c) For any fiscal year in which the amount appropriated to carry out this program equals or exceeds $10,500,000, the Secretary shall reserve a portion, and use the portion to make a grant for the eligible system serving the American Indian Consortium. The Secretary shall make the grant in an amount of not less than $50,000 for the fiscal year.

(d) Reallotment:

(1) For any fiscal year in which the amount appropriated to carry out this program equals or exceeds $5,500,000 and if the Secretary determines that any amount of an allotment to an eligible system within a State will not be expended by such system in carrying out the provisions of this part, the Secretary shall make such amount available to one or more of the eligible systems that the Secretary determines will be able to use additional amounts during such year for carrying out this part.

(2) Any reallotment amount made available to an eligible system for any fiscal year shall, for the purposes of this section, be regarded as an increase in the eligible system's allotment under this part for that fiscal year.

(Authority: Sections 12(c) and 509(c)–(e) of the Rehabilitation Act of 1973, as amended; 29 U.S.C. 709(c) and 794e(c)–(e))

Subpart D—What Conditions Must Be Met After an Award?

§381.30 How are services to be administered?

(a) Each eligible system shall carry out the protection and advocacy program authorized under this part.

(b) An eligible system may not award a grant or make a subaward to another entity to carry out, in whole or in part, the protection and advocacy program authorized under this part.

(c) An eligible system may contract with another agency, entity, or individual to carry out the PAIR program in whole or in part, but only if the agency, entity, or individual with whom the eligible system has contracted—

(1) Does not provide services under the Act or does not provide treatment, services, or habilitation to persons with disabilities; and

(2) Is independent of, and not connected financially or through a board of directors to, an entity or individual that provides services under the Act or that provides treatment, services, or habilitation to persons with disabilities.

(d) For purposes of paragraph (c) of this section, "services under the Act" and "treatment, services, or habilitation" does not include client assistance services under CAP, protection and advocacy services authorized under the protection and advocacy programs under part C of the DD Act and the PAIMI, or any other protection and advocacy services.

(Authority: Section 12(c) of the Rehabilitation Act of 1973, as amended; 29 U.S.C. 709(c))

§ 381.31 What are the requirements pertaining to the protection, use, and release of personal information?

(a) All personal information about individuals served by any eligible system under this part, including lists of names, addresses, photographs, and records of evaluation, must be held confidential.

(b) The eligible system's use of information and records concerning individuals must be limited only to purposes directly connected with the protection and advocacy program, including program evaluation activities. Except as provided in paragraph (c) of this section, an eligible system may not disclose personal information about an individual, directly or indirectly, other than in the administration of the protection and advocacy program, unless the consent of the individual to whom the information applies, or his or her guardian, parent, or other authorized representative or advocate (including the individual's advocate from the eligible system), has been obtained in writing. An eligible system may not produce any report, evaluation, or study that reveals any personally identifying information without the written consent of the individual or his or her representative.

(c) Except as limited in paragraph (d) of this section, the Secretary or other Federal or State officials responsible for enforcing legal requirements must be given complete access to all—

(1) Records of the eligible system receiving funds under this program; and

(2) All individual case records of clients served under this part without the consent of the client.

(d)(1) The privilege of a person or eligible system not to produce documents or provide information pursuant to paragraph (c) of this section is governed by the principles of common law as interpreted by the courts of the United States, except that, for purposes of any periodic audit, report, or evaluation of the performance of the eligible system established or assisted under this part, the Secretary does not require the eligible system to disclose the identity of, or any other personally identifiable information related to, any individual requesting assistance under the PAIR program.

(2) However, notwithstanding paragraph (d)(1) of this section, if an audit, monitoring review, State plan assurance review, evaluation, or other investigation has already produced independent and reliable evidence that there is probable cause to believe that the eligible system has violated its legislative mandate or misused Federal funds, the eligible system shall disclose, if the Secretary so requests, the identity of, or any other personally identifiable information (i.e., name, address, telephone number, social security number, or other official code or number by which an individual may be readily identified) related to, any individual requesting assistance under the PAIR program, in accordance with the principles of common law as interpreted by the courts of the United States.

(Authority: Sections 12(c) and 509(h) of the Rehabilitation Act of 1973, as amended; 29 U.S.C. 709(c) and 794e(h))

§ 381.32 What are the reporting requirements under this part?

Each eligible system shall provide to the Secretary, no later than 90 days after the end of each fiscal year, an annual report that includes information on the following:

(a) The types of services and activities undertaken by the eligible system and how these services and activities addressed the objectives and priorities developed pursuant to § 381.10(a)(6).

(b) The total number of individuals, by race, color, national origin, gender, age, and disabling condition, who requested services from the eligible system and the total number of individuals, by race, color, national origin, gender, age, and disabling condition, who were served by the eligible system.

(c) The types of disabilities represented by individuals served by the eligible system.

(d) The types of issues being addressed on behalf of individuals served by the eligible system.

(e) Any other information that the Secretary may require.

(Approved by the Office of Management and Budget under control number 1820–0018)

(Authority: Sections 12(c), 13, and 509(k) of the Rehabilitation Act of 1973, as amended; 29 U.S.C. 709(c), 710, and 794e(k))

§ 381.33 What are the requirements related to the use of funds provided under this part?

(a) Funds made available under this part must be used to supplement and not supplant the non-Federal funds that would otherwise be made available for the purpose for which Federal funds are provided under this part.

(b) In any State in which an eligible system is located within a State agency, that State or State agency may not use more than five percent of any allotment for the costs of administration of the eligible system supported under this part. For purposes of this paragraph, "costs of administration" include, but are not limited to, administrative salaries (including salaries for clerical and support staff), supplies, depreciation, the cost of operating and maintaining facilities, equipment, and grounds (e.g., rental of office space or equipment, telephone, postage, maintenance agreements), and other similar types of costs that may be incurred by the State or State agency to administer the eligible system.

(c) Funds paid to an eligible system within a State for a fiscal year, including reallotment funds, to carry out this program that are not expended or obligated prior to the end of that fiscal year remain available to the eligible system within a State for obligation during the succeeding fiscal year in accordance with sections 19 and 509(g) of the Act.

(d) For determining when an eligible system makes an obligation for various kinds of property or services, 34 CFR 75.707 and 76.707, as appropriate, apply to this program. If the appropriation for the PAIR program is less than $5,500,000, § 75.707 applies. If the appropriation for the PAIR program is equal to or greater than $5,500,000, § 76.707 applies. An eligible system is considered a State for purposes of § 76.707.

(e) Program income:

(1) Consistent with 2 CFR 200.80 and for purposes of this part, *program income* means gross income earned by the designated agency that is directly generated by an activity supported under this part.

(2)(i) The designated agency must use program income to supplement Federal funds that support program activities that are subject to this part. See, for example 2 CFR 200.307(e)(2).

(ii) Notwithstanding 2 CFR 200.305(a) and consistent with 2 CFR 200.305(b)(5), and to the extent that program income funds are available, all designated agencies, regardless of whether they are a State agency, must disburse those funds (including repayments to a revolving fund), rebates, refunds, contract settlements, audit recoveries, and interest earned on such funds before requesting additional funds from the Department.

(3) Any program income received during a fiscal year that is not obligated or expended prior to the beginning of the succeeding fiscal year in which the program income was received, remain available for obligation and expenditure by the grantee during that succeeding fiscal year.

(Authority: Sections 12(c), 19, and 509(f)(7), (g), and (i) of the Rehabilitation Act of 1973, as amended; 29 U.S.C. 709(c), 716, and 794e(f)(7), (g), and (i); and 20 U.S.C. 3474)

PART 385—REHABILITATION TRAINING

AUTHORITY: Sections 12(c), 301, and 302 of the Rehabilitation Act of 1973, as amended; 29 U.S.C. 709(c), 771, and 772; Pub. L. 111–256, 124 Stat. 2643; unless otherwise noted.

SOURCE: 81 FR 55614, Aug. 19, 2016, unless otherwise noted.

Subpart A—General

§ 385.1 What is the Rehabilitation Training program?

(a) *Purpose.* The Rehabilitation Training program is designed to—

(1) Ensure that skilled personnel are available to provide rehabilitation services to individuals with disabilities through vocational, medical, social, and psychological rehabilitation programs (including supported employment programs), through economic and business development programs, through independent living services programs, and through client assistance programs;

(2) Maintain and upgrade basic skills and knowledge of personnel employed, including personnel specifically trained to deliver rehabilitation services, including supported employment services and customized employment services, to individuals with the most significant disabilities, and personnel specifically trained to deliver services to individuals with disabilities whose employment outcome is self-employment, business ownership, or telecommuting, to provide state-of-the-art service delivery and rehabilitation technology services; and

(3) Provide training and information to individuals with disabilities, the parents, families, guardians, advocates, and authorized representatives of the individuals, and other appropriate parties to develop the skills necessary for individuals with disabilities to access the rehabilitation system and to become active decision makers in the vocational rehabilitation process.

(b) The Secretary awards grants and contracts on a competitive basis to pay part of the costs of projects for training, traineeships or scholarships, and related activities, including the provision of technical assistance, to assist in increasing the numbers of qualified personnel trained in providing vocational rehabilitation services and other services provided under the Act, to individuals with disabilities. Financial assistance is provided through multiple training programs, including:

(1) Rehabilitation Long-Term Training (34 CFR part 386).

(2) Innovative Rehabilitation Training (34 CFR part 387).

(3) Rehabilitation Short-Term Training (34 CFR part 390).

(4) Training of Interpreters for Individuals Who Are Deaf and Hard of Hearing and Individuals Who Are Deaf-Blind (34 CFR part 396).

(Authority: Sections 12(c), 301 and 302 of the Rehabilitation Act of 1973, as amended; 29 U.S.C. 709(c), 771 and 772)

§ 385.2 Who is eligible for assistance under these programs?

States and public or private non-profit agencies and organizations, including Indian tribes and institutions of higher education, are eligible for assistance under the Rehabilitation Training program.

(Authority: Sections 7(19), 301, and 302 of the Rehabilitation Act of 1973, as amended; 29 U.S.C. 705(19), 771 and 772)

§ 385.3 What regulations apply to these programs?

The following regulations apply to the Rehabilitation Training program:

(a) The Education Department General Administrative Regulations (EDGAR) as follows:

(1) 34 CFR part 75 (Direct Grant Programs).

(2) 34 CFR part 77 (Definitions That Apply to Department Regulations).

(3) 34 CFR part 79 (Intergovernmental Review of Department of Education Programs and Activities).

(4) 34 CFR part 81 (General Education Provisions Act—Enforcement).

(5) 34 CFR part 82 (New Restrictions on Lobbying).

(6) 34 CFR part 84 (Governmentwide Requirements for Drug-Free Workplace (Financial Assistance).

(7) 34 CFR part 86 (Drug-Free Schools and Campuses).

(8) 34 CFR part 97 (Protection of Human Subjects).

(9) 34 CFR part 98 (Student Rights in Research, Experimental Programs, and Testing.

(10) 34 CFR part 99 (Family Educational Rights and Privacy).

(b) The regulations in this part 385.

(c) [Reserved]

(d)(1) 2 CFR part 180 (OMB Guidelines to Agencies on Debarment and Suspension (Nonprocurement)), as adopted at 2 CFR part 3485; and

(2) 2 CFR part 200 (Uniform Administrative Requirements, Cost Principles, and Audit Requirements for Federal Awards) as adopted at 2 CFR part 3474.

(Authority: Sections 12(c) and 302 of the Rehabilitation Act of 1973, as amended; 29 U.S.C. 711(c) and 772)

§ 385.4 What definitions apply to these programs?

(a) The following definitions in 34 CFR part 77 apply to the programs under the Rehabilitation Training Program—

Applicant
Application
Award
Budget Period
Department
EDGAR
Grantee
Nonprofit
Private
Project
Project Period
Public
Secretary

(Authority: Section 12(c) of the Rehabilitation Act of 1973, as amended; 29 U.S.C. 709(c))

(b) The following definitions also apply to programs under the Rehabilitation Training program:

Act means the Rehabilitation Act of 1973, as amended (29 U.S.C. 701 *et seq.*).

Assistive technology means technology designed to be utilized in an assistive technology device or assistive technology service.

Assistive technology device means any item, piece of equipment, or product system, whether acquired commercially off the shelf, modified, or customized, that is used to increase, maintain, or improve functional capabilities of individuals with disabilities.

Assistive technology service means any service that directly assists an individual with a disability in the selection, acquisition, or use of an assistive technology device. The term includes—

(i) The evaluation of the needs of an individual with a disability, including a functional evaluation of the individual in the individual's customary environment;

(ii) Purchasing, leasing, or otherwise providing for the acquisition of assistive technology devices by individuals with disabilities;

(iii) Selecting, designing, fitting, customizing, adapting, applying, maintaining, repairing, or replacing of assistive technology devices;

(iv) Coordinating and using other therapies, interventions, or services with assistive technology devices, such as those associated with existing education and rehabilitation plans and programs;

(v) Training or technical assistance for an individual with disabilities, or, if appropriate, the family of an individual with disabilities;

(vi) Training or technical assistance for professionals (including individuals providing education and rehabilitation services), employers, or other individuals who provide services to, employ, or are otherwise substantially involved in the major life functions of individuals with disabilities; and

(vii) A service consisting of expanding the availability of access to technology, including electronic and information technology, to individuals with disabilities.

Community rehabilitation program means a program that provides directly or facilitates the provision of vocational rehabilitation services to individuals with disabilities, and that provides, singly or in combination, for an individual with a disability to enable the individual to maximize opportunities for employment, including career advancement—

(i) Medical, psychiatric, psychological, social, and vocational services that are provided under one management;

(ii) Testing, fitting, or training in the use of prosthetic and orthotic devices;

(iii) Recreational therapy;

(iv) Physical and occupational therapy;

(v) Speech, language, and hearing therapy;

(vi) Psychiatric, psychological, and social services, including positive behavior management;

(vii) Assessment for determining eligibility and vocational rehabilitation needs;

(viii) Rehabilitation technology;

(ix) Job development, placement, and retention services;

(x) Evaluation or control of specific disabilities;

(xi) Orientation and mobility services for individuals who are blind;

(xii) Extended employment;

(xiii) Psychosocial rehabilitation services;

(xiv) Supported employment services and extended services;

(xv) Services to family members when necessary to the vocational rehabilitation of the individual;

(xvi) Personal assistance services; or

(xvii) Services similar to the services described in paragraphs (i) through (xvi) of this definition.

Designated State agency means an agency designated under section 7(8) and 101(a)(2)(A) of the Act.

Designated State unit means

(i) Any State agency unit required under section 7(8) and 101(a)(2)(B) of the Act, or

(ii) In cases in which no State agency unit is required, the State agency described in section 101(a)(2)(B)(ii) of the Act.

Independent living core services means—

(i) Information and referral services;

(ii) Independent living skills training;

(iii) Peer counseling, including cross-disability peer counseling; and

(iv) Individual and systems advocacy.

Independent living services includes—

(i) Independent living core services; and

(ii)(A) Counseling services, including psychological, psychotherapeutic, and related services;

(B) Services related to securing housing or shelter, including services related to community group living, and supportive of the purposes of this Act and of the titles of this Act, and adaptive housing services (including appropriate accommodations to and modifications of any space used to serve, or occupied by, individuals with disabilities);

(C) Rehabilitation technology;

(D) Mobility training;

(E) Services and training for individuals with cognitive and sensory disabilities, including life skills training, and interpreter and reader services;

(F) Personal assistance services, including attendant care and the training of personnel providing these services;

(G) Surveys, directories, and other activities to identify appropriate housing, recreation opportunities, and accessible transportation, and other support services;

(H) Consumer information programs on rehabilitation and independent living services available under this Act, especially for minorities and other individuals with disabilities who have traditionally been unserved or underserved by programs under this Act;

(I) Education and training necessary for living in the community and participating in community activities;

(J) Supported living;

(K) Transportation, including referral and assistance for transportation;

(L) Physical rehabilitation;

(M) Therapeutic treatment;

(N) Provision of needed prostheses and other appliances and devices;

(O) Individual and group social and recreational services;

(P) Training to develop skills specifically designed for youths who are individuals with disabilities to promote self-awareness and esteem, develop advocacy and self-empowerment skills, and explore career options;

(Q) Services for children;

(R) Services under other Federal, State, or local programs designed to provide resources, training, counseling, or other assistance of substantial benefit in enhancing the independence, productivity, and quality of life of individuals with disabilities;

(S) Appropriate preventive services to decrease the need of individuals assisted under this Act for similar services in the future;

(T) Community awareness programs to enhance the understanding and integration of individuals with disabilities; and

(U) Such other services as may be necessary and not inconsistent with the provisions of this Act.

Individual with a disability means any individual who—

(i) Has a physical or mental impairment, which for that individual constitutes or results in a substantial impediment to employment;

(ii) Can benefit in terms of an employment outcome from vocational rehabilitation services provided pursuant to title I, III, or VI of the Rehabilitation Act of 1973, as amended; and

(iii) Has a disability as defined in section 7(20)(B) of the Act.

Individual with a significant disability means an individual with a disability—

(i) Who has a severe physical or mental impairment that seriously limits one or more functional capacities (such as mobility, communication, self-care, self-direction, interpersonal skills, work tolerance, or work skills) in terms of an employment outcome;

(ii) Whose vocational rehabilitation can be expected to require multiple vocational rehabilitation services over an extended period of time; and

(iii) Who has one or more physical or mental disabilities resulting from amputation, arthritis, autism, blindness, burn injury, cancer, cerebral palsy, cystic fibrosis, deafness, head injury, heart disease, hemiplegia, hemophilia, intellectual disability, respiratory or pulmonary dysfunction, mental illness, multiple sclerosis, muscular dystrophy, musculo-skeletal disorders, neurological disorders (including stroke and epilepsy), paraplegia, quadriplegia and other spinal cord conditions, sickle-cell anemia, specific learning disabilities, end-stage renal disease, or another disability or combination of disabilities determined on the basis of an assessment for determining eligibility and vocational rehabilitation needs.

Institution of higher education has the meaning given the term in section 101(a) of the Higher Education Act (20 U.S.C. 1001(a)).

Personal assistance services means a range of services provided by one or more persons designed to assist an individual with a disability to perform daily living activities on or off the job that the individual would typically perform if the individual did not have a disability. The services shall be designed to increase the individual's control in life and ability to perform everyday activities on or off the job.

Qualified personnel. (i) For designated State agencies or designated State units, means personnel who have met standards that are consistent with existing national or State approved or recognized certification, licensing, registration, or other comparable requirements that apply to the area in which

461

such personnel are providing vocational rehabilitation services.

(ii) For other than designated State agencies or designated State units, means personnel who have met existing State certification or licensure requirements, or, in the absence of State requirements, have met professionally accepted requirements established by national certification boards.

Rehabilitation services means services, including vocational, medical, social, and psychological rehabilitation services and other services under the Rehabilitation Act, provided to individuals with disabilities in performing functions necessary in preparing for, securing, retaining, or regaining an employment or independent living outcome.

Rehabilitation technology means the systematic application of technologies, engineering methodologies, or scientific principles to meet the needs of and address the barriers confronted by individuals with disabilities in areas that include education, rehabilitation, employment, transportation, independent living, and recreation. The term includes rehabilitation engineering, assistive technology devices, and assistive technology services.

State includes, in addition to each of the several States of the United States, the District of Columbia, the Commonwealth of Puerto Rico, the United States Virgin Islands, Guam, American Samoa, and the Commonwealth of the Northern Mariana Islands.

Stipend means financial assistance on behalf of individuals in support of their training, as opposed to salary payment for services provided within the project.

Supported employment means competitive integrated employment, including customized employment, or employment in an integrated work setting in which individuals are working on a short-term basis toward competitive integrated employment, that is individualized and customized consistent with the strengths, abilities, interests, and informed choice of the individuals involved, for individuals with the most severe disabilities—

(i)(A) For whom competitive integrated employment has not traditionally occurred; or

(B) For whom competitive employment has been interrupted or intermittent as a result of a severe disability; and

(ii) Who, because of the nature and severity of their disability, need intensive supported employment services from the designated State unit and extended services after transition in order to perform the work involved.

Supported employment services means ongoing support services, including customized employment, and other appropriate services needed to support and maintain an individual with most severe disability in supported employment, that are—

(i) Provided singly or in combination and are organized and made available in such a way as to assist an eligible individual in entering or maintaining integrated, competitive employment;

(ii) Based on a determination of the needs of an eligible individual, as specified in an individualized written rehabilitation program; and

(iii) Provided by the designated State unit for a period of time not more than 24 months, unless under special circumstances the eligible individual and the rehabilitation counselor or coordinator jointly agree to extend the time in order to achieve the rehabilitation objectives identified in the individualized plan for employment.

Vocational rehabilitation services means services provided to an individual with a disability in preparing for, securing, retaining, or regaining an employment outcome that is consistent with the strengths, resources, priorities, concerns, abilities, capabilities, interests, and informed choice of the individual, and services provided for the benefit of groups of individuals with disabilities. Vocational Rehabilitation Services for an individual with a disability may include—

(i) An assessment for determining eligibility and vocational rehabilitation needs by qualified personnel, including, if appropriate, an assessment by personnel skilled in rehabilitation technology;

(ii) Counseling and guidance, including information and support services to assist an individual in exercising informed choice;

(iii) Referral and other services to secure needed services from other agencies;

(iv) Job-related services, including job search and placement assistance, job retention services, follow-up services, and follow-along services;

(v) Vocational and other training services, including the provision of personal and vocational adjustment services, books, tools, and other training materials;

(vi) Diagnosis and treatment of physical and mental impairments;

(vii) Maintenance for additional costs incurred while the individual is receiving services;

(viii) Transportation;

(ix) On-the-job or other related personal assistance services;

(x) Interpreter and reader services;

(xi) Rehabilitation teaching services, and orientation and mobility services;

(xii) Occupational licenses, tools, equipment, and initial stocks and supplies;

(xiii) Technical assistance and other consultation services to conduct market analysis, develop business plans, and otherwise provide resources to eligible individuals who are pursuing self-employment or telecommuting or establishing a small business operation as an employment outcome;

(xiv) Rehabilitation technology, including telecommunications, sensory, and other technological aids and devices;

(xv) Transition services for individuals with disabilities that facilitate the achievement of employment outcomes;

(xvi) Supported employment services;

(xvii) Services to the family of an individual with a disability necessary to assist the individual to achieve an employment outcome;

(xviii) Post-employment services necessary to assist an individual with a disability to retain, regain, or advance in employment; and

(xix) Expansion of employment opportunities for individuals with disabilities, which includes, but is not limited to—

(A) Self-employment, business ownership, and entrepreneurship;

(B) Non-traditional jobs, professional employment, and work settings;

(C) Collaborating with employers, Economic Development Councils, and others in creating new jobs and career advancement options in local job markets through the use of job restructuring and other methods; and

(D) Other services as identified by the Secretary and published in the FEDERAL REGISTER.

[81 FR 55614, Aug. 19, 2016, as amended at 82 FR 31913, July 11, 2017]

Subpart B [Reserved]

Subpart C—How Does One Apply for a Grant?

§ 385.20 What are the application procedures for these programs?

The Secretary gives the designated State agency an opportunity to review and comment on applications submitted from within the State that it serves. The procedures to be followed by the applicant and the State are in 34 CFR 75.155 through 75.159.

(Authority: Sections 12(c) and 302 of the Rehabilitation Act of 1973, as amended; 29 U.S.C. 709(c) and 772)

Subpart D—How Does the Secretary Make a Grant?

§ 385.30 [Reserved]

§ 385.31 How does the Secretary evaluate an application?

(a) The Secretary evaluates applications under the procedures in 34 CFR part 75.

(b) The Secretary evaluates each application using selection criteria identified in parts 386, 387, and 390, as appropriate.

(c) In addition to the selection criteria described in paragraph (b) of this section, the Secretary evaluates each application using—

(1) Selection criteria in 34 CFR 75.210;

(2) Selection criteria established under 34 CFR 75.209; or

(3) A combination of selection criteria established under 34 CFR 75.209 and selection criteria in 34 CFR 75.210.

(Authority: Sections 12(c) and 302 of the Rehabilitation Act of 1973, as amended; 29 U.S.C. 709(c) and 772)

§ 385.33 What other factors does the Secretary consider in reviewing an application?

In addition to the selection criteria listed in § 75.210 and parts 386, 387, and 390, the Secretary, in making awards under this program, considers such factors as—

(a) The geographical distribution of projects in each Rehabilitation Training Program category throughout the country; and

(b) The past performance of the applicant in carrying out similar training activities under previously awarded grants, as indicated by such factors as compliance with grant conditions, soundness of programmatic and financial management practices and attainment of established project objectives.

(Authority: Sections 12(c) and 302(b) of the Rehabilitation Act of 1973, as amended; 29 U.S.C. 709(c) and 772(b))

Subpart E—What Conditions Must Be Met by a Grantee?

§ 385.40 What are the requirements pertaining to the membership of a project advisory committee?

If a project establishes an advisory committee, its membership must include individuals with disabilities or parents, family members, guardians, advocates, or other authorized representatives of the individuals; members of minority groups; trainees; and providers of vocational rehabilitation and independent living rehabilitation services.

(Authority: Section 12(c) of the Rehabilitation Act of 1973, as amended; 29 U.S.C. 709(c))

§ 385.41 What are the requirements affecting the collection of data from designated State agencies?

If the collection of data is necessary from individuals with disabilities being served by two or more designated State agencies or from employees of two or more of these agencies, the project director must submit requests for the data to appropriate representatives of the affected agencies, as determined by the Secretary. This requirement also applies to employed project staff and individuals enrolled in courses of study supported under these programs.

(Authority: Section 12(c) of the Rehabilitation Act of 1973, as amended; 29 U.S.C. 709(c))

§ 385.42 What are the requirements affecting the dissemination of training materials?

A set of any training materials developed under the Rehabilitation Training Program must be submitted to any information clearinghouse designated by the Secretary.

(Authority: Section 12(c) of the Rehabilitation Act of 1973, as amended; 29 U.S.C. 709(c))

§ 385.43 What requirements apply to the training of rehabilitation counselors and other rehabilitation personnel?

Any grantee who provides training of rehabilitation counselors or other rehabilitation personnel must train those counselors and personnel on the services provided under this Act, and, in particular, services provided in accordance with amendments made to the Rehabilitation Act by the Workforce Innovation and Opportunity Act of 2014. The grantee must also furnish training to these counselors and personnel regarding applications of rehabilitation technology in vocational rehabilitation services, the applicability of section 504 of this Act, title I of the Americans with Disabilities Act of 1990, and the provisions of titles II and XVI of the Social Security Act that are related to work incentives for individuals with disabilities.

(Authority: Sections 12(c), 101(a), and 302 of the Rehabilitation Act of 1973, as amended; 29 U.S.C. 709(c), 721(a) and 772)

§ 385.44 What requirement applies to the training of individuals with disabilities?

Any grantee or contractor who provides training shall give due regard to the training of individuals with disabilities as part of its effort to increase the number of qualified personnel available to provide rehabilitation services.

(Authority: Section 12(c) of the Rehabilitation Act of 1973, as amended; 29 U.S.C. 709(c)

§ 385.45 What additional application requirements apply to the training of individuals for rehabilitation careers?

(a) All applicants for a grant or contract to provide training shall demonstrate how the training they plan to provide will prepare rehabilitation professionals to address the needs of individuals with disabilities from minority backgrounds.

(b) All applicants for a grant shall include a detailed description of strategies that will be utilized to recruit and train persons so as to reflect the diverse populations of the United States, as part of the effort to increase the number of individuals with disabilities, individuals who are members of minority groups, who are available to provide rehabilitation services.

(Approved by the Office of Management and Budget under control number 1820–0018)

(Authority: Sections 21(a) and (b) and 302 of the Rehabilitation Act of 1973, as amended; 29 U.S.C. 718(a) and (b) and 772)

§ 385.46 What limitations apply to the rate of pay for experts or consultants appointed or serving under contract under the Rehabilitation Training program?

An expert or consultant appointed or serving under contract pursuant to this section shall be compensated at a rate subject to approval of the Commissioner which shall not exceed the daily equivalent of the rate of pay for level 4 of the Senior Executive Service Schedule under section 5382 of title 5, United States Code. Such an expert or consultant may be allowed travel and transportation expenses in accordance with section 5703 of title 5, United States Code.

(Authority: Section 302(b)(3) of the Rehabilitation Act of 1973, as amended; 29 U.S.C. 772(b)(3))

PART 386—REHABILITATION TRAINING: REHABILITATION LONG-TERM TRAINING

Subpart A—General

AUTHORITY: Sections 12(c) and 302 of the Rehabilitation Act of 1973, as amended; 29 U.S.C. 709(c) and 772, unless otherwise noted.

SOURCE: 81 FR 55619, Aug. 19, 2016, unless otherwise noted.

Subpart A—General

§ 386.1 What is the Rehabilitation Long-Term Training program?

(a) The Rehabilitation Long-Term Training program provides financial assistance for—

(1) Projects that provide basic or advanced training leading to an academic degree in one of those fields of study

identified in paragraph (b) of this section;

(2) Projects that provide a specified series of courses or program of study leading to award of a certificate in one of those fields of study identified in paragraph (b) of this section; and

(3) Projects that provide support for medical residents enrolled in residency training programs in the specialty of physical medicine and rehabilitation.

(b) The Rehabilitation Long-Term Training program is designed to provide academic training that leads to an academic degree or academic certificate in areas of personnel shortages identified by the Secretary and published in a notice in the FEDERAL REGISTER. These areas may include—

(1) Assisting and supporting individuals with disabilities pursuing self-employment, business ownership, and telecommuting;

(2) Vocational rehabilitation counseling;

(3) Rehabilitation technology, including training on its use, applications, and benefits;

(4) Rehabilitation medicine;

(5) Rehabilitation nursing;

(6) Rehabilitation social work;

(7) Rehabilitation psychiatry;

(8) Rehabilitation psychology;

(9) Rehabilitation dentistry;

(10) Physical therapy;

(11) Occupational therapy;

(12) Speech pathology and audiology;

(13) Physical education;

(14) Therapeutic recreation;

(15) Community rehabilitation program personnel;

(16) Prosthetics and orthotics;

(17) Rehabilitation of individuals who are blind or visually impaired, including rehabilitation teaching and orientation and mobility;

(18) Rehabilitation of individuals who are deaf or hard of hearing;

(19) Rehabilitation of individuals who are mentally ill;

(20) Undergraduate education in the rehabilitation services;

(21) Independent living;

(22) Client assistance;

(23) Administration of community rehabilitation programs;

(24) Rehabilitation administration;

(25) Vocational evaluation and work adjustment;

(26) Services to individuals with specific disabilities or specific impediments to rehabilitation, including individuals who are members of populations that are unserved or underserved by programs under this Act;

(27) Job development and job placement services to individuals with disabilities;

(28) Supported employment services and customized employment services for individuals with the most significant disabilities;

(29) Specialized services for individuals with significant disabilities;

(30) Other fields contributing to the rehabilitation of individuals with disabilities.

(Authority: Sections 12 and 302 of the Rehabilitation Act of 1973, as amended; 29 U.S.C. 709 and 772)

§ 386.2   Who is eligible for an award?

Those agencies and organizations eligible for assistance under this program are described in 34 CFR 385.2.

(Authority: Section 302(a) of the Rehabilitation Act of 1973, as amended; 29 U.S.C. 772(a))

§ 386.3   What regulations apply?

The following regulations apply to the Rehabilitation Training: Rehabilitation Long-Term Training program:

(a) The regulations in this part 386.

(b) The regulations in 34 CFR part 385.

(Authority: Section 302(a) of the Rehabilitation Act of 1973, as amended; 29 U.S.C. 772(a))

§ 386.4   What definitions apply?

The following definitions apply to this program:

(a) Definitions in 34 CFR 385.4.

(b) *Other definitions.* The following definitions also apply to this part:

Academic year means a full-time course of study—

(i) Taken for a period totaling at least nine months; or

(ii) Taken for the equivalent of at least two semesters, two trimesters, or three quarters.

Certificate means a recognized educational credential awarded by a grantee under this part that attests to the completion of a specified series of courses or program of study.

Professional corporation or professional practice means—

(i) A professional service corporation or practice formed by one or more individuals duly authorized to render the same professional service, for the purpose of rendering that service; and

(ii) The corporation or practice and its members are subject to the same supervision by appropriate State regulatory agencies as individual practitioners.

Related agency means—

(i) An American Indian rehabilitation program; or

(ii) Any of the following agencies that provide services to individuals with disabilities under an agreement or other arrangement with a designated State agency in the area of specialty for which training is provided:

(A) A Federal, State, or local agency.

(B) A nonprofit organization.

(C) A professional corporation or professional practice group.

Scholar means an individual who is enrolled in a certificate or degree granting course of study in one of the areas listed in §386.1(b) and who receives scholarship assistance under this part.

Scholarship means an award of financial assistance to a scholar for training and includes all disbursements or credits for student stipends, tuition and fees, books and supplies, and student travel in conjunction with training assignments.

State vocational rehabilitation agency means the designated State agency as defined in 34 CFR 361.5(c)(13).

(Authority: Section 12(c) of the Rehabilitation Act of 1973, as amended; 29 U.S.C. 709(c))f **Subpart B [Reserved]**

Subpart C—How Does the Secretary Make an Award?

§386.20 What additional selection criteria are used under this program?

In addition to the criteria in 34 CFR 385.31(c), the Secretary uses the following additional selection criteria to evaluate an application:

(a) *Relevance to State-Federal vocational rehabilitation service program.* (1) The Secretary reviews each application for information that shows that the proposed project appropriately relates to the mission of the State-Federal vocational rehabilitation service program.

(2) The Secretary looks for information that shows that the project can be expected either—

(i) To increase the supply of trained personnel available to State and other public or nonprofit agencies involved in the rehabilitation of individuals with disabilities through degree or certificate granting programs; or

(ii) To improve the skills and quality of professional personnel in the rehabilitation field in which the training is to be provided through the granting of a degree or certificate.

(b) *Nature and scope of curriculum.* (1) The Secretary reviews each application for information that demonstrates the adequacy of the proposed curriculum.

(2) The Secretary looks for information that shows—

(i) The scope and nature of the coursework reflect content that can be expected to enable the achievement of the established project objectives;

(ii) The curriculum and teaching methods provide for an integration of theory and practice relevant to the educational objectives of the program;

(iii) For programs whose curricula require them, there is evidence of educationally focused practical and other field experiences in settings that ensure student involvement in the provision of vocational rehabilitation, supported employment, customized employment, pre-employment transition services, transition services, or independent living rehabilitation services to individuals with disabilities, especially individuals with significant disabilities;

(iv) The coursework includes student exposure to vocational rehabilitation, supported employment, customized employment, employer engagement, and independent living rehabilitation processes, concepts, programs, and services; and

(v) If applicable, there is evidence of current professional accreditation by the designated accrediting agency in the professional field in which grant support is being requested.

(Authority: Section 12(c) and 302 of the Rehabilitation Act of 1973, as amended; 29 U.S.C. 709(c) and 772)

§ 386.21 What are the application procedures for these programs?

(a) *Application.* No grant shall be awarded or contract entered into under the Rehabilitation Long-Term Training program unless the applicant has submitted to the Secretary an application at such time, in such form, in accordance with such procedures identified by the Secretary and, and including such information as the Secretary may require, including—

(1) A description of how the designated State unit or units will participate in the project to be funded under the grant or contract, including, as appropriate, participation on advisory committees, as practicum sites, in curriculum development, and in other ways so as to build closer relationships between the applicant and the designated State unit and to encourage students to pursue careers in public vocational rehabilitation programs;

(2) The identification of potential employers that provide employment that meets the requirements in § 386.33(c); and

(3) An assurance that data on the employment of graduates or trainees who participate in the project is accurate.

(b) The Secretary gives the designated State agency an opportunity to review and comment on applications submitted from within the State that it serves. The procedures to be followed by the applicant and the State are in 34 CFR 75.155–75.159.

(Authority: Sections 12(c) and 302(b)(2) and (d) of the Rehabilitation Act of 1973, as amended; 29 U.S.C. 709(c) and 772(b)(2) and (d))

Subpart D—What Conditions Must Be Met After an Award?

§ 386.30 What are the matching requirements?

The grantee is required to contribute at least ten percent of the total cost of a project under this program. However, if the grantee can demonstrate that it has insufficient resources to contribute the entire match but that it can fulfill all other requirements for receiving an award, the Secretary may waive part of the non-Federal share of the cost of the

project after negotiations with Department staff.

(Authority: Section 12(c) of the Rehabilitation Act of 1973, as amended; 29 U.S.C. 709(c))

§ 386.31 What are the requirements for directing grant funds?

(a) A grantee must use at least 65 percent of the total cost of a project under this program for scholarships as defined in § 386.4.

(b) The Secretary may waive the requirement in (a) and award grants that use less than 65 percent of the total cost of the project for scholarships based upon the unique nature of the project, such as the establishment of a new training program or long-term training in an emerging field that does not award degrees or certificates.

(c) Before providing a scholarship to a scholar, a grantee must make good faith efforts to determine that the scholar is not concurrently receiving more than one scholarship under this program for the same academic term.

(Authority: Sections 12(c) and 302 of the Rehabilitation Act of 1973, as amended; 29 U.S.C. 709(c) and 772)

§ 386.32 What are allowable costs?

In addition to those allowable costs established in the Education Department General Administrative Regulations in 34 CFR 75.530 through 75.562, the following items are allowable under long-term training projects:

(a) Student stipends.

(b) Tuition and fees.

(c) Books and supplies.

(d) Student travel in conjunction with training assignments.

(Authority: Sections 12(c) and 302 of the Rehabilitation Act of 1973, as amended; 29 U.S.C. 709(c) and 772)

§ 386.33 What are the requirements for grantees in disbursing scholarships?

Before disbursement of scholarship assistance to an individual, a grantee—

(a)(1) Must obtain documentation that the individual is—

(i) A U.S. citizen or national; or

(ii) A permanent resident of the Commonwealth of Puerto Rico, the United States Virgin Islands, Guam, American Samoa, or the Commonwealth of the Northern Mariana Islands;

(2) Must confirm from documentation issued to the individual by the U.S. Department of Homeland Security that he or she—

(i) Is a lawful permanent resident of the United States; or

(ii) Is in the United States for other than a temporary purpose with the intention of becoming a citizen or permanent resident; and

(b) Must confirm that the applicant has expressed interest in a career in clinical practice, administration, supervision, teaching, or research in the vocational rehabilitation, supported employment, or independent living rehabilitation of individuals with disabilities, especially individuals with significant disabilities;

(c) Must obtain documentation, as described in § 386.40(a)(7), that the individual expects to seek and maintain employment in a designated State agency or in a related agency as defined in § 386.4 where

(1) The employment is in the field of study in which the training was received or

(2) Where the job functions are directly relevant to the field of study in which the training was received.

(d) Must ensure that the scholarship, when added to the amount of financial aid the scholar receives for the same academic year under title IV of the Higher Education Act, does not exceed the scholar's cost of attendance;

(e) Must limit scholarship assistance to no more than four academic years, unless the grantee provides an extension consistent with the institution's accommodations under section 504 of the Act; and

(f) Must obtain a Certification of Eligibility for Federal Assistance from each scholar as prescribed in 34 CFR 75.60, 75.61, and 75.62.

(Approved by the Office of Management and Budget under control number 1820–0018)

(Authority: Sections 12(c) and 302(b) of the Rehabilitation Act of 1973, as amended; 29 U.S.C. 709(c) and 772(b))

§ 386.34 What assurances must be provided by a grantee that intends to provide scholarships?

A grantee under this part that intends to grant scholarships for any academic year must provide the following assurances before an award is made:

(a) *Requirement for agreement.* No individual will be provided a scholarship without entering into a written agreement containing the terms and conditions required by this section. An individual will sign and date the agreement prior to the initial disbursement of scholarship funds to the individual for payment of the individual's expenses. An agreement must be executed between the grantee and scholar for each subsequent year that scholarship funds are disbursed and must contain the terms and conditions required by this section.

(b) *Disclosure to applicants.* The terms and conditions of the agreement between the grantee and a scholar will be fully disclosed in the application for scholarship.

(c) *Form and terms of agreement.* Prior to granting each year of a scholarship, the grantee will require each scholar to enter into a signed written agreement in which the scholar agrees to the terms and conditions set forth in § 386.40. This agreement must be in the form and contain any additional terms and conditions that the Secretary may require.

(d) *Executed agreement.* The grantee will provide an original signed executed payback agreement upon request to the Secretary.

(e) *Standards for satisfactory progress.* The grantee will establish, publish, and apply reasonable standards for measuring whether a scholar is maintaining satisfactory progress in the scholar's course of study. The Secretary considers an institution's standards to be reasonable if the standards—

(1) Conform with the standards of satisfactory progress of the nationally recognized accrediting agency that accredits the institution's program of study, if the institution's program of study is accredited by such an agency, and if the agency has those standards;

(2) For a scholar enrolled in an eligible program who is to receive assistance under the Rehabilitation Act, are the same as or stricter than the institution's standards for a student enrolled in the same academic program who is not receiving assistance under the Rehabilitation Act; and

(3) Include the following elements:

(i) Grades, work projects completed, or comparable factors that are measurable against a norm.

(ii) A maximum timeframe in which the scholar must complete the scholar's educational objective, degree, or certificate.

(iii) Consistent application of standards to all scholars within categories of students; *e.g.*, full-time, part-time, undergraduates, graduate students, and students attending programs established by the institution.

(iv) Specific policies defining the effect of course incompletes, withdrawals, repetitions, and noncredit remedial courses on satisfactory progress.

(v) Specific procedures for appeal of a determination that a scholar is not making satisfactory progress and for reinstatement of aid.

(f) *Exit certification.* (1) At the time of exit from the program, the grantee will provide the following information to the scholar:

(i) The name of the institution and the number of the Federal grant that provided the scholarship.

(ii) the total amount of scholarship assistance received subject to § 386.40(a)(7).

(iii) The scholar's field of study and the obligation of the scholar to perform the service obligation with employment that meets the requirements in § 386.40(a)(7)(i).

(iv) The number of years the scholar needs to work to satisfy the work requirements in § 386.40(a)(7)(ii).

(v) The time period during which the scholar must satisfy the work requirements in § 386.40(a)(8).

(vi) As applicable, all other obligations of the scholar in § 386.40.

(2) Upon receipt of this information from the grantee, the scholar must provide written and signed certification to the grantee that the information is correct.

(g) *Tracking system.* The grantee has established policies and procedures to determine compliance of the scholar with the terms of the signed payback agreement. In order to determine whether a scholar has met the terms and conditions set forth in § 386.40, the tracking system must include for each

employment position maintained by the scholar—

(1) Documentation of the employer's name, address, dates of the scholar's employment, name of supervisor, position title, a description of the duties the scholar performed, and whether the employment is full- or part-time;

(2) Documentation of how the employment meets the requirements in § 386.40(a)(7); and

(3) In the event a grantee is experiencing difficulty locating a scholar, documentation that the grantee has checked with existing tracking systems operated by alumni organizations.

(h) *Reports.* The grantee will make annual reports to the Secretary, unless more frequent reporting is required by the Secretary, that are necessary to carry out the Secretary's functions under this part.

(i) *Repayment status.* The grantee will immediately report to the Secretary whenever a scholar has entered repayment status under § 386.43(e) and provide all necessary documentation in support thereof.

(j) *Records.* The grantee will maintain accurate and complete records as outlined in paragraphs (g) and (h) of this section for a period of time not less than one year beyond the date that all scholars provided financial assistance under the grant—

(1) Have completed their service obligation or

(2) Have entered into repayment status pursuant to § 386.43(e).

(Approved by the Office of Management and Budget under control number 1820–0018)

(Authority: Sections 12(c) and 302(b) of the Rehabilitation Act of 1973, as amended; 29 U.S.C. 709(c) and 772(b))

§ 386.35   **What information must be provided by a grantee that is an institution of higher education to assist designated State agencies?**

A grantee that is an institution of higher education provided assistance under this part must cooperate with the following requests for information from a designated State agency:

(a) Information required by section 101(a)(7) of the Act which may include, but is not limited to—

(1) The number of students enrolled by the grantee in rehabilitation training programs; and

(2) The number of rehabilitation professionals trained by the grantee who graduated with certification or licensure, or with credentials to qualify for certification or licensure, during the past year.

(b) Information on the availability of rehabilitation courses leading to certification or licensure, or the credentials to qualify for certification or licensure, to assist State agencies in the planning of a program of staff development for all classes of positions that are involved in the administration and operation of the State vocational rehabilitation program.

(Approved by the Office of Management and Budget under control number 1820–0018)

(Authority: Sections 12(c) and 302 of the Rehabilitation Act of 1973, as amended; 29 U.S.C. 709(c) and 772)

§ 386.36 What is a grantee's liability for failing to provide accurate and complete scholar information to the Department?

The Department may recover, in whole or in part, from the grantee the debt amount and any collection costs described in §§ 386.40(d) and 386.43, if the Department:

(a) Is unable to collect, or improperly collected, some or all of these amounts or costs from a scholar and

(b) Determines that the grantee failed to provide to the Department accurate and complete documentation described in § 386.34.

(Authority: Sections 12(c) and 302 of the Rehabilitation Act of 1973, as amended; 29 U.S.C. 709(c) and 772)

Subpart E—What Conditions Must Be Met by a Scholar?

§ 386.40 What are the requirements for scholars?

(a) A scholar must—

(1) Be enrolled in a course of study leading to a certificate or degree in one of the fields designated in § 386.1(b);

(2) Receive the training at the educational institution or agency designated in the scholarship;

(3) Not accept payment of educational allowances from any other entity if that allowance conflicts with the scholar's obligation under section 302 of the Act and this part;

(4) Not receive concurrent scholarships for the same academic term from more than one project under this program;

(5) Enter into a signed written agreement with the grantee, prior to the receipt of scholarship funds, as required in § 386.34(c);

(6) Maintain satisfactory progress toward the certificate or degree as determined by the grantee;

(7) Upon exiting the training program under paragraph (a)(1) of this section, subsequently maintain employment on a full- or part-time basis subject to the provisions in paragraph (b) of this section—

(i)(A) In a State vocational rehabilitation agency or related agency as defined in § 386.4; and

(B)(1) In the field of study for which training was received, or

(2) Where the field of study is directly relevant to the job functions performed; and

(ii) For a period of at least the full-time equivalent of two years for every academic year for which assistance under this section was received subject to the provisions in paragraph (c) of this section for part-time coursework;

(8) Complete the service obligation within a period, beginning after the recipient exits the training program for which the scholarship was awarded, of not more than the sum of the number of years in the period described in paragraph (a)(7)(ii) of this section and two additional years;

(9) Repay all or part of any scholarship received, plus interest, if the individual does not fulfill the requirements of this section, except as provided for in § 386.41 for exceptions and deferrals; and

(10) Provide the grantee all requested information necessary for the grantee to meet the exit certification requirements in § 386.34(f) and, as necessary, thereafter for any changes necessary for the grantee to monitor the scholar's service obligation under this section.

(b)(1) The period of qualifying employment that meets the requirements of paragraph (a)(7) of this section may begin—

(i) For courses of study of at least one year, only subsequent to the completion of one academic year of the training for which the scholarship assistance was received.

(ii) For courses of study of less than one year, only upon completion of the training for which the scholarship assistance was received.

(2) The work completed as part of an internship, practicum, or any other work-related requirement necessary to complete the educational program is not considered qualifying employment.

(c) If the scholar is pursuing coursework on a part-time basis, the service obligation for these part-time courses is based on the equivalent total of actual academic years of training received.

(d) If a scholar fails to provide the information in paragraph (a)(10) of this section or otherwise maintain contact with the grantee pursuant to the terms of the signed payback agreement and enters into repayment status pursuant to § 386.43, the scholar will be held responsible for any costs assessed in the collection process under that section even if that information is subsequently provided.

(Authority: Sections 12(c) and 302(b) of the Rehabilitation Act of 1973, as amended; 29 U.S.C. 709(c) and 772(b))

§ 386.41 Under what circumstances does the Secretary grant a deferral or exception to performance or repayment under a scholarship agreement?

Based upon sufficient evidence to substantiate the grounds as detailed in § 386.42, a repayment exception to or deferral of the requirements of § 386.40(a)(7) may be granted, in whole or in part, by the Secretary as follows:

(a) Repayment is not required if the scholar—

(1) Is unable to continue the course of study or perform the work obligation because of a permanent disability that meets one of the following conditions:

(i) The disability had not been diagnosed at the time the scholar signed the agreement in § 386.34(c); or

(ii) The disability did not prevent the scholar from performing the require-

ments of the course of study or the work obligation at the time the scholar signed the agreement in § 386.34(c) but subsequently worsened; or

(2) Has died.

(b) Repayment of a scholarship may be deferred during the time the scholar is—

(1) Engaging in a full-time course of study in the field of rehabilitation at an institution of higher education;

(2) Serving on active duty as a member of the armed services of the United States for a period not in excess of four years;

(3) Serving as a volunteer under the Peace Corps Act;

(4) Serving as a full-time volunteer under title I of the Domestic Volunteer Service Act of 1973;

(5) Experiencing a temporary disability that affects the scholar's ability to continue the course of study or perform the work obligation, for a period not to exceed three years; or

(c) Under limited circumstances as determined by the Secretary and based upon credible evidence submitted on behalf of the scholar, the Secretary may grant an exception to, or deferral of, the requirement to repay a scholarship in instances not specified in this section. These instances could include, but are not limited to, the care of a disabled spouse, partner, or child or the need to accompany a spouse or partner on active duty in the Armed Forces.

(Authority: Sections 12(c) and 302(b) of the Rehabilitation Act of 1973, as amended; 29 U.S.C. 709(c) and 772(b))

§ 386.42 What must a scholar do to obtain an exception or a deferral to performance or repayment under a scholarship agreement?

To obtain an exception or a deferral to performance or repayment under a scholarship agreement under § 386.41, a scholar must provide the following:

(a) *Written application.* A written application must be made to the Secretary to request a deferral or an exception to performance or repayment of a scholarship.

(b) *Documentation.* Sufficient documentation must be provided to substantiate the grounds for all deferrals or exceptions, including the following, as appropriate.

(1) Documentation necessary to substantiate an exception under §386.41(a)(1) or a deferral under §386.41(b)(5) must include a letter from a qualified physician or other medical professional, on official stationery, attesting how the disability affects the scholar in completing the course of study or performing the work obligation. The documentation must be less than three months old and include the scholar's diagnosis and prognosis and ability to complete the course of study or work with accommodations.

(2) Documentation to substantiate an exception under §386.41(a)(2) must include a death certificate or other evidence conclusive under State law.

(3) Documentation necessary to substantiate a deferral or exception under 386.41(c) based upon the disability of a spouse, partner, or child must meet the criteria, as relevant, in paragraph (b)(1) of this section.

(Approved by the Office of Management and Budget under control number 1820–0018)

(Authority: Sections 12(c) and 302 of the Rehabilitation Act of 1973, as amended; 29 U.S.C. 709(c) and 772)

§ 386.43 What are the consequences of a scholar's failure to meet the terms and conditions of a scholarship agreement?

In the event of a failure to meet the terms and conditions of a scholarship agreement or to obtain a deferral or an exception as provided in §386.41, the scholar must repay all or part of the scholarship as follows:

(a) *Amount.* The amount of the scholarship to be repaid is proportional to the employment obligation not completed.

(b) *Interest rate.* The Secretary charges the scholar interest on the unpaid balance owed in accordance with 31 U.S.C. 3717.

(c) *Interest accrual.* (1) Interest on the unpaid balance accrues from the date the scholar is determined to have entered repayment status under paragraph (e) of this section.

(2) Any accrued interest is capitalized at the time the scholar's repayment schedule is established.

(3) No interest is charged for the period of time during which repayment has been deferred under §386.41.

(d) *Collection costs.* Under the authority of 31 U.S.C. 3717, the Secretary may impose reasonable collection costs.

(e) *Repayment status.* A scholar enters repayment status on the first day of the first calendar month after the earliest of the following dates, as applicable:

(1) The date the scholar informs the Secretary he or she does not plan to fulfill the employment obligation under the agreement.

(2) Any date when the scholar's failure to begin or maintain employment makes it impossible for that individual to complete the employment obligation within the number of years required in §386.40(a)(8).

(f) *Amounts and frequency of payment.* The scholar shall make payments to the Secretary that cover principal, interest, and collection costs according to a schedule established by the Secretary.

(Authority: Sections 12(c) and 302(b) of the Rehabilitation Act of 1973, as amended; 29 U.S.C. 709(c) and 772(b))

PART 387—INNOVATIVE REHABILITATION TRAINING

Subpart A—General

AUTHORITY: Sections 12(c) and 302 of the Rehabilitation Act of 1973, as amended; 29 U.S.C. 709(c), and 772, unless otherwise noted.

Source: 81 FR 55623, Aug. 19, 2016, unless otherwise noted.

Subpart A—General

§ 387.1 What is the Innovative Rehabilitation Training program?

This program is designed—

(a) To develop new types of training programs for rehabilitation personnel and to demonstrate the effectiveness of these new types of training programs for rehabilitation personnel in providing rehabilitation services to individuals with disabilities;

(b) To develop new and improved methods of training rehabilitation personnel so that there may be a more effective delivery of rehabilitation services to individuals with disabilities by designated State rehabilitation agencies and designated State rehabilitation units or other public or non-profit rehabilitation service agencies or organizations; and

(c) To develop new innovative training programs for vocational rehabilitation professionals and paraprofessionals to have a 21st century understanding of the evolving labor force and the needs of individuals with disabilities so they can more effectively provide vocational rehabilitation services to individuals with disabilities.

(Authority: Sections 12(c), 121(a)(7), and 302 of the Rehabilitation Act of 1973, as amended; 29 U.S.C. 709(c), 721(a)(7), and 772)

§ 387.2 Who is eligible for assistance under this program?

Those agencies and organizations eligible for assistance under this program are described in 34 CFR 385.2.

(Authority: Section 12(c) and 302 of the Rehabilitation Act of 1973, as amended; 29 U.S.C. 709(c) and 772)

§ 387.3 What regulations apply to this program?

(a) 34 CFR part 385 (Rehabilitation Training); and

(b) The regulations in this part 387.

(Authority: Sections 12(c) and 302 of the Rehabilitation Act of 1973, as amended; 29 U.S.C. 709(c) and 772)

§ 387.4 What definitions apply to this program?

The definitions in 34 CFR part 385 apply to this program.

(Authority: Sections 12(c) and 302 of the Rehabilitation Act of 1973, as amended; 29 U.S.C. 709(c) and 772))

§ 387.5 What types of projects are authorized under this program?

The Innovative Rehabilitation Training Program supports time-limited pilot projects through which new types of rehabilitation workers may be trained or through which innovative methods of training rehabilitation personnel may be demonstrated.

(Authority: Sections 12(c) and 302 of the Rehabilitation Act of 1973, as amended; 29 U.S.C. 709(c) and 772))

Subparts B–C [Reserved]

Subpart D—How Does the Secretary Make a Grant?

§ 387.30 What additional selection criteria are used under this program?

In addition to the criteria in 34 CFR 385.31(c), the Secretary uses the following additional selection criteria to evaluate an application:

(a) *Relevance to State-Federal rehabilitation service program.* (1) The Secretary reviews each application for information that shows that the proposed project appropriately relates to the mission of the State-Federal rehabilitation service program.

(2) The Secretary looks for information that shows that the project can be expected either—

(i) To increase the supply of trained personnel available to public and private agencies involved in the rehabilitation of individuals with disabilities; or

(ii) To maintain and improve the skills and quality of rehabilitation personnel.

(b) *Nature and scope of curriculum.* (1) The Secretary reviews each application for information that demonstrates the adequacy and scope of the proposed curriculum.

(2) The Secretary looks for information that shows that—

(i) The scope and nature of the training content can be expected to enable the achievement of the established project objectives of the training project;

(ii) The curriculum and teaching methods provide for an integration of theory and practice relevant to the educational objectives of the program;

(iii) There is evidence of educationally focused practicum or other field experiences in settings that assure student involvement in the provision of vocational rehabilitation or independent living rehabilitation services to individuals with disabilities, especially individuals with significant disabilities; and

(iv) The didactic coursework includes student exposure to vocational rehabilitation processes, concepts, programs, and services.

(Authority: Sections 12(c) and 302 of the Rehabilitation Act of 1973, as amended; 29 U.S.C. 709(c) and 772)

Subpart E—What Conditions Must Be Met by a Grantee?

§387.40 What are the matching requirements?

A grantee must contribute to the cost of a project under this program in an amount satisfactory to the Secretary. The part of the costs to be borne by the grantee is determined by the Secretary at the time of the grant award.

(Authority: Sections 12(c) and 302 of the Rehabilitation Act of 1973, as amended; 29 U.S.C. 709(c) and 772)

§387.41 What are allowable costs?

In addition to those allowable costs established under 34 CFR 75.530–75.562, the following items are allowable under Innovative Rehabilitation training projects—

(a) Student stipends;

(b) Tuition and fees; and

(c) Student travel in conjunction with training assignments.

(Authority: Sections 12(c) and 302 of the Rehabilitation Act of 1973, as amended; 29 U.S.C. 709(c) and 772)

PARTS 388–389 [RESERVED]

PART 390—REHABILITATION SHORT-TERM TRAINING

Subpart A—General

AUTHORITY: Sections 12(a) and (c) and 302 of the Rehabilitation Act of 1973, as amended; 29 U.S.C. 709(a) and (c) and 772, unless otherwise noted.

SOURCE: 81 FR 55624, Aug. 19, 2016, unless otherwise noted.

Subpart A—General

§390.1 What is the Rehabilitation Short-Term Training program?

This program is designed for the support of special seminars, institutes, workshops, and other short-term courses in technical matters relating to the vocational, medical, social, and psychological rehabilitation programs, independent living services programs, and client assistance programs.

(Authority: Sections 12(a)(2) and 302 of the Rehabilitation Act of 1973, as amended; 29 U.S.C. 709(a)(2) and 772)

§ 390.2 Who is eligible for assistance under this program?

Those agencies and organizations eligible for assistance under this program are described in 34 CFR 385.2.

(Authority: Section 302 of the Rehabilitation Act of 1973, as amended; 29 U.S.C. 772)

§ 390.3 What regulations apply to this program?

(a) 34 CFR part 385 (Rehabilitation Training); and

(b) The regulations in this part 390.

(Authority: Section 302 of the Rehabilitation Act of 1973, as amended; 29 U.S.C. 772)

§ 390.4 What definitions apply to this program?

The definitions in 34 CFR part 385 apply to this program.

(Authority: Section 12(c) of the Rehabilitation Act of 1973, as amended; 29 U.S.C. 709(c))

Subpart B—What Kinds of Projects Does the Department of Education Assist Under This Program?

§ 390.10 What types of projects are authorized under this program?

(a) Projects under this program are designed to provide short-term training and technical instruction in areas of special significance to the vocational, medical, social, and psychological rehabilitation programs, supported employment programs, independent living services programs, and client assistance programs.

(b) Short-term training projects may be of regional or national scope.

(c) Conferences and meetings in which training is not the primary focus may not be supported under this program.

(Authority: Section 12(a)(2) and 302 of the Rehabilitation Act of 1973, as amended; 29 U.S.C. 709(a)(2) and 772)

Subpart C [Reserved]

Subpart D—How Does the Secretary Make a Grant?

§ 390.30 What additional selection criterion is used under this program?

In addition to the criteria in 34 CFR 385.31(c), the Secretary uses the following additional selection criterion to evaluate an application:

(a) *Relevance to State-Federal rehabilitation service program.* (1) The Secretary reviews each application for information that shows that the proposed project appropriately relates to the mission of the State-Federal rehabilitation service programs.

(2) The Secretary looks for information that shows that the proposed project can be expected to improve the skills and competence of—

(i) Personnel engaged in the administration or delivery of rehabilitation services; and

(ii) Others with an interest in the delivery of rehabilitation services.

(b) *Evidence of training needs.* The Secretary reviews each application for evidence of training needs as identified through training needs assessment conducted by the applicant or by designated State agencies or designated State units or any other public and private nonprofit rehabilitation service agencies or organizations that provide rehabilitation services and other services authorized under the Act, whose personnel will receive the training.

(Authority: Section 12(c) of the Rehabilitation Act of 1973, as amended; 29 U.S.C. 709(c))

Subpart E—What Conditions Must Be Met by a Grantee?

§ 390.40 What are the matching requirements?

A grantee must contribute to the cost of a project under this program in an amount satisfactory to the Secretary. The part of the costs to be borne by the grantee is determined by the Secretary at the time of the award.

(Authority: Section 12(c) and 302 of the Rehabilitation Act of 1973, as amended; 29 U.S.C. 709(c) and 772)

§ 390.41 What are allowable costs?

(a) In addition to those allowable costs established in 34 CFR 75.530–

75.562, the following items are allowable under short-term training projects:

(1) Trainee per diem costs;

(2) Trainee travel in connection with a training course;

(3) Trainee registration fees; and

(4) Special accommodations for trainees with handicaps.

(b) The preparation of training materials may not be supported under a short-term training grant unless the materials are essential for the conduct of the seminar, institute, workshop or other short course for which the grant support has been provided.

(Authority: Section 12(c) and 302 of the Rehabilitation Act of 1973, as amended; 29 U.S.C. 709(c) and 772)

PART 395—VENDING FACILITY PROGRAM FOR THE BLIND ON FEDERAL AND OTHER PROPERTY

Subpart A—Definitions

AUTHORITY: Sec. 2, 49 Stat. 1559, as amended; 20 U.S.C. 107a.

SOURCE: 42 FR 15802, Mar. 23, 1977, unless otherwise noted. Redesignated at 45 FR 77369, Nov. 21, 1980, and further redesignated at 46 FR 5417, Jan. 19, 1981.

Subpart A—Definitions

§395.1 Terms.

Unless otherwise indicated in this part, the terms below are defined as follows:

(a) *Act* means the Randolph-Sheppard Vending Stand Act (Pub. L. 74–732), as amended by Pub. L. 83–565 and Pub. L. 93–516, 20 U.S.C., ch. 6A, Sec 107.

(b) *Blind licensee* means a blind person licensed by the State licensing agency to operate a vending facility on Federal or other property.

(c) *Blind person* means a person who, after examination by a physician skilled in diseases of the eye or by an optometrist, whichever such person shall select, has been determined to have

(1) Not more than 20/200 central visual acuity in the better eye with correcting lenses, or

(2) An equally disabling loss of the visual field as evidenced by a limitation to the field of vision in the better eye to such a degree that its widest diameter subtends an angle of no greater than 20°.

(d) *Cafeteria* means a food dispensing facility capable of providing a broad variety of prepared foods and beverages (including hot meals) primarily through the use of a line where the customer serves himself from displayed selections. A cafeteria may be fully automatic or some limited waiter or waitress service may be available and provided within a cafeteria and table or booth seating facilities are always provided.

(e) *Secretary* means the Secretary of the Rehabilitation Services Administration.

(f) *Direct competition* means the presence and operation of a vending machine or a vending facility on the same premises as a vending facility operated by a blind vendor, except that vending machines or vending facilities operated in areas serving employees the majority of whom normally do not have direct access (in terms of uninterrupted ease of approach and the amount of time required to patronize the vending facility) to the vending facility operated by a blind vendor shall not be considered to be in direct competition with the vending facility operated by a blind vendor.

(g) *Federal property* means any building, land, or other real property owned, leased, or occupied by any department, agency or instrumentality of the United States (including the Department of Defense and the U.S. Postal Service), or any other instrumentality wholly owned by the United States, or by any department or agency of the District of Columbia or any territory or possession of the United States.

(h) *Individual location installation or facility* means a single building or a self-contained group of buildings. In order for two or more buildings to be considered to be a self-contained group of buildings, such buildings must be located in close proximity to each other, and a majority of the Federal employees housed in any such building must regularly move from one building to another in the course of official business during normal working days.

(i) *License* means a written instrument issued by the State licensing agency to a blind person, authorizing such person to operate a vending facility on Federal or other property.

(j) *Management services* means supervision, inspection, quality control, consultation, accounting, regulating, in-service training, and other related services provided on a systematic basis to support and improve vending facilities operated by blind vendors. *Management services* does not include those services or costs which pertain to the on-going operation of an individual facility after the initial establishment period.

(k) *Net proceeds* means the amount remaining from the sale of articles or services of vending facilities, and any vending machine or other income accruing to blind vendors after deducting the cost of such sale and other expenses (excluding set-aside charges required to be paid by such blind vendors).

(l) *Nominee* means a nonprofit agency or organization designated by the State licensing agency through a written agreement to act as its agent in the provision of services to blind licensees under the State's vending facility program.

(m) *Normal working hours* means an eight hour work period between the approximate hours of 8:00 a.m., to 6:00 p.m., Monday through Friday.

(n) *Other property* means property which is not Federal property and on which vending facilities are established or operated by the use of any funds derived in whole or in part, directly or indirectly, from the operation of vending facilities on any Federal property.

(o) *Permit* means the official approval given a State licensing agency by a department, agency or instrumentality in control of the maintenance, operation, and protection of Federal property, or person in control of other property, whereby the State licensing agency is authorized to establish a vending facility.

(p) *Program* means all the activities of the licensing agency under this part related to vending facilities on Federal and other property.

(q) *Satisfactory site* means an area fully accessible to vending facility patrons and having:

(1) Effective on March 23, 1977 a minimum of 250 square feet available for the vending and storage of articles necessary for the operation of a vending facility; and

(2) Sufficient electrical plumbing, heating, and ventilation outlets for the

location and operation of a vending facility in accordance with applicable health laws and building codes.

(r) *Secretary* means the Secretary of Education.

(s) *Set-aside funds* means funds which accrue to a State licensing agency from an assessment against the net proceeds of each vending facility in the State's vending facility program and any income from vending machines on Federal property which accrues to the State licensing agency.

(t) *State* means a State, territory, possession, Puerto Rico, or the District of Columbia.

(u) *State vocational rehabilitation agency* means that agency in the State providing vocational rehabilitation services to the blind as the sole State agency under a State plan for vocational rehabilitation services approved pursuant to the provisions of the Rehabilitation Act of 1973 (29 U.S.C., ch. 16).

(v) *State licensing agency* means the State agency designated by the Secretary under this part to issue licenses to blind persons for the operation of vending facilities on Federal and other property.

(w) *United States* includes the several States, territories, and possessions of the United States, Puerto Rico, and the District of Columbia.

(x) *Vending facility* means automatic vending machines, cafeterias, snack bars, cart service, shelters, counters, and such other appropriate auxiliary equipment which may be operated by blind licensees and which is necessary for the sale of newspapers, periodicals, confections, tobacco products, foods, beverages, and other articles or services dispensed automatically or manually and prepared on or off the premises in accordance with all applicable health laws, and including the vending or exchange of changes for any lottery authorized by State law and conducted by an agency of a State within such State.

(y) *Vending machine*, for the purpose of assigning vending machine income under this part, means a coin or currency operated machine which dispenses articles or services, except that those machines operated by the United States Postal Service for the sale of postage stamps or other postal prod-

ucts and services, machines providing services of a recreational nature, and telephones shall not be considered to be vending machines.

(z) *Vending machine income* means receipts (other than those of a blind vendor) from vending machine operations on Federal property, after deducting the cost of goods sold (including reasonable service and maintenance costs in accordance with customary business practices of commercial vending concerns, where the machines are operated, serviced, or maintained by, or with the approval of, a department, agency, or instrumentality of the United States, or commissions paid (other than to a blind vendor) by a commercial vending concern which operates, services, and maintains vending machines on Federal property for, or with the approval of, a department, agency, or instrumentality of the United States.

(aa) *Vendor* means a blind licensee who is operating a vending facility on Federal or other property.

(bb) *Vocational rehabilitation services* means those services as defined in §1361.1(ee) (1) and (2) of this chapter.

Subpart B—The State Licensing Agency

§395.2 Application for designation as a State licensing agency; general.

(a) An application for designation as a State licensing agency may be submitted only by the State vocational rehabilitation agency providing vocational rehabilitation services to the blind under an approved State plan for vocational rehabilitation services under part 1361 of this chapter.

(b) Such application shall be:

(1) Submitted in writing to the Secretary;

(2) Approved by the chief executive of the State; and

(3) Transmitted over the signature of the administrator of the State agency making application.

§395.3 Application for designation as State licensing agency; content.

(a) An application for designation as a State licensing agency under §395.2 shall indicate:

(1) The State licensing agency's legal authority to administer the program, including its authority to promulgate rules and regulations to govern the program;

(2) The State licensing agency's organization for carrying out the program, including a description of the methods for coordinating the State's vending facility program and the State's vocational rehabilitation program, with special reference to the provision of such post-employment services necessary to assure that the maximum vocational potential of each blind vendor is achieved;

(3) The policies and standards to be employed in the selection of suitable locations for vending facilities;

(4) The methods to be used to ensure the continuing and active participation of the State Committee of Blind Vendors in matters affecting policy and program development and administration.

(5) The policies to be followed in making suitable vending facility equipment and adequate initial stock available to a vendor;

(6) The sources of funds for the administration of the program;

(7) The policies and standards governing the relationship of the State licensing agency to the vendors, including their selection, duties, supervision, transfer, promotion, financial participation, rights to a full evidentiary hearing concerning a State licensing agency action, and, where necessary, rights for the submittal of complaints to an arbitration panel;

(8) The methods to be followed in providing suitable training, including on-the-job training and, where appropriate, upward mobility training, to blind vendors;

(9) The arrangements made or contemplated, if any, for the utilization of the services of any nominee under § 395.15; the agreements therefor and the services to be provided; the procedures for the supervision and control of the services provided by such nominee and the methods used in evaluating services received, the basis for remuneration, and the fiscal controls and accounting procedures;

(10) The arrangements made or contemplated, if any, for the vesting in accordance with the laws of the State, of the right, title to, and interest in vending facility equipment or stock (including vending machines), used in the program, in a nominee to hold such right, title to, and interest for program purposes; and

(11) The assurances of the State licensing agency that it will:

(i) Cooperate with the Secretary in applying the requirements of the Act in a uniform manner;

(ii) Take effective action, including the termination of licenses, to carry out full responsibility for the supervision and management of each vending facility in its program in accordance with its established rules and regulations, this part, and the terms and conditions governing the permit;

(iii) Submit promptly to the Secretary for approval a description of any changes in the legal authority of the State licensing agency, its rules and regulations, blind vendor agreements, schedules for the setting aside of funds, contractual arrangements for the furnishing of services by a nominee, arrangements for carrying general liability and product liability insurance, and any other matters which form a part of the application;

(iv) If it intends to set aside, or cause to be set aside, funds from the net proceeds of the operation of vending facilities, obtain a prior determination by the Secretary that the amount of such funds to be set aside is reasonable;

(v) Establish policies against discrimination of any blind vendor on the basis of sex, age, physical or mental impairment, creed, color, national origin, or political affiliation;

(vi) Furnish each vendor a copy of its rules and regulations and a description of the arrangements for providing services, and take adequate steps to assure that each vendor understands the provisions of the permit and any agreement under which he operates, as evidenced by his signed statements:

(vii) Submit to an arbitration panel those grievances of any vendor unresolved after a full evidentiary hearing;

(viii) Adopt accounting procedures and maintain financial records in a manner necessary to provide for each vending facility and for the State's vending facility program a classification of financial transactions in such detail as is sufficient to enable evaluation of performance; and

(ix) Maintain records and make reports in such form and containing such information as the Secretary may require, make such records available for audit purposes, and comply with such provisions as the Secretary may find necessary to assure the correctness and verification of such reports.

(b) An application submitted under §395.2 shall be accompanied by a copy of State rules and regulations affecting the administration and operation of the State's vending facility program.

§395.4 State rules and regulations.

(a) The State licensing agency shall promulgate rules and regulations which have been approved by the Secretary and which shall be adequate to assure the effective conduct of the State's vending facility program (including State licensing agency procedures covering the conduct of full evidentiary hearings) and the operation of each vending facility in accordance with this part and with the requirements and conditions of each department, agency, and instrumentality in control of the maintenance, operation, and protection of Federal property, including the conditions contained in permits, as well as in all applicable Federal and State laws, local ordinances and regulations.

(b) Such rules and regulations and amendments thereto shall be filed or published in accordance with State law.

(c) Such rules and regulations shall include provisions adequate to insure that the right, title to, and interest in each vending facility used in the program and the stock will be vested in accordance with the laws of the State in only the following:

(1) The State licensing agency; or

(2) Its nominee, subject to the conditions specified in §395.15(b); or

(3) The vendor, in accordance with State determination.

(d) Notwithstanding the provisions of paragraph (c) of this section, any right, title to, or interest which existed on June 30, 1955, in stock may continue so long as:

(1) The interest is in the stock of a facility established under the program prior to July 1, 1955, and

(2) The vendor was licensed in the program (whether or not for the operation of the vending facility in question) prior to July 1, 1955.

§395.5 Approval of application for designation as State licensing agency.

When the Secretary determines that an application submitted by a State vocational rehabilitation agency under §395.2, and the accompanying rules and regulations indicate a plan of program operations which will stimulate and enlarge the economic opportunities for the blind, and which will meet all other requirements of this part, he shall approve the application and shall designate the applying State vocational rehabilitation agency as the State licensing agency.

§395.6 Vendor ownership of vending facilities.

(a) If a State licensing agency determines under §395.4(c) that the right, title to, and interest in a vending facility may be vested in the blind vendor, the State licensing agency shall enter into a written agreement with each vendor who is to have such ownership. Such agreement shall contain in full the terms and conditions governing such ownership in accordance with criteria in the State licensing agency's regulations, this part, and the terms and conditions of the permit. The criteria established to govern the determination that the title may be so vested shall contain reasonable provisions to enable a vendor to purchase vending facility equipment and to ensure that no individual will be denied the opportunity to become a vendor because of his inability to purchase the vending facility equipment or the initial stock;

(b) The State licensing agency shall establish in writing and maintain policies determining whether the vendor-owner or the State licensing agency shall be required to maintain the vending facility in good repair and in an attractive condition and replace worn-out or obsolete equipment; and if the former, such policies shall provide that upon such vendor-owner's failure to do so, the State licensing agency may make the necessary maintenance, replacement, or repairs and make equitable arrangements for reimbursement;

(c) Where the vendor owns such equipment and is required to maintain the vending facility in good repair and in an attractive condition and replace worn-out or obsolete equipment, or agrees to purchase additional new equipment, service charges for such purposes shall be equitably reduced and the method for determining such amount shall be established by the State licensing agency in writing;

(d) Where the vendor owns such equipment, the State licensing agency shall retain a first option to repurchase such equipment, and in the event the vendor-owner dies, or for any other reason ceases to be a licensee, or transfers to another vending facility, ownership of such equipment shall become vested in the State licensing agency for transfer to a successor licensee subject to an obligation on its part to pay to such vendor-owner or his estate, the fair value therein; and

(e) The vendor-owner, his personal representative or next of kin shall be entitled to an opportunity for a full evidentiary hearing with respect to the determination of the amount to be paid by the State licensing agency for a vendor's ownership in the equipment. When the vendor-owner is dissatisfied with any decision rendered as a result of such hearing, he may file a complaint with the Secretary under § 395.13 to request the convening of an ad hoc arbitration panel.

§ 395.7 The issuance and conditions of licenses.

(a) The State licensing agency shall establish in writing and maintain objective criteria for licensing qualified applicants, including a provision for giving preference to blind persons who are in need of employment. Such criteria shall also include provisions to assure that licenses will be issued only to persons who are determined by the State licensing agency to be:

(1) Blind;

(2) Citizens of the United States; and

(3) Certified by the State vocational rehabilitation agency as qualified to operate a vending facility.

(b) The State licensing agency shall provide for the issuance of licenses for an indefinite period but subject to suspension or termination if, after affording the vendor an opportunity for a full evidentiary hearing, the State licensing agency finds that the vending facility is not being operated in accordance with its rules and regulations, the terms and conditions of the permit, and the terms and conditions of the agreement with the vendor.

(c) The State licensing agency shall further establish in writing and maintain policies which have been developed with the active participation of the State Committee of Blind Vendors and which govern the duties, supervision, transfer, promotion, and financial participation of the vendors. The State licensing agency shall also establish procedures to assure that such policies have been explained to each blind vendor.

§ 395.8 Distribution and use of income from vending machines on Federal property.

(a) Vending machine income from vending machines on Federal property which has been disbursed to the State licensing agency by a property managing department, agency, or instrumentality of the United States under § 395.32 shall accrue to each blind vendor operating a vending facility on such Federal property in each State in an amount not to exceed the average net income of the total number of blind vendors within such State, as determined each fiscal year on the basis of each prior year's operation, except that vending machine income shall not accrue to any blind vendor in any amount exceeding the average net income of the total number of blind vendors in the United States. No blind vendor shall receive less vending machine income than he was receiving during the calendar year prior to January 1, 1974, as a direct result of any limitation imposed on such income under this paragraph. No limitation shall be imposed on income from vending machines, combined to create a vending facility, when such facility is maintained, serviced, or operated by a blind vendor. Vending machine income disbursed by a property managing department, agency or instrumentality of the United States to a State licensing agency in excess of the amounts eligible to accrue to blind vendors in accordance with this paragraph shall be retained by the appropriate State licensing agency.

(b) The State licensing agency shall disburse vending machine income to blind vendors within the State on at least a quarterly basis.

(c) Vending machine income which is retained under paragraph (a) of this section by a State licensing agency shall be used by such agency for the establishment and maintenance of retirement or pension plans, for health insurance contributions, and for the provision of paid sick leave and vacation time for blind vendors in such State, if it is so determined by a majority vote of blind vendors licensed by the State licensing agency, after such agency has provided to each such vendor information on all matters relevant to such purposes. Any vending machine income not necessary for such purposes shall be used by the State licensing agency for the maintenance and replacement of equipment, the purchase of new equipment, management services, and assuring a fair minimum return to vendors. Any assessment charged to blind vendors by a State licensing agency shall be reduced pro rata in an amount equal to the total of such remaining vending machine income.

§ 395.9 The setting aside of funds by the State licensing agency.

(a) The State licensing agency shall establish in writing the extent to which funds are to be set aside or caused to be set aside from the net proceeds of the operation of the vending facilities and, to the extent applicable, from vending machine income under § 395.8(c) in an amount determined by the Secretary to be reasonable.

(b) Funds may be set aside under paragraph (a) of this section only for the purposes of:

(1) Maintenance and replacement of equipment;

(2) The purchase of new equipment;

(3) Management services;

(4) Assuring a fair minimum of return to vendors; or

(5) The establishment and maintenance of retirement or pension funds, health insurance contributions, and provision for paid sick leave and vacation time, if it is so determined by a majority vote of blind vendors licensed by the State licensing agency, after such agency provides to each such vendor information on all matters relevant to such proposed purposes.

(c) The State licensing agency shall further set out the method of determining the charge for each of the above purposes listed in paragraph (b) of this section, which will be determined with the active participation of the State Committee of Blind Vendors and which will be designed to prevent, so far as is practicable, a greater charge for any purpose than is reasonably required for that purpose. The State licensing agency shall maintain adequate records to support the reasonableness of the charges for each of the purposes listed in this section, including any reserves necessary to assure that such purposes can be achieved on a consistent basis.

§ 395.10 The maintenance and replacement of vending facility equipment.

The State licensing agency shall maintain (or cause to be maintained) all vending facility equipment in good repair and in an attractive condition and shall replace or cause to be replaced worn-out and obsolete equipment as required to ensure the continued successful operation of the facility.

§ 395.11 Training program for blind individuals.

The State licensing agency shall ensure that effective programs of vocational and other training services, including personal and vocational adjustment, books, tools, and other training materials, shall be provided to blind individuals as vocational rehabilitation services under the Rehabilitation Act of 1973 (Pub. L. 93–112), as amended by the Rehabilitation Act Amendments of 1974 (Pub. L. 93–516). Such programs shall include on-the-job training in all aspects of vending facility operation for blind persons with the capacity to operate a vending facility, and upward mobility training (including further education and additional training or retraining for improved work opportunities) for all blind licensees. The State licensing agency shall further ensure that post-employment services shall be provided to blind vendors as vocational rehabilitation services as necessary to assure that the maximum vocational potential of such vendors is achieved and suitable employment is maintained within the State's vending facility program.

§ 395.12 Access to program and financial information.

Each blind vendor under this part shall be provided access to all financial data of the State licensing agency relevant to the operation of the State vending facility program, including quarterly and annual financial reports, provided that such disclosure does not violate applicable Federal or State laws pertaining to the disclosure of confidential information. Insofar as practicable, such data shall be made available in braille or recorded tape. At the request of a blind vendor State licensing agency staff shall arrange a convenient time to assist in the interpretation of such financial data.

§ 395.13 Evidentiary hearings and arbitration of vendor complaints.

(a) The State licensing agency shall specify in writing and maintain procedures whereby such agency affords an opportunity for a full evidentiary hearing to each blind vendor (which procedures shall also apply to cases under § 395.6(e)) dissatisfied with any State licensing agency action arising from the operation or administration of the vending facility program. When such blind vendor is dissatisfied with any action taken or decision rendered as a result of such hearing, he may file a complaint with the Secretary. Such complaint shall be accompanied by all available supporting documents, including a statement of the decision which was rendered and the reasons in support thereof.

(b) The filing of a complaint under paragraph (a) of this section with either the State licensing agency or the Secretary shall indicate consent by the blind vendor for the release of such information as is necessary for the conduct of a full evidentiary hearing or

the hearing of an ad hoc arbitration panel.

(c) Upon receipt of a complaint filed by a blind vendor which meets the requirements established by the Secretary, the Secretary shall convene an ad hoc arbitration panel which shall, in accordance with the provisions of 5 U.S.C. chapter 5, subchapter II, give notice, conduct a hearing, and render its decision which shall be final and binding on the parties except that such decision shall be subject to appeal and review as a final agency action for purposes of the provisions of 5 U.S.C. chapter 7.

(d) The arbitration panel convened by the Secretary to hear the grievances of blind vendors shall be composed of three members appointed as follows:

(1) One individual designated by the State licensing agency;

(2) One individual designated by the blind vendor; and

(3) One individual not employed by the State licensing agency or, where appropriate, its parent agency, who shall be jointly designated by the other members of the panel and who shall serve as chairman of the panel.

(e) If either the State licensing agency or the blind vendor fails to designate a member of an arbitration panel, the Secretary shall designate such member on behalf of such party.

(f) The decisions of an arbitration panel convened by the Secretary under this section shall be matters of public record and shall be published in the FEDERAL REGISTER.

(g) The Secretary shall pay all reasonable costs of arbitration under this section in accordance with a schedule of fees and expenses which shall be published in the FEDERAL REGISTER.

(h) The provisions of this section shall not require the participation of grantors of permits for the operation of vending facilities on property other than Federal property.

§ 395.14 The State Committee of Blind Vendors.

(a) The State licensing agency shall provide for the biennial election of a State Committee of Blind Vendors which, to the extent possible, shall be fully representative of all blind vendors in the State program on the basis of such factors as geography and vending facility type with a goal of providing for proportional representation of blind vendors on Federal property and blind vendors on other property. Participation by any blind vendor in any election shall not be conditioned upon the payment of dues or any other fees.

(b) The State Committee of Blind Vendors shall:

(1) Actively participate with the State licensing agency in major administrative decisions and policy and program development decisions affecting the overall administration of the State's vending facility program;

(2) Receive and transmit to the State licensing agency grievances at the request of blind vendors and serve as advocates for such vendors in connection with such grievances;

(3) Actively participate with the State licensing agency in the development and administration of a State system for the transfer and promotion of blind vendors;

(4) Actively participate with the State licensing agency in the development of training and retraining programs for blind vendors; and

(5) Sponsor, with the assistance of the State licensing agency, meetings and instructional conferences for blind vendors within the State.

§395.15 Use of nominee agreements.

(a) The State licensing agency may enter into an agreement whereby another agency or organization undertakes to furnish services to blind vendors. Such agreement shall be in writing and shall contain provisions which:

(1) Clearly insure the retention by the State licensing agency of full responsibility for the administration and operation of all phases of the program;

(2) Specify the type and extent of the services to be provided under such agreement;

(3) Provide that no set-aside charges will be collected from blind vendors except as specified in such agreement;

(4) Specify that no nominee will be allowed to exercise any function with respect to funds for the purchase of new equipment or for assuring a fair minimum of return to vendors, except to collect and hold solely for disposi-

tion in accordance with the order of the State licensing agency any charges authorized for those purposes by the licensing agency; and

(5) Specify that only the State licensing agency shall have control with respect to selection, placement, transfer, financial participation and termination of the vendors, and the preservation, utilization, and disposition of program assets.

(b) If the State licensing agency permits any agency or organization other than a vendor to hold any right, title to, or interest in vending facilities or stock, the arrangement shall be one permitted by State law and shall specify in writing that all such right, title to, or interest is held by such agency or organization as the nominee of the State licensing agency for program purposes and subject to the paramount right of the State licensing agency to direct and control the use, transfer, and disposition of such vending facilities or stock.

§395.16 Permit for the establishment of vending facilities.

Prior to the establishment of each vending facility, other than a cafeteria, the State licensing agency shall submit an application for a permit setting forth the location, the amount of space necessary for the operation of the vending facility; the type of facility and equipment, the number, location and type of vending machines and other terms and conditions desired to be included in the permit. Such application shall be submitted for the approval of the head of the Federal property managing department, agency, or instrumentality. When an application is not approved, the head of the Federal property managing department, agency, or instrumentality shall advise the State licensing agency in writing and shall indicate the reasons for the disapproval.

§395.17 Suspension of designation as State licensing agency.

(a) If the Secretary has reason to believe that, in the administration of the program, there is a failure on the part of any State licensing agency to comply substantially with the Act and this part, he shall so inform such agency in writing, setting forth, in detail, the areas in which there is such failure and giving it a reasonable opportunity to comply.

(b) If, after the lapse of a reasonable time, the Secretary is of the opinion that such failure to comply still continues and that the State licensing agency is not taking the necessary steps to comply, he shall offer to such agency, by reasonable notice in writing thereto and to the chief executive of the State, an opportunity for a hearing before the Secretary (or person designated by the Secretary) to determine whether there is a failure on the part of such agency to comply substantially with the provisions of the Act and of this part.

(c) If it is thereupon determined that there is a failure on the part of such agency to comply substantially with the Act and this part, appropriate written notice shall be given to such agency and to the chief executive of the State suspending such agency's designation as licensing agency effective 90 days from the date of such notice. A copy of such written notice shall be given to each department, agency, or instrumentality of the United States responsible for the maintenance, operation, and protection of Federal property on which vending machines subject to the requirements of § 395.32 are located in the State. Upon the suspension of such designation, vending machine income from vending machines on Federal property due for accrual to the State licensing agency under § 395.32 shall be retained in escrow by such department, agency, or instrumentality of the United States responsible for the maintenance, operation and protection of the Federal property on which such vending machines are located, pending redesignation of the State licensing agency or rescission of the suspension under paragraph (e) of this section.

(d) If, before the expiration of such 90 days, the Secretary (or person designated by him) determines that the State licensing agency is taking the necessary steps to comply, he may postpone the effective date of such suspension for such time as he deems necessary in the best interest of the program.

(e) If, prior to the effective date of such suspension, the Secretary (or person designated by him) finds that there is no longer a failure on the part of the State licensing agency to comply substantially with the provisions of the Act and this part, he shall so notify the agency, the chief executive of the State, and each Federal department, agency, or instrumentality required to place funds in escrow under paragraph (c) of this section, in which event the suspension of the designation shall not become effective and the requirement to place funds in escrow shall be terminated.

Subpart C—Federal Property Management

§ 395.30 The location and operation of vending facilities for blind vendors on Federal property.

(a) Each department, agency, or instrumentality of the United States in control of the maintenance, operation, and protection of Federal property shall take all steps necessary to assure that, wherever feasible, in light of appropriate space and potential patronage, one or more vending facilities for operation by blind licensees shall be located on all Federal property *Provided* that the location or operation of such facility or facilities would not adversely affect the interests of the United States. Blind persons licensed by State licensing agencies shall be given priority in the operation of vending facilities on any Federal property.

(b) Any limitation on the location or operation of a vending facility for blind vendors by a department, agency or instrumentality of the United States based on a finding that such location or operation or type of location or operation would adversely affect the interests of the United States shall be fully justified in writing to the Secretary who shall determine whether such limitation is warranted. A determination made by the Secretary concerning such limitation shall be binding on any department, agency, or instrumentality of the United States affected by such determination. The Secretary shall publish such determination in the FEDERAL REGISTER along with supporting documents directly relating to the determination.

(c) Priority in the operation of vending facilities in areas administered by the National Park Service or the National Aeronautics and Space Administration shall be given to blind vendors. Priority in the awarding of contracts for the operation of concessions in such areas when such concessions provide accommodations, facilities, and services of a scope or of a character not generally available in vending facilities operated by blind vendors shall be given in accordance with the provisions of the Concession Policy Act (Pub. L. 98–249, 16 U.S.C. 1) or the National Aeronautics and Space Act of 1958, as amended (Pub. L. 85–568, 42 U.S.C. 2473). The provisions of this part shall not apply when all accommodations, facilities, or services in such areas are operated by a single responsible concessioner.

§ 395.31 Acquisition and occupation of Federal property.

(a) Effective January 2, 1975, no department, agency, or instrumentality of the United States shall undertake to acquire by ownership, rent, or lease, or to otherwise occupy, in whole or in part, any building unless it is determined that such building includes a satisfactory site or sites for the location and operation of a vending facility by a blind vendor. In those cases where a purchase contract, an agreement to lease, or other similar commitment was entered into prior to January 2, 1975, the provisions of this paragraph shall not apply.

(b) Effective January 2, 1975, no department, agency, or instrumentality of the United States, shall undertake to occupy, in whole or in part, any building which is to be constructed, substantially altered, or renovated, or in the case of a building which is occupied on January 2, 1975 by a department, agency, or instrumentality of the United States, no such department, agency, or instrumentality shall undertake to substantially alter or renovate such building, unless it is determined that the design for such construction, substantial alteration, or renovation includes a satisfactory site or sites for the location and operation of a vending facility by a blind vendor. In those cases where a design contract or other similar commitment was entered into prior to January 2, 1975, the provisions of this paragraph shall not apply. For purposes of this paragraph, *substantial alteration or renovation of a building* means a permanent material change in the floor area of such building which would render such building appropriate for the location and operation of a vending facility by a blind vendor.

(c) The determination that a building contains a satisfactory site or sites under paragraph (a) or (b) of this section shall be made after consultation between the State licensing agency and the head of the department, agency, or instrumentality of the United States which is planning to acquire or otherwise occupy such building. In order to make such determination, effective on the publication date of this part each such department, agency, or instrumentality shall provide to the appropriate State licensing agency written notice of its intention to acquire or otherwise occupy such building. Such written notice shall be by certified or registered mail with return receipt and shall be provided as early as practicable but no later than 60 days prior to such intended action. The written notice shall indicate that a satisfactory site or sites for the location and operation of a vending facility by blind persons is included in the plans for the building to be acquired or otherwise occupied and shall further assure that the State licensing agency shall be afforded the opportunity to determine whether such building includes a satisfactory site or sites for a vending facility. The written notice shall further assure that the State licensing agency, subject to the approval of the head of the Federal property managing department, agency, or instrumentality, shall be offered the opportunity to select the location and type of vending facility to be operated by a blind vendor prior to the completion of the final space layout of the building. The receipt of such written notice shall be acknowledged in writing promptly by the State licensing agency but no later than within 30 days and the State licensing agency shall indicate at that time whether it is interested in establishing a vending facility. A copy of the written notice to the State licensing agency and the State licensing agency's acknowledgement shall be provided to the Secretary.

(d) When, after a written notice has been provided under paragraph (c) of this section, the State licensing agency determines that the number of persons using the Federal property is or will be insufficient to support a vending facility, and the Secretary concurs with such determination, the provisions of paragraphs (a) and (b) of this section shall not apply. The provisions of paragraphs (a) and (b) of this section shall also not apply when fewer than 100 Federal Government employees are or will be located during normal working hours in the building to be acquired or otherwise occupied or when such building contains less than 15,000 square feet of interior space to be utilized for Federal Government purposes in the case of buildings in which services are to be provided to the public.

(e) The operation of a vending facility established under pre-existing arrangements shall not be affected by the provisions of this section. The provisions of this section shall further not preclude future arrangements under which vending facilities to be operated by blind vendors may be established in buildings of a size or with an employee population less than that specified in paragraph (d) of this section: *Provided,* That both the State licensing agency and the Federal property managing department, agency or instrumentality concur in such establishment.

(f) Each department, agency, and instrumentality of the United States, when leasing property in privately owned buildings, shall make every effort to lease property capable of accommodating a vending facility. When, however, such department, agency, or instrumentality is leasing part of a privately owned building in which prior to the execution of the lease, the lessor or any of his tenants had in operation or had entered into a contract for the operation of a restaurant or other food facility in a part of the building not included in such lease and the operation of a vending facility by a blind vendor would be in proximate and substantial direct competition with such restaurant or other food facility, the provisions of paragraphs (a), (b), and (c) of this section shall not apply.

§ 395.32 **Collection and distribution of vending machine income from vending machines on Federal property.**

(a) The on-site official responsible for the Federal property of each property managing department, agency, or instrumentality of the United States, in accordance with established procedures of such department, agency, or instrumentality, shall be responsible for the collection of, and accounting for, vending machine income from vending machines on Federal property under his control and shall otherwise ensure compliance with the provisions of this section.

(b) Effective January 2, 1975, 100 per centum of all vending machine income from vending machines on Federal property which are in direct competition with a vending facility operated by a blind vendor shall accure to the State licensing agency which shall disburse such income to such blind vendor operating such vending facility on such property provided that the total amount of such income accruing to such blind vendor does not exceed the maximum amount determined under § 395.8(a). In the event that there is income from such vending machines in excess of the maximum amount which may be disbursed to the blind vendor under § 395.8(a), such additional income shall accrue to the State licensing agency for purposes determined in accordance with § 395.8(c).

(c) Effective January 2, 1975, 50 per centum of all vending machine income from vending machines on Federal property which are not in direct competition with a vending facility operated by a blind vendor shall accrue to the State licensing agency which shall disburse such income to the blind vendor operating such vending facility on such property. In the event that there is no blind vendor, such income shall accrue to the State licensing agency, except as indicated under paragraph (d) of this section. The total amount of such income disbursed to such blind vendor shall not exceed the maximum amount determined under §395.8(a). In the event that there is income from such vending machines in excess of the maximum amount which may accrue to the blind vendor under §395.8(a), such additional income shall accrue to the State licensing agency for purposes determined in accordance with §395.8(c).

(d) Effective January 2, 1975, 30 per centum of all vending machine income from vending machines, which are not in direct competition with a vending facility operated by a blind vendor and which are on Federal property at which at least 50 per centum of the total hours worked on the premises occurs during a period other than normal working hours, shall accrue to the State licensing agency which shall disburse such income to the blind vendor operating a vending facility on such property. In the event that there is no blind vendor on such property, such income shall accrue to the State licensing agency. The total amount of such income disbursed to such blind vendor shall not exceed the maximum amount determined under §395.8(a). In the event that there is income from such vending machines in excess of the maximum amount which may be disbursed to the blind vendor under §395.8(a), such additional income shall accrue to the State licensing agency for purposes determined in accordance with §395.8(c).

(e) The determination that a vending machine on Federal property is in direct competition with a vending facility operated by a blind vendor shall be the responsibility of the on-site official responsible for the Federal property of each property managing department, agency or instrumentality of the United States, subject to the concurrence of the State licensing agency.

(f) In the case of vending machine income which, prior to the effective date of this part, has been disbursed to a blind vendor by a property managing department, agency, or instrumentality from proceeds which accrued from operations subsequent to January 2, 1975, pursuant to agreements in effect prior to such time, such income may be deducted, at the discretion of such property managing department, agency or instrumentality, from vend-

ing machine income due to the State licensing agency under paragraphs (b), (c), or (d) of this section.

(g) The collection of vending machine income and its disbursement to the appropriate State licensing agency shall be conducted on at least a quarterly basis.

(h) All arrangements pertaining to the operation of vending machines on Federal property not covered by contract with, or by permits issued to, State licensing agencies, shall be renegotiated upon the expiration of the existing contract or other arrangement for consistency with the provisions of this section.

(i) The provisions of this section shall not apply to income from vending machines within operated retail sales outlets under the control of post exchange or ships' stores systems authorized under title 10 U.S.C.; to income from vending machines operated by the Veterans Canteen Service; or to income from vending machines not in direct competition with a blind vending facility at individual locations, installations, or facilities on Federal property the total of which at such individual locations, installations, or facilities does not exceed $3,000 annually.

(j) The provisions of this section shall not operate to preclude pre-existing or future arrangements, or regulations of departments, agencies, or instrumentalities of the United States, under which blind vendors or State licensing agencies may:

(1) Receive a greater percentage or amount of vending machine income than that specified in paragraphs (b), (c), and (d) of this section, or

(2) Receive vending machine income from individual locations, installations, or facilities on Federal property the total of which at such individual locations, installations, or facilities does not exceed $3,000 annually.

§ 395.33 Operation of cafeterias by blind vendors.

(a) Priority in the operation of cafeterias by blind vendors on Federal property shall be afforded when the Secretary determines, on an individual basis, and after consultation with the appropriate property managing department, agency, or instrumentality, that such operation can be provided at a reasonable cost, with food of a high quality comparable to that currently provided employees, whether by contract or otherwise. Such operation shall be expected to provide maximum employment opportunities to blind vendors to the greatest extent possible.

(b) In order to establish the ability of blind vendors to operate a cafeteria in such a manner as to provide food service at comparable cost and of comparable high quality as that available from other providers of cafeteria services, the appropriate State licensing agency shall be invited to respond to solicitations for offers when a cafeteria contract is contemplated by the appropriate property managing department, agency, or instrumentality. Such solicitations for offers shall establish criteria under which all responses will be judged. Such criteria may include sanitation practices, personnel, staffing, menu pricing and portion sizes, menu variety, budget and accounting practices. If the proposal received from the State licensing agency is judged to be within a competitive range and has been ranked among those proposals which have a reasonable chance of being selected for final award, the property managing department, agency, or instrumentality shall consult with the Secretary as required under paragraph (a) of this section. If the State licensing agency is dissatisfied with an action taken relative to its proposal, it may file a complaint with the Secretary under the provisions of § 395.37.

(c) All contracts or other existing arrangements pertaining to the operation of cafeterias on Federal property not covered by contract with, or by permits issued to, State licensing agencies shall be renegotiated subsequent to the effective date of this part on or before the expiration of such contracts or other arrangements pursuant to the provisions of this section.

(d) Notwithstanding the requirements of paragraphs (a) and (b) of this section, Federal property managing departments, agencies, and instrumentalities may afford priority in the operation of cafeterias by blind vendors on Federal property through direct negotiations with State licensing agencies whenever such department, agency, or instrumentality determines, on an individual basis, that such operation can be provided at a reasonable cost, with food of a high quality comparable to that currently provided employees: *Provided, however,* That the provisions of paragraphs (a) and (b) of this section shall apply in the event that the negotiations authorized by this paragraph do not result in a contract.

§ 395.34 Application for permits.

Applications for permits for the operation of vending facilities other than cafeterias shall be made in writing on the appropriate form, and submitted for the review and approval of the head of the Federal property managing department, agency, or instrumentality.

§ 395.35 Terms of permit.

Every permit shall describe the location of the vending facility including any vending machines located on other than the facility premises and shall be subject to the following provisions:

(a) The permit shall be issued in the name of the applicant State licensing agency which shall:

(1) Prescribe such procedures as are necessary to assure that in the selection of vendors and employees for vending facilities there shall be no discrimination because of sex, race, age, creed, color, national origin, physical or mental disability, or political affiliation; and

(2) Take the necessary action to assure that vendors do not discriminate against any person or persons in furnishing, or by refusing to furnish, to such person or persons the use of any vending facility, including any and all services, privileges, accommodations, and activities provided thereby, and comply with title VI of the Civil Rights Act of 1964 and regulations issued pursuant thereto.

(b) The permit shall be issued for an indefinite period of time subject to suspension or termination on the basis of compliance with agreed upon terms.

(c) The permit shall provide that:

(1) No charge shall be made to the State licensing agency for normal cleaning, maintenance, and repair of the building structure in and adjacent to the vending facility areas;

(2) Cleaning necessary for sanitation, and the maintenance of vending facilities and vending machines in an orderly condition at all times, and the installation, maintenance, repair, replacement, servicing, and removal of vending facility equipment shall be without cost to the department, agency, or instrumentality responsible for the maintenance of the Federal property; and

(3) Articles sold at vending facilities operated by blind licensees may consist of newspapers, periodicals, publications, confections, tobacco products, foods, beverages, chances for any lottery authorized by State law and conducted by an agency of a State within such State, and other articles or services as are determined by the State licensing agency, in consultation with the on-site official responsible for the Federal property of the property managing department, agency or instrumentality, to be suitable for a particular location. Such articles and services may be dispensed automatically or manually and may be prepared on or off the premises in accordance with all applicable health laws.

(d) The permit shall further provide that vending facilities shall be operated in compliance with applicable health, sanitation, and building codes or ordinances.

(e) The permit shall further provide that installation, modification, relocation, removal, and renovation of vending facilities shall be subject to the prior approval and supervision of the on-site official responsible for the Federal property of the property managing department, agency, or instrumentality, and the State licensing agency; that costs of relocations initiated by the State licensing agency shall be paid by the State licensing agency; and that costs of relocations initiated by the department, agency, or instrumentality shall be borne by such department, agency, or instrumentality.

(f) The operation of a cafeteria by a blind vendor shall be covered by a contractual agreement and not by a permit.

§ 395.36 Enforcement procedures.

(a) The State licensing agency shall attempt to resolve day-to-day problems pertaining to the operation of the vending facility in an informal manner with the participation of the blind vendor and the on-site official responsible for the property of the property managing department, agency, or instrumentality as necessary.

(b) Unresolved disagreements concerning the terms of the permit, the Act, or the regulations in this part and any other unresolved matters shall be reported in writing to the State licensing agency supervisory personnel by the Regional or other appropriate official of the Federal property managing department, agency, or instrumentality in an attempt to resolve the issue.

§ 395.37 Arbitration of State licensing agency complaints.

(a) Whenever any State licensing agency determines that any department, agency, or instrumentality of the United States which has control of the maintenance, operation, and protection of Federal property is failing to comply with the provisions of the Act or of this part and all informal attempts to resolve the issues have been unsuccessful, such licensing agency may file a complaint with the Secretary.

(b) Upon receipt of a complaint filed under paragraph (a) of this section, the Secretary shall convene an ad hoc arbitration panel which shall, in accordance with the provisions of 5 U.S.C. ch. 5, subchapter II, give notice, conduct a hearing and render its decision which shall be final and binding on the parties except that such decision shall be subject to appeal and review as a final agency action for purposes of the provisions of 5 U.S.C. ch. 7. The arbitration panel convened by the Secretary to hear complaints filed by a State licensing agency shall be composed of three members appointed as follows:

(1) One individual designated by the State licensing agency;

(2) One individual designated by the head of the Federal department, agency, or instrumentality controlling the Federal property over which the dispute arose; and

(3) One individual, not employed by the Federal department, agency, or instrumentality controlling the Federal

property over which the dispute arose, who shall be jointly designated by the other members of the panel and who shall serve as chairman of the panel.

(c) If either the State licensing agency or the head of the Federal department, agency, or instrumentality fails to designate a member of an arbitration panel, the Secretary shall designate such member on behalf of such party.

(d) If the panel finds that the acts or practices of any department, agency, or instrumentality are in violation of the Act or of this part, the head of any such department, agency, or instrumentality (subject to any appeal under paragraph (b) of this section) shall cause such acts or practices to be terminated promptly and shall take such other action as may be necessary to carry out the decision of the panel.

(e) The decisions of an arbitration panel convened by the Secretary under this section shall be matters of public record and shall be published in the FEDERAL REGISTER.

(f) The Secretary shall pay all reasonable costs of arbitration under this section in accordance with a schedule of fees and expenses which shall be published in the FEDERAL REGISTER.

§ 395.38   Reports.

At the end of each fiscal year, each property managing department, agency, or instrumentality of the United States shall report to the Secretary the total number of applications for vending facility locations received from State licensing agencies, the number accepted, the number denied, the number still pending, the total amount of vending machine income collected and the amount of such vending machine income disbursed to the State licensing agency in each State.

PART 396—TRAINING OF INTERPRETERS FOR INDIVIDUALS WHO ARE DEAF OR HARD OF HEARING AND INDIVIDUALS WHO ARE DEAF–BLIND

Subpart A—General

AUTHORITY: Sections 12(c) and 302(a) and (f) of the Rehabilitation Act of 1973, as amended; 29 U.S.C. 709(c) and 772(a) and (f), unless otherwise noted.

SOURCE: 81 FR 55625, Aug. 19, 2016, unless otherwise noted.

Subpart A—General

§ 396.1   What is the Training of Interpreters for Individuals Who Are Deaf or Hard of Hearing and Individuals Who Are Deaf-Blind program?

The Training of Interpreters for Individuals Who Are Deaf or Hard of Hearing and Individuals Who Are Deaf-Blind program is designed to establish interpreter training programs or to provide financial assistance for ongoing interpreter programs to train a sufficient number of qualified interpreters throughout the country in order to meet the communication needs of individuals who are deaf or hard of hearing and individuals who are deaf-blind by—

(a) Training interpreters to effectively interpret and transliterate between spoken language and sign language and to transliterate between spoken language and oral or tactile modes of communication;

(b) Ensuring the maintenance of the interpreting skills of qualified interpreters; and

(c) Providing opportunities for interpreters to raise their skill level competence in order to meet the highest standards approved by certifying associations.

(Authority: Sections 12(c) and 302(a) and (f) of the Rehabilitation Act of 1973, as amended; 29 U.S.C. 709(c) and 772(a) and (f))

§ 396.2 Who is eligible for an award?

Public and private nonprofit agencies and organizations, including institutions of higher education, are eligible for assistance under this program.

(Authority: Section 302(f) of the Rehabilitation Act of 1973, as amended; 29 U.S.C. 772(f))

§ 396.3 What regulations apply?

The following regulations apply to the Training of Interpreters for Individuals Who Are Deaf or Hard of Hearing and Individuals Who Are Deaf-Blind program:

(a) 34 CFR part 385 (Rehabilitation Training), sections—

(1) 385.3(a) and (d);

(2) 385.40 through 385.46; and

(b) The regulations under this part 396.

(Authority: Sections 12(c) and 302(f) of the Rehabilitation Act of 1973, as amended; 29 U.S.C. 709(c) and 772(f))

§ 396.4 What definitions apply?

(a) *Definitions in EDGAR.* The following terms defined in 34 CFR 77.1 apply to this part:

Applicant
Application
Award
Equipment
Grant
Nonprofit
Private
Project
Public
Secretary
Supplies

(b) *Definitions in the rehabilitation training regulations.* The following terms defined in 34 CFR 385.4(b) apply to this part:

Individual With a Disability
Institution of Higher Education

(c) *Other definitions.* The following definitions also apply to this part:

Existing program that has demonstrated its capacity for providing interpreter training services means an established program with—

(i) A record of training qualified interpreters who are serving the deaf, hard of hearing, and deaf-blind communities; and

(ii) An established curriculum that uses evidence-based practices in the training of interpreters and promising practices when evidence-based practices are not available.

Individual who is deaf means an individual who, in order to communicate, depends primarily upon visual modes, such as sign language, speech reading, and gestures, or reading and writing.

Individual who is deaf-blind means an individual—

(i)(A) Who has a central visual acuity of 20/200 or less in the better eye with corrective lenses, or a field defect such that the peripheral diameter of visual field subtends an angular distance no greater than 20 degrees, or a progressive visual loss having a prognosis leading to one or both of these conditions;

(B) Who has a chronic hearing impairment so severe that most speech cannot be understood with optimum amplification, or a progressive hearing loss having a prognosis leading to this condition; and

(C) For whom the combination of impairments described in paragraphs (i)(A) and (B) of this definition causes extreme difficulty in attaining independence in daily life activities, achieving psychosocial adjustment, or obtaining a vocation;

(ii) Who, despite the inability to be measured accurately for hearing and vision loss due to cognitive or behavioral constraints, or both, can be determined through functional and performance assessment to have severe hearing and visual disabilities that cause extreme difficulty in attaining independence in daily life activities, achieving psychosocial adjustment, or obtaining vocational objectives; or

(iii) Who meets any other requirements that the Secretary may prescribe.

Individual who is hard of hearing means an individual who, in order to communicate, needs to supplement auditory information by depending primarily upon visual modes, such as sign language, speech reading, and gestures, or reading and writing.

Interpreter for individuals who are deaf or hard of hearing means a qualified professional who uses sign language skills, cued speech, or oral interpreting skills, as appropriate to the needs of individuals who are deaf or hard of hearing, to facilitate communication between individuals who are deaf or hard of hearing and other individuals.

Interpreter for individuals who are deaf-blind means a qualified professional who uses tactile or other manual language or fingerspelling modes, as appropriate to the needs of individuals who are deaf-blind, to facilitate communication between individuals who are deaf-blind and other individuals.

Novice Interpreter means an interpreter who has graduated from an interpreter education program or enters the field through an alternate pathway, is at the start of his or her professional career with some level of proficiency in American Sign Language, and is working toward becoming a qualified professional.

Qualified professional means an individual who has—

(i) Met existing certification or evaluation requirements equivalent to the highest standards approved by certifying associations; and

(ii) Successfully demonstrated interpreting skills that reflect the highest standards approved by certifying associations through prior work experience.

Related agency means—

(i) An American Indian rehabilitation program; or

(ii) Any of the following agencies that provide services to individuals with disabilities under an agreement or other arrangement with a designated State agency in the area of specialty for which training is provided:

(A) A Federal, State, or local agency.

(B) A nonprofit organization.

(C) A professional corporation or professional practice group.

(Authority: Sections 12(c) and 302(f) of the Rehabilitation Act of 1973, as amended and Section 206 of Pub. L. 98–221; 29 U.S.C. 709(c) and 772(f) and 29 U.S.C 1905)

§ 396.5 What activities may the Secretary fund?

The Secretary may award grants to public or private nonprofit agencies or organizations, including institutions of higher educations, to provide assistance for establishment of interpreter training programs or for projects that provide training in interpreting skills for persons preparing to serve, and persons who are already serving, as interpreters for individuals who are deaf or hard of hearing, and as interpreters for individuals who are deaf-blind in public and private agencies, schools, and other service-providing institutions.

(Authority: Section 302(f) of the Rehabilitation Act of 1973, as amended; 29 U.S.C. 772(f))

Subpart B [Reserved]

Subpart C—How Does One Apply for an Award?

§ 396.20 What must be included in an application?

Each applicant shall include in the application—

(a) A description of the manner in which the proposed interpreter training program will be developed and operated during the five-year period following the award of the grant;

(b) A description of the communication needs for training interpreters for the population(s) or in the geographical area(s) to be served by the project;

(c) A description of the applicant's capacity or potential for providing training of interpreters for individuals who are deaf or hard of hearing and interpreters for individuals who are deaf-blind that is evidence-based, and based on promising practices when evidence-based practices are not available;

(d) An assurance that any interpreter trained or retrained under this program shall meet those standards of competency for a qualified professional, that the Secretary may establish;

(e) An assurance that the project shall cooperate or coordinate its activities, as appropriate, with the activities of other projects funded under this program;

(f) The descriptions required in 34 CFR 385.45 with regard to the training of individuals with disabilities, including those from minority groups, for rehabilitation careers; and

(g) Such other information as the Secretary may require.

(Approved by the Office of Management and Budget under control number 1820–0018)

(Authority: Sections 12(c), 21(c), and 302(f) of the Rehabilitation Act of 1973, as amended; 29 U.S.C. 709(c), 718(c), and 772(f))

Subpart D—How Does the Secretary Make an Award?

§ 396.30   How does the Secretary evaluate an application?

(a) The Secretary evaluates applications under the procedures in 34 CFR part 75.

(b) The Secretary evaluates each application using selection criteria in § 396.31.

(c) In addition to the selection criteria described in paragraph (b) of this section, the Secretary evaluates each application using—

(1) Selection criteria in 34 CFR 75.210;

(2) Selection criteria established under 34 CFR 75.209; or

(3) A combination of selection criteria established under 34 CFR 75.209 and selection criteria in 34 CFR 75.210.

(Authority: Section 302(f) of the Rehabilitation Act of 1973, as amended; 29 U.S.C. 772(f))

§ 396.31   What additional selection criteria are used under this program?

In addition to the criteria in 34 CFR 396.30(c), the Secretary uses the following additional selection criterion to evaluate an application. The Secretary reviews each application to determine the extent to which—

(a) The proposed interpreter training project was developed in consultation with State Vocational Rehabilitation agencies and their related agencies and consumers;

(b) The training is appropriate to the needs of both individuals who are deaf or hard of hearing and individuals who are deaf-blind and to the needs of public and private agencies that provide services to either individuals who are deaf or hard of hearing or individuals who are deaf-blind in the geographical area to be served by the training project;

(c) Any curricula for the training of interpreters includes evidence-based practices and promising practices when evidence-based practices are not available;

(d) There is a working relationship between the interpreter training project and State Vocational Rehabilitation agencies and their related agencies, and consumers; and

(e) There are opportunities for individuals who are deaf or hard of hearing and individuals who are deaf-blind to provide input regarding the design and management of the training project.

(Authority: Sections 12(c) and 302(f) of the Rehabilitation Act of 1973, as amended; 29 U.S.C. 709(c) and 772(f))

§ 396.32   What additional factors does the Secretary consider in making awards?

In addition to the selection criteria listed in § 396.31 and 34 CFR 75.210, the Secretary, in making awards under this part, considers the geographical distribution of projects throughout the country, as appropriate, in order to best carry out the purposes of this program. To accomplish this, the Secretary may in any fiscal year make awards of regional or national scope.

(Authority: Sections 12(c) and 302(f) of the Rehabilitation Act of 1973, as amended; 29 U.S.C. 709(c) and 772(f))

§ 396.33   What priorities does the Secretary apply in making awards?

(a) The Secretary, in making awards under this part, gives priority to public or private nonprofit agencies or organizations, including institutions of higher education, with existing programs that have demonstrated their capacity for providing interpreter training.

(b) In announcing competitions for grants and contracts, the Secretary may give priority consideration to—

(1) Increasing the skill level of interpreters for individuals who are deaf or hard of hearing and individuals who are deaf-blind in unserved or underserved populations or in unserved or underserved geographic areas;

(2) Existing programs that have demonstrated their capacity for providing interpreter training services that raise

the skill level of interpreters in order to meet the highest standards approved by certifying associations; and

(3) Specialized topical training based on the communication needs of individuals who are deaf or hard of hearing and individuals who are deaf-blind.

(Authority: Sections 12(c) and 302(f)(1)(C) of the Rehabilitation Act of 1973, as amended; 29 U.S.C. 709(c) and 772(f)(1)(C))

§ 396.34 What are the matching requirements?

A grantee must contribute to the cost of a project under this program in an amount satisfactory to the Secretary. The part of the costs to be borne by the grantee is determined by the Secretary at the time of the grant award.

(Authority: Section 12(c) and 302(f) of the Rehabilitation Act of 1973, as amended; 29 U.S.C. 709(c) and 772(f))

PART 397—LIMITATIONS ON USE OF SUBMINIMUM WAGE

Subpart A—General Provisions

Subpart B—Coordinated Documentation Procedures Related to Youth with Disabilities

Subpart C—Designated State Unit Responsibilities Prior to Youth with Disabilities Starting Subminimum Wage Employment

Subpart D—Local Educational Agency Responsibilities Prior to Youth with Disabilities Starting Subminimum Wage Employment

Subpart E—Designated State Unit Responsibilities to Individuals with Disabilities During Subminimum Wage Employment

Subpart F—Review of Documentation

AUTHORITY: Section 511 of the Rehabilitation Act of 1973, as amended; 29 U.S.C. 794g, unless otherwise noted.

SOURCE: 81 FR 55785, Aug. 19, 2016, unless otherwise noted.

Subpart A—General Provisions

§ 397.1 Purpose.

(a) The purpose of this part is to set forth requirements the designated State units and State and local educational agencies must satisfy to ensure that individuals with disabilities, especially youth with disabilities, have a meaningful opportunity to prepare for, obtain, maintain, advance in, or regain competitive integrated employment, including supported or customized employment.

(b) This part requires—

(1) A designated State unit to provide youth with disabilities documentation demonstrating that they have completed certain requirements, as described in this part, prior to starting subminimum wage employment with entities (as defined in § 397.5(d)) holding special wage certificates under section 14(c) of the Fair Labor Standards Act of 1938 (29 U.S.C. 214(c));

(2) A designated State unit to provide, at certain prescribed intervals for the duration of such employment, career counseling and information and referral services, designed to promote opportunities for competitive integrated employment, to individuals with disabilities, regardless of age, who are known to be employed at subminimum wage; and

(3) A designated State unit, in consultation with the State educational agency, to develop a process or utilize an existing process, to document completion of required activities under this part by a youth with a disability known to be seeking employment at subminimum wage.

(c) This part authorizes a designated State unit, or a representative of a designated State unit, to review individual documentation required to be maintained by these entities under this part.

(d) The provisions in this part work in concert with requirements in 34 CFR parts 300, 361, and 363, and do not alter any requirements under those parts.

(Authority: Sections 12(c) and 511 of the Rehabilitation Act of 1973, as amended; 29 U.S.C. 709(c) and 794g)

§ 397.2 What is the Department of Education's jurisdiction under this part?

(a) The Department of Education has jurisdiction under this part to implement guidelines for—

(1) Documentation requirements imposed on designated State units and local educational agencies, including the documentation process that the designated State unit must develop in consultation with the State educational agency;

(2) Requirements related to the services that designated State units must provide to individuals regardless of age who are employed at subminimum wage; and

(3) Requirements under § 397.31.

(b) Nothing in this part will be construed to grant to the Department of Education, or its grantees, jurisdiction over requirements set forth in the Fair Labor Standards Act, including those imposed on entities holding special wage certificates under section 14(c) of that Act, which is administered by the Department of Labor.

(Authority: Sections 12(c), 511(b)(3), 511(c), and 511(d) of the Rehabilitation Act of 1973, as amended; 709(c), 794g(b)(3), 794g(c), and 794g(d))

§ 397.3 What rules of construction apply to this part?

Nothing in this part will be construed to—

(a) Change the purpose of the Rehabilitation Act, which is to empower individuals with disabilities to maximize opportunities for achieving competitive integrated employment;

(b) Promote subminimum wage employment as a vocational rehabilitation strategy or employment outcome, as defined in 34 CFR 361.5(c)(15); or

(c) Be inconsistent with the provisions of the Fair Labor Standards Act, as amended before or after July 22, 2014.

(Authority: Sections 12(c) and 511(b) of the Rehabilitation Act of 1973, as amended; 29 U.S.C. 709(c) and 794g(b))

§ 397.4 What regulations apply?

(a) The regulations in 34 CFR part 300 governing the definition of transition services, and the Individualized Education Program requirements related to the development of postsecondary goals and the transition services needed to assist the eligible child in reaching those goals (§§ 300.320(b), 300.321(b), 300.324(c), and 300.43).

(b) The regulations in 34 CFR part 361 governing the vocational rehabilitation program, especially those regarding protection and use of personal information in 34 CFR 361.38; eligibility determinations in 34 CFR 361.42; individualized plans for employment in 34 CFR 361.45 and 34 CFR 361.46; provision of vocational rehabilitation services, including pre-employment transition services, transition services, and supported employment services in 34 CFR 361.48; ineligibility determinations in 34 CFR 361.43; informed choice in 34 CFR 361.52; and case closures in 34 CFR 361.56.

(c) The regulations in 29 CFR part 525 governing the employment of individuals with disabilities at subminimum wage rates pursuant to a certificate issued by the Secretary of Labor.

(d) The regulations in this part 397.

(Authority: Sections 12(c), 102(a) and (b), 103(a), and 113 of the Rehabilitation Act of 1973, as amended; 29 U.S.C. 709(c), 722(a) and (b), 723(a), and 733; sections 601(34) and 614(d)(1)(A)(i)(VIII) of the Individuals with Disabilities Education Act (20 U.S.C. 1401(34) and 1414(d)); and section 14(c) of the Fair Labor Standards Act (29 U.S.C. 214(c))

§ 397.5 What definitions apply?

(a) The following terms have the meanings given to them in 34 CFR 361.5(c):

(1) Act;

(2) Competitive integrated employment;

(3) Customized employment;

(4) Designated State unit;

(5) Extended services;

(6) Individual with a disability;

(7) Individual with a most significant disability;

(8) Individual's representative;

(9) Individualized plan for employment;

(10) Pre-employment transition services;

(11) Student with a disability;

(12) Supported employment;

(13) Vocational rehabilitation services; and

(14) Youth with a disability.

(b) The following terms have the meanings given to them in 34 CFR part 300:

(1) Local educational agency (§ 300.28);

(2) State educational agency (§ 300.41); and

(3) Transition services (§ 300.43).

(c) The following terms have the meanings given to them in 29 CFR 525.3 and section 6(a)(1) of the Fair Labor Standards Act (29 U.S.C. 206(a)(1)):

(1) *Federal minimum wage* has the meaning given to that term in section 6(a)(1) of the Fair Labor Standards Act (29 U.S.C. 206(a)(1)); and

(2) *Special wage certificate* means a certificate issued to an employer under section 14(c) of the Fair Labor Standards Act (29 U.S.C. 214(c)) and 29 CFR part 525 that authorizes payment of subminimum wages, wages less than the statutory minimum wage.

(d) *Entity* means an employer, or a contractor or subcontractor of that employer, that holds a special wage certificate described in section 14(c) of the Fair Labor Standards Act (29 U.S.C. 214(c)).

(Authority: Sections 7, 12(c), and 511(a) and (f) of the Rehabilitation Act of 1973, as amended; 29 U.S.C. 705, 709(c), and 794g(a) and (f); sections 601 and 614(d) of the Individuals with Disabilities Education Act, 20 U.S.C. 1401 and 1414(d); section 901 of the Elementary and Secondary Education Act of 1965, 20 U.S.C. 7801; and sections 6(a)(1) and 14(c) of the Fair Labor Standards Act, 29 U.S.C. 206(a)(1) and 29 U.S.C. 214(c))

Subpart B—Coordinated Documentation Procedures Related to Youth with Disabilities

§ 397.10 What documentation process must the designated State unit develop?

(a) The designated State unit, in consultation with the State educational agency, must develop a new process, or utilize an existing process, to document the completion of the actions described in § 397.20 and § 397.30 by a youth with a disability, as well as a process for the transmittal of that documentation from the educational agency to the designated State unit, consistent with confidentiality requirements of the Family Education Rights and Privacy Act (20 U.S.C. 1232g(b) and 34 CFR 99.30 and 99.31) and the Individuals with Disabilities Education Act (20 U.S.C. 1417(c) and 34 CFR 300.622).

(1) Such documentation must, at a minimum, contain the—

(i) Youth's name;

(ii) Determination made, including a summary of the reason for the determination, or description of the service or activity completed;

(iii) Name of the individual making the determination or the provider of the required service or activity;

(iv) Date determination made or required service or activity completed;

(v) Signature of the designated State unit or educational personnel making the determination or documenting completion of the required services or activity;

(vi) Date of signature described in paragraph (a)(1)(v) of this section;

(vii) Signature of designated State unit personnel transmitting documentation to the youth with a disability; and

(viii) Date and method (*e.g.*, hand-delivered, faxed, mailed, emailed, etc.) by which document was transmitted to the youth.

(2) In the event a youth with a disability or, as applicable, the youth's parent or guardian, refuses, through informed choice, to participate in the activities required by this part, such documentation must, at a minimum, contain the—

(i) Youth's name;

(ii) Description of the refusal and the reason for such refusal;

(iii) Signature of the youth or, as applicable, the youth's parent or guardian;

(iv) Signature of the designated State unit or educational personnel documenting the youth's refusal;

(v) Date of signatures; and

(vi) Date and method (*e.g.*, hand-delivered, faxed, mailed, emailed, etc.) by which documentation was transmitted to the youth.

(3) The documentation process must include procedures for the designated State unit to retain a copy of all documentation required by this part in a manner consistent with the designated State unit's case management system and the requirements of 2 CFR 200.333.

(b) The documentation process must ensure that—

(1) A designated State unit provides, in the case of a student with a disability, documentation of completion of appropriate pre-employment transition services, in accordance with § 361.48(a) of this chapter and as required by § 397.20(a)(1);

(2) In the case of a student with a disability, for actions described in § 397.30—

(i) The appropriate school official, responsible for the provision of transition services, must provide the designated State unit documentation of completion of appropriate transition services under the Individuals with Disabilities Education Act, including those provided under section 614(d)(1)(A)(i)(VIII) (20 U.S.C. 1414(d)(1)(A)(i)(VIII));

(ii) The designated State unit must provide documentation of completion of the transition services, as documented and provided by the appropriate school official in accordance with paragraph (b)(2) of this section, to the youth with a disability.

(c) The designated State unit must provide—

(1) Documentation required by this part in a form and manner consistent with this part and in an accessible format for the youth; and

(2)(i) Documentation required by paragraph (a)(1) of this section to a youth as soon as possible upon the completion of each of the required actions, but no later than—

(A) 45 calendar days after the determination or completion of the required activity or service; or

(B) 90 calendar days, if additional time is necessary due to extenuating circumstances, after the determination or completion of each of the required actions in § 397.20 and § 397.30(a). Extenuating circumstances should be interpreted narrowly to include circumstances such as the unexpected lengthy absence of the educational or designated State unit personnel necessary for the production of the documentation or the transmittal of that documentation due to illness or family emergency, or a natural disaster.

(ii) Documentation required by paragraph (a)(2) of this section, when a youth has refused to participate in an action required by this part, must be provided to the youth within 10 calendar days of the youth's refusal to participate.

(3) When transmitting documentation of the final determination or activity completed, as required by § 397.20 and § 397.30(a), the designated State unit must provide a coversheet that itemizes each of the documents that have been provided to the youth.

(Authority: Sections 12(c) and 511(d) of the Rehabilitation Act of 1973, as amended; 29 U.S.C. 709(c) and 794g(d))

Subpart C—Designated State Unit Responsibilities Prior to Youth With Disabilities Starting Subminimum Wage Employment

§ 397.20 What are the responsibilities of a designated State unit to youth with disabilities who are known to be seeking subminimum wage employment?

(a) A designated State unit must provide youth with disabilities documentation upon the completion of the following actions:

(1)(i) Pre-employment transition services that are available to a student with a disability under 34 CFR 361.48; or

(ii) Transition services under the Individuals with Disabilities Education Act (20 U.S.C. 1400 *et seq.*), such as transition services available to the individual under section 614(d) of that Act (20 U.S.C. 1414(d));

(2) Application for vocational rehabilitation services, in accordance with 34 CFR 361.41(b), with the result that the individual was determined—

(i) Ineligible for vocational rehabilitation services, in accordance with 34 CFR 361.43; or

(ii) Eligible for vocational rehabilitation services, in accordance with 34 CFR 361.42; and

(A) The youth with a disability had an approved individualized plan for employment, in accordance with 34 CFR 361.46;

(B) The youth with a disability was unable to achieve the employment outcome specified in the individualized plan for employment, as described in 34 CFR 361.5(c)(15) and 361.46, despite working toward the employment outcome with reasonable accommodations and appropriate supports and services, including supported employment services and customized employment services, for a reasonable period of time; and

(C) The youth with a disability's case record, which meets all of the requirements of 34 CFR 361.47, is closed.

(3)(i) Regardless of the determination made under paragraph (a)(2) of this section, the youth with a disability has received career counseling, and information and referrals from the designated State unit to Federal and State programs and other resources in the individual's geographic area that offer employment-related services and supports designed to enable the individual to explore, discover, experience, and attain competitive integrated employment.

(ii) The career counseling and information and referral services provided in accordance with paragraph (a)(3)(i) of this section must—

(A) Be provided by the designated State unit in a manner that facilitates informed choice and decision-making by the youth, or the youth's representative as appropriate;

(B) Not be for subminimum wage employment by an entity defined in § 397.5(d), and such employment-related services are not compensated at a subminimum wage and do not directly result in employment compensated at a subminimum wage provided by such an entity; and

(C) Be provided within 30 calendar days of a determination under paragraph (a)(2)(i) or (a)(2)(ii)(C) of this section for a youth known by the designated State unit to be seeking employment at subminimum wage.

(b) The following special requirements apply—

(1) For purposes of this part, all documentation provided by a designated State unit must satisfy the requirements for such documentation, as applicable, under 34 CFR part 361.

(2) The individualized plan for employment, required in paragraph (a)(2)(ii)(A) of this section, must include a specific employment goal consistent with competitive integrated employment, including supported or customized employment.

(3)(i) For purposes of paragraph (a)(2)(ii)(B) of this section, a determination as to what constitutes a "reasonable period of time" must be consistent with the disability-related and vocational needs of the individual, as well as the anticipated length of time required to complete the services identified in the individualized plan for employment.

(ii) For an individual whose specified employment goal is in supported employment, such reasonable period of time is up to 24 months, unless under special circumstances the individual and the rehabilitation counselor jointly agree to extend the time to achieve the employment outcome identified in the individualized plan for employment.

(Authority: Sections 7(5), 7(39), 12(c), 102(a) and (b), 103(a), 113, and 511(a) and (d) of the Rehabilitation Act of 1973, as amended; 29 U.S.C. 705(5), 705(39), 709(c), 722(a) and (b), 723(a), 733, and 794g(a) and (d))

Subpart D—Local Educational Agency Responsibilities Prior to Youth With Disabilities Starting Subminimum Wage Employment

§ 397.30 What are the responsibilities of a local educational agency to youth with disabilities who are known to be seeking subminimum wage employment?

(a) Of the documentation to demonstrate a youth with a disability's completion of the actions described in § 397.20(a), a local educational agency, as defined in § 397.5(b)(1), must provide the designated State unit with documentation that the youth has received transition services under the Individuals with Disabilities Education Act (20 U.S.C. 1400 *et seq.*), such as transition services available to the individual under section 614(d) of that Act (20 U.S.C. 1414(d)). The documentation must be provided to the designated State unit in a manner that complies with confidentiality requirements of the Family Education Rights and Privacy Act (20 U.S.C. 1232g(b) and 34 CFR 99.30 and 99.31) and the Individuals with Disabilities Education Act (20 U.S.C. 1417(c) and 34 CFR 300.622).

(b)(1) The documentation of completed services or activities required by paragraph (a) of this section must, at a minimum, contain the—

(i) Youth's name;

(ii) Description of the service or activity completed;

(iii) Name of the provider of the required service or activity;

(iv) Date required service or activity completed;

(v) Signature of educational personnel documenting completion of the required service or activity;

(vi) Date of signature described in paragraph (b)(1)(v) of this section; and

(vii) Signature of educational personnel transmitting documentation to the designated State unit; and

(viii) Date and method (*e.g.*, hand-delivered, faxed, mailed, emailed, etc.) by which document was transmitted to the designated State unit.

(2) In the event a youth with a disability or, as applicable, the youth's parent or guardian, refuses, through informed choice, to participate in the activities required by this part, such documentation must, at a minimum, contain the—

(i) Youth's name;

(ii) Description of the refusal and the reason for such refusal;

(iii) Signature of the youth or, as applicable, the youth's parent or guardian;

(iv) Signature of the educational personnel documenting the youth's refusal;

(v) Date of signatures required by paragraphs (b)(2)(iii) and (iv) of this section;

(vi) Signature of educational personnel transmitting documentation of the refusal to the designated State unit; and

(vii) Date and method (*e.g.*, hand-delivered, faxed, mailed, emailed, etc.) by which documentation was transmitted to the designated State unit.

(c)(1)(i) The educational personnel must transmit the documentation required by paragraph (b)(1) of this section to the designated State unit as soon as possible upon the completion of each of the required actions, but no later than—

(A) 30 calendar days after the completion of the required activity or service; or

(B) 60 calendar days, if additional time is necessary due to extenuating circumstances, after the completion of each of the required actions in paragraph (a) of this section. Extenuating circumstances should be interpreted narrowly to include the unexpected lengthy absence due to illness or family emergency of the educational personnel necessary to produce or transmit the documentation, or a natural disaster.

(ii) Documentation required by paragraph (b)(2) of this section, when a youth has refused to participate in an action required by this part, must be provided to the DSU within 5 calendar days of the youth's refusal to participate.

(2) When the educational personnel transmits the last documentation to the designated State unit regarding the services provided to the youth under paragraph (a) of this section, the educational personnel must provide a cover sheet that itemizes the documentation that has been provided to the designated State unit regarding that youth.

(d) The educational agency must retain a copy of all documentation provided to the designated State unit under this section in a manner consistent with the requirements of 2 CFR 200.333.

(Authority: Sections 12(c), 511(a)(2)(A), and 511(d) of the Rehabilitation Act of 1973, as amended; 29 U.S.C. 709(c), 794g(a)(2)(A), and (d))

§ 397.31 What are the contracting limitations on educational agencies under this part?

Neither a local educational agency, as defined in § 397.5(b)(1), nor a State educational agency, as defined in § 397.5(b)(2), may enter into a contract or other arrangement with an entity, as defined in § 397.5(d), for the purpose of operating a program for a youth under which work is compensated at a subminimum wage.

(Authority: Section 511(b)(2) of the Rehabilitation Act of 1973, as amended; 29 U.S.C. 794g(b)(2))

Subpart E—Designated State Unit Responsibilities to Individuals With Disabilities During Subminimum Wage Employment

§ 397.40 What are the responsibilities of a designated State unit for individuals with disabilities, regardless of age, who are employed at a subminimum wage?

(a) *Counseling and information services.* (1) A designated State unit must provide career counseling and information and referral services, as described in § 397.20(a)(3), to individuals with disabilities, regardless of age, or the individual's representative as appropriate, who are known by the designated State

unit to be employed by an entity, as defined in § 397.5(d), at a subminimum wage level.

(2) A designated State unit may know of an individual with a disability described in this paragraph through the vocational rehabilitation process, self-referral, or by referral from the client assistance program, another agency, or an entity, as defined in § 397.5(d).

(3) The career counseling and information and referral services must be provided in a manner that—

(i) Is understandable to the individual with a disability; and

(ii) Facilitates independent decision-making and informed choice as the individual makes decisions regarding opportunities for competitive integrated employment and career advancement, particularly with respect to supported employment, including customized employment.

(4) The career counseling and information and referral services provided under this section may include benefits counseling, particularly with regard to the interplay between earned income and income-based financial, medical, and other benefits.

(b) *Other services.* (1) Upon a referral by an entity, as defined in § 397.5(d), that has fewer than 15 employees, of an individual with a disability who is employed at a subminimum wage by that entity, a designated State unit must also inform the individual within 30 calendar days of the referral by the entity, of self-advocacy, self-determination, and peer mentoring training opportunities available in the community.

(2) The services described in paragraph (b)(1) of this section must not be provided by an *entity* as defined in § 397.5(d).

(c) *Required intervals.* (1) For individuals hired at subminimum wage on or after July 22, 2016, the services required by this section must be carried out once every six months for the first year of the individual's subminimum wage employment and annually thereafter for the duration of such employment.

(2) For individuals already employed at subminimum wage prior to July 22, 2016, the services required by this section must be carried out once by July

22, 2017, and annually thereafter for the duration of such employment.

(3)(i) With regard to the intervals required by paragraphs (c)(1) and (2) of this section for purposes of the designated State unit's responsibilities to provide certain services to individuals employed at subminimum wage, the applicable intervals will be calculated based upon the date the individual becomes known to the designated State unit.

(ii) An individual with a disability may become "known" to the designated State unit through self-identification by the individual with a disability, referral by a third-party (including an *entity* as defined in §397.5(d)), through the individual's involvement with the vocational rehabilitation process, or any other method.

(d) *Documentation.* (1)(i) The designated State unit must provide documentation to the individual as soon as possible, but no later than—

(A) 45 calendar days after completion of the activities required under this section; or

(B) 90 calendar days, if additional time is necessary due to extenuating circumstances, after the completion of the required actions in this section. Extenuating circumstances should be interpreted narrowly to include circumstances such as the unexpected lengthy absence of the designated State unit personnel, due to illness or other family emergency, who is responsible for producing or transmitting the documentation to the individual with a disability, or a natural disaster.

(ii) Documentation required by paragraph (d)(3) of this section, when an individual has refused to participate in an activity required by this section, must be provided to the individual within 10 calendar days of the individual's refusal to participate.

(2) Such documentation must, at a minimum, contain the—

(i) Name of the individual;

(ii) Description of the service or activity completed;

(iii) Name of the provider of the required service or activity;

(iv) Date required service or activity completed;

(v) Signature of individual documenting completion of the required service or activity;

(vi) Date of signature described in paragraph (d)(2)(v) of this section;

(vii) Signature of designated State unit personnel (if different from that in paragraph (d)(2)(v) of this section) transmitting documentation to the individual with a disability; and

(viii) Date and method (*e.g.*, hand-delivered, faxed, mailed, emailed, etc.) by which document was transmitted to the individual.

(3) In the event an individual with a disability or, as applicable, the individual's representative, refuses, through informed choice, to participate in the activities required by this section, such documentation must, at a minimum, contain the—

(i) Name of the individual;

(ii) Description of the refusal and the reason for such refusal;

(iii) Signature of the individual or, as applicable, the individual's representative;

(iv) Signature of the designated State unit personnel documenting the individual's refusal;

(v) Date of signatures; and

(vi) Date and method (*e.g.*, hand-delivered, faxed, mailed, emailed, etc.) by which documentation was transmitted to the individual.

(4) The designated State unit must retain a copy of all documentation required by this part in a manner consistent with the designated State unit's case management system and the requirements of 2 CFR 200.333.

(e) *Provision of services.* Nothing in this section will be construed as requiring a designated State unit to provide the services required by this section directly. A designated State unit may contract with other entities, *i.e.*, other public and private service providers, as appropriate, to fulfill the requirements of this section. The contractor providing the services on behalf of the designated State unit may not be an entity holding a special wage certificate under section 14(c) of the Fair Labor Standards Act (29 U.S.C. 214(c)) as defined in 397.5(d).

(Authority: Sections 12(c) and 511(c) and (d) of the Rehabilitation Act of 1973, as amended; 29 U.S.C. 709(c) and 794g(c) and (d))

Subpart F—Review of Documentation

§ 397.50 What is the role of the designated State unit in the review of documentation under this part?

(a) The designated State unit, or a contractor working directly for the designated State unit, is authorized to engage in the review of individual documentation required under this part that is maintained by an *entity*, as defined in 397.5(d), under this part. The contractor referred in this section may not be an entity holding a special wage certificate under section 14(c) of the Fair Labor Standards Act (29 U.S.C. 214(c)).

(b) If deficiencies are noted during a documentation review conducted under paragraph (a) of this section, the designated State unit should report the deficiency to the U.S. Department of Labor's Wage and Hour Division.

(Authority: Sections 12(c) and 511(e)(2)(B) of the Rehabilitation Act of 1973, as amended; 29 U.S.C. 709(c) and 794g(e)(2)(B))

PARTS 398–399 [RESERVED]

Made in United States
Troutdale, OR
10/23/2023

13954174R00281